W9-CCF-077

BRITISH COLUMBIA HANDBOOK

INCLUDING VANCOUVER, VICTORIA, AND THE CANADIAN ROCKIES

BRITISH COLUMBIA HANDBOOK

INCLUDING VANCOUVER, VICTORIA, AND THE CANADIAN ROCKIES
FOURTH EDITION

JANE KING & ANDREW HEMPSTEAD

MOON
TRAVEL
HANDBOOKS

BRITISH COLUMBIA HANDBOOK
FOURTH EDITION

Published by
Moon Publications, Inc.
P.O. Box 3040
Chico, California 95927-3040, USA

Printed by
Colorcraft Ltd.

© Text and photographs copyright Jane King and Andrew Hempstead, 1998. All rights reserved.

© Illustrations and maps copyright Moon Publications, Inc., 1998. All rights reserved.

Some photos and illustrations are used by permission and are the property of the original copyright owners.

ISBN: 1-56691-104-4
ISSN: 1096-097X

Editor: Don Root
Map Editor: Gina Wilson Birtcil
Production & Design: Carey Wilson
Cartography: Bob Race, Chris Folks, and Mike Morgenfeld
Index: Deana Shields

Front cover photo: Mt. Robson, BC by Bill Terry, courtesy of Photo Network

Distributed in the United States and Canada by Publishers Group West

Printed in China

Please send all comments, corrections, additions, amendments, and critiques to:

**BRITISH COLUMBIA HANDBOOK
MOON TRAVEL HANDBOOKS
P.O. BOX 3040
CHICO, CA 95927-3040, USA
e-mail: travel@moon.com
www.moon.com**

Printing History
1st Edition — 1989
4th Edition — January 1998

All rights reserved. No part of this book may be translated or reproduced in any form, except brief extracts by a reviewer for the purpose of a review, without written permission of the copyright owner.

Although the author and publisher have made every effort to ensure that the information was correct at the time of going to press, the author and publisher do not assume and hereby disclaim any liability to any party for any loss or damage caused by errors, omissions, or any potential travel disruption due to labor or financial difficulty, whether such errors or omissions result from negligence, accident, or any other cause.

CONTENTS

ABBREVIATIONS

C$—Canadian dollars
cm—centimeter
CPR—Canadian Pacific
  Railway
d—double
4WD—four-wheel drive
Hwy.—Highway
km—kilometer

kph—kilometers per hour
mm—millimeter
no.—number
NWMP—North West Mounted
  Police
p.o.—post office
Pt.—Point
RCMP—Royal Canadian
  Mounted Police

RV—recreational vehicle
s—single
t—triple
tel.—telephone number
UNESCO—United Nations
  Educational, Scientific, and
  Cultural Organization

MAPS

— — — INTERNATIONAL BOUNDARY
— · — · — PROVINCE BOUNDARY
— ·· — ·· — OTHER BOUNDARY
▬▬▬▬ MAIN HIGHWAY
——— SECONDARY ROAD
——— OTHER ROAD
— — — UNPAVED ROAD
— · — · — FOOT TRAIL
WATER

BRIDGE
PASS
— — — — FERRY ROUTE
RAILROAD
TRANSCANADA HIGHWAY
HIGHWAY ROUTE NUMBER
○ CITY, TOWN
○ SMALL TOWN
SKI AREA

■ POINT OF INTEREST
● HOTEL/ACCOMMODATION
⛺ CAMPING
▲ MOUNTAIN
PARK
C.G. = CAMPGROUND
N.P. = NATIONAL PARK
P.P. = PROVINCIAL PARK
H.P. = HISTORIC PARK
P.R.A. = PROVINCIAL
RECREATION AREA

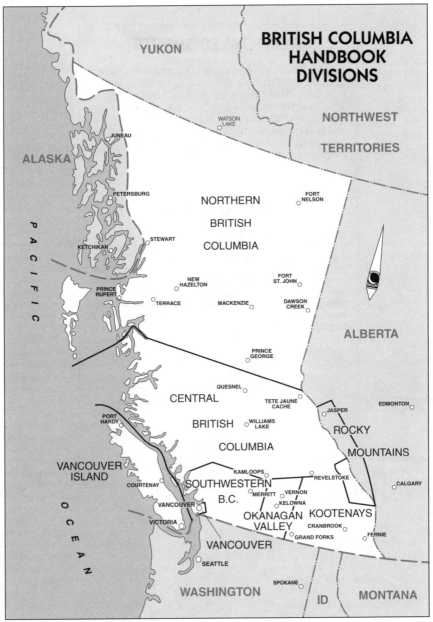

BRITISH COLUMBIA HANDBOOK DIVISIONS

YUKON

NORTHWEST

TERRITORIES

WATSON LAKE

ALASKA

JUNEAU

PETERSBURG

FORT NELSON

NORTHERN

BRITISH

COLUMBIA

STEWART

KETCHIKAN

P A C I F I C

PRINCE RUPERT

NEW HAZELTON

FORT ST. JOHN

TERRACE

MACKENZIE

DAWSON CREEK

ALBERTA

PRINCE GEORGE

QUESNEL

CENTRAL

TETE JAUNE CACHE

EDMONTON

JASPER

BRITISH

WILLIAMS LAKE

ROCKY

PORT HARDY

COLUMBIA

MOUNTAINS

VANCOUVER ISLAND

KAMLOOPS

SOUTHWESTERN

REVELSTOKE

CALGARY

COURTENAY

MERRITT

VERNON

B.C.

KELOWNA

O C E A N

VANCOUVER

KOOTENAYS

OKANAGAN VALLEY

CRANBROOK

VICTORIA

GRAND FORKS

FERNIE

VANCOUVER

SEATTLE

WASHINGTON

SPOKANE

ID

MONTANA

© MOON PUBLICATIONS, INC.

ACKNOWLEDGMENTS

A heartfelt thank you goes out to all the people who helped create *British Columbia Handbook:* to the British Columbians who shared their knowledge of B.C. and their insight; to all the well-trained staff of Travel InfoCentres and National and Provincial Parks throughout British Columbia; and to all the travelers/readers who took the time to write to us offering suggestions to make each updated edition more comrehensive.

DROP US A LINE

Although we have strived to produce the most up-to-date guidebook humanly possible, things change—restaurants and accommodations open and close, attractions come and go, and prices go up. If you come across a great out-of-the-way place, a new restaurant or lodging, or you think a particular hike warrants a mention, please write to us. Letters from tour operators and British Columbians in the tourism and hospitality industries are also appreciated. When writing, be as accurate as possible; write notes on the road or even send brochures. Write to:

British Columbia Handbook
c/o Moon Publications, Inc.
P.O. Box 3040
Chico, CA 95927 USA

BOB RACE

INTRODUCTION

British Columbia, the westernmost province of Canada, stretches from the Pacific Ocean to the towering heights of the Rocky Mountains. Sandwiched in between lies some of this planet's most magnificent scenery—an enormous variety of terrain including spectacular mountain ranges, glaciers, plains, river valleys, lakes, rugged coastline, and hundreds of islands.

The province's largest city is **Vancouver,** a splendid conglomeration of old and new architectural marvels, parks and gardens, and sheltered beaches lying along the shores of Burrard Inlet in the southwestern corner of the province. The provincial capital is old-world **Victoria,** perched at the southeastern tip of **Vancouver Island,** just across the Strait of Georgia from Vancouver. Victoria boasts an intriguing mixture of old-English architecture, customs, and traditions, along with modern attractions, cosmopolitan restaurants, and an infectious joie de vivre.

But most of British Columbia lies away from the cities, in the surrounding vastness. The protected coastal waterways, the rugged west coast of Vancouver Island, the famous Canadian Rockies and many other mountain ranges, the remote northern wilderness, and the intriguing Queen Charlotte Islands provide experiences you'll never forget, along with enough ooh-and-aah scenery to keep even the most jaded jet-setter in awe. In these wild areas, you'll find endless opportunities for hiking or climbing, viewing the abundant wildlife, fishing in the hundreds of lakes and rivers, skiing any of the dozens of resorts, or immersing yourself in native culture.

THE LAND

British Columbia is Canada's third-largest province in area, behind Ontario and Quebec. Covering 948,596 square kilometers, it's four times larger than Great Britain, two and a half times as large as Japan, larger than all U.S. states except Alaska, and larger than California, Oregon, and Washington combined. The province is long north-to-south, relatively narrow east-to-west, and lies between the 49th and 60th parallels. Its largest city, Vancouver, is on the same latitude as Paris and the same longitude as San Francisco. To the south are the U.S. states of Washington, Idaho, and Montana; to the west the Pacific Ocean and the narrow panhandle of southeast Alaska. To the north are Canada's Yukon Territory and Northwest Territories; to

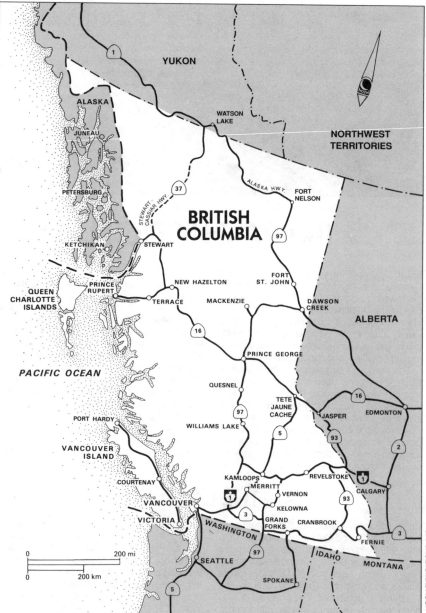

the east, across the Continental Divide, lies the Canadian province of Alberta. The land within those borders is dominated by mountain ranges, which trend northwest-southeast and are highest in the south.

Mountains

British Columbia occupies part of the mountainous terrain that runs down the entire western margin of the Americas. It lies mainly in the Cordilleran Region, which is composed of Precambrian to Cenozoic rock formed into mountain ranges, deep intermountain troughs, and wide plateaus.

The landscape is dominated by three parallel mountain ranges and a series of parallel valleys. Along the west coast are the steep **Coast Mountains,** containing 4,016-meter **Mt. Waddington,** the highest peak completely in British Columbia. The province's highest point is shared with Alaska; 4,663-meter **Mt. Fairweather** (sixth highest in Canada) is part of the **St. Elias Range,** a north-

Mt. Robson (3,954 meters) is the highest peak in the Canadian Rockies.

ern extension of the Coast Mountains that straddles the B.C./Alaska border in the extreme northwest corner of the province. The province's eastern border is defined by the lofty **Rocky Mountains,** which reach a high point in B.C. at 3,954-meter **Mount Robson,** astride the Alberta border. In the south of the province between the Coast Mountains and the Rockies lie the **Kootenays,** the collective name for the **Monashee, Selkirk,** and **Purcell Mountains.** These ranges rise to peak elevations of just over 3,000 meters and are separated by deep valleys and long, narrow lake systems. Only the highest of the Kootenays—including some glaciated peaks in the Selkirks and Purcells—are snow-covered year-round. In the north half of the province, the ranges are lower, wider, and less well defined, rising from vast plateaus that extend hundreds of kilometers in all directions.

Waterways

The province enjoys more than its share of waterways. Some 11,000 rivers and creeks and 6,000 lakes contribute to British Columbia's two million hectares of freshwater surface area. The Rocky Mountain Trench contains the headwaters of the **Kootenay, Columbia, Fraser, Peace,** and **Liard Rivers,** the former three draining eventually into the Pacific Ocean and the latter two flowing into the mighty Mackenzie River and into the Arctic Ocean. The province's longest river (Canada's fifth longest) is the Columbia, which runs for 2,000 km through B.C. and Washington.

Islands

Many small islands and a number of large ones, including Vancouver Island (largest and closest to the mainland) and the Queen Charlotte Islands, lie along the deeply indented coastline, effectively protecting the mainland from much of the wind- and wave-battering action of the Pacific Ocean.

CLIMATE

Precipitation in British Columbia is strongly influenced by the lay of the land and the waft of the wind—resulting in an astonishing variation in rainfall from place to place. For example, Kam-

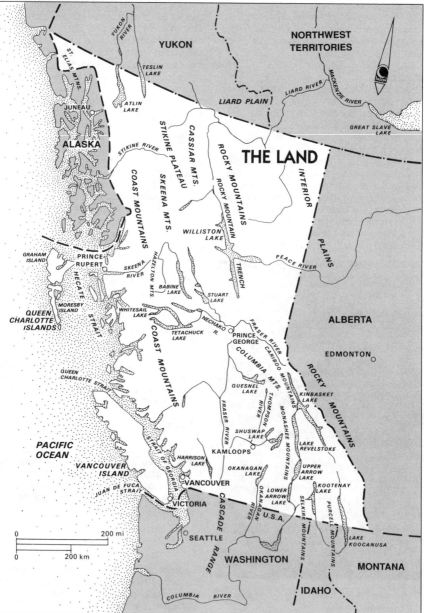

THE LAND

© MOON PUBLICATIONS, INC.

loops, in the sheltered Thompson River Valley in the interior, receives only 250 mm of precipitation annually, whereas the west coast of Vancouver Island averages 2,740 millimeters.

The amount of precipitation any given area receives is greatly determined by its location on the windward or lee sides of the major mountain ranges—the windward side usually cops most of the downpour. Hence, the western side of the Coast Range is wet; the Interior Plateau on the east side of the Coast Range is relatively dry; and the western, windward side of the Rockies along the Alberta border is once again wet.

The province's varied topography also makes for radically varying temperatures, which rise or fall with changes in elevation, latitude, slope aspect, and distance from the ocean. The **coastal zone** is influenced by polar maritime air, which causes cool and relatively dry summers and mild, wet winters. Most of **interior B.C.** is influenced by both continental and maritime air, resulting in colder, relatively dry winters and hot, dry summers. And the **northeast** region is influenced by polar continental and arctic air masses, making for extremely cold, snowy winters and short, cool, and wet summers.

Travel Seasons

Summer is by far the most popular time to visit British Columbia. Daytime temperatures in Vancouver average a pleasant 22° C, while the province's hotspot, the Southern Okanagan, experiences temperatures in the 30's on many days. Summer in the province sees the parks come alive with campers, the lakes and streams with anglers, the mountains with hikers, the woods with wildlife, and the roadsides with stalls selling fresh produce. Wherever you travel in summer, try to make accommodation reservations in advance.

Temperatures through spring and fall are, naturally, cooler than summer, but in many ways these are prime travel periods. June and September are especially pleasant, as crowds are minimal and wildlife is most active.

The main attraction of winter is skiing. Most ski resorts open well before Christmas, with Whistler/Blackcomb open from early November. Winter temperatures along the coast remain relatively mild (on only a few occasions each year does snow fall in downtown Vancouver); Van-

couver Island is a particularly popular winter destination for those from the eastern provinces. The interior and northern latitudes of the province are a different story—the average daily winter temperature is well below freezing, with temperatures of 40 below not uncommon.

In general, no matter what season you visit British Columbia, take layers of clothing to suit a variety of temperatures, and always have a windbreaker and raincoat handy.

FLORA

Two colors invariably jump to mind when you say "British Columbia": green and blue. Just about everywhere you travel in B.C. you see trees, trees, and more trees—around 60% of the province is forested. But the types of trees differ in each geographic and climatic region. **Western hemlock** predominates on the Queen Charlotte Islands, central and western Vancouver Island, and the west coast of the mainland. The Queen Charlottes' rainforest is thickly covered in spongy pale-green moss, which grows alongside **coastal Douglas fir.** In the region's subalpine areas you'll find **mountain hemlock.**

Engelmann spruce is common throughout the interior at subalpine elevations. The interior also supports a mixture of **Douglas fir** and **ponderosa pine** in the south; **interior western hemlock** in the southeast; **Cariboo aspen** and **lodgepole pine** in the central reaches; **subboreal spruce, birch,** and **willow** in the north; and **boreal white spruce** and **black spruce** in the northeast.

The official tree of British Columbia is the **western red cedar**—a valuable resource for the province. The official provincial floral emblem is the **Pacific dogwood,** a small tree sporting huge clusters of cream-colored flowers in spring, and bright foliage and red berries in autumn. The tree is a protected plant in British Columbia; it's a punishable offense to pick or destroy it.

In summer, British Columbia turns on a really magnificent floral display. Wildflowers of every color of the rainbow pop up on the roadsides—white and yellow daisies, purple lupines, pale pink and dark pink wild roses, bloodred Indian paintbrush, orange and black lilies, red and white clover, yellow buttercups, to name but a handful. And if you venture off the beaten track and up into the alpine meadows, the floral beauty is hard to believe. You can pick up a wildflower guide at most any local bookshop, and most of the national park visitor centers stock brochures on wildflower identification.

FAUNA

British Columbia is one of the best provinces in Canada for wildlife-watching. Thanks to a diverse topography that provides a wide variety of habitat, more species of birds and mammals are found here than in any other province or territory in the country.

Mammals

Within the province's boundaries live 112 species of mammals (74 of which are found exclusively in B.C.), including 25% of the world's grizzly bears, 60% of the mountain goats, and 75% of the Stone sheep. Moose, elk, deer, and black bears are all common. And because B.C.'s far-flung cities and towns have wilderness backyards, you may even encounter wildlife without trying; drivers need to be prepared to take avoidance measures when an animal suddenly appears in the roadway and decides to play chicken.

Offshore B.C. is home to an abundance of marine mammals. Thousands of Pacific gray whales cruise the coast twice a year. Porpoises, dolphins, and killer and humpback whales can be seen frolicking in coastal waters, and colonies of seals and sea lions can be viewed by boat or kayak.

Birds

The lower mainland is a migration stop for the million-odd birds that travel the Pacific flyway each year. Huge populations of waterfowl winter at Boundary Bay near Vancouver, and large concentrations can also be seen around Fort St. James, Cranbrook, Prince George, and Lac La Hache. The province is home to half of the world's populations of both trumpeter swans and blue grouse, as well as a quarter of the world's bald eagles. You'll see beautiful Canada and snow geese, trumpeter and whistling swans, and all kinds of ducks. British Columbia's official bird is the often-cheeky, vibrant blue and black **Steller's jay,** found throughout the province.

Fish

Many an angler experiences "real" fishing for the first time in B.C. and gets happily hooked, as it were. Of the 72 species of fish found in British

RACHEL TAYLOR

WILDLIFE AND YOU

British Columbia's abundance of wildlife is one of its biggest drawcards. To help preserve this unique resource, obey fishing and hunting regulations and use common sense.

- **Do not feed the animals.** Many animals may seem tame, but feeding them endangers yourself, the animal, and other visitors, as animals become aggressive when looking for handouts.

- **Store food safely.** When camping keep food in your vehicle or out of reach of animals. Just leaving it in a cooler isn't good enough.

- **Keep your distance.** Although it's tempting to get close to animals for a better look or a photograph, it disturbs the animal and, in many cases, can be dangerous.

- **Drive carefully.** The most common cause of premature death for larger mammals is being hit by cars.

Columbia, 22 are considered sport fish. The two varieties most sought-after by anglers are **salmon,** found in tidal waters along the coast, and **trout,** inhabiting the freshwater lakes and rivers of interior British Columbia.

Safety Tips

If you're lucky enough to encounter wildlife, keep a safe distance, particularly if young animals are present—the protective mother will not be far away. Never harass or feed wild animals, and resist the temptation to move in for an award-winning close-up photo; wild animals are unpredictable, so use a telephoto lens from farther back instead.

When planning a hike in the backcountry, ask local park- or forest-service staff about the likelihood of encountering wildlife along your intended route, and heed their advice. Often it's a good idea to take a noisemaker—a few rocks in a soft-drink can or a bell—or let out a loud yell every now and again to let wildlife know you're coming. The animals will usually avoid you, however, you may encounter the odd inquisitive black bear, fearless grizzly, or sudden cougar, all of which need to be left well alone. If a bear rears up, or growls with ears back, move slowly behind a tree or rock, or stand your ground and stay still. If an attack seems inevitable, drop to the ground in a hunched-up position, covering your neck, and play dead. Do not run—a bear can easily outrun a human.

The national parks hand out brochures on bears—read them! Also keep all food in airtight containers, locked in a vehicle, or strung from a high tree branch far from your tent. Tasty food odors openly invite wildlife to your area, like ringing a dinner gong and yelling "Food's on!" For more information, write **Wildlife Branch, Ministry of Environment, Lands and Parks,** 780 Blanshard St., Victoria, BC V8V 1X5.

HISTORY

EXPLORATION AND COLONIZATION

By Sea

Only 200 years ago the northwest coast of North America was one of the world's least explored areas. Its geography presented some formidable natural barriers to penetration from either the east (the lofty Rocky Mountains) or the west (long stretches of ocean away from other land masses). In the second half of the 18th century, curiosity and a common desire to discover rich natural resources lured Russian, Spanish, British, and American explorers and fur traders to the new and challenging land. In 1774, the ship of Mexican **Juan Perez** was the first vessel to explore the coastline and trade with the natives. He was quickly followed by Spaniard **Don Juan Francisco de la Bodega y Quadra,** who took possession of the coast of Alaska for Spain. England's **James Cook** arrived in 1778 to spend some time at Nootka, trading with the natives while he overhauled his ship. Cook received a number of luxuriantly soft sea-otter furs, which he later sold at a huge profit in China. This news spawned a fur-trading rush that began in 1785 and continued for 25 years. Ship after loaded ship called in along the coast, trading iron, brass, copper, muskets, cloth, jewelry, and rum with the natives in exchange for furs. The indigenous people were eager to obtain the foreign goods, but were also known for driving a hard bargain. The traders took the furs directly to China to trade for silk, tea, spices, ginger, and other luxuries. In 1789, Bodega y Quadra established a settlement at Nootka, but after ongoing problems with the British (who also claimed the area), he gave up the settlement to **Capt. George Vancouver** in 1793.

By Land

In the meantime, adventurous North West Company fur traders were crossing the Rockies in search of waterways to the coast. The first European to reach the coast via the Peace, Fraser, and West Road Rivers was **Alexander Mackenzie**—you can still see the rock in the Dean Channel (off Bella Coola) where he inscribed "Alexander Mackenzie from Canada by land 22nd July 1793." Not far behind came other famous explorers, including **Simon Fraser,** who followed the Fraser River to the sea in 1808, and **David Thompson,** who followed the Columbia River to its mouth in 1811. Today the names of these men grace everything from rivers to motels. In the early 19th century, the North West Company established trading posts in New Caledonia (the name Simon Fraser gave to the northern interior). These posts were taken over by Hudson's Bay Company after amalgamation of the two companies in 1821.

The Native Response

The fur trade brought prosperity to the indigenous society, which was organized around wealth, possessions, and potlatches. The Hudson's Bay Company had no interest in interfering with the natives and, in general, treated them fairly. This early contact with Europeans resulted in expanded trade patterns and increased commerce between coastal and interior tribes. It also spurred the production of indigenous arts and crafts to new heights, as chiefs required more carved headgear, masks, costumes, feast dishes, and the like for the increasingly frequent ceremonial occasions that came with increased wealth.

However, commerce between the Europeans and locals also caused the indigenous tribes to abandon their traditional homesites and instead to cluster around the forts for trading and protection. In addition, the Europeans introduced muskets, alcohol, and disease (most significantly smallpox), all of which took their toll. Christian missionaries soon arrived and tried to ban the natives' traditional potlatches. But not until land-grabbing white colonists showed up did major conflicts arise between native peoples and whites. Those land-ownership conflicts proved tenacious, continuing to this day.

Vancouver Island

The Imperial Government decided in 1849 that Vancouver Island should be colonized to confirm British sovereignty in the area and forestall any American expansion. Though mostly content to leave the island in the hands of the Hudson's Bay Company, the Brits nevertheless sent **Richard Blanshard** out from England to become the island colony's first governor. Blanshard soon resigned, and was replaced in 1851 by **James Douglas,** chief factor of the Hudson's Bay Company. Douglas had long been in control of the island, and his main concerns were to maintain law and order and to purchase land from the natives. He made treaties with the tribes in which the land became the "entire property of the white people forever." In return, tribes retained use of their village sites and enclosed fields, and could hunt and fish on unoccupied lands. Each indigenous family was paid a pitiful compensation.

In 1852, coal was discovered near Nanaimo and English miners were imported to develop the deposits. Around the same time, loggers began felling the enormous timber stands along the Alberni Canal, and the Puget Sound Agricultural Association (a subsidiary of Hudson's Bay Company) developed several large farms in the Victoria region. By the 1850s, the town of Victoria, with its moderate climate and fertile soil, had developed into an agreeable settlement.

LAW, ORDER, AND GOLD

Firsts

In 1856 the first parliament west of the Great Lakes was elected, and Dr. J.S. Helmcken became Speaker. (Today you can still see his house in Victoria.) Only two years later this still relatively unexplored and quiet part of the world was turned upside down with the first whispers of "gold" on the mainland, along the banks of the Fraser River. As the news spread, miners—mostly Americans—arrived by the shipload at Victoria, increasing the town's population from several hundred to more than 5,000. Fur trading faded as gold mining jumped to the forefront. Realizing that enormous wealth could be buried on the mainland, the British Government quickly responded by creating the mainland colony, British Columbia, in 1858. Governor James Douglas of Vancouver Island also became governor of B.C., giving up his Hudson's Bay Company position to serve both colonies. In 1866 the two colonies were combined into one.

Cariboo Gold

The lucrative Cariboo gold rush resulted in construction of the Cariboo Wagon Road, an amazing engineering feat that opened up British Columbia's interior. Completed in 1865, the road connected Yale with Barkerville, one of the richest and wildest gold towns in North America. Mule trains and stagecoaches plied the route, and roadhouses and boomtowns dotted its entire length. Among the colorful characters of this era was Judge Begbie, an effective chief of law and order during a time when law and order might as easily have been nonexistent.

In addition to the gold miners, groups of settlers soon began arriving in the Cariboo. One such group, a horde known as the **Overlanders,** left Ontario and Quebec with carts, horses, and oxen in summer 1862, intent on crossing the vast plains and the Rockies to British Columbia. One detachment rafted down the Fraser River, the other down the North Thompson. Both arrived in Kamloops in autumn that same year. Some continued north up the Cariboo Gold Trail, but others headed for the coast, having had more than their fill of adventure on the trip across.

Rapid Development

In addition to the Cariboo Wagon Road, other trails opened up more of the province in the early 1860s. The Hope-Princeton and Dewdney Trails into the Kootenays led to settlement in B.C.'s eastern regions. Salmon canning was also developed in the 1860s, and several canneries on both the lower Fraser and Skeena Rivers had the world market in their pockets. (You can still see one of the old canneries near Prince Rupert today.)

It wasn't until 1862 that Burrard Inlet—site of today's city of Vancouver—sprang onto the map with the building of a small lumber mill on the north shore. The region's tall, straight trees became much in demand. More lumber mills started up, and a healthy export market developed in only a few years. Farmers began to move into the area, and by the end of the 1860s a small town had been established. "Gassy Jack" Deighton started a very popular saloon on the south shore of Burrard Inlet near a lumber camp, and for some time the settlement was locally called Gastown.

After the townsite was surveyed in 1870, the name was changed to Granville. Then in 1886, the town was officially renamed Vancouver, in honor of Capt. George Vancouver. At this time, New Westminster was the official capital of the colony of British Columbia, much to the concern and disbelief of Vancouver Islanders who strongly believed Victoria should have retained the position. Two years later the capital reverted to Victoria, where it has remained ever since.

Confederation and Beyond

The next big issue to concern British Columbia was confederation. The eastern colonies had become one large dominion, and B.C. residents were invited to join. London and Ottawa both wanted B.C. to join to assist in counterbalancing the mighty U.S. power to the south. After much

PROVINCIAL ARCHIVES OF BRITISH COLUMBIA

The arrival of the first train on May 23, 1887, heralded Vancouver's emergence as the major metropolis of western Canada.

public debate, the southwesternmost colony entered the Confederation as the Province of British Columbia in July 1871—on the condition that the west coast be connected to the east by railway. Many roads were built during the 1870s, but it was the completion of the transcontinental railway in 1885 that really opened up B.C. to the rest of the country. Other railways followed, steamships plied the lakes and rivers, more roads were built, and industries—including logging, mining, farming, fishing, and tourism—started to develop.

Within the last century, B.C. has moved from roads to major multilane highways, from horses to ferries, and from gold mining to sportfishing. Yet it still attracts explorers—backcountry hikers and mountain climbers in search of untrammeled wilderness, plenty of which remains.

ECONOMY AND GOVERNMENT

ECONOMY

British Columbia's economy has always relied on resource-based activities, The first indigenous people hunted the region's abundant wildlife and fished in its trout- and salmon-filled rivers. Then whites arrived on the scene, reaping a bounty by cutting down forests for timber and slaughtering sea otters for their fur. Luckily, the province is blessed with a wealth of natural resources. In addition to timber and wildlife, B.C. holds rich reserves of minerals, petroleum, natural gas, and coal, and water for hydroelectric power is plentiful.

As increasing populations have put ever-increasing demands on these resources, conservation measures have become necessary. The province has imposed fishing and hunting seasons and limits, a freeze on rezoning agricultural land, and mandatory reforestation regulations, and has restrained hydroelectric development to protect salmon runs. By protecting its superb physical environment, the province will continue to attract outdoor enthusiasts and visitors from around the world, ensuring a steady stream of tourism revenues. But the ongoing battle between concerned conservationists and profit-motivated developers continues.

Forestry
Nearly half of British Columbia—some 43 million hectares—is forested, primarily in coniferous softwood (fir, hemlock, spruce, and pine). These forests provide about half the country's marketable wood and about 25% of the North American inventory. Along the coast the hemlock species is dominant; in the interior are forests of spruce and lodgepole pine. Douglas fir, balsam, and western red cedar are the other most valuable commercial trees. The provincial government owns 94% of the forestland, private companies own five percent, and the national government owns the remaining one percent. Private companies log much of the provincially owned forest under license from the government.

Forestry has been the mainstay of the economy in this century. But pressures on the industry are steadily increasing as the demand grows to preserve the forests for wildlife, recreation, and as a resource for following generations.

Mining
Mining for metals (such as copper, gold, zinc, silver, molybdenum, and lead), industrial minerals (sulphur, asbestos, limestone, gypsum, and others), structural materials (sand, gravel, dimension stone, and cement), and coal (most of which is exported to Japan and other Asian markets) makes up another major segment of the economy. In northeastern B.C., drilling for petroleum and natural gas also helps fuel the economy.

Tourism
Tourism has rapidly ascended in economic importance; it's now the second-largest industry and the province's largest employer. This segment of the economy should continue to grow, as more and more people become aware of B.C.'s outstanding scenery, its numerous national, provincial, historic, and regional parks, and the bountiful outdoor-recreation activities available in the province year-round.

Agriculture

Cultivated land is sparse in mountainous B.C.—only four percent of the province is arable. Nevertheless, provincial agriculture is diverse. Dairy farming predominates in the lower Fraser Valley, on southeast Vancouver Island, and in the north Okanagan-Shuswap areas. Cattle farms are mainly found in the Cariboo, Chilcotin, Kamloops, Okanagan, and Kootenay regions. Orchard crops and grapes grow in the Okanagan Valley, while berries flourish in the lower Fraser Valley. Poultry farms, vegetables, bulbs, and ornamental shrubs are found near Vancouver and Victoria; and the area around Dawson Creek is the provincial grain basket, supporting a mixture of farms and livestock ranches. The province's agriculture industry provides an estimated 55-60% of the food required for British Columbia's needs.

Fishing

The province's commercial fish farms produce oysters, five species of salmon (the most valuable crop), and trout. Commercial fishing, one of B.C.'s principal industries, concentrates on salmon, herring, halibut, cod, and sole. Canned and fresh fish are exported to markets all over the world—the province is considered the most productive fishing region in Canada. Japan is the largest export market, followed by the European Common Market countries (excluding the U.K.), the U.S., and the United Kingdom.

Recreational salt- and freshwater sportfishing for salmon, steelhead, and trout is also very popular. More than 250 licensed freshwater angling guides scattered throughout the province eagerly offer their services and expertise to both resident and nonresident fishing enthusiasts.

Industry

The sawmill and pulp-and-paper industries have long led B.C.'s manufacturing rolls, but increasingly prominent are the fabric, clothing, sports-and-rec equipment, and outdoor-furniture industries. The film industry is also developing; more and more Hollywood production companies are discovering the beauty of B.C., its studio facilities, on-site production crews, and support services, as well as the favorable exhange rate.

Shipping and Maritime Commerce

The province boasts year-round ports, deep-sea international shipping lanes, log-towing vessels, specialized freight and passenger steamers, and all the requisite marine facilities. The U.S. and Japan are B.C.'s main export and import trading partners.

GOVERNMENT

Canada is a constitutional monarchy. Its system of government is based on England's, and

commercial halibut fishermen at work

ANDREW HEMPSTEAD

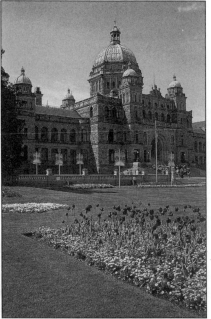

ANDREW HEMPSTEAD

parliament buildings, Victoria

session of each Parliament to make sure parliamentary rules are followed. A bill goes through three grueling sessions in the legislature—a reading, a debate, and a second reading. When all the fine print has been given the royal nod, the bill then becomes a law.

In the B.C. legislature, the lieutenant governor is at the top of the ladder. Under him are the members of the **Legislative Assembly.** Assembly members are elected for a period of up to five years, though an election for a new assembly can be called at any time by the lieutenant governor or on the advice of the premier. In the Legislative Assembly are the premier, the cabinet ministers and backbenchers, the **leader of the official opposition,** other parties, and independent members. Elections must be held every five years. All Canadian citizens and B.C. residents 19 years old and over can vote, providing they've lived in the province for at least six months.

The two main political parties are the **Social Credit Party,** which tends to advocate free enterprise and government restraint, and the **New Democratic Party,** which stands for moderate socialism and government economic and social involvement. After an election, the leader of the majority party becomes provincial premier and forms a government, selecting elected members of his or her party to head a variety of government ministries; these politicians make up the **Executive Council** or **Cabinet.** The leader of the official opposition and his or her party members form a check system by questioning government policies and actions and presenting alternatives.

Some of the responsibilities of the Legislature include administration of justice and oversight of property rights, civil rights, municipal government, crown lands, forests, water resources, and education. The laws of B.C. are administered by the cabinet, premier, and lieutenant governor, and interpreted by a **judiciary** made up of the Supreme Court of B.C., Court of Appeal, and County or Provincial Courts.

the British monarch is also king or queen of Canada. However, because it's an independent nation, the British monarchy and government have no control over the political affairs of Canada. An appointed **governor general** based in Ottawa represents the Crown, as does a **lieutenant governor** in each province. Both roles are mainly ceremonial, but their **royal assent** is required to make any bill passed by Cabinet into law.

Elected representatives debate and enact laws affecting their constituents. The head of the federal government is the **prime minister,** and the head of each provincial government is its **premier.** The **speaker** is elected at the first

THE PEOPLE

When British Columbia became a Canadian province in 1871, its population was only 36,000—27,000 of them natives. With the completion of the Canadian Pacific Railway in 1885, immigration during the early 20th century, and the rapid industrial development after WW II, the provincial population burgeoned. Between 1951 and 1971 it doubled. Today nearly 3.5 million people live in British Columbia, most of them in the southwest (more than a third in the metropolitan area of Vancouver) and on southern Vancouver Island. Overall this works out to a density of only three persons per square kilometer.

Indigenous Peoples

The coast and interior valleys of British Columbia were first occupied by native people some time after the last ice age. The interior bands were nomadic and depended heavily on hunting. They built huge 90-meter-long log houses and 20-meter-long dugout canoes, and developed a distinctive and highly decorative arts style featuring animals, mythical creatures, and oddly shaped human forms believed to be supernatural ancestors.

Prior to "discovery" by whites, Canada's west coast supported several indigenous popula-

TOTEM POLES

JANE AND BRUCE KING

Traveling through British Columbia you can't help but notice all the totem poles that decorate the landscape. Unfortunately, many have been snatched up by museums and personal collectors from around the world.

All totem poles are made of red (or occasionally yellow) cedar, and all are erected as validation of a public record or documentation of an important event. Five types of poles are believed to have evolved in the following order: house post (an integral part of the house structure), mortuary (erected as a chief's or shaman's grave post, often with the bones or ashes in a box at the top), memorial (commemorating special events), frontal (a memorial or heraldic pole), and shame poles. None is an object of worship; each tells a story or history of a person's clan or family. The figures on the pole represent either a mythical character or a zoomorphic clan symbol.

Ninstints, on the Queen Charlotte Islands, is regarded as the world's best example of an ancient Haida totem village. Throughout the south of these islands are numerous other abandoned villages with totem poles. More modern totems can be viewed at **Stanley Park,** Vancouver; **Thunderbird Park,** Victoria; **Alert Bay,** Cormorant Island; and **Kitwancool,** at the south end of the Stewart-Cassiar Highway. The **Museum of Anthropology** in Vancouver also has an excellent collection.

tions, including the **Kwakiutl, Bella Coola, Nootka, Haida,** and **Tlingit tribes.** These coastal bands lived comfortably off the land and the sea, hunting deer, beaver, bear, and sea otters, fishing for salmon, cod, and halibut, and harvesting edible kelp.

West-coast native society emphasized the material wealth of each chief and his tribe, displayed to others during special events called potlatches. The potlatch ceremonies were held to mark important moments in tribal society, such as marriages, puberty celebrations, deaths, or totem-pole raisings. The wealth of a tribe became obvious when the chief gave away enormous quantities of gifts to his guests—the nobler the guest, the better the gift. The potlatch exchange was accompanied by much feasting, speech-making, dancing, and entertainment, all of which could last many days. Stories performed by hosts garbed in elaborate costumes and masks educated, entertained, and affirmed each clan's historical continuity.

But then white settlers arrived and demanded land; villages and sites used by each local band were marked off as reserves, and the natives were expected to live only there. Urged by a strong church lobby that considered potlatches heathen affairs, the government banned potlatching in 1884—the ban lasted until 1951. During this time the costumes, masks, songs, dances, ritual items, and oratory began to disappear. These two factors, plus the influence of guns, alcohol, and disease introduced by whites, started the breakdown of indigenous society.

Today the native peoples of the north Pacific coast have adopted the technology and the ways of the European, though they still remain a distinct group, contributing to and enriching the culture of British Columbia. A social barrier still exists between the native and the nonnative. Much of the traditional social organization is gone, and many of the old obligations based on kinship and heredity have changed or disappeared (e.g., the chief is now elected). Yet native artisans continue to produce traditional woodworks and other handicrafts.

Nonnatives

British Columbia is a young province; almost 40% of its population is under the age of 40. Most British Columbians are of British origin, followed by those of German, Chinese, and French descent. To really get the British feeling, just spend some time in Victoria—a city that has retained its original English customs and traditions from days gone by.

Asians have made up a significant percentage of the population since the mid-1800s, when they came in search of gold. More recently, the province saw an influx of settlers from Hong Kong in anticipation of the 1997 transfer of control of that city from Britain to China.

Language

The main language spoken throughout the province is English, though almost six percent of the population also speaks French, Canada's second official language. All government information is written in both English and French throughout Canada.

The natives of British Columbia fall into 10 major ethnic groups by language: Nootka (west Vancouver Island), Coast Salish (southwest B.C.), Interior Salish (southern interior), Kootenay (in the Kootenay region), Athabascan (in the central and northeast regions), Bella Coola and Northern Kwakiutl (along the central west coast), Tsimshian (in the northwest), Haida (on the Queen Charlotte Islands), and Inland Tlingit (in the far northwest corner of the province). However, most natives still speak English more than their mother tongue.

ON THE ROAD
RECREATION

The great outdoors: British Columbia certainly has plenty of it. The province encompasses some 948,600 square kilometers of land area and a convoluted coastline totalling 25,000 kilometers. With spectacular scenery around every bend, millions of hectares of parkland, and an abundance of wildlife, the province is an outdoorsperson's fantasy come true. Hiking, mountain climbing, fishing, hunting, boating, canoeing, whitewater rafting, scuba diving, downhill and cross-country skiing—it's all here. For specific recreation information, contact **Tourism British Columbia,** P.O. Box 9830, Stn. Provincial Government, Victoria, BC V8W 9W5, tel. (250) 387-1642 or (800) 663-6000.

PARKS

Some of B.C.'s most outstanding scenic delights, wildlife reserves, and places of historic interest are protected as national, provincial, or historic parks. They range in size from less than one hectare to nearly a million hectares, providing almost unlimited recreation opportunities.

National Parks
British Columbia holds six national parks. **Pacific Rim National Park** protects a stretch of Vancouver Island's rugged west coast, offering long beaches, remote islands, and the famous West Coast Trail to explore. In the east of the province, **Kootenay** and **Yoho National Parks** form a part of the UNESCO Rocky Mountains World Heritage Site; the two spectacular mountain parks lie just across the Continental Divide from the more famous Banff and Jasper National Parks in neighboring Alberta. Also protecting a mountainous landscape are **Glacier** and **Mount Revelstoke National Parks** along the Trans-Canada Highway. The most remote of B.C.'s national parks is **Gwaii Haanas** on the Queen Charlotte Islands. No roads access this park, which encompasses the southern half of an archipelago renowned the world over for ancient Haida villages.

The cost of entering a national park is $5 per person per day to a maximum of $10 per vehicle; a **Great Western Pass** valid for one year in all British Columbia and Alberta National Parks costs $35 per person to a maximum of $70 per vehicle.

Provincial Parks

British Columbia boasts close to 500 provincial parks, which range in size from one hectare to nearly one million. Many are day-use areas, others have campgrounds, but all have one thing in common—they protect a particularly scenic area, a unique natural feature, a wildlife habitat, or maybe a fish-filled lake.

Among the best of these parks are: **Cypress Provincial Park,** on Vancouver's city limits and offering great views; **Carmanah Pacific Provincial Park,** protecting a magnificent stand of old-growth forest; **Manning Provincial Park,** a high alpine area of snowcapped peaks and colorful flower-filled meadows; **Kokanee Glacier Provincial Park,** named for its spectacular icefield; **Mount Assiniboine Provincial Park,** a rugged Rocky Mountain wilderness perfect for extending hiking trips; **Mount Robson Provincial Park,** protecting the Canadian Rockies' highest peak; **Bowron Lake Provincial Park,** famous for its wilderness canoe route; and **Naikoon Provincial Park,** on the Queen Charlotte Islands.

In recent years, the government has continued to set aside land in provincial parks, recreation areas, wilderness areas, and wilderness conservancies. The establishment of these preserves has mostly been due to lobbying by local environmental groups, such as the Valhalla Wilderness Society. Recent additions to the park system that were aided by such lobbying efforts include **Valhalla Provincial Park,** a remote wilderness area in the heart of the Kootenays; **Khutzeymateen Provincial Park,** an important coastal grizzly bear habitat; and, in the province's extreme northwest corner, **Tatshensheni-Alsek Wilderness Park,** part of an 8.5-million-hectare UNESCO World Heritage Site.

Forest Service Lands

Over half of British Columbia is forested and under the control of the Forest Service. Many recreation areas have been provided on forest land; these have limited facilities. Get more information on Forest Service recreation areas, forest roads, safety, and possible fire closures from Forest Service offices or information centers throughout the province.

OUTDOOR SPORTS

Hiking

Just about everywhere you go in British Columbia you'll find good hiking opportunities—from short, easy walks in city and regional parks to long, strenuous hikes in wilderness parks.

The national parks in the **Rocky Mountains** are great places to hike. You'll find short trails leading to waterfalls, lakes, rock formations, and viewpoints, and longer trails wandering high into alpine meadows tangled with wildflowers, past turquoise lakes, and up to snow-dusted peaks providing breathtaking views. Alpine huts are provided at regular intervals along wilderness trails.

Perhaps the best-known of British Columbia's hikes lies not in the Rockies but along the wild and remote west shore of Vancouver Island; backpackers return time and again to the **West Coast Trail,** an unforgettable, 77-km trek through Pacific Rim National Park.

In addition to the national parks, the provincial parks contain outstanding scenery and wildlife, crystal-clear lakes and rivers, and established trails that are generally well maintained and easy to follow.

To get the most out of a hiking trip, peruse the hiking section of any major bookstore—many books have been written on British Columbian hiking trails. Before setting off on a longer hike, study the trail guides and a topographical map of the area. Leave details of your intended route and itinerary with a relative or friend. And try to travel in groups of at least two in the backcountry, in case anyone needs help.

The **Great B.C. Adventure Company,** P.O. Box 39116, Vancouver, BC V6R 1G0, tel. (604) 684-7284, runs guided hikes throughout the summer for clients of all fitness levels. Among the company's offerings: a seven-day package on the West Coast Trail.

Cycling

Cycling is a great way to explore British Columbia. The casual pace allows riders time to stop and appreciate the scenery, wildlife, and flowers that can easily be overlooked at high speeds. Some of the most popular areas for cycling trips are the **Southern Gulf Islands** between Vancouver Island and the mainland (quiet, laid-back, loads of sunshine, rural scenery, and lots of artists), the **east coast of Vancouver Island** (following the Strait of Georgia past lazy beaches and bustling towns), the **Kootenays** (forest-clad mountains, deep lakes, curious old gold- and silver-mining communities, and ghost towns—good mountain-bike country), and the **Rockies** (outstanding mountain scenery second to none, abundant wildlife often right beside the highways, hot springs, and hiking trails). Rocky Mountain routes suit the intermediate to advanced cyclist.

For information on touring, racing, books, bicycle routes, or clubs, contact **Cycling B.C.,** Suite 332, 1367 W. Broadway, Vancouver, BC V6H 4A9, tel. (604) 737-3034; the **Outdoor Recreation Council of B.C.,** Suite 334, 1367 W. Broadway, Vancouver, BC V6H 4A9, tel. (604) 737-3034; or the **B.C. Safety Council,** tel. (250) 420-4110. The Outdoor Recreation Council also publishes a series of maps covering much of British Columbia. These maps can by purchased directly from the council or at many sporting-goods stores and bookstores.

Several companies in the province offer cycling trips and tours, among them: **Benno's Adventure Tours,** 3/1975 Maple St., Vancouver, BC V6J 3S9, tel. (604) 738-5105, which offers eight-day trips through B.C. and the Canadian Rockies, with bus lifts between the most spectacular sections; **Whistler Backroads Moun-**

tain Bike Adventures, P.O. Box 643, Whistler, BC V0N 1B0, tel. (604) 923-3111; **Okanagan Cycle Tours,** 2/516 Papineau St., Penticton, BC V2A 4X6, tel. (250) 493-BIKE; and **Rocky Mountain Cycle Tours,** P.O. Box 1978, Canmore, AB T0L 0M0, tel. (403) 678-6770 or (800) 661-2453.

Canoeing, Kayaking, and Whitewater Rafting

Canoes are a traditional form of transportation along British Columbia's numerous lakes and rivers. You can rent one at many of the more popular lakes, but if you bring your own you can slip into any body of water whenever you please, taking in the scenery and viewing wildlife from water level. One of the most popular canoe routes is in **Bowron Lake Provincial Park,** where a 117-km-long circuit leads through a chain of lakes in the Cariboo Mountains. Shorter but no less challenging is the **Powell Forest Canoe Route,** on the Sunshine Coast. Other, less-traveled destinations include **Slocan Lake, Wells Gray Provincial Park,** and the **Stikine River.** For information on canoe routes, courses, and clubs, contact the **Outdoor Recreation Council of B.C.,** Suite 334, 1367 W. Broadway, Vancouver, BC V6H 4A9, tel. (604) 737-3058.

Anywhere suitable for canoeing is also prime kayaking territory, although most keen kayakers look for whitewater excitement. The best wilderness kayaking experiences are in the north, where access can be difficult but crowds are

Experience the thrills of whitewater rafting on British Columbia's many rivers.

WILD WATER ADVENTURES

minimal. The **Stikine River** is challenging, with one stretch—the Grand Canyon of the Stikine—successfully run only a handful of times. The province's long coastline is great for sea kayaking, and rentals are available in most coastal communities. The **Gulf Islands** are ideal for kayakers of all experience levels, while destinations such as **Desolation Sound,** the **Broken Group Islands,** and the **Queen Charlotte Islands** are the domain of experienced paddlers.

The best and easiest way to experience a whitewater-rafting trip is with a qualified guide. Most companies offer half- and full-day trips, and many also offer extended trips. Close to Vancouver, the **Green, Fraser, Nahatlatch,** and **Thompson Rivers** are run commercially. In the Rockies, the **Kicking Horse River** provides the thrills.

Freshwater Fishing

The province's freshwater anglers fish primarily for trout—mostly rainbow trout, but also Dolly Varden, lake, brook, brown, and cutthroat trout. One particular type of rainbow trout, the large anadromous **steelhead,** is renowned as a fighting fish and considered by locals to be the ultimate fishing challenge. Salmon are also abundant in the province; several seagoing species come up B.C.'s rivers to spawn, and a landlocked, freshwater species—the kokanee—inhabits B.C.'s lakes.

Fishing guides, tours, lodges (from rustic to luxurious), and packages are available throughout the province; one is sure to suit you. Expect to pay from $30 an hour or $100-300 a day for a guide, and up to several thousand dollars for several days at a luxury lodge with all meals and guided fishing included.

Fishing licenses are required, and prices vary according to your age and place of residence. Canadian residents pay $24 for a freshwater adult license, good for one year. Nonresidents pay $41 for a one-year license, or $25 for a six-day license. Separate licenses are required for steelhead and Kootenay Lake rainbow trout. For more information contact Recreational Fisheries, Ministry of Environment, Lands, and Parks, Parliament Buildings, Victoria, BC V8V 1X4, tel. (250) 387-4573, and request the *British Columbia Freshwater Fishing Regulations Synopsis.*

Ocean Fishing

The several species of **Pacific salmon** inhabiting provincial waters are highly prized by anglers. The chinook salmon in particular is the trophy fish of choice. The largest chinooks—those weighing in excess of 12 kg—are sometimes called tyee salmon. Canuck, coho, and pink salmon are mainstays of British Columbia's tidal sport fishery. Other species sought by saltwater fishermen include halibut, rockfish, cod, perch, snapper, sea-run cutthroat trout, and flatfish.

The Queen Charlotte Islands and the Vancouver Island communities of Campbell River, Duncan, Courtenay, and Port Alberni are among the most popular saltwater fishing destinations in the province.

A resident tidal-water sportfishing license, good for one year, costs $39 for adults and seniors, under 16 free. Nonresident licenses are $21 for five days. When fish-tagging programs are on, you may be required to make a note of the date, location, and method of capture, or to record on the back of your license statistical information on the fish you catch. Read the current rules and regulations. For further information contact the **Department of Fisheries and Oceans,** Station 415, 555 W. Hastings St., Vancouver, BC V6B 5G3, tel. (604) 666-6331.

Boating

British Columbia's 25,000 km of coastline, in particular the sheltered, island-dotted Strait of Georgia between Vancouver Island and the mainland, is a boatie's paradise. Along it are sheltered coves, sandy beaches, beautiful marine parks, and facilities specifically designed for boaters—many accessible only by water. One of the most beautiful marine parks is **Desolation Sound,** north of Powell River—locals claim it's one of the world's best cruising grounds. Many of the enormous freshwater lakes inland are also excellent places for boating.

For the entire rundown on facilities for boaters, pick up a copy of the invaluable *Pacific Yachting Cruising Services Directory,* put out by *Pacific Yachting* magazine. In it are lists of boatbuilders, boatyards, charter companies, boating schools, chart and map sources, sail makers, water taxis, yacht clubs, marinas, and boater-oriented resorts for each coastal region, along with an abundance of other useful information. If you can't find one in the Visitor Info Centres, write to Special Interest Publications, Division of Maclean Hunter, Suite 900, 1130 W. Pender St., Vancouver, BC V6E 4A4. For more detailed information on boating in the province, and for details on vessel entry points and customs regulations, contact **BC Parks,** 2nd Floor, 800 Johnson St., Victoria, BC V8V 1X4, tel. (250) 387-5002.

Scuba Diving

Some of the world's most varied and spectacular cold-water diving lies off the coast of British Columbia. Diving is best in winter, when you can expect up to 40 meters visibility. The diverse marinelife includes sponges, anemones, soft corals, rockfish (china, vermilion, and canary), rock scallops, and cukes. Plenty of shipwrecks also dot the underwater terrain. First of all, get your hands on the British Columbia diver's bible, *141 Dives in the Protected Waters of Washington and British Columbia,* by Betty Pratt-Johnson. *Diver* magazine is another good source of local information; its scuba directory lists retail stores, resorts, charter boats, and other services. Then head for Vancouver, where a quick flip through the telephone directory lets you know that scuba diving is alive and well in this community. The city's many scuba shops have everything you need, and they're excellent sources of information on all the best spots along Georgia Strait. They can also usually tell you who is chartering what, and when.

The most popular dive sites are off the Gulf Islands, Nanaimo, Campbell River, Telegraph Cove, Port Hardy, and Powell River (the scuba-diving capital of Canada). Many of the coastal communities along Vancouver Island and the Sunshine Coast have dive shops with gear rentals and air tanks, and many can put you in touch with charter dive boats and guides.

Hunting

Bear, moose, elk, bighorn sheep, deer, and waterfowl are all hunted in British Columbia. Nonresidents hunting big game must be accompanied by a licensed B.C. guide. A nonresident of B.C. who is a resident of Canada may go with a B.C. resident instead of hiring a guide, subject to certain restrictions; contact BC Environment for details. You don't need to hire a guide if you're hunting small game or game birds.

Nonresident hunting licenses are available only from the Wildlife Branch, Ministry of Environment, Land, and Parks, 780 Blanshard St., Victoria, BC V8V 1X4, tel. (250) 387-9739. Before hunting, be sure to read the latest *British Columbian Hunting and Trapping Regulations Synopsis,* available from the above office or from sporting goods stores.

Golfing

British Columbia's climate is ideal for golfing, especially on Vancouver Island, where the sport can be enjoyed year-round. Many of the province's 250 courses are set in spectacular mountain, ocean, or lake settings. Municipal courses offer the lowest green fees, generally $5-15, but the semiprivate, private, and resort courses usually boast the most spectacular locations.

On Vancouver Island, the venerable **Royal Colwood Golf Club** is one of the province's oldest courses, and is regarded as among the top 10 courses in all of Canada. Not far away, on the coast at Oak Bay, the private **Victoria Golf Club** provides a great golfing experience if you can get a game.

In Whistler Valley you'll find **Chateau Whistler, Whistler, Nicklaus North,** and **Big Sky.** Green fees at these four great resort courses range $60-110.

The biggest concentration of golf courses in the interior is in the Okanagan Valley, with the top four there being **Summerland Golf and Country Club, Gallagher's Canyon Golf Resort, Quail Ridge Golf and Country Club,** and **Predator Ridge Golf Resort.**

Skiing

Most of the developed winter recreation areas are in the southern third of the province. Whether you're a total beginner or an advanced daredevil, British Columbian ski resorts have a slope to suit you. The price of lift tickets is generally reasonable, and at the smaller, lesser-known resorts, you don't have to spend half your day lining up for the lifts.

The major resorts are: **Grouse Mountain,** in Vancouver; **Whistler** and **Blackcomb,** north of Vancouver; **Forbidden Plateau** and **Mount Washington,** on Vancouver Island; **Apex Alpine,** near Penticton; **Big White,** southeast of Kelowna; **Silver Star,** near Vernon; **Sun Peaks,** north of Kamloops; **Whitewater** and **Red Mountain,** near Nelson; **Snow Valley,** near Fernie; **Kimberley Mountain,** near Kimberley; **Panorama Mountain,** near Invermere; **Ski Smithers,** near Smithers; and **Powder King,** north of Prince George.

Alternatives to resort skiing are also available. If you're an intermediate or advanced skier, you can go heli-skiing in the mind-boggling scenery and deep, untracked powder of the Coast and Chilcotin Ranges, the central Cariboo Mountains, the Bugaboos, and the Rockies. One of the largest operators, **CMH Heli-Skiing,** P.O. Box 1660, Banff, AB T0L 0C0, tel. (403) 762-7100, offers complete packages that

include accommodations and a guaranteed 100,000 vertical feet of skiing.

Another, less-expensive alternative is to hook up with one of the many Sno-Cat operations in the province. Sno-Cats are tracked, all-terrain vehicles that can transport skiers up through the snow to virgin ski slopes in high-country wilderness. Revelstoke is the Sno-Cat capital of the province. Many lodges offer package ski tours, which can be arranged through travel agents or through Tourism British Columbia offices.

Cross-country skiers can strap on their skis and blaze their own trails just about anywhere—particularly good skiing is found around the communities along the Yellowhead Highway and in

the Rockies. Many downhill resorts offer ski-touring packages and guided trips, too.

For more information on all the ski facilities in the province, call Tourism British Columbia, tel. (800) 663-6000, and request the latest *Ski Vacations* booklet.

ENTERTAINMENT

Museums
The best way to gain an appreciation of British Columbia's unique and colorful history is by visiting its museums. Almost every town has a small museum showcasing the surrounding area, but it's the larger facilities that attract the most attention. In the capital, Victoria, don't miss the **Royal British Columbia Museum**, a magnificent facility that catalogs the province's entire natural and human history. In Vancouver, the **Museum of Anthropology** boasts a fantastic collection of totem poles and other native artifacts. Outside of the major cities, museums generally reflect local heritage; pick of the bunch are the **Historic O'Keefe Ranch** outside Vernon, the **Museum of Northern British Columbia** in Prince Rupert, and the **Haida Gwaii Museum** out on the Queen Charlotte Islands.

Performing Arts
British Columbia's largest city boasts a lively performing-arts community; more than 30 theater groups call Vancouver home, and the city also supports an opera, an orchestra, and Ballet British Columbia. The city's magnificent **Ford Centre** hosts world-class productions. In addition to Vancouver, Victoria, Kamloops, and Prince George also have noteworthy performing-arts communities.

Spectator Sports
Canada's favorite winter spectator sport is **ice hockey.** Vancouver is home to the Canucks, a National Hockey League (NHL) franchise that figures in the play-off series most years. Van-

couver also has a franchise in the National Basketball League and a farm team for the California Angels baseball team. The CART Indy auto-racing series makes an annual stop in Vancouver.

SHOPPING FOR NATIVE ARTS AND CRAFTS

Indigenous artistry tends to fall into one of two categories: "arts" such as woodcarving and painting, argillite carving, jade and silverwork, and totem restoration (all generally attended to by the men); and "handicrafts" such as basketry, weaving, beadwork, skinwork, sewing, and knitting (generally created by the women). Today, all of these arts and crafts contribute significant income to native communities.

Painting and woodcarving are probably the most recognized artforms of the northern west-coast tribes. Throughout B.C.—in museums and people's homes, outdoors, and of course in all the shops—you can see brightly colored carved totems, canoes, paddles, fantastic masks, and ceremonial rattles, feast dishes, bowls, and spoons. Fabulous designs, many featuring animals or mythical legends, are also painstakingly painted in bright primary colors on paper. You can buy limited-edition, high-quality prints of these paintings at many Indian craft outlets. They are more reasonable in cost than carvings, yet just as stunning when effectively framed.

Basketry comes in a variety of styles and materials. Watch for decorative cedar-root (fairly rare) and cedar-bark baskets, still made on the west coast of Vancouver Island; spruce-root baskets from the Queen Charlotte Islands; and beautiful, functional, birch-bark baskets from the Hazelton area, between Prince George and Prince Rupert.

Beaded and fringed moccasins, jackets, vests, and gloves are available at most craft outlets. And all outdoorspersons should con-

DOVER PUBLICATIONS, INC.

sider forking out for a heavy, water-resistant, raw sheep-wool sweater; they're generally white or gray with a black design, and much in demand because they're warm, good in the rain, rugged, and last longer than one lifetime. One of the best places to get your hands on one is the Cowichan Valley on Vancouver Island, although you can also find them in the Fraser Valley from Vancouver to Lytton and in native craft outlets. Expect to pay around $90-160 for the real thing, more in tourist shops.

Carved argillite (black slate) miniature totem poles, brooches, ashtrays, and other small items, highly decorated with geometric and animal designs, are created exclusively by the Haida on the Queen Charlotte Islands; the argillite comes from a quarry near Skidegate and can only be used by the Skidegate band. You can find argillite carvings in Skidegate and in craft shops in Prince Rupert, Victoria, and Vancouver. Silverwork is also popular, and some of the best is created by the Haida. Particularly notable is the work of Bill Reid, a Haida artist living in Vancouver. Jade jewelry can be seen in the Lillooet and Lytton areas.

FESTIVALS AND EVENTS

British Columbia seems to have at least one festival or event going on somewhere in the province every day of the year. To make sure you don't miss anything, stop by one of the province's many Visitor Info Centres at the beginning of your trip and pick up a current copy of *Arts and Entertainment,* a brochure produced by Tourism BC.

Many of the most popular festivals are held during summer, the peak visitor season, but special events and artistic performances take place year-round. Many towns hold winter events featuring zany happenings such as snow golf, bed races on ice, and anything they can come up with that's good for a laugh. The following section lists some provincial event highlights; see the festivals and events sections of the particular town listings in this book for more.

Vancouver and Vicinity

In late May or early June, start off the season with the **Vancouver Children's Festival** at Vanier Park. Around the last week of June, check out the **du Maurier International Jazz Festival,** held at venues all across town. July is a festival-filled month, starting on the first with **Canada Day** celebrations at scattered locations. The following week the **Vancouver Folk Festival** comes to town. Also in July, look for the Nanaimo-to-Vancouver **Bathtub Race** and the **White Rock Sandcastle Competition,** at White Rock Beach. Abbotsford hosts the **Abbotsford International Airshow** in August.

Vancouver Island

In Victoria, one of the biggest summer events is the **Victoria International Festival,** a multicultural shindig at McPherson Playhouse and various other locations in town. The event runs mid-July to late August. North of Victoria, events to watch for include **Chorfest,** a weekend of choral music at Port Alberni, and a **Bluegrass Festival** at Coombs, both in May. In May and June, the **B.C. Festival of the Arts** comes to Duncan.

July is a very busy month. Ganges, on Salt Spring Island, throws its **Festival of Arts;** Courtenay presents **Summer Music From Courtenay;** Ucluelet and Tofino celebrate their **Pacific Rim Summer Festival;** and the walls of Chemainus come alive during the **Chemainus Festival of Murals.** In July and August, Nanaimo presents the very popular **Shakespeare Plus.** In August, attend the artistic **Filberg Festival,** a juried craft show at Comox, or kick up your heels at the **Hornby Midsummer Festival** on Hornby Island.

Okanagan and the Kootenays

In the Okanagan, major events include the **Penticton Peach Festival** in late July; the **Kelowna International Festival of the Arts** in September; and the delicious **Okanagan Wine Festival,** held throughout the valley in late September and early October.

In the Kootenays, June's big events include Castlegar's **Sunfest** and Cranbrook's **Sam Steele Days.** In July, Kimberley attracts a mass of accordion players and appreciators to the annual **International Old Time Accordion Championship.** Rossland gets into the event action with **Rossland Golden City Days** in September.

Central and Northern British Columbia

In the Cariboo, kids take center stage in June; take them to the **South Cariboo Children's Festival** at 100 Mile House, and the **Children's Festival** at Williams Lake. In July the **Country Bluegrass Festival** is held on the Indian Grounds in Kamloops, and the city also celebrates **Sunfest,** with tons of beach events.

If you're up north in summer, check out Prince Rupert's **Fine Arts Festival** in May, and Dawson Creek's **Tentertainment** in June. Also in June, Prince Rupert celebrates **Seafest** with a multitude of zany water-based events; Chetwynd presents its annual **Peace Country Bluegrass Music Festival;** and Smithers gets into the folk-music action with a **Midsummer Festival.** The first weekend of July, Williams Lake hosts one of the province's biggest **rodeos.** Also in July, Dawson Creek celebrates

Mile Zero Days. In August, check out **Simon Fraser Days** in Prince George, and the **International Airshow** at Vanderhoof.

Holidays

British Columbia celebrates 10 statutory holidays, on which most businesses are closed. But you can always find open some restaurants, pubs, and a few stores selling basic necessities.

The officially recognized holidays are: **New Year's Day** (1 January), **Good Friday** (late March or early April), **Victoria Day** (the 24 May weekend, or the closest Monday; celebrated in Victoria), **Canada Day** (1 July), **B.C. Day** (the first Monday in August), **Labour Day** (the first Monday in September), **Thanksgiving** (early October), **Remembrance Day** (11 November), **Christmas** (25 December), and **Boxing Day** (26 December).

ACCOMMODATIONS, CAMPING, AND FOOD

HOTELS AND MOTELS

The best guide to hotels and motels is the free *Accommodations* book put out annually by Tourism BC. It's available at all information centers or by calling (604) 663-6000 or (800) 663-6000. The book lists hotels, motels, lodges, resorts, bed and breakfasts, and campgrounds. It contains no ratings, simply listings with facilities and rates.

All rates quoted in this handbook are for a double room in the high season (summer, except in ski towns). Expect to pay less for downtown accommodations on weekends, and less outside of the busy July-August period. To all rates quoted, you must add the following taxes: an eight-percent Hotel and Motel Room Tax, a two-percent Tourism Tax, and a seven-percent Goods and Services Tax. The latter is refundable to non-Canadian visitors.

Prices for a basic motel room in a small town start at $35 s, $40 d. In Vancouver and Victoria expect to pay from double this amount for the least expensive rooms. The most luxurious lodgings in the province—the Pan Pacific Hotel Van-

couver, Victoria's grand old Empress Hotel, or any one of Whistler's resort hotels, for example—charge over $200 per night for a basic room. Room rates outside the two major cities fluctuate greatly. For example, few lodgings on Vancouver Island charge less than $60, but along the TransCanada Highway, in places like Kamloops and Revelstoke, you can pay as little as $40 for a room. Try to plan ahead for summer travel and book as far in advance as possible, especially for accommodations in Vancouver and Prince Rupert, on Vancouver Island, and on the Queen Charlotte Islands.

BED AND BREAKFASTS

Bed-and-breakfast accommodations are found throughout British Columbia, and staying at a B&B is a great way to meet British Columbians. Prices in Vancouver and Victoria generally range $40-110 s, $50-130 d, which includes either a continental or cooked breakfast. Bed and breakfast agencies maintain lists of offerings, including city homes, rural homes, homes with sea views, or farms where you can join in the activities. Call and tell them what you're looking for and the price you're prepared to pay, and they'll find the right place for you. Get details from the following associations: **AAA Home Away From Home B&B Agency,** 1441 Howard Ave., Vancouver, BC V5B 3S2, tel. (604) 294-1760; **AB&C B&B of Vancouver,** 4390 Frances St., Vancouver, BC V5C 2R3, tel. (604) 298-8815 or (800) 488-1941; **All Seasons Bed and Breakfast Agency,** 9858 5th St., Suite 101, Sidney, BC V8L 2X7, tel. (250) 655-7173; **Beachside B&B Registry,** 4208 Evergreen Ave., West Vancouver, BC V7V 1H1, tel. (604) 922-7773 or (800) 563-3311; **City and Sea Bed and Breakfast Registry,** 102/701 Esquimalt Rd., Victoria, BC V9A 3L5, tel. (250) 388-5556; and **Westway Accommodation Registry,** P.O. Box 48950, Bentall Centre, Vancouver, BC V7X 1A8, tel. (604) 273-8293. Many bed and breakfasts are listed in the *Accommodations* guide, and local information centers can also provide information.

HOSTELS

Staying in hostels is an enjoyable and inexpensive way to travel through the province. Generally, you need to provide your own sleeping bag and gear, but most supply extra bedding (if needed) at no charge.

Hostelling International operates 15 hostels in British Columbia, including two in Vancouver and one in each of the following locations: Victoria, Salt Spring Island, Chemainus, Alert Bay, Whistler, Penticton, Kelowna, Nelson, Fernie, Yoho National Park, Squilax, Kamloops, and along the Stewart-Cassiar Highway at Iskut. For a dorm bed, members of Hostelling International pay $10-17 per night, nonmembers pay $14-20; single and double rooms are often available, but are more expensive.

CAMPGROUNDS

Almost every town in British Columbia has at least one campground, often with showers and water, electricity, and sewer hookups. Prices range $6-14 in smaller towns, and up to $25 in the cities and more popular tourist destinations. If you're planning a summer trip to Vancouver Is-

land, the Sunshine Coast, Whistler, or the Okanagan Valley, you should try to book in advance. At other times and places, advance reservations aren't usually necessary.

National parks provide some of the nicest campgrounds in B.C. All have picnic tables, fire grates, toilets, and fresh drinking water, although only some provide showers. Prices range $7-17 depending on facilities and services. They are all open through summer, with each park having one area designated for winter camping. Parks Canada now charges $6 per person per night for backcountry camping in national parks.

Many **provincial parks** have campgrounds; rates range $6-15.50 a night depending on facilities, most of which are basic. Reserve a spot at the most popular provincial parks by calling BC Parks' Discover Camping hotline at (800) 689-9025. Reservations are taken between 1 March and 15 September, for dates up to three months in advance. The reservation fee is $6 per night, to a maximum of $18, and is in addition to applicable camping fees.

The least expensive camping spots are at the hundreds of **Forest Service Recreation Sites** scattered throughout British Columbia. Few are signposted and facilities comprise nothing more than pit toilets and a few picnic tables. For a list of site locations, pick up a Forest Service recreation map from local information centers.

Commercial and provincial park campgrounds are listed in Tourism BC's invaluable *Accommodations* guide, available at all information centers or by calling (800) 663-6000.

FOOD AND DRINK

British Columbia is not world-renowned for its culinary delights, but the province does offer excellent **Pacific Northwest cuisine,** meaning an abundance of seafood and fresh produce prepared with an Asian influence. Otherwise, Canadian food is similar to American food—in general, bland and not very interesting. Burgers, hot dogs, chicken-in-a-box, and ready-made sandwiches are available across the province. In the large cities, you'll also find fine-dining restaurants and gourmet continental cuisine. Vancouver is the best place to eat; the city's 2,000-plus restaurants serve a wide variety of ethnic foods

ANDREW HEMPSTEAD

Kokanee, British Columbia's best-loved beer, is brewed in Creston.

and standard Canadiana at a complete range of prices. Victoria also enjoys its share of good restaurants, but has the reputation for serving predominantly British food in as British an atmosphere as you could imagine outside of Britain.

Drink

British Columbian **wine** is highly regarded, having won awards throughout the world. The province is best known for icewines, made by a process in which the grapes aren't harvested until *after* the first frost; the frost splits the skins and the fermentation process begins with the grapes still on the vine. The largest concentration of vineyards is in the Okanagan Valley, where you'll find more than 30 wineries ranging from large-scale commercial operations to small plots of grapes grown on hobby farms. Vancouver Island is also home to a number of wineries. Expect to pay $14-20 for a bottle of locally produced wine.

All the popular Canadian and American beers are available at bars and liquor stores. **Kokanee,** brewed in Creston and widely available throughout British Columbia, is a fine-tasting beer that should be taken on all camping trips.

TRANSPORTATION

GETTING THERE

Air

Vancouver International Airport is British Columbia's main gateway and Canada's second-busiest airport. Regularly scheduled service to and from Vancouver is offered by major airlines throughout the world, including **Air Canada, American Airlines, British Airways, Canadian Airlines, Cathay Pacific, Continental, Delta Airlines, Japan Air Lines, KLM, Korean Air, Lufthansa, Qantas, Singapore Airlines,** and **United Airlines.**

In today's topsy-turvy world of air travel, the first step in getting to British Columbia is to find yourself a travel agent who takes the time to call around, does some research to get you the best fare, and helps you take advantage of any available special offers or promotional deals. The next best attack is to call the airlines in person (in the U.S. most have toll-free telephone numbers) and compare fares; ask if they have any specials. Also look in the travel sections of major newspapers—particularly in the Sunday editions—where budget fares and package deals are frequently advertised.

The further in advance you buy your ticket, the lower the cost, but expect a number of potentially nasty restrictions on the cheaper fares. Advance-Purchase Excursion (APEX) fares are the cheapest, and usually require payment 7-28 days in advance. Traveling in the off-season always saves you money, so try to pick dates that are out of the high-season period (summer) at both ends. All flights vary tremendously in price according to the time of year and the specials the airlines are currently running.

Rail

VIA Rail provides passenger-train service right across Canada. Rail travel opened up the province to the world a little over 100 years ago, but had lost much of its appeal by the beginning of this decade thanks to drastically reduced airfares. Today, however, improved service, a refitting of carriages, and a competitive pricing structure have helped trains regain popularity.

At Jasper (Alberta) the westbound transcontinental line divides, with one set of tracks continuing slightly north and west to Prince Rupert and the other heading southwest to Vancouver. Service on both routes operates three times a week in either direction and provides four classes of travel: **Coach, Manor, Chateau Sleeping Car,** and **Silver and Blue.** Silver and Blue class is the most luxurious, providing extra amenities and use of a dome car reserved exclusively for passengers in this class.

Discounts of 25-40% apply to travel in all classes Oct.-June. Those over 60 and under 25 receive a 10% discount that can be combined with other seasonal fares. Students receive a 50% discount year-round. Check for advance-purchase restrictions on all discount tickets. The **Canrailpass** allows unlimited travel anywhere on the VIA Rail system for 13 days within any given 30-day period. During high season (15 May-15 September) the pass is $535; the rest of the year it's $365. Even if you plan limited train travel the pass is an excellent deal; the regular Toronto-Edmonton one-way fare alone is $375.57.

Pick up a train schedule at any VIA Rail station or call (800) 561-8630 within western Canada; in other Canadian locations contact your local VIA Rail Station. In the U.S. call (800) 561-3949 or any travel agent. Other general sales agents include Walshes World, 92 Pitt St., Sydney, tel. (02) 9232-7499 or (800) 22-7122; Walshes World, 2nd Floor, Dingwall Building, 87 Queen St., Auckland, tel. (09) 379-3708; Canada Reise Dienst, Rathausplatz 2, 2070 Ahrensburg/Hamburg, tel. 4904102-51167; Long-Haul Leisurail, P.O. Box 113, Peterborough PE1 1LE, England, tel. (0733) 33-5599.

Rocky Mountaineer Railtours, tel. (604) 606-7245 or (800) 665-7245, runs a luxurious rail trip between Vancouver and Banff or Jasper, through the spectacular interior mountain ranges of British Columbia. Fare is $565 per person one-way. Travel is in either direction, and the trains run during daylight hours only so you don't miss anything. Rates include overnight accommodations in Kamloops, two breakfasts, two lunches, and light snacks. During value season (late May and late September), fares are reduced $100. A single supplement of $50 applies to all trips.

Bus

Bus travel throughout Canada is easy with **Greyhound,** tel. (604) 482-8747 or (800) 661-8747. The company offers TransCanada Highway service from Toronto, Winnipeg, Regina, and Calgary (Alberta), through Kamloops to Vancouver, as well as a more southerly route from Calgary through Cranbrook and the Kootenays to Vancouver. Among the northern routes: Edmonton and Jasper (Alberta) southwest to Vancouver or west to Prince Rupert; and Grande Prairie (Alberta) northwest through Dawson Creek to Whitehorse (Yukon). From the thousands of depots throughout North America, you can go just about anywhere you desire. Reservations are not necessary—just turn up when you want to go, buy your ticket, and kick back. As long as you use your ticket within 30 days, you can stop over wherever the bus stops and stay as long as you want.

When calling for information, ask about any special deals—sometimes they offer excursion fares to certain destinations that save you money if you buy a roundtrip ticket, other times they offer good prices if you buy your ticket a month in advance. The **Greyhound Canada Pass** is valid on all Greyhound routes in Canada. It is sold in periods of seven days ($212), 15 days ($277), 30 days ($373.43), and 60 days ($480.43). It must be purchased seven days in advance and is nonrefundable. You can buy the pass at any depot.

Ferry

One of the most pleasurable ways to get your first view of British Columbia is from sea level. Many scheduled ferry services cross from Washington State to Victoria, on Vancouver Island, but no ferries run to Vancouver. The *Royal Victorian,* tel. (206) 625-1880 or (250) 480-5555, cruises across Juan de Fuca Strait to Victoria, departing Seattle's Pier 48 mid-May to mid-October daily at 1 p.m. The fare is $60 for a vehicle with driver, $27 per passenger. The *Victoria Clipper* is a fast passenger-only service connecting Seattle's Pier 69 with Victoria's Inner Harbour. The service runs year-round, with up to five sailings daily in summer; adults US$55-63 one-way, US$89-104 roundtrip. Discounts apply for seniors and for tickets booked more than 14 days in advance. The same company also provides a ferry service from Seattle via the San Juan Islands for US$65 each way. For details call (206) 448-5000, (250) 382-8100, or (800) 888-2535.

From further north in Washington State, at Anacortes, **Washington State Ferries,** tel. (206) 464-6400 or (250) 381-1551, runs a once-daily ferry service to Sidney, on Vancouver Island 32 km north of Victoria. The one-way fare is adults US$7.90, car and driver US$36.60. Reservations must be made at least 24 hours in advance.

The least expensive ferry to Victoria is from Port Angeles on Washington's Olympic Peninsula. The *MV Coho* makes this crossing twice daily, four times daily in summer. The one-way fare is adults $8.90 (US$6.50), children $4.45 (US$3.25), cars $37.50 (US$27). Checks and credit cards are not accepted, and reservations are not taken. Call Black Ball Transport at (206) 457-4491 or (250) 386-2202 for estimated waiting times. Also plying this route is the *Victoria Express,* tel. (250) 361-9144 or (800) 633-1589, a passenger-only summer service with roundtrip fares of adults $20, children $10.

GETTING AROUND

The best way to get around British Columbia is via your own vehicle—be it a car, RV, motorbike, or bicycle. It's easy to get around by bus and train, but you can't get off the beaten track and, let's face it, that's exactly where most of British Columbia is. It's also easy to get around by air—all the larger airports are served by scheduled intraprovincial flights, and air-charter services fly out of many of the smaller ones.

Air

Canadian Regional, tel. (604) 279-6611 or (800) 665-1177, and **Air BC,** tel. (604) 668-5515 or (800) 663-3721, both offer an extensive network of air service to all major cities and towns. Smaller carriers include **North Vancouver Air,** tel. (604) 278-1608, serving major Vancouver Island centers; **Pacific Coastal Airlines,** tel. (604) 273-8666, flying daily between Vancouver and Powell River; and **Central Mountain Air,** tel. (604) 270-9111 or (800) 663-3905, with flights throughout the north of the province.

Rail

As well as the **VIA Rail** service between Jasper and Vancouver and Jasper and Prince Rupert (see "Getting There," above), three other passenger services run within British Columbia. **B.C. Rail** provides daily service between Vancouver and Prince George, where a transfer can be made to the VIA Rail line. Excursion fares are offered on this route between Vancouver and Whistler and between Whistler and Lillooet. B.C. Rail also operates the **Royal Hudson Steam Train,** between North Vancouver and Squamish. For general information, call (604) 984-5246 or (800) 663-8238. VIA Rail's **Malahat Train,** 450 Pandora Ave., Victoria, tel. (250) 383-4324 or (800) 561-8630, runs daily up the east coast of Vancouver Island between Victoria and Courtenay, making a pleasant daytrip from the capital or a good alternative to scheduled buses.

Bus

British Columbia by bus is a snap. Just about all the cities have local bus companies providing transportation in town and, in many cases, throughout their local region—check the transportation sections of each individual chapter for more details. **Greyhound** operates daily bus service to just about anywhere in the province. You don't need to make reservations—just buy your ticket and go. All scheduled services are nonsmoking. The bus depot in Vancouver is at

1150 Station St., tel. (604) 482-8747 or (800) 661-8747.

The one part of the province where Greyhound doesn't operate is Vancouver Island. There, **Island Coach Lines,** tel. (250) 385-4411 or (800) 318-0818, serves all of the island, running up the east coast to Port Hardy and out to the west coast at Tofino. Getting to the island itself is easy with **Pacific Coach Lines,** tel. (604) 662-8074, which provides bus service between Victoria and both Vancouver city center and Vancouver International Airport. **Maverick Coach Lines,** tel. (604) 662-8051, connects Vancouver with the Sunshine Coast, Squamish, Whistler, and Nanaimo.

Bigfoot's Backpacker Adventure Express, a bus service especially for backpackers, offers once-weekly service between Vancouver and Banff. The bus departs Vancouver Monday at 4 p.m., arriving in Banff Wednesday afternoon. The return trip departs Banff Wednesday at 4 p.m., arriving back in Vancouver Friday evening. The pace is leisurely, with time spent at major natural attractions en route and one night spent camping, the other at a hostel. The fare is $84 each way ($10 extra for bicycles), including all camping equipment. The company also offers a two-day Whistler Experience, departing Vancouver Saturday at 9 a.m. and returning the following afternoon; $45 round trip. For bookings call (604) 488-0484 or book through Vancouver or Banff hostels.

Ferry

Chances are, at some stage of your British Columbia adventure, you'll use the services of **BC Ferries,** 1112 Fort St., Victoria, BC V8V 4V2, tel. (250) 386-3431 or, toll-free in B.C., (888) BC-FERRY. All fares listed for "cars" in this book cover cars and trucks up to 20 feet long and under seven feet high (or under six feet eight inches high on a few routes). Larger vehicles such as RVs pay more. Also note that prices listed for all types of vehicles, including cars, motorcycles, bicycles, canoes, and kayaks, are in addition to the passenger price; the vehicle's driver/rider/porter is not included in the vehicle fare.

Vancouver has two major ferry terminals. From **Tsawwassen,** south of downtown, ferries run regularly across the Strait of Georgia to the Vancouver Island centers of Swartz Bay (32 km

north of Victoria) and Nanaimo. From **Horseshoe Bay,** west of downtown Vancouver, ferries ply the strait to Nanaimo. On weekends and holidays, the one-way fare on all routes between the mainland and Vancouver Island is adults $8, cars $30, motorcycles $15, bicycles $2.50, canoes and kayaks $4; rates for all motor vehicles are slightly lower on weekdays.

Also from Horseshoe Bay, ferries run across Howe Sound to **Langdale,** gateway to the Sunshine Coast; roundtrip fare is adults $7, cars $25.75, motorcycles $13, bicycles $2.50, canoes and kayaks $4.

From Powell River, at the north end of the Sunshine Coast, ferries depart for Comox (Vancouver Island), making it possible to visit both the island and the Sunshine Coast without returning to Vancouver.

BC Ferries also provides regular services from both Vancouver Island and the mainland to the Southern Gulf Islands of **Salt Spring, North Pender, Mayne, Galiano,** and **Saturna.** Other islands in the Strait of Georgia linked to Vancouver Island by ferry include: **Thetis** and **Kuper** (from Chemainus), **Gabriola** (from Nanaimo), **Lasqueti** (from Parksville), **Denman** and **Hornby** (from Buckley Bay), **Quadra** and **Cortes** (from Campbell River), and **Malcolm** and **Cormorant** (from Port McNeil). Fares for travel to these islands range adults $4-5, cars $10.75-17.25.

Prepaid vehicle reservations are required on all sailings to the Southern Gulf Islands from Tsawwassen (Vancouver). Limited reservations are available for the routes between the mainland and Vancouver Island. No reservations are taken for the other routes listed above, so you can expect a wait in summer.

From **Port Hardy** at the northern tip of Vancouver Island, a ferry runs north up the coast to **Prince Rupert.** From the end of May through September the ferry goes every other day, from October through April once a week, and during May twice a week. Peak one-way fare is adults $102, children 5-11 $51, cars $210, kayaks and canoes $17.50, bicycles $6.50. Reservable cabins are available, as are discounts for B.C. seniors. The trip takes 15 hours, and links up with the **Alaska Marine Highway,** tel. (250) 627-1744 or (800) 642-0066, in Prince Rupert. Also from Prince Rupert, ferries run out to the **Queen Charlotte Islands;** one-way fare is adults $23,

ANDREW HEMPSTEAD

As the sign says, take care when driving along roads frequented by logging trucks.

children 5-11 $11.50, cars $87, kayaks and canoes $7, bicycles $6; discounts for B.C. seniors. These longer sailings require reservations, which should be made as far in advance as possible.

A number of interior lakes and rivers are crossed by ferries owned and operated by the government. Of course, no service is available between freezeup and breakup, but the rest of year, expect daily service from 6 a.m. until at least 10 p.m. Some of the ferries are small, capable of carrying just two vehicles, while others can transport up to 50. Passage is free on all these ferries, including the 45-minute sailing across Kootenay Lake between Balfour and Kootenay Bay—the world's longest free ferry trip.

Car and RV Rental
All major car rental companies have outlets at Vancouver International Aitport, in downtown Vancouver, and in Victoria. Many companies also have cars available in towns and cities

throughout the province. Try to book in advance, especially in summer. Expect to pay from $55 a day for a small economy car.

Major rental companies include: **Avis,** tel. (800) 879-2847; **Budget,** tel. (800) 268-8900; **Discount,** tel. (800) 263-2355; **Dollar,** tel. (800) 465-0045; **Enterprise,** tel. (800) 325-8007; **Hertz,** tel. (800) 263-0600; **National Tilden,** tel. (800) 387-4747; and **Thrifty,** tel. (800) 367-2277. Cheaper used cars are available from only $35 a day plus 15 cents a kilometer from Rent-a-wreck, call (604) 876-7155 in Vancouver for more information and reservations. You may also get a good deal in Vancouver from **ABC Rent-a-car,** tel. (604) 273-6622 or (800) 464-6422, and **Lo Cost,** tel. (604) 689-9664, or in Victoria from **Ada Rent a Used Car,** tel. (250) 474-3455.

You might want to consider renting a campervan or other recreational vehicle for your trip. With one of these apartments-on-wheels, you won't need to worry about finding accommodations each night. Even the smallest units aren't cheap, but they can be a good deal for longer-term travel or for families or two couples traveling together. The most compact units start at $80 per day with the first 100 km free. Rental agencies in Vancouver include: **C.C. Canada Camper RV Rentals,** tel. (604) 327-3003; **Cruise Canada,** tel. (604) 946-5775 or (800) 327-7799 or, in the U.S., (800) 327-7778; and **Go Vacations,** tel. (800) 387-3998.

Driving in British Columbia
United States and International driver's licenses are valid in Canada. All highway signs in British Columbia give distances in kilometers and speeds in kilometers per hour. Unless otherwise posted, the maximum speed limit on the highways is 100 kph (62 mph).

Use of safety belts is mandatory, and motorcyclists must wear helmets. Infants and toddlers weighing up to nine kilograms (20 pounds) must be strapped into an appropriate children's car seat. Use of a child car seat for larger children weighing 9-18 kilograms (20-40 pounds) is required of B.C. residents and recommended to nonresidents. Before venturing off into the wilds, U.S. residents should ask their vehicle insurance company for a Canadian Non-resident Inter-provincial Motor Vehicle Liability Insurance Card. You may also be asked to prove vehicle ownership, so carry your vehicle registration form. If you're involved in an accident with a B.C. vehicle, contact the nearest Insurance Corporation of British Columbia (ICBC) office; tel. (604) 661-2800 in Vancouver or (250) 383-1111 in Victoria.

If you're a member in good standing of an automobile association, take your membership card—the Canadian AA provides members of related associations full services, including free maps, itineraries, excellent tour books, road-and weather-condition information, accommodations reservations, travel agency services, and emergency road services. For more information write British Columbia Automobile Association, 999 W. Broadway Ave., Vancouver, BC V5Z 1K5, tel. (604) 268-5600.

Note: drinking and driving (with a blood-alcohol level of .08% or higher) in B.C. can get you imprisonment for up to five years on a first offense, and will cost you your license for at least 12 months.

OTHER PRACTICALITIES

VISAS AND OFFICIALDOM

Entry for U.S. Citizens
United States citizens and permanent residents need only present some form of identification that proves citizenship and/or residency, such as a birth certificate, voter-registration card, driver's license with photo, or alien card (essential for aliens to reenter the U.S.). It never hurts to carry your passport as well.

Other Foreign Visitors
All other foreign visitors must have a valid passport, and may need a visa or visitor permit depending on their country of residence and the vagaries of international politics. At present, visas are not required for citizens of the U.S., British Commonwealth, or Western Europe. The standard entry permit is for six months, and you may be asked to show onward tickets or proof of sufficient funds to last you through your intended stay. Extensions ($60 per person) are available from the Department of Citizenship and Immigration offices in Vancouver and Victoria.

Employment and Study
Anyone wishing to work or study in Canada must obtain authorization *before* entering Canada. Authorization to work will only be granted if no qualified Canadians are available for the work in question. Applications for work and study are available from all Canadian embassies and must be submitted with a nonrefundable processing fee. The Canadian government has a reciprocal agreement with Australia for a limited number of **holiday work visas** to be issued each year. Australian citizens under the age of 26 are eligible; contact your nearest Canadian embassy or consulate.

Entry by Private Aircraft or Boat
If you're going to be entering Canada by private plane or boat, contact Customs in advance for a list of official ports of entry and their hours of operation. Write Revenue Canada, Customs and Excise, Regional Information Unit, 333 Dunsmuir St., Vancouver, BC V6B 5R4, or call (604) 666-0545. Canadian airports with customs clearance are also listed on the *Canada Flight Supplement,* available from the Canada Map Office, 615 Booth St., Ottawa, Ontario K1A 0E9, Canada, tel. (613) 952-7000. This office also sells aeronautical charts for $15 each. The publication *Air Tourist Information-Canada (TP771E)* lists all B.C.'s airports and has other necessary information for visiting pilots; it's available from Transport Canada, AAN DHD, Ottawa, Ontario K1A 0N8, Canada, tel. (613) 991-9970.

BOB RACE

GST

Canada imposes a seven-percent **goods and services tax (GST)** on most consumer purchases. Nonresident visitors can get a rebate for the GST they pay on short-term accommodations and on most consumer goods bought in the country and taken home. Items not included in the GST rebate program include: gifts left in Canada, meals and restaurant charges, campground fees, services such as dry cleaning and shoe repair, alcoholic beverages, tobacco, automotive fuels, groceries, agricultural and fish products, prescription drugs and medical devices, and used goods that tend to increase in value, such as paintings, jewelry, rare books, and coins.

The rebate is available on services and retail purchases that total at least $100 and were paid for within 60 days prior to your exit from the country. Rebates can be claimed any time within one year from the date of purchase. You'll need to include with your claim all receipts and vouchers that prove the GST was paid. Most visitors apply for the rebate at duty-free shops (also called Visitor Rebate Centres) when exiting the country. The duty-free shops can rebate up to $500 on the spot. For rebates over $500, you'll need to mail your completed GST rebate form directly to Revenue Canada, Customs and Excise, Visitors' Rebate Program, Ottawa, Ontario K1A 1J5. You can also submit rebate forms for amounts less than $500 directly to Revenue Canada. Rebate checks from Revenue Canada are issued in Canadian funds. For more info, call toll-free from anywhere in Canada (800) 668-4748; from outside Canada phone (613) 991-3346.

Customs

You can take the following into Canada duty-free: reasonable quantities of clothes and personal effects, 50 cigars and 200 cigarettes, 200 grams of tobacco, 1.14 liters of spirits or wine, food for personal use, and gas (normal tank capacity). Pets from the U.S. can generally be brought into Canada, with certain caveats. Dogs and cats must be over three months old and have a rabies certificate showing date of vaccination. Birds can be brought in only if they have not been mixing with other birds, and parrots need an export permit because they're on the endangered species list.

Handguns, automatic and semiautomatic weapons, and sawn-off rifles and shotguns are not allowed entry into Canada. Visitors with firearms must declare them at the border; restricted weapons will be held by customs and can be picked up on exit from the country. Those not declared will be seized and charges may be laid. It is illegal to possess any firearm in a national park unless it is dismantled or carried in an enclosed case. Up to 5,000 rounds of ammunition may be imported but should be declared on entry. For further information on firearms regulations contact Revenue Canada, Customs and Excise, Regional Information Unit, 333 Dunsmuir St., Vancouver, BC V6B 5R4, tel. (604) 666-0545.

On reentering the U.S., if you've been in Canada more than 48 hours you can bring back up to US$400 worth of household and personal items, excluding alcohol and tobacco, duty-free. If you've been in Canada less than 48 hours, you may bring in only up to $200 worth of such items duty-free.

MONEY

Canadian currency is based on dollars and cents, with 100 cents equal to one dollar. **All prices quoted in this handbook are in Canadian dollars and cents unless otherwise noted.** The exchange rate is roughly US$1= C$1.35. American dollars are accepted at many tourist areas, but don't expect a favorable exchange rate.

Coins come in denominations of one, five, 10, and 25 cents, and one and two dollars. The 11-sided, gold-colored, one-dollar coin is known as a "loonie" for the bird featured on it. The unique two-dollar coin is silver with a gold-colored insert. The most common notes are $2, $5, $10, $20, and $50. A $100 bill does exist but is uncommon.

Prices quoted by merchants may or may not include the goods and services tax (seven percent), so always ask if the tax is extra when you're given a quote.

The safest way to carry money is in the form of traveler's checks from a reputable and well-known U.S. company such as American Express, Visa, or Bank of America; those are also the easiest checks to cash. Cash only the amount you need when you need it. Banks offer the best exchange rates, but other foreign-currency exchange outlets are available. It's also a good idea to start off with a couple of traveler's checks in Canadian dollars so you're never caught without *some* money if you don't make it to a bank on time.

Visa and MasterCard credit cards are also readily accepted throughout British Columbia. By using credit cards you eliminate the necessity of thinking about the exchange rate—the transaction and rate of exchange on the day of the transaction will automatically be reflected in the bill from your credit-card company.

Costs

The cost of living in British Columbia is similar to all other Canadian provinces, but higher than in the United States. By planning ahead, having a tent or joining Hostelling International, and being prepared to cook your own meals it is possible to get by on well under $50 per person per day. Gasoline is sold in liters (3.78 liters equals one U.S. gallon) and is generally 55-65 cents a liter for regular unleaded; surprisingly, Vancouver is one of the most expensive places to fill your gas tank.

Tipping charges are not usually added to your bill. You are expected to add a tip of 15% to the total amount for waiters and waitresses, barbers and hairdressers, taxi drivers, and other such service providers. Bellhops, doormen, and porters generally receive $1 per item of baggage.

HEALTH

British Columbia is a healthy place. To visit, you don't need to get any vaccinations or booster shots. And when you arrive you can drink the water from the faucet and eat the food without worry.

Backcountry travelers should take a few extra precautions. It's always wise to boil or filter water from streams and lakes, just to be on the safe side. Be aware of poison oak, which causes itchy open blisters and sores a short time after contact, and keep your eyes peeled for rattlesnakes. If you bathe in hot springs, keep your head above water and *do not* let the water enter

your nose, ears, or mouth—a variety of parasites thrive in the hot water.

AIDS and other venereal and needle-communicated diseases are as much of a concern here as anywhere in the world today. Take exactly the same precautions you would at home—use condoms, and don't share needles.

It's a good idea to get health insurance or some form of coverage before heading to Canada if you're going to be there for a while, but check that your plan covers foreign services. Hospital charges vary from place to place, but can start at around $1,000 a day, and some facilities impose a surcharge for nonresidents. Some Canadian companies offer coverage specifically aimed at visitors; for an example, request a brochure from Hospital Medical Care, 1012 W. Georgia St., Vancouver, BC V6E 2Y2, tel. (604) 684-0666.

If you're on medication take adequate supplies with you, and get a prescription from your doctor to cover the time you will be away. You may not be able to get a prescription filled at Canadian pharmacies without visiting a Canadian doctor, so don't wait till you've almost run out. If you wear glasses or contact lenses, ask your optometrist for a spare prescription in case you break or lose your lenses, and stock up on your usual cleaning supplies.

If you need an ambulance, call the number listed on the inside front cover of the local telephone directory, and if you're unsure of your whereabouts ask the operator for assistance. All the cities and most of the large towns have local hospitals—look in each individual chapter of this book for locations and telephone numbers.

Be aware that some of B.C.'s highways snake for many kilometers through high mountain areas. In the Rockies particularly, roads can climb into the thin-air heights, reaching elevations of up to 1,774 meters. If you or your passengers can't handle high elevations well, read a good topographical map before you set off and try to find a low-lying route to your destination.

Visitors with Disabilities

For information on travel considerations in British Columbia for the physically handicapped, contact the Canadian Paraplegic Association, 780 Southwest Marine Dr., Vancouver, BC V6P 5Y7, tel. (604) 324-3611.

Winter Travel Considerations

Travel through the province during winter months should not be undertaken lightly. Before setting out in a vehicle, check antifreeze levels, and always carry a spare tire and blankets or sleeping bags.

Frostbite occurs in varying degrees. Most often it leaves a numbing, bruised sensation and the skin turns white. Exposed areas of skin such as the nose and ears are most susceptible, particularly when cold temperatures are accompanied by high winds.

Hypothermia occurs when the body fails to produce heat as fast as it loses it. Cold weather combined with hunger, fatigue, and dampness creates a recipe for disaster. Symptoms are not always apparent to the victim. The early signs are numbness, shivering, slurring of words, dizzy spells, and, in extreme cases, violent behavior, unconsciousness, and even death. The best treatment is to get the patient out of the cold, replace wet clothing with dry, slowly give hot liquids and sugary foods, and place the victim in a sleeping bag. Prevention is a better strategy; dress for cold in layers, including a waterproof outer layer, and make sure to wear a warm wool cap or other headgear.

SERVICES, COMMUNICATIONS, AND MEASUREMENTS

Postal Services

Canadian **postage stamps** must be used on all mail posted in Canada. First-class letters and postcards within Canada are 45 cents, to the U.S. 49 cents, to foreign destinations 90 cents. Prices increase along with the weight of the mailing. You can buy stamps at post offices, automatic vending machines, most hotel lobbies, railway stations, airports, bus terminals, and at many retail outlets and some newsstands. Visitors can have their mail sent to them c/o General Delivery, Main Post Office, in the city or town you request, British Columbia, Canada. The post office will hold the mail for 15 days, then return it to the sender.

Telephones and Electricity

The **area code** for Vancouver and the lower mainland, including the Sunshine Coast, as far north as Whistler, and east to Hope, is **604.** The rest of the province, including all of Vancouver Island, is **250.** These prefixes must be dialed for all long-distance calls, including those made within the province. The country code for Canada is 1, the same as the United States. Public phones accept five-, 10-, and 25-cent coins; local calls are

---

TOURISM OFFICES

As well as **Tourism BC,** tel. (604) 663-6000 or (800) 663-6000, the following regional offices will assist in planning your trip to British Columbia:

Vancouver, Coast and Mountains Tourism (includes the Sunshine Coast and Whistler), 204/1755 W. Broadway, Vancouver, BC V6J 4S5; tel. (604) 739-9011 or (800) 667-3306.

Tourism Victoria, 812 Wharf St., Victoria, BC V8W 1T3; tel. (250) 953-2033 or (800) 663-3883.

Tourism Association of Vancouver Island, 302/45 Bastion Square, Victoria, BC V8W 1J1; tel. (250) 382-3551.

Okanagan Tourism Association, 1332 Water St., Kelowna, BC V1Y 9P4; tel. (250) 860-5999.

Kootenay Country Tourist Association, 610 Railway St., Nelson, BC V1L 1H4; tel. (250) 352-6033 or (800) 661-6603.

Rocky Mountain Visitors' Association, P.O. Box 10, Kimberley, BC V1A 2Y5; tel. (250) 427-4838.

High Country Tourism Association (Central British Columbia), 2/1490 Pearson Pl., Kamloops, BC V1S 1J9; tel. (250) 372-7770 or (800) 567-2275.

Cariboo Tourism Association, P.O. Box 4900, Williams Lake, BC V2G 2V8; tel. (250) 392-2226 or (800) 663-5885.

North by Northwest Tourism Association (Burns Lake, Terrace, and Prince Rupert), P.O. Box 1030, Smithers, BC V0J 2N0; tel. (250) 847-5227.

Peace River–Alaska Highway Tourist Association, P.O. Box 6850, Fort St. John, BC V1J 4J3; tel. (250) 785-2544.

HEADING FURTHER AFIELD?

Tourism Yukon: tel. (403) 667-5340; http://www.touryukon.com

Alaska Division of Tourism: tel. (907) 465-2010

Alberta Tourism: tel. (403) 427-4321 or (800) 661-8888

Northwest Territories Economic Development and Tourism: tel. (403) 873-7200 or (800) 661-0788; http://www.edt.gov.nt.ca

Nunavut Tourism: tel. (819) 979-6551 or (800) 491-7910

Tourism Saskatchewan: tel. (306) 787-2300 or (800) 667-7191; http://www.sasktourism.sk.ca

Travel Manitoba: tel. (204) 945-3777 or (800) 665-0040; http://www.gov.mb.ca/itt/travel/explore/index.html

25 cents and most long-distance calls cost at least $2.50 for the first minute. **Electrical voltage** in British Columbia is 120 volts AC.

Time and Measurements

British Columbia is mostly in the **Pacific time zone,** one hour before mountain time and three hours before eastern time. The East Kootenays and the Dawson Creek area are in the mountain time zone.

The province is officially on the **metric system,** though you still hear everyone talking in pounds and ounces, miles, and miles per hour (see the metric conversion chart in the back of this book).

Business Hours

Shops throughout British Columbia are generally open Mon.-Fri. 9 a.m.-5 p.m. and Saturday 9 a.m.-1 p.m. Major malls stay open all weekend.

If you're in a city or large town, you can always find a store open for essentials, as well as restaurants and fast-food outlets. Most **banks** are open Mon.-Fri. 10 a.m.-3:30 p.m.

MAPS AND INFORMATION

Maps

Specialty bookstores are the best places to search out or order maps. In Vancouver, try **World Wide Books and Maps,** 736A Granville St., tel. (604) 687-3320; in Victoria, check out **Crown Publications,** 521 Fort St., tel. (250) 386-4636. These stores stock many topographical maps, and can order specific maps and marine charts for you.

Information

General information on just about everything in the province can be obtained from **Tourism British Columbia,** P.O. Box 9830, Stn. Provincial Government, Victoria, BC V8W 9W5, tel. (250) 387-1642 or (800) 663-6000. As well as being a great source of tourist information, the agency produces the invaluable *Accommodations* guide and a road map.

Each town of any size in B.C. has a **Visitor Info Centre;** hours vary, but most are open June-August. When these are closed, head to the local chamber of commerce for information. Most chamber offices are open Mon.-Fri. year-round.

BOB RACE

VANCOUVER
INTRODUCTION

Let your mind fill with images of dramatic, snow-capped mountains rising vertically from a city's backyard. Century-old inner-city buildings and steel-and-glass skyscrapers facing the sheltered shores of a large wide inlet. Manicured suburbs perching along the edge of the sea, fringed by golden sandy beaches. Lush tree-filled parks and brilliant flower gardens overflowing with color. Flocks of Canada geese overhead, noisily honking to one another as they fly toward the setting sun. These are the magnificent images of Vancouver.

If you view this gleaming mountain- and sea-dominated city for the first time on a beautiful sunny day, you're bound to fall for it in a big way. See it on a dull, dreary day when the clouds are low and Vancouver's backyard mountains are hidden and you may come away with a slightly less enthusiastic picture—you'll have experienced the "permagray," as residents are quick to call it with a laugh.

But even gray skies can't dampen the city's vibrant, outdoorsy atmosphere. By day, the active visitor can enjoy boating right from downtown, or perhaps venture out to one of the nearby provincial parks for hiking and skiing. More urban-oriented visitors can savor the aromas of just-

brewed coffee and freshly baked bread wafting from cosmopolitan sidewalk cafes, join in the bustle at seaside markets, bake on a local beach, or simply relax and do some people-watching in one of the city's tree-shaded squares. By night, Vancouver's myriad fine restaurants, nightclubs, and performing-arts venues beckon visitors to continue enjoying themselves on into the wee hours.

Rain or shine, night or day, Vancouver is an alluring and unforgettable city.

HISTORY

The first Europeans to set eyes on the land encompassing today's city of Vancouver were gold-seeking Spanish traders who sailed through the Strait of Georgia in 1790. Despite the fact that the forested wilderness they encountered was seemingly impenetrable, it had been inhabited by the Salish Indians for some 5,000 years.

Not to be outdone, the Brits sent Capt. George Vancouver to the area in 1792. Vancouver cruised through the Strait of Georgia in search of a northwest passage to the Orient,

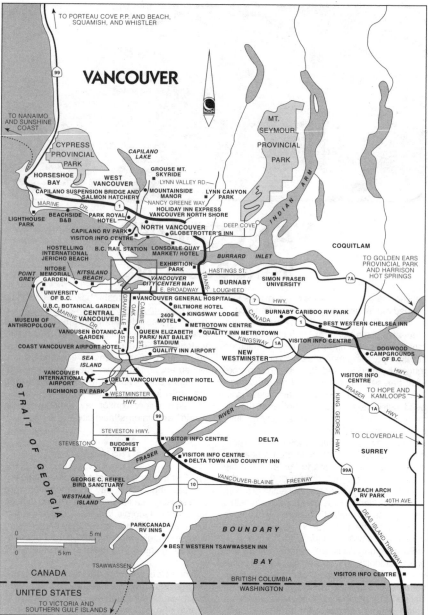

TO PORTEAU COVE P.P. AND BEACH,
SQUAMISH, AND WHISTLER

VANCOUVER

TO NANAIMO
AND SUNSHINE
COAST

CYPRESS
PROVINCIAL
PARK

CAPILANO
LAKE

MT.
SEYMOUR
PROVINCIAL
PARK

HORSESHOE
BAY

WEST
VANCOUVER

GROUSE MT.
SKYRIDE

LYNN VALLEY RD.

CAPILANO SUSPENSION BRIDGE AND
SALMON HATCHERY

MOUNTAINSIDE
MANOR

LYNN CANYON
PARK

MARINE DR.

NANCY GREENE WAY

HOLIDAY INN EXPRESS
VANCOUVER NORTH SHORE

LIGHTHOUSE
PARK

BEACHSIDE
B&B

PARK ROYAL
HOTEL

NORTH VANCOUVER

DEEP COVE

CAPILANO RV PARK
VISITOR INFO CENTRE

GLOBETROTTER'S INN

INDIAN ARM

B.C. RAIL STATION

LONSDALE QUAY
MARKET/ HOTEL

BURRARD   INLET

COQUITLAM

HOSTELLING
INTERNATIONAL
JERICHO BEACH

EXHIBITION
PARK

HASTINGS ST.

TO GOLDEN EARS
PROVINCIAL PARK
AND HARRISON
HOT SPRINGS

POINT
GREY

NITOBE
MEMORIAL
GARDEN

KITSILANO
BEACH

VANCOUVER
CITY CENTER MAP

SIMON FRASER
UNIVERSITY

7A

E. BROADWAY

BURNABY

LOUGHEED

UNIVERSITY
OF B.C.

U.B.C. BOTANICAL GARDEN

VANCOUVER GENERAL HOSPITAL

7   HWY.

CANADA

MUSEUM OF
ANTHROPOLOGY

MARINE DR.

CENTRAL
VANCOUVER

BILTMORE HOTEL

KINGSWAY LODGE

BURNABY CARIBOO RV PARK

1

VANDUSEN BOTANICAL
GARDEN

2400
MOTEL

METROTOWN CENTRE

BEST WESTERN CHELSEA INN

COAST VANCOUVER AIRPORT HOTEL

GRANVILLE ST.

OAK ST.

CAMBIE ST.

QUEEN ELIZABETH
PARK/ NAT BAILEY
STADIUM

QUALITY INN METROTOWN

KINGSWAY

1A

VISITOR INFO CENTRE

DOGWOOD
CAMPGROUNDS
OF B.C.

SEA
ISLAND

QUALITY INN AIRPORT

NEW
WESTMINSTER

VANCOUVER
INTERNATIONAL
AIRPORT

DELTA VANCOUVER AIRPORT HOTEL

VISITOR INFO
CENTRE

S T R A I T

RICHMOND RV PARK

WESTMINSTER
HWY.

RICHMOND

TO HOPE AND
KAMLOOPS

1A   HWY.

99

RIVER

DELTA

KING GEORGE HWY.

FRASER   HWY.

O F

STEVESTON HWY.

STEVESTON

BUDDHIST
TEMPLE

VISITOR INFO CENTRE

FRASER

TO CLOVERDALE

SURREY

G E O R G I A

GEORGE C. REIFEL
BIRD SANCTUARY

VISITOR INFO CENTRE

DELTA TOWN AND COUNTRY INN

99A

WESTHAM
ISLAND

10

VANCOUVER-BLAINE   FREEWAY

PEACH ARCH
RV PARK

40TH AVE.

17

DEAS ISLAND THRUWAY

0   5 mi

0   5 km

PARKCANADA
RV INNS

B O U N D A R Y

CANADA

BEST WESTERN TSAWWASSEN INN

BAY

VISITOR INFO CENTRE

TSAWWASSEN

UNITED STATES

BRITISH COLUMBIA
WASHINGTON

TO VICTORIA AND
SOUTHERN GULF ISLANDS

© MOON PUBLICATIONS, INC.

Vancouver skyline

BREWSTER

charting Burrard Inlet and claiming the land for Great Britain in the process. As stories of an abundance of fur-bearing mammals filtered east, the fur companies went into action. The North West Company sent fur-trader/explorer Simon Fraser overland to establish a coastal trading post. In 1808 he reached the Pacific Ocean via the river that was later named for him, and built a fur fort on the riverbank east of today's Vancouver. In 1827, the Hudson's Bay Company established its own fur fort on the Fraser River, 48 km east of present-day Vancouver. Neither of these two outposts spawned a permanent settlement.

Vancouver is Born
It wasn't until the discovery of gold up the Fraser River in the late 1850s that settlement really took hold in the area. The town of New Westminster, just southeast of present-day Vancouver, was declared British Columbia's first capital in 1866.

The settlement of Vancouver began with the establishment of a brickworks ("Bricks? Why on earth make bricks when we've got all these trees?" said the Woodcutters' Union spokesman) on the south side of Burrard Inlet. Sawmills and related logging and lumber industries followed, and soon several boomtowns were carved out of the wilderness. The first was Granville (now downtown Vancouver), which the original settlers called Gastown after one of its earliest residents, notorious saloon owner "Gassy Jack"

Deighton. In 1886 Granville, pop. 1,000, became the City of Vancouver. Not long thereafter, fire roared through the timber city. Just about everything burned to the ground, but with true pioneering spirit Vancouver was rebuilt at lightning speed.

A Growing City
In 1887, the struggling city got a boost with the arrival of the first transcontinental railroad. Selected as the western terminus for Canadian Pacific Railway, Vancouver suddenly became Canada's transportation gateway to the Orient and an important player in the development of international commerce around the Pacific Rim. Additionally, the opening of the Panama Canal in 1915 created the perfect outlet for transporting the province's abundant renewable resources to North America's east coast and Europe, resulting in further development of the port facilities and a population boom. Granville Island and the far reaches of Burrard Inlet sprawled with industry, the West End developed as a residential area, the University of British Columbia grew in stature, and the opening of the Lions Gate Bridge encouraged settlement on the north side of Burrard Inlet.

Today, Vancouver is Canada's third-largest city, holding a multicultural population of 1.5 million in its greater metropolitan area. It's also the largest port on North America's west coast, boasting 27 specialized terminals that handle more tonnage than any other port in Canada.

SIGHTS

GETTING ORIENTED

Vancouver isn't a particularly easy city to find your way around, although an excellent transit system helps immensely. **Downtown** lies on a spit of land bordered to the north and east by Burrard Inlet, to the west by English Bay, and to the south by False Creek, which almost cuts the city center off from the rest of the city. Due to the foresight of city founders, almost half of the downtown peninsula has been set aside as parkland.

South and west from downtown, between Burrard Inlet and the Fraser River, is **Central Vancouver.** Here lies the trendy beachside suburb of **Kitsilano** (known as "Kits" to the locals) and **Point Grey,** home of the University of British Columbia. To the east, the residential sprawl continues, through the suburbs of **Burnaby, New Westminster,** and **Coquitlam** which have a combined population of well over 250,000.

Farther south, the low-lying Fraser River delta extends all the way south to the border. Between the north and south arms of the river is **Richmond,** home of **Vancouver International Airport.** South of the south arm is the mostly industrial area of **Delta,** as well as **Tsawwassen,** departure point for ferries to Vancouver Island.

Southeast of the Fraser River lies **Surrey,** another of those never-ending suburbs, this one with a population of 300,000. The sprawl continues east from Surrey. With Vancouver growing at an incredible rate, and as development to the south and north are restricted—by the international border and the Coast Mountains—there's no where to go but east. From Surrey, the Trans-Canada Highway passes through the Fraser River Valley and towns such as **Langley** (pop. 80,000), **Abbotsford** (pop. 105,000), and **Chilliwack** (pop. 60,000)—all now part of the city sprawl.

Across Burrard Inlet to the north of downtown, **North Vancouver** is a narrow developed strip backed up to the mountains and connected to the rest of the city by the Lions Gate Bridge. To its west are **Horseshoe Bay,** departure point for Sunshine Coast and Vancouver Island ferries, and **West Vancouver,** an upscale suburb.

DOWNTOWN

Canada Place

The stunning architectural curiosity with the billowing white teflon-coated "sails" on Burrard Inlet—the one that looks as if it might weigh anchor and cruise off into the sunset at any moment—is Canada Place, Vancouver's convention center and cruise-ship dock. Built as the Canada Pavilion for Expo86, the impressive building at the foot of Burrard Street also houses the luxurious Pan Pacific Hotel (the glass marvel with domed top), restaurants, shops, and an IMAX theater. Start your self-guided tour at the information booth near the main entrance, then allow at least an hour to wander through the complex. Don't miss walking the outside promenade—three city blocks long—for splendid views of the harbor, North Vancouver, the Coast Mountains, and docked cruise ships.

Vancouver Art Gallery

Francis Rattenbury, architect of Victoria's Empress Hotel and many other masterpieces, designed Vancouver's imposing classic courthouse, which now houses Vancouver Art Gallery, 750 Hornby St., tel. (604) 662-4700. The exterior retains its original 1911 design while the interior was renovated in 1983 by Arthur Erickson, a prominent Vancouver architect.

The gallery houses a large collection of works by renowned B.C. artist Emily Carr, as well as the work of other Canadian and international artists. Guided tours are available. Kids will enjoy the children's gallery, while adults will appreciate the special-events program, including a lecture series, films, and concerts. The gift shop sells a wide selection of art books, jewelry, and gifts, and the gallery cafe is always crowded.

Summer hours are Mon.-Sat. 10 a.m.-5 p.m. (until 9 p.m. on Thursday), Sunday noon-5 p.m. Between October and May, the gallery is closed Monday and Tuesday. Admission is adults $6, seniors $4, children under 12 free.

VANCOUVER VIEWS

Commercial

For immediate orientation from downtown and a 360-degree bird's-eye view, catch the high-speed, stomach-sinking glass elevator up the outside of 40-story Harbour Centre Tower, 555 W. Hastings St., tel. (604) 689-0421. The ride takes less than a minute, and ends at **The Lookout,** an enclosed room 167 meters above street level. The elevator runs daily 8:30 a.m.-10:30 p.m. in summer, and daily 10:30 a.m.-9 p.m. the rest of the year. Costs is adults $7, seniors and children $6.

On the north side of the city, take the **Skyride Gondola,** Nancy Greene Way, tel. (604) 984-0661, up the slopes of **Grouse Mountain** for a view over the entire city and beyond; adults $14.50, seniors $12.50, children $5.95. From the summit, **Grouse Mountain Helicopters,** tel. (604) 525-1484, offers a 10-minute, $40-per-person joy-flight providing views from even higher elevations.

Free

Visitors on a budget can find plenty of free ways to enjoy a city panorama. Downtown, wander around the **Canada Place** promenade for neck-straining views of the city close up, as well as North Vancouver and the rugged mountains to the north. In Stanley Park, stroll the 10-km-long **Seawall Prom-** enade to appreciate the skyline to the east, the busy shipping lanes of First Narrows to the north, and the sandy beaches of English Bay to the west. Sunsets from **English Bay Beach,** in the West End, are delightful. Relax on the beach or soak up the sunset from the lounge in the Sylvia Hotel or the outdoor terrace of the Teahouse Restaurant.

While Grouse Mountain Gondola accesses the best-known viewpoint north of Burrard Inlet, the panorama from **Cypress Provincial Park,** up Cypress Bowl Rd., is no less spectacular. On the way back down, take Marine Dr. west to **Lighthouse Park,** from where English Bay, Stanley Park, and Kitsilano Beach are laid out in all their glory. **Seymour Provincial Park,** east of the gondola, provides views across the city from afar, but from a wilderness area with plenty of hiking opportunities. For a look at the skyline and sparkling Canada Place from sea level, take the SeaBus across Burrard Inlet to **Lonsdale Quay.**

South of downtown, the **Kitsilano** foreshore provides that well-known view of the city skyline backed by the Coast Mountains. The south side of the city is relatively flat. The high point is 152-meter-high **Little Mountain,** in Queen Elizabeth Park, where the city skyline and abruptly rising mountains provide a stark contrast to the residential sprawl of Central Vancouver all around.

The view from Harbor Centre Tower is spectacular.

JANE AND BRUCE KING

Mining and Forestry Displays

The **Mining Association of B.C.** has a small exhibit at 840 W. Hastings St., tel. (604) 681-4321. A large three-dimensional map of the province shows mineral deposits and current mining operations, while other displays show the importance of the industry to the province. Open Mon.-Fri. 8:30 a.m.-4:30 p.m. Also downtown, the **Forest Alliance of B.C. Information Centre,** 1055 Dunsmuir St., tel. (604) 685-7507, is a good place to learn about the forestry industry through interactive displays, computer programs, information boards describing the various woods and wood products, and a quiet area stacked with relevant literature. It's open Mon.-Fri. 8 a.m.-5 p.m.

Gastown

Named for the owner of the city's first saloon, Gastown is a marvelous place to spend a few hours. "Gassy Jack" Deighton, an English boat pilot, offered locals all the whiskey they could drink in return for helping him build a saloon beside Burrard Inlet in 1867. The town and industry that grew around the saloon was officially named Granville in 1869, but it has always been known as Gastown. The district's tree-lined cobblestone streets and old gas lamps front brightly painted restored buildings that house galleries, restaurants, and an abundance of gift and souvenir shops. Most walking tours of Gastown start at the top (city center) end, a five-minute walk from Canada Place.

On the corner of Water and Cambie Sts. is a **steam clock** built by a local clock maker and powered by an underground steam system originally put in place to heat the buildings along Water Street. Watch for the burst of steam every 15 minutes as the clock chimes to the Westminster theme. Continue east along Water St. to the 1899 **Dominion Hotel,** then half a block south down Abbott St. to **Blood Alley Square,** the hangout of many infamous turn-of-the-century rogues.

Further along Water St., at Carrall St., is a **statue of Gassy Jack.** The bronze statue stands in front of the **Alhambra Hotel,** which occupies the site of Gassy Jack's original saloon. The Alhambra was built in 1886 from bricks used as ballast in ships that sailed into Burrard Inlet.

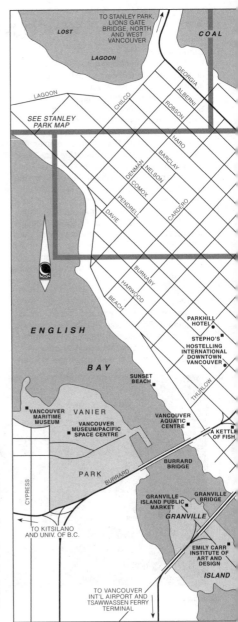

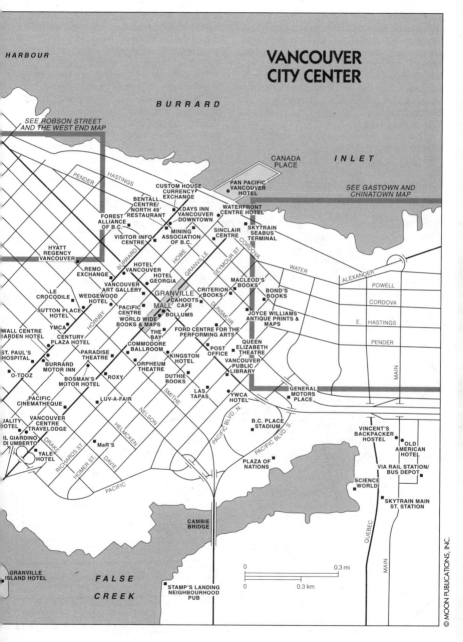

VANCOUVER
CITY CENTER

HARBOUR

BURRARD

INLET

CANADA
PLACE

SEE ROBSON STREET
AND THE WEST END MAP

SEE GASTOWN AND
CHINATOWN MAP

PENDER

HASTINGS

CUSTOM HOUSE
CURRENCY
EXCHANGE

PAN PACIFIC
VANCOUVER
HOTEL

BENTALL
CENTRE/
NORTH 49°
RESTAURANT

DAYS INN
VANCOUVER
DOWNTOWN

WATERFRONT
CENTRE HOTEL

FOREST
ALLIANCE
OF B.C.

MINING
ASSOCIATION
OF B.C.

SINCLAIR
CENTRE

SKYTRAIN
SEABUS
TERMINAL

VISITOR INFO
CENTRE

HYATT
REGENCY
VANCOUVER

BURRARD

HOWE

GRANVILLE

SEYMOUR ST

CORDOVA

WATER

ALEXANDER

REMO
EXCHANGE

HOTEL
VANCOUVER

MACLEOD'S
BOOKS

POWELL

LE
CROCODILE

VANCOUVER
ART GALLERY

HOTEL
GEORGIA

CRITERION
BOOKS

BOND'S
BOOKS

CORDOVA

WEDGEWOOD
HOTEL

GRANVILLE
MALL

CAHOOTS
CAFE

DUNSMUIR

E. HASTINGS

SUTTON PLACE
HOTEL

HORNBY

PACIFIC
CENTRE

BOLLUMS

JOYCE WILLIAMS
ANTIQUE PRINTS &
MAPS

PENDER

WALL CENTRE
GARDEN HOTEL

YMCA

WORLD WIDE
BOOKS & MAPS

THE
BAY

FORD CENTRE FOR THE
PERFORMING ARTS

CENTURY
PLAZA HOTEL

COMMODORE
BALLROOM

QUEEN
ELIZABETH
THEATRE

MAIN

ST. PAUL'S
HOSPITAL

PARADISE
THEATRE

KINGSTON
HOTEL

POST
OFFICE

VANCOUVER
PUBLIC
LIBRARY

BURRARD
MOTOR INN

ORPHEUM
THEATRE

O-TOOZ

BOSMAN'S
MOTOR HOTEL

ROXY

SMITHE

DUTHIE
BOOKS

GENERAL
MOTORS
PLACE

PACIFIC
CINEMATHEQUE

LUV-A-FAIR

NELSON

LAS
TAPAS

YWCA
HOTEL

JALITY
HOTEL

VANCOUVER
CENTRE
TRAVELODGE

HELMCKEN

B.C. PLACE
STADIUM

VINCENT'S
BACKPACKER
HOSTEL

IL GIARDINO
DI UMBERTO

DRAKE

MaR'S

PACIFIC BLVD N.

PACIFIC BLVD S.

OLD
AMERICAN
HOTEL

YALE
HOTEL

RICHARDS ST

HOMER ST

DAVIE

PLAZA OF
NATIONS

VIA RAIL STATION/
BUS DEPOT

PACIFIC

SCIENCE
WORLD

SKYTRAIN MAIN
ST. STATION

CAMBIE
BRIDGE

QUEBEC

MAIN

GRANVILLE
ISLAND HOTEL

FALSE

CREEK

STAMP'S LANDING
NEIGHBOURHOOD
PUB

0   0.3 mi

0   0.3 km

© MOON PUBLICATIONS, INC.

Chinatown

The second-largest Chinese community in North America and one of the largest outside Asia, Vancouver's Chinatown is an exciting place any time of year. But it's especially lively during a Chinese festival or holiday, when thronging masses follow the ferocious dancing dragon, avoid exploding firecrackers, sample tasty tidbits from outside stalls, and pound their feet to the beat of the drums.

Chinatown lies several blocks southeast of Gastown, along East Pender St. between Carrall and Gore Streets. Its commercial center is the block bordered by Main, East Pender, Gore, and Keefer Streets. Stroll through the neighborhood

to admire the architecture—right down to the pagoda-roofed telephone booths—or to seek out one of the multitude of restaurants. You'll find genuine Cantonese-style cuisine at the east end and tamer Chinese-Canadian dishes at the west.

The district's intriguing stores sell a mind-boggling array of Chinese goods—wind chimes, soy sauce, teapots, dried mushrooms, delicate paper fans, and much, much more. Along Main St. are a number of shops selling ginseng, sold by the Chinese ounce (38 grams). Cultivated ginseng costs from $10 an ounce, while wild ginseng goes for up to $400 an ounce. In addition to selling the herb in a variety of forms, the staff at **Ten Ren Tea and Ginseng Co.,** 550

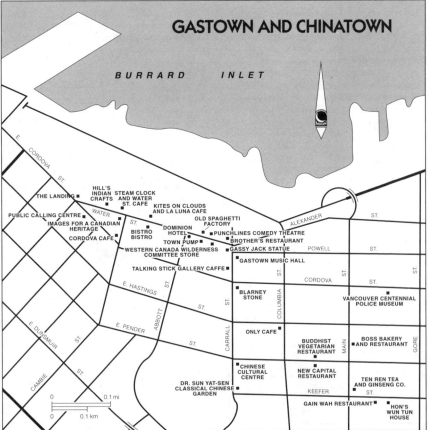

Main St., tel. (604) 684-1566, explains ginseng preparation methods to buyers and offers tea tastings as well.

The **Chinese Cultural Centre,** 50 E. Pender St., tel. (604) 687-0729, sponsors exhibitions and displays ranging from bonsai to watercolor paintings; admission varies according to what's going on. Gardening enthusiasts won't want to miss the peaceful and harmoniously designed **Dr. Sun Yat-sen Classical Chinese Garden,** 578 Carrall St. at the back of the Cultural Centre, tel. (604) 662-3207. Designed by artisans from Suzhou, China—a city famous for its green-thumbed residents—the garden features lime-stone rockeries, a waterfall and tranquil pools, and a variety of beautiful trees and plants hidden away behind tall walls. This was the first authentic classical Chinese garden to be built outside China. It's open daily from 10 a.m.; admission is adults $5, seniors and students $3.50. Tours are conducted six times daily. During summer, "Enchanted Evenings" held on the first Friday of each month give visitors a chance to tour the gardens and taste teas from around the world.

To get to Chinatown from downtown catch bus no. 19 or 22 east along Pender Street. Try to avoid East Hastings St. at all times; it's Vancouver's skid row, inhabited by unsavory characters day and night.

Vancouver Centennial Police Museum
This museum, 240 E. Cordova St., tel. (604) 665-3346, catalogs the history of Vancouver's police and the notorious criminals they chased. Formerly the city morgue, the museum houses a variety of historic police equipment, some intriguing seized items, and re-creations of the city's most famous crime scenes. Summer hours are Mon.-Sat. 11:30 a.m.-4:30 p.m., the rest of the year Mon.-Fri. 11:30 a.m.-4:30 p.m. Admission is adults $2, seniors and children $1. To get there, avoid walking E. Hastings St. for safety's sake and instead take bus no. 4 or 7 north up from Granville Mall.

WEST END

Pretty, park-fringed **English Bay Beach** is part of the section of Vancouver that locals call the West End. The golden sands, tree-shaded grass roadsides, and sidewalks are popular places to find poodle walkers, joggers, cyclists, and sun worshippers. Behind the beach lie ritzy condos and apartment blocks, homes with tidy gardens up quiet backstreets, and Denman Street's trendy cafes and restaurants. On Sunday, large numbers of Vancouverites congregate here for brunch and an afternoon stroll along the bay. The more energetic head for the north end of the beach to walk the Seawall Promenade beside magnificent Stanley Park.

Robson Street
If you like to shop in trendy boutiques, sample European delicacies, and sip cappuccinos at sidewalk cafes, saunter along this colorful and exciting street linking downtown to the West End. Once the center of a predominantly German neighborhood, Robson Street is also known as **Robsonstrasse.** At 1610 Robson (the west end), **Robson Public Market** occupies an impressive atrium-topped building filled with meat, seafood, dairy products, fruits and veggies, nuts, flowers, craft vendors, fresh juice and salad bars, and an international food fair. To get there catch bus no. 3, which runs west along Robson St. from Granville Mall. Between the market and Burrard St. is the trendy Robsonstrasse shopping area.

Roedde House Museum
Built in 1893, this restored house at 1415 Barclay St. (take Broughton St. off Robson St.), tel. (604) 684-7040, is a classic example of Vancouver's Edwardian architecture. The two-story residence was designed by Francis Rattenbury, architect of Victoria's Empress Hotel. It's furnished in period style and open to the public. Tours of the house are conducted Monday, Wednesday, and Friday at 2 p.m.

The house is on **Barclay Heritage Square,** a precinct of eight houses from the same era, each looking much as they would have when first built, right down to the style of surrounding gardens.

Stanley Park
Beautiful Stanley Park, a lush 405-hectare tree- and garden-carpeted peninsula jutting out into Burrard Inlet, is a sight for sore eyes in any weather—an enormous peaceful oasis sand-

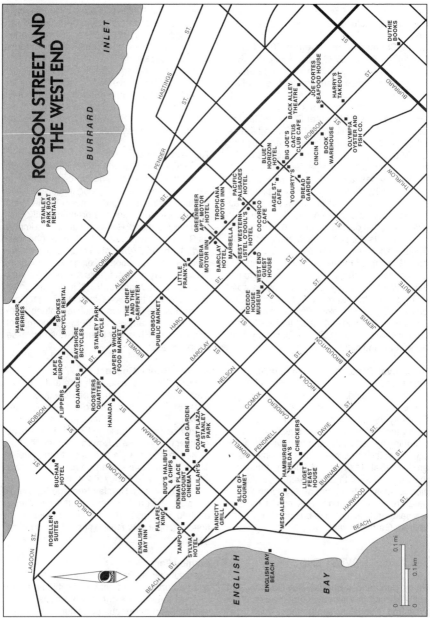

ROBSON STREET AND
THE WEST END

BURRARD INLET

BURRARD

© MOON PUBLICATIONS, INC.

wiched between city center's skyscrapers and commotion and North Vancouver at the other end of Lions Gate Bridge. It was named after Lord Stanley, Canada's governor-general from 1888 to 1893, who had the foresight to preserve the peninsula as a park for "the use and enjoyment of all peoples of all colors, creeds, and customs for all time."

Walk the 10-km **Seawall Promenade** or cycle or drive the perimeter via **Stanley Park Drive** to take in beautiful water and city views. Several stops of interest are found along the way, including Lost Lagoon Bird Sanctuary, totem poles, the Nine o'clock Gun, the *Girl in Wetsuit* statue, and the Teahouse Restaurant. Sauntering along any of the peaceful, forested trails crisscrossing the park or traversing the yellow-iris-edged shoreline of Lost Lagoon, you'll spy some of the resident waterfowl. Mallards, Canada geese, and swans abound, and fluffy ducklings and goslings are everywhere in spring.

Vancouver Aquarium, in the east of the park, tel. (604) 685-3364, is North America's third-largest aquarium. Among the more than 8,000 aquatic animals on display: orcas, beluga whales, sea lions, seals, halibut, crocodiles, sharks, and piranhas. The complex also holds a

rehabilitation center for rescued marine mammals and the Wildlife Crime Busters exhibit, displaying techniques used to catch poachers. It's all open in summer, daily 9:30 a.m.-8 p.m.; the rest of the year, daily 10 a.m.-5:30 p.m. Admission is adults $9.50, seniors $8.25, children $6.25. Don't miss the adjacent **children's zoo** where you can see everything from cheeky river otters hamming it up to lethargic polar bears panting in the sun. It's open daily 10 a.m. till dusk; admission free. Also near the aquarium, immediately east of the Royal Vancouver Yacht Club, is **Dead Man's Island,** the burial place of the last of the Coast Salish people.

Horse-drawn trams leave regularly from the park entrance on a 30-minute tour; adults $14, children $11. In summer, the city bus system also operates within the park; catch bus no. 19 on Pender St., then transfer onto bus no. 52 (Stanley Park Loop). The latter operates on good weather weekends and holidays; no service on weekdays or rainy days.

SOUTH OF DOWNTOWN

B.C. Place Stadium
Another Vancouver landmark, this 60,000-seat stadium at 777 Pacific Blvd., tel. (604) 669-2300, is the world's largest air-supported domed stadium. At Gate A is the **B.C. Sports Hall of Fame and Museum,** tel. (604) 687-5520. Displays in the Hall of Champions catalog the careers of British Columbia's greatest sports achievers. Memorabilia, old photographs, and a few videos commemorate the greats, while the Participation Gallery allows you to run, jump, climb, row, and throw, testing yourself against professional athletes. It's open Tues.-Sun. 10 a.m.-5 p.m.; admission is adults $6, seniors and children $4. The stadium also serves as the home of the B.C. Lions, one of the top Canadian Football League teams, and is the venue for major shows, concerts, and other big events. For coming events call (604) 661-7373. To get there, take the SkyTrain to Stadium Station, or take buses 15 or 17 south on Burrard Street.

Science World British Columbia
The impressive, 17-story, gleaming silver golf ball on the southeast side of city center, 1455

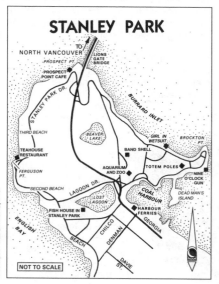

STANLEY PARK

NOT TO SCALE

© MOON PUBLICATIONS, INC.

Quebec St., tel. (604) 268-6363, was Expo Centre during Expo86. Then it housed restaurants, shops, and the world's largest Omnimax theater. Today the Vancouver landmark is home to Science World, a museum providing changing exhibitions that "introduce the world of science to the young and the young at heart." Numerous hands-on displays make it great fun for all ages.

Science World is open daily 10 a.m.-5 p.m.; admission is adults $9, seniors and children $5.50. The Omnimax theater is still here, and costs extra. The most enjoyable way to get to Science World is aboard a False Creek Ferry, from Granville Island or the Aquatic Centre. If you don't want to take the ferry, you can drive to the west end of Terminal Ave.—plenty of parking is available—or take the SkyTrain to Main Street Station, then walk across the street.

Granville Island

Prior to the 1970s, Granville Island was the dowdy, all-but-abandoned center of Vancouver's maritime industries. Now the refurbished, jazzed-up island is *the* place to go on a bright sunny day—allow at least several hours or an entire afternoon for this hive of activity. The triangular island lies in the middle of False Creek, immediately south of downtown.

Start at **Granville Island Information Centre,** 1592 Johnson St., tel. (604) 666-5784; open daily 9 a.m.-6 p.m., closed Monday in winter. The center offers a ton of local information, as well as displays and an audio-visual presentation detailing the island's colorful history.

After a preliminary stop at the info center, you can spend the better part of a day just walking around the island looking at the marina, the gift shops, the restaurants, and the theaters. Among the highlights are the **Emily Carr Institute of Art and Design,** 1399 Johnston St., tel. (604) 844-3800, where two galleries are worth perusing, and the colorful **Granville Island Public Market,** open daily 9 a.m.-6 p.m. Inside the market you'll find all kinds of things to eat—from fresh fruit and vegetables to prepared ready-to-go meals—as well

as unique jewelry and crafts, potted plants, and cut flowers. Grab a tasty bite and take it out onto the wharf to enjoy all the False Creek harbor activity—in summer the water teems with sailboats, small ferries, and barges. You can rent your own rowboat, kayak, or windsurfer right here. For details of the best shopping the island has to offer, see "Shopping" under "Recreation," below.

To get to the island by boat, jump aboard one of the small **False Creek Ferries.** The boats run regularly between the island, Vancouver Aquatic Centre at Sunset Beach ($1.75), and Vanier Park ($3). To get to the island by land, take a no. 50 (False Creek) bus from Howe St. to the stop under Granville Bridge at the entrance to the island, or take a Granville Island bus from downtown. Parking on the island is monstrous, at best, especially on weekends when locals do their fresh-produce shopping. If you do find a spot, it'll have a three-hour maximum stay.

CENTRAL VANCOUVER

Vancouver's three largest museums and a number of public gardens lie in Central Vancouver, a largely residential area of the city south of downtown and extending west to Point Grey and the University of British Columbia.

Vancouver Museum

Regional history from Precambrian times to the present comes to life at Vancouver Museum, 1100 Chestnut St. in Vanier Park, tel. (604) 736-4431. The West Coast archaeology and culture galleries hold ravishing masks, highly patterned woven blankets, and fine baskets. The Discovery and Settlement Gallery details European exploration of British Columbia—both by land and by sea. After browsing through the forestry and mill-town displays and the metropolis of Vancouver exhibit, you'll end up in the gallery of changing exhibitions where you never know what you'll find. The complex also holds a

DOVER PUBLICATIONS, INC.

gift shop and a self-serve restaurant overlooking Vanier Park. It's open in summer, daily 10 a.m.-9 p.m.; the rest of the year, Tues.-Sun. 10 a.m.-5 p.m. Admission is adults $6, children $3.

To reach the museum catch bus no. 22 on Burrard St. and get off after Burrard Bridge at the Cornwall and Chestnut St. stop, or catch a ferry to Vanier Park from Granville Island or the Aquatic Centre at Sunset Beach. If you're driving, you'll find plenty of free parking.

Above the museum is the **Pacific Space Centre,** tel. (604) 738-7827, a planetarium where you can galaxy-gaze Tues.-Fri. at 3 p.m. and 8 p.m., and weekends and holidays at noon, 1:30 p.m., 3 p.m., and 8 p.m. Admission is adults $6, seniors and children $4. The Space Centre also presents a popular laser rock music show Tues.-Sun. at 9:30 p.m., with additional shows on Friday and Saturday night; $8 per person, buy your ticket in advance to ensure a seat. Next to the museum is the **Gordon Southam Observatory,** open Fri.-Sat. 7:30 a.m.-midnight and Sat.-Sun. 1-4 p.m. when the skies are clear; admission is free.

Vancouver Maritime Museum

Just a five-minute stroll from Vancouver Museum is Vancouver Maritime Museum, 1905 Ogden Ave. (the end of Cypress Ave.) in Vanier Park, tel. (604) 257-8300. British Columbia's seafaring legacy is the focus here. Exhibits chronicle everything from the province's first sea explorers and their vessels to today's oceangoing adventurers, modern fishing boats, and fancy ships. Kids will love the Children's Maritime Discovery Centre and its model ships, computer terminals, and telescopes for viewing ships out in the harbor. The historic RCMP vessel, *St. Roch,* is dry-docked within the building, and admission includes a tour. Now a National Historic Site, the *St. Roch* was the first patrol vessel to successfully negotiate the infamous Northwest Passage. When you're through inside the museum, you can wander down behind it to view an international fleet of vessels docked in Heritage Harbour.

The museum is open daily 10 a.m.-5 p.m. Admission is adults $5, seniors and children $2.50. From downtown, take bus no. 22 south on Burrard St. or walk down Burrard St. to the Aquatic Centre and hop aboard a False Creek Ferry.

Museum of Anthropology

Containing the world's largest collection of arts and crafts of the Pacific Northwest native peoples, this excellent museum on the campus of the University of British Columbia, 6393 Northwest Marine Dr., tel. (604) 822-3825, should not be missed. Designed by innovative Canadian architect Arthur Erickson, the ultramodern concrete-and-glass building perches on a high cliff overlooking the Pacific Ocean and mimics the post-and-beam structures of the Coastal Salish.

The entrance is flanked by panels that create the shape of a Bent-box, which the Salish believed contained the meaning of life. Once inside, a ramp lined with impressive sculptures by renowned modern-day carvers leads to the Great Hall, a cavernous 18-meter-high room dominated by towering totem poles collected from along the coast and interspersed with other ancient works. Other displays include intricate carvings, baskets, and ceremonial masks, fabulous jewelry, and European ceramics. The museum's research collections are uniquely accessible. Instead of being stored in musty boxes out back and available only to crusty old anthropologists, the collections are stored in the main museum— in row upon row of glass-enclosed cabinets and in drawers that visitors are encouraged to open. Details of each piece are noted in handy catalogs.

Outside, a deliciously scented woodland path on the left side of the museum leads to a reconstructed Haida village and a number of contemporary totem poles with descriptive plaques.

In summer, the museum is open daily 11 a.m.-5 p.m., and till 9 p.m. on Tuesday nights. The rest of year, the museum is closed Monday but other hours remain the same. Admission is adults $6, seniors and children $3.50, everyone free on Tuesdays in the off-season. To get there, take bus no. 4 or 10 south along Granville Mall. If you have your own vehicle, go armed with a fistful of quarters and park in the lot beside the museum.

Other Sights on the University Campus

The University of British Columbia opened in 1925 and now enrolls over 30,000 students annually. The campus enjoys a spectacular coastal location, surrounded by over 750 hectares of parkland laced with hiking trails. Many of the trails provide access to the beach. If you're interested in learning more about the university, join one of the student-led tours which leave the Student Union Building daily through summer at 10 a.m. and 1 p.m.

About 300 meters south of the Museum of Anthropology is the serene **Nitobe Memorial Garden,** tel. (604) 822-6038, a traditional Japanese garden of shrubs and miniatures spread over one hectare. It's open in summer, daily 10 a.m.-6 p.m., weekdays only the rest of the year. Admission is $2.50.

Also on campus is the **UBC Botanical Garden,** 6804 Marine Dr., tel. (604) 822-9666. Set among coastal forest, the 28-hectare garden dates to the turn of the century and features a large rhododendron collection, vegetables, fruits, and nuts suited to the coastal climate, and a display of mountain plants from the world's continents. It's open every day of the year, 10 a.m.-6 p.m. Admission is adults $4.25, seniors $2.

On the east side of campus, a three-iron from the University golf course, is the **B.C. Golf Museum,** 2545 Blanca St., tel. (604) 222-4653, housing a collection of golfing memorabilia and extensive archives. It's open year-round, Tues.-Sun. noon-4 p.m.; admission is free.

VanDusen Botanical Garden

This 22-hectare garden at 5251 Oak St., tel. (604) 878-9274, is the city's answer to Victoria's Butchart Garden, albeit on a smaller scale. Feast your eyes on over 1,000 varieties of rhododendrons, as well as on roses, all kinds of botanical rarities, an Elizabethan hedge maze, and a children's topiary garden featuring animal shapes. The complex includes a shop selling cards, perfumes, soaps, potpourri, and all kinds of gifts with a floral theme, and popular **Sprinklers Restaurant,** tel. (604) 261-0011, where the light and airy decor, picture windows, and garden view bring the outside inside. Sprinklers is open daily, 11:30 a.m.-3 p.m. for a reasonably priced lunch, and 5:30-9 p.m. for a more expensive, dressier dinner; reservations recommended.

The garden is open in summer, daily 10 a.m.-9 p.m.; the rest of the year, daily 10 a.m.-4 p.m. Admission is adults $5, seniors $2.50. To get there by bus, take no. 17 south along Burrard Street. Oak Street runs parallel to Granville Street; access to the garden is on the corner of E. 33rd Avenue.

Queen Elizabeth Park

Less than two km from the VanDusen Botanical Garden, this 53-hectare park is a gardener's paradise of sweeping lawns, trees, flowering shrubs, formal flower gardens, and masses of rhododendrons—a vivid spectacle in May and June. The park sits atop 152-meter **Little Mountain,** the city's highest point, so magnificent views of Vancouver and the Coast Mountains are an added bonus. Admission to the park is free.

Within the park is the magnificent **Bloedel Floral Conservatory,** tel. (604) 257-8570, a glass-domed structure rising 40 meters and enclosing a temperature-controlled, humid tropical

Bloedel Observatory in Queen Elizabeth Park

JANE AND BRUCE KING

jungle. Inside you'll find a profusion of exotic flowering plants and a resident avian population including multihued parrots. The conservatory is open daily 10.a.m.-5 p.m., until 9 p.m. in summer. Admission is adults $3, seniors and children $1.50; The main entrance is by the junction of East 33rd Ave. and Cambie St.; to get there from downtown take bus no. 15 south on Burrard Street.

FARTHER SOUTH

Steveston
South of Central Vancouver in Richmond, historic Steveston Fishing Village is a lively spot worth a visit. For an introduction to the town's heritage, check out **Steveston Museum**, in the Royal Bank building at 3811 Moncton St., tel. (604) 271-6868. It's open Mon.-Sat. 9:30 a.m.-5 p.m. Then you can visit one of the many fishing-supply outlets or head for **Steveston Landing** on Bayview Road. The landing is lined with boutiques and restaurants, and bustles with activity in summer. Below the landing, fishing boats sell the day's catch. Shrimp are especially good value (avoid the headless ones) at around $4 per pound. To watch all the action, grab a seat on the deck of **Shady Island Seafood,** 3800 Bayview Rd., tel. (604) 275-6587, where daily specials are around $7, a bowl of incredibly good clam chowder is $4.50, and burgers with fries start at $6. Farther along the harborfront you'll find the **Gulf of Georgia Cannery National Historic Site,** 12138 4th Ave., tel. (604) 664-9009, and an old shipyard now transformed into an interpretive center.

To get to Steveston, take bus no. 401, 406, or 407 south on Howe Street. If you're driving, take Hwy. 99 to the Steveston Hwy. exit, passing by a magnificent Buddhist temple before entering Steveston town center.

George C. Reifel Bird Sanctuary
Like Steveston, this great attraction is missed by most visitors. The 350-hectare sanctuary protects low-lying Westham Island, a stopover for thousands of migratory birds in spring and fall. In the middle of a wide delta at the mouth of the Fraser River, the island is a world away from surrounding city life.

The best time for a visit is during the spectacular snow goose migration, which runs from early November to mid-December. Otherwise, you'll see abundant migratory bird life anytime between October and April. The island also serves as a permanent home for many bird species, including bald eagles, peregrine falcons, herons, swans, and owls.

Within the sanctuary are many kilometers of trails, an observation tower, free birdseed, and a couple of picnic areas. It's open year-round, daily 10 a.m.-4 p.m. Admission is adults $3.25, seniors and children $1. To get there, take Hwy. 99 south through Central Vancouver, then take Hwy. 17 south toward the Tsawwassen ferry terminal. Follow signs north along Robertson Rd. and over a short bridge to the sanctuary.

NORTH VANCOUVER AND VICINITY

To explore the many outdoor attractions north of Burrard Inlet, take the SeaBus from Waterfront Station to **Lonsdale Quay** (adults $1.50 each way). At the lively quay, a small information booth dispenses valuable information, and transit buses depart regularly for all the sights listed below. Locals come here to meet friends over coffee, or to stock up at a farmers' market full of fresh fruit and veggies, fish, meats, bread, flowers, and plants. Some take time out from shopping for a quick bite to eat, a cool drink, and a stunning harbor view from one of many in- or outdoor tables. The quay also features many gift shops and boutiques, restaurants, and the Lonsdale Quay Hotel (see "North Vancouver and Vicinity" under "Other Parts of the City" in the Accommodations and Camping section, below).

Capilano Suspension Bridge
The first bridge across the Capilano River opened in 1899. That remarkable wood-and-hemp structure spanned 137 meters across the deep canyon. Today, several bridges later, the canyon is spanned by a wood-and-wire suspension bridge a fearsome 70 meters above the Capilano River. Allow 30 minutes to walk the bridge and the nature trails on the far side, view the totem-pole carvers in action in summer, and browse the requisite gift shop. Admission is a bit steep—adults $8.25, seniors $7—but it's one

of Vancouver's most popular sights. (If you don't want to spend the money, you can get much of the same thrill by crossing the free bridge in Lynn Canyon Park; see below). The Capilano Suspension Bridge is open in summer, daily 8:30 a.m.-dusk; the rest of the year, daily 9 a.m.-5 p.m. For more information call (604) 985-7474. To get there by car, cross Lions Gate Bridge, turn east onto Marine Dr. then immediately north onto Capilano Rd., continuing to 3735 Capilano, on your left. By bus, take no. 246 north on Georgia St. or jump aboard the SeaBus and take bus no. 236 from Lonsdale Quay.

Capilano Salmon Hatchery and Regional Park

If you've always wanted to know more about the miraculous life cycle of a salmon, or want some facts to back up your fish stories, visit this hatchery on the Capilano River, two km upstream from the suspension bridge (turn onto Capilano Park Rd. from Capilano Rd.), tel. (604) 666-1790. Along with educational displays and nature exhibits you can see what the fish see from an underwater point of view. From July through October, magnificent adult coho and chinook salmon fight their way upriver to the hatchery. It's open daily 8 a.m.-4 p.m. Admission is free.

The hatchery is within **Capilano River Regional Park,** which extends north to **Cleveland Dam.** The dam was built in 1954 to form Capilano Lake—Vancouver's main drinking-water supply. Within the park are many kilometers of hiking trails, including one that leads all the way down to where the Capilano River drains into Burrard Inlet; seven km (two hours) each way.

Grouse Mountain

Continuing north, Capilano Rd. becomes Nancy Greene Way and ends at the base of the **Skyride Gondola,** tel. (604) 984-0661. For an excellent view of downtown Vancouver, Stanley Park, the Pacific Ocean, and as far south as Mount Baker (Washington), take the almost-vertical eight-minute ride on the gondola to the upper slopes of 1,250-meter Grouse Mountain. Tickets are adults $14.50, seniors $12.50, children $5.95. Ask about a discount with your BC Transit DayPass. The gondola runs year-round, departing every 10 minutes 10 a.m.-10 p.m. in summer.

Facilities at the top include the casual **Mountain Bistro,** where you can drink in some high-elevation sunshine along with the view on the outdoor deck (open daily 11 a.m.-10 p.m.); the fancy **Grouse Nest Restaurant,** which provides free Skyride tickets with dinner reservations (open daily 5:30 p.m.-9:30 p.m.); and a picnic area. In addition, three chairlifts continue higher up the mountain, and paved paths and nature trails skirt mountain meadows. Of the many possible hikes, the one-km **Blue Grouse Interpretive Trail** is the easiest and most enjoyable, winding around a lake and through a rainforest. More ambitious hikers will have ready access to the rugged West Coast Range.

For a bit of extra excitement when you get to the top, get a bird's-eye view of Vancouver with a **Grouse Mountain Helicopter Tour,** tel. (604) 525-1484. The chopper tour costs $40 per person for five minutes, $60 for 10 minutes. Flights lift off daily, 11 a.m. to sunset. In July the **World Invitational Hang Gliding Championship** takes to the air from the slopes of Grouse Mountain, and in summer you can often watch hang-gliding demonstrations. In winter, skiers can choose from beginner to advanced runs on the slopes of Grouse Mountain, with the added magic of night skiing (see "Skiing" under "Recreation," below).

To get to the gondola by bus from downtown, take the SeaBus to Lonsdale Quay, then take bus no. 236 to the end of the road.

Cypress Provincial Park

This 3,012-hectare park northwest of downtown encompasses a high alpine area in the North Shore Mountains. Even the road up to the park is worthwhile for the views; the roadside Highview Lookout provides a stunning panorama of the city. After passing a couple more lookouts, the road enters the park, ending at Cypress Bowl ski area. From the ski area parking lot, well-marked hiking trails radiate out like spokes, through alpine meadows and to low peaks with views across Howe Sound. With a vivid imagination, maybe you'll spot *Say-noth-kai,* the two-headed sea serpent of native Salish legend, believed to inhabit the sound. On a clear day you can also make out the cone of Mt. Baker, one of a row of Pacific Coast volcanoes. It's to the southeast, in Washington state.

Another concentration of hiking trails surrounds the old Hollyburn Lodge, in the park's southeast corner. Among many short hikes possible here, a six-km (one-way) trail leads to the 1,325-meter summit of Hollyburn Mountain. The trail gains 450 meters in elevation; allow 2.5 hours each way.

Aside from the ski resort, the park's only facilities are the picnic areas dotting the access road. Camping is permitted only in the backcountry. (For information on skiing within the park, see "Skiing" under "Recreation," later in this chapter).

To get to the park, take the TransCanada Hwy. 12 km west of Lions Gate Bridge and turn north onto Cypress Bowl Road.

Lighthouse Park

On a headland jutting into Howe Sound, 70-hectare Lighthouse Park lies eight km west of the Lions Gate Bridge. Trails lead through the park to coastal cliffs and a lighthouse that guides shipping into narrow Burrard Inlet. Views from the lighthouse grounds are spectacular, extending west over the Strait of Georgia and east to Stanley Park and the Vancouver skyline. Get there along Marine Dr. or aboard bus no. 250 from Georgia Street.

Horseshoe Bay

The pretty little residential area of Horseshoe Bay offers plenty to see and do while you wait for the Vancouver Island or Sunshine Coast ferry. If you and your trusty vehicle are catching one of the ferries, buy your ticket at the car booth, move your automobile into the lineup, then explore the town. Several restaurants, a bakery, a supermarket, a pub, and a couple of good delis cater to the hungry and thirsty. A stroll along the beautiful waterfront marina is a good way to cool your heels and dwindle away some waiting time.

Lynn Canyon Park

On its way to Burrard Inlet, Lynn Creek flows through a deep canyon straddled by this 240-hectare park. Spanning the canyon is the "other" suspension bridge. The one here, built in 1912, is half as wide as its more famous counterpart over the Capilano River, but it's a few meters higher and, best of all, it's free. An ancient forest of Douglas fir surrounds the impressive canyon and harbors a number of hiking trails. Also visit **Lynn Canyon Ecology Centre,** tel. (604) 981-3103, where displays, models, and free slide shows and films explore plant and animal ecology. The center is open daily 10 a.m.-5 p.m.; admission is free.

Lynn Canyon Park is seven km east of the Capilano River. To get there by car, take the Lynn Valley Rd. exit off Hwy. 1, east of the Lions Gate Bridge. By public transport, take the SeaBus to Lonsdale Quay, then bus no. 228 or 229.

Farther upstream is **Lynn Headwaters Regional Park,** a remote tract of wilderness on the edge of the city. Contact the Ecology Centre for more information.

Mount Seymour
Provincial Park and Vicinity

Hikers and skiers flock to this 3,508-hectare park 20 km northeast of downtown. The park lies off Mt. Seymour Parkway, which spurs east off the TransCanada Highway just north of Burrard Inlet. The long and winding access road to the park climbs steadily through an ancient forest of western hemlock, cedar, and Douglas fir to a small facility area at an elevation of 1,000 meters. From the parking lot, trails lead to the summit of 1,453-meter Mt. Seymour; two km (one-way), allow one hour.

If you continue along Mount Seymour Parkway instead of turning north toward the park, you end up in the scenic little village of **Deep Cove** on the west shore of Indian Arm (off the northeast end of Burrard Inlet)—an excellent spot for a picnic. Take your sack lunch to the waterfront park and watch the fishing and pleasure boats coming and going in the bay. More adventurous visitors can swim, kayak, or scuba dive.

Golden Ears Provincial Park

Encompassing 55,590 hectares of the Coast Mountains northeast of Vancouver, this park extends from the Alouette River, near the suburb of Maple Ridge, north to Garibaldi Provincial Park. To get to the main facility areas, follow Hwy. 7 east out of the city for 40 km to Maple Ridge, then follow signs north. Much of the park was logged for railway ties in the 1920s, but today the second-growth montane forest—dominated by western hemlock—has almost erased the early human devastation.

The park access road follows the Alouette River into the park, ending at Alouette Lake. The river and lake provide fair fishing, but the park's most popular activity is hiking. **Lower**

Falls Trail begins from the end of the road and leads 2.7 km (one-way) along Gold Creek to a 10-meter-high waterfall; allow one hour each way. Across Gold Creek, **West Canyon Trail** climbs 200 meters over 1.5 km (allow 40 minutes each way) to a viewpoint of Alouette Lake. This trail begins from the West Canyon parking lot, where you'll also find a 12-km trail along the west bank of Gold Creek to Panorama Ridge and to the summit of the park's namesake, the

Golden Ears. The name comes from the way the setting sun reflects off the twin peaks of Mt. Blanchard. This trail gains 1,500 meters, making it an extremely strenuous hike best undertaken as an overnight trip.

A number of riverside and lakeside picnic areas line the park access road, and at road's end are two large campgrounds, each with hot showers, flush toilets, picnic tables and fire rings; $15.50 per night.

RECREATION

BICYCLING

Stanley Park is a mecca for cyclists; among its network of bike paths is the popular Seawall Promenade, which hugs the coast for 10 km. On the south side of English Bay, a cycle path runs from Vanier Park to Point Grey and the university, passing all the city's best beaches on the way. On the north side of Burrard Inlet, hard-core mountain-bike enthusiasts tackle the rough trails of Cypress Provincial Park and Grouse Mountain.

Near the entrance to Stanley Park, where Robson and Denman Streets meet, you'll find a profusion of bike-rental shops; expect to pay from $5 per hour or $15 per day for the most basic bike, $12 per hour or $36 per day for a good mountain bike.

WATER SPORTS

Swimming and Sunbathing
All of Vancouver's best beaches are found along the shoreline of English Bay. Closest to downtown is **English Bay Beach,** at the end of Denman Street. Flanked by a narrow strip of parkland and a wide array of cafes and restaurants, this is *the* beach for peoplewatching. From English Bay Beach the Seawall Promenade leads north to **Second** and **Third Beaches,** both short, secluded stretches of sand. To the south is **Sunset Beach,** most popular with families.

Swimmers take note: Even at the peak of summer, the water here only warms up to about 17° C, tops. If that doesn't sound very enticing,

continue to the south end of Sunset Beach to **Vancouver Aquatic Centre,** 1050 Beach Ave., tel. (604) 665-3424. Inside is a 50-meter heated pool, saunas, whirlpools, and a small weight room. Admission is adults $3.50, seniors $2.

On the south side of English Bay, **Kitsilano Beach** offers spectacular views back across the bay to downtown and the mountains beyond. Again, for those who find the ocean temperatures a bit cool, take a dip in the adjacent public pool; $3. The beach and pool are an easy walk from both Vanier Park and a False Creek Ferries dock. Continuing west along Marine Dr. you'll come to **Jericho Beach,** with more great mountain views, then **Locarno** and **Spanish Banks Beaches.**

Canoeing and Kayaking
Granville Island is the center of action for paddlers, and the calm waters of adjacent False Creek make the perfect place to practice your skills. For the widest choice of equipment, head to **Adventure Fitness,** 1510 Duranleau St., tel. (604) 687-1528, or **Ecomarine Ocean Kayak Centre,** 1668 Duranleau St., tel. (604) 689-7575. Both rent single sea kayaks from $14 for two hours or $25 for 24 hours, and double sea kayaks and canoes from $19 for two hours, $30 for 24 hours. The companies also teach kayaking, run day trips to spectacular **Indian Arm** of Burrard Inlet, and lead overnight trips to destinations through the Southern Gulf Islands.

Fishing, Boating, and Yachting
Most keen anglers will want to head further afield for the best fishing opportunities, but a few runs of salmon occur within city limits, and

JANE AND BRUCE KING

It's a lot of fun putt-putting about False Creek by ferry—and inexpensive, too.

rainbow trout, kokanee, and Dolly Varden inhabit the larger mountain lakes north of the city. Boat-rental outlets include **Stanley Park Boat Rentals,** Coal Harbour Marina, 566 Cardero St., tel. (604) 682-6257; and **Granville Island Boat Rentals,** 1696 Duranleau St., tel. (604) 682-6287. These outlets sell bait and tackle and can direct you to the fishing hot spots. One charter operator that comes highly recommended is **Hi-liner Fishing Adventures,** 985 Crosscreek Rd., West Vancouver, tel. (604) 926-8184.

Yachties should head for **Cooper Boating Centre,** 1620 Duranleau St., Granville Island, tel. (604) 687-4110, which offers basic cruising courses, bareboat charters, and extended sailing trips. Rates for bareboat charters start at $1,125 for seven days aboard a 27-foot yacht. Low-season rates are considerably less. For an extra $100, you can take a skipper along for the first day.

Scuba Diving

Scuba diving might not be the best-known recreational activity in the Vancouver area, but the diving in the Strait of Georgia is world-class, reflected in the city's high number of dive shops—over 20 at last count. Unfortunately, a plankton bloom reduces visibility considerably through the warmer months so the best time of year for diving is winter, when the water is at its most frigid. Most winter divers slip into a six-millimeter wetsuit or a drysuit; these can be rented from most dive shops. During winter, visibility is in-

credible, especially offshore. Hundreds of colorful marine species live in nearby waters, and wrecks litter the seabed. At Porteau Beach, north of Horseshoe Bay, wrecks have even been placed just offshore for shore divers to enjoy. **Rowand's Reef Scuba Shop,** 1512 Duranleau St., Granville Island, tel. (604) 669-3483, is a full-service dive shop offering rentals, sales, organized diving trips, and dive-certification courses throughout the year.

SKIING

While Vancouver is the gateway to world-renowned Whistler/Blackcomb (see "Skiing" under "Whistler and Vicinity" in the Southwestern British Columbia chapter), the city boasts three other downhill ski resorts on its back doorstep. They don't offer the terrain or facilities of Whistler, and their low elevations can create unreliable conditions. But a day's skiing at any one of the three sure beats being stuck in the hustle and bustle of the city on a cold winter's day.

Grouse Mountain

Towering above North Vancouver, the cut slopes of this ski area can be seen from many parts of the city, but as you'd expect, on a clear day views from *up there* are much more spectacular. To get there, take Capilano Rd. north from the Trans-Canada, following it onto Nancy Greene Way, from where a gondola lifts you up 1,000 vertical meters to the slopes. Four chairlifts and a couple of T-bars serve a vertical rise of 300 meters. Advanced skiers shouldn't get too excited about a day's skiing here—even the runs with names like Inferno and Purgatory are pretty tame. But skiing the slopes of Grouse Mountain after dark is an experience you won't soon forget. Most runs are lit and overlook the city of Vancouver, laid out in all its brilliance far below. Facilities at the resort include a rental shop, ski school, and a couple of dining choices. Lift tickets are $30 per day. For more information call (604) 984-0661; for a snow report call (604) 986-6262.

Cypress Bowl

Located in Cypress Provincial Park, this ski area offers about 25 runs on a vertical rise of 580 meters. Its four double chairs open a wide variety of terrain, most suited to beginners and intermediates. Spectacular views take in Howe Sound and Vancouver Island. Another highlight of Cypress Bowl is the night skiing; many runs are lit until 11 p.m. Other facilities include a rental shop, ski school, cafe, and lounge. Lift tickets are $35 per day. Cypress Bowl also caters to cross-country skiers; of the resort's 16 km of groomed trails, most are set around the historic Hollyburn Lodge and lit for night skiing.

To get to the ski area, take the TransCanada Hwy. 12 km west from Lions Gate Bridge and turn north on Cypress Bowl Road. If you don't feel like driving up the mountain, catch the shuttle bus that departs hourly from Cypress Mountain Sports in Park Royal Mall, West Vancouver; $8 roundtrip. Cypress Mountain Sports also rents equipment and offers an overnight repair service. For ski area and shuttle bus information, call (604) 926-5612; for a snow report call (604) 926-6007.

Seymour Ski Country

With the highest base elevation of Vancouver's three ski areas, Seymour's snow is somewhat reliable, but the area's relatively gentle terrain will be of interest only to beginning and intermediate skiers. Four chairlifts serve 20 runs and a vertical rise of 365 meters. The emphasis is on learning at this hill, and a line of instructors always awaits your business. On-hill facilities include a massive day lodge with rental shop. Lift tickets are $28 per day.

The ski area is in Mt. Seymour Provincial Park. To get there, head north off the Trans-Canada Hwy. 15 km east of the Lions Gate Bridge, following the Mt. Seymour Parkway to Mt. Seymour Road. For resort information call (604) 924-1056; for a snow report call (604) 986-3444.

SPECTATOR SPORTS

Ice Hockey

The **Vancouver Canucks** have been a National Hockey League franchise since 1970. After playing at the Pacific Coliseum for 25 years they recently moved to General Motors Place, across from B.C. Place Stadium on Griffith Way. The team has been meeting with mixed success in recent seasons, but since the signing of some big names, home games attract sellout crowds. The season runs from October to April; ticket prices range $24-61. For more information call (604) 899-4600 or 899-4610.

Basketball

In 1995 Vancouver was awarded a franchise with the National Basketball Association, becoming the 29th team in the NBA and giving basketball-mad Vancouverites the opportunity to see the sport's biggest names demolish their home team. The **Grizzlies** share a home with the Canucks, playing at General Motors Place, 800 Griffith Way, tel. (604) 899-4666 or 899-4670.

Baseball

Baseball fans will love Nat Bailey Stadium, home to the **Vancouver Canadians,** a farm team for the California Angels. The field is a throwback to the heydays of baseball, featuring real grass and an old-style scoreboard that must be changed manually. The team plays in the AAA Pacific Coast League; the season runs April-October. Ticket prices range $6.50-8.50. The ballpark is on the corner of Ontario St. and 33rd Ave., adjacent to Queen Elizabeth Park in Central Vancouver, tel. (604) 872-5232.

Football

The **B.C. Lions,** tel. (604) 589-7627, are Vancouver's Canadian Football League franchise. American-football fans might be surprised by some of the plays—the rules are slightly different than those of the NFL. And no, you're not imagining things, the playing field is larger than those used in the game's American version. Home games are played at B.C. Place Stadium, on the south side of downtown at the corner of Robson and Beatty Sts., tel. (604) 669-2300. The season runs June through November; tickets range $13.50-43.

Motor Racing
The streets of Vancouver come alive on the first weekend of September during the **Molson Indy,** the grand finale of the CART Indy Series. The road circuit is set up on the south side of downtown along Pacific Boulevard. Ticket prices for the main Sunday race are $35; events earlier in the weekend are a little cheaper. For further information call (604) 280-4639 or 684-4639.

Horse Racing
Thoroughbred racing takes place in Exhibition Park at **Hastings Park Racecourse,** six km east of downtown on the corner of Renfrew and McGill Sts., tel. (604) 254-1631. Full betting and a variety of dining facilities are offered. The season runs April-October, with the first race starting at 1:30 p.m. on weekends and 6:30 p.m. on Wednesday and Friday.

ARTS AND ENTERTAINMENT

There's never a dull moment in Vancouver. For complete listings of all that's happening around the city, pick up the free *Georgia Strait* (weekly) or *Terminal City* (fortnightly), or buy a copy of one of the two daily newspapers, the *Province* or the *Vancouver Sun.*

Theater
Vancouver has theaters all over the city—for professional plays, amateur plays, comedy, and "instant" theater. One of the great joys of summer in the city is sitting around the main bandshell in Stanley Park watching **Theatre under the Stars,** Mon.-Sat. at 7 p.m.; $16 per person. For details of what's on call (604) 687-0174.

The **Ford Centre for the Performing Arts,** 777 Homer St., tel. (604) 280-2222, opened in November 1995 to host the biggest musical hits.

Designed by renowned architect Moshe Safdie, the modern wonder features a five-story glass lobby flanked by granite walls. The trilevel theater seats over 1,800 and boasts North America's largest stage. Matinees cost from $50 while evening shows range $55-90. One-hour tours of the complex depart from the lobby Mon.-Sat. at 10 a.m.; $4 per person.

The **Arts Club,** tel. (604) 687-1644, always offers excellent theater productions at its two locations: the Arts Club Theatre Granville Island, 1585 Johnston St., or the adjacent Arts Club Review. Productions range from drama to comedy to improv. Tickets run $8-25; book in advance and pick up your tickets at the door 30 minutes prior to showtime.

Since its inception in 1964, the **Vancouver Playhouse,** 543 W. 7th Ave. in Central Vancouver, tel. (604) 665-3050, has grown to become the city's largest theater company. Six productions are performed each year, and tickets are all under $15. Also in Central Vancouver, **Vancouver Little Theatre,** 3102 Main St., tel. (604) 876-4165, features productions by national and international companies, as well as works by up-and-coming local artists. Expect to pay $8-15.

For university productions, head out to **Frederic Wood Theatre,** on the UBC campus, tel. (604) 822-2678. Performances run throughout the academic year; admission is generally around $10. **Back Alley Theatre,** 751 Thurlow St., tel. (604) 688-7013, puts on a variety of shows for $12 weekdays, $15 weekends, and $7 for Monday and Tuesday's rookie nights.

Music and Dance
The Queen Elizabeth Theatre, in the Queen Elizabeth Complex at 630 Hamilton St., is the home of **Vancouver Opera,** tel. (604) 682-2871, and the primary venue for **Ballet British Columbia,** tel. (604) 732-5003. Tickets to the opera begin at $30, while ballet tickets range $18-45; call Ticketmaster at (604) 280-3311. The theater also hosts a variety of music recitals and stage performances.

The historic Orpheum Theatre, on the corner of Smithe and Seymour Sts., dates to 1927 and houses its original Wurlitzer organ. Now fully restored, the theater provides excellent acoustics for the resident **Vancouver Sym-**

phony **Orchestra,** tel. (604) 684-9100, as well as for concerts by the professional **Vancouver Chamber Choir,** tel. (604) 738-6822, the amateur **Vancouver Bach Choir,** tel. (604) 921-8012, and a variety of other musical groups.

Cinemas

Cinemas are located in all the major shopping malls and elsewhere throughout the city. Combined, **Cineplex Odeon Cinemas,** tel. (604) 434-2463, and **Famous Players Theatres,** tel. (604) 681-4255, operate 17 cinemas in Vancouver. Call the respective numbers or check the two daily papers for locations and screenings. Admission to first-run screenings is about $8.

The **Paradise Theatre,** 919 Granville St., tel. (604) 681-1732, features commercial hits for the bargain-basement price of $4. If you're staying at a Robson Street or West End accommodation, head over to **Denman Place Discount Cinema,** corner of Denman and Comox Sts., tel. (604) 683-2201, for first- and second-run hits for $2.50-5. For foreign and fringe films, check out **Pacific Cinematheque,** 1131 Howe St., tel. (604) 688-8202. At the far end of Canada Place, the **CN IMAX Theatre,** tel. (604) 682-4629, provides spectacular movie entertainment and special effects on a massive screen. Ticket prices range $6.50-11.

Fun Parks

Kids will be kids, so even with an overabundance of outdoor-recreation opportunities, you may still want to spend time with the tribe at an old-fashioned fun park.

Playland, Exhibition Park, corner E. Hastings and Cassiar Sts., tel. (604) 255-5161, features plenty of old-fashioned amusements, including a merry-go-round, a wooden roller coaster, a games arcade, and a petting zoo. It's open in summer, daily 11 a.m.-10 p.m.; April-June and Sept.-Oct., weekends only and shorter hours. Admission is adults $24, children $21, which includes unlimited rides. To get there from downtown, take bus no. 14 or 16 north along Granville Mall.

Bars and Pubs

Ever since "Gassy Jack" Deighton set up the city's first liquor outlet (a barrel of whiskey set atop a crude plank "bar") in the area that be-

came known as Gastown, Vancouver has had its favorite watering holes. Local liquor laws require bars to serve food, so most are also good places for an inexpensive feed.

In the historic Landing building at 375 Water St., **Steamworks Pub and Brewery,** tel. (604) 689-2739, is the perfect place to relax with a beer from the in-house brewery. The atmosphere is casual yet stylish, and you'll have great views across Burrard Inlet. Hours are 11:30 a.m.-10 p.m. daily. In the same part of the city, but toward Chinatown, the lively **Blarney Stone** pub, 216 Carrall St., tel. (604) 687-4322, frequently resounds with rowdy impromptu Irish sing-alongs. Toward the West End, **Joe Fortes Seafood House,** 777 Thurlow St., tel. (604) 669-1940, boasts a great bar, complete with a wide range of beers and a condensed menu from the adjacent restaurant.

Checkers, 1755 Davie St., West End, tel. (604) 682-1831, is another popular bar, this one with a distinctive checkered decor and live rock on weekends. The small but always lively **Stamp's Landing Neighbourhood Pub** overlooks False Creek at 610 Stamp's Landing (just east of Granville Island), tel. (604) 879-0821. Aside from beer and liquor, Stamp's offers delicious tasty snacks to keep you going, live music on weekends, and great sunset views overlooking the harbor. Across Burrard Inlet from downtown, the **Rusty Gull Neighbourhood Pub,** 175 E. 1st St. in North Vancouver, tel. (604) 988-5585, features over a dozen locally brewed beers. Another favorite north of Burrard Inlet, **Queens Cross Neighbourhood Pub** on Upper Lonsdale at the corner of Queens Rd., tel. (604) 980-7715, is a favorite local hangout for lunch, after-work drinks, conversation, and evening meals.

Nightclubs

Nightclubs change names and reputations with regularity, so check with the free entertainment newspapers for the latest hot spots. Along with the cover charge, drink prices can be outrageous, so be prepared to overspend your budget if you plan on drinking and dancing the night away.

The city's most popular Top 40 nightclub is the **Big Bam Boo,** 1236 W. Broadway, Kitsilano, tel. (604) 733-2220. It's open Wed.-Sun. from 8 p.m. Cover charge is just $4 and drinks are reasonably priced, which attracts droves of students from the nearby UBC campus. Downtown, the **Commodore Ballroom,** 870 Granville St., tel. (604) 681-7838, features numerous video screens and a massive dance floor that becomes a mass of bodies on the Tuesday and Friday disco nights. Live bands perform on other nights. Cover charge is $6-10.

Denizens of the alternative-music scene might want to check out **MaR's,** 1320 Richards St., tel. (604) 662-7077, or **Luv-a-fair,** around the corner at 1275 Seymour St., tel. (604) 685-3288. At least, those are the recommendations of a couple of drugged-out, weird-looking, dance-music types I bumped into at a downtown cafe.

Rock

The world's biggest rock acts usually include Vancouver on their world tours, and the city's thriving local rock industry supports live bands at a variety of venues. Most big-name acts play the Orpheum or Queen Elizabeth Theatres. At the classic **Roxy,** 932 Granville St., tel. (604) 331-7999, bands play rock 'n' roll music from the 1960s and '70s. It's open nightly from 7 p.m.; cover charges range $3-7. For live bands, dancing, video, and a piano lounge head for the **Town Pump,** 66 Water St. in Gastown, tel. (604) 683-6695. In the same part of the city is the historic **Gastown Music Hall,** 6 Powell St., tel. (604) 685-1333, offering a dance floor and tiered seating. It's predominately a rock venue, but you might also catch blues or country acts on stage.

Jazz, Blues, and Comedy

The **Hot Jazz Society,** 2120 Main St., Central Vancouver, tel. (604) 873-4131, presents live jazz on a regular basis; cover charge is $6-9. The **Coastal Jazz and Blues Society,** tel. (604) 682-0706, maintains a listing of all the city's jazz and blues events.

Serious blues lovers should head to the historic **Yale Hotel,** 1300 Granville St., tel. (604) 681-9253, which has hosted some of the greatest names in the business. The hotel offers plenty of room for everyone, whether you want get up and dance or shoot pool down the back. Sunday is the only night without live performances, although a jam session starts up about 3 p.m. on Saturday and Sunday afternoons. Drinks are expensive and a $7 cover charge is collected Thurs.-Sat. nights. Closer to downtown, the **Wedgewood Hotel,** 845 Hornby St., tel. (604) 689-7777, features a resident blues guitarist performing nightly in the hotel's stylish lounge. No cover, but the drinks aren't cheap.

Punchlines Comedy Theatre, next to the Old Spaghetti Factory at 15 Water St. in Gastown, tel. (604) 684-3015, presents "the best" in stand-up comedy Saturday and Sunday at 9 p.m. and 11 p.m. Admission is around $10. The cover charge is much lower during the week, such as on Tuesday's amateur night ($3.50). **Yuk Yuk's,** 750 Pacific Blvd. S (Plaza of Nations), tel. (604) 687-5233, offers comedy nights Wed.-Saturday. Admission costs $3 on Wednesday (amateur night), $6 on Thursday, $11 on Friday and Saturday nights.

SHOPPING

Vancouver has shopping centers, malls, and specialty stores everywhere. Head to Gastown for native arts and crafts; Robson Street for boutique clothing; Granville Mall for department stores; Granville Island for everything from ships' chandlery to kids' clothing; Yaletown for the trendy clothes of local designers; East Hastings Street for army-surplus stores and pawnbrokers; Chinatown for Eastern foods; and the junction of Main Street and 49th Avenue in Central Vancouver for Indian goods.

Before you set out, drop in at Vancouver Visitor Info Centre, 200 Burrard St., and ask for their free *Shopping Guide.* In addition to listing all the department stores and specialty shops you're likely to want to visit, the guide contains handy fold-out maps of downtown Vancouver and greater Vancouver, with all the shops and malls marked.

Gastown

Sandwiched between the many cafes, restaurants, and tacky souvenir stores along Water Street are other stores selling Vancouver's best selection of native arts and crafts. One of the largest outlets, **Hill's Indian Crafts,** 165 Water St., tel. (604) 685-4249, sells $10 T-shirts, towering $12,000 totem poles, and everything in between, including genuine Cowichan sweaters and carved ceremonial masks. Also featuring traditional native art is **Images for a Canadian Heritage,** 164 Water St., tel. (604) 685-7046.

The **Inuit Gallery of Vancouver,** 345 Water St., tel. (604) 688-7323, is in The Landing, a waterfront warehouse built in 1905 and completely restored to a stylish arcade featuring such luminaries as Polo–Ralph Lauren. The gallery exhibits the work of Inuit and northwest coast native artists and sculptors. Among the highlights are many soapstone pieces by carvers from Cape Dorset.

Down the street from Hill's Indian Crafts, **Kites on Clouds,** 131 Water St., tel. (604) 669-5677, sells hundreds of different kites, from the simplest designs to elaborate constructions priced at over $200. The **Western Canada Wilderness Committee Store,** 20 Water St., tel. (604) 683-8220, features environmentally friendly souvenirs including shirts, posters, and calendars. A couple of blocks from Water St. in the Sinclair Centre is **Dorothy Grant,** 757 W. Hastings St., tel. (604) 681-0201, a clothing store named for its owner. Dorothy and her husband are renowned for their contemporary Haida-inspired designs. The **Sinclair Centre** itself is a local landmark; its four historic buildings now hold galleries, boutiques, and food outlets.

Granville Island

Arts and crafts galleries on Granville Island include **Wickaninnish Gallery,** 1666 Johnston St., tel. (604) 681-1057, selling stunning native art, jewelry, carvings, weaving, and original paintings; **Gallery of B.C. Ceramics,** 1359 Cartwright St., tel. (604) 669-5645, showcasing the work of the province's leading potters and sculptors; and **Forge and Form,** 1334 Cartwright St., tel. (604) 684-6298, which creates and sells a variety of gold and silver jewelry. A few blocks south of Granville Island at **Jade World,** 1696 W. 1st Ave., tel. (604) 733-7212, you can watch master carvers create works of art in jade. It's open Mon.-Fri. 8 a.m.-4:30 p.m.

Duranleau St. is home to many maritime-based businesses, adventure-tour operators, and charter operators. The **Quarterdeck,** 1660 Duranleau St., tel. (604) 683-8232, stocks everything from marine charts to brass shipping bells. **The Ocean Floor,** 1525 Duranleau St., tel. (604) 681-5014, sells a similar range of treasures, including sea shells and model ships. To buy a

sea kayak or canoe (from $1,000 secondhand), head to **Adventure Fitness,** 1528 Duranleau St., tel. (604) 687-1528, or **Ecomarine Ocean Kayak Centre,** 1668 Duranleau St., tel. (604) 689-7575. Both shops also carry related equipment, books, and nautical charts. Before heading over to Vancouver Island, divers pick up gear at **Rowand's Reef Scuba Shop,** 1512 Duranleau St., tel. (604) 669-3483.

Department Stores, Plazas, and Malls

Despite looking pretty dowdy these days, **Granville Mall** nevertheless forms the heart of the downtown shopping precinct; the two-block stretch of Granville St. is closed to private vehicles, though buses and taxis still pass through. Here you'll find the city's two largest department stores: **The Bay,** 674 Granville St., tel. (604) 681-6211, a Canadian chain that evolved from the historic Hudson's Bay Company, and **Eaton's,** 701 Granville St., tel. (604) 685-7112. Both stores emphasize Canadian goods, from souvenirs to household appliances. Eaton's is the largest tenant in **Pacific Centre,** tel. (604) 688-7236, which features over 200 shops, a massive food court, and a three-story-high waterfall.

Across Lions Gate Bridge in West Vancouver are a couple of shopping centers worth a mention. In a scenic location at Marine Dr. and Taylor Way, **Park Royal Shopping Centre,** tel. (604) 925-9576, holds over 190 shops and three department stores. It's open seven days a week. Also on the north side of Burrard Inlet is **Lonsdale Quay Market,** tel. (604) 985-6261, the terminus of the SeaBus from downtown. This bustling center features a great fresh food market on the first floor and a range of boutiques and galleries on the second.

British Columbia's largest shopping complex, **Metrotown Centre,** tel. (604) 438-2444, houses more than 200 shops. It's on the Kingsway in Burnaby; get there from downtown on the Sky-Train.

FESTIVALS AND EVENTS

Spring

Generally starting during the last week of May and running for a full week is the **Vancouver Children's Festival** at Vanier Park; it's a kid's

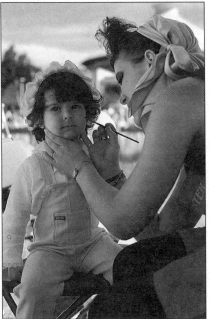

JANE AND BRUCE KING

face-painting at the Children's Festival, Vanier Park

paradise, with face painting, costumes, and fancy-hat competitions. Bring your camera! You'll need to buy tickets in advance for the special events—plays, puppetry, mime, sing-alongs, storytelling, etc.—but the rest of the fun and frivolity is free. For more information call (604) 687-7697.

After the 1996 success of combined performances by the CBC Vancouver Orchestra, Vancouver Symphony, and the New Music Ensemble, the merging of musics is now an annual event; the **Vancouver New Music Festival** takes place through the first week of May. Call Ticketmaster, tel. (604) 280-3311, for venues and ticketing. One of British Columbia's biggest rodeos is the **Cloverdale Rodeo and Exhibition,** held the third weekend of May. All rodeo events—saddle bronc, bareback, bull riding, steer wrestling, and calf roping—and a Western trade show take place at the rodeo grounds

in Cloverdale (between Surrey and Langley), tel. (604) 576-9461.

Summer
The **Canadian International Dragon Boat Festival,** tel. (604) 688-2382, comes to False Creek on the two middle weekends of June. In addition to the races, a variety of cultural activities take place in the Plaza of Nations. The last week of June Vancouver taps its feet to the beat of the annual **du Maurier International Jazz Festival,** when more than 600 musicians from countries around the world gather to perform traditional and contemporary jazz at various venues around the city. Part of the festival is a two-day street party in historic Gastown. Get your tickets early; if you want to go to a number of events, buy a jazz pass from ticket outlets. The jazz festival hotline is (604) 682-0706.

July 1 is Canada Day. The main celebrations—music, dancing, and fireworks—are held at Canada Place, but if you head out to the **Steveston Salmon Festival** you'll come across a massive salmon barbecue. The second week of July, Jericho Beach Park draws lots of folks to the **Vancouver Folk Music Festival.** In addition to the wonderful music, the festival features storytelling, dance performances, and live theater. For ticket details call the Vancouver Folk Music Society at (604) 602-9798. A hilarious mid-July event that brings Vancouverites out to the beach in force is the zany, internationally famous **Bathtub Race** from Nanaimo (Vancouver Island) to Kitsilano Beach. Call (800) 663-7337 for details. The **Vancouver International Comedy Festival,** tel. (604) 683-0883, takes place the last week of July at venues throughout the city.

Fall
During the second week of September, the **Vancouver International Fringe Festival,** tel. (604) 873-3646, schedules alternative-theater performances by artists from around the world. The **Vancouver International Film Festival** is held the second and third weeks of October and features the very best movies from the Pacific Rim, Canada, Great Britain, Russia, and more than 35 other countries at several theaters. For more details call (604) 685-0260. The following week, literary types congregate on Granville Island for

the **Vancouver International Writers Festival,** tel. (604) 681-6330.

Winter

Through the month of December, VanDusen Botanical Garden is transformed each evening by 20,000 lights and a nativity scene. New Year's Eve is celebrated with **First Night,** an alcohol-free party through downtown streets, while New Year's Day brings the **Polar Bear Swim** down at English Bay Beach. The information hotline for the latter event is (604) 732-2304, but all you really need to know is that the water will be *very* cold. Still, over 1,000 brave souls take to the water each year.

A more sensible winter event is **Ocean Cruising Adventures,** hosted by the Vancouver Maritime Museum through February. The lecture series features talks and presentations by local sailors.

ACCOMMODATIONS AND CAMPING

Whether you're looking for a campsite, hostel, bed-and-breakfast inn, motel, or luxury hotel, Vancouver has accommodations to suit your whim and budget. **Vancouver Visitor Info Centre,** 200 Burrard St., tel. (604) 683-2000, is the best place to get all the accommodations information in one shot. The center maintains accommodation listings for Vancouver and the entire province, and stocks a good selection of brochures provided by the lodgings. The staff will make bookings, too.

Before arriving in Vancouver, wise travelers will obtain a copy of Tourism BC's free guide, *British Columbia Accommodations,* using it to make advance reservations at their lodgings of choice. If you show up in late spring or summer without reservations, you may find all the best places, and definitely all the most reasonable, booked for the season. To request a copy of the guide, contact **Tourism British Columbia,** Parliament Buildings, Victoria, BC V8V 1X4, tel. (250) 387-1642 or (800) 663-6000. You can also make reservations through the **Discover British Columbia** hotline, tel. (800) 663-6000.

All rates quoted below are for high season (summer). Expect to pay less on weekends, especially for downtown accommodations, and outside of the busy July-August period. Like the rest of the province, the 10% provincial accommodation tax *and* the seven percent goods and services tax must be added; the latter is refundable to visitors from outside the country.

The price categories listed below are as follows: **Moderate,** $75-110 d; **Expensive,** $111-200 d; and **Very Expensive,** over $200 d.

DOWNTOWN

Moderate

Moderately priced accommodations in the downtown area are limited. One of the few choices is the **Kingston Hotel,** 757 Richards St., tel. (604) 684-9024, a small hotel with a European atmosphere. Most rooms share a bathroom. Amenities include a sauna, laundry, TV rental, and guest parking. Rates start at $60 s, $75 d,

including a continental breakfast. Weekly and off-season rates are available. The **Dominion Hotel,** 210 Abbott St., tel. (604) 681-6666, is in Gastown, a five-minute walk from downtown along Water Street. The old hotel dates to 1899, has a bar downstairs, and is popular with international travelers. Rooms are $85 s or d through summer, $65 the rest of the year. A similar distance from the business district but toward Granville Island is **Burrard Motor Inn,** 1100 Burrard St., tel. (604) 681-2331 or (800) 663-0366, which charges from $75 s, $85 d. Three blocks east of Burrard Motor Inn is **Bosman's Motor Hotel,** 1060 Howe St., tel. (604) 682-3171, which offers rooms from $100 s, $110 d. A few blocks farther south, and a five-minute walk to a False Creek Ferries wharf, is **Vancouver Centre TraveLodge,** 1304 Howe St., tel. (604) 682-2767 or (800) 665-2080. Rooms are clean and comfortable but this accommodation has seen better days, making the rates of $95 s, $105 d a little steep.

Expensive

Accommodations in this price range are scattered between the business district and Granville Island. Least expensive of the city-center hotels is **Days Inn Vancouver Downtown,** 921 W. Pender St., tel. (604) 681-4335 or (800) 329-7466. The 85 rooms are small, and surrounding high-rises block any views. But each room is decorated in bright and breezy pastel colors, and tea- and coffee-makers are provided; $125 s, $135 d. Also centrally located is **Hotel Georgia,** 801 Georgia St., tel. (604) 682-5566 or (800) 663-1111. Facilities are limited, but service is of a high standard and the rooms are well-furnished. Rates from $145 s, $175 d.

Century Plaza Hotel, 1015 Burrard St., tel. (604) 687-0575 or (800) 663-1818, offers over 200 rooms, each with a kitchen. Amenities include an indoor pool and a downstairs restaurant. Nightly rates are $120 s, $140 d, but weekly discounts are offered. At the elegantly furnished **Quality Hotel–The Inn at False Creek,** 1335 Howe St., tel. (604) 682-0229 or (800) 663-8474, a few rooms can be had for $130 s or d, but the one-bedroom suites, each with a full-kitchen, are the best value at $150 s or d.

The **Parkhill Hotel,** 1160 Davie St., tel. (604) 685-1311 or (800) 663-1525, is close to downtown and offers views over a residential area to English Bay. Rooms are spacious and have private balconies, and guests have use of a pool and fitness room. Rates are $165 s, $185 d.

Very Expensive

Canadian Pacific, best-known for landmark accommodations like the Empress Hotel in Victoria and the Banff Springs Hotel in Banff, operates two properties in the city. The copper-roofed **Hotel Vancouver,** 900 W. Georgia St., tel. (604) 684-3131 or (800) 441-1414, is the company's Vancouver flagship and a downtown landmark—you can't help but notice the distinctive green roof, the gargoyles, and the classic, gothic château-style architecture of this grand old lady. Everything here is on a grand scale, from the cavernous marble-lined lobby to the high ceilings and well-sized rooms. Facilities include restaurants, a comfortable lounge, an indoor pool, saunas, a weight room, health facilities, 24-hour room service, ample parking, and a large staff to attend to your every whim. Rooms run $245-260 s or d.

The other Canadian Pacific property is the relatively new, 23-story **Waterfront Centre Hotel,** 900 Canada Place Way, tel. (604) 691-1991 or (800) 828-7447, linked by a concourse to Canada Place. The 489 rooms are all spacious, and over half of them enjoy stunning harbor views. Many of the artworks found throughout the hotel were specially commissioned for the property. Rates are from $215 s or d.

For all the modern conveniences along with unbeatable city and harbor views, head for the sparkling **Pan Pacific Vancouver Hotel,** Canada Place, tel. (604) 662-8111 or (800) 937-1515 from the U.S., (800) 663-1515 from Canada. Opened for Expo86, the 13-story Pan Pacific was the most expensive hotel ever built in western Canada at the time. It's part of the landmark Canada Place, whose teflon sails fly over busy, bustling sidewalks and a constant flow of cruise ships. The hotel lobby is up a massive escalator that begins at the city end of Canada Place. Each of the 467 rooms boasts modern furnishings and stunning views. Facilities include a pool, an extra-charge health club, the Sails Restaurant, and the Cascades Lounge. Both the restaurant and lounge offer great views. Rooms start at $250 s or d.

One block from the city end of Robson Street is the superluxurious, European-style **Sutton Place Hotel,** 845 Burrard St., tel. (604) 682-5511 or (800) 961-7555, which offers a glass-enclosed pool, a gym, restaurants, and a beauty center; from $245 per night. The 34-story **Hyatt Regency Vancouver,** 655 Burrard St., tel. (604) 683-1234 or (800) 233-1234, towers above the Royal Centre Mall. Needless to say, most of the 600-plus rooms have views. Standard rate is $230 s or d, but weekend rates are considerably lower.

The millionaire owner of the **Wall Centre Garden Hotel,** 1088 Burrard St., tel. (604) 331-1000 or (800) 663-9255, spared no expense in construction, styling the hotel with the best of everything. Many of the furnishings were specially commissioned. Facilities include a couple of restaurants, a health club, indoor pool, and half-hectare garden. Rates are $250 s or d.

ROBSON STREET

Moderate

Most accommodations on Robson Street fall into the "Expensive" category, but one exception is the European-style **Barclay Hotel,** 1348 Robson St., tel. (604) 688-8850. Built in the 1920s, this three-story hostelry holds 80 medium-size rooms and a stylish lobby with lounge area. Rates of $85 s or d include a continental buffet breakfast, making the Barclay a good value.

Expensive

A number of accommodations on Robson Street fall into the expensive category but do provide a lot for the money. The **Greenbrier Apartment Motor Hotel,** 1393 Robson St., tel. (604) 683-4558, looks a bit rough on the outside, but rooms have recently been refurbished and each has a large living area, full kitchen, and separate bedroom. Rates are $118 s, $128 d. The **Riviera Motor Inn,** 1431 Robson St., tel. (604) 685-1301, offers similar facilities, as well as harbor or city views from the upper floors. All rooms are large and comfortably furnished; from $128 s or d. Up the hill one block from the Riviera, the **Tropicana Motor Inn,** 1361 Robson St., tel. (604) 687-6631, provides an indoor pool and many rooms with kitchenettes for $119 s or d. The **Blue Horizon Hotel,** 1225 Robson St., tel. (604) 688-1411 or (800) 663-1333, is a fairly standard accommodation, but has modern furnishings, large rooms (some with harbor views), a small pool, a fitness room, and a street-level restaurant that serves good breakfasts. Rates are from $145 s or d.

One of the better Robson St. accommodations is **Pacific Palisades Hotel,** 1277 Robson St., tel. (604) 688-0461 or (800) 663-1815. The hotel was formerly a luxury apartment building, so each of the 230 rooms is very spacious. Don't be put off by the dull exterior or tiny lobby; the rooms are well-furnished and many have views. Amenities include a lounge and stylish restaurant, a fitness center, lap pool, daily newspapers, and a variety of business services. Rates are $155 s, $170 d; kitchenettes an extra $10. Across the road is **Best Western Listel O'-Doul's Hotel,** 1300 Robson St., tel. (604) 684-8461 or (800) 663-5491, a full-service lodging with rates from $180 s, $200 d.

WEST END

The few accommodations at the west end of downtown are near some fine restaurants, close to Stanley Park and English Bay, and a 25-minute walk along bustling Robson Street from downtown proper.

Overlooking English Bay, the **Sylvia Hotel,** 1154 Gilford St., tel. (604) 681-9321, is a local landmark sporting a brick and terra-cotta exterior covered with Virginia creeper. Built in 1912 as an apartment building, the Sylvia was the tallest building on this side of town until 1958. Rates range $75-150 s or d, with the more expensive rooms featuring fantastic views and a full kitchen. Another less-expensive choice is the **Buchan Hotel,** in a quiet residential area at 1906 Haro St., tel. (604) 685-5354 or (800) 668-6654. Rooms are small, but the atmosphere is friendly and Stanley Park is only one block away; from $65 s or d. **Coast Plaza at Stanley Park,** 1733 Comox St., tel. (604) 688-7711 or (800) 663-1144, is actually closer to English Bay than

Stanley Park, but is a well-priced, full-service hotel with 267 rooms on 35 levels. Amenities include a health club, pool, restaurants, and a nightclub. Rates are from $119 s, $139 d. Slightly more expensive is **Rosellen Suites,** 2030 Barclay St., tel. (604) 689-4807, where each of the 30 units features modern furnishings, a separate living and dining area, and a full kitchen. Rates start at $130 for a one-bedroom unit and $180 for a two-bedroom unit.

OTHER PARTS OF THE CITY

North Vancouver and Vicinity
Without a doubt, the pick of accommodations on the north side of Burrard Inlet is the **Park Royal Hotel,** 540 Clyde Ave., West Vancouver, tel. (604) 926-5511. The Tudor-style accommodation is set on the banks of the Capilano River—you can fish for salmon and steelhead right on the property—and is surrounded by well-maintained gardens. Inside you'll find an English-style pub, a lounge area with fireplace, and 30 cozy rooms, each with a brass bed. Rates are a reasonable $140-260 s or d which includes tea and coffee and a daily newspaper. Book *well* ahead to be assured of a room at this popular place. To get there from downtown, take the Lions Gate Bridge over Burrard Inlet, turn left over the Capilano River, turn right onto Taylor Way, then take the next right, Clyde Avenue.

If you don't have transportation, and don't want to stay right downtown, **Lonsdale Quay Hotel,** 123 Carrie Cates Ct., North Vancouver, tel. (604) 986-6111, is a good choice. It's above lively Lonsdale Quay Market and the SeaBus Terminal, only 12 minutes to downtown by water. Amenities include restaurants, a fitness center, a sauna and whirlpool, a nightclub with entertainment, shops, and covered parking. Rates are from $165 s, $200 d, more for harbor views. Less expensive is **Holiday Inn Express Vancouver North Shore,** 1800 Capilano Rd., tel. (604) 987-4461 or (800) 663-4055, where well-furnished rooms and a complimentary breakfast are included in the rates of $99 s or d.

Horseshoe Bay Motel, 6588 Royal Ave., tel. (604) 921-7454, is right by the BC Ferries terminal, from where ferries depart for the Sunshine Coast and Nanaimo. It's within easy walking distance of numerous cafes and restaurants, and the nearby Horseshoe Bay Marina makes a pleasant place for an evening stroll. Rooms are $75 s or d.

Granville Island

Granville Island Hotel, 1253 Johnston St., tel. (604) 683-7373 or (800) 663-1840, attracts a trendy, fun-loving, jet-setter crowd looking for action. The hotel overlooks False Creek from Granville Island, just south of city center. Most of the rooms have water views. Amenities include a jacuzzi, sauna, restaurant, lounge, pub (always crowded in the evenings), and disco. Elsewhere on the island, within easy striking distance of the hotel, are theaters, restaurants, art galleries, shops, and a public market. Rooms run $190 s or d. If you object to loud, pounding music till 2 a.m., be sure to ask for a room far from the disco.

Central Vancouver, Burnaby, and Coquitlam

If you have your own transportation, the lodgings south of downtown are worth consideration. They're generally less expensive than the downtown hotels and you won't have to worry about parking.

Closest to downtown is the nine-story **Biltmore Hotel,** 395 Kingsway, tel. (604) 872-5252 or (800) 663-5713. Many rooms have city views; $89 s or d. Other choices on Kingsway include **Kingsway Lodge,** 2075 Kingsway, tel. (604) 876-5531, $69 s, $75 d; **2400 Motel,** 2400 Kingsway, tel. (604) 434-2464, $65-79 s or d; and **Quality Inn Metrotown,** 3484 Kingsway, tel. (604) 433-8255, which has a pool, cafe, restaurant, and lounge; $105 s, $110 d.

If you're coming into the city on the Trans-Canada Hwy., you'll find a cluster of motels just west of where the highway crosses the Fraser River. **Best Western Chelsea Inn,** 725 Brunette Ave. (take Exit 40B), tel. (604) 525-7777 or (800) 528-1234, features a heated outdoor pool, jacuzzi, restaurant, laundry, and large rooms, each with a lounge and coffee-making facilities; $85 s, $95 d. At the next major intersection heading toward the city, **Best Western Coquitlam Inn,** 319 North Rd., tel. (604) 931-9011, is more expensive, but its rooms face a cavernous atrium filled with plants, a pool, and a jacuzzi. Rates start at $139 s, $149 d.

Richmond (Vancouver International Airport)

The following accommodations, as well as the two in Tsawwassen, are good choices for those visitors who want to commute directly between the airport and ferry terminal without going into downtown Vancouver. All accommodations listed below offer complimentary airport shuttles.

Closest to the airport is **Delta Vancouver Airport Hotel,** 3500 Cessna Dr., tel. (604) 278-1241 or (800) 877-1133, offering a high standard of service and all the facilities of an international-style hostelry; from $200 s or d. **Coast Vancouver Airport Hotel,** 1041 Southwest Marine Dr., tel. (604) 263-1555 or (800) 663-1144, is good value with large rooms, a fitness center, lounge, and restaurant; $80 s, $90 d. Also on the downtown side of the Fraser River is **Quality Inn Airport,** 725 Southeast Marine Dr., tel. (604) 321-6611 or (800) 663-6715, which charges from $112 s or d.

Tsawwassen (BC Ferries Terminal)

The closest accommodation to the departure point for ferries to Vancouver Island is the **Best Western Tsawwassen Inn,** four km east of the terminal along Hwy. 17, tel. (604) 943-8221 or (800) 943-8221. Amenities include both an indoor and outdoor pool, a fitness center, restaurant, and complimentary ferry shuttle. Summer rates are $90 s, $100 d, less the rest of the year. Halfway between the airport and ferry terminal, at the junction of Hwys. 17 and 99, is **Delta Town and Country Inn,** tel. (604) 946-4404, which charges from $85 s, $95 d.

BED AND BREAKFASTS

If you want to meet locals and prefer the idea of staying in someone's home rather than an impersonal hotel room, stay in a bed and breakfast. B&Bs sprouted all over Vancouver just before Expo86, and today can be found all across the greater metropolitan area. Styles run the gamut—heritage homes, modern townhouses, rural farmhouses, a hammock in a backyard. Some have private baths, others shared facilities; some have swimming pools and saunas, others are on the beach or close to city attractions. Expect to pay $40-80 s, $50-120 d, including breakfast.

Most bed and breakfasts belong to an association or are listed with an agency. Associations and agencies with the largest Vancouver representations include: **AAA Home Away From Home B&B Agency,** 1441 Howard Ave., Vancouver, BC V5B 3S2, tel. (604) 294-1760; **AB&C B&B of Vancouver,** 4390 Frances St., Vancouver, BC V5C 2R3, tel. (604) 298-8815 or (800) 488-1941; **Beachside B&B Registry,** 4208 Evergreen Ave., West Vancouver, BC V7V 1H1, tel. (604) 922-7773 or (800) 563-3311; and **Westway Accommodation Registry,** P.O. Box 48950, Bentall Centre, Vancouver, BC V7X 1A8, tel. (604) 273-8293.

West End

Only one block from Robson Street is **West End Guest House,** 1362 Haro St., tel. (604) 681-2889. Built at the turn of the century, this inn has been lovingly refurbished and furnished with brass beds and antiques to retain its original Victorian charm. Each of the seven rooms has a private bathroom, television, and telephone, and guests can relax in either the comfortable lounge or on the outdoor terrace. Rates start at $95 s, $115 d, which includes a full breakfast and light snacks through the day.

Toward Stanley Park and nestled among towering apartment blocks is **English Bay Inn,** 1968 Comox St., tel. (604) 683-8002, a quiet retreat from the pace of the city. The decor is stylish, in an old-fashioned way. Highlights include a lounge area with log fireplace, and a small garden out the back. Rates start at $160 s or d, and the luxurious two-room suite goes for $275.

North Vancouver and Vicinity

Close to Grouse Mountain Gondola, **Mountainside Manor,** 5909 Nancy Greene Way, North Vancouver, tel. (604) 990-9772, is a great place to unwind—especially in the outdoor hot tub. The views are spectacular, the decor modern. During summer, the four rooms are $85-135 s or d. **Deep Cove B&B,** 2590 Shelley Rd., tel. (604) 929-3932, is also in North Vancouver, not in Deep Cove as the name suggests. Set on a large property adjoining a residential area, the atmosphere is informal and relaxing. Amenities include an outdoor hot tub, lounge, and billiard table. The two guest rooms, each

with private bathroom, rent for $75 s, $85 d. If you're prepared to spend a bit more money (and to book well ahead), **Beachside B&B,** 4208 Evergreen Ave., West Vancouver, tel. (604) 922-7773, is an excellent choice. Set on the waterfront at Sandy Cove (access off Marine Dr.), views extend across the sound to Stanley Park and the downtown skyline. Rates are $115 s or d.

Central Vancouver

South of False Creek you'll find a profusion of bed and breakfasts. Many lie in quiet residential areas, yet are close to public transportation. **Pillow 'n Porridge Guest House,** 2859 Manitoba St., tel. (604) 879-8977, only three blocks from City Hall, occupies a heritage house dating to the turn of the century. Each of the four bedrooms is furnished with antiques from around the world, and guests are served a hearty breakfast—with delicious porridge to start, of course. Rooms with shared bathroom are $85 s, $95 d; those with private bathroom are $95 s, $115 d.

Farther west, in the suburb of Kitsilano, is **Penny Farthing Inn,** 2855 W. 6th Ave., tel. (604) 739-9002, another heritage house with four antique-filled rooms. The least expensive rooms are $75 while the suite, complete with mountain views, a brass bed, and separate lounge area, is $155 s or d. Also in Kitsilano, **Kenya Court Guest House,** 2230 Cornwall Ave., tel. (604) 738-7085, enjoys great views over Kitsilano Beach and English Bay to the snowcapped mountains beyond. All rooms have views, and guests congregate each morning for breakfast in a glass-enclosed rooftop room. Rates range $85-105 s or d.

HOSTELS AND DORMS

Hostelling International

Opened in summer 1996, **Hostelling International Downtown Vancouver,** 1114 Burnaby St., tel. (604) 684-4565, is part of the new wave of facilities run by the world's largest and longest running network of backpacker accommodations. Gone are the midnight curfews, daily chores, and crowded rooms. This modern complex offers shared and private rooms (a maximum of four beds in each dormitory), a large

*Hostelling International
Jericho Beach*

JANE AND BRUCE KING

kitchen, library, games room, and bike rentals. Members of Hostelling International pay $19, nonmembers $23.

If you don't need to stay right downtown, **Hostelling International Jericho Beach,** 1515 Discovery St. (near the intersection of Northwest Marine Dr. and W. 4th Ave.), Point Grey, tel. (604) 224-3208, is a good alternative choice. The location is fantastic—in scenic and safe parkland behind Jericho Beach, across English Bay from downtown and linked to extensive biking and walking trails. Inside the huge white building with snazzy blue trim are separate dorms for men and women, rooms for couples and families, a living area with television, and a kitchen. Additional amenities include a cafeteria open for breakfast and dinner (good food, reasonable prices), a handy information board (the place to look if you need a ride, want to buy or sell a vehicle, or meet up with friends), lockers, left-luggage service ($5 a bag per week), and limited free parking. Members pay $16 per night, nonmembers $20. The family rooms must be reserved at least a week ahead. Reservations are recommended, and the maximum stay is five consecutive nights.

Other Backpacker Accommodations
Privately owned backpacker lodges in Vancouver come and go with predictable regularity. Many should be avoided, but a couple of them have been around for years and are excellent in all respects. **Globetrotter's Inn,** 170 W. Es-

planade, North Vancouver, tel. (604) 988-2082, is across the road from Lonsdale Quay and the SeaBus Terminal (with regular ferry connections to downtown), and near to restaurants, a couple of pubs, and a movie theater. Facilities include a small lounge, fully equipped kitchen, free laundry, and a pool table. Each dorm room holds a maximum of four beds. Rates for the dorm beds are $16, private rooms are $32 s, $40-45 d; weekly rates available. The office is open in summer 8 a.m.-11 p.m., the rest of the year 8 a.m.-8 p.m. Call ahead to be sure of a bed.

On the other side of downtown, behind City Hall between Cambie and Yukon Sts., is **Paul's Guest House,** 345 W. 14th Ave., Central Vancouver, tel. (604) 872-4753. Paul's is recommended by travelers as a friendly, clean, and comfortable place to stay. The host speaks many languages, cooks breakfast for the guests, and arranges airport transfers; single beds from $23-35 s.

Okay, onto the bad ones. At **Vincent's Backpackers Hostel,** 927 Main St., tel. (604) 682-2441, the rooms are sparse and small, the kitchen is disgusting, and the grubby lounge area is perpetually filled with a scruffy bunch of travelers gripping Lonely Planet guides and boasting of their courage at walking through the neighborhood after dark. I didn't even bother asking the rates while researching this edition, but it's probably about $12 a night for a sagging dorm bed. Across the road is the **Old American Hotel,** 928 Main St., tel. (604) 688-

0112, which provides cheap long-term accommodations and is managed by a chain-smoking heifer who makes the enterprising Vincent seem like the Host from Heaven. Monthly rates are $175 for a dorm bed, $350 for a single room, and $500 for a double room.

YWCA Hotel

In October 1995 the YWCA opened a brand new lodging for female travelers, couples, and families at 733 Beatty St., tel. (604) 895-5830 or (800) 663-1424. It's farther from the business core than the old Burrard Street property, but the modern facilities and choice of nearby restaurants more than compensate for the extra distance. More than 150 rooms are spread over 12 stories. Each room has a telephone, and some have televisions. Communal facilities include three kitchens, three lounges, and two laundries. Guests also have use of the YWCA fitness center, which houses a pool and gym. Rooms with shared bathroom facilities are $51-61 s, $62-74 d; those with a private bathroom are $65 s, $88 d.

YMCA

Though not as modern as the YWCA, the 110-room YMCA, 955 Burrard St., tel. (604) 681-0221, enjoys a good downtown location, only two blocks from busy Robson Street and all the restaurants and nightlife. Amenities include a coin-op laundry, television rental ($2 per day), a weight room, racquetball, sauna, and two lap pools. No cooking facilities are available, but the in-house cafe, Johnny T's, is open daily from breakfast to 4 p.m. Parking up the alley beside the building costs $3.75 for 24 hours; it's supervised during the day. Rooms, none with private bathroom, are available for men, women, and couples. Beds range $23.50-29 per person (plus $5 key deposit). Linen is provided and weekly rates are available.

UBC Housing and Conference Centre

Summer accommodations are available at the University of British Columbia, out at Point Grey, 16 km west of city center. Options include dorm beds, single rooms with shared bathrooms, and one- or two-bedroom suites or studio suites with private bathrooms and kitchenettes. A restaurant is close by, and a swimming pool, sauna, whirlpool, and tennis and fitness center are on campus; $22-60 s, $79-95 d. For further information and reservations, contact UBC Conference Centre, 5961 Student Union Blvd., tel. (604) 822-1010.

Simon Fraser University

Although it's about 20 km east of downtown Vancouver, Simon Fraser University offers inexpensive dorm rooms to travelers in summer. The hilltop campus is known for its modern architecture and excellent city views. Stop by or write SFU Housing and Conference Services, Room 212, McTaggart-Cowan Hall, Burnaby (Vancouver, BC V5A 1S6), or call the office at (604) 291-4503. Single or twin fully furnished townhouse units with shared bathrooms are available May-Aug.; $19-26 s, $42 and up d. The university is between Hwys. 7 and 7A in Burnaby. To get there by bus, catch no. 10 or 14 on Granville Mall (get a transfer ticket and ask the driver to tell you where to get off), then transfer to bus no. 135.

CAMPGROUNDS

You won't find any campgrounds in the city center area, but a limited number dot the suburbs along the major approach routes. Before trekking out to any of them, ring ahead to check for vacancies.

North

The closest campground to inner-city attractions is **Capilano RV Park,** 295 Tomahawk Ave., North Vancouver, tel. (604) 987-4722. To get there from downtown, cross Lions Gate Bridge, turn right on Marine Dr., right on Capilano Rd., and right on Welch Street. From Hwy. 1/99 in West Vancouver, exit south on Taylor Way toward the shopping center and turn left over the Capilano River. It's about an hour walk to downtown from the campground, over Lions Gate Bridge and through Stanley Park. Although limited spots are available for tents, the park is really intended for vehicle camping and RVs. It gets crowded in summer; advance prepaid reservations are required for July and August. If you want a tent site, call ahead and ask if they have any grassy areas left. A tent site runs $22; a site with electricity, water, and sewer hookups is $32.

South

Large **Richmond RV Park,** 15 km (20 minutes) south of downtown at 6200 River Rd., tel. (604) 270-7878, is a great place for those looking to stay in shape. It lies just across the road from the Fraser River, and atop the dike separating the river from the road is an eight-km-long footpath. The path is extremely popular with local walkers, joggers, dog exercisers, cyclists, and even seaplane and jet enthusiasts—the seaplane terminal is within sight, and the campground is just off the final flight path for Vancouver International Airport. Grassy banks and strategic benches along the path encourage quiet reflection on a bright sunny day. Tent sites at the campground are $16, while serviced sites range $17-23. Facilities include free showers, a coin-op laundry, and a games room.

Parkcanada RV Inns, on Hwy. 17 (take the 52nd St. exit), tel. (604) 943-5811, is convenient to the BC Ferries terminal at Tsawwassen, a 30-minute drive south of city center. The park is busy throughout summer. Amenities include a heated pool, store, laundromat, lounge, and free showers. Unserviced sites, suitable for tents, are $14; serviced sites range $17-23. **Peace Arch RV Park,** 14601 40th Ave., tel. (604) 594-7009, is between the suburbs of White Rock and Delta, 10 km from Douglas border crossing on Hwy. 99. The well-tended facilities include a heated pool, games room, and laundry. Sites in the tenting area are $18.50 while hookups range $20-25.

East

Surrounded by Burnaby Lake Regional Park, **Burnaby Cariboo RV Park,** 8765 Cariboo Pl., Burnaby, tel. (604) 420-1722, offers luxurious fa-cilities—an indoor heated pool, jacuzzi, sundeck, an adult lounge, and much more. Sites in the walk-in tenting area cost $21 per night; hookups are $25-33. The park is 17 km east of downtown. To get there, take the Cariboo exit from the TransCanada Hwy., turn right at the first traffic light, then make the first left, then first right into Cariboo Place.

Farther east, **Dogwood Campgrounds of B.C.,** 15151 112th Ave. (take Exit 50 north off the TransCanada Hwy., then head west on 112th Ave.), Surrey, tel. (604) 583-5585, is 35 km east of Vancouver and close to the Sky-Train station at Whalley. Hookups are $30-35.

Provincial Parks

Of the provincial parks on the north side of the city, the only one with a campground is **Golden Ears,** 40 km from downtown near the suburb of Maple Ridge. To get there, take Hwy. 7 from downtown through Coquitlam and Pitt Meadows to Maple Ridge and follow the signs north on 232nd Street. The park holds almost 400 sites in two campgrounds near Alouette Lake. The campgrounds are linked by hiking trails. Facilities include hot showers, flush toilets, and a picnic table and fire ring at each site; $15.50 per night.

Traveling north on Hwy. 99 toward Whistler, **Porteau Cove Provincial Park,** 20 km north of Horseshoe Bay, offers 60 sites in a pleasant treed setting with mountain views. All sites are $15.50. If you're traveling the TransCanada Hwy., the closest provincial park campground is at **Cultus Lake,** 100 km east of downtown and seven km south of the highway service center of Chilliwack (Exit 119). All sites are $15.50, which includes the use of hot showers.

FOOD

With well over 2,000 restaurants and hundreds of cafes and coffeehouses, Vancouver is a gastronomical delight. The city is home to over 60 different cultures, so you won't be surprised to find a smorgasbord of ethnic restaurants. In addition, many eateries specialize in a culinary style known as Pacific Northwest cuisine, which combines fresh local produce, seafood, and ethnic ingredients in a healthy, low-fat way.

One thing that will soon become apparent to first-time visitors is the amount of coffee consumed by the locals; specialty coffeehouses are *everywhere*. Seattle-based Starbucks Coffee Co. alone has 70 Vancouver outlets. Stroll Robson Street, Denman Street, and West 4th Avenue for the biggest concentrations of coffeehouses. Robson and Denman Streets also offer a cosmopolitan choice of cafes and restaurants, as does historic Gastown. For Chinese food, head to Chinatown, naturally. Restaurants throughout the city specialize in seafood; for the freshest, straight from the trawlers, head to Steveston on the city's southern outskirts.

NORTH AMERICAN

Fine Dining
To enjoy one of the best restaurant settings in Vancouver, head to **The Prow,** tel. (604) 684-1339, named for its position at the head of Canada Place. Considering the superb views and elegant surroundings, prices are very reasonable. Local seafood is prominently featured, and except for a couple of the finest beef cuts, all dinner entrees are under $20. Lunch is less expensive; salads start at $8 with entrees $10-13. Open daily for lunch and dinner.

More Casual
Also at Canada Place is **Five Sails,** in the Pan Pacific Vancouver Hotel, tel. (604) 662-8111. It's open for dinner only, and the fabulous setting and harbor views are reflected in the prices. The menu features items as varied as a traditional Mongolian dish to local seafood; main

dishes range $22-38 while the table d'hôte selections are better value at $30-42.

Nearby **North 49° Restaurant,** 200 Burrard St., tel. (604) 669-0360, is right beside the main information center on the Plaza Level of the Bentall Four building. The menu in this casual eatery offers around 100 items, including spit-roasted chicken, pork, and lamb cooked in the middle of the main dining area. Other dishes feature the cuisine of Italy, Greece, and Spain.

Overlooking English Bay in Stanley Park is the **Teahouse Restaurant,** 7501 Stanley Park Rd., tel. (604) 669-3281, originally built as barracks for army troops in the 1920s. Today the building contains an intimate restaurant with elegant surroundings and a game and seafood menu making use of all the best local ingredients. Expect to pay from $12 for lunch and from $15 for dinner. Open daily.

Pacific Northwest
Head for the West End to find the city's finest Pacific Northwest cuisine. **Liliget Feast House,** 1724 Davie St., tel. (604) 681-7044, serves authentic First Nations food, including smoked oolichans, bannock bread, seaweed and wild rice, watercress salad, smoked salmon, seafood or caribou barbecued over an alderwood fire, and steamed fern shoots. A narrow stairway leads down to a cavernous room styled on a traditional longhouse. Cedar columns rise from the stone floor, native artwork adorns the walls, and traditional music plays softly in the background. Dining here isn't particularly cheap; main dishes run $15-19 and feast platters for two that let you sample a variety of delicacies ring in at $45-55. But it's an experience you won't forget in a hurry. Open daily from 5 p.m.; last seating at 9:30 p.m.

A few blocks away, you'll find contemporary Pacific Northwest cuisine at **Delilah's,** 1739 Comox St., tel. (604) 687-3424. One of Vancouver's favorite restaurants, Delilah's features an elegant setting and well-prepared dishes that take advantage of seasonal produce and locally harvested seafood. The fixed-price two-course dinner costs from $20, depending on the season; a five-course feast is also offered.

The innovative menu and extensive by-the-glass wine list at nearby **Raincity Grill,** 1193 Denman St., tel. (604) 685-7337, have gained the restaurant numerous awards. The menu changes with the season, but always includes seafood and various game dishes. Wednesday is the "Chef's Surprise," featuring whatever the chef picked up at the local market that morning. Lunch entrees are $9-16, dinner ranges $14-22. Make reservations for dinner.

Mexican and Cajun

In a sprawling converted residence just off Denman Street, **Mescalero,** 1215 Bidwell St., tel. (604) 669-2399, has high ceilings, an ocher-colored interior, and Santa Fe–style furnishings. The atmosphere is casual—the staff has a good time while still being attentive. Tapas are the most popular menu items, but also featured are a variety of Mexican grills from $15-20. Open daily for lunch and dinner.

Las Margaritas, 1999 W. 4th Ave. at Maple, Kitsilano, tel. (604) 734-7117, is open for lunch (around $8) and dinner ($10-12), and boasts "mild or wild, we can add all the octane you wish." The decor is vintage south-of-the-border—white stucco walls, Mexican hats, tile floor, and tile-topped tables. It's a good place to take your taste buds for a buzz. Get some chips and salsa, throw back a couple of margaritas, and pretend you're in Mexico.

The venerable **Mulvaney's,** 1535 Johnston St., Granville Island, tel. (604) 685-6571, is the place to go for Cajun and Creole dishes. Entrees range $10-20. Open weekdays for lunch, daily from 5:30 p.m. for dinner, and on Sunday for brunch from 10 a.m.

SEAFOOD SPECIALISTS

One of Vancouver's finest seafood restaurants is **A Kettle of Fish,** near the Burrard Bridge at 900 Pacific St., tel. (604) 682-6853. The casual decor features cafe-style seating and abundant greenery, while the menu swims with schools of piscatory pleasures. New England clam chowder ($4.50) is one of over 20 appetizers, while entrees such as grilled snapper ($14) or a seafood platter for two ($32) make up the main menu. It's open for lunch Mon.-Fri. and for dinner daily.

Joe Fortes Seafood House, 777 Thurlow St. (half a block off Robson St.), tel. (604) 669-1940, is named after one of Vancouver's best-loved heroes, a swimming coach and lifeguard at English Bay. This restaurant is a city institution and is always busy. The comfortable interior offers elegant furnishings, bleached-linen tablecloths, and an oyster bar where you can relax while waiting for your table. At lunch, the specialty grilled fish goes for $14-18. The dinner menu is slightly more expensive. Open daily for lunch and dinner, but closed each afternoon 3-5 p.m. While the oysters at Joe's are hard to beat, those at **Olympia Seafoods,** just off Robson at 820 Thurlow, tel. (604) 685-0716, come pretty close.

Flippers, 1829 Robson St. (one block off Denman St.), tel. (604) 685-7560, is a pleasant restaurant with unpretentious decor and a small seafood-only menu. The halibut here is grilled to perfection for $15. Open daily for dinner. **Bud's Halibut and Chips,** 1007 Denman St., tel. (604) 683-0661, offers takeout or casual dining at one of the few tables.

On the north side of Burrard Inlet, try **Salmon House on the Hill,** 2229 Folkstone Way, West Vancouver, tel. (604) 926-3212, where the house-specialty salmon is barbecued over an open alderwood pit. The intriguing interior is full of northwest coast native arts and crafts—including a dugout canoe suspended over the main dining area—and provides a great view of West Vancouver, Stanley Park, and downtown. Out front, a rhododendron garden blooms its bloomers off in May. Enjoy drinks and appetizers ($5-8) or afternoon tea and dessert ($5-6—the Chocolate Paradise is sinfully scrumptious) in the bistro bar, or a full meal in the adjoining restaurant. Lunch averages $9-15, dinner entrees run $15-24. The Salmon House is open for

LOUISE FOOTE

lunch Mon.-Sat. 11:30 a.m.-2:30 p.m., for dinner daily from 5 p.m., and for Sunday brunch 11 a.m.-2:30 p.m. Make dinner reservations unless you plan on eating at 5 p.m. or after 9 p.m. To get there, take the 21st St. exit off Upper Levels Hwy. to Folkstone Way, then follow the signs.

ASIAN

For Chinese food, you can't go wrong in Chinatown. Just look for any restaurant packed with locals. The most authentic cuisine is at the east end; at the west end, the food seems to have been appropriately westernized. The **Boss Bakery and Restaurant,** 532 Main St., tel. (604) 683-3860, is always crowded and sells a great selection of Chinese- and western-style pastries. **Gain Wah Restaurant,** 218 Keefer St., tel. (604) 684-1740, is noted for inexpensive congee, a simple soup of water extracted from boiling rice. A bowl of congee costs $1.50, with flavorings an additional 25 cents to $2. The friendly staff will be willing to help you decide on a dish. **Hon's Wun Tun House,** 230 Keefer St., tel. (604) 688-0871, is a large, bright, and modern restaurant that attracts a younger Chinese crowd. The **New Capital Restaurant,** downstairs at 158 E. Pender St., tel. (604) 681-1828, serves daily lunch and dinner buffets; the selection isn't great, and it's noisy and crowded, but for $7 at lunch and $8 at dinner you can eat as much as you want.

For tasty and authentic Chinese cuisine in Central Vancouver head to **Bill Kee Restaurant,** 8 W. Broadway at Ontario St., tel. (604) 874-8522. The decor isn't fancy, but the food is good, plentiful, and reasonably priced. At lunch one dish is around $5, at dinner around $8, including bottomless cups of hot Chinese tea. It's open daily between 10:30 a.m. and the wee hours; eat in or take out.

For inexpensive, no-frills Japanese food head to **Hanada,** 823 Denman St., tel. (604) 685-1136. The atmosphere is nothing special but the service is efficient and all the traditional Japanese dishes are offered at reasonable cost, with no entrees over $11. The contemporary **Tanpopo,** 1122 Denman St., tel. (604) 681-7777, features a wide range of Japanese dishes averaging $12 at lunch and $18 at dinner.

Renowned for sushi is **Tojo's Restaurant,** 777 W. Broadway, tel. (604) 872-8050. Japanese entrees are also available; various teriyakis range $15-35.

A well-recommended restaurant serving Indian and Asian dishes is **Woodlands Natural Food Restaurant,** upstairs at 2582 W.Broadway (at Trafalgar St.), tel. (604) 733-5411. Here you can get a main course for $8-10, or try the "buffet by weight," at which you fill your plate then weigh it, paying $1.50 per 100 grams. Open daily 8 a.m.-10 p.m.

FRENCH

For Vancouver's finest French cuisine, go to the small, intimate **Le Crocodile,** 909 Burrard St., tel. (604) 669-4298. Entrees range $14-22. Open for lunch Mon.-Fri. and daily for dinner. Make reservations for weekend dining. **The Chef and the Carpenter,** 1745 Robson St., tel. (604) 687-2700, serves up great country-French cuisine in an intimate yet relaxed atmosphere. Portions are large, but save room for the delicious desserts. Entrees range $15-19. Open weekdays for lunch and daily for dinner (reservations required).

ITALIAN

Of Vancouver's many Italian restaurants, one of the best is **Il Giardino di Umberto,** on the south side of downtown at 1382 Hornby St., tel. (604) 669-2422. The light, bright furnishings and an enclosed terrace make the perfect environment to indulge in the featured Tuscan cuisine. Expect to pay $12-16 for lunch entrees, $14-30 for dinner entrees. Open Mon.-Fri. noon-2:30 p.m., and Mon.-Sat. 6-11 p.m.

Little Frank's, 1487 Robson St., tel. (604) 687-7210, offers inexpensive Italian food and a neat decor, with tables crowded together in typical Italian style. All pastas on the menu are under $12, while meat and seafood dishes are a bit more. It's open Mon.-Fri. for lunch, and daily for dinner. At **CinCin,** 1154 Robson St., tel. (604) 688-7338, the house specialty is wood-fired pizza, but you can also order pastas and a variety of grills.

The unique decor at **Brothers Restaurant,** in Gastown at 1 Water St., tel. (604) 683-9124, features monastery-like surroundings of wood, brick, stained glass, chandeliers, and monkish murals. Enjoy delicious soups (try the Boston clam chowder), salads, sandwiches, and a variety of entrees ($8-14)—all served by waiters appropriately dressed in monk attire, and accompanied by congregational sing-alongs and laser light shows. The daily lunch specials are good value, as are the early dinner deals available Mon.-Thurs. before 6 p.m.

The **Old Spaghetti Factory,** in Gastown at 53 Water St., tel. (604) 684-1288, is a family-style favorite offering lunch entrees from $6 and dinner entrees from $10, including salad, bread, dessert, and coffee. This place is worth a visit for the eclectic array of furnishings, from old lamps to a 1904 trolley car.

SPANISH

Diners at **Marbella,** 1368 Robson St., tel. (604) 681-1175, eat from stylish tiled tables, listen to traditional music, and generally immerse themselves in the culture of Spain. The 20 tapas range $2.50-5 each, while the rest of the menu features entrees from $13. Try the Spanish-style soup at lunch. Open Tues.-Sat. for lunch, and Tues.-Sun. for dinner. Another place for Spanish food is the extremely inexpensive **Las Tapas,** 760 Cambie St., tel. (604) 669-1624.

OTHER ETHNIC

Expect to wait for a table at **Stepho's,** 1124 Davie St., tel. (604) 683-2555, one of Vancouver's best-value restaurants. Locals line up here for all the favorite Greek dishes. Portions are generous and nothing on the menu costs over $10. Try the delicious baklava ($3.50). Stepho's is open daily noon-11:30 p.m. In the lower level of the Pacific Palisades Hotel, the cavernous **Monterey Lounge and Grill,** 1277 Robson St., tel. (604) 684-1277, features a Mediterranean-inspired menu to suit all tastes.

Kafe Europa, 735 Denman St. (near the corner of Robson St.), tel. (604) 683-4982, is a small, elegant restaurant featuring Central European recipes such as beef goulash and chicken paprika, prepared with local produce and game. Most entrees are under $15 and a few are under $10. Open Tues.-Sun. for dinner.

VEGETARIAN

In Chinatown, the **Buddhist Vegetarian Restaurant,** 137 E. Pender St., tel. (604) 683-8816, serves up inexpensive vegetarian food in bland surroundings.

A throwback to the hippie era of the 1960s is **Naam,** 2724 W. 4th Ave., Kitsilano, tel. (604) 738-7151, a particularly good natural-food restaurant boasting large servings, excellent service, and an easy-going atmosphere that has become legendary. It's open 24 hours a day, every day of the week. Veggie burgers start at $5, full meals range $6.50-9.

CAFES AND BISTROS

Gastown Gourmet
Gastown is the most tourist-oriented part of Vancouver, yet has many fine eating establishments that attract locals as well. At 375 Water St., adjacent to the SeaBus terminal, is The Landing, a restored warehouse now housing elegant boutiques and a couple of good-value eateries. Here you'll find **Pastel's,** tel. (604) 684-0176, which serves up a good $4 breakfast special and $7 Sunday brunch, and the **Landing Cafe,** tel. (604) 682-0970, dishing up breakfast and lunch with harbor views.

Some of Gastown's best coffee is ground and brewed at **La Luna Cafe,** 131 Water St., tel. (604) 687-5862. The cafe's striking yellow-and-black decor, daily papers, great coffee, and inexpensive light snacks (pizza wedges for $2.50) make this a pleasant escape from busy Water Street. Simple surroundings show off innovative artworks at **Cordova Cafe,** 307 W. Cordova St., tel. (604) 683-5637. Light meals are good value—a bowl of chili is $4, a Greek salad is $5, and the daily soup-and-sandwich special is $6. At the extreme east end of Gastown is the **Talking Stick Gallery Caffe,** 221 Carrall St., tel. (604) 683-3979, a funky little cafe that most visitors miss as it's a block off busy Water Street.

Breakfast is inexpensive (from $3.50) and newspapers are supplied.

At Gastown's busiest intersection, beside the crowd-drawing steam clock, is **Water St. Cafe,** 300 Water St., tel. (604) 689-2832. Sidewalk tables make for good peoplewatching, while the stylish interior is well suited to a quiet meal. The menu offers good pasta, chicken, and salads for around $12, and delicious specialties such as grilled Pacific salmon for a bit more. In the same vicinity, with similar decor and menu choices, is **Bistro Bistro,** 162 Water St., tel. (604) 682-2162.

Vancouver's oldest restaurant is the **Only Cafe,** 20 E. Hastings St., tel. (604) 681-6546, serving bargain-basement seafood Mon.-Sat. noon-7 p.m. The setting is very 1950s, and there are no bathrooms, but the fish and chips and chowders are all delicious and there's always a line.

Robson Street

Linking downtown to the West End, Robson Street holds the city's largest concentration of eateries. In addition to a number of fine-dining restaurants, dozens of cafes sprinkle the sidewalks with outdoor tables—perfect for people-watching. The listings below start closest to downtown and work their way out toward Stanley Park.

For thick and healthy sandwiches and rolls head to Harry's Takeout, 1087 Robson St., tel. (604) 331-0046. It's open daily 9 a.m.-9 p.m., and despite the name, you can also eat-in. Juice lovers might want to detour six blocks southwest down Thurlow Street and turn left on Davie for **O-Tooz,** 1068 Davie St., tel. (604) 689-0208, specializing in freshly squeezed juices, healthy shakes, salads, and low-fat bakery items.

The menu at the **Cactus Club Cafe,** 1136 Robson St., tel. (604) 687-3278, features mostly Southwestern dishes (and a great Caesar salad), but the decor of this busy restaurant is, well, different. It's covered with cow kitsch, from the black-and-white seating to the papier-mâché cows hanging from the ceiling. Open daily noon-1:30 a.m. **Yogurty's,** 1194 Robson St., tel. (604) 681-2113, offers yogurt in a bowl or cone from $3 a serving. Across the road, the place with the cafe tables spread over the sidewalk is **Big Joe's,** 1189 Robson St., tel. (604) 689-2470, named for legendary English Bay lifeguard Joe Fortes.

Bagel St. Cafe, 1218 Robson St. (corner of

All kinds of tasty delicacies are found at Robson Public Market.

Bute St.), tel. (604) 688-6063, sells a wide variety of bagels to take out or eat in. Across the street on the first floor of Blue Horizon Hotel is **Inlets Bistro,** 1225 Robson St., tel. (604) 688-1411, a stylish place featuring breakfast specials for around $6 and a wide-ranging menu with entrees from $12. Farther west, **Cocorico Cafe,** 1290 Robson St., tel. (604) 687-5155, serves up a wide range of patisserie items, while **Caper's Whole Food Market,** 1675 Robson St., tel. (604) 687-5288, sells groceries for the health-conscious. Caper's also has an in-house bakery and a large cafe with tables spread around the balcony.

It's been said that Vancouver is addicted to coffee, and walking along Robson St. it would be hard to disagree. The street harbors multiple outlets of the main coffeehouse chains, including **Starbucks,** at 1099, 1100, and 1702 Robson, and **Blenz** at 345 and 1201 Robson. But the best spot in this part of the city for coffee and a light snack is the **Bread Garden,** half a block off busy Robson St. at 812 Bute St., tel. (604) 688-3213. It's open 24 hours a day, and always busy—so much so that patrons often need to take a number and wait for service. The coffee is great, as are the freshly baked muffins and pastries. Salads and healthy sandwiches are also available.

West End and Stanley Park

At the English Bay end of Denman Street, a number of small eateries serve quick snacks to go, but also put a couple of tables out on the sidewalk. Among the best of these: **Falafel King,** 1110 Denman St., tel. (604) 669-7278, offering Greek salads and falafels from $4; and **Slice of Gourmet,** 1152 Denman St., tel. (604) 689-1112, where you can get a slice of mouthwatering pizza and a small salad for $5.

The **Bread Garden,** 1040 Denman St., tel. (604) 685-2996, is a busy cafe open 24 hours. For chicken cooked to perfection, head to **Roosters Quarter,** 836 Denman St., tel. (604) 689-8023, a casual eatery chock-full of chicken memorabilia. A full chicken with accompanying vegetables and fries (for two) is a reasonable $17.

At the street's north end is **Bojangles,** 785 Denman St., tel. (604) 687-3622, a small cafe on a busy intersection. Its few sidewalk tables and inside counters are perfect places for watching in-line skaters practice their new-found skills (or lack of them) as they leave surrounding rental shops.

Hamburger Hilda's, 1726 Davie St., tel. (604) 687-8090, serves the best burgers in town for under $5. On the northern tip of Stanley Park, **Prospect Point Cafe** is the perfect place to pick up a drink or light snack and soak up harbor views.

Downtown

Though much of downtown's business-district dining is sacrificed to the foodcourt scene, small, trendy **Cahoots Cafe,** two blocks east of Granville Mall at 565 Dunsmuir St., tel. (604) 681-7634, is an exception. Popular with locals, the cafe serves cooked breakfasts from $3 and healthy eating the rest of the day.

TRANSPORTATION

GETTING THERE

Air

Vancouver International Airport is on Sea Island, 15 km south of Vancouver city center. Over 10 million passengers annually pass through the terminal. A new International Terminal opened in May 1996, and is linked to the Domestic Terminal by a concourse. The three-level complex holds coffee shops and restaurants, car rental agencies, a post office, currency exchanges, newsstands, gift shops, and duty-free shops. Numerous information boards provide a quick airport orientation, and an **information booth** on level three offers tourist brochures, bus schedules, and taxi information.

The **YVR Airporter,** tel. (604) 244-9888, leaves Level 2 every 30 minutes between 6:30 a.m. and 11:30 p.m. daily, shuttling passengers between the airport and more than 20 downtown accommodations. The one-way fare is adults $9, seniors $7, children $5, with a slight discount offered for a roundtrip purchase. Buy tickets from the driver or from the ticket office in front of the International Terminal, Level 2. To get to town by public transport, jump aboard bus no. 100 (Midway Connector) on Level 3 (basic fare $1.50) and get off at 70th St. and Granville, then take bus no. 20 (Vancouver) to downtown. A cab from the airport to downtown runs around $32.

Pacific Coach Lines, tel. (604) 662-8074, runs a regular service between the airport and downtown Victoria ($26.50 one-way, $50 roundtrip) while **Perimeter Transportation,** tel. (604) 266-5386, provides a twice-daily service between the airport and Whistler ($32 one-way).

Short-term parking at the airport is $2 per hour or $10 per day. Many companies offer long-term parking within a few kilometers of the airport. **Park 'N Fly,** Miller Rd., tel. (604) 270-9476, charges $7.50 per day, $42 per week, $112 per month.

International carriers serving Vancouver International Airport include: **Air Canada, British**

Airways, Canadian, Cathay Pacific, Continental, Japan Airlines, KLM, Lufthansa, and **Singapore Airlines.** For onward travel connections, contact **Canadian Regional,** tel. (604) 279-6611, or **Air BC,** tel. (604) 688-5515, both flying to destinations throughout western Canada; **Baxter Aviation,** tel. (604) 683-6525, offering seaplane service to Nanaimo; and **North Vancouver Air,** tel. (604) 278-1608, serving Vancouver Island and Powell River.

Rail

The **VIA Rail** station, 1150 Station St., is a $7 cab ride or 30-minute walk from downtown. Inside the station you'll find a currency exchange, cash machines, lockers, a newsstand, information boards, and a McDonalds restaurant. VIA Rail runs passenger trains from Vancouver to Kamloops, Jasper, and on to eastern Canada three times a week in each direction. Pick up a train schedule in the station or call (800) 561-3949 from the U.S. or (800) 561-8630 from western Canada. From other Canadian locations, contact the nearest VIA Rail Station.

The **Rocky Mountaineer** is the only rail service to Banff ($565) and Calgary ($625). It's a luxurious summer-only rail trip through the spectacular interior of British Columbia, stopping overnight in Kamloops; fares include accommodations in Kamloops. For information and reservations call (604) 606-7245 or (800) 665-7245.

B.C. Rail's **Cariboo Prospector** makes a scenic daily run from North Vancouver to Squamish, Whistler, and Lillooet; it also continues to Prince George several times a week. The B.C. Rail station is at 1311 W. 1st St., North Vancouver. For current fares and schedules, call (604) 984-5246 or (800) 663-8238.

Bus

The **Greyhound** bus depot is in the VIA Rail station at 1150 Station St., tel. (604) 482-8747 or (800) 661-8747. You can't make reservations—just buy your ticket and go. Sample one-way fares from Vancouver: Kamloops $43.32, Penticton $46.76, Cranbrook $85.17, Banff $97.32, Jasper $97.50, Prince George $83.56, Prince Rupert $170.24, and Whitehorse $301.33. Always ask if excursion tickets are available to your destination of choice. Major credit cards are accepted. If you are planning extensive bus

travel, the **Greyhound Canada Pass** (see "Transportation" in the On the Road chapter) is a good deal.

From the same depot, **Maverick Coach Lines,** tel. (604) 662-8051, runs bus service to Vancouver Island (Nanaimo $26.65 one-way), the Sunshine Coast (Gibsons $13.65, Sechelt $19.55, Powell River $32.25), Squamish ($8), Whistler ($15.50), and Pemberton ($19.75).

Ferry

From **Tsawwassen Ferry Terminal,** 30 km south of Vancouver, ferries run to the Southern Gulf Islands and Swartz Bay, 32 km north of Victoria, and to Nanaimo on Vancouver Island. For information, call **BC Ferries** at (250) 386-3431 or, toll-free in B.C., (888) BCFERRY.

To get to the terminal from downtown by car, follow Hwy. 17 south—in summer this road gets crazy with traffic. Buses also link the ferry terminal with downtown; catch no. 601 from downtown, or no. 640 from the ferry terminal, transferring from one to the other at Ladner Exchange (ask the driver for a transfer ticket); $1.50-3 depending on the time of day. To get to Vancouver International Airport from the ferry terminal, catch a no. 640 bus to Ladner Exchange, then a no. 601 to Massey Exchange, then a no. 404 or no. 405 to the airport.

In high season (June to September), the ferries run about once an hour, 7 a.m.-10 p.m. The rest of the year they run a little less frequently. The crossing takes around 90 minutes. Expect a wait in summer, particularly if you have an oversized vehicle (each ferry can accommodate far fewer large vehicles than standard-size cars and trucks). Limited reservations are accepted. Peak one-way fare for the trip over to Vancouver Island, either to Swartz Bay or Nanaimo, is adults $8, children 5-11 $4, cars $30, motorcycles $15, bicycles $2.50, canoes and kayaks $4.

The other ferry route linking the mainland to Vancouver Island runs between Horseshoe Bay and Nanaimo. Horseshoe Bay is on the north side of Burrard Inlet, a 20-minute drive northwest of downtown. You don't save any money on this route—the fares are the same as above—and the wait is often longer. This is also the departure point for ferries to the Sunshine Coast.

SkyTrain is a fast, efficient, and entertaining way to see some of Vancouver.

JANE AND BRUCE KING

GETTING AROUND

BC Transit

BC Transit, tel. (604) 521-0400, operates an extensive network of **bus, SkyTrain,** and **SeaBus** routes that can get you just about anywhere you want to go within the city. The free brochure, *Discover Vancouver on Transit,* is available from all city information centers and is an invaluable source of information. The brochure includes details of many attractions and how to reach them by public transportation.

During rush hours (Mon.-Fri. 5:30-9:30 a.m. and 3-6:30 p.m.), the city is divided into three zones and bus fares vary $1.50-3 for each sector. At other times, travel anywhere in the city costs $1.50 one-way. A **DayPass** is available weekdays after 9:30 a.m. and all weekend. It costs $4.50 and allows unlimited travel for one day anywhere on the BC Transit system. Pay the driver (exact change only) for bus travel or purchase tickets from machines at any SkyTrain station or SeaBus terminal. Buses run to all corners of the city between 5 a.m. and 2 a.m. every day of the year. Transfers are valid for 90 minutes of travel in one direction. Throughout summer, bus no. 52 runs around Stanley Park for free.

SkyTrain is a computer-operated light-rail transit system that runs along 25 km of elevated track from downtown Vancouver through New Westminster and over the Fraser River to Whalley. It stops at 20 stations along its 37-minute route.

The four city-center stations are underground but are clearly marked at each street entrance.

The SeaBus passenger ferry scoots across Burrard Inlet, linking downtown Vancouver to North Vancouver in just 12 minutes. The downtown terminus is Waterfront Station, beside Canada Place and a five-minute walk from the Vancouver Visitor Info Centre. The terminal in North Vancouver is at Lonsdale Quay, from where you can catch BC Transit buses to most north-shore sights.

Vancouver Trolley Company

From the main pick-up point at 157 Water St., this company operates an old-fashioned trolley through the streets of downtown Vancouver. The two-hour loop stops at 15 tourist attractions, from Stanley Park in the north to Science World in the south. Trolleys run April-Oct., daily 9 a.m.-4 p.m., coming by each stop every half hour. Tickets are adults $17, children $9. For more information call (604) 451-5581.

Disabled Passengers

BC Transit's **Handydart** buses provide door-to-door wheelchair-accessible service for about the same price you'd pay on regular buses. You'll need to book in advance at (604) 430-2692. Many other city buses have wheelchair lifts, and all Sky-Train stations as well as the SeaBus are fully wheelchair accessible. The best source of further information is the *Rider's Guide to Accessible Transit,* available by calling (604) 521-0400.

A number of wheelchair-accommodating taxicabs are available from **Vancouver Taxi,** tel. (604) 871-1111. The fares are the same as regular taxis.

Taxi

Cabs are easiest to catch outside major hotels or transportation hubs. Fares in Vancouver are a uniform $2.60 flag charge plus $1.35 per kilometer. Trips within downtown usually run under $8. The trip between the airport and downtown is about $35. Major companies include: **Black Top,** tel. (604) 731-1111; **Vancouver Taxi,** tel. (604) 871-1111; and **Yellow Cabs,** tel. (604) 681-1111.

Car Rental

Vancouver is full of car-rental agencies offering a wide range of vehicles, prices, and deals. Some throw in extras such as coupon books giving you discounts at attractions and certain restaurants.

One of the most recognized low-cost agencies is **Rent-a-wreck,** tel. (604) 688-0001, where basic compact cars rent from $39.95 a day plus 15 cents a kilometer, with the first 200 km free. Obviously you're not getting a new car, and it may be a gas-guzzler, but the rates are low. Most agencies provide free airport and downtown hotel pick-up and drop-off services. Agencies include: **ABC Rent-a-car,** tel. (604) 873-6622 or (800) 464-6422; **Avis,** tel. (604) 606-2847 or (800) 879-2847; **Budget,** tel. (604) 668-7000 or (800) 268-8900; **Discount,** tel. (604) 876-3161 or (800) 263-2355; **Dollar,** tel. (604) 689-5303 or (800) 465-0045; **Enterprise,** tel. (604) 872-1600 or (800) 325-8007; **Hertz,** tel. (604) 688-2411 or (800) 263-0600; **National Tilden,** tel. (604) 685-6111 or (800) 387-4747; and **Thrifty,** tel. (604) 606-1666 or (800) 367-2277.

Bicycle

Downtown Vancouver is not particularly bicycle friendly but nearby areas such as Stanley Park and the coastline west of Kitsilano are perfect places for pedal power. The main concentration of rental shops surrounds the corner of Robson and Denman Streets, two blocks from Stanley Park. Expect to pay from $5 per hour or $15 per day for the most basic bike and $12 per hour or $36 per day for a good mountain bike. Most of the shops also rent in-line skates and tandem bikes. Try: **Bayshore Bicycles,** 745 Denman St., tel. (604) 688-2453; **Spokes Bicycle Rental,** 1798 W. Georgia St., tel. (604) 688-5141; or **Stanley Park Cycle,** 1741 Robson St., tel. (604) 608-1908.

Tours

If you don't have a lot of time to explore Vancouver on your own, or just want an introduction to the city, consider one of the many tours available—they'll maximize your time and get you to the highlights with minimum stress. **Gray Line of Vancouver,** tel. (604) 879-3363, offers a large variety of tours. The basic 3.5-hour City Tour, which includes Stanley Park, Grouse Mountain, Chinatown, Gastown, Robson Street, and English Bay, costs $36 per person. Other options with Gray Line include a downtown tour aboard an old English double-decker bus, $20; a 10-hour tour to Whistler, $52; and a 12-hour tour to Vancouver Island, $92.

More personalized tours are run by **Rockwood Adventures,** tel. (604) 926-7705. On its two-hour Stanley Park tour, guides describe local natural and human history and take you to all the best viewpoints; $20 per person. The company also offers a guided walk along the Capilano River with a visit to a fish hatchery; four hours, $35 per person.

From June to September, **Harbour Ferries,** tel. (604) 688-7246, offers a 90-minute tour of Vancouver's bustling harbor on the paddle wheeler MV *Constitution.* Tours depart from the north foot of Denman St.; adults $15, seniors and students $13.

SERVICES AND INFORMATION

SERVICES

Emergency Services
For emergencies call 911 or contact: **Vancouver Hospital,** 855 W. 12th Ave., tel. (604) 875-4111; **St. Paul's Hospital,** 1081 Burrard St., tel. (604) 682-2344; **Lions Gate Hospital,** 231 E. 15th St., tel. (604) 988-3131; or **B.C. Children's Hospital,** 4480 Oak St., tel. (604) 875-2345. **Seymour Medical Clinic,** 1530 W. 7th Ave., tel. (604) 738-2151, is open 24 hours. For emergency dental help, call (604) 946-9526 or the 24-hour clinic at Burnaby, tel. (604) 524-3674. For the **RCMP** call (604) 264-3111.

Post Offices
Vancouver's **main post office** is at 349 W. Georgia St., tel. (604) 662-5725. It's open Mon.-Saturday. **Postal Station A,** 757 W. Hastings St., and the branch at **Bentall Centre,** 595 Burrard St., are also open on Saturdays. Smaller branches are located in some drugstores—ask a local for the nearest.

Money Exchange
Custom House Currency Exchange is at 355 Burrard St., tel. (604) 482-6000. Also downtown is **Remo Exchange,** 789 Burrard St. (at Robson St.), tel. (604) 685-4921. **Thomas Cook Foreign Exchange** operates a small money-changing facility in the lobby of the Pan Pacific Vancouver Hotel, Canada Place, tel. (604) 641-1229. Another option for currency exchange is the banks, which can deal with most common transactions.

Telephones
Local calls from public phones cost a quarter; long distance calls are much more expensive. The area code for Vancouver and the southwest mainland is 604, while the rest of the province, including Vancouver Island, is 250. The **Public Calling Centre,** 470 W. Cordova St., tel. (604) 687-2040, is designed especially for visitors. From its private booths you can call anywhere in North America for 50 cents a minute or anywhere in the world at posted, discounted rates; pay by cash or credit card. The center can also be used for sending and receiving faxes.

Film and Processing
One-hour film processing is offered by dozens of outlets throughout Vancouver. For high-quality color-print film processing and overnight slide developing, take your precious films to **Totemcolor,** 119 E. 1st St., North Vancouver, tel. (604) 986-2271.

BOOKS, MAGAZINES, AND NEWSPAPERS

Vancouver Public Library
In November 1995, after two years of construction and a cost of $100 million, Vancouver Public Library, 350 W. Georgia St., tel. (604) 331-3600, opened its doors to the public. The magnificent new nine-story facility is a far cry from the city's first library, which opened with a grant of £250 back in 1887. Its facade contains a glass-walled promenade rising six stories above a row of stylish indoor shops and cafes. Once inside, you'll soon discover that the city also found enough money to stock the shelves; the library holds over one million books. To help you find that one book you're searching for, use the self-guided tour brochure available at the information desk. It's open year-round, Mon.-Wed. 10 a.m.-9 p.m., Thurs.-Sat. 10 a.m.-6 p.m., and also Sunday 1-5 p.m. from October to April.

General Bookstores
Per capita, residents of Vancouver buy more books than the residents of any other North American city. And they buy them from a huge number of bookstores scattered throughout the city. The city's largest bookstore is **Bollums,** 650 W. Georgia St., tel. (604) 687-0083, right in the heart of downtown. With over 90,000 titles, newspapers from around the world, and sections devoted entirely to both Vancouver and British Columbia authors, you should be able to find what you're looking for. The hours should

suit you as well: Mon.-Thurs. 8 a.m.-10 p.m., Fri.-Sat. 8 a.m.-midnight, Sunday 10 a.m.-10 p.m. **Duthie Books** has six outlets in the city, among them: 345 Robson St. (Library Square), tel. (604) 602-0610; 919 Robson St., tel. (604) 684-4496; and 4255 Arbutus St., tel. (604) 738-1833. To save a few bucks on current titles or pick up new books at bargain prices, search out the **Book Warehouse** at either 1150 Robson St., tel. (604) 685-5711, or 632 W. Broadway, Central Vancouver, tel. (604) 872-5711. On Granville Island, **Blackberry Books,** 1663 Duranleau St., tel. (604) 685-6188, stocks a wide range of touristy-type coffee-table books and a wide range of western Canadiana.

World Wide Books and Maps, downtown at 736A Granville St. (downstairs), tel. (604) 687-3320, has the city's best stock of travel guides and maps. It's open seven days a week. Also specializing in travel is the **Travel Bug,** 2667 W. Broadway, Kitsilano, tel. (604) 737-1122. For environmentally aware literature head for the **Western Canada Wilderness Committee Store,** 20 Water St., Gastown, tel. (604) 683-8220.

Secondhand and Antiquarian Bookstores

Vancouver has some fantastic secondhand bookstores, including a few specializing entirely in nonfiction. The largest concentration lies along W. Pender St. between Richards and Hamilton Streets. **Macleod's Books,** 455 W. Pender St., tel. (604) 681-7654, stocks a wide range of antiquarian titles, including many of the earliest works on western Canada. Across the road, **Criterion Books,** 434 W. Pender St., tel. (604) 685-2224, stocks newer titles, but the western Canada section is just as good. One block east is **Joyce Williams Antique Prints and Maps,** 346 W. Pender St., tel. (604) 688-7434. On the corner of W. Hastings and Hamilton Sts. are **Bond's Books,** tel. (604) 688-5227, specializing in Canada and the Arctic, and **Stephen C. Lunsford Books,** tel. (604) 681-6830, with plenty of old Canadian nonfiction titles. All of the above bookstores are closed Sunday.

Newspapers and Periodicals

In addition to the two daily newspapers—the *Province* and the *Vancouver Sun*—many free publications are distributed throughout the city. The weekly *Georgia Strait* features articles on local issues, as well as a full entertainment rundown for Vancouver. The *Westender,* also a weekly, spotlights downtown issues and has good restaurant reviews. The fortnightly *Terminal City* and, for the younger set, *Sunny Side Up* both have offbeat articles and music and entertainment diaries. *Coast* focuses on outdoor recreation in the region, while the quarterly *Common Ground* is dedicated to health and personal development.

INFORMATION CENTERS

Downtown

The city's main information center is **Vancouver Visitor Info Centre,** just up from Canada Place at 200 Burrard St., tel. (604) 683-2000. The specially trained staff provides free maps, brochures, and public transportation schedules, books sightseeing tours, makes accommodations reservations, and sells the invaluable BC Transit Day-Pass along with postcards, stamps, and film. The center is open May-Sept., daily 8 a.m.-6 p.m.; the rest of the year, Mon.-Sat. 8:30 a.m.-5:30 p.m. In summer, information booths also operate in Stanley Park and downtown on the corner of Granville and Georgia Streets. On Granville Island, **Granville Island Information Centre,** 1592 Johnson St., tel. (604) 666-5784, is open daily 9 a.m.-6 p.m. in summer; closed Monday the rest of the year.

South

If you approach Vancouver from the south, **White Rock Visitor Info Centre** is just north of the border at 15150 Russell Ave., tel. (604) 536-6844. If you miss it, try **Delta Visitor Info Centre,** 6201 60th Ave. (take the Delta exit and follow the signs), tel. (604) 946-4232, or **Richmond Visitor Info Centre,** to the east just past the George Massey Tunnel crossing the Fraser River, tel. (604) 271-8280. All three centers are open daily in summer, weekdays only the rest of the year. **Vancouver International Airport** has information centers on Level 1 and Level 3; both are open every day of the year, 6:30 a.m.-11:30 p.m.

North

North Vancouver Visitor Info Centre, 131 E. 2nd St., tel. (604) 987-4488, is open daily in summer, Mon.-Fri. only the rest of the year. A more handy source of information north of the harbor is the small booth by the bus station at Lonsdale Quay.

East

If you're approaching the city from the east, **Coquitlam Visitor Info Centre,** 1180 Pinetree Way, tel. (604) 464-2716, is a convenient stop along the TransCanada Hwy. on the west side of the Fraser River. Off the TransCanada Hwy. is **Surrey Visitor Info Centre,** 15105 105th Ave., tel. (604) 581-7130; closed weekends outside of the busy summer season. Farther out along the Trans-Canada Hwy. are: **Langley Visitor Info Centre,** 20420 Fraser Hwy., tel. (604) 530-6656; **Fort Langley Visitor Info Centre,** 23325 Mavis Ave., tel. (604) 888-1477; **Abbotsford Visitor Info Centre,** 2462 McCallum Rd., tel. (604) 859-9651; and **Chilliwack Visitor Info Centre,** 44150 Luckakuck Way, tel. (604) 858-8121. If you're traveling into the city on the north side of the Fraser River, along the Lougheed Hwy. from Harrison Hot Springs, stop at **Mission Visitor Info Centre,** 34033 Lougheed Hwy., tel. (604) 826-6914, or, closer to the city, **Maple Ridge Visitor Info Centre,** 22238 Lougheed Hwy., tel. (604) 463-3366.

LOUISE FOOTE

VANCOUVER ISLAND

Vancouver Island, the largest isle in North America's Pacific, stretches for more than 450 superb kilometers off the west coast of mainland British Columbia. A magnificent chain of rugged snowcapped mountains, sprinkled with lakes and rivers and pierced by a number of deep inlets, effectively divides the island into two distinct sides: dense, rain-drenched forest and remote surf- and wind-battered shores on the west, and well-populated, sheltered, beach-fringed lowlands on the east. At the northern and southern tips lie large regions of low, rolling hills.

Much of the lushly green island is covered with dense forests of Douglas fir, western red cedar, and hemlock. The climate, stabilized by the Pacific Ocean and warmed by the Japanese current, never really gets too hot or too cold, but be prepared for cloudbursts, especially in winter.

Victoria, the provincial capital, lies at the southern tip of the island and is connected to the much-larger city of Vancouver by regular ferry services. Its deeply entrenched British traditions make Victoria unique among North American cities. The rest of the island draws scenery buffs, outdoor adventurers, wildlife watchers, and students of northwest Native American art and culture.

Backpackers head west from Victoria to Port Renfrew, the starting point of the **West Coast Trail.** Island-hoppers take Hwy. 17 north up the

Saanich Peninsula to Swartz Bay, jump on a ferry, and cruise the scenic **Southern Gulf Islands.** Other explorers head north up the Island Highway, Rt. 1/19, which follows the Strait of Georgia all the way to the island's northern tip. The old highway is gradually being replaced by the Inland Island Highway (to be completed by 2000), but to take in the best the island has to offer, stick to the old route. Along the way you'll pass sandy beaches, resorts, and old logging, mining, and fishing towns that now base their existence to a large degree on tourism.

At Parksville, Hwy. 4 turns off west and leads through "oooh" and "aaah" mountain scenery to the relatively untamed west coast. There you'll find picture-perfect fishing villages, driftwood-littered sand for as far as you can see, and **Pacific Rim National Park,** the only national park on the island. Also on the west coast is **Tofino,** a base for sea kayaking and whalewatching on Clayoquot Sound. Farther north up Hwy. 19, at Campbell River, Hwy. 28 cuts west to Gold River, passing through enormous **Strathcona Provincial Park.**

North of Campbell River lies a surprisingly large area mostly untouched by civilization—in fact, today you can still find maps of the island that fizzle out above Campbell River. Does life exist farther north? Anything to see or do? Can birds fly? Travel kilometer after kilometer along

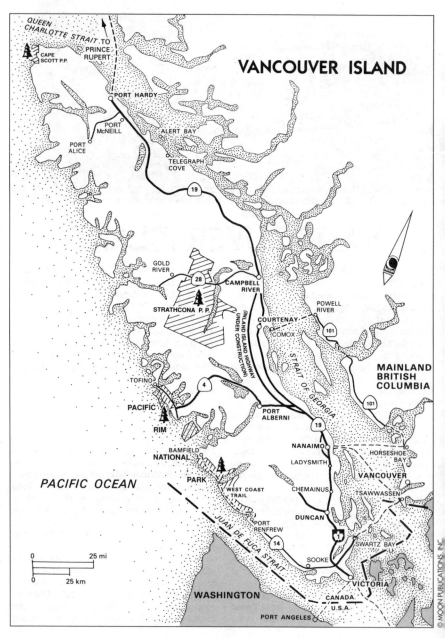

Hwy. 19 through impressive mountain scenery where the road itself, rest areas at all the very best views, and some unfortunate stretches of clear-cutting are the only human signatures on the landscape. Avail yourself of excellent camping spots, hiking trails, lakes perfect for canoeing and fishing, and more than a smattering of indigenous art and culture along the way. Unique **Telegraph Cove,** a boardwalk village known for its fishing and whalewatching activities, and intriguing **Alert Bay** on Cormorant Island are definitely worthwhile side trips on your way north. Finally, you'll come to road's end at **Port Hardy,** the largest community on the north island and the terminus for ferries to Prince Rupert and Alaska.

VICTORIA

Victoria, the elegant capital of British Columbia, boasts a mild climate, friendly people, and a distinct holiday atmosphere somewhat unusual for a capital city. Standing proudly at the southern tip of Vancouver Island, the fashionable city of 350,000 projects an intriguing mixture of images, old and new. Well-preserved century-old buildings line inner-city streets; ancient totem poles sprout from shady parks; restored historic areas house trendy shops, offices, and exotic restaurants; double-decker buses and horse-drawn carriages compete for summer trade; and the residents keep alive the original traditions and atmosphere of Merry Olde England.

Many people view the city for the first time from the Inner Harbour, coming in by boat the way people have for almost 150 years. On rounding Laurel Point, Victoria sparkles into view. Ferries, fishing boats, and seaplanes bob in the harbor, backdropped by manicured lawns and flower gardens, quiet residential suburbs, and striking inner-city architecture. Despite the pressures that go with city life, easygoing Victorians still find time for a stroll along the waterfront, a round of golf, or a typically English high tea.

Victoria has so many attractions, both free and commercial, that if you want to see *everything* you'd better give yourself a few extra days. The best way to get to know this beautiful city is on foot. All the downtown attractions are within a short walk of each other, and the more remote sights are easily reached by bus. In summer various tours are offered, giving you the choice of seeing Victoria by horse-drawn carriage, bus, boat, bicycle, limo—you name it! But if you still feel the need to have a car readily available, note that parking is plentiful just a few blocks from the Inner Harbour.

The city relies on tourism as its economic mainstay. High season is May through October and low season falls in winter when the weather can be less appealing. In spring, the city jumps to life and shakes out the welcome mat; enormous baskets of daffodils and other blooming bulbs are hung from all the lampposts, turning downtown into one big flower garden. Summer is the busiest time—time to enjoy the hustle and bustle of a city full of visitors, and to join in the plethora of warm-weather activities the city offers. If you prefer a more laid-back atmosphere, don't mind the possibility of rain and nippy sea breezes, and like meeting relaxed locals enjoying their few months of peace and quiet, take advantage of the lower prices, grab your windbreaker and brolly, and discover Victoria in the off-season.

HISTORY

In 1792, Capt. George Vancouver sailed through the Strait of Georgia, noting and naming Vancouver Island. But this had little effect on the many indigenous communities living along the shoreline. Europeans didn't see and exploit the island's potential for another 50 years, when the Hudson's Bay Company established control over the entire island and the mainland territory of "Columbia."

Fort Victoria

Needing to firmly establish British presence on the continent's northwest coast, the Hudson's Bay Company built Fort Victoria—named after Queen Victoria—on the southern tip of Vancouver Island in 1843. Three years later, the Oregon Treaty fixed the U.S./Canada boundary at the 49th parallel, with the proviso that the section of Vancouver Island lying south of that line would be retained by Canada. To forestall any claims that the U.S. may have had on the area, the British government set about settling the island. In 1849, the island was gazetted as a Crown colony and leased back to the Hudson's Bay Company. Gradually land around Fort Victoria was opened up by groups of British settlers brought to the island by the company's subsidiary, Puget Sound Agricultural Company. Several large company farms were developed, and Esquimalt Harbour became a major port for British ships.

The Growth of Victoria
In the late 1850s gold strikes on the mainland's Thompson and Fraser Rivers brought thousands of gold miners into Victoria, the region's only port and source of supplies. Overnight, Victoria became a classic boomtown, but with a distinctly British flavor; most of the company men, early settlers, and military personnel firmly maintained their homeland traditions and celebrations. Even after the gold rush ended, Victoria remained an energetic bastion of military, economic, and political activity, and was officially incorporated as a city in 1862. In 1868, two years after the colonies of Vancouver Island and British Columbia were united, Victoria was made capital. Through the two World Wars, Victoria continued to grow. The commencement of ferry service between Tsawwassen and Sidney in 1903 created a small population boom, but Victoria has always lagged well behind Vancouver in the population stakes.

AROUND INNER HARBOUR

Initially this harbor extended further inland; prior to the construction of the massive stone causeway that now forms the marina, the area on which the impressive Empress Hotel now stands was a deep, oozing mudflat. Walk along the lower level, then up the steps in the middle to come face-to-face with an unamused Capt. James Cook; the bronze statue commemorates the first recorded British landing, in 1778, on the territory that would later become British Columbia. Above the northeast corner of the harbor

is the **Victoria Visitor Info Centre,** 812 Wharf St., tel. (250) 953-2033, the perfect place to start your city exploration. Be sure to return to the Inner Harbour after dark, when the parliament buildings are outlined in lights and the Empress Hotel is floodlit.

Empress Hotel
The pompous, ivy-covered Empress Hotel was designed in 1908 by the well-known architect Francis Rattenbury, who also designed the parliament buildings, the CPR steamship terminal (now housing the wax museum), and Crystal Garden. It's worthwhile walking through the hotel lobby to gaze—head back, mouth agape—at the interior razzle-dazzle, and to watch people-watching people partake in traditional afternoon tea (see "Food," below). Browse through the conservatory and gift shops, drool over the menus of the various restaurants, see what tours are available, and exchange currency if you're desperate (banks give a better exchange rate).

Empress Hotel

Parliament Buildings

Satisfy your lust for governmental, historic, and architectural knowledge all in one go by taking a free tour of the harborside Provincial Legislative Buildings, aka the parliament buildings. These prominent buildings were designed by Francis Rattenbury and completed in 1897. The exterior is British Columbia Haddington Island stone, and if you walk around the buildings you'll no doubt spot a stern or gruesome face staring down from the stonework.

On either side of the main entrance stand statues of Sir James Douglas, who chose the location of Victoria, and Sir Matthew Baillie Begbie, who was in charge of law and order during the gold-rush period. Atop the copper-covered dome stands a gilded statue of Capt. George Vancouver, the first mariner to circumnavigate Vancouver Island. Walk through the main entrance and into the memorial rotunda, look skyward for a dramatic view of the central dome, then continue upstairs to peer into the legislative chamber, the home of the democratic government of British Columbia. Free guided tours are offered many times a day in summer, less frequently (Mon.-Fri. only) in winter. The time of each tour changes daily according to the goings-on inside; for current times, call the tour office at (250) 387-3046.

Laurel Point

For an enjoyable short walk from downtown, continue along Belleville Street from the parliament buildings, passing a conglomeration of modern hotels, ferry terminals, and some intriguing architecture dating back to the late 19th century. A path leads down through a shady park to Laurel Point, hugging the waterfront and providing good views of Inner Harbour en route. If you're feeling really energetic, continue to **Fisherman's Wharf Park** and the crowded marina.

Commercial Attractions

Oodles of ways to trim bulging wallets confront you in Victoria, some excellent, some routine. Along the waterfront on Belleville Street, across the road from the parliament buildings, is the former CPR steamship terminal, now the **Royal London Wax Museum,** 470 Belleville St., tel. (250) 388-4461. This building, completed in 1924, was also designed by Francis Ratten-

bury. The museum features around 300 wax figures direct from London. It's open daily 9:30 a.m.-6 p.m., until 9 p.m. in summer; adults $7, seniors $6.25, children $3. On the water beside the wax museum, **Undersea Gardens,** 490 Belleville St., tel. (250) 382-5717, boasts more than 5,000 marine specimens in their "natural" habitat, as well as performing scuba divers and Armstrong the giant octopus. It's open in summer, daily 10 a.m.-7 p.m.; the rest of the year, daily 10 a.m.-5 p.m. Admission is adults $7, children $3.50. Behind the Empress Hotel is **Miniature World,** 649 Humboldt St., tel. (250) 385-9731, another of Victoria's many commercial attractions; adults $7, children $5.

Royal British Columbia Museum

Canada's most visited museum and easily one of North America's best, the Royal British Columbia Museum, 675 Belleville St., tel. (250) 387-3701, is a must-see attraction for even the most jaded museum-goer. Its fine natural-history displays are extraordinarily true to life, complete with appropriate sounds and smells. Come face-to-face with an ice-age woolly mammoth, stroll through a coastal forest full of deer and tweeting birds, meander along a seashore or tidal marsh, then descend into the open ocean—a very real trip not recommended for claustrophobics.

Human history is also explored here in creative ways. Take a tour through time via the time capsules; walk along a turn-of-the-century street; and experience hands-on exhibits on industrialization, the gold rush, and the exploration of B.C. by land and sea. The Archaeology Gallery, First Peoples Gallery, Totem Pole and Art Gallery, and Kwakiutl Indian Bighouse complete the tour.

A gift shop stocks an excellent collection of books on Canadiana, wildfe, history, and native Indian art and culture, along with postcards and tourist paraphernalia. Next door, the tearoom is always crowded.

The museum is open in summer, daily 9:30 a.m.-7 p.m.; the rest of the year, daily 9 a.m.-5 p.m. Admission is a very worthwhile adults $7, children $4.

In front of the museum, the 27-meter-high **Netherlands Centennial Carillon** was a gift to the city from British Columbia's Dutch community. The tower's 62 bells range in weight from

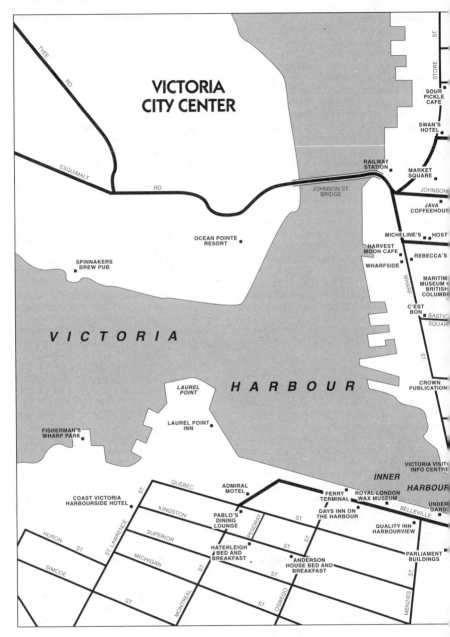

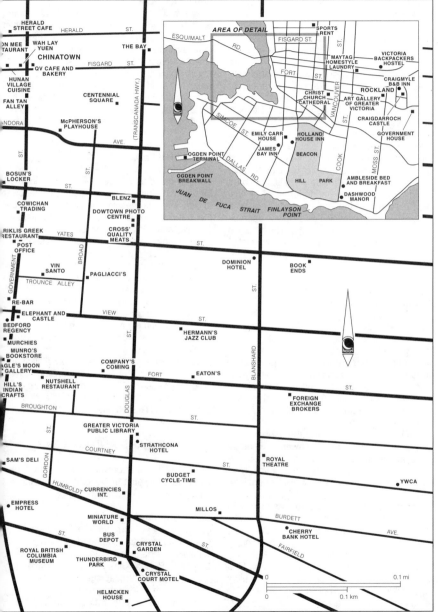

HERALD STREET CAFE

HERALD ST.

ON MEE TAURANT

WAH LAY YUEN

THE BAY

CHINATOWN

QV CAFE AND BAKERY

FISGARD ST.

HUNAN VILLAGE CUISINE

CENTENNIAL SQUARE

FAN TAN ALLEY

ANDORA

McPHERSON'S PLAYHOUSE

AVE.

(TRANSCANADA HWY.)

BOSUN'S LOCKER

ST.

COWICHAN TRADING

BLENZ

DOWTOWN PHOTO CENTRE

RIKLIS GREEK RESTAURANT

YATES

CROSS' QUALITY MEATS

POST OFFICE

BROAD

ST.

VIN SANTO

PAGLIACCI'S

TROUNCE ALLEY

GOVERNMENT

RE-BAR

VIEW

ELEPHANT AND CASTLE

ST.

BEDFORD REGENCY

MURCHIES

ST.

HERMANN'S JAZZ CLUB

MUNRO'S BOOKSTORE

AGLE'S MOON GALLERY

COMPANY'S COMING

FORT

HILL'S INDIAN CRAFTS

NUTSHELL RESTAURANT

EATON'S

BROUGHTON

DOUGLAS

ST.

FOREIGN EXCHANGE BROKERS

GREATER VICTORIA PUBLIC LIBRARY

ST.

COURTNEY

STRATHCONA HOTEL

GORDON

SAM'S DELI

ROYAL THEATRE

ST.

HUMBOLDT

BUDGET CYCLE-TIME

CURRENCIES INT.

YWCA

EMPRESS HOTEL

MILLOS

BURDETT

MINIATURE WORLD

BUS DEPOT

CHERRY BANK HOTEL

AVE.

ST.

ROYAL BRITISH COLUMBIA MUSEUM

CRYSTAL GARDEN

FAIRFIELD

THUNDERBIRD PARK

CRYSTAL COURT MOTEL

0   0.1 mi

HELMCKEN HOUSE

0   0.1 km

AREA OF DETAIL

ESQUIMALT

RD.

FISGARD ST.

SPORTS RENT

ST.

FORT

ST.

VICTORIA BACKPACKERS HOSTEL

MAYTAG HOMESTYLE LAUNDRY

CRAIGMYLE B&B INN

CHRIST CHURCH CATHEDRAL

VANCOUVER

ROCKLAND

ART GALLERY OF GREATER VICTORIA

CRAIGDARROCH CASTLE

SIMCOE

ST.

EMILY CARR HOUSE

HOLLAND HOUSE INN

ST.

GOVERNMENT HOUSE

MOSS ST.

OGDEN POINT TERMINAL

DALLAS

RD.

JAMES BAY INN

BEACON

HILL   PARK

COOK

AMBLESIDE BED AND BREAKFAST

OGDEN POINT BREAKWALL

DASHWOOD MANOR

JUAN   DE   FUCA   STRAIT   FINLAYSON POINT

© MOON PUBLICATIONS, INC.

eight to 1,500 kilograms, and toll at 15-minute intervals, daily 7 a.m.-10 p.m.

Thunderbird Park and Helmcken House

Beside the Royal British Columbia Museum, on the corner of Belleville and Douglas Sts., lies Thunderbird Park, a small green spot chockablock with authentic totem poles intricately carved by northwest coastal natives.

Walk through the park to the historic Helmcken House, tel. (250) 361-0021, the oldest house in Victoria still standing on its original site. It was built by Dr. J.S. Helmcken, pioneer surgeon and legislator, who arrived in Victoria in 1850 and aided negotiating the union of British Columbia with Canada in 1870. Inside you'll find restored rooms decorated with period furniture, as well as a collection of the good doctor's gruesome surgical equipment (which will help you appreciate modern medical technology). The house is open in summer, daily 11 a.m.-5 p.m.; the rest of the year, daily noon-4 p.m. Admisson is adults $4, seniors or students $3, children $2.

Crystal Garden

Designed by Francis Rattenbury and built by Percy James, the Crystal Garden, 713 Douglas St., tel. (250) 381-1213, opened in 1925 as the largest saltwater pool in the British Empire. It held tearooms, ballrooms, and a promenade, and was the venue for flower shows, craft shows, and big-band dancing, along with swimming, of course. In 1971, rising maintenance costs forced its closure. The provincial government then bought it and turned it into a two-story conservatory.

Today's visitors will find themselves surrounded by lush greenery, flowering plants, a waterfall, and the cacophony of an enormous variety of exotic birds from South America, New Guinea, and Australia. Wood carvings from New Guinea peek out of the lush undergrowth, coral-colored flamingos strut their stuff at a series of placid pools, and iguanas, monkeys, squirrels, wallabies, and marmosets cavort nearby. Sip afternoon tea on the humid upper floor, close your eyes, and you'll swear you're in the tropics. The garden is open daily 9 a.m.-6 p.m., till 9 p.m. in summer. Admission is adults $7, seniors and children $5. An English tea, served 2:15-4:15 p.m., costs extra.

Emily Carr House

Artist Emily Carr was born in this typical upper-class Victorian-era home at 207 Government St., tel. (250) 383-5843. Carr moved to the mainland at an early age, escaping the confines of the capital to draw and write about the British Columbian natives and the wilderness in which she lived. She is best remembered today for her painting. The house is open mid-May to mid-October, daily 9 a.m.-5 p.m. Admission is adults $4, seniors and students $3, children $2.

Beacon Hill Park

This large, hilly city park—a lush, sea-edged oasis of grass and flowers—extends from the back of the museum along Douglas Street out to cliffs that offer spectacular views of Juan de Fuca Strait and, on a clear day, the distant Olympic Mountains. Add a handful of rocky points to scramble on and many protected pebble-and-sand beaches and you've found yourself a perfect spot to indulge your senses. Catch a sea breeze (along with numerous hang gliders, windsurfers, and kite-fliers) and gaze at all the strolling, cycling, dog-walking, and pram-pushing Victorians passing by. On a bright sunny day you'll swear that most of Victoria is here, too. The park is within easy walking distance from downtown, and can also be reached by bus no. 5. For a tidbit of history, walk through the park to rocky Finlayson Point, once the site of an ancient fortified native village. Between 1878 and 1892 two enormous guns protected the point against an expected but unrealized Russian invasion.

ROCKLAND AND OAK BAY

This historic part of downtown lies behind the Inner Harbour, east of Douglas Street, and is easily accessible on foot.

Christ Church Cathedral

On the corner of Quadra and Courtney Sts., Christ Church Cathedral, tel. (250) 383-2714, is the seat of the Bishop of the Diocese of British Columbia. Built in 13th-century Gothic style, it's one of Canada's largest churches. Self-guided tours are possible Mon.-Fri. 8:30 a.m.-5 p.m. and Sunday 7:30 a.m.-8:30 p.m. In summer, the cathedral sponsors free choral recitals each Saturday at 4 p.m. The park next to the cathedral is a shady haven to rest weary feet, and the gravestones make fascinating reading.

Art Gallery of Greater Victoria; Government House

From Christ Church Cathedral, walk up Rockland Ave. through the historic Rockland district, passing stately mansions and colorful gardens on tree-lined streets. Turn left on Moss St. and you'll come to the 1889 Spencer Mansion and its modern wing that together make up the Art Gallery of Greater Victoria, 1040 Moss St., tel. (250) 384-4101. The gallery contains Canada's finest collection of Japanese art, a range of contemporary art, and a variety of traveling exhibits, as well as a Japanese garden with a Shinto shrine. The Gallery Shop sells art books, reproductions, and handcrafted jewelry, pottery, and glass. Hours are Mon.-Sat. 10 a.m.-5 p.m., Thursday 10 a.m.-9 p.m., and Sunday 1-5 p.m. Admission is adults $4, seniors and children $3; free for everyone Thursday 5-9 p.m.

Continue up Rockland Ave. to Government House on the right. The green velvet lawns and picture-perfect flower gardens are open to the public throughout the year.

Craigdarroch Castle

A short walk up (east) from the art gallery along Rockland Ave. and left on Joan Cres. brings you to the baronial mansion known as Craigdarroch Castle, 1050 Joan Cres., tel. (250) 592-5323. From downtown take bus no. 11 (Uplands) or no. 14 (University). The architectural masterpiece was built in 1890 for Robert Dunsmuir, a wealthy Victorian industrialist and politician who died just before the building was completed. For all the nitty-gritties, tour the mansion with volunteer guides who really know their Dunsmuir, then admire at your leisure all the polished wood, stained-glass windows, period furnishings, and the great city views from upstairs. Admission and tour costs adults $6, seniors and children $4.50. Open in summer, daily 9 a.m.-7:30 p.m.; the rest of the year, daily 10 a.m.-5 p.m.

Marine Drive

Take Belleville St. along the Inner Harbour, then take Montreal St. to Dallas Rd. and the oceanfront following the blue Scenic Drive signs. East of Douglas St., Dallas Rd. becomes Marine Dr. and hugs the coastline to Oak Bay. This route takes you through quiet residential areas, past small pebble beaches covered in driftwood, and into the ritzy mansion district east of downtown, where the residents have manicured gardens, sea views, and live "behind the tweed curtain," because they are "so British."

Continue through the velvet greens of Victoria Golf Club on Gonzales Point, stopping if you'd like at Oak Bay Marina and the Royal Victoria Yacht Club at Cadboro Bay. The route borders the east side of the **University of Victoria.** Head west for the city center, or north up the

Craigdarroch Castle

JANE AND BRUCE KING

Saanich Peninsula (see below) toward famous **Butchart Gardens, Butterfly Gardens,** Sidney, and the terminal at the tip of the peninsula, where ferries depart for the beautiful Southern Gulf Islands and Vancouver.

OLD TOWN

The oldest section of Victoria lies several blocks north of the city center between Wharf and Government Streets. Start by walking north from the Inner Harbour along historic Wharf Street, where Hudson's Bay Company furs were loaded onto ships bound for England, gold seekers arrived in search of fortune, and shopkeepers first established businesses. Cross the road to cobblestoned **Bastion Square,** lined with old gas lamps and decorative architecture dating from the 1860s to 1890s. This was the original site chosen by James Douglas in 1843 for Fort Victoria, the Hudson's Bay Company trading post. At one time the square held a courthouse, jail, and gallows. Today restored buildings house trendy restaurants, cafes, nightclubs, and fashionable offices.

Maritime Museum of British Columbia
At the top (east) end of Bastion Square, the Maritime Museum of British Columbia, tel. (250) 385-4222, traces Victoria's seafaring history through displays of dugout canoes, model ships, Royal Navy charts, figureheads, photographs, naval uniforms, and bells. One room is devoted to exhibits chronicling the circumnavigation of the world. The museum is open daily 9:30 a.m.-4:30 p.m., until 6 p.m. in summer. Admission is adults $6, seniors $5, children $4.

Other Old Town Sights
Centennial Square, bounded by Government St., Douglas St., Pandora Ave., and Fisgard St., is lined with many buildings dating from the 1880s and '90s, refurbished in recent times for all to appreciate. Don't miss the 1878 **City Hall** (fronting Douglas St.) and the imposing Greek-style building of the Hudson's Bay Company. Continue down Fisgard St. into colorful **Chinatown,** one of Canada's oldest Chinese enclaves. It's a delicious place to breathe in the aroma of authentic Asian food wafting from the many restaurants. Chinese prospectors and laborers

first brought exotic spices, plants, and a love of intricate architecture and bright colors to Victoria in the 19th century. Poke through the dark little shops along Fisgard St., where you can find everything from fragile paper lanterns and embroidered silks to gingerroot and exotic canned fruits and veggies, then cruise Fan Tan Alley, the center of the opium trade in the 1800s. Walk south along Store St. and Wharf St. back to Bastion Square.

WEST OF DOWNTOWN

Point Ellice House and Garden
Built in 1861, this restored mansion sits amid beautiful gardens on Point Ellice, less than two km from the Inner Harbour. The house's second owner, a successful entrepreneur and politician, bought the house in 1868 and entertained many distinguished guests there. Original Victorian-era artifacts clutter every nook and cranny of the interior.

The house, tel. (250) 380-6506, is open mid-May to mid-September, daily 10 a.m.-5 p.m. Admission is adults $4, seniors $3, children $2. To get there from the Inner Harbour, jump aboard a **Victoria Harbour Ferry,** tel. (250) 480-0971 ($2.50 each way), or take Government or Douglas Sts. north from downtown, turn left on Bay St., and turn left again on Pleasant Street.

Craigflower Manor and Schoolhouse
Cross the Point Ellice Bridge from Point Ellice House and follow Craigflower Rd. west, turning right on Admirals Rd., to come to the site of Craigflower Farm. The farm was developed in the 1850s by the Puget Sound Agricultural Co., a subsidiary of the Hudson's Bay Company. The employment of colonists by this farm and three others helped in the transition of the area from a fur-trade camp to a permanent settlement.

Built in 1856 with native materials, the farm's manor house was the center of social life for Victorian residents and the navy officers from Esquimalt. Step into your time machine, dial in 1860, and enter the house to discover furniture, lace bedspreads, bed warmers, cooking pots, books, and all sorts of things that belonged to the original family. An appropriately dressed guide lets you in on all the family secrets—how the family kept their food cold without a refrigerator, cooked without a microwave, and kept the entire house (except the nanny's room) warm in winter. See all the glamorous and hideous wallpaper designs that were "in" throughout the years, and much more.

Across Gorge Waterway from the farmhouse is Craigflower Schoolhouse, built in 1854-55 from lumber obtained from a steam-powered sawmill at Craigflower Farm. The men employed to build it were notoriously drunk, the evidence of which is quite obvious when you tour the interior; note the sloping doorframes and tilted fireplace. Canada's oldest surviving schoolhouse, it operated 1855-1911. The single schoolroom served children from the farm and nearby district, and the upper floor provided living quarters for the teacher's family and student boarders.

Both historic sites are open in summer, daily noon-4 p.m.; spring and fall, Thurs.-Mon. noon-4 p.m. Admission is adults $4, seniors $3, children $2. Get there from the corner of Douglas and Yates Sts. on bus no. 14, or from the Inner Harbour aboard the **Victoria Harbour Ferry,** tel. (250) 480-0971. For more information call (250) 592-5323.

Anne Hathaway's Cottage; Olde England Inn
The Stratford-upon-Avon cottage of Anne Hathaway, William Shakespeare's wife, has been recreated at 429 Lampson St., tel. (250) 388-4353; catch bus no. 24 (Munro) from downtown and return on no. 24 (Colville). The cottage is authentically furnished with 16th-century antiques. It's open for tours in summer, daily 9 a.m.-9 p.m.; the rest of the year, daily 10 a.m.-5 p.m. Admission is adults $7, seniors and children $4.50.

Next to the cottage is the **Olde England Inn** (see "West Side" under "Hotels and Motels Outside of Downtown," below) and a series of Tudor-style buildings that make up an English village. If you feel like splurging, the food at the inn is excellent and oh so English. For an even bigger splurge, stay in one of the inn's antique-furnished rooms. Each one has a fireplace and a draped four-poster bed so high you need a stool to clamber up .

Fort Rodd Hill National Historic Site
Clinging to a headland at the entrance to Esquimalt Harbour west of downtown, this picturesque site at 603 Fort Rodd Hill Rd., Colwood, tel. (250) 363-4662, comprises **Fort Rodd,** built in 1898 to protect the fleets of ships in the harbour, and **Fisgard Lighthouse,** which dates to 1873. It's an interesting place to explore; audio stations bring the sounds of the past alive, workrooms are furnished as they were at the turn of the century, and the lighthouse has been fully restored and is open to visitors. The grounds are open daily 10 a.m.-5:30 p.m. Admission is adults $3, seniors $2.25, children $1.50. To get there from downtown, take the Old Island Hwy. (Gorge Rd.) and turn left on Belmont Road. By bus, take no. 50 from downtown then transfer to no. 52.

Goldstream Provincial Park
Lying just 20 km from the heart of Victoria, this 390-hectare park straddles Hwy. 1 northwest of downtown. The park's main natural feature is the Goldstream River, which flows north into the Finlayson Arm of Saanich Inlet. Forests of ancient Douglas fir and western red cedar flank the river, while at higher elevations forests of lodgepole pine flourish.

The park's highlight event occurs in November and December, when chum, coho, and chinook salmon fight their way upriver to spawn themselves out on the same shallow gravel bars where they were born four years previously. From the picnic area parking lot two km north of the campground turnoff, a trail leads 400 meters (10 minutes) along the Goldstream River to **Freeman King Visitor Centre,** where the life cycle of salmon is described. The center is open daily 9 a.m.-5 p.m.

Beyond the visitor center, the **Marsh Trail** leads 200 meters (five minutes) to the mouth of the Goldstream River and the head of Finlayson Arm, a great birdwatching spot. One of the park's longer hikes is the **Goldmine Trail,** which begins from a parking lot on the west side of Hwy. 1 halfway between the campground and picnic area. This trail winds two km (45 minutes) each way through a mixed forest of lodgepole pine, maple, and western hemlock, passing the site of a short-lived goldrush and coming to **Niagara Falls,** a poor relation of its eastern namesake but still a picturesque flow of water. For details about camping in Goldstream Provincial Park, see "North" under "Campgrounds," below.

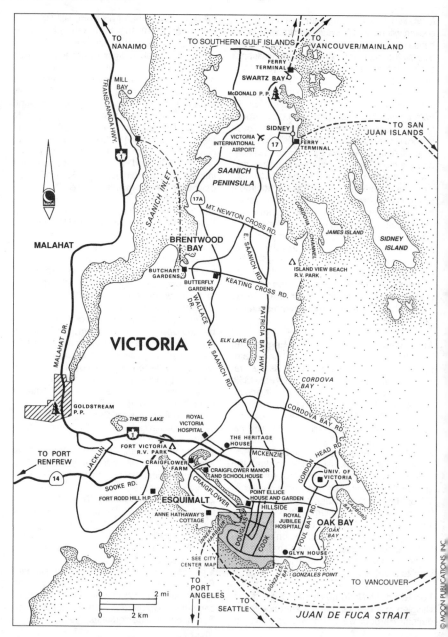

By Ferry to the Saanich Peninsula

Continuing north from Goldstream Provincial Park, you'll come to **Mill Bay,** where a ferry departs regularly for **Brentwood Bay** on the other side of Saanich Inlet. Brentwood Bay is home to the famous Butchart Gardens. The ferry runs in both directions nine times daily between 7:30 a.m. and 6 p.m. Peak one-way fares for the 25-minute crossing are adults $3.75, children $2, cars $10, bicycles 75 cents. For details call **BC Ferries** at (250) 386-3431 or, toll-free in B.C., (888)-BCFERRY.

SAANICH PENINSULA

Butchart Gardens

These delightful gardens on Tod Inlet are Victoria's best-known attraction. They're approximately 20 km north of downtown at 800 Benvenuto Dr., Brentwood Bay, tel. (250) 652-4422 or 652-5256 (recorded information).

A Canadian cement pioneer, R.P. Butchart built a mansion near his quarries. He and his wife, Jennie, traveled extensively, collecting rare and exotic shrubs, trees, and plants from around the world. By 1904, the quarries had been abandoned, and the couple began to beautify them by transplanting their collection into a number of formal gardens interspersed with concrete footpaths, small bridges, waterfalls, ponds, and fountains. The gardens now contain more than 5,000 varieties of flowers, and the extensive nurseries test-grow some 35,000 new bulbs and more than 100 new roses every year.

Many a gardener would give both hands to be able to work in these gardens. Go there in spring, summer, or early autumn to treat your eyes and nose to a marvelous sensual experience. In winter, when little is blooming and the entire landscape is green, the basic design of the gardens can best be appreciated, and you can watch innumerable teams of gardeners mowing, weeding, checking out the tourists, transplanting, and reorganizing like crazy.

Also on the premises are several tearooms and restaurants, and a gift shop specializing in, you guessed it, floral items. The gardens are open every day of the year from 9 a.m., closing in summer at 8:30 p.m. and in winter at 4 p.m. Admission in summer is adults $12, juniors (13-17) $7, children (5-12) $3; admission is much lower in winter. Take Hwy. 17 north to the Brentwood–Butchart Gardens turnoff, turn left on Keating Crossroad and follow the signs, or catch a no. 74 or 75 bus from downtown. Many guided tours of Victoria also include the gardens.

Butterfly Gardens

At Butterfly Gardens, corner of Benvenuto and W. Saanich Rds., tel. (250) 652-3822, you can view and photograph some of the world's most spectacular butterflies at close range. Thousands of these beautiful creatures—species from around the world—live here, flying freely around the enclosed gardens and feeding on the nectar provided by colorful tropical plants. The gardens are open daily 10 a.m.-5 p.m.; admission is adults $7, seniors $6, children $4.

Sidney

The small town of Sidney lies on the east side of the Saanich Peninsula, overlooking the Strait of Georgia. As well as being the departure point for ferries to the San Juan Islands (Washington), it's a pleasant spot to spend a sunny day exploring the colorful marina and the many outdoor cafes. From the marina, the **Sidney Harbour Shuttle,** tel. (250) 655-5211, runs four tours daily around the harbor and to a couple of the inner Gulf Islands; $11 per person.

RECREATION

Biking

For those keen on getting around by bike, it doesn't get much better than the bike path following the coastline of the peninsula on which Victoria lies. From downtown, ride down Government St. to Dallas Rd., where you'll pick up the separate bike path running east along the coast to the charming seaside suburb of Oak Bay. From there, Oak Bay Rd. will take you back into the heart of the city for a roundtrip of 20 km. You can rent bikes at **Sports Rent,** just north of downtown at 611 Discovery St., tel. (250) 385-7368; from $6 per hour, $20 per day.

Swimming and Sunbathing

The best beaches are east of downtown. At **Willows Beach,** Oak Bay, most of the summer crowds spend the day sunbathing, although a few hardy individuals brave a swim; water temperature here tops out at around 17° C (63° F). Closer to downtown, at the foot of Douglas St., the foreshore is mostly rocky, but you can find a couple of short sandy stretches here and there. **Elk Lake,** toward the Saanich Peninsula, and **Thetis Lake,** west of downtown along Hwy. 1, are also popular swimming and sunbathing spots. **Crystal Pool,** one km north of downtown at 2275 Quadra St., tel. (250) 380-7946, has an Olympic-size pool as well as diving facilities, a kids' pool, sauna, and whirlpool.

Kayaking
Ocean River Sports, Market Square, 1437 Store St., tel. (250) 381-4233 or (800) 909-4233, sells and rents kayaks and other equipment, offers kayaking courses, and organizes day and overnight trips through the Gulf Islands and Queen Charlotte Islands. **Sports Rent,** 611 Discovery St., tel. (250) 385-7368, rents canoes, kayaks, and a wide range of other outdoor equipment. Expect to pay about $30 per day and from $120 per week for a canoe or kayak.

Scuba Diving
Close to downtown Victoria lie a number of good dive sites, notably the Odgen Point breakwall. For the lowdown on local diving and rentals head to **PSD Underwater Sports,** downtown at 2519 Douglas St., tel. (250) 386-3483.

To access the great diving in the Straits of Georgia and Juan de Fuca you'll need to charter a boat. One particularly interesting site lies in the shallow waters off Sidney, just north of Victoria, where a 110-meter destroyer escort was scuttled especially for divers. In Sidney, **Deep Cove Ocean Sports,** 10990 Madrona Dr., tel. (250) 656-0060, rents equipment and organizes charters out to the wreck.

Whalewatching
The whalewatching hot spots on Vancouver Island are Tofino for gray whales and Telegraph Cove for orcas, but a number of operators also offer whalewatching day-trips out of Victoria,

April-October. **Ocean Explorations,** tel. (250) 383-6722, focuses on finding orcas from seven-meter inflatable boats. Trips last two to three hours and cost $55-75. The departure point is Dock A, in front of the Empress Hotel. **Sea Quest DSV Adventures,** tel. (250) 655-9256, is based in Sidney, north of downtown, and offers orca-watching cruises on the Strait of Georgia.

ARTS AND ENTERTAINMENT

Theater
Originally called the Pantages Theatre, the **McPherson Playhouse,** 3 Centennial Square (corner of Pandora Ave. and Government St.), is a grand old theater hosting a variety of performing arts. For schedules and tickets call (250) 386-6121. Dating to the early 1900s, the **Royal Theatre,** 805 Broughton St., tel. (250) 386-6121, hosts stage productions and a variety of musical recitals. Performing arts on a smaller scale can be appreciated at the **Belfry Theatre,** 1291 Gladstone St., tel. (250) 385-6815, which offers live theater Oct.-April; tickets cost $18 per person.

Music and Dance
Pacific Opera Victoria, tel. (250) 385-0222 or 382-1641, performs three productions each year (usually through the winter months) in the McPherson Playhouse. Tickets run $16-55. The **Victoria Operatic Society,** tel. (250) 381-1021, presents opera year-round; call for current schedule.

orca (killer whale)

BOB RACE

At the free Symphony Splash on the first Sunday of August, the **Victoria Symphony Orchestra** performs on a barge moored at the Inner Harbour. This kicks off the performing-arts season, with regular performances through to May at the Royal Theatre and other city venues. Tickets range $10-15. For details call (250) 385-9771.

Bars and Nightclubs
Victoria's many English-style pubs usually feature a wide variety of beers, congenial atmos-

phere, and inexpensive meals. Converted from an old warehouse to a pub is **Swans Hotel,** 506 Pandora St., tel. (250) 361-3310, which brews its own beer. As well as being a dining hot spot, it's a popular hangout for local business-people and gets busy weeknights 5-8 p.m. Open daily from 11 a.m. Farther from downtown, relax with an ale or two at **James Bay Inn,** 270 Government St., tel. (250) 384-7151, or **Toad in the Hole,** corner Burnside and Harriett Rds., View Royal, tel. (250) 386-8623. Offering magnificent water views is **Spinnakers Brew Pub,** lying across the Inner Harbour from downtown at 308 Catherine St., tel. (250) 386-2739. A casual atmosphere, modern decor, and great food make this place well worth the diversion. Open daily 11 a.m.-2 p.m.

Downstairs in Swans Hotel is **Pier 42,** 1605 Store St., tel. (250) 381-7437, a Top 40 nightclub with a large dance floor and plenty of bright lights; discs are spun Wed.-Sun. from 8 p.m. Nearby in the Wharfside complex, **Uforia,** 1208 Wharf St., tel. (250) 381-2331, also has a dance floor, with different styles of music played on different nights. This place attracts a younger crowd; cover charge $3 after 9:30 p.m.

Jazz, Blues, and Rock

Hermann's Jazz Club, 753 View St., tel. (250) 388-9166, is the city's lone all-jazz venue. As the name suggests, it's mostly Dixieland jazz, with acts performing Mon.-Saturday. Meals from $10, drinks from $3.50, no cover charge. **The Planet,** 15 Bastion Square, tel. (250) 385-5333, was formerly Harpo's, a legendary live-music venue. The new club continues the tradition with a line-up of jazz, blues, and rock. Performances nightly except Sunday; cover charge $5-15. **Legends,** in the Strathcona Hotel, corner Courtney and Douglas Sts., tel. (250) 383-7137, comes alive with live rock 'n' roll six days a week (closed Sunday); $5 cover charge.

SHOPPING

Victoria is a shopper's delight. Most shops and all major department stores are generally open Mon.-Sat. 9:30 a.m.-5:30 p.m., and stay open for late-night shopping Thursday and Friday night until 9 p.m. The touristy shops around the Inner Harbour and along Government Street are generally open Sundays. Government Street is the main strip of tourist and gift shops. The bottom end, behind the Empress Hotel, is where you'll pick up all those tacky T-shirts and such. Farther up the street are more stylish shops, such as **James Bay Trading Co.,** 1102 Government St., tel. (250) 388-5477, which specializes in native arts from coastal communities; **Eagle's Moon Gallery,** 1010 Government St., tel. (250) 361-4184, which displays and sells the simple but stunning art of Tsimshian artist Henry Roy Vickers, a Vancouver Island native; **Hill's Indian Crafts,** 1008 Government St., tel. (250) 385-3911, selling a wide range of authentic native souvenirs; and **Cowichan Trading,** 1328 Government St., tel. (250) 383-0321, featuring Cowichan sweaters.

In Old Town, the colorful, two-story **Market Square** complex was once the haunt of sailors, sealers, and whalers, who came ashore looking for booze and brothels. Shops here specialize in everything from holographs to condoms. Walk out of Market Square on Johnson Street to find a range of camping-supply stores and the excellent **Bosun's Locker,** 580 Johnson St., tel. (250) 386-1308, filled to the brim with nautical goodies.

Malls line all routes into the city. Besides those at the malls, major department stores in town include **The Bay,** 1701 Douglas St., and **Eaton's,** between Government and Douglas Sts. at Fort Street.

FESTIVALS AND EVENTS

The first of Victoria's many music-related festivals is the **TerrifVic Jazz Party,** the third week of April, when performers from around the world come together at downtown venues. In May, the **Luxton Pro Rodeo** comes to the Luxton Fairgrounds north of downtown. As well as the rodeo, the event includes a midway, a display of antique farm equipment, and a dance. The last weekend of May, the western theme continues with the **Mill Bay Country Music Festival,** and the Inner Harbour comes alive as the finishing point for the **Swiftsure Lighthouse Classic,** a yacht race through local waterways.

The **Victoria Fringe Festival** is a celebration of fringe theater with over 50 companies performing at venues throughout the city. All tickets are under $8. For dates and venues call the Intrepid Theatre Company at (250) 383-2663. Another event that spans weeks rather than days is the **Victoria International Festival,** which runs from mid-July to late August. Showcasing a variety of performing arts, venues are spread throughout the city. For details contact the McPherson Playhouse at (250) 386-6121.

The first Sunday in August brings the unique **Symphony Splash,** when the local symphony orchestra performs from a barge moored in the Inner Harbour to masses crowded around the shore. The **Luxton Fall Fair,** held the first weekend of September, highlights the island's agricultural roots with fun events and machinery displays.

HOTELS AND MOTELS DOWNTOWN

Finding a room in Victoria can be difficult during the summer months, when gaggles of tourists compete for a relative paucity of motel rooms. All the best lodgings are in smaller boutique hotels offering only a few dozen rooms. Most of the major worldwide hotel chains are not represented downtown—the city has no Four Seasons, Hilton, Hotel Inter-Continental, Hyatt, Marriott, Raddison, Regent, or TraveLodge. In the off-season, rooms are discounted up to 50%, but again, occupancy rates are high as Canadians flock to the country's winter hot-spot. All things considered, you'd be wise to make reservations as far ahead as possible, no matter what time of year you plan to visit.

The price categories listed below are as follows: **Inexpensive,** under $75 d; **Moderate,** $75-110 d; **Expensive,** $111-200 d; and **Very Expensive,** over $200 d.

Inexpensive
One of the least expensive places to stay close to the Inner Harbour is the **Cherry Bank Hotel,** in a quiet location at 825 Burdett Ave., tel. (250) 385-5380 or (800) 998-6688. Aside from a choice of rooms in either the original or new wings, the hotel offers a bar and lounge, and a restaurant known for excellent ribs (see "Food," below). The rooms have no TV or phone. High-season rates are $50-67 s, $58-73 d, including an excellent cooked breakfast.

Moderate
Tucked away behind the Empress Hotel is the **Crystal Court Motel,** 701 Belleville St., tel. (250) 384-0551, with 60 rooms, half with kitchenettes; rates from $72 s, $75 d. One block from busy Douglas St. is the 1876 **Dominion Hotel,** 759 Yates St., tel. (250) 384-4136 or (800) 663-6101, Victoria's oldest hotel. Millions of dollars have been spent restoring the property with stylish wooden beams, brass trim and lamps, ceiling fans, and marble floors reliving the Victorian era. Yet staying at the Dominion is still reasonably priced. Advertised rates are $100 s, $110 d but special deals are generally offered, such as accommodation and a three-course dinner for $89 d.

In the heart of the city center, the **Strathcona Hotel,** 919 Douglas St., tel. (250) 383-7137 or (800) 663-7476, attracts a younger crowd—three of the city's most popular drinking holes are downstairs. Rooms are sparsely furnished but clean and comfortable. In summer, rates are $74 s, $84 d, but the rest of the year rates are reduced considerably.

At **Harbour Towers Hotel,** 345 Quebec St., tel. (250) 385-2405 or (800) 663-5896, most of the 185 rooms have water views, and each features a private balcony; from $90 s, $100 d. Farther west, three blocks from the Inner Harbour, is the **Admiral Motel,** 257 Belleville St., tel. (250) 388-6267. All the rooms have kitchens, parking is free, and the managers are friendly; from $75 s, $95 d.

Dating to 1907 and once home to artist Emily Carr, **James Bay Inn,** 270 Government St., tel. (250) 384-7151 or (800) 836-2649, is five blocks from the harbor and within easy walking distance of all city sights and Beacon Hill Park. Some rooms have private baths and color television, and the popular pub downstairs serves hearty breakfasts; $95-105 s or d.

Expensive
Right at harborside, **Quality Inn Harbourview,** 455 Belleville St., tel. (250) 386-2421 or (800) 228-5151, features a large indoor pool with a

glass ceiling; $120-180 s or d. Also with a prime location is the four-story **Days Inn on the Harbour,** 427 Belleville St., tel. (250) 386-3451 or (800) 325-2525; $120-179 s or d. The **Swans Hotel,** 506 Pandora Ave., tel. (250) 361-3310 or (800) 668-7926, is part of a restaurant/pub complex that was originally a waterfront grain storehouse. Each of the 29 split-level suites holds a loft, full kitchen, dining area, and bedroom. The furnishings are simple and casual, but the rates of $135 s or d are still great value. In the off-season these same rooms are under $100 per night.

On a quiet residential street behind the parliament buildings is **Holland House Inn,** 595 Michigan St., tel. (250) 384-6644, a boutique hotel owned by local artist Lance Olsen. The house dates to 1934 and has been restored in a casual yet elegant style. Each of the 10 antique-filled rooms has a four-poster bed and private bath. Rooms range $110-225 s, $120-235 d, which includes a delicious cooked breakfast.

In the oldest section of downtown, surrounded by the city's best dining and shopping opportunities, is the **Bedford Regency,** 1140 Government St., tel. (250) 384-6835 or (800) 665-6500, featuring 40 luxuriously appointed rooms restored to their 1930s' art deco glory. Rates start at $135 s, $150 d.

The **Laurel Point Inn,** 680 Montreal St., tel. (250) 386-8721 or (800) 663-7667, sits on a point of land jutting into the Inner Harbour three blocks west of Government Street. Each of the 200 rooms has a water view and private balcony. Amenities include an indoor pool, beautifully landscaped gardens, a sauna, and a small gym; from $180 s or d.

Farther around the bay, but within easy walking distance of downtown, is **Coast Victoria Harbourside Hotel,** 146 Kingston St., tel. (250) 360-1211 or (800) 663-1144. This hotel is only a few years old, so furnishings are new and modern. The least expensive rooms, $145 s or d, have views and small balconies, but for an extra $25, you get a much larger room with a wide balcony.

Very Expensive

Completely restored in 1989, the grand old **Empress Hotel,** 721 Government St., tel. (250) 384-8111 or (800) 441-1414, is Victoria's best-loved accommodation. Covered in ivy and with only magnificent gardens separating it from the Inner Harbour, it's also in the city's best location. Designed by Francis Rattenbury in 1908, the Empress is another of the grand Canadian Pacific hotels. Rooms aren't particularly large, but each is filled with Victorian period furnishings and antiques. The least expensive rooms start at $200 but for a harbor view expect to pay from $265. Rates are reduced considerably outside of summer. Parking is $10 per day.

Across the Inner Harbour from downtown, and offering stunning city views, is the luxurious **Ocean Pointe Resort,** 45 Songhees Rd., tel. (250) 360-2999 or (800) 667-4677. Opened in 1992, this hotel offers all the services of a spa resort with the convenience of downtown just a short ferry trip away. Facilities include a large health club, indoor glass-enclosed pool, spa and massage services, tennis, lounge, and restaurant. Rates are $170-399 s or d.

HOTELS AND MOTELS OUTSIDE OF DOWNTOWN

West Side

Heading west out of downtown are the suburbs of Esquimalt, View Royal, and Langford, where Hwy. 1 turns north. In Esquimalt, the **Olde England Inn,** 429 Lampson St., tel. (250) 388-4353, provides accommodations on the grounds of Anne Hathaway's Cottage, a tourist attraction (see "West of Downtown," above). The grounds are delightful and boast an excellent restaurant, but on busy days the crowds are bad. Rooms are furnished in period style, but aren't particularly large; from $85 s or d.

About the same distance from downtown, along Gorge Rd., is a string of inexpensive motels, including **Fountain Inn,** 356 Gorge Rd. E, tel. (250) 385-1361, from $50 s, $55 d; and **Canterbury Flag Inn,** 310 Gorge Rd. E, tel. (250) 382-2151 or (800) 952-2151, which has a pool, restaurant, and rates from $75 s or d. Both can be recommended.

South of Hwy. 1 in the suburb of Langford is **Westwind Plaza Hotel,** 741 Goldstream Ave., tel. (250) 478-8334, which offers a cafe, pub, and rooms of a reasonable standard for $50 s, $56 d.

Malahat

This small community is strung out along the Saanich Inlet 25 km from downtown Victoria, making it a good place to spend the night for those who want to get an early start on northward travel. **Malahat Oceanview Motel,** Hwy. 1, tel. (250) 478-9231, offers rooms with views from private balconies; $50 s, $58 d. **Malahat Chalet,** 265 Malahat Dr., tel. (250) 478-3386, offers four units, each of which is well furnished and has a comfortable bed. Rates of $65-105 s, $90-110 d include breakfast. For a splurge, consider **Aerie Resort,** 600 Ebedora Lane, tel. (250) 743-7115, high above the waters of Saanich Inlet and surrounded by well-manicured gardens and interesting hiking trails. Each of the large rooms features a king-sized bed, private balcony, jacuzzi, lounge with fireplace, and luxurious bathroom. The resort also has an indoor pool, outdoor hot tub, tennis courts, and a restaurant. Rates start at $175 s or d including breakfast. To get there take the Spectacle Lake Provincial Park turnoff from Hwy. 1, then take the first right and follow the winding road up to the resort.

Saanich Peninsula

Highway 17, the main route between downtown Victoria and the BC Ferries terminal at Swartz Bay, holds many motels suited to travelers arriving or departing from the airport or ferry terminal. **Western 66 Motel,** flanking the highway at 2401 Mt. Newton Cross Rd., tel. (250) 652-4464 or (800) 463-4464, has a large variety of affordable rooms, complimentary coffee in the lobby each morning, and a family restaurant on the premises; $50 s, $65 d. At the same intersection is **Quality Inn Waddling Dog,** 2476 Mt. Newton Cross Rd., tel. (250) 652-1146 or (800) 567-8466, styled as an old English guesthouse complete with an English pub; $99 s or d.

On the road into downtown Sidney is **Cedarwood Motel,** 9522 Lochside Dr., tel. (250) 656-5551. The rooms are fairly standard, but the setting is glorious, highlighted by a garden with outdoor seating overlooking the Strait of Georgia. Rates start at $99 s or d.

Dunsmuir Lodge, 1515 McTavish Rd., tel. (250) 656-3166 or (800) 255-4055, is a bit off the beaten track, but provides clean and comfortable modern accommodations in a bushland setting with distant ocean views. Guests have use of a restaurant and two cozy lounges. Rooms start at $89 s, $99 d, while the suites are a reasonable $99 s, $119 d.

BED AND BREAKFASTS

Victoria's bed and breakfasts are even more abundant than tour operators in the height of the season—over 300 at last count. Prices range from reasonable to outrageous. Check the brochures at the Visitor Info Centre, but if you're looking for something specific you may want to call one of the following agencies: **AAA Home Away From Home B&B Agency,** 1441 Howard Ave., Vancouver, BC V5B 3S2, tel. (604) 294-1760; **All Seasons Bed and Breakfast Agency,** 9858 5th St., Suite 101, Sidney, BC V8L 2X7, tel. (250) 655-7173; **City and Sea Bed and Breakfast Registry,** 102/701 Es-

The Captain's Palace is a great accommodation in an even better location.

ANDREW HEMPSTEAD

quimalt Rd., Victoria, BC V9A 3L5, tel. (250) 388-5556; or **Westway Accommodation Registry,** P.O. Box 48950, Bentall Centre, Vancouver, BC V7X 1A8, tel. (604) 273-8293. Otherwise, you can't go wrong staying at one of the personally selected places below.

Downtown

Overlooking the Inner Harbour is **Captain's Palace,** 309 Belleville St., tel. (250) 388-9191, a magnificent 16-room bed and breakfast dating to 1897. The house has been elegantly restored, with stained-glass windows, a magnificent fireplace, lots of exposed wood, crystal chandeliers under a gabled roof, and antiques decorating every corner. Afternoon tea is served in a comfortable lounge area off the lobby, and the restaurant has a nice veranda. Through summer rooms are $135-250, while the rest of year rates range $85-155 s or d.

A few blocks back from the Inner Harbour is **Andersen House Bed and Breakfast,** 301 Kingston St., tel. (250) 388-4565. Built late last century for a retired sea captain, the house features large high-ceilinged rooms that all overlook the garden. Rates start at $125 s, $135 d. In the same residential area of downtown is **Haterleigh Bed and Breakfast,** 243 Kingston St., tel. (250) 384-9995. Beautifully restored to its early 1900s' glory, each of the six rooms features a luxurious bathroom; from $165 s or d.

Beacon Hill Park and Vicinity

Dashwood Manor, 1 Cook St., tel. (250) 385-5517 or (800) 667-5517, a 1912 Tudor-style heritage house on a bluff overlooking Juan de Fuca Strait, enjoys a panoramic view of the entire Olympic mountain range. The 14 rooms are elegantly furnished, and host Derek Dashwood will happily recount the historic details of each room. Rates range from $135 s or d up to $265 for the "Oxford Grand," which holds a chandelier, stone fireplace, and antiques. Just around the corner is **Ambleside Bed and Breakfast,** 1121 Faithful St., tel. (250) 383-9948, a 1920s' heritage home with two light and bright guest rooms; from $95 s, $105 d. **Glyn House,** 154 Robertson St., tel. (250) 598-0064, a three-minute walk from Gonzales Beach (southeast of city center), also provides a bed and breakfast in an early 1900s' home.

The rooms have period furnishings and private bathrooms; from $75 s, $95 d.

Rockland and Oak Bay

In the quiet residential area of Rockland, **Craigmyle B&B Inn,** 1037 Craigdarroch Rd., tel. (250) 595-5411, is a beautiful old home full of character, comfortable furnishings, and lots of original stained-glass windows. It's within walking distance of the city and stands directly in front of Craigdarroch Castle. Rooms include singles, doubles, and family suites, all with bathrooms. A comfy living room with a television, a bright sunny dining area, and friendly owners make this a real home-away-from-home. Rates are $70 s, $85-90 d.

East of Government House in the suburb of Oak Bay, the Tudor-style, vintage 1912 **Oak Bay Guest House,** 1052 Newport Ave., tel. (250) 598-3812 or (800) 575-3812, offers 11 antique-filled rooms, each with a private balcony and a bathroom. A lounge area off the main lobby holds a small library, as well as tea- and coffee-making facilities. Rates of $110-170 s or d, include a delicious four-course breakfast.

North of Downtown

Heritage House, 3808 Heritage Lane, tel. (250) 479-0892, a beautiful 1910 mansion surrounded by trees and gardens, sits in a quiet residential area near Portage Inlet, five km northwest of city center. Friendly owners Larry and Sandra Gray have lovingly restored the house to its former glory. Guests choose from several outstanding rooms, one with a view of Portage Inlet from a private veranda. The three bathrooms are shared. Enjoy the large communal living room and a cooked breakfast in the elegant dining room. It's very busy in summer, but quieter Nov.-April. Reservations are necessary year-round. Rates are $60-75 s, $85-110 d, minimum two nights. Heritage Lane is not shown on any Victoria maps; from city center, take Douglas St. north to Burnside Rd. E (bear left off of Douglas). Just across the TransCanada Hwy., Burnside makes a hard left (if you continue straight instead you'll be on Interurban Rd.). Make the left turn, and continue down Burnside to just past Grange Road. The next lane on the right is Heritage Lane.

HOSTELS AND DORMS

Hostels

In the heart of downtown Victoria's oldest section is **Hostelling International Victoria,** 516 Yates St., tel. (250) 385-4511. The totally renovated hostel enjoys a great location only a stone's throw from the harbor. Separate dorms and bathroom facilities for men and women are complemented by two fully equipped kitchens, a large meeting room, lounge, library, games room, travel services, and an informative bulletin board. Members of Hostelling International pay $15 per night, nonmembers $19; private rooms range $34-42 s or d. If you're traveling up the island or exploring the rest of the province, ask at the office for the list of mini-hostels. These are not members of Hostelling International but private homes or small commercial hotels offering low-budget accommodations geared toward backpackers.

Victoria Backpackers Hostel, a one-km walk from downtown at 1418 Fernwood Rd., tel. (250) 386-4471, provides cooking and laundry facilities, free coffee, bicycle rentals, and parking. A dorm bed is $12, a private room is $38. Another good choice is **Selkirk Guest House,** 934 Selkirk Ave., tel. (250) 389-1213, an attractive historic home on the Gorge Waterway. It's a 15-minute bus ride from city center, but the friendly hosts make all feel welcome. Cost is $15 for a dorm bed or $35 s, $40 d.

YWCA

A few blocks east of the harbor, the **YMCA/YWCA of Victoria,** 880 Courtney St., tel. (250) 386-7511, offers exercise facilities for both sexes, but the accommodation is for women only. The small, clean rooms share bathrooms. No cooking facilities are available, but the ground-floor cafe is good (it's usually crowded at lunchtime). Rates are $34 s, $49 twin.

University of Victoria

When University of Victoria students leave on summer vacation, their campus dormitory rooms become available to travelers. The rooms are sparse, and each has one or two single beds with shared bathroom and kitchen facilities. Rates are $32-75 s, $45-90 twin, which includes linen and a full breakfast. The rooms are at the corner of Sinclair and Finnerty Roads; for details call Housing and Conference Services at (250) 721-8396.

CAMPGROUNDS

West

Closest camping to downtown is **Fort Victoria RV Park,** 340 Island Hwy., tel. (250) 479-8112, six km northwest of city center on Hwy. 1A. This campground provides hookups (no official tent sites), free showers, laundry facilities, and opportunities to join charter salmon-fishing trips. During the summer, sites are $26. A little farther west is **Thetis Lake Campground,** 1938 Hwy. 1, tel. (250) 478-3845, featuring pleasant shaded tent sites, coin-operated showers, laundry facilities, and swimming in Thetis Lake; unserviced sites $15, hookups $16-20. Just beyond Thetis Lake, take the Millstream Rd. exit and continue north two km to **All Fun Recreation Park,** 2207 Millstream Rd., tel. (250) 474-4546, which offers water slides, go-carts, a driving range, and race track around 100 campsites in a rather uninspiring setting; $18-24 per night.

North

One of the most beautiful provincial parks where camping is permitted is **Goldstream Provincial Park,** 19 km northwest of downtown along Hwy. 1. The campground offers free hot showers, but limited facilities in winter. Sites are $15.50 per night, no hookups. Good hiking trails and many other recreational opportunities are available in the area. In Malahat, seven km farther north along Hwy. 1, is **KOA Victoria West,** tel. (250) 478-3332. Facilities include free showers, an outdoor pool, laundry, store, and games room. Unserviced sites are $22, hookups $24-28. Continuing north, you'll come to **Malahat Tent and RV Park,** right beside the highway, tel. (250) 478-5452, with facilities and prices similar to the KOA.

Saanich Peninsula

If you're coming from or heading for the ferry terminal, consider staying at **McDonald Provincial Park,** near the tip of the Saanich Peninsula 31 km north of the city center. Facilities are limited (no showers or hookups); campsites are $9.50 per night. Also on the peninsula, halfway between downtown Victoria and Sidney, is **Island View Beach RV Park,** Homathko Dr., tel. (250) 652-0548, right on the beach three km east of Hwy. 17. Sites are $14-20 and you'll need quarters for the showers.

FOOD

Coffeehouses and Cafes
Murchies, 1110 Government St., tel. (250) 381-5451, is a large coffeehouse on Victoria's busiest downtown street. Overlooking a cobbled pedestrian mall, quiet **C'est Bon,** 10 Bastion Square, tel. (250) 381-1461, serves a range of coffees, pastries, and muffins. Nearby **Re-bar,** 50 Bastion Square, tel. (250) 361-9223, offers a funky atmosphere in a below-street-level setting, along with healthy eating at reasonable prices. **Java Coffeehouse,** 537 Johnson St., tel. (250) 381-2326, is painted all-black and furnished to match. On the second story of Market Square, 560 Johnson St., the **Bavarian Bakery,** tel. (250) 388-5506, sells a wide range of bakery delights.

In a corner of the Wharfside complex, **Nasty Jacks,** 1208 Wharf St., tel. (250) 360-1808, is named for a South Seas pirate who spent the 1860s in Victoria. It's open all day, every day; breakfasts start at $4 but the cafe is best known for Nasty Stacked Sandwiches from $5. Around the corner from Chinatown, the small **Sour Pickle Cafe,** 1623 Store St., tel. (250) 384-9390, comes alive with funky music and an enthusiastic staff. The menu offers bagels from $1.40, full cooked breakfasts from $4, soup of the day $2, healthy sandwiches $4-5, and delicious single-serve pizza for around $6. Open Mon.-Fri. 7:30 a.m.-4:30 p.m.

While tourists flock to the cafes and restaurants of the Inner Harbour and Government Street, Douglas Street remains the haunt of lunching workers. **Blenz,** 1328 Douglas St., tel. (250) 995-2456, serves up delicious coffees in modern surroundings with a few tables positioned for peoplewatching. As this strip is away from the tourists, it's the place for a cheap eat. **Company's Coming,** 670 Fort St., tel. (250) 383-7044, is a coffee shop and bakery where you can get a coffee and muffin for $2. **Cross' Quality Meats,** 1312 Douglas St., tel. (250) 384-2631, is even cheaper—a coffee and muffin to go is $1.

Casual Dining
Wharfside Eatery, 1208 Wharf St., tel. (250) 360-1808, is a bustling waterfront restaurant with a maritime theme and family atmosphere. Behind a small cafe section and a bar is the main dining room, where many tables have water views. The menu features soups, salads, pizza from a wood-fired oven, a variety of meat dishes, and fresh local seafood. Sunday brunch, $8-10, is very popular. Right across from the information center, and drawing tourists like a magnet, is **Sam's Deli,** 805 Government St., tel. (250) 382-8424. Many places nearby have better food, but Sam's boasts a superb location and cheerful atmosphere. The ploughman's lunch, a staple of English pub dining, costs $7, while sandwiches range $4-7 and salads are all around $5. Open daily 7:30 a.m.-10 p.m.

For a sit-down lunch and an excuse to eat in the Empress Hotel, head to the **Bengal Lounge,** 721 Government St., tel. (250) 384-8111, which serves meals Mon.-Sat. 11 a.m.-6:30 p.m. Prices range from $5 for soup to $8.50 for open sandwiches and $10-15 for main courses. The Empress's less formal **Garden Cafe** serves light meals daily 7 a.m.-9:30 p.m.

Away from the tourist-clogged streets of the Inner Harbour, and right at sea level, is **Barb's Place,** on Fisherman's Wharf at the end of St. Lawrence St., tel. (250) 384-6515. The specialty is fish and chips to go, but the seafood chowder is also good. Open daily from 8 a.m.

Afternoon Tea
Afternoon tea is served just about everywhere in Victoria—it's a local tradition. The one in the main lobby of the **Empress Hotel,** 721 Government St., tel. (250) 384-8111, is the dressiest affair (no jeans, shorts, tennis shoes, etc.);

keep in mind that you're taking part in one of the oldest Victorian rituals. It's so popular with tourists that reservations are necessary for the 1 p.m., 2:30 p.m., and 4 p.m. sittings. Sample English honey crumpets, homemade scones with cream and jam, sandwiches, Empress cakes, and an Empress blend tea for $19.50 per person. Also downtown, afternoon tea is served at the **Bedford Regency,** 1140 Government St., tel. (250) 384-6835.

Pub Meals

Right in the heart of downtown is the **Elephant and Castle,** corner Government and View Sts., tel. (250) 383-5858. This English-style pub features exposed beams, oak paneling, and traditional pub decor. A few umbrella-shaded tables line the sidewalk out front. All the favorites, such as steak and kidney pie and fish and chips, range $7-14. Open daily for lunch and dinner.

Across from the waterfront is **Swans Hotel,** 506 Pandora St., tel. (250) 361-3310, an English-style pub that brews its own beer and serves delicious food. As well as the typical pub pews, the hotel has covered a section of the sidewalk with a glass-enclosed atrium. The **James Bay Inn,** 270 Government St., tel. (250) 384-7151, also serves up typical English pub food at reasonable prices. Look for traditional dishes such as kippers and poached eggs for breakfast, ploughman's lunches, and roast beef with Yorkshire pudding or steak and kidney pie in the evening; dinner entrees start at $9.50. The **Toad in the Hole,** corner Burnside and Harriett Rds., View Royal, tel. (250) 386-8623, enjoys a jovial pub atmosphere, a fireplace (cozy in winter), and a large local clientele. Expect good meals, friendly service, and prices in the $7-13 range.

While all the above pubs exude the English traditions for which Victoria is famous, **Spinnakers Brew Pub,** 308 Catherine St., Esquimalt, tel. (250) 386-2739, is in a class by itself. It was Canada's first in-house brew pub, and is as popular today as when it first opened. The crowds come for the beer, but also for great food served up in a casual, modern atmosphere. It's open daily from 11 a.m.

Ribs

The restaurant at the Cherry Bank Hotel, **Cherry Bank Spare Rib House,** 825 Burdett Ave.,

tel. (250) 385-5380, provides plenty to see and do while you wait for your ribs, seafood, or chicken. The restaurant springs to life as the honky-tonk piano player starts pounding out one old-fashioned tune after another and the air fills with voices, hands clapping, feet tapping, and tables and chairs jiving. The food is excellent; main courses run $10-19 and come with salad, potato, vegetable, and garlic bread. Open daily for lunch and dinner, with early-bird specials Mon.-Fri. 5-6 p.m.

Healthy Eating

For a quiet dinner in the heart of the city, **Nutshell Restaurant,** 627 Fort St., tel. (250) 383-6142, is a good choice, with dishes ranging from grilled salmon to vegetarian; expect to pay $8-14 for an entree. **Green Cuisine,** in Market Square on Johnson St., tel. (250) 385-1809, takes the vegetarian theme even further, with a vegan menu that uses no oils, sugars, or refined flours. A small buffet is offered, but the regular menu provides many varied choices, from chili to fruit juices. Open daily.

Mexican

On the waterfront side of Market Square is **Cafe Mexico,** 1425 Store St., tel. (250) 386-1425. The atmosphere is very casual, with Mexican paraphernalia hanging everywhere and loud music playing. A large buffet lunch is served Mon.-Fri. from 11:30 a.m. The regular menu is extensive, ranging from $2.50 salsa dips to $11-15 gourmet dishes.

Italian

One of the most popular restaurants in town is **Pagliacci's,** 1011 Broad St., tel. (250) 386-1662, known for hearty Italian food, homemade bread, great desserts, and loads of atmosphere. Small and always busy, the restaurant attracts a lively local crowd; you'll inevitably have to wait for a table during the busiest times. Pastas range $10-14. This is also one of the few late-night restaurants in Victoria; open daily 11:30 a.m.-midnight. A jazz trio plays Wed.-Sun. nights.

The **Herald Street Cafe,** 546 Herald St., tel. (250) 381-1441, is also good, with a menu comparable to Pagliacci's but more extensive. Housed in a heritage building in Old Town, the atmosphere is casual, with artworks adorning the walls and flowering plants everywhere. Open Wed.-Sat. for lunch, and daily for dinner.

Along a narrow sidestreet among boutiques and galleries is **Vin Santo,** 620 Trounce Alley, tel. (250) 480-5560. While small and intimate, this bistro-style restaurant has a floor-to-ceiling glass front for watching the parade of people walking past. The Northern Italian cuisine makes good use of local produce. Most lunch entrees are under $10, while dinner ranges $12-18. Open daily.

Other European Restaurants

A good place to go for Greek food, and live entertainment on weekends, is **Periklis Greek Restaurant,** 531 Yates St., tel. (250) 386-3313. Main courses range $12-25, and almost anything can be happening on the floor—from exotic belly dancers to crazy Greek dancing. For a more subdued atmosphere, head to **Millos,** 716 Burdett Ave., tel. (250) 382-4422, which also presents belly dancing some nights. Beyond the west end of Belleville St. is **Pablo's Dining Lounge,** 225 Quebec St., tel. (250) 388-4255, a long-time Victorian favorite serving a variety of European cuisines. Atmosphere in the Edwardian house is relaxed yet intimate and the dishes are all well-prepared and well-presented. Entrees range $15-26. Open daily from 5 p.m.

Chinese

Victoria's small Chinatown surrounds a short, colorful strip of Fisgard St. between Store and Government Streets. Near the top (east) end of Fisgard is **QV Cafe and Bakery,** 1701 Government St., tel. (250) 384-8831, offering inexpensive western-style breakfasts in the morning and Chinese delicacies the rest of the day. One of the least expensive places in the area is **Wah Lai Yuen,** 560 Fisgard St., tel. (250) 381-5355, a large, simply decorated, well-lit restaurant with fast and efficient service. The wonton soups (from $3) are particularly good, or try the hearty chicken hot pot ($7), or scallops and broccoli ($12.50). Open daily 10 a.m.-9 p.m.

Named for the Chinese province renowned for hot and spicy food, **Hunan Village Cuisine,** 546 Fisgard St., tel. (250) 382-0661, offers entrees ranging $8-15. It's open Mon.-Sat. for lunch, and daily for dinner. Down the hill a little is

Don Mee Restaurant, 538 Fisgard St., tel. (250) 383-1032, specializing in the cuisine of Canton. Entrees run about $6 each, while four-course dinners for two or more diners are a good deal at under $12 per person. Open Mon.-Fri. for lunch, and daily for dinner.

Two Out of Town Splurges

The following two restaurants are out of town but well worth the drive. Both also provide accommodations. **Sooke Harbour House,** 34 km west of downtown at 1528 Whiffen Spit Rd., tel. (250) 642-3421, provides one of British Columbia's finest dining experiences in a magnificent setting atop a seaside bluff. Originally a private residence, three of the largest rooms have been converted to a restaurant. Most dishes feature seafood, prepared to perfection with vegetables and herbs picked from the surrounding garden. Dinner entrees range $16-30. Open daily from 5:30 p.m.; make reservations before driving out.

The restaurant at the **Aerie Resort,** in Malahat north of Victoria, tel. (250) 743-7115, is equally popular with those looking for a splurge. In a delightful setting, surrounded by forest and grazing wildlife, diners are treated to French cuisine, elegant atmosphere, and service that oozes professionalism. Main courses are around $25-30, and a seven-course feast is offered for $55 per person. Open daily 5-10 p.m.

GETTING THERE

Air

Victoria International Airport is on the Saanich Peninsula 20 km north of the city center. The terminal building houses a cocktail lounge, cafe, and various rental car agencies. P.B.M. Transport, tel. (250) 475-2010, operates the **Airporter** bus between the airport and major downtown hotels every 30 minutes; $13 per person each way. A taxi costs approximately $45 to downtown.

Air Canada, tel. (250) 360-9074 or (800) 663-3721, **Canadian Airlines,** tel. (250) 382-6111 or (800) 665-1177, and various regional connectors fly to Victoria from most western Canada cities and Seattle. **Horizon Air,** tel.

(800) 547-9308, flies daily into Victoria International Airport from Seattle.

Also from Seattle, **Kenmore Air,** tel. (206) 486-1257 or (800) 543-9595, offers scheduled floatplane flights between the north end of Lake Washington and Victoria's Inner Harbour; US$93 one-way, US$159 roundtrip.

A variety of smaller airlines, including those with floatplanes and helicopter services, provide a direct link between Victoria and Vancouver, landing on or beside the Inner Harbour. These include **Harbour Air,** tel. (250) 384-2215 or (800) 665-0212, and **Helijet Airways,** tel. (250) 382-6222. **South Island Air,** tel. (250) 642-2156 or (800) 305-7055, offers floatplane pick-up on the Inner Harbour with charters to downtown Vancouver, Vancouver International Airport, Nanaimo, or anywhere a floatplane can get down.

Bus

The main Victoria **bus depot** is behind the Empress Hotel at 710 Douglas Street. **Pacific Coach Lines,** tel. (604) 662-8074 or (250) 385-4411, operates bus service between the Vancouver bus depot and downtown Victoria, via the Swartz Bay ferry. In summer the coaches run hourly 6 a.m.-9 p.m.; $22.50 one-way, $42 roundtrip.

Pacific also runs three daily buses from Vancouver International Airport directly to Victoria; $26.50 one-way, $50 roundtrip. If you take the ferry over independently, you can catch a **Victoria Regional Transit System** bus, tel. (250) 382-6161, from the Swartz Bay ferry terminal to downtown for $2.25.

Ferry

From Tsawwassen (Vancouver): Ferries run regularly across the Strait of Georgia from Tsawwassen, 30 km south of Vancouver, to the **Swartz Bay Ferry Terminal,** 32 km north of Victoria. Through summer, ferries run hourly 7 a.m.-10 p.m.; the rest of the year slightly less frequently. The crossing takes 90 minutes. You can expect a wait in summer; limited vehicle reservations are accepted. Peak fares are adults $8, children 5-11 $4, cars $30, motorcycles $15, bicycles $2.50, canoes and kayaks $4. For information, call **BC Ferries** at (250) 386-3431 or, toll-free in B.C., (888) BCFERRY.

From Seattle: Clipper Navigation offers a fleet of five foot-passengers-only ferries connecting Seattle's Pier 69 with Victoria's Inner Harbour. Its turbojet catamaran, the *Victoria Clipper IV,* is North America's fastest passenger ferry, traveling at speeds of up to 45 knots (over 80 kph). This speedy vessel makes the crossing in two hours and costs adults US$63 one-way, US$104 roundtrip. The company's other vessels make the trip in 2.5 hours and cost adults US$55 one-way, US$89 roundtrip. The service runs year-round. In summer, up to five sailings a day are offered, with some stopping off at Friday Harbor in the San Juan Islands (US$65 one-way, through to Victoria). All vessels feature spacious seating arrangements, writing tables, complimentary tea and coffee, and light snacks. Discounts apply outside of the busy summer months and to tickets purchased 14 or more days in advance. Seniors also get a break, and children travel for half price. Clipper Navigation also offers reasonably priced accommodations and tour packages in Victoria (from US$99 including transportation from Seattle; high season). For further information, call (800) 888-2535, or drop by one of their offices: at Pier 69, Seattle, tel. (206) 448-5000, or at the Inner Harbour terminal on Belleville St., tel. (250) 382-8100.

Victoria Line operates the *Royal Victorian* between Seattle's Pier 48 and Victoria's Ogden Point Terminal. This ferry carries both passengers and vehicles, and runs mid-May to mid-October, departing Seattle daily at 1 p.m. and Victoria at 7:30 a.m. and taking 4.5 hours each way. Facilities include a buffet restaurant, cafe, bar, solarium, and a gift shop with duty-free shopping. The fare is $60 for a vehicle with driver, or $27 per passenger. For reservations call Victoria Line at (206) 625-1880, (250) 480-5555, or (800) 668-1167.

From Anacortes: Washington State Ferries, tel. (206) 464-6400 or (250) 381-1551, runs a regular ferry schedule between Anacortes and the San Juan Islands, with the 8 a.m. sailing continuing to Sidney, on the Saanich Peninsula 32 km north of Victoria. The one-way fare is adults US$7.90, car and driver US$36.60. Reservations must be made at least 24 hours in advance.

From Port Angeles: The **MV** *Coho* crosses Juan de Fuca Strait in just over 90 minutes, arriving in Victoria's Inner Harbour. It makes four crossings daily in each direction from mid-May to mid-October; two crossings daily the rest of the year. Advance reservations are not accepted—phone a day or so before your planned departure for estimated waiting times. The one-way fare is adults $8.90 (US$6.50), children $4.45 (US$3.25), cars $37.50 (US$27). Checks and credit cards are not accepted. For details call Black Ball Transport Inc. at (250) 386-2202 in Victoria, or (206) 457-4491 in Port Angeles.

Also making the run from Port Angeles to Victoria's Inner Harbour is the *Victoria Express,* tel. (250) 361-9144 or (800) 633-1589, a passenger-only service that runs from June to mid-October, three times daily in each direction; adults $20 roundtrip, children $10.

MAJOR ROUTES UP THE ISLAND FROM VICTORIA

From downtown Victoria, take Douglas St. north for three km to Hwy. 1, which jogs westward through Victoria's residential suburbs before turning north and running up the east side of the island to Nanaimo (113 km), Courtenay (220 km), Campbell River (260 km), and Port Hardy (495 km). It's not necessary to return to Victoria to get back to the mainland; ferries operate between Nanaimo and Vancouver, Comox and the Sunshine Coast, and Port Hardy and Prince Rupert.

Rail

VIA Rail's Malahat train departs Victoria for Courtenay Mon.-Sat. at 8:15 a.m. and Sunday at noon, and departs Courtenay for Victoria Mon.-Sat. at 1:15 p.m. and Sunday at 5:15 p.m. Several stops are made along the way. This route is so scenic that many make the train trip a one-day excursion, going as far as Namaimo and spending a few hours in the city before returning. The one-way fare from Victoria to Chemainus is $14.98, to Nanaimo $19.26, and to Courtenay $32.10. Make reservations as far ahead as possible in summer, and buy your ticket the day before departure. For more information, stop in

at the station, 450 Pandora Ave., tel. (250) 383-4324 or (800) 561-8630.

Bus

Island Coach Lines, tel. (250) 385-4411 or (800) 318-0818, serves all of Vancouver Island. For current schedules, stop in at the Victoria depot, 710 Douglas St. at the corner of Belleville Street. Sample one-way fares from Victoria are: Nanaimo, $16.10; Port Alberni, $27.60; Tofino, $43.70; Campbell River, $36.80; Port Hardy, $77.85. Six buses daily depart Victoria for Nanaimo, with one continuing to Tofino, three to Campbell River, and one to Port Hardy (departs Victoria at 6:20 a.m. and arrives Port Hardy at 4:30 p.m.).

GETTING AROUND

Bus

Most of the inner-city attractions can be reached on foot. However, the excellent **Victoria Regional Transit System** is an excellent bus network and it's easy to jump on and off and get everywhere you want to go. Pick up an *Explore Victoria by Bus* brochure at the information center for details of all the major sights, parks, beaches, and shopping areas, and the buses needed to reach them. Bus fares for travel within Zone 1, which covers most of the city, are adults $1.50, seniors and children $1. Zone 2 covers outlying areas such as the Swartz Bay ferry terminal; adults $2.25, seniors and children $1.50. Transfers are good for travel in one direction within 90 minutes of purchase. A Day-Pass, valid for one day's unlimited bus travel, costs adults $5, seniors and children $4. For general bus information call (250) 382-6161.

Taxi

Taxis operate on a meter system, charging $2.75 at the initial flag drop plus around $1.50 per kilometer. Call **Blue Bird Cabs** at (250) 382-4235; **Empress Taxi** at (250) 381-2222; or **Victoria Taxi** at (250) 383-7111.

Car Rental

It's best to call around and compare prices for cars—some lesser-known agencies advertise cheaper daily rates than others, but their cars are often used, old, large, and less economical, and usually must be returned to Victoria. Renting by the week is better, and you often get a number of kilometers free. If you don't want to return the car to Victoria, you'll probably have to pay a drop charge; usually the farther up the island you go, the higher the fee. For a used car in the low season, rates start around $30 a day, plus 15 cents per kilometer, plus gas. As with accommodations and many attractions, prices are higher in peak tourist periods. Rental car agencies in Victoria include: **Ada Rent a Used Car,** tel. (250) 474-3455; **Avis,** tel. (250) 386-8468 or (800) 879-2847; **Budget,** tel. (250) 953-5300 or (800) 268-8900; **Enterprise,** tel. (250) 475-6900 or (800) 325-8007; **Hertz,** tel. (250) 656-2312 or (800) 263-0600; **National Tilden,** tel. (250) 386-1213 or (800) 387-4747; **Rent-a-wreck,** tel. (250) 384-5343; **Sigmar,** tel. (250) 388-6686 or (800) 325-8007; and **Thrifty,** tel. (250) 383-3659 or (800) 367-2277.

Bicycle

Victoria doesn't have the great network of bicycle paths that Vancouver boasts, but bike-rental shops are nevertheless plentiful. Try: **Sports Rent,** 611 Discovery St., tel. (250) 385-7368; **James Bay Bicycle Works,** 1A-507 Simcoe St., tel. (250) 380-1664; or **Oak Bay Bicycle,** 1968 Oak Bay Ave., tel. (250) 598-4111. Expect to pay from around $6 an hour, $20 per day.

Tours

The place to jump aboard a tour is beside the Inner Harbour along Belleville Street. From here, the buses of **Gray Line of Victoria,** tel. (250) 388-5248, depart on a wide variety of tours through the city and beyond. They're a great way to get yourself oriented while also learning some city history. In summer, the 90-minute Grand City Tour departs from Belleville Street every half hour 9:30 a.m.-7 p.m.; adults $14, children $7. If you're coming over from Vancouver for just one day, consider taking a **Gray Line of Vancouver** tour across on the ferry. The 12-hour excursion costs $92.

Victoria Harbour Ferry, tel. (250) 480-0971, offers boat tours of the harbor and beyond. The company's funny looking boats each seat around 20 passengers, and depart regularly 10

a.m.-10 p.m. from below the Empress Hotel. The 45-minute loop tour allows passengers the chance to get on and off at will; adults $10, children $5. You can also travel just pieces of the entire loop for $2.50 per sector.

SERVICES AND INFORMATION

Emergency Services

In a medical emergency call 911 or contact **Royal Jubilee Hospital,** 1900 Fort St., tel. (250) 370-8000, or **Victoria General Hospital,** 35 Helmcken Rd., tel. (250) 727-4212. For non-urgent cases, a handy facility is **James Bay Medical Treatment Centre,** 230 Menzies St., tel. (250) 388-9934. The **Cresta Dental Centre** is at 3170 Tillicum Rd. (at Burnside St.), tel. (250) 384-7711. **Shopper's Drug Mart,** at 1222 Douglas St., tel. (250) 381-4321, is open daily 7 a.m.-7 p.m.

Other Services

The main post office is on the corner of Government and Yates Streets. To change your money to the colorful Canadian variety, head to any of the major banks or to **Currencies International,** 724 Douglas St., tel. (250) 384-6631; or **Custom House Currency Exchange,** 815 Wharf St., tel. (250) 389-6001. **Downtown Photo Centre,** 1314 Douglas St., tel. (250) 383-8111, offers full photographic services, including 24-hour slide developing. **Maytag Homestyle Laundry** is at 1309 Cook St., tel. (250) 386-1799.

Books and Bookstores

Greater Victoria Public Library is at 735 Broughton St., at the corner of Courtney St., tel. (250) 382-7241. It's open Mon.-Fri. 9 a.m.-6 p.m., Saturday 9 a.m.-1 p.m. **Crown Publications,** 521 Fort St., tel. (250) 386-4636, is a specialty bookstore with a great selection of western Canadiana and maps. Right downtown, **Munro's Bookstore,** 1108 Government St., tel. (250) 382-2464, stocks a wide selection of all types of books. For new books at discounted prices, head to **Book Ends,** 907 Yates St., tel. (250) 380-0740.

Tourist Information

Tourism Victoria runs the bright, modern **Victoria Visitor Info Centre,** 812 Wharf St. on the Inner Harbour, tel. (250) 953-2033 or (800)

663-3883. The friendly staff can answer most of your questions. They also book accommodations, tours and charters, restaurants, entertainment, and transportation, all at no extra cost; sell local bus passes and map books with detailed area-by-area maps; and stock an enormous selection of tourist brochures. Also collect the free *Accommodations* publication and the free local news and entertainment papers—the best way to find out what's happening in Victoria while you're in town. The center is open year-round, daily 9 a.m.-5 p.m. Coming off the ferry from Vancouver, stop in at **Sidney Visitor Info Centre,** three km south of the terminal, tel. (250) 656-0525; open daily 9 a.m.-5 p.m. For **weather forecasts** call (250) 656-3978; or for **marine weather** forecasts call (250) 656-7515.

a relaxing way to tour Victoria

BILL MARSHALL

VICINITY OF VICTORIA

Two highways lead out of Victoria: Hwy. 14 heads west and Hwy. 1 heads north. Highway 14 is a spectacular coastal route that ends in **Port Renfrew,** 104 km from Victoria. Along this ocean-hugging stretch of road are provincial parks, delightful oceanfront lodgings, and a panorama that extends across Juan de Fuca Strait to the snowcapped peaks of the Olympic Mountains in Washington state. Port Renfrew is the southern terminus of the rugged and re- mote, 77-km **West Coast Trail,** which chal- lenges hikers from around the world each sum- mer. Highway 1 leads north from Victoria to **Dun- can, Chemainus,** and **Ladysmith,** each with its own particular charm. West of Duncan are massive **Cowichan Lake,** an inland paradise for anglers and boaters, and **Carmanah Pacific Provincial Park,** protecting a valley full of ancient Sitka spruce that miraculously escaped logging.

HIGHWAY 14 TO PORT RENFREW

The 104-km trip along Hwy. 14 between Victoria and Port Renfrew can easily be enjoyed as a day-trip. Plenty of diversions line the route, and those with time can also follow a logging road north from Port Renfrew to Cowichan Lake, west of Duncan.

Sooke

About 34 km from Victoria, Sooke (pop. 4,500) is a logging, fishing, and farming center known for its good salmon fishing. **Sooke Regional Museum** lies just beyond Sooke River Bridge on the corner of Sooke and Phillips Rds., tel. (250) 642-6351. When you've finished admiring the historic arti- facts, relax on the grassy area in front or wander around the back to count all 478 growth rings on the cross-section of a giant spruce tree. The mu- seum is open Tues.-Sun. 9 a.m.-5 p.m., and also houses the **Sooke Visitor Info Centre.**

Continuing toward Jordan River

The road from Sooke takes you past gray peb- bly beaches scattered with shells and driftwood, past **Gordon's Beach** to 59-hectare **French Beach Provincial Park** (about 20 km from Sooke). Here you can wander down through the trees to watch Pacific breakers crashing up on the beach—and keep an eye open for orcas and gray whales. It's a great place for a windswept walk, a picnic, or camping ($9.50 per night; pit toilets provided). An information board at the park entrance posts fairly detailed maps and articles on area beaches, points of in- terest, plants, and wildlife.

Continuing west, the highway winds up and down forested hills for another 12 km or so,

Gray whales migrate past the coast of Vancouver Island in April, en route to Alaska.

BOB RACE

passing evidence of regular logging as well as signposted forest trails to sandy beaches. Along this stretch of coast are two great accommodations. The first, three km beyond French Beach, is **Point No Point Lodge,** tel. (250) 646-2020, which features 20 beautiful log cabins, each with views, a full kitchen, and fireplace. Explore the shore out front, relax on the nearby beach, or scan the horizon for migrating whales, with the Olympic Mountains as a backdrop. Rates range $85-160 s or d and meals are available in the lodge restaurant. Two km farther west is **Fossil Bay Resort,** tel. (250) 646-2073, offering six oceanfront cottages, each with a hot tub, private balcony, fireplace, king size bed, and full kitchen; $169 s or d. These two places are understandably popular, so make reservations well in advance, especially for weekends.

Jordan River

When you emerge at the small logging town of Jordan River, take time to take in the smells of the ocean and the surrounding windswept landscape. The town comprises only a few houses, a local logging operation, and a small recreation area. The recreation area lies on a point at the mouth of the Jordan River. It's not the best camping spot you'll ever come across, but no signs prohibit overnight stays; surfers often spend the night here, waiting for the swells to rise and the long right-handed waves known as Jordans to crank up. Note: **Sports Rent,** 611 Discovery St., Victoria, tel. (250) 385-7368, rents surfboards and wetsuits for $15 per day.

LOUISE FOOTE

butter clam

Across the road from the ocean is **Shakies,** a popular burger stand, and a little farther along is **Breakers,** a small cafe with great ocean views.

China Beach Provincial Park

This 61-hectare park lies three km west of Jordan River. From the parking lot off Hwy. 14, a 700-meter trail leads through Sitka spruce to pebbly China Beach, which is strewn with driftwood and backed by a couple of protected picnic sites. The park is the trailhead for the 73-km **Juan de Fuca Marine Trail,** which ends at Port Renfrew.

Port Renfrew

This small seaside community clings to the rugged shoreline of Port San Juan, 104 km from Victoria. An eclectic array of houses leads down the hill to the waterfront. Follow the signs to **Botanical Beach,** a fascinating tidal-pool area where low tide exposes all sorts of marine creatures at the foot of scoured-out sandstone cliffs. The road to the beach is rough and can be impassable in winter.

Accommodations are available at the waterfront **Port Renfrew Hotel,** tel. (250) 647-5541, a good base for West Coast Trail hikers. Rooms are sparse but clean and facilities include hot showers, a laundry, restaurant, and bar; from $40 s, $50 d. **Orca II Bed and Breakfast** is one block from the water at 44 Tsonoquay St., tel. (250) 647-5528. Rooms are simply furnished and bathrooms are shared, but the owners are friendly and provide a wealth of information on fishing (they operate a charter boat), kayaking, and the West Coast Trail; $40 s, $55 d. Beyond town, at the mouth of the San Juan River, **Port Renfrew Marina and RV Park,** tel. (250) 647-5430, offers open tent sites but no showers; $12-14. Boat charters and fishing gear are available.

San Juan Valley

If you don't want to return to Victoria along Hwy. 14, and you're eventually heading north up the island, consider taking the gravel road from Port Renfrew through the San Juan Valley to **Lake Cowichan.** The road's usually in good condition, but find out from locals the present conditions and whether logging is active in the area—logging trucks don't give way, *you* do. Make sure you have enough gas, and drive with your headlights on so the trucks see you from a good distance. You'll find free campgrounds at **Fairy Lake,** six km from Port Renfrew, and **Lizard Lake,** 12 km farther along the road; both offer limited facilities.

THE WEST COAST TRAIL

The magnificent West Coast Trail meanders 77 km along Vancouver Island's untamed western shoreline, through the West Coast Trail unit of **Pacific Rim National Park.** It's one of the world's great hikes, exhilaratingly challenging, incredibly beautiful, and very satisfying—many hikers come back to do it again. The very quickest hikers can complete the trail in four days, but by allowing six, seven, or eight days you'll have time to fully enjoy the adventure. The trail extends from the mouth of the Gordon River near Port Renfrew to Pachena Bay, near the remote fishing village of Bamfield on Barkley Sound. Along the way you'll wander along beaches, steep clifftops, and slippery banks; ford rivers by rope, suspension bridge, or ferry; climb down sandstone cliffs by ladder; cross slippery boardwalks, muddy slopes, bogs, and deep gullies; and balance on fallen logs. But for all your efforts you're rewarded with panoramic views of sand and sea, dense lush rainforest, waterfalls cascading into deep pools, all kinds of wildlife—gray whales, eagles, sea lions, seals, and a variety of seabirds—and the constant roar and hiss of the Pacific surf pummeling the sand.

History

This stretch of the coast, the southernmost section of Pacific Rim National Park, was nicknamed "Graveyard of the Pacific" due to the great number of shipwrecks that occurred along here. After the SS *Valencia* ran aground in 1906 and most of the passengers and crew drowned or died from exposure, the Canadian government constructed a lifesaving trail to help future survivors penetrate the dense coastal forest. The trail followed a rugged telegraph route toward Victoria that connected lighthouses and towns and was kept open by telegraph linesmen and lighthouse keepers. Since the trail was incorporated into Pacific Rim National Park in the mid-1960s, it has gained enormous popularity. A quota system is now in use to prevent degradation of the fragile coastal environment.

Hiking Conditions

The trail can be hiked in either direction, so take your choice. The first two days out from Gor-

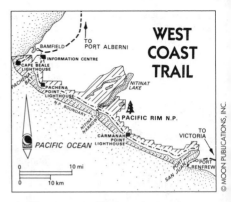

WEST COAST TRAIL

© MOON PUBLICATIONS, INC.

don River traverse difficult terrain, meaning more enjoyable hiking for the remaining days. The first two days out from Pachena Bay are relatively easy, meaning a lighter pack for the more-difficult section. Transportation to both trailheads is good, but if you leave your vehicle at Port Renfrew and return by bus or boat, you won't have to shuttle a vehicle out to remote Bamfield. Pachena Bay lies 11 km from Bamfield, and taxis operate between the two points.

Two major water crossings en route necessitate ferry service. One is at the Gordon River outside of Port Renfrew; call Norm Smith at (250) 647-5430. Fare is $5-10 per person. The other ferry, midway along the trail, crosses Nitinat Narrows, the treacherous mouth of tidal Nitinat Lake. It's sponsored by the park and runs 15 April-30 Sept., daily 9 a.m.-5 p.m.; $5 per person. These crossings cannot be made without the ferry services.

Hikers must be totally self-sufficient, as no facilities exist along the route. Go with at least two other people, and travel as light as possible. Wear comfortable hiking boots, and take a stove, at least 15 meters of strong light rope, head-to-toe waterproof gear (keep your spare clothes and sleeping bag in a plastic bag), a small amount of fire starter for an emergency, suntan lotion, insect repellent, a first-aid kit (for cuts, burns, sprains, and blisters), and waterproof matches. Also take enough cash to pay for boat crossings (allow $15) and transportation at the end of the trail (reservations required). Rainfall is least likely in the summer; July is generally the driest month, but be prepared for rain, strong winds, thick fog, and muddy trail conditions even then. The trail is closed 1 Oct.-15 April. Not only is traveling through this period treacherous due to guaranteed bad weather and no trail maintenance, but the rivers can't be crossed.

Trail-Use Permits

A quota system is in effect on the trail to reduce the environmental impact caused by overuse. Between 15 April and 30 September only 52 hikers a day are issued permits to start down the trail (26 from each end). Reservations for 40 of the 52 slots are accepted starting 1 March for the following season; call Tourism BC at (604) 663-6000 or (800) 663-6000 between 6 a.m.-6 p.m. (Pacific standard time) daily. The nonrefundable reservation fee is $25 per person, which includes a waterproof trail map. The remaining 12 spots a day are allocated on a first-come, first-served basis (six from each end; no reservation fee), but expect a wait of up to three days in summer. Once at Port Renfrew or Bamfield, all hikers must head for the registration office to obtain a trail-use permit, which costs an additional $60 per person. These permits are compulsory and checked regularly, and you'll need to show one in order to board the two ferries along the trail.

Transportation

Getting to and from either end of the trail has been made much easier by a number of companies who cover just about every routing. With your own transportation, leave your vehicle at either end of the trail and take one of the two following options.

Port Renfrew to Bamfield: The **Pacheenaht Bus Service,** tel. (250) 647-5521, offers a direct link between the two trailheads, a four-hour trip over 200 km of rough logging roads. Trips aren't regularly scheduled—this is really only a charter service. The fare is $40 per person each way, with a minimum rate of $160, and if the van must return to Port Renfrew without passengers, the fare is doubled. A more interesting way to return to your point of origin—if the seas are cooperating—is aboard the 13-meter boat of **West Coast Express Charters,** tel. (250) 647-5409; $50 per person each way.

Victoria to Port Renfrew: The **West Coast Trail Connector,** operated by Knight Limou-

sine Service Ltd., tel. (250) 475-3010, offers daily service between Victoria and Port Renfrew. It can be combined with the West Coast Express (see above) for roundtrip transportation to both ends of the trail.

Port Alberni to Bamfield: To get to the northern end of the trail from Port Alberni, catch the delightful **MV *Lady Rose,*** tel. (250) 723-8313 or (800) 663-7192, departing Alberni Harbour Quay on Tuesday, Thursday, and Saturday at 8 a.m. and arriving Bamfield at 12:30 p.m. the same day. The fare is $19 each way. **Western Bus Lines** run a two-hour shuttle service departing Port Alberni Monday at 12:30 p.m. and Friday at 10:30 a.m., and departing Bamfield the same day at 3 p.m. and 1 p.m., respectively. It's also possible to be picked up or dropped off right at Pachena Bay with this service. The fare is $17 each way. From Port Alberni, buses depart from a depot at 4521 10th Ave., tel. (250) 723-3341.

Victoria to Bamfield: The **West Coast Trail Express,** tel. (250) 477-8700 (call between 5 p.m. and 9 p.m.), provides a daily except Tuesday and Thursday bus service between downtown Victoria and Bamfield, departing Victoria at 7 a.m. and departing Bamfield (also picks up at Pachena Bay) at 1 p.m. The fare is $46.73 each way.

Information

The first step in planning to hike the West Coast Trail is to request the free ***West Coast Trail Hiker Preparation Guide*** from park headquarters; write to Superintendent, Pacific Rim National Park, P.O. Box 280, Ucluelet, BC V0R 3A0, or call the office at (250) 726-7721. The invaluable guide covers everything you need to know, including an overview of what to expect, instructions on how to apply for a trail-use permit, a list of equipment you should take, a list of relevant literature, tide tables, and advertisements for companies offering trailhead transportation.

Seasonal park information centers are in Port Renfrew, tel. (250) 647-5434, and Pachena Bay, tel. (250) 728-3234. The recommended topographic map *West Coast Trail, Pacific Rim National Park—Port Renfrew to Bamfield* is available at most specialty map stores, as well as at the information centers (registration offices) at each end of the trail. The cost of a trail-use permit includes this map.

Reference books for trail preparation include *Official Guidebook to Pacific Rim National Park* (order through park headquarters), *Pacific Rim Explorer,* by Bruce Obee (Whitecap Books, North Vancouver), and *The West Coast Trail and Nitinat Lakes* (Sierra Club of Western Canada, Victoria).

DUNCAN

Duncan, self-proclaimed "City of Totems," lies at the junction of Hwys. 1 and 18, about 60 km north of Victoria. The small city of 5,500 serves the surrounding farming and forestry communities of the Cowichan Valley. Native carvers, many from the local Cowichan band, have created some 60 intricate and colorful totem poles here. Look for the poles along the main highway near the information center, beside the railway station in the old section of town, by City Hall, and inside local businesses.

Sights

Duncan's main attraction is the excellent **British Columbia Forest Museum Park,** one km north of town, tel. (250) 746-1251. Here you can catch a ride on an old steam train and puff back in time, through the forest and past a farmstead, a logging camp, and Somenos Lake. Then check out the forest museum, working sawmill, re-stored planer mill, blacksmith's shop, and the variety of forestry and lumber displays. The park is also a pleasant place to wander—through shady glades of trees (most identified) or over to the pond where you'll find a gaggle of friendly geese awaiting a tasty morsel. It's open May-Sept., daily 9:30 a.m.-6 p.m.; admission is adults $7, seniors $6, children $4.

Follow the signs off the main highway to the city center for a quick wander around the renovated **Old Town.** (Free, two-hour parking is available by the old railway station on Canada Avenue.) Start your totem-pole hunt here or just wander down the streets opposite the railway station to appreciate some of the pleasing older architecture, such as City Hall on the corner of Kenneth and Craig Streets. Two distinctly different native carvings stand side by side behind City Hall—a Native American carving and a New Zealand Maori carving donated by Duncan's sister city, Kaikohe. On the south side of downtown, head to the **Native Heritage Centre,** 200 Cowichan Way, tel. (250) 746-8119, for a taste of the arts, crafts, legends, and traditions of northwest coast native peoples; admission $7.

Practicalities

Motels line the highway through town. Best value of the bunch is **Island Welcome Inn,** south of the river at 5325 Hwy. 1, tel. (250) 748-0331; $40 s, $47 d. Also south of the river is the turnoff to **Duncan RV Park and Campground,** 2950 Boys Rd., tel. (250) 748-8511, which is one block west of the highway, right beside the river. Sites are $12-19; full hookups available.

Always crowded with locals, **Arbutus Cafe,** on the corner of Kenneth and Jubilee Sts., tel. (250) 746-5443, concocts a great shrimp salad for $7, sandwiches and hamburgers for $4-7, and specialty pies for $3.75.

Stop at **Duncan-Cowichan Visitor Info Centre,** on the main highway by Coronation St., tel. (250) 746-4636, for the complete rundown on the area. The center staff provides information on local hiking and fishing, and on traveling the logging roads beyond Lake Cowichan. They also offer a map showing the location of all Duncan's totem poles. Hours are Mon.-Sat. 9 a.m.-5 p.m.

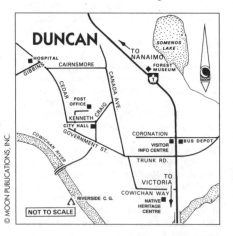

LAKE COWICHAN AND VICINITY

Don a good pair of walking shoes, grab your swimsuit, sleeping bag, fishing pole, and frying pan, and head west from Duncan to Lake Cowichan, Vancouver Island's second-largest lake. The massive, 32-km-long inland waterway, called *Kaatza* ("The Big Lake") by natives, is a popular spot for canoeing, water-skiing, swimming, and especially fishing—the lake and river are well stocked with kokanee and trout (steelhead, rainbow, brown, and cutthroat). Boat-launching facilities and excellent campsites are found at regular intervals along the lakeshore. Numerous logging roads, some paved, encircle the lake (75 km roundtrip) and provide hikers access into the adjacent wilderness, which includes the legendary **Carmanah Valley** (see "Carmanah Pacific Provincial Park," below).

Practicalities

The sleepy lakeside village of **Lake Cowichan** (pop. 3,200) lies on the eastern arm of Cowichan Lake, 30 km from Duncan. **Southshore Motel,** right in town at 266 Southshore Rd., tel. (250) 749-6482, offers comfortable, well-furnished motel rooms for $45 s, $55 d, including use of the barbecue and laundry facilities. Also downtown is **Sturgess Place Lodge,** 68 Stanley Rd., tel. (250) 749-4464, which features nine kitchen-equipped units, some right on the river, for $65-80 s or d. The finest accommodation in the region is **Sahtlam Lodge and Cabins,** 5720 Riverbottom Rd. W, tel. (250) 748-7738, set right on the Cowichan River halfway between Duncan and the lake. The cabins are spread across the property, and each is equipped with an old-style fireplace, woodstove, and full kitchen. Rates of $120 s, $135 d include breakfast; discounts are offered on multinight stays.

Campers have the choice of staying at **Lakeview Park,** three km west of Lake Cowichan, $15 per night, or **Gordon Bay Provincial Park,** on the south side of the lake 23 km farther west, $14.50 per night. Both campgrounds have hot showers.

Rail's End Pub, 109 Southshore Rd., tel. (250) 749-6755, has a good family-style restaurant overlooking the outlet of Cowichan Lake;

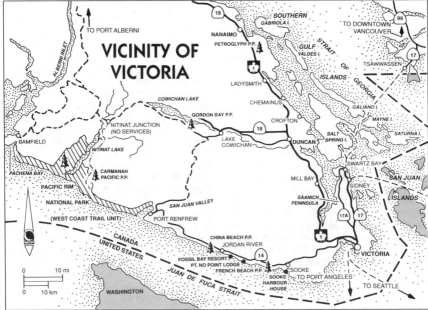

open daily from 11 a.m. On the waterfront is **Cowichan Lake Visitor Info Centre,** 125 Southshore Rd., tel. (250) 749-3244, open daily in summer, Mon.-Sat. 9 a.m.-4 p.m., Sunday 1-4 p.m. The center is a good source of information on fishing conditions and on the logging roads leading to the Carmanah Valley and Port Renfrew. Next door is the **Kaatza Station Museum,** at the end of a rail line that once linked the lake to the main line up Vancouver Island's east coast.

Carmanah Pacific Provincial Park

Eyed by logging companies for many years, the remote **Carmanah Valley** was protected with provincial-park status in 1990. For environmentalists, creation of the park was a major victory—this mist-shrouded valley extending all the way to the rugged west coast holds an old-growth forest of absolute wonder. Man's impact in the valley has been almost nonexistent. Many thousand-year-old Sitka spruce trees—some of the world's oldest— rise up to 95 meters off the damp valley floor here. Others lie where they've fallen, their slowly decaying, moss- and fern-cloaked hulks providing homes for thousands of small mammals and insects. Facilities in the park are limited to one primitive camping area at the end of the access road. From the road's-end parking lot, a rough 1.3-km trail (30 minutes each way) descends to the valley floor and Carmanah Creek. From the creek, trails lead upstream to the Three Sisters (2.5 km; 40 minutes) and Grunt's Grove (four km; 70 minutes) and downstream to the Fallen Giant (2.4 km; 40 minutes) and Heaven Grove (2.6 km; 45 minutes).

It's possible to reach the park via logging roads from Port Renfrew in the south and Port Alberni in the north, but the easiest access is gained by taking Hwy. 18 west from Duncan. Follow the south shore of Cowichan Lake to Nitinat Main, a logging road that leads south to Nitinat Junction (no services). There the road is joined by a logging road from Port Alberni. From this point Nitinat Main continues south to a bridge across the Caycuse River. Take the first right after crossing the river. This is Rosander Main, a rough road that dead-ends at the park boundary. The park is signposted from Nitinat Junction, but the signs are small and easy to miss.

A great way to visit the valley without the worry of finding your own way is with Cindy Storie on a **Freedom Adventure Tour,** tel. (250) 480-9409 (or book through Victoria International Hostel). Cindy's tours start in Victoria at 8 a.m. and return sometime after 7 p.m.—a long but rewarding day spent exploring one of the province's hidden treasures. Trips depart Sunday and Wednesday; $50 per person. For general park information, stop in at **BC Parks,** 800 Johnson St., 2nd Floor, Victoria; tel. (250) 387-5002. '

NORTH TOWARD NANAIMO

Chemainus

Continuing north from Duncan, the next place well worth a visit is the small town of Chemainus (pop. 600), which bills itself as "The Little Town that Did." Did what, you ask? Well, Chemainus has always been a sleepy little mill town; its first sawmill dates back to 1862. In 1982, MacMillan Bloedel shut down the town's antiquated mill that employed 400 people, replacing it a year later with a modern mill employing only 155 people. Chemainiacs did not want their town to die. Needing tourists, they hired local artists to cover many of the town's plain walls with larger-than-life murals depicting the town's history and culture. The result was outstanding. In 1983, the town received a First Place award at a downtown revitalization competition held in New York.

Follow the signs to Chemainus from Hwy. 1 and park at **Chemainus Visitor Info Centre,** 9758 Chemainus Rd., tel. (250) 246-3944 (open May-Sept., daily 9 a.m.-5 p.m.), where you'll see the first enormous mural—a street scene. From there you can explore the rest of Chemainus on foot, following the yellow footprints into town. Walk down to shady, waterfront **Heritage Park,** passing a mural information booth (where there's a small replica of the waterwheel that powered the original 1862 sawmill) and a detailed map of the town. Then wander through the park to the small museum on Maple Street.

Chemainus Tours operates horse-drawn carriage rides around town, passing all the murals along the route. The rides depart from Waterwheel Park every half-hour; adults $5, seniors $4, children $3.

Ladysmith

Ladysmith's main claim to fame is its location straddling the 49th parallel, the invisible boundary line separating Canada from the United States. After much bargaining, Canada got to keep all of Vancouver Island despite the 49th parallel chopping the island in two. Ladysmith was originally designed as a dormitory and recreation town for Nanaimo coal miners. Today the pretty little waterfront village is home to foresters and commercial fishermen. If you appreciate old-style architecture, wander through town to see many of the original buildings still in use.

SOUTHERN GULF ISLANDS

This group of islands lies in the Strait of Georgia, off the southeastern coast of Vancouver Island and just north of Washington's San Juan Islands, which are part of the same archipelago. Five of the islands—**Salt Spring, North Pender, Galiano, Mayne,** and **Saturna**—are populated. The largest of the islands, Salt Spring, is home to more than triple the population of the other four combined.

The islands' mild, almost Mediterranean climate, beautiful pastoral scenery, and prolific marinelife (sea lions, bald eagles, harbor seals, killer whales, blue herons, cormorants, and diving ducks, among other species) seem to attract creative people in search of life in the slow lane. However, these appealing qualities have also lured swarms of hikers, campers, cyclists, canoeists, fishermen, beachcombers, island-hoppers, and art lovers. Fortunately, those looking for solitude need only grab a boat and head north. Bronzed boaters, cruising from one provincial marine park or marina to the next, claim that the crystal-clear waters and sheltered bays here make the Southern Gulf Islands one of the world's finest cruising regions.

Getting There and Around

BC Ferries operates scheduled services among the Southern Gulf Islands, and out to the islands from both the B.C. mainland and Vancouver Island. See the transportation sections for the individual islands listed below for specific ferry information. If you're catching the ferry between Tsawwassen and the Southern Gulf Islands you need to make reservations. From Swartz Bay, Crofton, Chemainus, and Nanaimo, no reservations are necessary.

All ferries take cars, motorcycles, bicycles, canoes, and kayaks. Keep in mind that some of the islands are large, and if you don't have your own transportation you'll only see the ferry terminal area or have to fork out for a taxi (available on some islands) to see the rest. Traveling the islands by bicycle or sea kayak is both feasible and rewarding.

Other Practicalities

You'll find plenty of campsites in the provincial parks on the islands. In summer, grab a campsite by midafternoon; no reservations. Also available are bed-and-breakfast lodgings, resorts, and hotels—book ahead in winter, and far ahead in summer—as well as pubs, coffee shops, and restaurants.

Before you head for the islands, get the latest rundown from the Information Centre in downtown Victoria, from the Saanich Peninsula InfoCentre on Hwy. 17 near the Swartz Bay Ferry Terminal, or from Tourism Vancouver Island, 302-45 Bastion Square, Victoria, tel. (250) 382-3551. You might also want to pick up a copy of *The Gulf Islands Explorer,* published by Whitecap Books, 351 Lynn Ave., North Vancouver, BC V7J 2C4, available in most good bookstores.

SALT SPRING ISLAND

Largest of the Southern Gulf Islands, Salt Spring (pop. 8,000) lies close to the coast of Vancouver Island, immediately north of Saanich Inlet. Ferries link the south and north ends of the island to Vancouver Island, and a myriad of roads converge on the service town of **Ganges.** The laid-back island is home to a large number of artisans, along with hobby farmers, retirees, and those attracted to island life.

Salt Spring Island Visitor Info Centre is on the north side of the island in Ganges, at 121 Lower Ganges Rd., tel. (250) 537-5252. It's open in summer, daily 8 a.m.-6 p.m.; the rest of the year, Mon.-Fri. 8:30 a.m.-4:30 p.m.

Vesuvius Bay

ANDREW HEMPSTEAD

Sights and Recreation

From the Fulford Harbour ferry terminal, take Beaver Point Rd. east to 486-hectare **Ruckle Provincial Park.** The access road ends at Beaver Point, from where trails lead north along the coastline, providing great views across to North Pender Island.

Along the road north to Ganges, small **Mt. Maxwell Provincial Park** protects the slopes of its namesake mountain. From the 588-meter summit, views extend south across the island to Vancouver Island and east to the other Gulf Islands. South of Mt. Maxwell is 704-meter **Mt. Bruce,** the island's highest peak. A rough unsealed road off Musgrave Rd. leads to the summit.

Although the island offers good hiking opportunities, it's better-known for water-oriented activities such as kayaking , boating, and fishing. Rent kayaks from **Saltspring Kayaking,** tel. (250) 653-4222, with outlets at Fulford Harbour and Ganges, or **Salt Spring Marine Rentals,** Salt Spring Marina, tel. (250) 537-9100 or (800) 334-6629. The latter also rents boats and offers fishing charters.

For a different perspective of the island, organize a horseback-riding excursion with **Salt Spring Guided Rides,** tel. (250) 537-5761; $25 per hour per person, 2-6 people, by reservation only.

Accommodations and Camping

Bed and breakfasts are abundant on the island—with over 50 at last count. Make reservations as far in advance as possible, especially for week-

ends. Call direct or book through the **Canadian Gulf Islands B&B Reservation Service,** 637 Southwind Rd., Montague Harbour, Galiano Island, BC V0N 1P0, tel. (250) 539-5390.

In the south is one of the island's premier accommodations, **Pauper's Perch Bed and Breakfast,** 225 Armand Way, tel. (250) 653-2030, a magnificent modern home set on two hectares high above sea level, with views extending west to Vancouver Island. Each of the three rooms has a large jacuzzi, balcony, and private entrance. The rates of $115-155 s, $125-165 d include a full breakfast. A few bucks cheaper on the island's southern end is **Log House B&B,** by Cusheon Lake at 490 Horel Rd., tel. (250) 537-1104; $70 s, $80 d. Regular motel rooms are offered at the **Fulford Inn,** 2661 Fulford-Ganges Rd., tel. (250) 653-4432 or (800) 652-4432; $50 s or d. Continuing north is **Captain's Hideway,** 162 Harrison Ave., tel. (250) 537-9595, where just one room is offered, but it's a beauty. It has its own kitchen and living area, and overlooks a private dock where a rowboat is available for guest use. The rate of $55 s, $65 d includes breakfast. **Maple Ridge Cottages** lie on St. Mary Lake at 301 Tripp Rd., tel. (250) 537-5977. Each has a kitchen, private deck, and fireplace, and guests are allowed complimentary use of canoes. Rates range $70-95 s or d.

The campground in **Ruckle Provincial Park** holds 70 sites in a forest of Douglas fir right by the water. All sites are a short walk from the parking lot, making this place unsuitable for RVs; $9,50 per night. On the north side of the island on St. Mary Lake are two commercial campgrounds: **Lakeside Gardens Resort,** tel. (250) 537-5773, offers sites with full hookups for $22, along with showers and a beach with boat rentals; while **Cedar Beach Resort,** tel. (250) 537-2205, has no showers or hookups, but charges only $15 per site.

Transportation
Closest of the Southern Gulf Islands to Vancouver Island, Salt Spring is served by **BC Ferries,** tel. (250) 386-3431 or, toll-free in B.C., (888) BCFERRY. Ferries run 10-12 times daily between Swartz Bay and Fulford Harbour, and even more frequently between Vesuvius Bay, at the island's north end, and Crofton. Fares for travel on either route are the same, and as all prices are for the roundtrip you can leave the island from either end at no extra charge. Peak roundtrip fares are adults $5, children $2.50, cars $17.25, canoes and kayaks $2.25, bicycles $1.50.

From the B.C. mainland, at least two sailings a day leave the Tsawwassen terminal (south of downtown Vancouver), tel. (604) 669-1211, bound for Long Harbour on the east side of Salt Spring Island. The night sailings are nonstop (or stop just once) while all others make multiple stops, extending the 80-minute trip to three hours. The peak one-way fare from Tsawwassen to Salt Spring Island is adults $8.50, children $4.25, cars $34.50, bicycles $3.25, canoes and kayaks $4.50.

Long Harbour is also the departure point for interisland travel. Sailings to North Pender Island are direct; to all other islands at least one stop is required. Peak fares for all interisland travel are the same: adults $2.50, children $1.25, cars $6, bicycles 75 cents, canoes and kayaks $1.75.

NORTH PENDER ISLAND

A short ferry ride from Salt Spring Island's Long Harbour ferry terminal, this 24-square-km island has many great little beaches and provides ocean access at over 20 points. One of the nicest spots is **Hamilton Beach** on Browning Harbour. This is also the main service area, from where roads radiate out to all points of the

island. One road leads across a rickety old wooden bridge to **South Pender Island,** site of **Beaumont Provincial Marine Park.**

Pender Island Visitor Info Centre is east of the ferry terminal, up the hill. The small booth is open through summer, daily 9 a.m.-6 p.m.

Accommodations and Camping
The least expensive way to enjoy an overnight stay on North Pender Island is to camp at **Prior Centennial Provincial Park,** six km south of the Otter Bay ferry terminal. Sites are primitive, with no showers or hookups, but the location is excellent; $9.50 per night. The island's premier accommodation is **Cliffside Inn On-the-sea,** on Armadale Rd. three km from the ferry terminal, tel. (250) 629-6691. Each room is elegantly furnished and a wide balcony takes advantage of the waterfront location. Rates start at $115 s, $125 d, including breakfast.

Transportation
Up to seven times a day ferries depart the Swartz Bay terminal, tel. (250) 386-3431, for North Pender Island. Most sailings are direct (40 minutes) although a couple of the early-morning trips go via Galiano and Mayne Islands (over two hours), so check the timetable carefully before boarding. The peak roundtrip fare is adults $5, children $2.50, cars $18.25, canoes and kayaks $2.50, bicycles $1.50. Sailings from the Tsawwassen ferry terminal, tel. (604) 669-1211, depart twice daily; adults $8.50, children $4.25, cars $34.50, bicycles $3.25, canoes and kayaks $4.50. The peak one-way fare between North Pender Island and any of Salt Spring, Mayne, Galiano, and Saturna Islands is adults $2.50, children $1.25, cars $6, canoes and kayaks $1.75, bicycles 75 cents.

GALIANO ISLAND

This long and narrow island, 27 km from north to south but only a few km wide, lies north of Salt Spring Island. Most of the population lives in the south, around the ferry terminal at Sturdies Bay. Right at the terminal is **Galiano Island Visitor Info Centre,** tel. (250) 539-2233; open in summer only, daily 9 a.m.-5 p.m.

ANDREW HEMPSTEAD

Sea kayaking is a great way to experience the Southern Gulf Islands.

Sights and Recreation

One of the best ways to explore local waterways is with **Galiano Island Sea Kayaks,** tel. (250) 539-2442. Three-hour guided tours, either early in the morning or at at sunset, are $40. Another tour takes in the local marinelife on a six-hour paddle for $60. Those with previous experience can rent a kayak; $33 per day for a single or $55 for a double.

Climbing out of Sturdies Bay, Porlier Pass Rd. crosses through **Montague Harbour Provincial Park,** which protects 97 coastal hectares. The park offers a variety of short hikes, through forests of Douglas fir and along the shoreline.

Accommodations and Camping

Sutil Lodge at Montague Harbour, tel. (250) 539-2930, is a historic fishing lodge set on eight waterfront hectares. Each of the seven rooms is decorated with a heritage theme, and guests

have use of a communal lounge area and the dining room where breakfast is served. Days can be spent exploring the nearby park, kayaking, or cruising aboard the lodge's catamaran. Rates start at $65 s, $75 d. Another historic lodging, within walking distance of the ferry terminal, is **Bellhouse Inn,** 29 Farmhouse Rd., tel. (250) 539-5667 or (800) 970-7464. Rooms are large, and most feature a hot tub, private balcony, and fireplace. Rates start at $90 s, $110 d, including a full breakfast.

Farther north, in a spectacular location, is **Hill House B&B,** 90 Ganner Dr., tel. (250) 539-3322. The one room offered has a private entrance, large balcony with panoramic views, and modern furnishings. A full breakfast is included in the rates of just $95 s or d.

The only campground on Galiano Island is at **Montague Harbour Provincial Park,** 10 km from the ferry. As with all provincial park campgrounds through the Southern Gulf Islands, the location is superb and the facilities are limited to picnic tables, pit toilets, and drinking water; $12 per night.

Transportation

BC Ferries, tel. (250) 386-3431 or, toll-free in B.C., (888) BCFERRY, schedules four sailings daily between Swartz Bay and Mayne Island; peak roundtrip fare is adults $5, children $2.50, cars $18.25, canoes and kayaks $2.50, bicycles $1.50. From the B.C. mainland, Galiano Island is the first stop for the Gulf Islands ferries, which depart at least twice daily from the Tsawwassen terminal, tel. (604) 669-1211. Peak one-way fare is adults $8.50, children $4.25, cars $34.50, canoes and kayaks $4.50, bicycles $3.25. Galiano Island is linked to Mayne Island by four sailings daily, with a couple of those continuing to the other islands. All interisland travel is charged at the same rate: adults $2.50, children $1.25, cars $6, canoes and kayaks $1.75, bicycles 75 cents.

MAYNE ISLAND

Separated from Galiano Island by a narrow channel, Mayne Island is just 21 square kilometers in area. Roads lead from the ferry dock at Village Bay to all corners of the island. "Village" Bay has no village; all commercial facilities are at nearby **Miners Bay,** which got its name during the Cariboo gold rush when miners used the island as a stopping point. Island beaches are limited to those at Oyster Bay, but visitors can enjoy interesting shoreline walks, or take the road to the low summit of Mount Park for panoramic views.

Accommodations

Overlooking Miners Bay, two km east of the ferry terminal, is **Tinkerers' Bed and Breakfast,** 417 Georgina Point Rd., tel. (250) 539-2280. This delightful old house sits right on the bay, and makes a great base for exploring the area on foot or bike (bike rentals available). Rooms are smallish and simply furnished, but guests have use of a communal lounge and the relaxing gardens. Rates are $60-80 s, $70-90 d; the least expensive rooms share bathroom facilities.

Set on four hectares overlooking a protected waterway, less than two km south of the ferry terminal, is **Oceanwood Country Inn,** 630 Dinner Bay Rd., tel. (250) 539-5074. Each of the 12 rooms has its own character; some have a private balcony, others a deck or jacuzzi, and the largest features a split-level living area, luxurious bathroom, and private deck with hot tub. Rates start at $120 s, $130 d; rooms with ocean views range $230-295. A cooked breakfast and tea and coffee throughout the day are included. Mayne Island has no designated camping areas.

Transportation

From Swartz Bay, **BC Ferries,** tel. (250) 386-3431 or, toll-free in B.C., (888) BCFERRY, schedules four sailings daily to Mayne Island; peak roundtrip fare is adults $5, children $2.50, cars $18.25, canoes and kayaks $2.50, bicycles $1.50. Sailings from the Tsawwassen ferry terminal, tel. (604) 669-1211, depart at least once daily, with a stop at Galiano Island en route; the peak one-way fare is adults $8.50, children $4.25, cars $34.50, canoes and kayaks $4.50, bicycles $3.25. Regular interisland sailings are offered from Saturna, North Pender, and Galiano Islands. The peak fare for all interisland travel is

adults $2.50, children $1.25, cars $6; canoes and kayaks $1.75, bicycles 75 cents.

SATURNA ISLAND

Most remote of the populated Southern Gulf Islands, Saturna protrudes into the heart of Georgia Strait and features a long rugged northern coastline. From the ferry dock at **Lyall Harbour,** the island's main road follows this stretch of coast for 14 km, ending at East Point.

Accommodations

Most accommodations on Saturna Island are in private home bed and breakfasts. The island has no campgrounds. Right at the ferry terminal is **Lyall Harbour B&B,** 121 East Point Rd., tel. (250) 539-5577. Each of the three guest rooms is spacious and features modern furnishings, a fireplace, and a deck with ocean views; $80 s, $85 d. Also within walking distance of Lyall Harbour is **Saturna Lodge,** 130 Payne Rd., tel. (250) 539-2254. Right on the water, this modern accommodation offers seven guest rooms, a restaurant, lounge, and jacuzzi; $80 s, $90 d, including breakfast.

Transportation

Although Saturna is the most difficult of the main islands to reach by ferry, fares are no higher than on other routes. Direct ferries are available, but you might want to take one of the other ferries and explore one or more of the other islands on the way out to Saturna. Peak one-way fare on any interisland route is adults $2.50, children $1.25, cars $6, canoes and kayaks $1.75, bicycles 75 cents. Two to three sailings daily come direct from the Swartz Bay ferry terminal, tel. (250) 386-3431; peak roundtrip fare is adults $5, children $2.50, cars $18.25, canoes and kayaks $2.50, bicycles $1.50. Sailings to Saturna from the Tsawwassen ferry terminal, tel. (604) 669-1211, depart twice daily, but require a transfer at Mayne Island. The peak one-way fare is adults $8.50, children $4.25, cars $34.50, canoes and kayaks $4.50, bicycles $3.25.

NANAIMO AND VICINITY

Nanaimo (pronounced nan-NYE-mo) sprawls lazily up and down the hilly coastal terrain between sparkling Nanaimo Harbour and Mt. Benson, on the east coast of Vancouver Island. With a population of 74,000, it's the island's second-largest city and one of the 10 largest cities in British Columbia. It's also a vibrant city enjoying a rich history, mild climate, wide range of visitor services, and a direct ferry link to both of Vancouver's ferry terminals.

Until 1997, the main highway up Vancouver Island passed right through downtown Nanaimo, creating chaos on the narrow winding roads. The new **Nanaimo Parkway** alleviates this problem, bypassing the city to the west along a 21-km route that branches off the old highway five km south of downtown, rejoining it 18 km north of downtown.

History
Five native bands lived here (the name Nanaimo is a derivative from the Salish word *Sney-Ny-Mous,* or "Meeting Place"), and it was they who innocently showed dull, black rocks to Hudson's Bay Company employees in 1852. For most of the next century, mines in the area exported huge quantities of coal. Eventually, oil-fueled ships replaced the coal burners, and by 1949 most of the mines had closed. Surprisingly, no visible traces of the mining boom remain in Nanaimo, aside from a museum (built on top of the most productive mine) accurately depicting those times, and a sturdy fort (now a museum) built in 1853 in case of a native attack.

Nanaimo was officially incorporated in 1874, which makes it the province's third-oldest town. When the coal mines closed, forestry and fishing became mainstays of the city. Today Nanaimo is also a major deep-sea shipping port.

SIGHTS

Downtown Nanaimo lies in a wide bowl sloping down to the waterfront, where forward thinking by early town planners has left wide expanses of parkland. Down near the water, the Civic Arena building makes a good place to park your car and go exploring on foot. Right in front of the Civic Arena is **Swy-A-Lana Lagoon,** a unique man-made tidal lagoon full of interesting marinelife. Up in downtown proper, many historic buildings still stand, most around the corner of Front and Church Sts. and along Commercial Street. Look for hotels dating to last century, the Francis Rattenbury-designed courthouse, and various old commercial buildings. Up Fitzwilliam St. are the 1893 St. Andrew's Church and the 1883 railway station.

The Bastion
Overlooking the harbor at the junction of Bastion and Front Sts. stands the Bastion, a well-pro-

Nanaimo's downtown area has been rejuvenated, but the distinguished old buildings still stand.

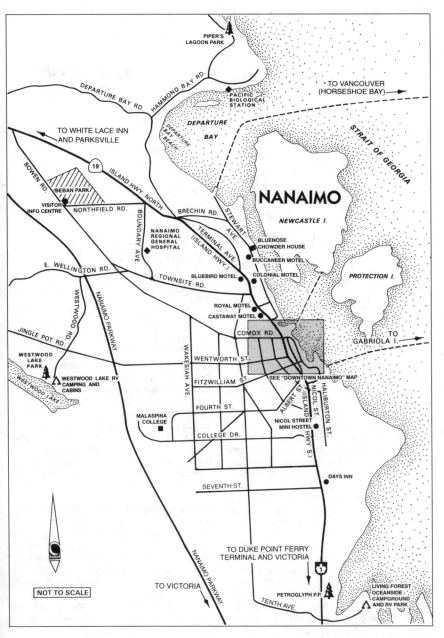

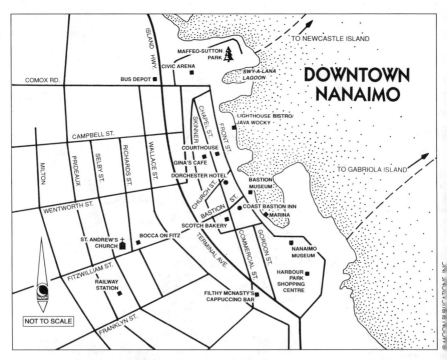

TO NEWCASTLE ISLAND

ISLAND HWY.

MAFFEO-SUTTON PARK

CIVIC ARENA

COMOX RD.

BUS DEPOT

SWY-A-LANA LAGOON

DOWNTOWN NANAIMO

CHAPEL ST.

SKINNER

FRONT ST.

LIGHTHOUSE BISTRO/ JAVA WOCKY

CAMPBELL ST.

RICHARDS ST.

SELBY ST.

WALLACE ST.

COURTHOUSE

GINA'S CAFE

DORCHESTER HOTEL

CHURCH ST.

BASTION MUSEUM

TO GABRIOLA ISLAND

MILTON

PRIDEAUX

WENTWORTH ST.

BASTION ST.

COAST BASTION INN

MARINA

SCOTCH BAKERY

ST. ANDREW'S CHURCH

BOCCA ON FITZ

COMMERCIAL ST.

GORDON ST.

NANAIMO MUSEUM

FITZWILLIAM ST.

RAILWAY STATION

TERMINAL AVE.

HARBOUR PARK SHOPPING CENTRE

FILTHY MCNASTY'S CAPPUCCINO BAR

NOT TO SCALE

FRANKLYN ST.

tected fort built in 1853 by the Hudson's Bay Company to protect employees and their families against an attack by natives. Originally used as a company office, arsenal, and supply house, today the fort houses the **Bastion Museum,** open in summer, daily 10 a.m.-5 p.m. For the benefit of tourists, a group of local university students dressed in appropriate gunnery uniforms and led by a piper parades down Bastion Street daily at noon in summer. The parade ends at the Bastion, where the three cannons are fired out over the water. It's the only ceremonial cannon firing west of Ontario. For a good vantage point, be there early.

Nanaimo Museum

In Piper Park, just across Front St. from the Bastion and up the stairs, is Nanaimo Museum, 100 Cameron St., tel. (250) 753-1821. Walk around the outside to appreciate harbor, city, and mountain views, as well as replica petroglyphs of animals, humans, and spiritual crea-

tures. Then allow at least an hour for wandering through the two floors of displays inside, which focus on life in early Nanaimo and include topics such as local geology, native peoples, and pioneers. An exhibit on the coal-mining days features a realistic coal mine from the 1850s. Don't miss the impressive native carvings by James Dick. Displays are changed regularly, so something's always new. The museum is open in summer, daily 9 a.m.-6 p.m.; the rest of the year, Tues.-Sat. 9 a.m.-4 p.m.

Newcastle Island Provincial Marine Park
Newcastle Island is a magnificent chunk of wilderness separated from downtown Nanaimo by a narrow channel. It's mostly forested, and ringed by sandstone cliffs and a few short stretches of pebbly beach. Wildlife inhabitants include deer, raccoons, beavers, and over 50 species of birds.

When Europeans arrived and began mining coal, they displaced natives who had lived on the island for centuries. Coal was mined until 1883, and sandstone—featured on many of Nanaimo's historic buildings—was quarried here until 1932. The pavilion and facilities near the ferry dock date to the 1940s. Back then, the island was a popular holiday spot, at one point even boasting a floating hotel.

A 7.5-km trail (allow 2-3 hours) encircles the island, leading to picturesque Kanaka Bay, Mallard Lake, and a lookout offering views east to the snowcapped Coast Mountains. Ferries depart for the island regularly from Maffeo-Sutton Park, in front of the Civic Arena. The roundtrip fare is adults $4.25, seniors and children $3.25, bicycles $1.50. For ferry details call (250) 753-5141.

Other Parks

On the road into downtown Nanaimo from the south, two km north of the new Nanaimo Parkway intersection, **Petroglyph Provincial Park** features a short trail leading to ancient petroglyphs (rock carvings). Petroglyphs are found throughout the province and are common along the coastal waterways. They were made with stone tools, and recorded important ceremonies and events. The designs at this park were carved thousands of years ago, and are believed to represent human beings, animals (real and supernatural), bottom fish, and the rarely depicted sea wolf, a mythical creature part wolf and part killer whale.

West of downtown (take Wentworth St. then Jingle Pot Rd. across the Nanaimo Parkway), **Westwood Lake Park** surrounds the crystal-clear waters of its namesake lake. The park is inhabited by a resident flock of Canada geese, who are tame enough to snatch food from your fingers and flap back to the lake. North of downtown along Hammond Bay Rd. is **Piper's Lagoon Park**, encompassing an isthmus and a rocky headland that shelter a shallow lagoon. A trail from the parking lot leads to the

headland, where you'll have views of the mainland across the Strait of Georgia. It's a great spot for birdwatching or, when the wind's howling, watching colorful windsurfers chasing each other across the water.

RECREATION

Harbor Cruise

The obvious way to appreciate the harbor aspect of Nanaimo is by boat. To arrange a cruise, wander down to the marina below the Bastion and inquire among the fishing and sightseeing charter boats, or stop by the Nanaimo Visitor Info Centre and ask for a list of local guides and charters, plus current prices.

One vessel, the **Bastion City,** takes passengers on 2.5-hour narrated cruises of the harbor and adjacent islands. During the cruise, you might spot a variety of wildlife, including sea lions—who come into the harbor in March and early April to feed on abundant schools of herring—seals, orcas, bald eagles, blue herons, and cormorants. Cruises cost adults $25, seniors $21, children $14; call (250) 753-2852 for reservations and information.

NANAIMO'S WORLD CHAMPIONSHIP BATHTUB RACE

On the fourth Sunday of every July the Strait of Georgia comes alive for the World Championship Bathtub Race, the grand finale of Nanaimo's annual Marine Festival. The idea for the race was conceived back in 1967, when the chairman of the city's Canada Centennial Committee, Frank Ney, was asked to come up with a special event for the occasion. Bathtub racing was born over a cup of coffee, and Ney went on to be elected mayor of Nanaimo.

Competitors fit a modified bathtub with a 7.5-horsepower outboard motor and try to navigate it as fast as possible across the 35-km stretch of Georgia Strait between Nanaimo and Kitsilano Beach, Vancouver. The racers are escorted by hundreds of boats of the more regular variety, loaded with people just waiting for the competitors to sink! Every bathtubber wins a prize—a golden plug for entering, a small trophy for making it to the other side of the strait, and a silver plunger for the first tub to sink! These days, the sport and the festivities around it have grown enormously, attracting tens of thousands of visitors to Nanaimo. And "tubbing," as the locals call it, has spread to other provincial communities where preliminary races qualify entrants for the big one.

Bungee Jumping

Nanaimo is home to North America's only bridge-based commercial bungee jump. People flock here from afar to have their ankles tied and connected to "Bungee Bridge" by a long elastic rope. Next they dive head first 45 meters down almost to the surface of Nanaimo River, rebounding until momentum dissipates. To receive this thrill of a lifetime you have to part with $95 (plus tax), and if you have any cash left over, you'll find must-have T-shirts, hats, posters, videos, stickers, and other souvenirs to prove to the world that you really did it, and of course there's nothing stopping you from simply buying a T-shirt and letting the world draw its own conclusions.This is also a thoroughly entertaining spectator sport, with good viewing areas and plenty of parking provided. The site is 13 km south of downtown. For details and reservations call **Bungy Zone** at (250) 753-5867 or (800) 668-7771.

Arts and Entertainment

Lovers of the arts will find Nanaimo to be quite the cultural center. Over on the campus of Malaspina University-College, **Nanaimo Art Gallery**, 900 5th St., tel. (250) 755-8790, displays works of art, primarily of Canadian origin. At the gift shop you can buy arts and crafts by local island artists. The center is open Mon.-Sat. 10 a.m.-5 p.m., Sunday noon-5 p.m.

During the **Nanaimo Festival** in July and August, professional theater companies perform nightly. Original Canadian plays, musicals, and comedies, as well as the plays of William Shakespeare, are presented in contemporary settings by world-renowned actors. Nanaimo has been called the "Stratford of western Canada." For a brochure of scheduled events call the festival office at (250) 754-7587, or the College Theatre box office at (250) 755-8700. Also presenting live theater is **Nanaimo Theatre Group**, 2373 Rosstown Rd., tel. (250) 758-7246.

The best place in Nanaimo for a quiet drink in a relaxing atmosphere is the **Lighthouse Pub**, 50 Anchor Way, tel. (250) 754-3212, built out over the water in front of downtown. For nautical atmosphere, head over to the **Dinghy Dock Floating Marine Pub**, moored at Protection Island, tel. (250) 753-2373; ferries depart regularly from Nanaimo Boat Basin.

Events

The year kicks off in early April with the **Sea Lion Festival**, which coincides with the end of the Dec.-April herring run through the Strait of Georgia. Attracted by the fish, hundreds of sea lions congregate on log booms for a quick and easy feed. Festivities include boat trips out on the water, onshore entertainment, and educational displays. The **Heritage Days** festival in late June celebrates the city's past with concerts and historical displays. July's **Marine Festival** is best-known for the World Championship Bathtub Race (see the Special Topic), but also includes a Silly Boat Regatta, a variety of races, a street fair, and fireworks.

ACCOMMODATIONS AND CAMPING

Hotels and Motels

Across from the waterfront and within easy walking distance of downtown, the Departure Bay ferry terminal, and the information center is **Buccaneer Motel**, 1577 Stewart Ave., tel. (250) 753-1246. The rooms aren't particularly large, but are clean, comfortable, and very well priced at $45 s, $55 d. Look for discount coupons at the information center. The **Bluebird Motel**, 995 Terminal Ave., tel. (250) 753-4151, is also inexpensive ($46 s, $55 d), but it's on a busy road three km north of downtown beyond the information center. Across the road from the Bluebird is the slightly cheaper, nine-room **Colonial Motel**, 950 Terminal Ave., tel. (250) 754-4415. Coming into the city from the south, **Days Inn Harbourview**, 809 Island Hwy. S, tel. (250) 754-8171 or (800) 329-7466, features a large indoor pool, restaurant, and laundry; from $69 s, $79 d.

As you'd expect, accommodations right downtown are more expensive. The **Coast Bastion Inn**, 11 Bastion St., tel. (250) 753-6601 or (800) 663-1144, is a full-service hotel with an exercise room, cafe and restaurant, and water views from every room. Rates are $99 s, $109 d. The **Best Western Dorchester Hotel**, 70 Church St., tel. (250) 754-6835 or (800) 661-2449, also offers water views, as well as a rooftop terrace; from $105 s or d.

Seven km north of downtown, the three-story **Long Lake Inn**, 4700 Island Hwy. N, tel. (250)

758-1144 or (800) 565-1144, overlooks a beautiful lake. The inn boasts a short stretch of private beach along the lakeshore; canoe rentals are available. Other amenities include an exercise room, sauna, spa, and a delightful waterfront cafe. Rooms are modern, and many have water views; from $110 s or d.

Hostel

On the main road into town from the south, **Nicol Street Mini Hostel,** 65 Nicol St., tel. (250) 753-1188, enjoys a convenient location three blocks from the train station and seven blocks from the bus depot. The hostel operates year-round, providing dormitory-style accommodations, as well as campsites, a kitchen, laundry, TV room, and bicycle rentals. Guests can get discounts at many local restaurants and attractions. All beds are $17; camping out back costs $8 per person.

Campgrounds

Three commercial campgrounds lie within 10 km of city center, but the nicest surroundings are in the provincial park out on **Newcastle Island** (see "Sights," above), connected to downtown by regular ferry service. The island isn't suitable for RVers, but it's ideal for those with a lightweight tent. Facilities include picnic tables and a barbecue shelter. If you don't want to cook, you can eat at the restaurant on the island. Sites are $9.50. For details call the park office at (250) 391-2300.

The closest of the commercial campgrounds to downtown is **Westwood Lake RV Camping and Cabins,** 380 Westwood Rd., tel. (250) 753-3922. It's right on the edge of beautiful Westwood Lake, and offers fishing, canoe rentals, a few short hiking trails, a barbecue area, games room, laundry, and hot showers. Unserviced sites are $15, hookups $18, cabins $50-55.

Beside the braided mouth of the Nanaimo River south of downtown is **Living Forest Oceanside Campground,** 6 Maki Rd., tel. (250) 755-1755, set on 21 forested hectares; $15-17 per night. **Brannen Lake Campsites,** 4220 Biggs Rd., tel. (250) 756-0404, offers sunny or shady lakeside sites on an operating beef ranch. To get there, head north of town, turn left on Mostar Rd., then right on Biggs Road. Sites are $14-16 per night.

FOOD

First things first. This is the place to try a delicious chocolate-topped **Nanaimo Bar** (80 cents). Head to the **Scotch Bakery,** 87 Commercial St., tel. (250) 753-3521, for the best in town. Line up, buy your cakes, grab a coffee, and relax at the tables provided.

Cafes and Cheap Eats

Right on the harbor, in the Pioneer Waterfront Plaza, is **Javawocky,** 90 Front St., tel. (250) 753-1688, a modern coffeehouse with all the usual coffee drinks, great milk shakes, inexpensive cakes and pastries, and light lunchtime snacks. Want some real island atmosphere? Try **Filthy McNasty's Cappuccino Bar,** 14 Commercial St., tel. (250) 753-7011, for good food, a good crowd, and good prices. McNasty's also hosts a jazz jam on Wednesday night and live music with Sunday brunch. It's open daily 8 a.m.-10 p.m. Up Fitzwilliam St. from the center of town, in the Old Quarter, are a couple of quiet little cafes including **Bocca on Fitz,** 427 Fitzwilliam St., tel. (250) 753-1799, offering healthy sandwiches and freshly squeezed juices, and **Sweet Revenge,** 321 Wesley St., tel. (250) 755-1444, for coffees, healthy snacks, and not-so-healthy desserts.

Head down to the marina on Front St. for seafood straight from the fishing boats. You can buy fish, prawns, crabs, or whatever's been caught, or walk out the wharf to **Troller's,** which cooks up fish and chips for $6.

Restaurants

Dinghy Dock Floating Marine Pub, tel. (250) 753-2373, offers a unique dining experience; the floating restaurant is moored at nearby Protection Island. Well-known for great food and plenty of seagoing atmosphere, the pub also hosts live entertainment on Friday and Saturday nights from May to September. It's open daily 11 a.m.-11 p.m., later on weekends. To get to the restaurant, take a ferry from Nanaimo Boat Basin. Ferries depart hourly 9:10 a.m.-11:10 p.m.; for ferry information call (250) 753-8244.

In the seaplane terminal on the waterfront (below the Bastion), **Lighthouse Bistro,** 50 Anchor Way, tel. (250) 754-3212, offers wonderful harbor views, exciting seaplane action, and good food. The seafood chowder is excellent, and served with delicious bread. Also on the menu are tasty appetizers, salads, burgers, sandwiches, croissants, pasta dishes, and good daily specials. Expect to pay $7-10 for a lunch entree, $13-20 at dinner. It's open daily 11 a.m.-11 p.m.

Another good choice for a seafood feast is **Bluenose Chowder House,** 1340 Stewart Ave., tel. (250) 754-6611. Locals rave about the clam chowder with garlic bread, chowder topped with shrimp, or plain old fish and chips. You also get terrific views, whether you eat inside or out on the deck in summer. Open Tues.-Sun. 11 a.m.-9 p.m., until 10 p.m. Fri.-Saturday. For some of the best Mexican food on the island, head for **Gina's Cafe,** behind the courthouse at 47 Skinner St., tel. (250) 753-5411; open daily for lunch and dinner.

TRANSPORTATION

Getting There

It's possible to get to Nanaimo by airplane, train, or bus, but most people arrive by car up Hwy. 1 from Victoria or by ferry from the mainland. **BC Ferries,** tel. (250) 386-3431 or, toll-free in B.C., (888) BCFERRY, operates a regular service between Vancouver and Nanaimo. In summer, ferries leave Vancouver's Tsawwassen terminal eight times a day for the two-hour trip to Nanaimo's new Duke Point terminal, 20 minutes south of downtown. Ferries from Vancouver's Horseshoe Bay terminal leave 10 times a day, arriving at Nanaimo's Departure Bay terminal after a 95-minute crossing. Slightly fewer sailings are offered the rest of the year. The peak one-way fare on either route is adults $8, cars $30, motorcycles $15, bicycles $2.50, canoes and kayaks $4. Limited reservations are taken.

Baxter Aviation, tel. (250) 754-1066, flies daily between Vancouver and the seaplane base in downtown Nanaimo; $58 one-way. **Kenmore Air,** tel. (800) 543-9595, offers seaplane service between Seattle's Lake Washington and Nanaimo; US$135 northbound, US$141.50 southbound, US$276.50 roundtrip.

The **Island Coach Lines** bus depot is at the rear of the Tally-Ho Island Inn on the corner of Terminal Ave. and Comox Rd., tel. (800) 753-4371. One-way fares from Nanaimo include: Victoria $16.10, Port Alberni $7.15, Tofino $31.40, Campbell River $26.55, Port Hardy $61.65.

A great way to travel up the island is with **VIA Rail.** Its Malahat train departs Victoria Mon.-Sat. at 8:15 a.m. and on Sunday at noon, running as far north as Courtenay. Get off at Nanaimo, spend a couple of hours exploring the city or Newcastle Island, then jump aboard the return service to Victoria that same afternoon; $19.26 one-way, $38.52 roundtrip. The station is on Selby St., up the hill from downtown, tel. (250) 383-4324 or (800) 561-8630.

Getting Around

Nanaimo Regional Transit System buses run daily. The main routes radiate from the Gordon St. Exchange (below the Bastion) north along Hammond Bay Rd., west to Westwood Lake, and south as far as Chase River. The adult fare is $1.30; an all-day pass is $3.15. For schedule information call (250) 390-4531.

Rental car agencies in Nanaimo include: **Avis,** tel. (250) 753-1111; **Budget,** tel. (250) 754-7368; **National Tilden,** tel. (250) 758-3509; and **Rent-a-wreck,** tel. (250) 753-6461.

SERVICES AND INFORMATION

The **post office** is on Front St. in the Harbour Park Shopping Centre; open Mon.-Fri. 8:30 a.m.-5 p.m. **Nanaimo Regional General Hospital** is at 1200 Dufferin Cres., tel. (250) 754-2141. If you need a **pharmacy** head for Pharmasave in Beaufort Centre, across from Nanaimo Regional General Hospital, tel. (250) 753-2212. For maps, nautical charts, and books about Vancouver Island, visit **Nanaimo Maps and Charts,** 8 Church St., tel. (250) 754-2513.

Nanaimo Visitor Info Centre, 2290 Bowen Rd., tel. (250) 756-0106 or (800) 663-7337, is on the grounds of Beban Park, northwest of downtown. It's open in summer, daily 8 a.m.-8 p.m.; the rest of the year, Mon.-Fri. 9 a.m.-5 p.m., Sat.-Sun. 10 a.m.-4 p.m. A small seasonal information center operates in the Bastion, right downtown, through summer.

GABRIOLA ISLAND

Like the Southern Gulf Islands, Gabriola (pop. 2,500) is partly residential, but also holds large expanses of forest, abundant wildlife, and long stretches of unspoiled coastline. The ferry from Nanaimo docks at Descanso Bay, on the east side of the island.

Take Taylor Bay Rd. north from the ferry terminal to access the island's best beaches, including those within five-hectare **Gabriola Sands Provincial Park.** Walk out to the park's southern headland to view sandstone cliffs eroded into interesting shapes by eons of wave action. The island is encircled by the North and South Roads, which combine for a 30-km loop perfect for a leisurely bike ride. You'll find many scenic spots to pull off—at petroglyphs, secluded bays, and lookouts. The island's southeast corner is protected by **Drumbeg Provincial Park,** where a short trail through dense forest leads to a secluded bay.

Practicalities

The least expensive way to overnight on the island is by camping at **Gabriola Campground,** 595 Taylor Bay Rd., tel. (250) 247-2079. Facilities are limited (no showers or hookups) but it's a great little spot right on the ocean; $14 per night.

Surf Lodge, 885 Berry Point Rd. (a continuation of Taylor Bay Rd.), tel. (250) 247-9231, features large rooms set on a waterfront property with a saltwater pool and restaurant; from $50-80 s or d. The island's nicest accommodation is **Marina's Hideaway,** 943 Canso Dr., tel. (250) 247-8854, a bed and breakfast overlooking Northumberland Channel one km from the ferry terminal. Each of the two guest rooms in this magnificent waterfront home has a private entrance and balcony. Rates are $85 s, $95 d.

BC Ferries, tel. (250) 386-3431 or, toll-free in B.C., (888) BCFERRY, schedules 15 sailings daily between the terminal off Front St. in Nanaimo (downtown, across from Harbour Park Shopping Centre) and Gabriola Island. The trip takes 20 minutes each way. The peak roundtrip fare is adults $4, children $2, cars $10.75, canoes and kayaks $2. For a taxi, call **Gabriola Cabs,** tel. (250) 247-9348. Basic services are available at Folklife Village, a little over one km from the ferry terminal on North Road. There you'll find a cafe, grocery store, and **Gabriola Island Visitor Info Centre,** tel. (250) 247-9332, which is open mid-May to mid-September, daily 9 a.m.-6 p.m.

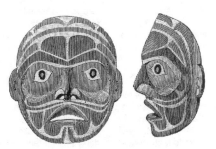

DOVER PUBLICATIONS, INC.

CENTRAL VANCOUVER ISLAND

From Nanaimo, it's 35 km northwest up Hwy. 19 to one of Vancouver Island's main highway junctions, where Hwy. 4 spurs west to Port Alberni and the island's west coast. Follow Hwy. 4 to its end to reach **Pacific Rim National Park,** a long, narrow park protecting the wild coastal strip and some magnificent sandy beaches, and **Tofino,** a picturesque little town that makes the perfect base for sea kayaking, whalewatching, or fishing excursions.

Continuing north from the junction, you can take either the new Inland Island Highway or the old coast-hugging route, which passes some of Canada's best beaches and the resort towns that have sprung up around them. Approximately halfway up the island is the **Comox Valley,** a popular year-round destination where you'll find more great beaches and fishing, and great downhill skiing on the back doorstep during the colder months.

HIGHWAY 4
TOWARD PORT ALBERNI

Englishman's Falls Provincial Park

After turning off Hwy. 19, make your first stop here, where Englishman River—full of steelhead, cutthroat, and rainbow trout—cascades down from high Beaufort Range snowfields in a series of beautiful waterfalls. Within the park you'll find a picnic area, easy hiking trails to both the upper and lower falls, crystal-clear swimming holes, and plenty of campsites among tall cedars and lush ferns ($9.50 per night; no showers).

To get there, turn off Hwy. 4 on Errington Rd., three km west of the highway junction, and continue another nine km, following signs.

Coombs

This small community comprises a row of old-fashioned country stores scattered around **Coombs Emporium and Frontier Town.** The shops sell everything from pottery planters, jewelry, and assorted knickknacks to tasty snacks and cool drinks. Check out **Wood and Bone**

Crafts for a unique souvenir, and cast your eyes toward the grass-covered roof of **Old Country Market,** where several goats can be seen contentedly grazing, seemingly oblivious to the amused, camera-clicking visitors. Coombs is also home to **Butterfly World,** tel. (250) 248-7026, housing 1,000 free-flying butterflies, and **Emerald Forest Bird Garden,** tel. (250) 248-7282.

Little Qualicum Falls
Provincial Park and Vicinity

This 440-hectare park lies along the north side of the highway, 10 km west of Coombs. The park's main hiking trail leads alongside the Little Qualicum River to a series of plummeting waterfalls. Take your fishing pole along the riverside trail and catch a trout, stop for an exhilarating dip in one of the icy emerald pools, and stay the night in a sheltered riverside campsite ($12 per night; no showers).

The source of the Little Qualicum River is **Cameron Lake,** a large, deep-green, trout-filled body of water just outside the western park boundary. Magnificent old-growth forest encircles the lake, and at the west end is 136-hectare **MacMillan Provincial Park.** Here a 500-meter trail leads to majestic **Cathedral Grove,** a stand of 200- to 600-year-old Douglas firs that grow up to 70 meters high and 1.5 meters wide.

Mount Arrowsmith Regional Park

South of the highway, along a sometimes-rough 27-km logging road, this 489-hectare park offers several trails leading to the summit of 1,818-meter Mt. Arrowsmith. In winter, a few old lifts crank up at **Mt. Arrowsmith Ski Hill,** tel. (250) 723-1300; lift tickets are $23.

PORT ALBERNI AND VICINITY

If you hit Port Alberni on a cloudy day, you won't know what you're missing—until the sky lifts! Then beautiful tree-mantled mountains suddenly appear, and Alberni Inlet and the Somass River turn a stunning deep blue. Situated at the

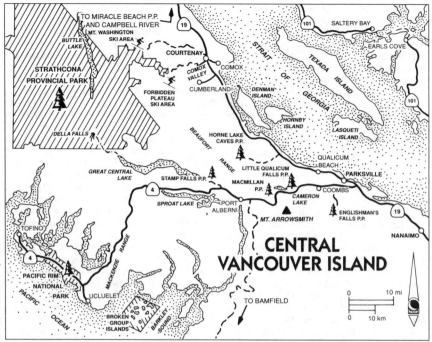

head of the island's longest inlet, Port Alberni is an industrial town of 19,500 centered around the forestry industry. The town's three mills—lumber, specialty lumber, and pulp and paper—are its main sources of income. The mills belch evil-smelling steam into the atmosphere, but residents reckon that you get used to the odor; it's worst in winter when trapped under low clouds. The town is also a port for pulp and lumber freighters, deep-sea vessels, and commercial fishing boats.

Despite all the industry, Port Alberni has much to offer, including a couple of interesting museums, nearby provincial parks, and a modern marina filled with both charter fishing boats and tour boats offering cruises to Barkley Sound.

Sights

Follow the signs from Hwy. 4 to brightly decorated **Alberni Harbour Quay** at the end of Argyle Street. For a great view of the quay, harbor, marina, inlet, and surrounding mountains, climb the clock tower. Also on the quay is the **Forestry Information Centre,** tel. (250) 724-7890, where you can view interpretive displays on logging, milling, and replanting, and arrange tours through local industry. It's open in summer, daily 10 a.m.-6 p.m.; the rest of the year, Wed.-Fri. noon-4:30 p.m., Sat.-Sun. 10 a.m.-6 p.m. Through summer a **steam train** runs along the waterfront Sat.-Sun. 11 a.m.-4 p.m.; adults $3, children $2.

Find out more about the origins of the famous West Coast Trail, see a collection of native artifacts, or tinker with a variety of operating motorized machines from the forestry industry at the **Alberni Valley Museum,** on the corner of 10th Ave. and Wallace St., tel. (250) 723-2181. It's open Tues.-Sat. 10 a.m.-5 p.m.; admission by donation.

MV *Lady Rose*

This vintage Scottish coaster has been serving the remote communities of Alberni Inlet and Barkley Sound for over 50 years as a supply and passenger service. But because of the spectacular scenery along the route, the cruise is also one of the island's biggest tourist attractions. Depending on the time of year, orcas and gray whales, seals, sea lions, porpoises, river otters, bald eagles, and all sorts of seabirds join you on your trip through magnificent Barkley Sound. The vessel is also a great way to reach the remote fishing village of Bamfield (see below) and the only way to reach the Broken Group Islands (see the Special Topic).

Year-round, the MV *Lady Rose* departs Alberni Harbour Quay Tuesday, Thursday, and Saturday at 8 a.m., reaching Kildonan at 10 a.m. and Bamfield at 12:30 p.m., then departing Bamfield at 1:30 p.m. and docking back in Port Alberni at 5:30 p.m. In summer, sailings are also made to Bamfield on Sunday, with a special stop for kayakers in the Broken Group Islands. If you want to stay longer in Bamfield, accommodations are available (see "Practicalities" under "Bamfield," below). June-Sept. an extra route is added to the schedule, with the vessel departing Monday, Wednesday, and Friday at 8 a.m. for the Broken Group Islands, arriving at Ucluelet at 1 p.m. for a one-hour layover before returning to Port Alberni around 6:30 p.m. One-way fares from Port Alberni are: Kildonan $12, Bamfield $19, Broken Group Islands $20, Ucluelet $22. Children under 16 travel for half price. For further details call (250) 723-8313 or (800) 663-7192. In summer the *Lady Rose* does a roaring business—book as far ahead as possible.

Fishing
Along with at least one other Vancouver Island town, Port Alberni claims to be the "Salmon capital of the world." The fishing in Alberni Inlet is certainly world-class, but probably no better than a handful of other places on the island.

coho salmon

The main salmon runs occur in fall, when hundreds of thousands of salmon migrate up Alberni Inlet to their spawning grounds.

The best way to get the rundown on fishing charters is by heading down to the full-service **Port Alberni Marina,** 5104 River Rd., tel. (250) 723-8022; open daily, in summer dawn to dusk, in winter 9 a.m.-5 p.m. The owners, local fishing guides, have put together all kinds of printed information on local fishing. They know all the best spots, and know how to catch the lunkers. Expect to pay $300 for two people, $330 for three for a six-hour guided morning charter; $200 for two, $220 for three, for a four-hour guided afternoon charter. The marina also rents boats (from $15 per hour or $90 per day, plus gas) and fishing rods ($12 per day), sells bait and tackle, and provides information about sportfishing/accommodations packages in the region.

The annual **Port Alberni Salmon Festival** fishing derby each Labour Day weekend (first Monday in September) draws anglers from afar in the hopes of winning over $65,000 in prize money. Crowds of fishing enthusiasts gather to watch thousands of pounds of salmon being weighed in at Clutesi Haven Marina, and multitudes of salmon-eaters throng to a three-day salmon barbecue.

Della Falls
Located in the remote southern section of **Strathcona Provincial Park** (see "Highway 28" under "Northern Vancouver Island," later in this chapter), difficult-to-reach Della Falls is accessible only from Port Alberni. The 440-meter waterfall northwest of town is one of the highest in North America, and getting to it requires a lot of effort: first by boat or canoe along Great Central Lake, then by a rough 16-km hike (eight-hours each way) up the Drinkwater Creek watershed.

Accommodations and Camping
Whether you're in search of a tent site with water views, a

BOB RACE

cozy bed and breakfast, or a luxurious motel room, Port Alberni has something to suit, although Port Alberni motels are generally more expensive than those on other parts of the island.

On the main road through town is **Esta Villa Motel,** 4014 Johnston Rd., tel. (250) 724-1261 or (800) 724-0844, a small accommodation with comfortable rooms for $57 s, $62 d. Within walking distance of the quay is **Bluebird Motel,** 3755 3rd Ave., tel. (250) 723-1153, which charges $49 s, $56 d. Similarly priced is **Southwind Motor Inn,** 4850 Beaver Creek Rd., tel. (250) 723-1300, across Kitsuksus Creek from downtown on the way out to the west coast. Right downtown, the **Coast Hospitality Inn,** 3835 Redford St., tel. (250) 723-8111 or (800) 663-1144, is part of the upmarket Coast Hotels and Resorts chain. Each of the large rooms is air-conditioned and features a comfortable bed and a writing desk; $114 s, $120 d.

The local municipal campground is in **Dry Creek Park,** south of downtown at the corner of 4th and Napier Streets. It's a pleasant little spot, within walking distance of the quay and with hookups and showers; $8-19 per night. Farther out is **China Creek Park Marina and Campground,** right on Alberni Inlet, tel. (250) 723-9812. This one offers a choice of open or wooded full-facility sites ($12-25 per site), a marina, sailboard rentals, great views of the inlet from a sandy log-strewn beach, and lots of bald eagles for company. To get there take 3rd Ave. south to Ship Creek Rd. and follow it for 14 km. **Stamp Falls Provincial Park,** northwest of Port Alberni, enjoys a beautiful location on the Stamp River; $9.50 per site. To get there follow Hwy. 4 west, and immediately after crossing Kitsuksus Creek take Beaver Creek Rd. north for 14 km.

Food

At any time of day, the best place to find something to eat is down at Alberni Harbour Quay. At the entrance to the quay is **Blue Door Cafe,** 5415 Argyle St., tel. (250) 723-8811, a small old-style place that's a real locals' hangout. Breakfasts are huge; an omelette with all the trimmings goes for $5-7 and bottomless self-serve coffee is an extra buck. Open daily from 5 a.m. On the quay itself, **Turtle Island Fish and**

Chips, 5440 Argyle St., tel. (250) 723-4227, features delicious salmon and chips for $7 as well as other seafood delicacies. Eat at the couple of tables supplied, or, better still, down on the grassy waterfront area.

Information

On the rise above town to the east is **Port Alberni Visitor Info Centre,** 2533 Redford St., tel. (250) 724-6535. This excellent facility is a great source of information on Pacific Rim National Park, transportation options to Bamfield, and all west coast attractions. It's open in summer, daily 8 a.m.-8 p.m.; the rest of the year, Mon.-Fri. 9 a.m.-5 p.m.

BAMFIELD

One of the island's most remote communities, this tiny fishing village lies along both sides of a narrow inlet on Barkley Sound. Most people arrive here aboard the **MV Lady Rose** from Port Alberni (see "Port Alberni and Vicinity," above), but the town is also linked to Port Alberni by a rough 100-km logging road. It's well worth the trip out for the day to go fishing, explore the seashore, or see the picturesque waterfront boardwalk, which is lined with a variety of little shops. Accommodations are available for those who want to stay longer. Bamfield is also the northern terminus of the **West Coast Trail** (see "Vicinity of Victoria," earlier in this chapter).

Practicalities

At the far end of the boardwalk is **Bamfield Inn,** tel. (250) 728-3354, one of the village's original buildings and now beautifully restored. The inn holds a guest lounge and an elegant restaurant, and also serves as the base for a variety of charter operators. Rates are $80-120 s or d. Accessed via a short boat trip is **Sherry's B&B,** tel. (250) 728-2323, which features beautiful natural surroundings, an outdoor hot tub, and a canoe for guest use. Rates of $45 per person include transfers and a cooked breakfast.

Get to Bamfield aboard the MV *Lady Rose,* tel. (250) 723-8313 or (800) 663-7192. This historic vessel departs Port Alberni's quay year-round on Tuesday, Thursday, and Saturday at 8 a.m., departing Bamfield for the return journey that same afternoon at 1:30 p.m. The fare is $19 each way.

WEST FROM PORT ALBERNI

Highway 4 west from Port Alberni meanders through unspoiled mountain wilderness, and you won't find a gas station or store for at least a couple of hours. The highway skirts the north shore of large Sproat Lake, whose clear waters draw keen trout and salmon anglers, campers, and photographers to 39-hectare **Sproat Lake Provincial Park** in summer. Provided they're not out squelching a fire, you can also see the world's largest water bombers—Martin Mars Flying Tankers—tied up here. Used to fight wildfires, these massive flying beasts—36 meters long and with a wingspan over 60 meters—skim across the lake, each filling its tank with 27 tons of water.

Ninety-one km from Port Alberni, Hwy. 4 splits, leading eight km south to Ucluelet or 34 km north through Pacific Rim National Park to Tofino.

UCLUELET

A small town of 1,800 on the northern edge of Barkley Sound, Ucluelet (pronounced yoo-CLOO-let) was first established centuries ago by the Nu-chal-nulth people as a fishing village. In the native language, the town's name means "People with a Safe Landing Place." During the last century or so, Ucluelet has also been a fur sealers' trading post and a logging and sawmill center. But fishing remains the steady mainstay, as evidenced by the town's resident fishing fleet and several fish-processing plants.

Today Ucluelet is obviously also benefitting from the tourism industry, netting a good share of all the west coast visitors. Many of these visitors also come for the fishing, particularly for chinook salmon (Feb.-Sept.) and halibut (May-July). The fall runs of chinook can yield fish up to 20 kilograms, and the town's busy charter fleet offers deep-sea fishing excursions as well as whalewatching trips.

fishing boats at Ucluelet

JANE AND BRUCE KING

Onshore attractions include the **lighthouse** near the end of Peninsula Rd., one of the most accessible along Canada's west coast, and **He-tin-kis Park,** where a short trail leads through a littoral rainforest to a small stretch of rocky beach.

Practicalities

A unique accommodation in town is offered by **Canadian Princess Resort** on Peninsula Rd., tel. (250) 726-7771 or (800) 663-7090. Here you can spend the night aboard the 75-meter steamship, *Canadian Princess,* which is permanently anchored in Ucluelet Harbour. The least expensive rooms aboard this historic gem are small and share bathroom facilities, but they're still good value at $49 s, $59 d. The resort also offers modern, expensive onshore rooms.

On the high side of Peninsula Rd. is **Peninsula Motor Inn,** tel. (250) 726-7751, which is basic and charges $50 s, $60 d. **Little Beach Resort,** 1187 Peninsula Rd., tel. (250) 726-4202, is a pleasant and quiet little spot within walking distance of a small sandy beach. Its 19 units go for $60-85 s or d. Fisherfolk congregate at **Island West Fishing Resort,** 160 Hemlock St., tel. (250) 726-4624, which has its own marina right on the inlet and serves as the base of operations for a wide range of charter boats. The resort also has a good restaurant and pub. In the height of summer, rooms—each with full kitchen—run $86 s, $89 d. Waterfront RV parking (not suitable for tents) costs $16-25.

Besides the pub and restaurant at Island West Fishing Resort, local eateries include **Blueberries,** up the hill at 1627 Peninsula Rd., tel. (250) 726-7707, which offers light meals daily until around 5 p.m., and **Peninsula Cafe,** in the front of the Peninsula Motor Inn at 1648 Peninsula Rd., tel. (250) 726-7751, which sports red vinyl booths and faded logging posters, and offers a Chinese and western menu (burgers from $3, entrees from $6.50).

Ucluelet Visitor Info Centre is just off Peninsula Rd. at 227 Main St., tel. (250) 726-4641. It's open daily in summer, and Mon.-Fri. only the rest of the year.

PACIFIC RIM NATIONAL PARK

Named for its location on the edge of the Pacific Ocean, this park encompasses a long and narrow strip of coast that has been battered by the sea for eons. The park comprises three "units," each very different in nature and each accessed in different ways. The section at the end of Hwy. 4 is the **Long Beach Unit,** named for an 11-km stretch of beach that dominates the landscape. Accessible by vehicle, this is the most popular part of the park and is particularly busy in July and August. To the south, in Barkley Sound, the **Broken Group Islands Unit** (see the Special Topic) encompasses an archipelago of 100 islands, accessible by the MV *Lady Rose* from Port Alberni. Farther south still is the **West Coast Trail Unit,** named for the famous 77-km-long hiking trail between Port Renfrew and Bamfield (see "Vicinity of Victoria," earlier in this chapter).

Flora and Fauna
Like the entire west coast of Vancouver Island, Pacific Rim National Park is dominated by littoral (coastal) rainforest. Closest to the ocean, clinging to the rocky shore, a narrow windswept strip of Sitka spruce is covered by salty water year-round. These forests of spruce are compact and low-growing, but form a natural windbreak for the old-growth forests of western hemlock

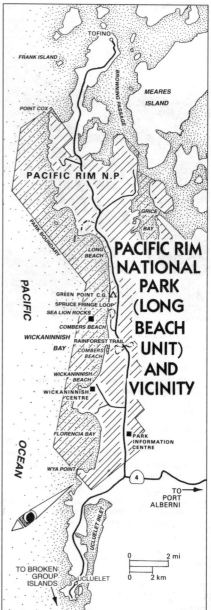

PACIFIC RIM N.P.

PACIFIC RIM NATIONAL PARK (LONG BEACH UNIT) AND VICINITY

© MOON PUBLICATIONS, INC.

ANDREW HEMPSTEAD

The driftwood-strewn beaches of Pacific Rim National Park are great for beachcombing.

and western red cedar farther inland. The old-growth forests are strewn with fallen trees, and lushly carpeted with mosses, shrubs, and ferns.

The ocean off western Canada reputedly holds more species of marinelife than any other temperate coast. Gray whales migrate up the coast each spring; seals and porpoises inhabit the park's waters year-round; sea lions overwinter on rocky offshore outcrops; and salmon spawn in the larger creeks through late fall. The tidal zone is the best place to search out smaller sea creatures—anemones, shellfish, and starfish are all colorful residents of the rocky shoreline.

The park's largest land mammal is the black bear, some of which occasionally wander down to the beach in search of food. Also present are blacktail deer, raccoons, otters, and mink. Bald eagles are year-round residents, but it's the migratory birds that arrive in the largest numbers—in spring and fall, thousands of Canada geese, pintails, mallards, and black brants converge

on the vast tidal mudflats of **Grice Bay,** in the north of the park beyond the golf course.

Climate

Pacific Rim National Park receives heavy rainfall (3000 millimeters annually), and the weather here can only be described as extremely changeable. It can be windy and wet in the morning, yet warm and dry in the afternoon—always carry extra clothes and raingear while exploring the park. In summer the average temperature is 15° C, and dense morning fog usually clears in the afternoon. In winter the park experiences a good proportion of its annual rainfall, and the average temperature is 6° C. In spring you can expect 10° C days, 6° C days in autumn.

Long Beach

Ensconced between rocky headlands here lies more than 11 km of hard-packed white sand, covered in twisted driftwood, shells, and the occasional Japanese glass fishing float. Dense rainforest and the high snowcapped peaks of the Mackenzie Range form a beautiful backdrop, while offshore lie craggy surf-battered isles that are home to a myriad of marinelife. You can access the beach at many places, but first stop at the **Wickaninnish Centre,** tel. (250) 726-4212, which overlooks the entire beach from a protected southern cove. This is the place to learn about the natural and human history of both the park and the ocean through a variety of exhibits and spectacular hand-painted murals. The center is open mid-March to mid-October, daily 10:30 a.m.-6 p.m.

Through summer Long Beach attracts hordes of visitors. Most just wander along the beach soaking up the smells and sounds of the sea, but some brave the cool waters for swimming or surfing. The waves here are reputed to be Canada's best; rent boards and wetsuits in Ucluelet and Tofino. In winter, hikers dress for the harsh elements and walk the surf-pounded beach in search of treasures, admiring the ocean's fury during the many ferocious storms.

Hiking

The most obvious place for a walk is Long Beach, but a number of other options are worth consideration. From the Wickaninnish Centre, an 800-meter trail (15 minutes each way) leads south around a windswept headland, passing a number of small coves and Lismer Beach, then descending a boardwalk to pebbly **South Beach.** Back up the hill, the **Wickaninnish Trail** leads 2.5 km (50 minutes each way) over to Florencia Bay. The beach along the bay can also be accessed by road off the Wickaninnish Centre access road. Continuing northwest toward Tofino, the **Rainforest Trail** traverses an old-growth littoral rainforest in two, one-km loops (allow 20 minutes for each). Farther north, at the back of the Combers Beach parking lot, is the trailhead for the 1.5-km (30-minute) **Spruce Fringe Loop.** This trail leads along the beach past piles of driftwood and through a forest of Sitka spruce.

Campgrounds

The park's one official campground fills up *very* fast every day through summer. But it's in a marvelous location behind **Green Point,** a beautiful bluff above the beach. Facilities include drive-in sites, washrooms, picnic tables, and plenty of firewood, but no showers or hookups. Mid-March to mid-October, sites are $18 per night; the rest of the year they're $8 per night. The walk-in campground at Schooner Cove, still marked on many maps, is now closed. The closest commercial campgrounds are in Ucluelet and Tofino.

Services and Information

There are no stores or gas stations in the park, but supplies and gas are available in Ucluelet and Tofino. The **Wickaninnish Restaurant,** in the Wickaninnish Centre, tel. (250) 726-7706, overlooks the wide sweeping bay for which it's named. It's not particularly cheap (lunch entrees $9-18), but the views are magnificent and even if you don't indulge in a full meal, it's a

THE BROKEN GROUP ISLANDS

These 100 or so forested islands in the mouth of Barkley Sound, south of Ucluelet, once held native villages and some of the first trading posts on the coast. Now they're inhabited only by wildlife, and visited primarily by campers paddling through the archipelago in canoes and kayaks. The islands offer few beaches, so paddlers come ashore in the many sheltered bays.

Marinelife abounds in the cool and clear waters; seals, porpoises, and gray whales are present year-round. Birdlife is also prolific. Bald eagles, blue herons, and cormorants are permanent residents, and large numbers of loons and Canada geese stop by on their spring and fall migration routes.

The archipelago extends almost 15 km out to sea from Sechart. The protected islands of **Hand, Gibraltar, Dodo,** and **Willis** all hold campsites and are good destinations for novice paddlers. Farther out, the varying sea conditions make a higher level of skill necessary. Predictably, a westerly wind blows up early each afternoon through summer, making paddling more difficult.

Everyone planning a trip to the islands should buy Marine Chart 3670 from Canadian Hydrographic Service, Chart Sales and Distribution Office, Institute of Ocean Services, 9860 W. Saanich Rd., P.O. Box 6000, Sidney, BC V8L 4B2; $9. The chart includes detailed navigational information on the islands and park, as well as a handy description of campsite facilities. Some islands are marked as having drinking water, but sources are unreliable so plan on bringing your own.

The best way to reach the Broken Group Islands is aboard the **MV *Lady Rose*** from Port Alberni or Ucluelet. Based in Port Alberni, this historic vessel departs Alberni Harbour Quay June-Sept., Monday, Wednesday, and Friday at 8 a.m., dropping canoeists and kayakers at the abandoned **Sechart Whaling Station.** The *Lady Rose* then continues to Ucluelet, departing that village at 2 p.m. and making another stop at Sechart before returning to Port Alberni. In July and August, an additional Sunday sailing departs Port Alberni at 8 a.m., stopping at Sechart and returning directly to Port Alberni. The one-way fare between Port Alberni and Sechart is $19; between Ucluelet and Sechart it's $12.50.

The company that operates the boat also rents canoes and kayaks ($30 and $30-45 per day, respectively), which are left at Sechart so you don't have to pay a transportation charge. If you bring your own canoe or kayak, the transportation charge is $15-20 each way. The trip out on this boat is worthwhile just for the scenery, with the Ucluelet sailing passing right through the heart of the archipelago. For further information and reservations (necessary in summer), call (250) 723-8313 or (800) 663-7192. From Ucluelet, **Subtidal Adventures,** tel. (250) 726-7336, offers day-trips out to the islands.

great place to sip a coffee while watching the ocean. Sunday brunch is particularly popular. The restaurant is open mid-March through mid-October, daily 10:30 a.m.-6 p.m.

The **Park Information Centre,** tel. (250) 726-4212, is on the north side of Hwy. 4 just inside the park boundary (coming from Port Alberni, turn right toward Tofino at the Ucluelet/Tofino highway junction). It holds a number of exhibits and displays, and lots of information. Open daily mid-March to mid-June, 10 a.m.-6 p.m.; mid-June through August, 8 a.m.-8 p.m.; September to mid-October, 10 a.m.-6 p.m. For more information, contact the Superintendent, Pacific Rim National Park, P.O. Box 280, Ucluelet, BC V0R 3A0, tel. (250) 726-7721.

Park Fee

You're not charged a fee just to travel straight through the park to Tofino, but if you stop anywhere en route a strictly enforced charge applies. A one-day permit is $5 per person to a maximum of $10 per vehicle, and an annual **Great Western Pass,** good for entry to all 11 of western Canada's national parks, is $35 per person to a maximum of $70 per vehicle.

TOFINO

The bustling fishing village of Tofino sits at the very end of a long narrow peninsula, with the only road access to the outside world being winding Hwy. 4. The closest town of any size is Port Alberni, 130 km to the east (allow at least two hours); Victoria is 340 km distant.

Originally the site of a native Clayoquot village, Tofino was one of the first points in Canada to be visited by Captain Cook. It was named in 1792 for Don de Vincent Tofino, a hydrographer with a Spanish expedition. Aside from contact with fur traders and whalers, the entire district remained basically unchanged for almost 100 years.

Fishing has always been the mainstay of the local economy, but Tofino is also a supply center for the several hundred hermits living along the secluded shores of the sound and for the hordes of visitors that come in summer to visit Pacific Rim National Park, just to the south. In winter it's a quiet, friendly community with a population of fewer than 1,200. In summer the population

swells to several times that size and the village springs to life—fishing boats pick up supplies and deposit salmon, cod, prawns, crabs, halibut, and other delicacies of the sea, and cruising, whalewatching, and fishing boats, along with seaplanes, do a roaring business introducing visitors to the natural wonders of the west coast.

The town lies on the southern edge of sheltered **Clayoquot Sound,** known worldwide for an ongoing fight by environmentalists to save the world's largest remaining coastal temperate forest. Around 200,000 hectares of this old-growth forest remains, with logging eating away at the amount every year. An influx of environmentally conscious residents over the last decade has added flavor to one of the west coast's most picturesque and relaxing towns. And due to a large number of aware residents who like Tofino exactly the way it is, it's unlikely that high-rise hotels or fast-food chains will ever spoil this peaceful coastal paradise.

Sun, Sand, and Surf

If you fancy a long walk along a fabulous shell-strewn stretch of white sand, like to sit on craggy rocks watching the waves disintegrate into white spray, or just want a piece of sun all your own to lie in and work on your tan, head for **Chesterman Beach,** just south of Tofino. From that beach, at low tide you can walk all the way out to **Frank Island** to watch the surf pound the exposed side while the tide creeps in and cuts you off from civilization for a few hours. The turnoff (not marked) to Chesterman Beach is Lynn Rd., on the right just past the Dolphin Motel as you leave Tofino. Follow the road and park at one of three small parking lots; the parking lot at the corner of Lynn and Chesterman Beach Rds. is closest to Frank Island. Surfers wanting to hit the water should head south of town to **Live To Surf,** 1182 Hwy. 4, tel. (250) 725-3363. The shop rents surfboards for $25 per day and wetsuits for $18. They'll tell you where the best surf can be found, and if there's no surf, they'll tell you how good it was last week.

Whalewatching

Each spring around 20,000 gray whales migrate between Baja and Alaska, passing through the waters off Tofino between March and May. Most of them continue north, but some stay in local waters through summer. Their feeding grounds are about 30 km up the coast at **Maquinna Marine Park,** accessible by a 20-minute boat trip. During the spring migration and some feeding periods, gray whales are also frequently sighted in the calm inland waters around **Meares Island,** just off Tofino.

Whalewatching is one of the most popular activities in town, and a variety of companies search out whales to watch them cruise up the coast, diving, surfacing, and spouting. On the whalewatching trips, you'll likely spy other marinelife as well; look for sea lions and puffins sunning themselves on offshore rocks, dolphins and harbor seals frolicking in the bays and inlets, and majestic bald eagles gracefully swooping around in the sky or perching in the treetops.

Trips depart March-Oct. and generally last 2-3 hours. Expect to pay about $50 per person. Shop around and compare prices with: **Chinook Charters,** 450 Campbell St., tel. (250) 725-2360 or (800) 665-3646; **Jamie's Whaling Station,** 606 Campbell St., tel. (250) 725-3919 or (800) 667-9913; **Remote Passages,** 568 Campbell St., tel. (250) 725-3330 or (800) 666-9833; **Sea Trek,** 441 Campbell St., tel. (250) 725-4412 or (800) 811-9155; and the **Whale Centre,** 411 Campbell St., tel. (250) 725-2132 (head to the Whale Centre to see a 13-meter-long gray whale skeleton).

Sea Kayaking
Exploring the waters around Tofino by sea kayak has become increasingly popular in recent years. **Tofino Sea Kayaking Company,** 320 Main St., tel. (250) 725-4222 or (800) TOFINO4, has designed tours to meet the demand and suit all levels of experience. Excursions

range from a four-hour paddle to Meares Island ($50 per person) to an overnight trip to a remote lodge ($270 per person). The company's experienced staff will also help adventurous, independent paddlers plan an itinerary—many camping areas lie within a one-day paddle of Tofino. Single kayak rentals are $43 for one day or $35 per day for two or more days. Double kayaks are $74 and $65, respectively. Rental prices include all the accessories. At the company base, right on the harbor, is a shop selling provisions, accessories (such as marine charts), and a wide range of local literature. Also here are a coffee shop and a few rooms renting for $60 per room per night.

Hot Spring
Pamper yourself and take a boat or floatplane to **Hotsprings Cove,** Vancouver Island's only hot spring. Water bubbles out of the ground at a temperature of 87° C (189° F), tumbles over a cliff, then drops down through a series of pools—each large enough for two or three people—and into the sea. Lobsterize yourself silly in the first pool, or go for the ultimate in hot/cold torture by immersing yourself in the last pool, where at high tide you'll be slapped by breathtakingly refreshing ocean waves.

Several companies along Campbell Street offer excursions out to the hot springs. Shop around for the best deal, but expect to pay around $70-80 for a six- to seven-hour trip departing around 10 a.m., with about three hours ashore at the hot springs and the chance to see whales en route. Companies offering this trip include: **Chinook Charters,** 450 Campbell St., tel. (250) 725-2360 or (800) 665-3646; **Jamie's**

BOB RACE

Whaling Station, 606 Campbell St., tel. (250) 725-3919 or (800) 667-9913; **Remote Passages,** 568 Campbell St., tel. (250) 725-3330 or (800) 666-9833; **Sea Trek,** 441 Campbell St., tel. (250) 725-4412 or (800) 811-9155; and the **Whale Centre,** 411 Campbell St., tel. (250) 725-2132. Even with all these operators, business is brisk, so book ahead if possible. **Tofino Airlines,** based at the 1st St. dock, tel. (250) 725-4454, offers a scenic 15-minute flight to the hot springs by floatplane; from $95 per person roundtrip, minimum three persons.

Eagle Aerie Gallery

This gallery, 350 Campbell St., tel. (250) 725-3235, features the excellent paintings, prints, and sculptures of Roy Henry Vickers, a well-known and highly respected Tsimshian artist. You can watch a video about the artist, then browse among the artworks—primarily native Canadian designs and outdoor scenes with clean lines and brilliant colors. If you fall for one of the most popular paintings but can't afford it, you can buy it in card or poster form. The gallery itself is built on the theme of a west coast native longhouse, with a carved and painted exterior and interior totem poles. Open in summer, daily 9 a.m.-8 p.m.; the rest of the year, daily 9:30 a.m.-5:30 p.m. Vickers is also featured in Victoria at **Eagle's Moon Gallery,** 1010 Government St., tel. (250) 361-4184.

Pacific Rim Whale Festival

Tofino and Ucluelet join together each spring to put on the annual Pacific Rim Whale Festival, which features educational shows and special events in the adjacent national park, a native song and dance festival, crab races, plays at the local theater, dances, concerts, and a multitude of events and activities in celebration of the gray whale spring migration. The festival takes place the last two weeks of March and the first week of April. To receive a Pacific Rim Whale Festival package, including a calendar of events, whale-watching information, and accommodations brochures, write the festival office at P.O. Box 476, Tofino, BC V0R 2Z0, or call (250) 725-3414.

Accommodations and Camping

Tofino boasts plenty of accommodations, both in town and on the outskirts. But getting a room or a campsite in summer can be difficult if you just turn up, so book as far ahead as possible. Without exception, all accommodations offer deeply discounted off-season rates.

The best choice in town is **Cable Cove Inn,** 201 Main St., tel. (250) 725-4236 or (800) 663-6449. The inn is tucked away in a quiet location overlooking a small cove, yet it's only a couple of hundred meters from the center of town. Each of the six rooms features a private deck and a fireplace, and is well-furnished in a casual yet elegant style. The least-expensive room is $95 s or d while the others, ranging $125-175, each have a jacuzzi. Outside of summer, rooms range $65-125. A continental breakfast is included in these rates. Book well in advance to be assured of a room.

Of Tofino's regular motels, least expensive is **Dolphin Motel,** on the highway into town, tel. (250) 725-3377, which charges $48 s, $53 d. Continuing into town, **Tofino Swell Lodge** is just off the highway at 341 Olsen Rd., tel. (250) 725-3274. Above a busy marina, this small motel offers well-decorated rooms, shared use of a fully equipped kitchen and living room (complete with stereo, TV, and telescope), and incredible views of Tofino Inlet, tree-covered Meares Island, and distant snowcapped mountains. Summer rates are $68-90 s or d.

In the best location in town, right beside the main dock, is **Himwitsa Lodge,** 300 Main St., tel. (250) 725-3319 or (800) 899-1947. No expense has been spared in the four massive upstairs suites, each with hot tub, comfortable lounge and writing area, television and video cassette player, fully equipped kitchen, and private balcony with spectacular ocean views. Summer rates are $185 s or d, $145 the rest of the year.

All Tofino's campgrounds are on the beaches south of town. Best of the bunch is **Bella Pacifica Campground,** tel. (250) 725-3400, which is right on MacKenzie Beach and offers protected tent sites, full hookups, hot showers, and a laundry. Sites are $20-27. Another choice is **Crystal Cove Beach Resort,** also on MacKenzie Beach, tel. (250) 725-4213.

Food

Tofino has grocery stores, fish and seafood stores, bakeries, and a variety of cafes and restaurants, many of them serving locally caught seafood. The **Common Loaf Bake Shop,** 180 1st St., tel. (250) 725-3915, is a favorite with locals (cinnamon rolls $1.35); sit outside or upstairs, where you'll have a magnificent view down Tofino's main street and across the sound. It's open daily 8 a.m.-6 p.m. Another popular cafe is the **Coffee Pod,** along the main highway at 4th St., tel. (250) 725-4246, serving healthy sandwiches, salads, and a variety of cakes and pastries.

The best views in town are from the **Sea Shanty,** 300 Main St., tel. (250) 725-2902, part of the Himwitsa Lodge complex above the marina. Breakfasts are around $7, pastas $13-15, and seafood delicacies—the bulk of the menu—over $17.

In Weigh West Marine Resort's **Blue Heron Dining Room,** 634 Campbell St., tel. (250) 725-3277, you can savor delicious clam chowder with garlic toast for $6.50, and seafood or steak dinners for $13-19. In the same complex is a pub with inexpensive meals and water views. The **Loft,** 346 Campbell St., tel. (250) 725-4241, is open daily 7 a.m.-8 p.m. in summer for breakfast ($4-9), lunch ($6-11), and dinner ($9-21). The house specialty is west coast seafood, the atmosphere is relaxed, and the service is smart.

Transportation, Services, and Information
Island Coach Lines, tel. (250) 725-3101 or (800) 318-0818, runs one bus daily between Victoria and Tofino. The bus departs Victoria at 8:05 a.m. and Nanaimo at 11 a.m. before heading west along Hwy. 4, arriving in Tofino at 3:30 p.m. The return service departs Tofino at 4:10 p.m., arriving back in Nanaimo at 8:05 p.m. and Victoria at 11 p.m. The one-way fare from Victoria is $43.70, from Nanaimo $31.40.

Though it doesn't offer any scheduled flights, **Tofino Airlines,** based at the foot of 1st St., tel. (250) 725-4454, provides a variety of scenic floatplane flights and charters; around $40 per person for a 20-minute flight.

The **post office,** a **laundromat,** and **Tofino General Hospital,** tel. (250) 725-3212, are all on Campbell Street. **Tofino Visitor Info Centre,** 346 Campbell St., tel. (250) 725-3414, is open in summer, daily 9 a.m.-9 p.m.; the rest of the year, Mon.-Fri. 11 a.m.-4 p.m.

PARKSVILLE TOWARD COURTENAY

Back on the east side of the island, the new Inland Island Highway north of the Hwy. 4 junction bypasses a stretch of coast that has developed as a popular holiday area, with many beaches, resorts, and waterfront campgrounds. The new route rejoins Hwy. 19 at Mud Bay.

Parksville
The coastline between Parksville (pop. 10,000) and Qualicum Beach is fringed with golden sand. Parksville Beach claims "the warmest water in the whole of Canada." When the tide goes out along this stretch of the coast, it leaves a couple of kilometers of sand exposed to the sun. When the water returns, voilà—sand-heated water. **Rathtrevor Beach Provincial Park,** a 348-hectare chunk of coastline just south of Parksville, features a fine two-km-long sandy beach, a wooded upland area, nature trails, and birdwatching action that's particularly good in early spring, when seabirds swoop in for an annual herring feast. Plenty of campsites are available, but in summer you'll need to line up early in the morning to stake your claim; $9.50-15.50 per night. Also on Rathtrevor Beach is **Gray Crest Seaside Resort,** 1115 East Island Hwy., tel. (250) 248-6513 or (800) 663-2636, offering 43 modern, kitchen-equipped units, some with a fireplace and jacuzzi; $98-149 s or d. Many other motels line this strip of coast, but none are particularly cheap. On the south side of Parksville, **Arbutus Grove Motel,** 1182 East Island Hwy., tel. (250) 248-6422, offers basic but clean and comfortable accommodations for $65 s or d.

On the southern outskirts of town, the **Parksville Visitor Info Centre,** 1275 East Island Hwy., tel. (250) 248-3613, is open in summer, daily 8 a.m.-8 p.m.; the rest of the year, Mon.-Fri. 9 a.m.-5 p.m. Adjacent to the information center is **Craig Heritage Park,** tel. (250) 248-6966, comprising historic buildings such as a post office and church; admission is free.

Qualicum Beach
This small beach community (pop. 7,000) is generally quieter than Parksville, but it shares the same golden sands of Georgia Strait and attracts the same droves of beachgoers, sun

worshippers, anglers, and golfers on summer vacation. The beachfront highway through town is lined with motels, resorts, and RV parks. The attractive downtown area, locally known as "the Village," is off the main highway and up a steep hill to the west. If you appreciate high-quality arts and crafts, detour off the main drag at this point and head for the **Old Schoolhouse Gallery and Art Centre,** 122 Fern Rd. W, tel. (250) 752-6133. The gallery occupies a beautifully restored 1912 building, while working artist studios below allow you a chance to see woodcarving, printmaking, pottery, weaving, painting, and fabric art in progress. Don't miss a stop at the gallery shop, where all kinds of original handcrafted treasures are likely to lure a couple of dollars out of your wallet.

At **Old Dutch Inn,** across from the water at 2690 West Island Hwy., tel. (250) 752-6914 or (800) 661-0199, facilities include an indoor pool, sauna and whirlpool, restaurant, and high-standard rooms for $80 s, $90 d. Farther north, 19 km from Qualicum Beach at Qualicum Bay, **Shady Shores Beach Resort,** 6695 West Island Hwy., tel. (250) 757-8595, enjoys a secluded location below the highway and right on the water. Rooms range $60-80 and each has a fully equipped kitchen. For the complete rundown on this stretch of the coast, stop in at **Qualicum Beach Visitor Info Centre,** on the waterfront side of the highway, tel. (250) 752-9532.

Horne Lake Caves Provincial Park

Continue 11 km beyond Qualicum Beach and turn off at the Horne Lake Store, following the road for 16 km to this intriguing park where the Qualicum River drains into Horne Lake. The park encompasses a system of caves at the base of the Beaufort Range, and also offers good swimming and fishing, canoe rentals, and camping for $15 per night. Several different guided tours of the caves are offered. The 90-minute tour of Riverbend Cave includes a short walk as well as underground exploration and explanation; $15 per person. Two caves are open for exploration without a guide. There's no charge for entering these caves, but you'll need a helmet and light source, which can be rented. All caves are open mid-June to September, daily 10 a.m.-4 p.m. For details call (250) 757-8687.

Denman Island

Island-hoppers can catch the Denman Island ferry from **Buckley Bay** for a one-km, 10-minute trip across Baynes Sound to this quiet rural island. Fishing, boating, and scuba diving are prime draws here, and you'll also find good beaches, parks, and an artisan community.

Just a short walk from the ferry, the downtown area boasts a number of turn-of-the-century heritage buildings. On the opposite side of the island, 23-hectare **Fillongley Provincial Park** features forested trails, long stretches of beach, and campsites for $9.50. At **Boyle Point Park** in the south, an 800-meter loop trail (20 minutes roundtrip) leads to a lookout with views across to Chrome Island, where a lighthouse stands.

Get to Denman Island with **BC Ferries,** tel. (250) 386-3431 or, toll-free in B.C., (888) BC-FERRY. The service runs hourly 7 a.m.-11 p.m. Peak roundtrip fare is adults $3.50, children $1.75, cars $9.25, canoes and kayaks $1.75.

Hornby Island

Every hour, 8 a.m.-6 p.m., a small ferry departs the southern end of Denman Island for Hornby Island, a short, 10-minute run across Lambert Channel. The fares are the same as the Buckley Bay–Denman Island run. This small, seldom-visited island has great beaches, especially along crescent-shaped Tribune Bay, where the longest stretch of sand is protected by 95-hectare **Tribune Bay Provincial Park.** Continue beyond that park and take St. John's Point Rd. to 287-hectare **Helliwell Provincial Park,** on a rugged, forested headland where trails lead to high bluffs.

Neither of those provincial parks permit camping. Instead, stay at **Tribune Bay Campsite,** tel. (250) 335-2359, on the beach; tent sites $17, electrical hookups $23. Right by the ferry dock is **Hornby Island Resort,** 4305 Shingle Spit Rd., tel. (250) 335-0136, which offers a small beach, tennis courts, boat rentals, a restaurant and pub, and a laundry. Rooms are $65 s, $70 d; campsites $14-21 per night.

THE COMOX VALLEY

The three communities of **Courtenay, Cumberland,** and **Comox** lie in the beautiful Comox

FORBIDDEN PLATEAU

This high plateau west of the Comox Valley was "forbidden" according to native legend. The village of Comox was threatened by Cowichan warriors many moons ago, so the Comox men sent their women and children up the mountain to be out of harm's way. When the danger was over, the men went up to collect their families but they had disappeared without a trace—and were never seen again. Not knowing how or why the party disappeared off the face of the planet, the plateau became for the Comox a fearful and forbidden place. But judging by the number of skiers and hikers who explore Forbidden Plateau and return to tell the tale, the legend has been put to rest.

Valley, nestled between Georgia Strait and high snowcapped mountains to the west. Welcome to the "Recreational Capital of Canada," where you can enjoy beaches, excellent downhill and cross-country skiing, fishing, golfing, and camping. The valley lies almost halfway up the island, 220 km from Victoria, but is also linked to the mainland by ferry.

Courtenay Sights

The valley's largest town and a commercial center for local farming, logging, fishing, and retirement communities, Courtenay (pop. 19,000) sprawls around the head of Comox Harbour. It's not particularly scenic but has a few interesting sights and plenty of accommodations. It was named for Capt. George Courtenay, who led the original surveying expedition of the area in 1848.

As you enter Courtenay from the south, you pass all sorts of restaurants, the information center, and motel after motel. Continue into the heart of town and you come to the pleasing downtown area with its cobbled streets, old-fashioned lamps, brick planters full of flowers, and numerous shops. The main attraction downtown is **Courtenay and District Museum,** 360 Cliffe Ave., tel. (250) 334-3611. It's housed in the 1928 Native Sons Hall, one of the world's largest vertical-log cabins. Step back in time to visually relive the history of the Comox Valley from prehistoric times to the present. Among the ex-

hibits are 80-million-year-old fossils of the Puntledge River elasmosaur, a series of realistic dioramas, and a replica of a bighouse containing many native artifacts and items, some formerly belonging to prominent chiefs. Finish up in the gift shop, which is well stocked with local arts and crafts. The museum is open May-Aug., daily 10 a.m.-4:30 a.m.; the rest of the year, Tues.-Sat. 10 a.m.-4:30 p.m.

From downtown, cross the bridge to the totem pole–flanked entrance to **Lewis Park,** at the confluence of the Puntledge and Tsolum Rivers. The two rivers join here to form the very short Courtenay River.

Comox Sights

In the small community of Comox, six km east of Courtenay, **Filberg Heritage Lodge and Park,** Comox Ave. at Filberg Rd., tel. (250) 339-2715, is worth a visit. The beautifully landscaped three-hectare grounds stretch along the waterfront and are open dawn to dusk year-round. The lodge dates to 1929 and is open in summer, daily 11 a.m.-5 p.m.; admission $2. You can visit with a variety of farm animals at the petting zoo, then savor lunch or afternoon tea in the Filberg Teahouse. In early August, the four-day **Filberg Festival** features gourmet food, free entertainment, and unique arts and crafts from the best of B.C.'s artisans.

For insight into Canadian Air Force history, browse through **CFB Comox Air Force Museum,** at the entrance to Comox Air Force Base at the end of Ryan Rd., tel. (250) 339-8162. It's open in summer, Wed.-Sun. 10 a.m.-4 p.m.; the rest of the year, Sat.-Sun. 10 a.m.-4 p.m.

North of the ferry terminal, **Seal Bay Nature Park** protects one of the region's few undeveloped stretches of coastline. Trails lead through a lush forest of Douglas fir and ferns to a pleasant rocky beach. The park is on Waveland Rd.; take Anderton Rd. north from downtown Comox.

Summer Recreation

The heart of 210,000-hectare **Strathcona Provincial Park** is accessed from Hwy. 28 west of Campbell River, but from Courtenay a gravel road climbs 35 km to **Forbidden Plateau,** a high alpine area in the extreme east of the park. The road ends at Mt. Washington Ski Area (see below) from where the one-km Battleship Lake

Trail (30 minutes each way) climbs onto the plateau's lower elevations. To really experience the alpine environment, continue up to the plateau proper and an extensive network of trails and backcountry campgrounds.

Comox Valley Kayaks, 2020 Cliffe Ave., tel. (250) 334-2628, offers sea-kayaking lessons for $35 per person, full-day guided trips from $55, and a variety of overnight trips from $240. Or rent a kayak for some exploration by yourself, around the local waterways or out on nearby Denman and Hornby Islands; $25-35 for three hours, $35-55 per day. The company also rents canoes—great for nearby Comox Lake—for $20 per day.

Skiing

In winter, you may be surprised to find all the least-expensive motels and a good proportion of the fanciest hotels in Comox Valley fully booked. Off-season for the rest of Vancouver Island is high season here, as hordes of skiers from the island and the mainland come to plant their poles on the slopes of two nearby ski resorts.

Mt. Washington, 35 km northwest of Courtenay, attracts the third-largest number of skiers of any British Columbian ski area. With a large self-contained base village, an annual snowfall of 10 meters, and winter temperatures that never get too cold, the resort's popularity is no wonder. Five chairlifts serve 370 hectares with the vertical rise a respectable 500 meters and the longest run just under two km.

Lift tickets are adults $36, seniors $28.50, and children $19.50. A cross-country pass to the groomed trails of Paradise Meadows is $10. Add to these prices the road-improvement tax that pays for sealing the access road; adults $2, children 50 cents.

Along with over 4,000 beds, the base village contains a number of restaurants and bars, a ski school, and a couple of rental shops. For general resort information call (250) 338-1386; for snow reports call (250) 338-1515 (or 604-657-2734 from Vancouver); for accommodations call (800) 699-6499.

To the south, accessed along a different road, is **Forbidden Plateau Ski Area,** the island's first ski resort. It's a small day-use-only area great for families. You'll find a wide variety of terrain, fabulous views, a day lodge and ski school, a chairlift, three T-bars, a rope tow, and a beginner's handletow. The lifts run Fri.-Sun. only. Downhill skiers pay $27 per day adults, $17 children; cross-country skiers pay $8 per day, which includes use of the chairlift to reach the beginning of the advanced trails. Ski and snowboard rentals are $27 per day, and lessons are available. For resort information call (250) 334-4744; for ski reports call (250) 338-1919.

Accommodations and Camping

The valley's least expensive motels are strung out along the highway (Cliffe Ave.) as you enter Courtenay from the south. Rates here are generally lower than on other parts of the island. The least expensive choice is **Anco Motel,** 1885 Cliffe Ave., tel. (250) 334-2451, with a heated outdoor pool; $45 s, $50 d, kitchens an extra $5. Offering excellent value on the same side of town is **Quality Inn—Kingfisher,** 4330 South Island Hwy., tel. (250) 338-1323 or (800) 663-7929, where the 30 rooms, each with a private balcony, are separated from the water by a grassy area and large heated pool. A lounge with outdoor seating sits right on the water, while the main building houses a seafood restaurant. Rates of $80 s, $90 d include a continental breakfast.

After crossing the Courtenay River on the Island Hwy., continue north one km to **Washington Inn,** 1001 Ryan Rd., tel. (250) 338-5441 or (800) 663-0191. This large hostelry features an indoor pool, sauna and whirlpool, lounge, and Mexican restaurant, all in a parkland setting. Rooms are large, and though simply furnished, offer good value at $69-99 s or d. In Comox, **Port Augusta Motel,** 2082 Comox Ave., tel. (250) 339-2277 or (800) 663-2141, is close to everything and charges $60 s, $65 d.

Campers have a couple of choices in the Comox Valley. Along Lazo Rd., east of Comox, is **Seaview Tent and Trailer Park,** tel. (250) 339-3946, within walking distance of the beach. Unserviced sites are $12, hookups $13-18. Just north of the ferry terminal, **King Coho Fishing Resort,** 1250 Wally Rd., tel. (250) 339-2039, is popular with anglers. Its facilities include a boat ramp, boat rentals, guided charters, a tackle shop, and a weigh station. Sites, some right on the waterfront, are $13-20.

Food

In downtown Courtenay, **Leung Grocery,** 456 5th St., tel. (250) 334-3824, is a local favorite serving inexpensive food at a well-worn formica counter. Across the road in more salubrious surroundings is **Union Street Grill,** 477 5th St., tel. (250) 897-0081. It's remarkably inexpensive, yet the portions are large. Breakfasts are around $5, lunches $4-7, and dinners from $7. Sunday brunch, from 10 a.m., is very popular. Another place for a cheap eat is **Betty's Place,** on the waterfront below the information center, tel. (250) 897-1410. Close to the museum, the large and friendly **Bar None Cafe,** 244 4th St., tel. (250) 334-3112, serves a vegetarian-based menu, fresh juices, and good coffee; open daily 8 a.m.-8 p.m.

Occupying one of Courtenay's original residences, the **Old House Restaurant,** 1760 Riverside Lane, tel. (250) 338-5406, sits among landscaped gardens right on the river. Downstairs is a casual restaurant/pub with a large outdoor deck, while upstairs is a more formal eatery with the ambience of an elegant country lodge. Both are open daily for lunch and dinner, with the Sunday brunch buffet (10 a.m.-2 p.m.; $15) filling the restaurant with hungry patrons.

Transportation

Getting to Courtenay by public transportation is easy. The most scenic way to arrive from Victoria is aboard the **VIA Rail Malahat train,** tel. (250) 383-4324 or (800) 561-8630. This service terminates in Courtenay, departing Victoria Mon.-Sat. at 8:15 a.m., Sunday at noon; $32.10 each way. **Island Coach Lines,** tel. (250) 334-2475 or (800) 318-0818, runs buses three times daily between Victoria and Courtenay ($31.55), continuing north to Campbell River.

BC Ferries, tel. (250) 386-3431 or, toll-free in B.C., (888) BCFERRY, offers sailings four times daily between Comox and Powell River, allowing mainlanders easy access to midisland beaches and ski slopes and saving visitors to northern Vancouver Island from having to backtrack down to Nanaimo or Victoria. The regular one-way fare for this 75-minute sailing is adults $7, cars $24, motorcycles $12, bicycles $2.50, canoes and kayaks $3.50. Roundtrip travelers can save 15% by buying the **Circlepac** ticket, good for roundtrip travel from mainland British Columbia as well as ferry connections along the Sunshine Coast.

Get around the valley with the **Comox Valley Transit System,** tel. (250) 334-2475. Scheduled services run Mon.-Sat. around Courtenay, out to Cumberland, and around Comox Harbour to Comox; $1.25 per sector. A rural service is also offered out to the ferry terminal ($2.50), but call ahead.

Information

Comox Valley Visitor Info Centre, 2040 Cliffe Ave., tel. (250) 334-3234, is on the main highway leading into Courtenay—look for the totem pole out front. It's open in summer, daily 8:30 a.m.-6 p.m.; the rest of the year, Mon.-Fri. 9 a.m.-6 p.m. Information is also available at **Cumberland Visitor Info Centre,** 2755 Dunsmuir Ave., tel. (250) 336-8313.

NORTH TOWARD CAMPBELL RIVER

An enjoyable place to pitch a tent, 137-hectare **Miracle Beach Provincial Park** is about three km off the main highway, 23 km north of Courtenay. Highlights include a wooded campground, sandy beach, good swimming and fishing, and a variety of nature trails. Look for porpoises and seals at the mouth of Black Creek, orcas in the Strait of Georgia, black-tailed deer, black bear, and raccoons in the park, and seabirds and crabs along the shoreline. In summer you can take a nature walk with a park naturalist, participate in a clambake or barbecue, or watch demonstrations and films at the Miracle Beach Nature House. Campsites cost $17 per night.

The road through the park ends at **Miracle Beach Resort,** tel. (250) 337-5171, offering tent sites with water views from $17, hookups from $21.

A few km north of Miracle Beach is **Salmon Point Resort,** 2176 Salmon Point Rd., tel. (250) 923-6605, also offering great views of the Strait of Georgia and the snowcapped peaks of the Coast Mountains. Facilities are excellent, and include a pool, a couple of recreation rooms (one for adults only), fishing guide service and tackle, heated bathrooms, hot showers, and a laundry. All campsites are set among small stands of pines; $18-26. Cabins start at $75 per night.

NORTHERN VANCOUVER ISLAND

The northern section of Vancouver Island is mountainous, heavily treed, dotted with lakes, riddled with rivers and waterfalls, and almost completely unsettled. Just one main highway serves the region, though hundreds of kilometers of logging roads penetrate the dense forests. The gateway to the north is **Campbell River,** a small city that proudly calls itself the "Salmon Capital of the World." From this point north, the Island Highway follows a winding route over mountains and through valleys, first hitting the coast near **Telegraph Cove,** one of Canada's most photogenic communities and the departure point for orca-watching trips to the nutrient-rich waters of Johnstone Strait and Robson Bight. The island's northernmost town is **Port Hardy,** terminus for ferries heading north to

Prince Rupert and the gateway to the wild west coast and **Cape Scott Provincial Park.**

CAMPBELL RIVER

This scenic resort town of 31,000, another self-proclaimed "Salmon Capital of the World," stretches along Discovery Passage 260 km north of Victoria and 235 km southeast of Port Hardy. Views from town—of tree-covered Quadra Island and the magnificent white-topped mountains of mainland British Columbia—are superb, but most visitors come for the superior fishing. It's the underwater topography that creates the prime angling conditions; Georgia Strait ends just south of Campbell River and Discov-

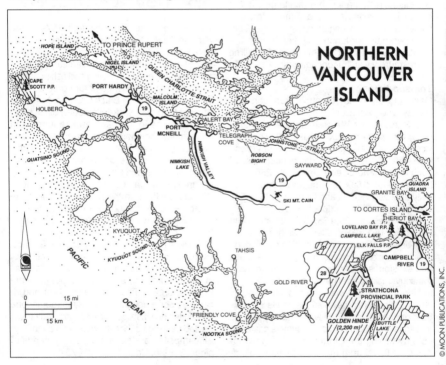

NORTHERN VANCOUVER ISLAND

© MOON PUBLICATIONS, INC.

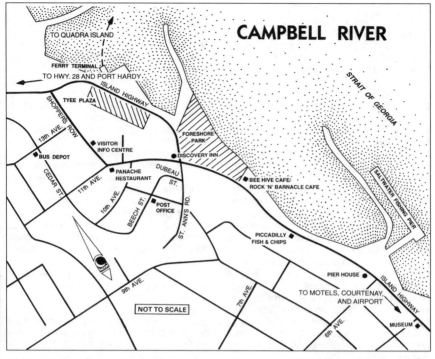

ery Passage begins. The waterway suddenly narrows to a width of only two km between Vancouver and Quadra Islands, causing some of the strongest tides on the coast, attracting bait fish, and forcing thousands of migrating salmon to concentrate off Campbell River, much to every fisherman's delight.

Sights

The best place to absorb some of the local atmosphere is **Campbell River Saltwater Fishing Pier.** The 180-meter-long pier is fun to walk on whether you're into fishing or not. Its benches and protected shelters allow proper appreciation of the marina, strait, mainland mountains, and fishing action, even on wet and windy days. The pier also sports built-in rod holders, fish-cleaning stations, and colorful signs describing the fish you're likely to catch. Anglers of all sizes and ages spin cast for salmon, bottomfish, and

the occasional steelhead, hauling them up in nets on long ropes. Rod rentals are available at the pier for $3 per hour, $8 per half-day, $15 per day. Don't forget, you also need a license.

Campbell River and District Museum, at the corner of Island Hwy. and 5th Ave., tel. (250) 287-3103, sits on four hectares overlooking Discovery Passage. First check out the photos and interesting written snippets that provide a look at Campbell River's early beginnings. Then feast your eyes on mystical artifacts, masks, exciting artwork, baskets, woven articles, carved-wood boxes, colorful button blankets, petroglyphs, and totem poles. The staff offers special cultural- and natural-history programs in summer. Finish up in the gift shop where you can buy stunning native prints, masks, postcards, and other paraphernalia. Open May-Aug., daily 9 a.m.-5 p.m.; the rest of the year, Tues.-Sun. noon-4 p.m. Admission is $2.

Fishing

Salmon are pursued year-round in this area, but May-Oct. is peak season. Steelhead and freshwater cutthroat trout can also be caught year-round in the many freshwater lakes and rivers in the area, but the peak season for steelhead is Jan.-April, for freshwater trout March-May. Start your research on fishing guides, equipment, and locations at the Visitor Info Centre. The staff stocks hundreds of brochures and will be happy to give you advice and point you in the right direction. Fishing from the Saltwater Fishing Pier is the easiest way to try to hook a big one, but you can also hire a professional guide through the information center.

If you're fishing between 15 July and 15 September, you may want to try qualifying for **Tyee Club** membership. This exclusive club, famous among anglers around the world, has been dedicated to upholding the traditional methods of sportfishing since 1924. Several rules must be followed in order to become a member. You have to preregister your intent to fish under club rules; troll from a rowboat in the mouth of the Campbell River without using a motor; use a rod between six and nine feet long, an artificial lure, and a line not more than 20 pounds pretested breaking weight; then catch a trophy-size tyee (a chinook weighing over 14 kilograms). For more information, call the club at (250) 287-2724.

Accommodations and Camping

As Campbell River is a resort, every kind of accommodation you could possibly want is here, from campgrounds and RV parks to luxury hotels and exclusive fishing lodges.

Along the highway south of town are several motels separated from Discovery Channel by only the road. Least expensive of these is **Big Rock Motel,** 1020 Island Hwy., tel. (250) 923-4211, with small rooms for $45 s, $55 d and a few kitchenettes for $65. Continuing north you'll come to the three-story, Bavarian-themed **Bachmair Apartment Hotel,** 492 Island Hwy., tel. (250) 923-2848. Each room has a kitchen and a balcony with water views; good value at $79 s, $89 d. **Super 8 Motel,** 340 Island Hwy., tel. (250) 286-6622 or (800) 800-8000, offers a heated indoor pool and jacuzzi. A continental breakfast is included in the rates of $75 s, $80 d.

Through Campbell River to the north is **Friendship Inn Motel,** 3900 Island Hwy., tel. (250) 287-9591, good value at $44 s, $52 d (head to the adjacent gas station for great potato wedges). Right downtown, **Coast Discovery Inn,** 975 Shopper's Row, tel. (250) 287-7155 or (800) 663-1144, is a full-service hotel with a fitness room, restaurant, and pub; from $90 s, $100 d.

Bed and breakfast accommodations are provided by **Pier House,** across from the Saltwater Fishing Pier at 670 Island Hwy., tel. (250) 287-2943. The old antique-filled house has a library and five rooms with shared or private bathrooms. Rates range $50-65 s, $65-75 d, including a cooked breakfast.

Many campgrounds line the highway south of town, but although they're close to the water, the surroundings are generally nothing special. One of the better choices is **Campbell River Fishing Village and RV Park,** 260 Island Hwy., tel. (250) 287-3630, with sites for $19-22. Less commercial options with limited facilities include **Elk Falls Provincial Park,** six km west of town on Hwy. 28, and **Loveland Bay Provincial Park,** on the shore of Campbell Lake 20 km west of town; $9,50 and $6, respectively.

Food

One of the best places to go for a meal is the **Bee Hive Cafe,** overlooking the marina at 915 Island Hwy., tel. (250) 286-6812. The house specialty is seafood, including clam chowder for $3.95 and fish and chips for around $8. Also on the menu are the usual burgers and salads, and cooked breakfasts ranging $5-9. It's open daily 6:30 a.m.-8 p.m.

Another good place for inexpensive seafood is **Piccadilly Fish and Chips,** along the Island Hwy. opposite the marina, tel. (250) 286-6447. This place is difficult to miss—it's an old English double-decker bus parked by the highway. Eat upstairs or take your meal across the road to Foreshore Park.

Down on the waterfront, on the second floor of the two-story complex that houses the Bee Hive Cafe, is **Rock 'n' Barnacle Restaurant,** 915 Island Hwy., tel. (250) 286-6812. It offers good views and an upbeat, modern decor. The least expensive entrees, a variety of pastas, are $12. Salmon, cooked however you prefer, goes for $14. Open daily 5:30-10 p.m.

Another good place for dinner is **Panache Restaurant,** right downtown at 1040 Shopper's Row, tel. (250) 830-0025. The appetizers feature local seafood, but the rest of the menu has something to suit all tastes. Entrees range $15-22. It's open Mon.-Sat. from 6 p.m.

Transportation

Campbell River Airport, off Erickson Rd. 20 km south of downtown, is served by **Air B.C.,** tel. (250) 287-2419, and **Canadian Regional,** tel. (800) 663-3721. For transportation between the airport and accommodations, call the **Campbell River Airporter** at (250) 286-3000. From Victoria, **Island Coach Lines** operates three buses daily to Campbell River ($36.80 one-way), with one continuing north to Port Hardy (departs Campbell River at 12:20 p.m.; $40.95). The bus depot, tel. (250) 287-7151, is on Cedar St. behind the Royal Bank.

Get around town by **Campbell River Transit System,** departing from Tyee Plaza via Shopper's Row. Pick up a schedule in the information center or call (250) 287-RIDE; $1.25 per sector. Rental car agencies in Campbell River include: **Avis,** tel. (250) 923-1234; **Budget,** tel. (250) 923-4283; **National Tilden,** tel. (250) 923-7278; and **Rent-a-wreck,** tel. (250) 287-8353.

Services and Information

Park in the large parking lot of Tyee Plaza and you're within easy walking distance of all services, including the **post office** on Beech Street. Within the plaza itself are banks, supermarkets, restaurants, a laundromat, and a bookstore. Island Images gift shop in the plaza also has a post office outlet. The **hospital** is at 375 2nd Ave., tel. (250) 287-7111.

At the front of the Tyee Plaza parking lot is **Campbell River Visitor Info Centre,** 1235 Shopper's Row, tel. (250) 287-4636. Aside from tons of brochures, free tourist papers, and information on both the local area and Vancouver Island in general, the knowledgeable staff can answer just about any question on the area you could think up. It's open in summer, daily 8 a.m.-8 p.m.; the rest of the year, Mon.-Fri. 9 a.m.-5 p.m.

QUADRA ISLAND

A 10-minute ferry ride from downtown Campbell River takes you to this beautiful island, separated from the mainland by Discovery Passage. The ferry docks in the south of the island, where most of the island's population resides. This narrow peninsula widens in the north to a vast unpopulated area where wildlife such as black-tailed deer, raccoons, and squirrels are abundant. Marinelife around the shoreline is also widespread; orcas cruise Discovery Passage and seals and sea lions are commonly spied in surrounding waters. Since Captain Vancouver first stepped ashore at Cape Mudge in 1792 to visit a native village, the island has seen much nonnative activity. It was settled well before the Campbell River area.

From the ferry, take Cape Mudge Rd. south to **Kwagiulth Museum,** in Cape Mudge Village, tel. (250) 285-3733. This excellent facility displays a wide variety of ceremonial dresses used in potlatches, as well as masks and other native artifacts. It's open in summer, Mon.-Sat. 10 a.m.-4:30 p.m.; the rest of the year, Tues.-Sat. 10 a.m.-4:30 p.m. Wander over to the park across from the museum to see petroglyphs.

At the island's southern tip, **Cape Mudge Lighthouse** was built in 1898 to prevent shipwrecks in the wild surging waters around the point. On the east coast is **Heriot Bay,** the name of both a cove and the island's largest community. The bay is protected from the elements by narrow Rebecca Spit, site of **Rebecca Spit Marine Park.** Roads lead north from Heriot Bay to the island's wild northern reaches. There you can go hiking: to the low summit of **Chinese Mountain** (three km; allow one hour each way); around **Morte Lake** (five km; allow 90 minutes for the loop), and out to **Newton Lake** from Granite Bay (four km; 75 minutes each way).

Practicalities

Adjacent to Cape Mudge Lighthouse is **Tsa-Kwa-Luten Lodge,** tel. (250) 285-2042 or (800) 665-7745. Built by the local Kwagiulth people, the centerpiece of this magnificent waterfront lodge is the foyer, built in the style of a Big House (a traditional meeting place) in locally milled woods. Each of the large rooms is decorated in northwest native theme, and each has a private balcony with water views. Rates are a reasonable $85 s, $90 d. The lodge coordinates fishing charters and cultural activities, and its restaurant specializes in native foods. A more inexpensive option is **Heriot Bay Inn,** Heriot Bay Rd., tel. (250) 285-3322, where rates start at $75 s or d including a full breakfast in the restaurant. The inn also offers a campground; $10-17 per night with full hookups.

BC Ferries, tel. (250) 386-3431 or, toll-free in B.C., (888) BCFERRY, offers services from Campbell River to the island, every hour on the hour 6 a.m.-11 p.m. Roundtrip fare is adults $3.50, children $1.75, cars $9.50, canoes and kayaks $2, bicycles free. To get around the island, rent a bike from **Island Cycle,** tel. (250) 285-3627, or catch a cab from **Tony's Taxi,** tel. (250) 285-3598.

CORTES ISLAND

Accessible by ferry from Quadra Island, Cortes Island (pronounced Cortez—it was named by an early Spanish explorer) is a relatively remote place, closer to the mainland than to Vancouver Island. Few visitors venture out here. A couple of parks are among the island highlights. **Man-

Orcas frequent the waters of Robson Bight.

son's Landing Provincial Park** is a beautiful little spot sandwiched between a large tidal lagoon and the forested shoreline of **Hague Lake.** And in the south of the island is **Smelt Bay Provincial Park,** another great spot for swimming, beachcombing, and taking in the unique island environment.

Practicalities

Accommodations on the island are limited, so unless you plan to camp, make reservations before coming over. **Smelt Bay Provincial Park,** 25 km from the ferry terminal, offers campsites for $9,50 per site. Closer to the terminal, **Gorge Harbour Marina Resort,** Hunt Rd., tel. (250) 935-6433, offers tent sites ($10) and full hookups ($17) beside the island's main marina, as well as four rooms ($60 s or d for bed and breakfast), bike and boat rentals, fishing charters, and a restaurant. Another accommodation choice is **Cortes Island Motel,** at Manson's Landing, tel. (250) 935-6363; $50 s, $60 d.

The ferry trip between Quadra and Cortes Islands takes 45 minutes. **BC Ferries,** tel. (250) 386-3431 or, toll-free in B.C., (888) BCFERRY, operates scheduled service between the islands six times daily, with the first departing Quadra Island at 9 a.m. and the last departing Cortes Island at 5:50 p.m. Peak roundtrip fare is adults $4.50, children $2.25, cars $11.75, canoes and kayaks $2, bicycles free.

HIGHWAY 28

Running from the east coast to the west coast through the northern section of magnificent **Strathcona Provincial Park,** Hwy. 28 is another island road worth traveling for the scenery alone. The first place to stop is 1,087-hectare **Elk Falls Provincial Park,** six km west of Campbell River. Here you can follow beautiful forest trails to waterfalls, go swimming and fishing, and stay the night (April-Oct.) in a wooded campsite; $9.50 per night, no showers. Not far beyond the park, the highway parallels Upper Campbell Lake for 20 km before splitting, with the main highway continuing west to Gold River and a side road following the east shore of Buttle Lake into Strathcona Provincial Park.

Strathcona Provincial Park

ANDREW HEMPSTEAD

Strathcona Provincial Park

British Columbia's oldest and Vancouver Island's largest park, Strathcona preserves a vast 231,000-hectare wilderness in the northern center of Vancouver Island. Within the park lie a number of superlative natural features, including: 2,220-meter **Golden Hinde,** the island's highest peak; 440-meter-high **Della Falls,** one of North America's highest waterfalls (see "Port Alberni and Vicinity" under "Central Vancouver Island," earlier in this chapter); and a 1,000-year-old, 93-meter-high Douglas fir, British Columbia's tallest known tree. The valleys are carpeted with Douglas fir and western red cedar, the high slopes with wildflowers—lupine, Indian paintbrush, moss campion, and kinnikinnick. Resident mammals include black bears, wolves, wolverines, cougars, marmots, deer, and the island's only herd of elk. The park's lakes are full of cutthroat trout, rainbow trout, and Dolly Varden. And all kinds of birds soar the skies here, including the provincial bird: the Steller's jay.

You'll get a taste of Strathcona's beauty along Hwy. 28, but to get into the park proper turn south off Hwy. 28 halfway between Campbell River and Gold River. This access road hugs the eastern shore of **Buttle Lake,** passing many well-marked nature walks and hiking trails. One of the first is the 500-meter trail (10 minutes each way) to **Lupin Falls,** which are more impressive than the small creek across from the parking lot would suggest. Continuing south

along the lakeshore past driftwood-strewn beaches, you'll come to the **Karst Creek Trail** (two km loop; allow 40 minutes), which passes through a karst landscape of sinkholes and disappearing streams. At the lake's southern end, where the road crosses Thelwood Creek, a six-km trail (2.5 hours each way) climbs a steep valley to **Bedwell Lake** and surrounding alpine meadows.

As the road continues around the lakeshore, look for **Myra Falls** across the water. After passing through the Westmin Resources mining operation, the road ends on the edge of an old-growth forest. From this point, explore on foot by taking the **Upper Myra Falls Trail** (three km; one hour each way) to a lookout point above the falls.

Apart from numerous picnic areas along the shore of Buttle Lake, the only facilities within the park are two campgrounds. **Buttle Lake Campground** is beside Buttle Lake, just west of the junction of Hwy. 28 and the park access road. **Ralph River Campground** is farther south, on the shore of Buttle Lake. Both have pit toilets, picnic tables, and fire rings, and both charge $9.50 per night.

Gold River

Lying beyond the western edge of Strathcona Provincial Park at the confluence of the Gold and Heber Rivers, the town of Gold River (pop. 2,200) was built in 1965 to house employees of a pulp mill. It was the first all-electric town in Canada. Today it has lodgings, restaurants, stores, gas stations, and banking facilities.

Peppercorn Trail Motel and RV Park, Mill Rd., tel. (250) 283-2443, charges $45 s or d for a very basic room and $18 for a campsite with hookups. Of a higher standard, but significantly more expensive, is **Ridgeview Motel,** 395 Donner Court, tel. (250) 283-2277; $75 s, $85 d.

Find out about things to see and do in the region at **Gold River Visitor Info Centre,** along the main road (Hwy. 28) at Muchalat Dr., tel. (250) 283-2418. It's open daily 9 a.m.-4:30 p.m.

Nootka Sound and Beyond

Continue 14 km from Gold River to the dock at the end of Hwy. 28 and take a cruise up beautiful Nootka Sound on the **MV Uchuck III,** a converted WW II minesweeper. The vessel's primary purpose is dropping supplies at remote west coast communities and logging camps, but paying customers are more than welcome and are made to feel comfortable by the hardworking crew. The main sailing departs year-round, every Tuesday at 9 a.m., arriving at **Tahsis** for a one-hour stopover at 1 p.m. before returning to the dock at 6 p.m.; adults $45, seniors $41, children $22.50. A second sailing departs year-round, Thursday at 7 a.m., heading out to the open ocean and up the coast to **Kyuquot.** This is an overnight trip, and accommodations are included in the price of $165 s, $270 d, children $65. A third sailing departs on Wednesdays in summer, visiting two points of historical interest: the spot where Capt. James Cook and his men first landed and made contact with the natives in 1778; and **Friendly Cove,** where in 1792 Capt. George Vancouver and Don Juan Francisco de la Bodega y Quadra negotiated possession of Nootka Sound territory. Fare for this sailing is adults $38, seniors $36, children $19. One-way fares are available to all the above points for those exploring by sea kayak. For further information and reservations call (250) 283-2325.

NORTH TO PORT MCNEILL

Highway 19, covering the 235 km between Campbell River and Port Hardy, is a good, fast road with plenty of straight stretches and not much traffic. Passing through kilometer after kilometer of relatively untouched wilderness, with only logged hillsides to remind you of the ugliness man can produce with such ease, it's almost as though you've entered another world, or at least another island. Stop at all the frequent rest areas for the very best views of deep blue mountains, white peaks, sparkling rivers and lakes, and cascading waterfalls.

Sayward

This small logging town (pop. 1,000) lies 15 km north of the Island Highway on Johnstone Strait. Down on the waterfront, the main attraction is the **log sort,** where cut logs from active logging areas are brought to be sorted for transportation south. A unique building in town houses the **Cable House Cafe,** tel. (250) 282-5532; the steel-frame building is made entirely from used logging cables.

Nimpkish Valley

Continuing toward the north end of the island, the highway is one moment flanked by steep snowcapped mountains and gorgeous lakes, the next by bleak, desolate logged areas. In the Nimpkish Valley you'll pass the turnoff to **Ski Mt. Cain,** a small community-operated ski area with two T-bars serving a vertical rise of 500 meters. The terrain is a good mix for all levels of ability, and the area's high snowfalls make it a hidden gem for hardcore powderhounds. For general information call (250) 949-9496; for a recorded snow report call (250) 956-2226.

Telegraph Cove

Most visitors come to Telegraph Cove to go whalewatching on Johnstone Strait (see the Special Topic), but the village itself is well worth the eight-km detour from the highway. Built around a deep sheltered harbor, it's one of the last existing "boardwalk" communities on the island. Many of the buildings stand on stilts and pilings over the water, and are linked by a boardwalk.

Fewer than 20 people live here year-round, but the population swells enormously during late spring and summer when whalewatching, diving, and fishing charters do a roaring trade, canoeists and kayakers arrive to paddle along Johnstone Strait, and the campground opens

WHALEWATCHING IN JOHNSTONE STRAIT

Over 50 whalewatching operations have sprung up around Vancouver Island in recent years, but the opportunity to view orcas (killer whales) close up in Johnstone Strait is unparalleled. These magnificent, intelligent mammals spend the summer in the waters around Telegraph Cove, and are most concentrated in **Robson Bight,** where they rub on the gravel beaches near the mouth of the Tsitka River.

Bill and Donna MacKay, and Jim Borrowman were involved in the establishment of Robson Bight as an ecological reserve, and know everything known to date about the whales. They operate **Stubbs Island Charters,** whose boats *Lukwa* and *Gikumi* depart Telegraph Cove on half-day whalewatching cruises daily from June to early October. The experienced crew takes you out to view the whales in their natural habitat and to hear their mysterious and beautiful sounds through the underwater hydrophone.

The cost of the cruise is adults $75, seniors and children $65. Make reservations as far ahead as possible by calling (604) 928-3185 or 928-3117. Dress warmly and don't forget your camera for this experience of a lifetime.

JIM BORROWMAN

for the season. Walk along the boardwalk passing cabins, an art gallery, and a small store selling groceries, fishing tackle and licenses, bait, gas, oil, and souvenirs.

Some of the cabins on the boardwalk can be rented by the night, but they generally need to be reserved well in advance. The cabins are simply furnished, have kitchens, and enjoy an incredible setting; from $70 s or d per night. Book through **Stubbs Island Charters,** tel. (250) 928-3185. **Telegraph Cove Resorts,** tel. (250) 928-3131,

opens in summer and provides wooded campsites a short walk from the cove, as well as showers, a laundromat, boat launch, and store. Sites are $18-22.

Port McNeill

The small coastal logging town of Port McNeill (pop. 3,000) lies on Broughton Strait 200 km from Campbell River. It's the regional headquarters for three logging companies and home of "the world's largest burl," on the main highway two km north of town at the entrance to MacMillan Bloedel's logging company office—you can't miss it. The center of town comprises a shopping plaza and industrial waterfront development. Stop at **Port McNeill Visitor Info Centre,** 1626 Beach Dr., tel. (250) 956-3131, for information on Alert Bay (see below).

ALERT BAY (CORMORANT ISLAND)

This fascinating village is the only settlement on crescent-shaped Cormorant Island, which lies in Broughton Strait 45 minutes by ferry from Port McNeill. The island's population of 700 is evenly split between natives and nonnatives.

Alert Bay holds plenty of history. Captain Vancouver landed there in the late 1700s, and it's been a supply stop for fur traders and gold miners on their way to Alaska, a place for ships to stock up on water, and home base to an entire fishing fleet. Today the village is one of the region's major fishing and marine service centers, and holds two fish-processing and -packing plants. Half the island is owned by the Kwakiutl, whose powerful art draws visitors to Alert Bay.

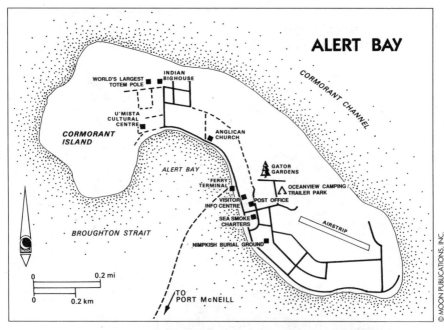

© MOON PUBLICATIONS, INC.

Sights

All the island's numerous attractions can be reached on foot or by bicycle. Start by wandering through the village to appreciate the turn-of-the-century waterfront buildings and the colorful totems decorating **Nimpkish Burial Ground.**

For an outstanding introduction to the fascinating culture and heritage of the Kwakiutl, don't miss the **U'Mista Cultural Centre** on Front St., tel. (250) 974-5403. Built to house a ceremonial potlatch collection confiscated by the federal government after a 1921 ban on potlatches, the center contains masks and other Kwakiutl art and artifacts. Take a guided tour through the center, then wander at leisure past the photos and colorful displays to watch two award-winning films produced by the center—one explaining the origin and meaning of the potlatch. The center also teaches local children the native language, culture, song, and dance. It's open year-round, Mon.-Fri. 9 a.m.-5 p.m., Saturday noon-5 p.m. Admission is adults $6, seniors $5, children $2.

Also on the north end of the island you'll find the **Indian Bighouse,** the **World's Largest Totem Pole** (the only way to photograph it is on your back), and the historic century-old **Anglican Church.** Take a boardwalk stroll through the intriguing ecological area called **Gator Gardens** to see moss-draped forests, ghostly blackwater swamps, and lots of ravens, bald eagles, and other birds. If you're still looking for something to do, consider a whalewatching cruise (June-Sept.) with **Sea Smoke Charters,** tel. (250) 974-5225; adults $75, children $65. The cruise lasts around six hours and includes a seafood lunch.

Practicalities

The island's least expensive accommodation is **Oceanview Camping and Trailer Park,** overlooking Broughton Strait, tel. (250) 974-5213; campsites are $10-15 per night. Other choices include **Orca Inn,** 291 Fir St., tel. (250) 974-5322, which charges $50 s or d, and **Ocean View Cabins,** 390 Poplar St., tel. (250) 974-5457, comprising 12 kitchen-equipped cabins from $50 per night.

BC Ferries, tel. (250) 386-3431 or, toll-free in B.C., (888) BCFERRY, runs to the island from Port McNeill many times daily. The peak roundtrip fare is adults $4.50, children $2.25. You can take a vehicle over for $11.75 roundtrip, but there's no real point as everything on the island is reachable on foot.

Across from the waterfront is **Alert Bay Visitor Info Centre,** 116 Fir St., tel. (250) 974-5213. It's open in summer, daily 9 a.m.-6 p.m.; the rest of the year, Mon.-Fri. 9 a.m.-5 p.m.

PORT HARDY

Port Hardy (pop. 5,400) lies along sheltered Hardy Bay, on the edge of Queen Charlotte Strait. It's the largest community north of Campbell River and the terminus for ferries sailing the Inside Passage to and from Prince Rupert. The ferry is the main reason most people drive this far north, but Port Hardy is also a good base from which to explore the wild and untamed northern tip of the island or fish for salmon in the sheltered waters of "King Coho Country."

Sights and Recreation
As you enter the Port Hardy area, take the scenic route to town via Hardy Bay Road. You'll pass several original chainsaw woodcarvings and skirt the edge of peaceful Hardy Bay before entering downtown via Market Street.

One of the most enjoyable things to do in town is to stroll along the **seawalk** to **Tsulquate Park,** where you can appreciate native carvings and do some beachcombing if the tide is out. A large number of bald eagles reside around the bay, and if you're lucky you'll see them swooping about in the neighborhood. Also along the seawalk, you'll pass **Watchman's Bay,** where another chainsaw woodcarving holds representations of the fishing, logging, and mining industries that support the town, and **Carrot Park** with its unusual "Mile Zero Trans Carrot" sculpture. For years the residents of northern Vancouver Island pleaded for a link with the populated south. Throughout the years various governments made promises and "dangled the carrot" but never came through with the money required to complete the task. Eventually north islanders launched a massive Carrot Campaign, using every means possible to spread the word of their plight. When the campaign became an item on national radio and television, the government relented, kicking in "the rest of the carrot."

Another interesting place to spend a little time is the small **Port Hardy Museum,** 7110 Market St., tel. (250) 949-8143. Browse through a variety of artifacts and an old photograph collection, finishing up in the gift shop where you can buy books, postcards, T-shirts with native designs, and crafts by local artists. The museum is open Tues.-Sat. noon-4:30 p.m.

At **Quatse River Hatchery,** on Byng Rd., tel. (250) 949-9022, you can observe incubation and rearing facilities for pink, chum, and coho salmon, and steelhead. The hatchery, open Mon.-Fri. 8 a.m.-4:30 p.m., is in the middle of a regional park on the scenic Quatse River. Good fishing on the river attracts droves of anglers year-round, but the Quatse is by no means the only fishing game in town. With so much water—both salt and fresh—surrounding Port Hardy, visiting fishermen probably won't know where to start. Ask at the local sporting-goods store on Market St. for the best fishing spots, or take a fishing charter (inquire at the information center for current guides and skippers).

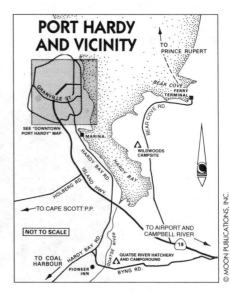

PORT HARDY AND VICINITY

© MOON PUBLICATIONS, INC.

Accommodations and Camping

Accommodations in Port Hardy are limited and often fill up, especially on the night prior to ferry departures. Book ahead. Right downtown, the least expensive choice is **North Shore Inn,** 7370 Market St., tel. (250) 949-8500. Although the rooms aren't particularly large, each has a balcony with water views; $58 s, $64 d. Also downtown is **Thunderbird Inn,** 7050 Rupert St., tel. (250) 949-7767, with a restaurant and pub; $78 s, $81 d.

Pioneer Inn, out of town at 4965 Byng Rd., tel. (250) 949-7271 or (800) 663-8744, has reasonable rates (very reasonable off-season rates) and an excellent coffee shop, licensed restaurant, and laundromat on the premises; $64 s, $76 d. Also out of town, and offering superb water views, is **Glen Lyon Inn,** beside the marina at 6435 Hardy Bay Rd., tel. (250) 949-7115. The rooms are large and well equipped, and the dining room on the premises is good; $70-82 s or d. Out at the airport, just 500 meters from the terminal, is **Airport Inn,** 4030 Byng Rd., tel. (250) 949-9434, which charges $75 s, $85 d.

The closest campground to the ferry terminal is **Wildwoods Campsite,** on Forestry Rd. about three km along Bear Cove Rd., tel. (250) 949-6753; unserviced sites $10, hookups $15. With much better surroundings is **Quatse River Campground,** three km south of town on Byng Rd., tel. (250) 949-2395. It's right by the salmon hatchery, and provides endless fishing opportunities, shady sites, showers, and a laundromat. Sites are $18 with electricity, $14 without.

Food

Port Hardy doesn't offer a large variety of dining options. The main breakfast hangout is the spacious **Family Bakery,** 7030 Market St., tel. (250) 949-8122, which opens at 4 a.m. Or head across the road and down the hill to **Captain Hardy's,** on Market St., tel. (250) 949-7133, where the advertised breakfast specials are small and come on plastic plates for about $3. The rest of the day, this place offers good fish and chips from $4.50.

For excellent lunches and dinners (try the chef salad with house dressing) go to the licensed dining room at the **Glen Lyon Inn** on Hardy Bay Road. If you're in luck, you'll see bald eagles feeding right outside the window. For more of a flashy affair and an excuse to dress up a little, try the **Sportsman's Steak House,** on Market St., tel. (250) 949-7811.

Getting There

Port Hardy Airport, 12 km south of town, is served by **Canadian Regional,** tel. (800) 665-1177, and **Pacific Coastal,** tel. (604) 273-8666 or (800) 663-2872. Airport facilities include parking ($2.50 per day), Budget and National Tilden rental car outlets, and a small cafe. The **Airporter,** tel. (250) 949-6300, offers twice-daily shuttle service between the airport and downtown accommodations; $5.50 each way.

Port Hardy Marina

ANDREW HEMPSTEAD

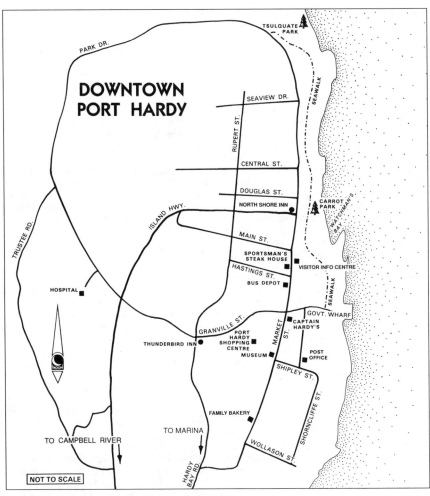

DOWNTOWN PORT HARDY

PARK DR.

TSULQUATE PARK

SEAVIEW DR.

SEAWALK

RUPERT ST.

CENTRAL ST.

DOUGLAS ST.

NORTH SHORE INN

ISLAND HWY.

CARROT PARK

WATCHMAN'S BAY

TRUSTEE RD.

MAIN ST.

SPORTSMAN'S STEAK HOUSE

HASTINGS ST.

VISITOR INFO CENTRE

BUS DEPOT

SEAWALK

HOSPITAL

GOVT. WHARF

GRANVILLE ST.

CAPTAIN HARDY'S

PORT HARDY SHOPPING CENTRE

MARKET ST.

THUNDERBIRD INN

MUSEUM

POST OFFICE

MOON

SHIPLEY ST.

SHORNCLIFFE ST.

FAMILY BAKERY

TO CAMPBELL RIVER

TO MARINA

WOLLASON ST.

HARDY BAY RD.

NOT TO SCALE

© MOON PUBLICATIONS, INC.

Island Coach Lines, tel. (250) 949-7532, operates once-daily bus service up the length of the island, departing Victoria at 6:20 a.m. and arriving in Port Hardy at 4:30 p.m., meaning an overnight stay if you're planning on continuing north aboard the ferry. In the other direction, the bus leaves Port Hardy at 8:30 a.m., arriving in Victoria at 5:30 p.m. The bus fare is $81.45 each way between Victoria and Port Hardy. Stops are made along the way. The depot is the North Island Transportation Ltd. ticket office at 7210 Market Street.

Continuing North by Ferry

Most people arriving in Port Hardy do so with the intention of continuing north by ferry to Prince Rupert and beyond. The ferry terminal is at Bear Cove, eight km from downtown Port Hardy. The *Queen of the North* departs Port Hardy at 7:30 a.m. on even-numbered days in June, July, and

September, and on odd-numbered days in August, arriving in Prince Rupert the same evening at 10:30 p.m. The service runs year-round, but departures are less-frequent outside of summer. Peak one-way fare is adults $102, children 5-11 $51, cars $210, kayaks and canoes $17.50, bicycles $6.50. Cabins are offered by reservation, and discount fares are offered to B.C. seniors. For reservations (necessary in summer) contact **BC Ferries,** tel. (250) 386-3431 or, toll-free in B.C., (888) BCFERRY.

Prince Rupert is the northern terminus of the BC Ferries network. From there, you can head east along the Yellowhead Highway and explore northern British Columbia or, international politics willing, jump aboard an Alaska Marine Highway ferry and continue north up the Inside Passage. (See "Alaska Marine Highway" under "Transportation" in the Prince Rupert section of the Northern British Columbia chapter.)

Real explorers might want to try another BC Ferries route, the "Discovery Coast Passage," which heads north from Port Hardy to Shearwater, then turns east up Dean Channel to Ocean Falls and Bella Coola. (See "Bella Coola" under "Cariboo Country" in the Central British Columbia chapter.) One-way adult fare for this summers-only service is $110 between Port Hardy and Bella Coola. For more information, call BC Ferries at (250) 386-3431 or, toll-free in B.C., (888) BCFERRY.

Getting Around
The local **bus and taxi depot,** 7210 Market St., tel. (250) 949-6300, is also the base for **North Island Transportation Ltd.** Head here for all your transportation needs; the company can arrange transportation to the ferry terminal or airport, and also acts as ticket agent for Island Coach Lines.

Information
Port Hardy Visitor Info Centre is by the waterfront at 7250 Market St., tel. (250) 949-7622.

It's open in summer, daily 8 a.m.-8 p.m.; the rest of the year, Mon.-Fri. 9 a.m.-5 p.m. The energetic staff will happily fill you in on everything there is to see and do in Port Hardy and the entire area. Collect maps (if you want to get off the beaten track, pick up the detailed Forest Service maps) and brochures and you're ready to explore.

CAPE SCOTT PROVINCIAL PARK

Cape Scott Provincial Park encompasses 15,070 hectares of rugged coastal wilderness at the northernmost tip of Vancouver Island. It's the place to go if you really want to get away from everything and everyone. Rugged trails, suitable for experienced hikers and outdoorspersons, lead through dense forests of cedar, pine, hemlock, and fir to 23 km of beautiful sandy beaches and rocky promontories and headlands.

To get to the park boundary, you have to follow 67 km of logging roads (remember that logging trucks always have the right of way), then hike in. Near the end of the road is a small Forest Service campground (free). The trail to **Cape Scott Lighthouse** (23 km; about eight hours each way) is relatively level, but you'll need stout footwear. A shorter and very popular trail leads to beautiful **San Josef Bay** at the southern boundary of the park (2.5 km; 45 minutes each way).

Before setting off for the park, go by the Port Hardy Visitor Info Centre and pick up the park brochure and detailed logging-road maps for the area. Be well-equipped for unpredictable weather, even in midsummer.

South of the park is rugged and remote **Raft Cove.** To get there turn off seven km before the park, following a rough 12-km logging road to a slight rise where the road ends. From this point, a narrow and rough trail leads 1.5 km to the cove.

BOB RACE

SOUTHWESTERN BRITISH COLUMBIA

INTRODUCTION

Once you've reluctantly decided to drag yourself away from Vancouver, you'll be confronted by a variety of things to see and do within a day's drive of the city.

Although British Columbia is best known for its mountains, a stretch of coastline northwest of Vancouver is a watery playground perfect for swimming, sunbathing on sandy beaches, canoeing and kayaking, beachcombing, scuba diving, boating, and fishing. Known as the **Sunshine Coast,** the region is reached by taking a ferry from Horseshoe Bay (west of North Vancouver) then continuing up Hwy. 101. The highway winds along the Strait of Georgia, passing seaside villages, provincial parks, and marine parks, and ending near **Powell River,** a large tourist town and service center. Powell River is the gateway to paddler's paradise at **Desolation Sound** and on the **Powell Forest Canoe Route.**

Spectacular Hwy. 99, the aptly named **Sea to Sky Highway,** leads you northeast out of Vancouver along the edge of island-dotted **Howe Sound.** You'll pass numerous provincial parks before coming to the resort town of **Whistler.** This year-round outdoor-sports mecca offers outstanding opportunities for hiking, biking, golfing, fishing, and other warm-weather pursuits. But it's best known for its two ski areas: Whistler and Blackcomb. The two mountains boast North America's second-highest and highest lift-served vertical rise, respectively.

From Vancouver two routes head east—you can zip along the TransCanada Highway on the south side of the wide **Fraser River,** or meander along slower Hwy. 7 on the north side of the river. Both highways take you through the lush, fertile, and obviously agricultural Fraser Valley, converging at **Hope.** After exploring Hope's spectacular canyon formations, you have another choice of routes: north along the Fraser River Canyon, northeast to Kamloops along the Coquihalla Highway, or east along Hwy. 3 to the picturesque lakes and alpine meadows of **Manning Provincial Park.**

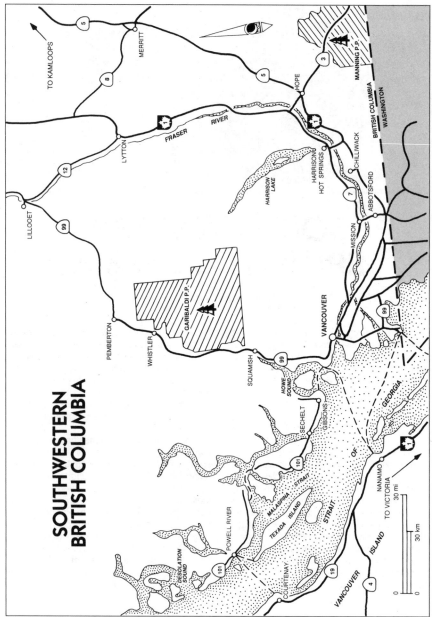

SOUTHWESTERN
BRITISH COLUMBIA

© MOON PUBLICATIONS, INC.

THE SUNSHINE COAST

The 150-km-long Sunshine Coast lies along the northeast shore of the Strait of Georgia between Howe Sound in the south and Desolation Sound in the north. This rare bit of sun-drenched Canadian coastline is bordered by countless bays and inlets, broad sandy beaches, quiet lagoons, rugged headlands, provincial parks, and lush fir forests backed by the snowcapped Coast Mountains. It's well worth visiting, whether on a day-trip from Vancouver, on the "circle route" to Vancouver Island and back, or on a relaxing extended vacation.

The twisty road north from Vancouver is punctuated by two short ferry rides and offers delightful glimpses of wilderness islands in the Strait of Georgia. Settlement began here in the late 19th century, and as you work your way up this stretch of the coastline you'll notice the odd assortment of place names left by Coast Salish natives and Spanish and British navigators.

Today the area is a recreation paradise. Boasting Canada's mildest climate, the Sunshine Coast enjoys moderately warm summers and mild winters, with only 940 mm of rain annually and 2,400 hours of sunlight—a few more hours than Victoria, the so-called provincial hot spot. Boaters and kayakers can cruise into a number of beautiful marine parks providing sheltered anchorage and campsites amid some of the most magnificent scenery along the west coast, or anchor at sheltered fishing-villages with marinas and all the modern conveniences.

Transportation

Although part of the mainland, a trip up the Sunshine Coast entails two trips with **BC Ferries,** tel. (604) 669-1211 or, toll-free in B.C., (888) BC-FERRY (no reservations taken). From **Horseshoe Bay,** west of North Vancouver, ferries regularly cross Howe Sound to **Langdale,** the gateway to the Sunshine Coast. From there, Hwy. 101 runs up the coast 81 km to **Earls Cove,** where another ferry crosses Jervis Inlet to **Saltery Bay.** From the terminal at Saltery Bay, Hwy. 101 continues 35 km to Powell River. The ferry charge is adults $7, children $3.50, cars $25.75, motorcycles $13, bicycles $2.50, canoes and kayaks $4, which includes one-way travel on both ferries or roundtrip travel on just one ferry.

From Powell River, you can return along the same route, or loop back on Vancouver Island via the **Powell River–Comox ferry;** adults $7, cars $24, motorcycles $12, bicycles $2.50, canoes and kayaks $3.50.

LANGDALE TO SALTERY BAY

Gibsons
A delightful hillside community of 4,000 at the mouth of Howe Sound, Gibsons offers recreation galore. Here you can try your hand at salmon fishing, windsurfing, or sailing (the recreational marine center has plenty of moorage and complete facilities for the seafarer); stroll along the picturesque harbor; hunt for antique treasures or arts and crafts in the village; or take the **Gibsons Seawalk,** a 10-minute, scenic meander (lit at night) between Government Wharf and Gibsons Marina in Lower Gibsons.

Elphinstone Pioneer Museum, 716 Winn Rd., tel. (604) 886-8232, features intriguing pioneer and Coastal Salish native displays, and holds what must be one of the largest seashell collections on the planet (some 25,000). In August locals participate in a couple of salmon derbies and revel at the annual **Sea Cavalcade,** which features a swimming race from nearby Keats Island to Gibsons, a parade, and fireworks.

On the main road, Cedars Inn, 895 Hwy. 101, tel. (604) 886-3008, features a heated outdoor pool, sauna, small exercise room, and restaurant; from $74 s or d. On the same stretch of road is **Sunny Crest Motel,** 835 Hwy. 101, tel. (604) 886-2419, with basic rooms from $45 s, $50 d.

Gibsons has a surprisingly good selection of eateries, most in the original part of town on a hill above the marina. For homestyle cooking at reasonable prices, try **Molly's Reach,** 647 School Rd., tel. (604) 886-9710, or the **Come Home Cafe,** 440 Marine Ave., tel. (604) 886-

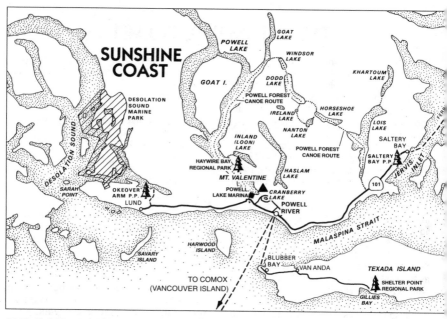

2831. Food is also offered at **Gramma's Marine Pub,** 1552 Marine Ave., tel. (604) 886-8215, a popular watering hole.

Gibsons Visitor Info Centre, 668 Sunnycrest Rd., tel. (604) 886-2325, is along the main road through town but easy to miss—it's tucked away behind a Chevron gas station. Open daily 9 a.m.-5 p.m.

Roberts Creek

About nine km northwest of Gibsons you'll find the small artistic community of Roberts Creek (take the lower road off Hwy. 101), where arts-and-crafts appreciators can often snatch up a bargain. Several bed-and-breakfast guesthouses are available; try **Huckleberry House,** 1495 Henderson Ave., tel. (604) 885-0603, a small kitchen-equipped cottage in a delightful treed setting for $100 s or d. **Roberts Creek Provincial Park,** 14 km northwest of Gibsons, holds hiking trails, waterfalls, a picnic ground, and pebbly beach. Campsites are $9.50 per night.

Nine km farther northwest is the gently curving arc of Davis Bay, home to **Bella Beach Inn,** 4748 Hwy. 101, tel. (604) 885-7191 or (800) 665-1925. This great accommodation has a beach, restaurant, and 32 units, most with a private balcony and separate sleeping area; from $69 s or d.

Sechelt and Vicinity

The native cultural center and regional service center of Sechelt (pop. 7,800) perches on the isthmus of the Sechelt Peninsula between the head of Sechelt Inlet and the Strait of Georgia. The town is supported by logging, fishing, and summer tourism.

One of the area's nicest spots is **Porpoise Bay Provincial Park,** four km north of Sechelt via East Porpoise Bay Road. The park offers open grassy areas among forests of fir and cedar, and a broad sheltered sandy beach along the eastern shore of Sechelt Inlet. Hiking trails connect the beach with a day-use area and campground, and a woodland trail meanders along the bank of Angus Creek, where chum and coho salmon spawn in fall. The park is a handy base for kayakers and canoeists exploring Sechelt Inlets Provincial Marine Recreation Area. Porpoise Bay and the nearby rivers are also noted for good sport-

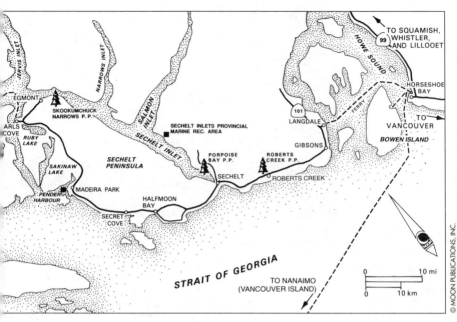

fishing, and oysters and clams are found along the inlet northwest of the park. The park campground ($14.50) has hot showers.

Back in Sechelt, the **Driftwood Inn,** 5454 Trail Ave., tel. (604) 885-5811, features large rooms from $69 s or d and a restaurant with water views. **Seasport Scuba,** 5567 Dolphin St., tel. (604) 885-9830, can help you with your diving needs. **Sechelt Visitor Info Centre,** tel. (604) 885-3100, is in the large Trail Bay Centre shopping complex along Hwy. 101. Open through summer 9 a.m.-6 p.m.; the rest of the year Mon.-Fri. 9 a.m.-5 p.m.

Pender Harbour
Along the shores of Pender Harbour lie the villages of Madeira Park, Garden Bay, and Irvines Landing. Boating and ocean-fishing are popular activities on this stretch of coast, and Ruby and Sakinaw Lakes—between Madeira Park and Earls Cove—are a trout fisherman's delight in season. Canoeists head for the chain of eight lakes between Garden Bay and Egmont, where those casting a line will find good fishing for cutthroat trout May-October.

Pender Harbour is also orca habitat. These highly intelligent gentle giants, also known as killer whales, travel in pods of up to 100. Feeding on salmon found year-round in these waters, they grow up to nine meters long, weighing as much as eight tons. Keep your eyes on the water and your camera ready to capture their triangular-shaped dorsal fins slicing through the water.

Skookumchuck Narrows Provincial Park
Just before Earls Cove, take the road north to Egmont, then the 3.5-km hiking trail (one-hour each way) along Sechelt Inlet to this 123-hectare park. Meaning "Turbulent Water" in Chinook, Skookumchuck protects Narrows and Roland Points and the 400-meter-wide, rock-strewn waterway between them. The tides of three inlets roar through this narrow passage four times a day. The resulting rapids and eddies boisterously boil and bubble to create fierce-looking whirlpools—fascinating to see when your feet are firmly planted on terra firma, but very dangerous for inexperienced boaters unfamiliar with the tides. It's a particularly amazing spectacle during extreme tides in spring, when the rapids may reach

Pacific whiteside dolphin

JIM BORROWMAN

as high as five meters and the water whooshes past at 20 kph. You'll also see abundant marine creatures in tidal pools here—it's a fascinating spot. Pull up a rock and enjoy the view.

Earls Cove

Earls Cove marks the end of this section of Hwy. 101. From here, BC Ferries offers regular service across Jervis Inlet to Saltery Bay. The 16-km crossing takes 50 minutes.

Saltery Bay and Vicinity

Less than two km from the Saltery Bay ferry terminal is 70-hectare **Saltery Bay Provincial Park,** one of the Sunshine Coast's diving hotspots. Waters off the park are accessible from the shore and are full of marinelife, including a three-meter bronze mermaid. The park also features good beaches and salmon fishing (from late April). Camping is $9.50 per night. Saltery Bay is named for a fish saltery that was located nearby in the early 1900s.

From Saltery Bay, it's 31 km of winding road to Powell River. Along the way you'll cross Lois River, the outlet for large Lois Lake, and pass a string of coastal communities that cling to the rocky shoreline of Malaspina Strait.

POWELL RIVER

Situated between Jervis Inlet and Desolation Sound along the edge of Malaspina Strait, Pow-

ell River (pop. 14,500) is almost surrounded by water. The town is actually a municipality made up of four communities. **Townsite,** the original "Powell River," is occupied by an ugly waterfront pulp mill and a number of boarded-up buildings. A few kilometers south is **Westview,** Powell River's main service center, home to the ferry terminal and information center as well as accommodations and restaurants. The other two official communities are **Wildwood,** north of Townsite, and **Cranberry,** east of Townsite.

Powell River was named in 1885 after Dr. Israel Powell, Superintendent of Indian Affairs for B.C., who led the movement that brought B.C. into confederation with Canada in 1871. During the early years of the 20th century, logging of the tall and slender local trees began in the forests around Lois, Horseshoe, and Nanton Lakes, producing exceptionally fine flagpoles that were exported to the rest of the world. In 1912, Powell River became the first town in western Canada to manufacture newsprint.

Today Powell River holds one of the world's largest pulp and paper mill complexes and is a thriving center for the region's abundant outdoor-recreation opportunities, including salmon fishing (good year-round), trout fishing, scuba diving, sailing, canoeing, kayaking, and hiking.

Sights

One of the best ways to explore Powell River is on foot, armed with the *Heritage Walk* brochure available at the information center. The first commercial building was the original 30-room **Powell River Hotel,** completed in 1911. Most of the other buildings you'll see in the Townsite, north of the ferry terminal, were built between 1911 and 1939. This old section of Powell River is a shadow of its former self, with most businesses having moved south to Westview. But the town's reason for being—the pulp and paper mill complex—remains here. The mill is operated by **MacMillan Bloedel,** and tours are available in summer, Mon.-Fri. four times a day. Call ahead at (604) 483-3722 for reservations and meeting details.

Visiting the excellent **Powell River Historical Museum** across the road from Willingdon Beach (watch for the sign) on Marine Ave., tel. (604) 485-2222, is like wandering back in time. Peruse the vast collection of photographs (the province's third-largest archives) and other displays to find out about this seashore community and to see what the area was like before the town was established. Also see well-preserved artifacts, native carvings and baskets, and even sand from around the world. It's open in summer, daily 10 a.m.-5 p.m.; the rest of the year, Mon.-Fri. only. Admission $2.

Hiking

While most visitors to Powell River spend their time enjoying water-oriented sports, the hiking

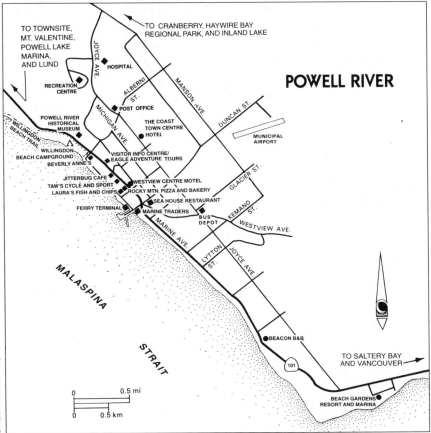

around town is also good—and chances are you'll have the trails to yourself.

From Powell River's municipal campground, the one-km **Willingdon Beach Trail** spurs north past interpretive boards describing natural features and the uses of old logging machinery. The trail ends at a viewpoint overlooking historic Townsite and the pulp operations. One of the most popular short local trails is the one-km hike up 182-meter-high **Mt. Valentine,** north of Cranberry. The trail leads to a stunning panoramic view of Malaspina Strait and the Strait of Georgia. Access is from the end of Crown Avenue: take Manson Ave. east to Cranberry St., turn left, then turn right on Crown.

Another trail loops around **Inland Lake,** north of Powell River between Powell and Haslam Lakes. The wheelchair-accessible trail is 13 km roundtrip, has bridges and boardwalks over swampy areas, and offers picnic sites at regular intervals. Minimal elevation gain is made; allow 3-4 hours. An interesting addition to this hike is a two-km spur leading to **Lost Lake;** follow the main trail clockwise from the parking lot 800 meters to the spur junction. To get to the trailhead from Westview, take Manson Ave. north for

five km, turn right on Cranberry St., then left on Haslam St., from where a signposted logging road leads north to the lake and a primitive campground.

Inquire at the local information center about the **Sunshine Coast Trail,** a volunteer project that when completed will extend 180 km from Saltery Bay to Sarah Point, north of Lund.

For those who'd prefer to explore the Powell River region with a guide, contact **Eagle Adventure Tours,** beside the Powell River Visitor Info Centre, 4690 Marine Ave., tel. (604) 485-2105.

Canoeing and Kayaking

The sheltered Sunshine Coast provides plenty of opportunities for good lake and ocean canoeing or kayaking. The most popular canoe trip is the **Powell Forest Canoe Route** (see Special Topic), while kayakers find solitude in Desolation Sound (see "Vicinity of Powell River," below).

Wolfson Creek Ventures, 9537 Nassichuk Rd., tel. (604) 487-9670, rents canoes for the Powell Forest Canoe Route. Prices range $23-30 for one day, or $19-26 per day for five or more days. The company also rents all the nec-

---

POWELL FOREST CANOE ROUTE

This four- to eight-day backcountry canoe route is a great way to get away from it all, surrounding yourself with tree-covered lowlands and rugged mountain peaks while slipping through fjordlike lakes. Take side trips and you can extend the water distance from 80 km to more than 150 km, or just do one or two sections of the trail—all the major lakes can be reached by road.

To reach the put-in at **Lois Lake,** take Hwy. 101 east of Powell River 20 km to a logging road that branches north off the highway. Follow that road for one km, then turn right on the Branch 41 logging road and follow it seven km to a primitive lakeside campground. The route includes paddling along part of Lois Lake, then the lengths of **Horseshoe, Dodd, Windsor,** and **Goat Lakes,** to **Powell Lake.** Powell Lake Marina is the most popular pull-out point.

In total, the route requires 80 km of paddling and 10 km of portaging. The longest single paddle is 28.5 km (but this can be broken up) and the longest portage is 2.5 km. Carry a tent, stove, and supplies, and stay at one of the 20 Forest Service

recreation sites and camping areas along the route. Don't forget your fishing rod and tackle—all the lakes are stocked with cutthroat trout, and some hold rainbow trout and kokanee.

The route's major outfitter is **Wolfson Creek Ventures,** south of Powell River at 9537 Nassichuk Rd., tel. (604) 487-9670. Canoe rentals range $23-30 for one day, $19-26 per day for five or more days. The company provides all accessories and free car parking, and shuttles paddlers to and from the route for $50. **Edgehill Store,** 5206 Manson Ave., tel. (604) 483-3909, and **Powell River Sea Kayaks,** based at the south end of Powell Lake, tel. (604) 483-2410, also provide canoe rentals at similar prices.

For a map and brochure describing the route in detail and to find out present water levels and campfire regulations contact the **Sunshine Coast District Forest Service,** 7077 Duncan St., Westview, tel. (604) 485-0700, or drop by **Powell River Visitor Info Centre,** 4690 Marine Ave., Westview, tel. (604) 485-4701.

essary accessories and fishing gear, provides free parking, and runs a shuttle service to and from the put-in ($50). Basic paddling courses start at $40, and fully guided overnight tours are available. Offering similar services and prices is **Edgehill Store,** 5206 Manson Ave., tel. (604) 483-3909.

Powell River Sea Kayaks, tel. (604) 483-2410, is based in a small shed overlooking the south end of Powell Lake, the terminus of the Powell Forest Canoe Route. Although this company rents canoes and can provide Powell Forest Canoe Route shuttles, kayaks are its specialty. Single and double kayaks for use around local waterways rent for $35-55 for one day, $60-90 for two days, additional days $20-35. Drop-offs at Okeover Arm, the gateway to the kayaker's paradise of Desolation Sound, cost $20 per person. Guided overnight sea-kayaking trips start at $200, and three-hour basic-kayaking classes run $35.

BOB RACE

Scuba Diving

Known as the "Diving Capital of Canada," the Strait of Georgia provides divers with exceptionally clear, relatively warm water and more than 100 exciting dives mapped by local experts. Conditions are particularly excellent in winter, when visibility reaches 30 meters. Expect to see underwater cliffs and abundant marinelife including sponges, giant octopuses, wolf eels, perch, ling cod, tubeworms, sea anemones, nudibranchs (including intriguing hooded nudibranchs), sea stars, crabs, and tunicates. Seals can be seen year-round, sea lions Nov.-April.

The highlight for wreck divers on the Sunshine Coast is the HMCS *Chaudiere,* sunk in 1993 to form an artificial reef. The hull provides a home for colorful marinelife, and giant holes have been cut through it to enable adventurous divers to do some inside exploration.

Diving gear is available at **Sunshine Coast Fitness & Sports,** 7074 Westminster, tel. (604) 485-6809, and **Good Diving & Kayaking,** 1436 Lund Hwy., tel. (604) 483-3223. Beach Gardens Resort (see "Hotels and Motels," below) is a popular diver's hangout.

Fishing

With ocean to the west and lakes to the east, Powell River is a fishing fantasy come true. Saltwater fishing for chinook salmon is good year-round, but particularly good in autumn and midwinter. Coho salmon usually arrive around April or May. Sport anglers also pursue red snapper, perch, flatfish, ling cod, and rockfish. Bring your own boat (launching ramps are free) or charter one with or without a guide and equipment. Dangle a line from the wharf, docks, or breakwaters, or hurl it out from the shore; a saltwater fishing license is required.

Cutthroat trout inhabit more than a dozen local lakes, most of which are accessible by logging road. Many of the lakes are stocked with rainbow trout and kokanee, and in a couple you can also catch Dolly Varden. Note that you need separate fishing licenses for freshwater and saltwater fishing. Local tackle stores include: **Marine Traders,** 6791 Wharf St., tel. (604) 485-4624, and **Taw's Cycle & Sport,** 4597 Marine Ave., tel. (604) 485-2555.

Hotels and Motels

Powell River doesn't have a great number of regular motels, so try to reserve a room in advance or plan to camp or stay at a more-expensive resort. A good cheapie is **Westview Centre Motel,** 4534 Marine Ave., tel. (604) 485-4023, with basic rooms for $48 s, $54 d. The **Coast Town Centre Hotel,** 4660 Joyce Ave., tel. (604) 485-3000, has all the facilities of a full-service hotel including a health club, restaurant, pub, and large courtyard complete with jacuzzi and gazebo. Rates range $80-109 s or d. **Beach Gardens Resort,** five km south of the ferry terminal at 7074 Westminster Ave., tel. (604) 485-6267 or (800) 663-7070, features an indoor swimming pool, sauna, tennis courts, a fitness room, and a marina with boat rentals and divers' air; it's a great place to meet fellow scuba enthusiasts. The resort's restaurant offers lunchtime buffets and a pub. Rooms, most with water views, range $90-160 s or d.

Bed and Breakfast

One of the most attractive and relaxing lodgings in Powell River is **Beacon Bed and Breakfast,** 3750 Marine Dr. (two km south of the ferry terminal), tel. (604) 485-5563, which overlooks Malaspina Strait, Texada Island, and the peaks of Vancouver Island. Within the two-story waterfront home are three guest rooms, each with ocean views. Facilities include a lounge area overlooking the water and an outdoor hot tub. Rates are from $65 s, $75 d; the large Sunset Suite goes for $95 s or d.

Campgrounds

Willingdon Beach Municipal Campground, on Marine Ave., tel. (604) 485-2242, enjoys a great waterfront location one km north of the ferry terminal. You'll find sheltered and very popular campsites along the beach, as well as a laundromat and washrooms with free hot showers. Basic tent sites are $11, full hookups $14-18.

Canoeists find **Haywire Bay Regional Park** handy. It's seven km north of town on Powell Lake, at one end of the Powell Forest Canoe Route. The park's campground offers hot showers, a sandy beach, and a boat launch. Sites are $8-10. It's accessible by boat or canoe from Powell Lake Marina, and also by road; from the ferry terminal drive up Duncan St., turn left on Manson Ave. and follow it for five km, then turn right on Cranberry St., and left on Haslam St., from where a signposted logging road (on the left) leads north four km to Haywire Bay.

Food

Beverly Anne's Cafe, 4715 Marine Ave., tel. (604) 485-7111, is a local breakfast favorite, but doesn't seem to have much atmosphere and the food isn't outstanding. Instead head to **Rocky Mountain Pizza and Bakery Co.,** 4471 Marine Ave., tel. (604) 485-9111, for great bakery items, coffee as strong (or as weak) as you like it, and daily newspapers. The rest of the day it's pizza, pizza, and more pizza.

Right by the ferry terminal is **Laura's Fish and Chips,** 4454 Willingdon Ave., tel. (604) 485-2252. It's a takeout only place, but the water-

front and a number of ideal picnic spots are just 100 meters away. At the entrance to Willingdon Beach, **Kathie's Kitchen** is always busy serving fish and chips, hamburgers, and the Sunshine Coast's best ice cream. The **Jitterbug Cafe,** 4643 Marine Ave. on the corner of Alexander St., tel. (604) 485-7797, occupies an old restored cottage with an outdoor deck offering views of Malaspina Strait. The menu offers pasta entrees from $8.50 and freshly prepared local seafood from $12. It's open for lunch Tues.-Sun. 11 a.m.-3 p.m., and for dinner Fri.-Sat. 5-8 p.m.

For a great view of the comings and goings of the Vancouver Island ferry, check out the **Sea House,** 4448 Marine Ave., tel. (604) 485-5163. It's open for lunch from noon, dinner from 5 p.m., serving delicious seafood fresh from local waters, as well as salads, pastas, and meat dishes. Atmosphere is casual in the restored heritage house.

Overlooking Powell Lake, north of town, the **Shinglemill Restaurant and Pub,** tel. (604) 483-2001, features dishes to suit all tastes; entrees $12-20. The nautically themed pub section offers expensive meals and great lake views. The restaurant is open daily for dinner while the pub is open daily 11 a.m.-11 p.m. Another popular place for seafood and fine cuisine is the **Beach Gardens Resort Hotel,** 7074 Westminster Ave., tel. (604) 485-6267, where the outdoor tables overlook Malaspina Strait. Sample their lunch buffet, salad bar, or bistro, or go for the formal sit-down dinner.

Transportation

Powell River Municipal Airport is east of town, off Duncan Street. **Pacific Coastal Airlines,** tel. (604) 483-2107 or, from Vancouver, (604) 273-8666, flies at least three times daily between Powell River and Vancouver's international airport; $95 one-way, $165 roundtrip. Also based at the municipal airport, **Suncoast Air,** tel. (604) 485-2915, and **Powell River Air Services,** tel. (604) 485-7172, offer reasonable charter rates (from $1 per kilometer) and flightseeing from $40 per person.

From the terminal in Westview, **BC Ferries** offers regular departures to Comox on Vancouver Island. One-way fares for the 75-minute sailing are adults $7, cars $24, motorcycles $12, bicycles $2.50, canoes and kayaks $3.50. A special

Circlepac fare has been designed expressly for those who want to explore both the Sunshine Coast and Vancouver Island on a loop trip. The fare includes passage on the ferry from Vancouver to Vancouver Island, on the ferry from Comox to Powell River, and on the two ferries along the Sunshine Coast, all at a savings of 15% off the individual one-way fares. BC Ferries also offers daily departures for **Texada Island** (see "Vicinity of Powell River," below); adults $4, cars $10.75, motorcycles $5.50, bicycles free, canoes and kayaks $2. You can't make reservations on any of these ferry services—just roll up and join the queue. For information call BC Ferries at (604) 669-1211 or, toll-free in B.C., (888) BCFERRY, or call the local terminal at (604) 485-2943.

The **bus depot**, on the corner of Joyce Ave. and Glacier St., is served by **Maverick Coach Lines**, tel. (604) 485-5030. Maverick runs twice daily in both directions between Powell River and Vancouver; $28 each way. **Sunshine Coast Transit System**, tel. (604) 885-3234, operates local bus service between Sunshine Coast communities; $1 per sector; no Sunday service.

Information

Powell River Visitor Info Centre is along the main strip of shops at 4690 Marine Ave., Westview, tel. (604) 485-4701. Coming off the ferry from Vancouver Island, drive up the hill to Marine Ave. and turn left; it's three blocks down on the right.

VICINITY OF POWELL RIVER

Texada Island

A 35-minute ferry trip from Powell River's Westview Terminal, Texada is one of the largest of the gulf islands (50 km from north to south), but the population is small and services limited. Originally home to a whaling station, the island has also been home to a couple of mining operations and a distillery that supplied liquor to the United States during prohibition.

From the ferry terminal at Blubber Bay, the island's main road winds south to **Van Anda,** a historic village that once boasted saloons, an opera house, and a hospital. Take a walk along Van Anda's Erickson Beach to appreciate the island's natural beauty. Continuing south, the road leads to Gillies Bay, and beyond to **Shelter Point Regional Park,** which has some short but enjoyable hiking trails and campsites for $12.

Get to the island with **BC Ferries,** tel. (604) 485-2943; adults $4, cars $10.75, motorcycles $5.50, bicycles free, canoes and kayaks $2. Ferries depart about every two hours, 8 a.m.-11 p.m.; no reservations taken.

Lund

Twenty-eight km north of Powell River, Hwy. 101 dead-ends on the old wooden wharf of Lund, a tiny fishing village founded in 1889 and named after the Swedish hometown of the first settlers. Lund lies on a secluded harbor backed by the magnificent peaks of the Coast Mountains. Although best known as the gateway to Desolation Sound, it's worth the trip out just for the relaxed atmosphere and surrounding beauty. Wander around the bustling marina, cruise over to Savary Island on a water taxi (tel. 604-483-9749; $6 roundtrip), or relax with a coffee at **Carvers Studio and Coffee House.** The historic **Lund Hotel,** tel. (604) 483-3187, offers small but comfortable rooms above a row of shops; $60 s, $68 d, senior discounts. Dine with all the locals in the downstairs cafe or with the tourists in the adjacent restaurant.

Okeover Arm

Forested four-hectare **Okeover Arm Provincial Park** park lies eight km east of Lund on the east side of Malaspina Peninsula. It's a small, rustic park with just a few undeveloped campsites (free), a pit toilet, and a kayak- and boat-launching ramp, but it's a great spot to camp if you're into canoeing or kayaking. The shallow, sheltered waters of Okeover Arm—a southern arm of Desolation Sound—provide the perfect environment for all kinds of prolific marinelife; try to time your visit with the receding tide. Access is via Malaspina Rd., off Hwy. 101 south of Lund.

North of the park on three hectares overlooking Okeover Arm, **Desolation Lodge,** 2694 Dawson Rd., tel. (604) 483-3592, offers five kitchen-equipped units, each unique, from $105 d. Fishing, canoeing, and kayaking are practically right out your door, and the setting is magnificent.

Desolation Sound Marine Park

Desolation Sound was named by Captain Vancouver after his visit in 1792—he was obviously unimpressed, as the name implies. Today, 8,256 hectares of the sound are protected in the largest of British Columbia's 50 marine parks. The park also preserves over 60 km of shoreline, a number of offshore islands, the Gifford Peninsula, and a section of mainland that includes Unwin Lake. A wilderness-seeker's paradise, the park is totally undeveloped and without road access. The sound is a popular yachtie hangout and a haven for sea kayakers, who need to be totally self-sufficient here.

Good Diving and Kayaking, under the Lund Hotel, tel. (604) 483-3223, rents kayaks for $30-55 per day; transport the kayaks to Okeover Arm (see above) and you're on your way. **Powell River Sea Kayaks,** on Powell Lake, tel. (604) 483-2410, offers similarly priced rentals and can organize drop-offs at Okeover Arm.

SEA TO SKY HIGHWAY

The spectacular, aptly named Sea to Sky Highway (Hwy. 99) runs 105 km between Horseshoe Bay and Whistler. With the almost-vertical tree-covered **Coast Mountains** to the east and island-dotted **Howe Sound** to the west, this cliff-hugging highway winds precariously through a dramatic glacier-carved landscape.

The weather certainly affects what you see and how you feel about this part of British Columbia. On sunny days everything seems to be bright blue, emerald green, and sparkling clean; only water trickling down the roadside cliffs gives you the clue that it rains a bit around here. On the other hand, after a string of dull drizzly days, impressive waterfalls, one after another, plummet down those same cliffs right beside you to abruptly disappear underneath the highway, and the scenery merges into a magnificent blue-and-gray blur.

Along the road expect some tight corners, narrow stretches, and enough traffic to keep your concentration at an optimum. Be aware of potential hazards in bad weather (washouts can occur), and if you want to go slowly to absorb everything, use the slow-lane pullouts.

HORSESHOE BAY TOWARD SQUAMISH

Porteau Cove Provincial Park

On the east shore of Howe Sound, Porteau Cove offers good swimming, fishing, and reportedly some of the best diving on this part of the coast. In addition, the area's strong winds and lack of waves make for perfect windsurfing conditions. The park holds boat-launching and scuba-diving facilities, an ecology information center, picnic tables, and a waterfront campground for tents and RVs. The campground is open year-round; $15.50 per site per night March-Oct., free the rest of the year.

Britannia Beach

Small Britannia Beach is worth a stop to visit the **B.C. Museum of Mining,** overlooking Howe Sound, tel. (604) 896-2233. In the early 1930s the Britannia Beach Mine was the British Empire's largest producer of copper, producing more than 600 million kilograms. Today it's not a working mine but a working museum. Ever wondered what it's like to slave away underground? Here's your chance to don a hard hat and raincoat, hop on an electric train, and travel under a mountain, without even getting your hands dirty. See a variety of fully functional mining equipment, along with demonstrations and displays on the techniques of mining. Then take a step into the past in the museum, where hundreds of photos and artifacts tell the story of the mine. Also here are a gift shop, restaurant, and gold-panning pool. Open mid-May to mid-October, Mon.-Fri. 10 a.m.-4:30 p.m., with extended hours of 10 a.m.-5 p.m. daily in July and August. Admission is adults $9.50, seniors and students $7.50, children under five free.

Continuing North

Straddling the highway, 24-hectare **Murrin Provincial Park** provides good boating, fishing, swimming, and walking trails, as well as steep cliffs that attract novice and intermediate rock climbers. The park has picnic tables but no campsites. Farther up the highway, stop at 87-hectare **Shannon Falls Provincial Park** to view the spectacular 335-meter-high namesake falls from a platform at the base. You can picnic here or hike a few trails. No campsites are available, but just across the road is **Klahanie Campground and RV Park,** tel. (604) 892-3435. This pleasant campground has sites for $15-22 and an adjacent restaurant with spectacular views (open daily 6:30 a.m.-9 p.m.).

SQUAMISH

Squamish (pop. 14,500) enjoys a stunning location at the head of Howe Sound, surrounded by snowcapped mountains. It's a natural deep-water port and a "nuclear-weapons-free zone." The name Squamish is a native Coast Salish word meaning "Mother of the Wind"—the town gets stiff breezes year-round, delighting today's sailors and windsurfers.

The first white settlers made their home in the valley in 1888, logging the local giant cedar and fir trees for a living. Squamish quickly became a logging town, then a railroad town; at one time it was the southern terminus for the Pacific Great Eastern rail line. Today lumber is still the lifeblood of the area—along **Mamquam Blind Channel** on the east side of town, you can see logs being boomed in preparation for towing to southern mills.

bald eagle

BOB RACE

Sights and Recreation

See around 50 vintage rail cars and engines at **West Coast Railway Heritage Park,** through Squamish on Centennial Way, one km from Hwy. 99, tel. (604) 898-9336. It's open May-Oct., daily 10 a.m.-5 p.m.; admission $5. Also in town is the **Squamish Valley Museum,** in a heritage house on 2nd Ave.; open Wed.-Sunday.

At Squamish Municipal Airport, **Glacier Air Tours,** tel. (604) 898-9016, offers sightseeing flights that include an exciting glacier landing.

Flights are offered daily during summer; reservations recommended. Call for fares. Golfers can enjoy an **18-hole golf course** in town, tel. (604) 898-9691, while hikers can choose from a great number of wilderness hiking trails (get details and maps at the information center). Experienced rock climbers flock to Squamish to conquer 762-meter-high **Stawamus Chief,** one of the world's largest granite monoliths. Other local recreation includes fishing, horseback riding, and bald-eagle watching in the Squamish Valley in autumn and winter.

Early in August, Squamish is mobbed by loggers from around the world who congregate for the annual **Squamish Days World Championship Logging Show.** Don't be too surprised to see people competing at racing up trees, rolling logs, and throwing axes. The show also includes an RV rally, Truck Loggers Rodeo, dances, pageants, and parades.

Practicalities

The best place to stay around Squamish is **Dryden Creek Resorts,** six km north of town (corner of Depot Rd.), tel. (604) 898-9726 or (800) 903-4690. It's set on six hectares of landscaped parkland with Garibaldi Provincial Park as a backdrop. Each of the six suite-style studios has a cedar ceiling, large skylights, and a fully equipped kitchen with handcrafted cabinets. Rates of $64 s or d include complimentary coffee and chocolates. The resort's campground offers a choice of forested or creekside sites; unserviced sites $15, hookups $18-21.

The cheapest place to stay downtown is the **Chieftain Hotel,** on Cleveland Ave., tel. (604) 892-5222. Rooms are just $40 s, $45 d, but rowdy locals downstairs tend to make the place noisy. Close by and much quieter is the **Garibaldi Inn,** 38012 3rd Ave., tel. (604) 892-5204; the rates are reasonable at $48 s, $56 d, $68 with a kitchen, but in summer it fills up fast.

In summer, the *Royal Hudson* steam train chugs up to Squamish and back from Vancouver. The train departs Wed.-Sun. at 10 a.m. from the

B.C. Rail terminal, 1311 W. 1st St., North Vancouver, tel. (604) 984-5246 or (800) 663-8238. Roundtrip fare is adults $36, seniors $32, children $10. A train/boat package is also offered, allowing visitors to take the train from Vancouver to Squamish, but return aboard the **MV Britannia,** which cruises back down Howe Sound to downtown Vancouver. Fare for this combo trip is adults $62, seniors $53, children $17.

For detailed information on Squamish, local provincial parks, and Whistler, follow the signs from the highway to **Squamish Visitor Info Centre,** 37950 Cleveland Ave., tel. (604) 892-9244. It's open in summer, daily 9 a.m.-5 p.m.; the rest of the year, Mon.-Fri. 9 a.m.-4 p.m.

NORTH TOWARD WHISTLER

Garibaldi Provincial Park
This beautiful park encompasses 195,000 hectares of pristine alpine wilderness east of Hwy. 99. Dominated by the snowcapped and glaciated Coast Mountains, the park reaches a high point at 2,678-meter **Mt. Garibaldi,** named in 1860 after Italian soldier and statesman Giuseppe Garibaldi. Other park features include 2,315-meter **Black Tusk,** the **Gargoyles** (eroded rock formations reached by a trail from the park's southern entrance), and a 1.5-km-long lava flow above the west side of **Garibaldi Lake.**

Garibaldi is a true wilderness park, with road access only up to the park boundary. From late July through early September, the hiking is fabulous—through forests of fir, red cedar, hemlock, and balsam, across high meadows crowded with spectacular wildflowers, and past bright blue lakes, huge glaciers, and jagged volcanic peaks and lava flows. If you're in the right spot at the right time, you may see black and grizzly bears, mountain goats, and deer. And you'll certainly spy lots of marmots, chipmunks, squirrels, and birds. In winter and spring the park is thickly blanketed in snow, luring experienced cross-country skiers. Snow can linger well into July, and the higher peaks are permanently mantled.

Between Squamish and Pemberton, five clearly marked entrance roads lead off Hwy. 99 to trailheads providing access into the five most popular areas of the park: **Diamond Head, Black Tusk/Garibaldi Lake, Cheakamus Lake, Singing Pass,** and **Wedgemount Lake.** Aside from these five areas, the rest of the park is untouched wilderness, only explored by mountaineers and experienced cross-country skiers. Backcountry tent sites are located along all major trails. For further park information contact the Garibaldi District Office, P.O. Box 220, Brackendale, BC V0N 1H0; tel. (604) 898-3678.

Alice Lake Provincial Park
Alice Lake, surrounded by a 400-hectare park of open grassy areas, dense forests, and impressive snowcapped peaks, is particularly good for canoeing, swimming, and fishing for small rainbow and cutthroat trout. Trails around the lake beckon hikers in summer and cross-country skiers in winter. A campground with showers and picnic tables is open year-round; $15.50 per night March-Oct., free the rest of the time. The park entrance is 13 km north of Squamish.

Brandywine Falls Provincial Park
If you like waterfalls, stop at this 143-hectare park 45 km north of Squamish and follow the 300-meter, five-minute trail from the parking lot. It's the kind of trail that excites all your senses—magnificent frosty peaks high above, dense lush forest on either side, a fast, deep river roaring along on one side, the pungent aroma and cushiness of crushed pine needles beneath your feet.

The trail takes you to a viewing platform to see 66-meter-high **Brandywine Falls,** where the waters plummet down a vertical lava cliff into a massive swirling plunge pool, then roar down a forest-edged river into a lake. It's most magnificent early in summer. The falls were named in the early part of this century by two railroad surveyors who made a wager on guessing the falls' height, the winner to receive bottles of, you guessed it, brandywine. From the trail to the falls you can also branch off on another trail that leads either to **Swim Lake** (400 meters; 10 minutes) or along the **Calcheak Trail** (four km; 70 minutes). Aside from hiking, the park is also a good spot for swimming and fishing. A campground near Hwy. 99 provides gravel campsites; $9.50 per night May-Oct., no charge the rest of the year.

WHISTLER AND VICINITY

Magnificent snowcapped peaks, dense green forests, transparent lakes, sparkling rivers, and a cosmopolitan village right in the middle of it all—welcome to Whistler (pop. 7,500), one of the world's great resort towns, just 120 km north of Vancouver.

Best-known among skiers, the town boasts the twin mountains of **Whistler** and **Blackcomb** towering over the valley floor. The two ski areas on those peaks offer almost 3,000 hectares of world-class skiing, including vast powder-filled bowls and some of the world's best-known steeps.

A ski season stretching from November to late May doesn't leave much time for summer recreation, but in recent years, the "off-season" has become almost equally busy. Among the abundant summertime recreation opportunities: lift-served hiking and glacier skiing; biking through the valley and mountains; water activities on five lakes; horseback riding; golfing on some of the world's best resort courses; and fishing, rafting, and jet-boating on the rivers. The more sedentary summer visitor can simply stay in bustling **Whistler Village** and enjoy a plethora of outdoor cafes and restaurants.

History
Amazing as it seems, until just a little over 30 years ago the only development here was a bunch of ramshackle holiday houses around the base of what was then known as London Mountain. Back then, the valley was linked to Vancouver by a rough and treacherous gravel road.

In 1966 the first lift was constructed up London Mountain, which soon became known as Whistler Mountain after the shrill call of marmots that lived around its summit. As road access improved, so did the lift system, and in 1980/81 Whistler Village took shape as the main base area. That same winter the first lifts opened on adjacent Blackcomb Mountain. Since then, Whistler has grown to become one of the world's great resort towns, with skiing, summer recreation, and services to match. Along with its infrastructure improvements, the valley has seen a population boom—a tenfold increase since 1975.

SKIING

No matter what your ability, the twin resorts of Whistler Mountain and Blackcomb Mountain combine to make a ski holiday you won't forget in a hurry. The ski areas are usually referred to collectively as "Whistler/Blackcomb," but in fact they are two distinct mountains separated by a steep-sided valley. Each one is served by lifts operated by a different company, but the lifts converge at Whistler Village and the lift tickets are interchangeable. Consistently rated as North America's No. 1 ski destination, Whistler and Blackcomb offer enough runs and lifts to keep you smiling all ski-season long.

The drawbacks of a ski vacation here are few, but should be noted. A low base elevation

LEANNA RATHKELLY/WHISTLER RESORT ASSOCIATION

Whistler Resort

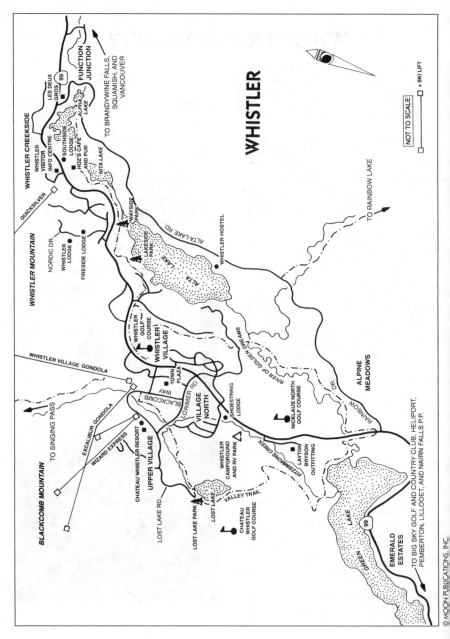

WHISTLER

© MOON PUBLICATIONS, INC.

and exposure to warm Pacific weather fronts can create slushy conditions any time of the season; rain is not uncommon. Also, lift tickets and accommodations are steeply priced, but this is less of a drawback for visiting Americans who, taking advantage of the favorable exchange rate, ski for around US$40 a day.

Whistler Mountain

Rising to a peak elevation of 2,182 meters, Whistler Mountain offers more than 100 marked ski runs, the longest being a quad-burning 11 km. The vertical rise of 1,530 meters is the second-largest in North America, behind only neighboring Blackcomb, and the total area of lift-served terrain is 1,480 hectares. From Whistler Village, a five-km-long gondola lifts skiers more than a vertical kilometer above the valley to east-facing slopes served by eight chairlifts and a T-bar. Over the back of the main mountain, 400 hectares of bowl skiing is served by the Harmony Express quad chairlift.

Lift tickets are adults $49, seniors and youths $39, children $22. The season runs from late November to the end of April, but early and late in the season snow cover on the bottom half of the mountain can be light. For general resort information call (604) 932-3434; for snow reports call (604) 932-4191 or, from Vancouver, (604) 687-6761; for accommodation packages call (604) 932-4222 or (800) 944-7853.

Blackcomb Mountain

Immediately north of Whistler Mountain is towering Blackcomb Mountain, a 1,342-hectare ski area over half of which is above the treeline. With a base elevation of 675 meters and lifts rising to 2,284 meters, it boasts a vertical rise of 1,609 meters (5,280 feet)—the longest of any ski area in North America. In addition to the slopes facing the village, the resort offers two massive powder-filled bowls on the back side. The slopes are served by a short gondola, six quad chairs, three double chairs, and assorted T-bars and rope tows. Of the over 100 marked runs, the longest stretches 10 km.

Lift tickets are adults $49, seniors and youths $39, children $22. The season runs from late November to late May, with the Horstman Glacier open for skiing for a few weeks of summer

(see the Special Topic). Night skiing is offered Wednesday and Saturday 5-9 p.m. For resort information call (604) 932-3141; for snow reports call (604) 932-4211.

Cross-country Skiing

Many kilometers of groomed trails wind through snow-covered terrain in the vicinity. Starting at Whistler Village and running the length of the valley, the **Valley Trail** is a paved walk/bikeway in summer (see "Hiking" under "Summer Recreation," below) that becomes a popular cross-country ski trail in winter.

Just northeast of the Village, **Lost Lake Park** offers trails for all ability levels on 15 km of set track, as well as a cozy warming hut at Lost Lake. Another good spot for cross-country skiing is **Whistler Golf Club.** Cross-country ski rentals are available from several shops in the Village.

Heli-skiing

Heli-skiing is offered by **Whistler Heli-skiing,** tel. (604) 932-4105, which takes strong intermediates and expert adventurers high into the Coast Mountains to ski fields of untracked powder. Rates of $415-550 include transportation to and from the heliport north of Whistler Village, a gourmet lunch, and the guide.

SUMMER RECREATION

At the Ski Areas

Both Whistler and Blackcomb Mountains offer a wide variety of on-slope summer recreation, including hiking, guided naturalist walks, mountain biking, horseback riding, or just riding the lifts to enjoy the mountainscape.

Rates for the sightseeing lifts on **Whistler Mountain,** tel. (604) 932-3434, are adults $18, seniors $15, children free. Summer lift hours are daily 10 a.m.-5 p.m., mid-June to September; 11 a.m.-4 p.m. during the first couple of weekends of June and October. Over 30 km of hiking trails wind around the mountain, including trails through the high alpine to destinations such as beautiful Harmony Lake (two km from the top of the gondola) or to the toe of a small glacier (2.5 km from the top of the gondola). Also on the mountain, you can rent snowshoes for $5 per hour to walk across areas of year-

SUMMER SKIING

Just because the calendar, thermometer, and sun's angle say it's summer doesn't mean skiing is months away. Blackcomb Mountain is one of just two North American resorts offering lift-served summer skiing. Between late June and early August, a T-bar on the Horstman Glacier opens daily noon-3:30 p.m.; $32 per person includes lift transportation from the valley floor. The slopes can get crowded, with local or national ski teams in training and with visitors enjoying the novelty of summer skiing. But if it gets too bad, just go back to the valley floor for golf or water sports.

round snowpack. Or for an adrenaline rush, take the gondola up, then bicycle down the mountain with **Whistler Backroads Mountain Bike Adventures,** tel. (604) 932-3111.

Over on **Blackcomb Mountain,** tel. (604) 932-3141, sightseeing lifts operate mid-June to Labour Day, daily 8 a.m.-4:30 p.m.; rates are the same as at Whistler Mountain. Other activities include hiking, guided naturalist walks, horseback riding, and summer skiing (see the Special Topic). And you can dine at the restaurant at the top of the Solar Coaster Express. Die-hard skiers will even find glacier skiing here early in the summer (see the Special Topic).

Even if it's a beautiful spring or summer day down in the valley, when you head up the mountain take a warm wind- and waterproof coat and wear hiking boots—tennis shoes just don't make the grade at the top.

Hiking

The easiest way to access the area's most spectacular hiking country is to take a sightseeing lift up Whistler or Blackcomb Mountain. But many other options are available. Walking around Whistler Valley you'll notice signposted trails all over the place. **Valley Trail** is a paved walkway/bikeway in summer, a cross-country ski trail in winter. It makes an almost complete tour of the valley, from Whistler Village to **Lost** and **Green Lakes,** along the **River of Golden Dreams** and past a couple of golf courses at **Alta, Nita,** and **Alpha Lakes,** and finally to Hwy. 99 in the Whistler Creekside area. If you'd

rather do a short walk, head for Lost Lake via the two-km trail from Parking Lot East at the back of Whistler Village, or via the free Whistler Transit System bus from the middle of the village. Once at the beautiful lake, you can saunter along the shore, picnic, swim, or, in winter, cross-country ski.

Between Whistler and Blackcomb Mountains, a gravel road leads five km to the trailhead for the **Singing Pass Trail.** From the parking lot, this trail follows the Fitzsimmons Creek watershed for 7.5 km (allow three hours each way) to Singing Pass, gaining 600 meters in elevation. From the pass, it's another two km (40 minutes) to beautiful **Russet Lake,** where you'll find a backcountry campground.

On the opposite side of the valley, an eight-km trail (3.5 hours each way) leads from Alta Lake Rd. just north of Whistler Hostel up Twenty One Mile Creek to **Rainbow Lake.** The elevation gain is a strenuous 850 meters.

Mountain Biking

The Whistler Valley is a perfect place to take a bicycle or mountain bike—you'd need months to ride all the trails here. Many of the locals have abandoned their cars for bikes, which in some cases are worth much more than their cars! You can see them scooting along **Valley Trail,** a paved walk/bikeway that links the entire valley and appears to be the resident bicyclists' freeway. Another popular place for mountain bikers is beautiful **Lost Lake,** two km northeast of Whistler Village.

If you didn't bring a bike, not to worry—they're for rent. Rental rates start at around $8 per hour, $30-45 per day. Or perhaps a guided bicycle tour of the local area sounds appealing—it's not a bad idea to have a guide at first. For all the details on tours and current rates, contact **Backroads,** tel. (604) 932-3111; **Blackcomb Ski and Sport,** tel. (604) 938-7788; **CanSki,** tel. (604) 938-7755; **Evolution,** tel. (604) 932-2967; **Mountain Riders,** tel. (604) 932-3659; **Sportstop,** tel. (604) 932-5495; **Whistler Bike Co.,** tel. (604) 938-9511; **Whistler Mountain Sport Shop,** tel. (604) 932-2311; or **Whistler Outdoor Experience Co.,** tel. (604) 932-3389.

Whistler is host to several major mountain-bike racing events each summer; find out more at the information center.

Water Sports

Sunbathers head for the public beaches along the shores of **Alta Lake**—watching all the windsurfers whipping across the water or beginners repeatedly taking a plunge is a good source of summer entertainment. Wayside Park at the south end of the lake has a beach, a canoe launch, an offshore pontoon, a grassy area with picnic tables, and hiking/biking trails. At Lakeside Park, also on Alta Lake, **Whistler Outdoor Experience Co.,** tel. (604) 932-3389, rents canoes for $14 an hour or $48 per half day, and kayaks for $12 an hour. They also offer a variety of adventure tours, including a 3.5-hour river-rafting trip for $65 per person, a one-hour jet-boat trip for $55 per person, and a three-hour horseback-riding trip for $55 per person. In winter they offer cross-country ski, heli-ski, and snowshoe adventures.

For a little whitewater excitement, try river rafting with **Whistler River Adventures,** tel. (604) 932-3532, which provides a variety of guided scenic and whitewater tours between the end of May and early September. Outings range from an easy float down the Green River for $45 per person, to the whitewater thrills of a full day trip on the Elaho River for $109. This company also offers a number of jet-boat adventures from $59.

Horseback Riding

At **Whistler Trail Riding,** tel. (604) 932-6623, you can sign up for a variety of horseback trips, including a one-hour trail ride for $25 per person, a three-hour ride for $60, an evening barbecue, a hayride, an overnight pack trip with gourmet campfire cooking, a fishing or hunting trip, and an entire holiday on horseback. To get there, follow the highway one mile north of Whistler Village, turn at Mons Rd., then branch left. **Whistler Outdoor Experience Co.,** tel. (604) 932-3389, also arranges horseback-riding excursions.

Golf

Whistler boasts four world-class championship golf courses, each having its own character and charm. The golfing season runs mid-May to October, so in late spring you can ski in the morning and golf in the afternoon.

Designed by Arnold Palmer, **Whistler Golf Club,** between Whistler Village and Alta Lake, tel. (604) 932-3280, offers large greens and narrow wooded fairways over a challenging layout; green fees are $60-75. Also near the village is **Chateau Whistler Golf Course,** Blackcomb Way, tel. (604) 938-2095. Designed by renowned golf-course architect Robert Trent Jones Jr., this course takes advantage of the rugged terrain of Blackcomb Mountain's lower slopes through holes that rise and fall with the lay of the land. Green fees are $90-110, which includes the use of a cart equipped with a computerized yardage meter.

Opened in 1995, **Nicklaus North,** just north of Whistler Village, tel. (604) 938-9898, is named for its architect, Jack Nicklaus. The open course holds numerous water hazards and boasts 360-degree mountain vistas. Green fees range $90-110. Farther up the valley is **Big Sky Golf and Country Club,** tel. (604) 894-6106 or (800) 668-7900, a lengthy par-72 course of over 7,000 yards; $70-85 per round.

Flightseeing

Nothing beats the spectacular sight of the Coast Mountain Range's majestic peaks, glaciers, icy-

TODD CLARK

blue lakes, and lush mountain meadows from an unforgettable vantage point high in the sky. **Whistler Air Service,** tel. (604) 932-6615, will take you aloft in a floatplane from Green Lake, three km north of Whistler Village. An 18-minute flight costs $59 per person; a 25-minute flight over the glaciers of Garibaldi Provincial Park goes for $69; and a 70-minute flight landing on a high alpine lake runs $129. You can also charter the whole plane (minimum four people) for a remote backcountry adventure.

Helicopter rides are also available, and will cost you from $80 per person for a 20-minute flight with either Whistler Air or **Mountain Helisports,** tel. (604) 932-2070. Both companies also offer heli-hiking and heli-picnic packages, and both base their choppers at a heliport 10 km north of Whistler Village.

ENTERTAINMENT AND EVENTS

Entertainment

Throughout the year you can usually find live evening entertainment in Whistler Village. At **Buffalo Bill's** in the Timberline Lodge, 4122 Village Green, tel. (604) 932-6613, expect anything from reggae to rock. Another of the hottest nightspots, **Tommy Africa's,** tel. (604) 932-6090, is popular with the younger crowd, pumping out high-volume reggae across the valley's most popular dance floor.

Head to **Savage Beagle,** tel. (604) 938-3337, nightly between 8 p.m. and 2 a.m. for dance, house, and alternative music. The **Garibaldi Lift Co. Bar & Grill,** tel. (604) 905-2220, features live entertainment most nights—often blues and jazz—and good food at reasonable prices. The **Boot,** in Shoestring Lodge, tel. (604) 932-3338, offers some of the cheapest drinks in the valley and offers occasional live music.

Blacks Pub, 4270 Mountain Sq., tel. (604) 932-6945, offers more than 90 international beers and a quiet atmosphere. Other watering holes include **Crystal's Lounge** in the Crystal Lodge, tel. (604) 932-2221, and the **Mallard Bar** at the Chateau Whistler Resort, tel. (604) 938-8000.

Events

Each weekend in June and daily through summer, the streets of Whistler come alive with a variety of street entertainment such as musicians, jugglers, and comedians. The last weekend of May is the official end of the ski season up on Blackcomb Mountain, with a **Slush Cup** and live music.

Canada Day, 1 July, is celebrated with a parade through Whistler Village. **Whistler Country, Roots, and Blues Festival,** the third weekend of July, brings together dozens of musicians for outdoor and indoor performances. The following weekend, the last in July, is the **Cactus Cup Mountain Bike Festival,** with demonstrations, lessons, guided rides, and racing.

On the second weekend of August, the valley hosts the **Whistler Classical Music Festival,** which includes a program of events ranging from Brass on a Raft to a concert by the Vancouver Symphony Orchestra high up on the slopes of Whistler Mountain. The **Alpine Wine Festival,** early in September, showcases the province's best wineries with daily winetasting at Pika's Restaurant, high on the slopes of Whistler Mountain. The streets come alive again the second weekend of September during the **Fall for Jazz Festival.**

During **Oktoberfest,** many restaurants and businesses dress themselves up in a Bavarian theme. The festival also features dancing in the streets, and, of course, a beer hall. Spring brings the **World Ski and Snowboard Festival,** held over 10 days early in April. Events include the World Technical Skiing Championships, junior races, a film festival, and snowboard competitions.

ACCOMMODATIONS AND CAMPING

Whistler's accommodations range from a hostel and inexpensive dorm beds to luxury resort hotels. It's just a matter of selecting one to suit your budget and location preference. Skiers may want to be right in Whistler Village or by the gondola base in Whistler Creekside so they can stroll out their door, strap on skis, and jump on a lift. Winter or summer, contact one of the following reservation agencies to inquire about package deals: **Whistler Resort,** tel. (604) 664-5625 or (800) 944-7853; **Rainbow Retreats Accommodations,** tel. (604) 932-2343; **Whistler Chalets and Accommodations,** tel. (604) 932-6699 or

(800) 663-7711. Most accommodations offer package rates for both winter (peak) and summer (slightly less expensive) seasons.

Hotels, Motels, and Resorts

One of Whistler's least expensive motels is **Southside Lodge**, 2102 Lake Placid Rd., tel. (604) 932-2554. It's four km south of Whistler Village, across from the information center and within walking distance of Whistler Creekside. With just six rooms and rates of $70-80 s or d year-round, you'll need to book in advance.

In Whistler Village itself, accommodations are naturally more expensive. Best value is **Hearthstone Lodge**, 4211 Sunshine Pl., tel. (604) 932-4161 or (800) 663-7711, offering 19 kitchenette units for $120-190 per night in the height of summer. **Crystal Lodge**, 4154 Village Green, tel. (604) 932-2221 or (800) 667-3363, is in the heart of the action, with all the best restaurants and shopping at the doorstep. Summer rates start at $99 s or d while in winter rooms run from $180. **Listel Whistler Hotel**, 4121 Village Green, tel. (604) 932-1133 or (800) 663-5472, is a self-contained resort complete with a pool, jacuzzi, laundry facility, restaurant, and bar. Rates are $95-199 s or d in summer.

On the edge of the village and adjacent to one of the valley's best golf courses is **Whistler Fairways Hotel and Resort**, 4005 Whistler Way, tel. (604) 932-2522 or (800) 663-5644. Each of the 200 spacious rooms is simply but stylishly decorated in pastel colors. Facilities include a heated outdoor pool, exercise room, jacuzzi, restaurant, and bar. Rates start at a reasonable $99 in summer and $119 in winter.

Part of the historic Canadian Pacific hotel chain is **Chateau Whistler Resort**, at the base of Blackcomb Mountain in Upper Village, tel. (604) 938-8000 or (800) 441-1414. This is Whistler's most luxurious lodging, with its own championship golf course, a health club with the best equipment money can buy, tennis courts, and all the facilities expected of one of the world's best accommodations. The massive lobby is decorated in the style of a rustic lodge, but the rooms couldn't be more different. Each is elegantly furnished and offers great mountain views. In the low season (late spring and fall) rooms start at $199 s or d; peak summer rates start at $299 s or d, winter rates at $325 s or d.

Whistler Hostel

Owned and operated by Hostelling International, this accommodation is on the western shores of Alta Lake (water laps the back of the building) and boasts magnificent mountain views. Meet people from around the world in the communal kitchen, dining area, and big, cozy living area, where you can delight in the view of the lake and the mountains without moving out of your tired muscles. It's understandably popular year-round; members $17.50 per night, nonmembers $22.50, or you can set a tent up for $13 per person. Call ahead to see if there's room; tel. (604) 932-5492. From town, it's quite a hike with a heavy pack. If you're driving into Whistler from the south, take Alta Lake Rd. to the left off Hwy. 99 and continue until the road parallels Alta Lake. Look for the sign on the lake side of the road, park your car in the lot, then follow the sign down over the railway tracks to the hostel. It's open daily for registration 4-10 p.m. At 9:30 a.m., 4 p.m., and 5:55 p.m., **Whistler Transit System** buses depart Whistler Village and run right past the hostel door.

Other Budget Accommodations

The **Shoestring Lodge**, 7124 Nancy Greene Dr., White Gold Estates (north of the Village on the right side of the highway), tel. (604) 932-3338, is one of the most reasonably priced lodges in Whistler, although rooms are small and it can get noisy. Soak in the sauna, relax in front of the open fire, or go for a cheap meal and a rip-roaring evening in the Boot Pub, all without leaving your home away from home. Dorm beds are $18-20 per person ($23-26 in winter); private rooms are $65-75 s or d ($85-95 in winter).

Scattered through Whistler are a number of club-owned lodges open to nonmembers when beds are available. They generally provide guests with use of a kitchen, a living or common room with a fireplace, laundry facilities, a games room, ski lockers, a ski-tuning room (you'll need your own tools), and a sauna and/or jacuzzi. You provide your own bedding and towels. Best of the bunch is UBC-owned **Whistler Lodge**, 2124 Nordic Dr., tel. (604) 932-6604. It has a large kitchen and lounge area, and an outdoor deck with barbecue facilities. Dorm beds are $18 in summer, slightly higher in winter. Down the hill a bit is **Fireside Lodge**, 2117

Nordic Dr., tel. (604) 932-4545, charging $25-30 for a dorm bed and $70-90 d for a private room.

Campgrounds

The closest provincial park campgrounds to Whistler are **Brandywine Falls,** 11 km south, and **Nairn Falls,** 28 km north. Both are open April-Nov. and charge $9.50 per night.

FOOD

Breakfast on the Mountain

Through the ski season, both resorts offer breakfast on the mountain, as well as the chance to hit the slopes before the lifts officially open. On **Blackcomb Mountain,** tel. (604) 938-7747, it's coffee and cakes in the Rendezvous Restaurant for $6, while over on **Whistler Mountain,** tel. (604) 932-3434, a full buffet breakfast in Pika's Restaurant is $12. These breakfast deals must be paid for in conjunction with a lift pass, and lifts open at 7:30 a.m. for diners.

Cafes

One of the best places in Whistler Village for breakfast is **Chalet Deli,** 4437 Sundial Place, tel. (604) 932-8345. Light breakfasts cost from $5 and the service is fast and efficient. The rest of the day the deli is a great choice for hamburgers and healthy sandwiches and salads. Open daily from 7:30 a.m. Scattered through the village are a number of coffeehouses, including **Starbucks,** tel. (604) 938-0611, **Moguls Coffee Bean,** tel. (604) 932-4845, and **Gourmet Deli & Cafe,** tel. (604) 932-3949. In Village North, get your fill of caffeine at **Grabbajabba,** tel. (604) 932-3213.

North American

For steaks, seafood, a salad bar, fresh hot bread, and plenty of food at a reasonable price, the **Keg,** at Whistler Village Inn, Sundial Place, tel. (604) 932-5151, is a sure thing. Expect to pay from $12 for an entree; open daily from 5:30 p.m. The rustic decor and great Canadian food at **Garibaldi Lift Co. Bar & Grill,** at the base of the Whistler Village gondola, tel. (604) 905-2220, has been a big hit since opening in 1995. The bar and sundeck are popular après-ski hangouts, and by around 8 p.m. everyone's

BOB RACE

back for dinner. For western-style atmosphere, head to the **Longhorn Saloon and Grill** in Carleton Lodge, tel. (604) 932-5999, or the **Rodeo Bar and Grill** at Listel Hotel, tel. (604) 932-1133. **Citta,** in Whistler Village, tel. (604) 932-4177, offers all the usual pizza, pasta, and salads at reasonable prices; open daily for lunch and dinner. Near Whistler Creekside, **Hoz's Cafe and Pub,** 2129 Lake Placid Rd., tel. (604) 932-4424, is renowned for good pub food, such as fish and chips from $8 and ribs from $14; open daily from 11:30 a.m.

Picking away at a bowl of nachos is a traditional après-ski activity in the bars around town, but for a full Mexican meal, head to **Mescalero,** in Whistler Village, tel. (604) 932-2002. The cantina-style decor is a bit over the top, but the food is well prepared and the portions generous. Open daily for lunch and dinner.

Continental

For great Greek food, **Zeuski's Taverna,** Town Plaza, Village North, tel. (604) 932-6009, is open daily for lunch and dinner and is always busy. For something different, sample their souvlaki cooked on the barbecue.

Restaurant entrepreneur Umberto Menghi operates numerous eateries in Vancouver and two restaurants in Whistler Village. Both are reasonably priced with menus influenced by the cuisine of Tuscany. Check out **Il Caminetto di Umberto,** tel. (604) 932-4442, and **Trattoria di Umberto,** in the Mountainside Lodge, tel. (604) 932-5858. **Ristorante Araxi,** Whistler Village, tel. (604) 932-4540, consistently wins awards for its traditional Italian menu. It also boasts an extensive wine list. One of the valley's finest restaurants is **Val d'Isere,** Whistler Village, tel. (604) 932-4666, open daily from 5:30 p.m. The atmosphere is elegant and intimate, with traditional French dishes the specialty. Expect to pay from $18 for an entree. More casual is **Les Deux Gros,** two km west of Whistler Creekside at Alta Lake Rd., tel. (604) 932-4611, dishing up classic French country fare Tues.-Sun. 5:30-10:30 p.m.

Asian
Reasonably priced Mongolian fare is on the menu at **Mongolie Grill,** Whistler Village, tel. (604) 938-9416; open daily from 3 p.m. **Whistler Garden** in Delta Whistler Resort, tel. (604) 938-9781, is a large Chinese restaurant featuring a dim sum lunch and a Cantonese-inspired regular menu; open daily.

TRANSPORTATION

Getting There
Vancouver International Airport, 130 km to the south, is the main gateway to Whistler. **Perimeter Transportation,** tel. (604) 266-5386 (Vancouver) or (604) 905-0041 (Whistler), provides twice-daily bus service between the two; $32 each way. **Maverick Coach Lines,** tel. (604) 255-1171 or (604) 932-5031, runs six buses daily between the main Vancouver bus depot at 1150 Station St. and Whistler Village; $15 one-way, $29 roundtrip.

In summer, **B.C. Rail** provides daily service to Whistler from 1311 W. 1st St., North Vancouver, tel. (604) 984-5246 or (800) 663-8238. The valley terminal is on Lake Placid Rd. near Whistler Creekside.

An inexpensive way to visit Whistler is with **Bigfoot's Backpacker Adventure Express,** tel. (604) 488-0484. Tours depart Vancouver each Saturday through summer, stopping at all the most scenic spots on the route up to Whistler. They spend the night under canvas and the following day enjoy all the activities the village has to offer, returning to Vancouver Sunday evening. The cost is $45 roundtrip, which includes transportation and camping equipment.

Getting Around
Once you're in Whistler, getting around is pretty easy—if you're staying in Whistler Village, every-thing you need is within easy walking distance. **Whistler Transit System,** tel. (604) 932-4020, operates extensive bus routes throughout the valley, daily 6 a.m.-midnight. Routes radiate from Village Exchange in Whistler Village south to Whistler Creekside and as far north as Emerald Estates on the shore of Green Lake. Three times daily (9:30 a.m., 4 p.m., and 5:55 p.m.), the Whistler Creekside service returns to the village via Alta Lake Rd., passing Whistler Hostel. Fare is $1.50 (exact change only) except for travel on the Village Loop, which is free (and probably the only thing in the valley that *is* free). An all-day pass costs adults $3.60, seniors $3. Through summer Whistler Transit runs a shuttle between the Village Exchange and Lost Lake every 15 minutes.

For a cab call **Sea to Sky Taxi,** tel. (604) 932-3333, or **Whistler Taxi,** tel. (604) 938-3333. Rental car agencies in Whistler include **Budget,** tel. (604) 932-1236, and **Thrifty,** tel. (604) 938-0302.

SERVICES AND INFORMATION

In Whistler Village you'll find a post office, banks, a currency exchange, laundromat, supermarket, and liquor store. To contact **Whistler Health Care Centre,** call (604) 932-4911.

On entering Whistler from the south, look for the sign to the east for **Whistler Visitor Info Centre,** 2097 Lake Placid Rd., Whistler Creekside, tel. (604) 932-5528. A map outside the center shows the Whistler Valley in detail, including hiking trails (with length and elevation gain), downhill and cross-country ski areas, overnight shelters, vehicle and tent campgrounds, fishing, hiking, picnic spots, canoe and kayak portages, and more. The center is open year-round, daily 9 a.m.-5 p.m. Other good sources of information are the free *Whistler Journal* (published every three months), which has a detailed map of Whistler Valley, and the weekly *Pique* newspaper.

THE GOLD NUGGET ROUTE

The route north between Whistler and Lillooet is best traveled in good weather—the scenery is so spectacular you don't want to miss *anything.* See white-topped peaks all around you and big glacier-colored rivers. If you have the time, stop at provincial parks along the way for always-good scenery and outdoor activities. **Nairn Falls Provincial Park** on the banks of Green River has a wooded trail leading to a waterfall. It's worth a stop to see the falls or to stay overnight at the campground; open April-Nov., $9.50 per site from May to October, free the rest of the year.

Pemberton

A small logging town and service center surrounded by mountains, trees, lakes, and rivers, Pemberton sits in the fertile Pemberton Valley 32 km north of Whistler. Best known for its potatoes, locals affectionately call the area "Spud Valley." It's only a short distance south of the Lillooet River, a main transportation route to the Cariboo during the 1860s' gold-rush days. Today's visitors mostly leave their gold pans at home, coming mainly to fish or to hike in the beautiful valleys around Pemberton.

North to Lillooet

From Pemberton you can take one of three routes to Lillooet. The most direct—the route once taken by fortune-seekers heading toward the Cariboo goldfields—is paved Hwy. 99, which zigzags 100 km through steep-sided mountains and over a high pass. The weather here can change rapidly, and even in summer you might find yourself traveling through a sudden snowstorm on the pass. However, the scenery makes the effort worthwhile. You'll see beautiful lakes, fast rivers, summer wildflowers, deep-blue mountains, steep ravines, never-ending forests, and vistas in every shade of green imaginable. Campgrounds and picnic areas mark all the best locations.

The second route (summer only) goes through Mount Currie along the Birkenhead River, passing the turnoff to 3,642-hectare **Birkenhead Lake Provincial Park.** The beautiful lake is surrounded by snowcapped peaks; campsites are $9.50. **Anderson Lake Resort,** 16 km beyond the park turnoff, tel. (604) 452-3232, is in a wooded lakeside location. The smallest cottages, each with a kitchen, are $50; camping is $15-18.

The third and longest route, over 200 km of mostly unpaved road (also summer only), climbs north through Pemberton Meadows, over Hurley Pass, and to the historic mining communities of **Gold Bridge** and **Bralorne.**

For information on **Lillooet,** the confluence of the three above routes, see "Cache Creek and Lillooet" in the "Cariboo Country" section of the Central British Columbia chapter.

EAST FROM VANCOUVER

TOWARD HOPE

When you leave Vancouver and head due east, you travel through the most built-up and heavily populated area of British Columbia, skirting modern cities, residential suburbs, and zones of heavy industry. However, it's not an unattractive area—the main roads follow the mighty Fraser River through a fertile valley of rolling farmland dotted with historic villages, and beautiful mountains line the horizon in just about any direction.

You have a choice of two major routes. The TransCanada Highway, on the south side of the Fraser River, speeds you out of southeast Vancouver through Abbotsford and scenic Chilliwack to Hope. **Cultus Lake Provincial Park,** 11 km south of Chilliwack, holds a warm-water lake surrounded by mountains—a good spot for swimming, picnicking, or camping. The park's campground is open year-round; $15.50 per night March-Oct., free the rest of the year. Slower, more picturesque Hwy. 7 meanders along the north side of the Fraser River through **Mission,** named after a Roman Catholic mission school built in 1861. The town is now known for its Benedictine monastery, which offers a retreat center open to the public. The highway then passes the road to **Harrison Hot Springs** and a resort at the base of Harrison Lake, and crosses over the Fraser River to Hope. In summer you can pick and choose from an endless number of road-

side stands selling fresh fruit at bargain prices—the raspberries in July are delectable.

Fort Langley

Fort Langley is off Hwy. 1, 40 km east of Vancouver. To find out all about the province's beginnings, stop at **Fort Langley National Historic Park,** 23433 Mavis St., Fort Langley, tel. (604) 888-4424. It's on the south bank of the Fraser River, one km north off Hwy. 1. Fort Langley was the first European settlement in the Fraser Valley—a trading post, provisions depot, and administrative center set up by the Hudson's Bay Company in 1827. The fort played a major role in the development of British Columbia. Out its gates have vamoosed native fur and salmon traders, adventurous explorers who opened up the interior, Company traders, and fortune seekers heading for the goldfields of the upper Fraser River. When British Columbia became a crown colony in 1858, the official proclamation was uttered here in the "big house." Today the restored trading post springs to life as park interpreters in period costumes animate the fort's history. Admission is adults $3, children $1.50, seniors and children under five free. It's open in summer, daily 10 a.m.-4:30 p.m.; closed Mon.-Tues. the rest of the year.

Kilby Historic Store and Farm

Off Hwy. 7 at the confluence of the Fraser and Harrison Rivers (look for the inconspicuous sign

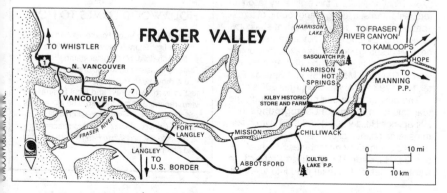

close to Harrison Mills), Kilby Historic Store and Farm, tel. (604) 796-9576, is off the beaten track and often missed by those unfamiliar with the area. The fascinating museum/country store is fully stocked with all the old brands and types of goods that were commonplace in the 1920s and '30s. On the two-hectare riverside grounds are farm equipment, farm animals, a gift shop, and a cafe serving delicious home-style cooking. It's open April-Nov., daily 11 a.m.-5 p.m. Around the corner, you can picnic, swim, fish, or use the boat launch at **Harrison Bay.**

Harrison Hot Springs

A popular resort self-described as "the Spa of Canada," Harrison Hot Springs (pop. 1,000) lies on the sandy southern shores of large **Harrison Lake,** 125 km east of Vancouver. The main attraction is the public hot pool, right downtown on the corner of Harrison Hot Springs Rd. and Esplanade Ave., tel. (604) 796-2244. Scalding 74° C mineral water is pumped from its source, cooled to a soothing 38° C, then pumped into the pool. One-time admission is adults $7, seniors and children $5, or you can swim and soak all day for $9 and $6, respectively. The pool is open in summer, daily 8 a.m.-9 p.m.; the rest of the year, daily 9 a.m.-9 p.m. The 70-km-long lake provides good swimming, sailing, canoeing, and fishing for trout and coho salmon. At the Harrison Hot Springs Hotel in summer, you can sign up for sailing lessons, rent sailboats or rowboats, or take a boat tour of the lake.

The town's most elegant lodging is the aforementioned **Harrison Hot Springs Hotel,** 100 Esplanade, tel. (604) 796-2244 or (800) 663-2266. Right on the lake, this eight-story resort offers restaurants, a lounge, and rooms of a reasonable standard, each with a private balcony. Rates of $114-200 s or d include use of the nearby hot springs pool. A less expensive option still within walking distance of the pools and lake is **Glencoe Motel,** 259 Hot Springs Rd., tel. (604) 796-2574, which charges $60 s or d.

The pick of three campgrounds along the road into town is **Bigfoot Campgrounds,** 670 Hot Springs Rd., tel. (604) 796-9767, which features large shaded sites, free showers, a laundry, and a games room; tent sites $14, hookups $16-20. **Harrison Hot Springs Visitor Info Centre** is beside the main road into town, tel.

(604) 796-3425. It's open in summer, daily 8 a.m.-6 p.m.

Through town to the north is 1,217-hectare **Sasquatch Provincial Park,** named for a tall, hairy, unshaven beast that supposedly inhabits the area. The park extends from a day-use area on the bank of Harrison Lake to two picturesque tree-encircled lakes, each with road access, short hiking trails, day-use areas, and campsites (no showers) for $9.50 a night.

HOPE AND VICINITY

Locals say "all roads lead to Hope"—and they're right. Set on a finger of land at the confluence of the Fraser and Coquihalla Rivers, 158 km east of Vancouver, Hope (pop. 7,000) really is a hub. The TransCanada Highway and Hwy. 7 from Vancouver, the Coquihalla Highway to Kamloops, and Hwy. 3 from the Okanagan all meet at Hope. Don't be put off by first impressions of the town itself. Surrounded by magnificent mountains and rivers, with a couple of great wilderness areas only a short drive away and an abundance of recreational opportunities, Hope is a great place to spend some time.

Simon Fraser, after whom the Fraser River was named, stopped in this area in 1808 after leading the first expedition south down Fraser River Canyon. By 1848 Fort Hope had been set up by the Hudson's Bay Company as a fur-trading post. With the discovery of gold in the canyon in 1858, Hope became a busy stopping point and meeting spot for adventurers and for-

HOLLYWOOD COMES TO HOPE

Late in 1981, Hollywood came north to Hope to film the first Rambo movie, *First Blood.* The multimillion-dollar blockbuster starring Sylvester Stallone transformed the quiet streets of Hope into a movie set. Buildings were constructed just to be blown away, and local businesses were renamed to suit the film. The wilderness action scenes were shot almost entirely in Coquihalla Canyon, east of town. More recently, *K-2, Shoot to Kill,* and *White Fang II* were filmed in and around Hope.

tune seekers. How did Hope get its name? No one really knows, but most theories revolve around various explorers or settlers feeling some kind of hope at reaching the river junction at which the town lies.

Town Sights

To find out more about the history of Hope, visit **Hope Museum,** 919 Water Ave., tel. (604) 869-7322, in the same building as the information center. The museum's comprehensive collection of pioneer artifacts is displayed in several recreated settings, including a kitchen, bedroom, parlor, schoolroom, and blacksmith shop. Other exhibits focus on local native crafts and on artifacts from the original Fort Hope and gold-rush days. Outside, climb on the Home Gold Mill, a restored gold-ore concentrator from the Coquihalla area. The museum is open May-June, daily 9 a.m.-5 p.m.; July-Aug., daily 8 a.m.-8 p.m.

While you're discovering the downtown area, check out the authentic **Japanese garden** in Memorial Park beside the town hall. The garden was constructed to commemorate Tashme, a WW II internment camp for Japanese-Canadians that was located east of Hope. Also don't miss the tree-stump art in Memorial Park. The eagle holding a salmon in its claws (in front of the district office) was carved from a tree with root rot, and it was one of the original tree-stump works of art. As the years go by, more and more carvings are added by chainsaw artist Pete Ryan. During summer look for him in the park, working on his latest creation.

Othello-Quintette Tunnels

These five huge tunnels through a steep gorge of **Coquihalla Canyon** were carved out of solid granite by the Kettle Valley Railway, completing a route for the company's steam locomotives between Vancouver and Nelson. The tunnels opened in 1916, but the line was plagued by snow, rock slides, and washouts, and closed for repairs more often than it was open. It was eventually abandoned in 1959. By 1962 the tracks and four steel bridges over the awesome Coquihalla River gorge had been removed. Today a short, tree-shaded walk takes you from the **Coquihalla Canyon Recreation Area** parking lot to the massive, dark tunnels, now a popular tourist attraction. Stroll through them and over the stur-

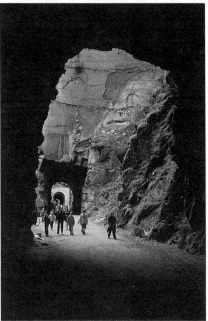

the Othello-Quintette tunnels

ANDREW HEMPSTEAD

dy wooden bridges to admire the gorge and the power and the roar of the Coquihalla River below.

To get to the tunnels from downtown, take Wallace St. to 6th Ave. and turn right. Turn left on Kawkawa Lake Rd., crossing the Coquihalla River Bridge and railway tracks. At the first intersection take the right branch, Othello Rd., and continue until you see a sign to the right (over a rise and easy to miss) pointing to the recreation area.

Skagit Valley Recreation Area

This remote wilderness of 32,570 hectares southeast of Hope is bordered to the east by Manning Provincial Park and to the south by the U.S./Canada border. Access is along the Silver-Skagit Rd., which branches south off Flood Hope Rd. four km southwest of Hope. This rough gravel road climbs steadily for 39 km to the park entrance, then continues 22 km farther to the international border and road's end at **Ross Lake Reservoir.**

Through the park, the road follows the Skagit River, which flows northward from Ross Lake Reservoir through a magnificent valley cloaked in spruce, pine, aspen, and maple. Black bears, cougars, wolves, coyotes, deer, beavers, and over 200 species of birds are all present within the park.

Outdoor enthusiasts can a hike a variety of trails suited mainly to overnight excursions. Skagit River Trail begins just east of where the park access road crosses the river, following the river downstream for 15 km (allow five hours) to a day-use area beside Hwy. 3. Fishing in the Skagit River is good for Dolly Varden and rainbow trout. The access road is dotted with day-use areas, including Shawatum, six km from the park entrance, which was the site of a bustling town with saloons, restaurants, a sawmill, and a daily newspaper—until it was discovered that the only gold found in the area had been planted.

Within the park are two campgrounds; **Silvertip** is three km from the park entrance, while **Ross Lake** is near the end of the road. Over the border, within the boundary of Ross Lake National Recreation Area, is **Hozomeen Campground.** All sites are $9.50. Another option for camping is **Silver Lake Provincial Park,** six km along the park access road from Hope; $6.

Hope Slide

On Hwy. 3, about a 15-minute drive southeast of Hope, the effects of one of nature's amazing forces can be seen. On 9 January 1965, a minor earthquake caused a huge section of mountain to come crashing down, filling the bottom of the Nicolum Creek Valley, destroying about three kilometers of the Hope-Princeton Highway, and killing four motorists. The highway, viewpoint, and parking area are built over the **Hope Slide,** but you can still see the slide's treeless boundaries along the south side of the valley.

Accommodations and Camping

Hope's newer accommodations are east of the TransCanada Highway on Old Hope–Princeton Way, but a couple of choices are found downtown. Best value is **Park Motel,** 832 4th Ave., tel. (604) 869-5891, charging $50 s, $55 d. Slightly more expensive is the much larger **Best Continental Motel,** 860 Fraser Ave., tel. (604) 869-9726, which also has a restaurant; $58 s, $62 d.

Out on Old Hope–Princeton Way, **Royal Lodge Motel,** tel. (604) 869-5358, has rooms for $50 s, $55 d, with kitchens an extra $5. The much newer **Alpine Motel,** tel. (604) 869-9931, offers large, comfortably furnished rooms, a pool, and a pleasant setting; from $60 s, $70 d. In a beautiful spot four km north of Hope, **Beautiful Lake of the Woods Resort,** TransCanada Hwy., tel. (604) 869-9211, is set on a lake with views of the surrounding mountainscape. Rooms are fairly basic, but facilities include a restaurant and canoe rentals. Rates are $50 s, $60 d.

Along the road up to the tunnels, **Coquihalla Campground,** Kawkawa Lake Rd., tel. (604) 869-7119, sits right beside the river. Most sites are surrounded by trees, and facilities include hot showers, a barbecue area, laundry, and games room. Unserviced sites are $15, hookups $18-20.50.

Food

For classic small-town atmosphere check out **Cariboo Cafe,** downtown at 241 Wallace St., tel. (604) 869-5413. The speckled laminex tables and lunch counter, frilly curtains, and walls adorned by a strange collection of faded photographs are the pinnacle of retro chic. Meanwhile, the apron-clad waitresses offer all the usual specials (from $6 for a hearty cooked breakfast and $5 for burgers) as they efficiently keep everyone's coffee topped up. Open daily from 6 a.m.

Chinese **Kan Yon Restaurant,** 800 3rd Ave., tel. (604) 869-2212, looks unremarkable from the outside, but dishes are well-prepared and portions generous. Combination dinners run $9-11 and most entrees are under $10. The **Home Restaurant,** in a stylish two-story building at 665 Old Hope–Princeton Way, tel. (604) 869-5241, is recommended for delicious entrees such as ribs, chicken, and steaks. Expect to pay around $20 per person for a three-course meal.

Information

Hope Visitor Info Centre is right downtown at 919 Water Ave., tel. (604) 869-2021. It's open daily 9 a.m.-5 p.m., with extended summer hours of 8 a.m.-8 p.m. The friendly staff can help you decide which of the routes to take out of Hope, but might also convince you to stay in town a little longer.

FRASER RIVER CANYON

From Hope, the old TransCanada Highway runs north along the west bank of the fast-flowing Fraser River. Although the new Coquihalla Highway is a much shorter option for those heading for Kamloops and beyond, the old highway offers many interesting stops and is by far the preferred route for those not in a hurry. Head north through downtown Hope, cross the Fraser River, take the first right and you're on your way.

The first worthwhile stop is 15-hectare **Emory Creek Provincial Park,** 15 km from Hope. Stopping at this quiet riverside park, it's hard to believe that a little over 100 years ago it was the site of Emory City, complete with saloons, a brewery, a large sawmill, and all the other businesses of a bustling frontier gold town. The city had virtually disappeared by the 1890s, and today no hint of its short-lived presence remains. Wander along riverside trails, try some fishing, or stay at one of the wooded campsites ($9.50).

Yale

This small town of 200 has quite a history. It started off as one of the many Hudson's Bay Company posts, then became a transportation center at the head of the navigable lower section of the Fraser River—the terminus of one of the largest sternwheeler operations on the west coast. Enormous Lady Franklin Rock blocked the upriver section to steamer traffic, so all goods heading for the interior had to be carried from

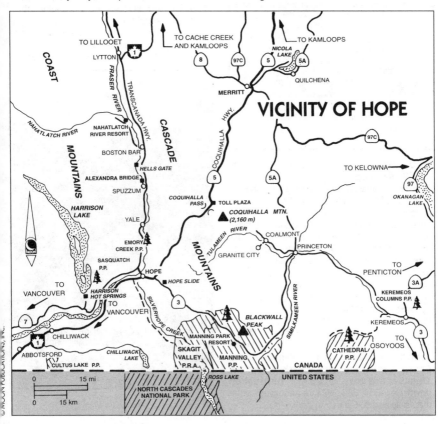

WHITEWATER RAFTING

The Thompson and Fraser Rivers offer some of Canada's most exciting whitewater rafting, and both are run commercially by a number of companies. The town of Lytton, at the confluence of the two rivers, is home to a couple of companies, with others spread south along the Trans-Canada Highway.

Whichever operator you go with, and whichever river you choose to run, you'll be in for the trip of a lifetime. The Thompson is known for its high water, the mighty Fraser for its spectacular canyon and obstacles such as Hell's Gate. Those looking for an extra thrill also run the Nahatlatch, a tributary of the Fraser.

All companies include a great lunch (such as a salmon barbecue) and all transfers, and charge around $90 for a full day. Other options are overnight trips (from $220) and week-long floats from deep in the interior (from $1,200).

From south to north, companies include: Fraser River Raft Expeditions, Yale, tel. (604) 863-2336 or (800) 363-7238; REO Rafting, Boston Bar, tel. (604) 867-9252 or (800) 736-7238; Kumsheen Raft Adventures, Lytton, tel. (604) 455-2296 or (800) 663-6667; and Hyak Wilderness Adventures, Lytton, tel. (604) 734-8622 or (800) 663-7238.

Alexandra Bridge

The treacherous Fraser Canyon posed a major transportation obstacle between the trails from the south and the interior. Several routes across the river were attempted, including a canoe crossing, a cable ferry, and the 1848 Anderson Bridge trail from Fort Yale to Spuzzum.

The gold rush of the 1850s and the onslaught of gold miners and mule trains on the route increased the need for a safe river crossing. In 1863, Alexandra Bridge, 22 km north of Yale, was completed. However, with the successful completion of the Canadian Pacific Railway line through the canyon, the bridge and the Cariboo Wagon Road fell into disrepair.

The popularity of the automobile forced engineers to construct a new suspension bridge in 1926. The new bridge used the original abutments and lasted right up to 1962, when it was replaced by today's bridge on Hwy. 1. **Alexandra Bridge Provincial Park** now protects a section of the old Cariboo Wagon Road, in-

Alexandra Bridge

this point by wagon train along the famous Cariboo Wagon Road.

In 1858 Yale was a flourishing gold-rush town of 20,000, filled with tents, shacks, bars, gambling joints, and shops. But when the gold ran out so did most of the population, and Yale dwindled to the small forestry and service center that it has been for 100 years. If you want to find out more about Yale's historic past, the gold rush, the Cariboo Wagon Road, and railway construction, visit the **Yale Museum,** on Douglas St., tel. (604) 863-2324, and the adjacent historic 1863 **St. John's Church.** The museum is open in summer, Wed.-Sat. 9:30 a.m.-5:30 p.m.

Stay in town at inexpensive **Fort Yale Motel,** tel. (604) 863-2216; $35 s, $40 d. Or head back down the highway 12 km to the campground at **Emory Creek Provincial Park.** Along the TransCanada Hwy. is a small **information booth,** tel. (604) 863-2324, open through summer daily 9 a.m.-6 p.m.

cluding the old bridge. The trail down to the bridge makes a good place to get out and stretch your legs.

Hell's Gate

At well-known Hell's Gate, the Fraser River powers its way through a narrow, glacially carved, 34-meter-wide gorge. When Simon Fraser saw this section of the gorge in 1808 he called it "the Gates of Hell" and the name stuck. In 1914 a massive rock slide rocketed down into the gorge, blocking it even further and resulting in the almost-total obliteration of the sockeye salmon population. In 1944 giant concrete fishways were built to slow the waters and allow the spawning salmon to jump upstream—the river soon swarmed with salmon once again. Today you can cross the canyon aboard the 25-passenger **Hell's Gate Airtram,** tel. (604) 867-9277, which runs through summer, daily 9 a.m.-5 p.m.; adults $9, seniors $8, children $6. Across the river you can browse through landscaped gardens, learn more about the fishway and salmon, or sink your teeth into a fresh salmon at the **Salmon House Restaurant** (same telephone number as the Airtram).

Boston Bar

Another small town with a gold-rush history, Boston Bar is today a popular whitewater rafting mecca for those brave enough to float the Fraser River's roaring rapids. A bridge crossing at Boston Bar accesses the **Nahatlatch River,** renowned for whitewater kayaking. Along quieter stretches of this river are some great fishing spots, three lakes, and numerous primitive campgrounds. **Nahatlatch River Resort,** 15 km along this road, tel. (604) 867-9252 or (800) 736-7238, offers a few campsites for $12 and tent cabins from $50. The resort is also the base for **REO Rafting,** which offers day-trips down the Nahatlatch River from $90 per person. The company also has an office in Boston Bar beside the highway.

COQUIHALLA HIGHWAY

Opened in late spring 1986, the Coquihalla Highway is the most direct link between Hope and the interior of British Columbia. It saves at least two hours by cutting 72 km from the trip between Hope and Kamloops and bypassing the TransCanada Highway's narrow, winding stretch along the Fraser River Canyon. Along the 190-km route are many worthwhile stops, but only one that's compulsory—a toll plaza at Coquihalla Pass where $10 is collected from each vehicle.

The highway ascends and descends through magnificent mountain and river scenery to dry semiarid grasslands. You'll cruise through the valleys of the Lower Coquihalla River and Boston Bar Creek, climb to the 1,240-meter summit of Coquihalla Pass near Coquihalla Lake, descend along the Coldwater River, then climb the Coldwater's eastern valley slope to Merritt. From Merritt the highway climbs the valleys of the Nicola River and Clapperton Creek to join the Trans-Canada Highway eight km west of Kamloops.

Merritt

This town of 8,000 in the Nicola Valley, 115 km north of Hope, provides the only services along the Coquihalla Highway. It's also the exit point for those heading east to the Okanagan on the Okanagan Connector.

Make your first stop off the highway at **Merritt Visitor Info Centre,** on a high point east of the highway, tel. (250) 378-2281. Upstairs in this large log building is an intriguing forestry exhibition, and behind the building is the **Godey Creek Hiking Trail,** which takes you 1.4 km (25 minutes) each way to a lookout cabin. The center is open year-round, daily 9 a.m.-5 p.m.

Each July, **Merritt Mountain Music Festival** attracts tens of thousands of country-music lovers for a weekend of concerts featuring the biggest names in country music. For information and ticketing call (604) 860-1470.

Since the Coquihalla Highway opened, many motels have been built around Merritt. But by far the best choice is one of the originals, the **Quilchena Hotel,** on Nicola Lake, 23 km east of town on Hwy. 5A, tel. (250) 378-2611. Built in 1908, this grand old three-story hostelry features a cafe, restaurant, and antiques-decorated rooms. The hotel sits beside a beautiful lake where you can rent a boat and go fishing. Rates are $69-79 s or d.

MANNING PROVINCIAL PARK

This spectacular 71,000-hectare park in the Cascade Mountains, 64 km east of Hope along Hwy. 3, stretches down to the Canada/U.S. border. Hwy. 3 makes a "U" through the park—from the northwest to south to northeast corners. But to really appreciate the park, you need to get off the highway—take in the beautiful bodies of water, drive up to a wonderful stretch of high alpine meadows, or hike on the numerous trails. Within the park are two major watersheds; the Skagit River flows west to the Fraser River, and the Similkameen River flows east into the Columbia River. The many tributaries of these two rivers flow down from the highest peaks of the rain-drenched Cascade Mountains, through dense subalpine forests of Engelmann spruce, Douglas fir, western red cedar, and hemlock to the valley through which Hwy. 3 runs. Wildlife is abundant, including populations of black bear, moose, elk, coyote, and beaver.

cutthroat trout

Summer Recreation

A highlight of the park is the paved road immediately across Hwy. 3 from Manning Park Resort; the road climbs steadily to **Cascade Lookout,** a viewpoint offering a magnificent 180-degree panoramic view. Beyond the lookout, the road turns to gravel and continues climbing for nine km, ending at a parking lot beneath 2,063-meter Blackwall Peak. From this area of flower-filled alpine meadows, views extend over the park's remote northern boundary. Take time to soak up the color by taking one of the short trails originating from the parking lot. Or hike **Heather Trail** (10 km each way; allow three hours) to Three Brothers Mountain. If you're there between late July and mid-August, you won't believe what you'll see—a rich yellow, orange, and white carpet of wildflowers as far as you can see.

Along Hwy. 3 are a number of short self-guided nature trails, including a 700-meter walk (20 minutes) through a stand of ancient western red cedars. The trailhead is Sumallo Grove day-use area, 10 km east of where Hwy. 3 enters the park from the west. Just east of the Visitor Information Centre, on the south side of the road, is the 500-meter (10-minute) **Beaver Pond Trail.** If you notice anyone arriving on foot in this parking lot with worn soles, a bent back, and a great big smile on their face, give them a pat on the back—they may have just completed one of the world's greatest long-distance hikes. The **Pacific Crest Trail** runs 3,860 km from the U.S./Mexican border to this small and undistinguished trailhead.

During the summer months you can fish in rivers, streams, and lakes for Dolly Varden and rainbow trout (get a license first) or explore **Lightning Lake** in a canoe; lakeside rentals cost $10 per hour. At **Manning Park Corral,** next to Manning Park Resort, tel. (250) 840-8844, you can go on a one-hour trail ride for $20, or spend all day on horseback with a hearty trailside lunch thrown in for $100.

BOB RACE

Skiing

Manning Provincial Park gets plenty of dry snow for good downhill and cross-country skiing. At **Ski Manning,** 11 km west of Manning Park Resort along Gibson Pass Rd., downhill enthusiasts can take advantage of a 437-meter vertical rise served by two chairlifts, a T-bar, and a rope tow. Most runs are for intermediate skiers, but novices and experts will also find suitable terrain. Lift tickets are adults $29, seniors $19, children $18, under six free. On-hill facilities include a cafeteria, ski school, and ski rentals (from $20 for a full day). A free shuttle bus transfers guests to the ski area from Manning Park Resort, which offers winter packages from $115 for two nights' accommodations and two days' skiing. In winter, RVers can stay in one of the ski area's upper parking lots. For ski resort and packages information call (250) 840-8822; for ski conditions call the Vancouver Snowphone at (604) 689-7669.

Along with 190 km of wilderness trails, there are 30 km of groomed skiing trails available for $10 per day. Cross-country skis rent for $14 per day.

Manning Park Resort

In the heart of the park on Hwy. 3, Manning Park Resort, tel. (250) 840-8822, is a full-service lodging providing comfortable hotel rooms, cabins, and triplexes, as well as a dining room, self-serve cafeteria, small grocery store, and an open fireside lounge. Other facilities include saunas, a TV room, indoor recreational games, tennis courts, a coin-operated laundry, and a gift shop. Through summer, rooms in the main lodge are $79 s or d, and chalets with kitchens range $89-109. The rest of the year rates are reduced, with rooms from $54.

Campgrounds

The park's four campgrounds hold a total of 355 sites; in summer, get in early to be assured of snagging one. Each campground provides drinking water and toilets. Firewood is available for a fee. The most popular is **Lightning Lake,** which has showers, and is two km west of Manning Park Resort on Gibson Pass Rd.; $15.50 per night. Others include **Coldspring Campground,** on Hwy. 3 two km west of the resort; **Hampton Campground,** on Hwy. 3 four km east of the resort; and **Mule Deer Campground,** a further four km east. These three charge $9.50 per night.

Information

The park's **Visitor Information Centre** is one km east of Manning Park Resort, tel. (250) 840-8836. Inside you'll find displays on recreation opportunities and on the area's natural and cultural history, as well as maps and detailed information about park facilities. The center is open in summer, daily 8:30 a.m.-4:30 p.m.; weekdays only the rest of the year. In July and August park interpreters offer guided walks, interesting slide shows, and evening talks at the amphitheater on Gibson Pass Rd.; scan information boards around the park or inquire at the Visitor Information Centre to see what's on.

CONTINUING TOWARD THE OKANAGAN VALLEY

From the eastern boundary of Manning Provincial Park, Hwy. 3 follows the Similkameen River north to Princeton, then turns sharply to the southeast to Osoyoos, at the southern end of the Okanagan

Valley, a total distance of 158 km. Between the pak and Princeton, stop along the highway at **Similkameen Falls,** where the Similkameen River rushes over a narrow escarpment. The adjacent campground costs $9.50 per night.

Princeton

At the confluence of the Similkameen and Tulameen Rivers, surrounded by low tree-covered hills, lies the small friendly ranching town of Princeton (pop. 3,000). **Princeton and District Pioneer Museum,** 167 Vermilion Ave., tel. (250) 295-7588, features pioneer artifacts from Granite City (see below), Chinese and Interior Salish artifacts, and a good fossil display; open Mon.-Fri. 1-5 p.m. Another local attraction is **Castle Park,** on the northeast side of town, where the 75-year-old stone-and-concrete ruins of a cement plant lie beside twinkling One Mile Creek. Around, through, and over these magnificent ruins grow trees, wild roses, lilacs, and lupines. Take a look at the concrete paths and steps leading down from the back of the administrative building to the ruins—the concrete is loaded with fossilized shells. The ruins are now part of a commercial campground and tours are run throughout summer. To get there from Princeton, cross the bridge at the north end of Bridge St., turn right on Old Hedley Rd., cross Hwy. 5, turn left on Five Mile Rd., then continue until the sign to the park leads you right. You'll pass a small lake before coming to the park entrance.

Just a short stroll from downtown, **Riverside Motel,** 307 Thomas Ave. at the north end of Bridge St., tel. (250) 295-6232, was built in 1934 as a hunting and fishing lodge. The aptly named motel is right beside the river, and in the height of summer the water level drops to expose a small beach and shallow swimming hole. Ask the owner to show you a photo of the place taken in 1937—the cabins still look exactly the same. Each comfortable log cabin has a toilet, a shower, and a kitchen with a fridge, stove, cooking utensils, crockery, and cutlery. Rates are a very reasonable $30-38 s, $36-44 d. **Princeton Castle RV Park,** on Hwy. 5A three km north of town, tel. (250) 295-7988, features sites alongside a small creek in a treed setting. Sites are $14-16.

For a meal, head downtown to **Sunflower Cafe,** in the Princeton Hotel at 258 Bridge St., tel. (250) 295-3355. The sunflowers may be fake and the atmosphere far from riveting, but for $5 you'll get a good cooked breakfast or a burger and fries. **Princeton Visitor Info Centre** is at the west entrance to town, tel. (250) 295-3103, and is open year-round 8:30 a.m.-4:30 p.m.; daily in summer, Mon.-Fri. only the rest of the year.

Coalmont

If you want to see some impressive canyon scenery off the main tourist drag, cross the river at the north end of Princeton's Bridge Street and turn left, heading west toward Coalmont (about 18 km) and Granite City (20 km). Coalmont came to the forefront when gold-rush activity moved from Granite City (see below) to this village in 1911. Today, you can't help but notice that the town's residents have a sense of humor. The welcoming sign states that Coalmont has no industry but plenty of activity in the form of sleeping and daydreaming. It also claims Coalmont has a hot, cold, wet, and dry climate, warns traveling salesmen to stay away, and advises single women that their safety is not guaranteed due to the predominance of bachelors. The attractive old **Coalmont Hotel** (circa 1911) still stands, along with quite a number of homes—some with backyards crammed with eclectic collections of rusting mine machinery.

Granite City

At the stop sign in Coalmont, continue straight ahead to Granite Creek, turn left on Hope St., right over the creek, then follow the road until you reach the remains of Granite City, a ghost town. After the discovery of a gold nugget in Granite Creek back in 1885, a 13-saloon gold-rush city sprang to life on this spot. Soon it was the third-largest city in the province, supporting a population of over 2,000. It's on the right just after the first road intersection, but it's easy to miss because there isn't much left—just a few fallen-down cabins among wild lilac bushes and trees. It's up to your imagination to re-create the good ol' days.

If you continue along Rice Rd. you'll end up at the B.C. Forest Service's **Granite Creek Recreation Site,** a gorgeous place to picnic or camp. Free, tree-shaded campsites with picnic tables line the creek in a large daisy- and cow-filled meadow. Pit toilets are nearby.

Continuing East from Princeton on Highway 3

From Princeton, Hwy. 3 takes you on a scenic route through the beautiful **Similkameen River Valley,** which holds lots of places to camp, in either provincial parks or private campgrounds. Between Princeton and Keremeos the road follows the **Dewdney Trail,** a 468-km mule track used in the 1860s to connect Hope with the Kootenay goldfields. This stretch itself has also been a major mining area, supplying a fortune in gold, silver, nickel, and copper over the years. Notice the changes in vegetation as you progress east—from tall, tree-covered mountains between Hope and Princeton, through rolling hills covered in sagebrush and lush irrigated orchards around Keremeos, to desert (complete with lizards, cactus, and rattlesnakes) around Osoyoos on the Canada/U.S. border.

Cathedral Provincial Park

Wilderness hikers and mountaineers should not miss the turnoff to this spectacular 33,272-hectare park just west of Keremeos. A 21-km gravel road leads into the park, ending one km beyond the base camp for privately owned **Cathedral Lakes Lodge.** Guests get a lift 16 km uphill to the resort, everyone else has to walk. For this reason most park visitors stay at the resort, which provides accommodations, meals, use of canoes, a recreation room and hot tub, and transportation to and from the base camp. The minimum stay is a two-day package; original cabins are $115-140 per night while rooms in the main lodge are $170-190. For reservations call (250) 226-7560 or 492-1606.

About 50 km of wilderness trails lead from the resort to a variety of striking and enticingly named rock formations, including Stone City, Giant Cleft, Devil's Woodpile, Macabre Tower, Grimface Mountain, Denture Ridge, and Smokey the Bear. Wander through meadows waving with dainty alpine flowers, climb peaks for tremendous views, fish for trout in sparkling turquoise lakes, capture on film immense glacier-topped mountains. For general park information, call (250) 494-0321.

Keremeos

As you approach mountain-surrounded Keremeos from the west, the road is lined with lush irrigated orchards and fruit stands, one after another, which is probably what inspired the town's claim to fame as the "Fruit Stand Capital of Canada." Keremeos has one of the longest growing seasons in the province. Try a tastebud-tingling fruit-juice shake in summer; recommended is the second-to-last stand as you head east out of town. Harvest dates are mid-June to mid-July for cherries; mid-July to early August for apricots; mid-July to early September for peaches; mid-August to mid-September for pears; early August to mid-October for apples; early- to mid-September for prunes; early September to early October for grapes.

The town's main historic attraction is the **Grist Mill,** tel. (250) 499-2888, a restored water-powered mill built in 1877. This is where pioneer Similkameen Valley settlers used to grind locally produced wheat into flour. Take a guided tour of the mill any day of the week from mid-May to October (closed the rest of the year), then try your hand at the many informative and entertaining hands-on displays in the museum and visitor center, or relax in the tearoom overlooking the gardens. Admission is $4. To get there, go through town on the main highway, turn north on Hwy. 3A toward Penticton, then right at the Historic Site sign on Upper Bench Road.

Another local highlight, although it takes some effort to reach, is 20-hectare **Keremeos Columns Provincial Park.** The park is named for a 90-meter cliff of remarkable hexagonal basalt columns rising from a lava base just outside the park boundary. The columns were supposed to be in the park but because of a surveying accident actually stand on private land. Access the viewpoint by taking a steep eight-km logging road off Hwy. 3 about four km north of town (turn right at the Keremeos cemetery), then take another steep eight-km hike (allow at least three hours one-way) across private property; ask for permission and trail details at the house at the end of the paved road.

In the mood for a bit of winetasting? Head for **St. Laszlo Vineyards** on Hwy. 3 about one km east of Keremeos, tel. (250) 499-5600. This winery produces 18 varieties of wine from their vineyard of American and French hybrids and exotic vinifera grapes.

DOVER PUBLICATIONS, INC.

BOB RACE

OKANAGAN VALLEY

This warm, sunny valley 400 km east of Vancouver extends 180 km between the U.S./Canada border in the south and the TransCanada Highway in the north. Lush orchards and vineyards, fertile irrigated croplands, low rolling hills, and a string of beautiful lakes line the valley floor, where you'll also find 40 golf courses, dozens of commercial attractions, and lots and lots of people—especially in summer.

The Okanagan Valley's three main cities—**Penticton, Kelowna,** and **Vernon**—are spread around long, narrow **Okanagan Lake,** and collectively hold the bulk of interior British Columbia's population. Numerous smaller communities also ring the lakeshore, doubling or tripling in size between May and September when hordes of vacationers turn the valley into one big resort. Most of these summer pilgrims are Canadians from cooler climes, who come in search of guaranteed sunshine, lazy days on a beach, and a take-away tan. In winter, the valley draws pilgrims of another sort—skiers on their way to the world-class slopes flanking the valley.

All the credit for developing the Okanagan into Canada's fruit basket goes to the original planter, Father Charles Pandosy, a French oblate priest who established a mission in the Kelowna area in 1859. Within a couple of years he had successfully introduced apple trees to the district. The trees positively blossomed under his care, thanks to the valley's long five-and-a-half-month growing season, over 2,000 hours of sunshine a year, relatively mild winters, and the ready availability of water. Soon fruit orchards of all types were springing up everywhere, and today the Okanagan Valley region produces 30% of Canada's apples, 60% of its cherries, 20% of its peaches, half of its pears and prunes, and all the apricots in the country.

OSOYOOS

This town of 4,200 is nestled on the west shore of **Osoyoos Lake,** Canada's warmest freshwater lake. The town also boasts Canada's highest year-round average temperature. Away from the valley floor and its many orchards, the landscape is surprisingly arid, including small tracts of desert complete with sand, cacti, sagebrush, lizards, snakes, and other desert dwellers.

For a bird's-eye view of the lake, take Hwy. 3 west from town 12 km, then follow a 20-km gravel road to the 1,874-meter summit of **Mt. Kobau.** Short trails there lead to viewpoints of the Similkameen and Okanagan Valleys. Along the section of Hwy. 3 before the turnoff, watch for the **spotted lake** on the south side of the road. As summer progresses and the lake's water evaporates, high concentrations of magnesium, calcium, and sodium crystallize, forming colorful circles.

Practicalities

In summer, Osoyoos Lake attracts hordes of boaters, water-skiers, anglers, windsurfers, and sun worshippers, so getting accommodations can be difficult. **Avalon Motel,** on Hwy. 3 between the information center and downtown, tel. (250) 495-6334 or (800) 264-5999, is a clean and comfortable accommodation with smallish rooms for $42 s, $47 d. Boasting a great location down on the lakeshore is **Holiday Inn Sunspree Resort,** Hwy. 3, tel. (250) 495-7223 or (800) 216-6246, which was totally renovated for the summer of 1997. It offers 85 rooms, many overlooking the resort's private beach, as well as a rooftop garden, fitness center, boat rentals, and a restaurant. Rates start at $89 s or d. Also on the lakeshore are several older resort motels, including **Desert Motor Inn,** 7702 62nd Ave., tel. (250) 495-6525, which charges $65-89

per room; and **Poplars Motel,** 6404 67th St., tel. (250) 495-6035, with a private beach and rooms from $75. **Haynes Point Provincial Park** protects an extremely narrow low-lying spit that juts into Osoyoos Lake south of downtown. Camping in the park is $14.50 per night.

Walk down Main Street and take your pick from various cafes and the usual smattering of Italian and Chinese restaurants. **Beans Desert Cafe,** 8323 Main St., tel. (250) 495-7742, features a good range of coffee concoctions in a modern setting. More-traditional fare is offered down on the spit at **Osoyoos Burger House,** where hamburgers cost $3.50-6.

In a patrking lot at the corner of Hwys. 3 and 97 is **Osoyoos Visitor Info Centre,** tel. (250) 495-7142 or (888) 676-9667. It's open 8:30 a.m.-4:30 p.m., daily in summer and Mon.-Fri. the rest of the year.

PENTICTON

One of the Okanagan's three major population centers, Penticton (pop. 33,000) lies between the north end of Skaha Lake and the south end of Okanagan Lake. The city gets its name from the nomadic Salish natives, in whose tongue Penticton means "Place To Stay Forever."

Approaching from the south, you'll see a roadside plaque honoring pioneer Thomas Ellis, who arrived in the valley in 1886, built a great cattle empire, and planted the area's first orchard. Today fruit orchards are everywhere. Penticton's nickname is Peach City; the annual **Penticton Peach Festival** celebrates the harvest in mid-August with a week of sailboat races, parades, games, and entertainment. The second week of September, the **Penticton Harvest and Grape Fall Fair** is another fruitful event.

SIGHTS AND RECREATION

Along Okanagan Lake

Wander west along the tree-shaded shores of Lake Okanagan to see the **SS Sicamous,** the last Canadian Pacific Railway sternwheeler to work on Okanagan Lake. The Sicamous operated from 1914 to 1951; now it rests on the lakeshore at the end of the beach and houses a

museum. It's open in summer daily 7 a.m.-7 p.m.; admission $3. The adjacent **rose garden** is worth a stroll to see perfect blooms and manicured lawns, and to read all the stats on **Okanagan Lake Dam** and flood-control system. Next to the rose garden are a **miniature golf course** and a bicycle-rental outfit (see "Transportation" under "Other Practicalities," below).

If you wander east from the tourist center along Lakeshore Dr., you'll come to the **Art Gallery of the South Okanagan,** 11 Ellis St., tel. (250) 493-2928; open Tues.-Fri. 10 a.m.-5 p.m., Sat.-Sun. 1-5 p.m. The craft shop is a good place to pick up creative treasures and handmade souvenirs. If you're visiting on a Sunday you can get in on afternoon tea. Continue east from the gallery and you'll arrive at the local **marina**—another enjoyable spot for a lakeside stroll.

Penticton Museum

This museum, 785 Main St., tel. (250) 492-6025, houses an excellent collection of Western Canadiana, covering natural history, local native peoples, the fur-trading days, railways, early Chinese residents, and sternwheelers. It also features an enormous taxidermy section, mining, ranching, and ghost-town artifacts and trea-

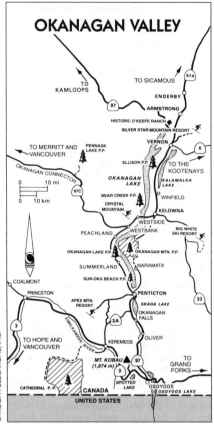

OKANAGAN VALLEY

TO KAMLOOPS

TO SICAMOUS

97A

ENDERBY

97

ARMSTRONG

HISTORIC O'KEEFE RANCH

SILVER STAR MOUNTAIN RESORT

VERNON

TO MERRITT AND VANCOUVER

PENNASK LAKE P.P.

ELLISON P.P.

6

TO THE KOOTENAYS

OKANAGAN CONNECTOR

OKANAGAN LAKE

KALAMALKA LAKE

0   10 mi

97C

0   10 km

BEAR CREEK P.P.

WINFIELD

CRYSTAL MOUNTAIN

KELOWNA

WESTSIDE

PEACHLAND

WESTBANK

BIG WHITE SKI RESORT

OKANAGAN LAKE P.P.

OKANAGAN MTN. P.P.

COALMONT

SUMMERLAND

NARAMATA

SUN-OKA BEACH P.P.

PRINCETON

PENTICTON

APEX MTN. RESORT

SKAHA LAKE

33

OKANAGAN FALLS

3A

SIMILKAMEEN RIVER

3

TO HOPE AND VANCOUVER

KEREMEOS

OLIVER

MT. KOBAU (1,874 m)

97

3

TO GRAND FORKS

CATHEDRAL P.P.

SPOTTED LAKE

OSOYOOS

OSOYOOS LAKE

CANADA

UNITED STATES

© MOON PUBLICATIONS, INC.

sures, and assorted militaria. Allow at least an hour or two in here. The museum is open Mon.-Sat. 10 a.m.-5 p.m.

Commercial Attractions

For some local mining history visit **Bill Barlee's Old West Museum,** 954 Eckhardt Ave., tel. (250) 492-5116. It's open in summer, daily 10 a.m.-6 p.m. The $3 admission price includes a map of the old goldfields. **Okanagan Game Farm,** eight km south of Penticton on Hwy. 97, tel. (250) 497-5405, contains over 1,000 animals from around the world, including lions, bears, giraffes, and snakes. Admission is adults $8, children $6, under five free. Open daily 8

a.m.-dusk. From Penticton north you'll no doubt notice that water-slide mania has hit the Okanagan hard—even the TraveLodge in Penticton has an indoor water slide. If you're in the mood for a bit of slip slidin' away, try **Wonderful Waterworld,** 225 Yorkton Ave., tel. (250) 492-8121; open daily, adults $14, children $10.

Skiing

Sunniest of the Okanagan ski resorts is **Apex Mountain Resort,** 33 km west of Penticton, which provides 605 vertical meters and 56 runs over 222 hectares. The slopes are served by a T-bar and two chairlifts, one of which—the Quick-draw quad—zips skiers to the summit of 2,178-meter Beaconsfield Mountain and opens up most of the expert terrain. Among base-area facilities are restaurants, lounges, a day lodge, grocery and liquor store, free outdoor hot tubs, an ice rink, ski school, and ski shop with rentals. The resort is open daily December to mid-April, with one run open for night skiing on Wednesday, Friday, and Saturday. Lift tickets are adults $38, seniors $24, children $21; kids under seven free. For ski-area information call (250) 492-2880; for accommodation packages call (800) 387-2739.

Cross-country skiers head to Apex Mountain's 12 km of trails around the base area, or to **Nickel Plate Nordic Centre,** six km from the ski area, featuring 30 km of groomed trails and 20 km of backcountry trails.

On-mountain accommodations are available at **Holiday Inn Sunspree Resort,** tel. (250) 292-8121 or (800) 387-2739, which charges from $64.50 per person (room only). Many Penticton accommodations offer great ski packages from $42 per person.

Events

Penticton seems to have festivals, parades, events, or competitions going on throughout the year. The biggest event is the annual **Peach Festival,** held on the second week of August; it's a tradition going back more than 50 years. Events include peach tasting, the crowning of Miss Penticton, a classic auto show, a sand-castle competition, fireworks, and nightly entertainment in Gyro Park.

Other annual happenings include **Mid-Winter Break-Out** in February; the **Blossom Festival** in April or early May; the **Highland Games** and

Okanagan Summer School of the Arts in July; the **Ironman Canada Triathlon** and **B.C. Square Dance Jamboree** in August; and the **Okanagan Wine Festival** in October.

ACCOMMODATIONS AND CAMPING

Hotels and Motels
Several lodgings are on Lakeshore Drive, close to both the lake and downtown. **Club Paradise**

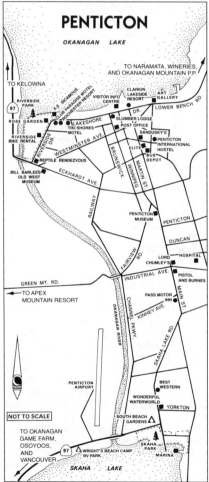

PENTICTON

Motel, 1000 Lakeshore Dr., tel. (250) 493-8400, is the least expensive lodging by the lake. It's been renovated out front, but the back is still a bit of a mess. Nevertheless, the rooms are clean, comfortable, and air-conditioned; from $54 s or d. **Rochester Resort,** 970 Lakeshore Dr., tel. (250) 493-1128, charges similar prices to the Club Paradise. At **Tiki Shores Beach Resort,** 914 Lakeshore Dr., tel. (250) 492-8769, all rooms have kitchens, and some have a private rooftop terrace. Amenities include a pool and hot tub. Rates start at $89 s or d.

For a million-dollar lake view, consider the six-story **Clarion Lakeside Resort,** 21 Lakeshore Dr. W, tel. (250) 493-8221 or (800) 663-9400, the only accommodation right on the lake. The full-service hotel has over 200 rooms, an indoor pool overlooking the lake, a whirlpool, saunas, tennis courts, lounges, and a restaurant; $94-195 s or d.

Another bunch of motels lies south of downtown, within walking distance of Skaha Lake. Least expensive of these is **Pass Motor Inn,** 2307 Skaha Lake Rd., tel. (250) 492-0323 or (800) 670-8062, which charges from $45 s, $50 d. **Best Western Inn at Penticton,** 3180 Skaha Lake Rd., tel. (250) 493-0311 or (800) 668-6746, offers an indoor pool in tropical surroundings, an outdoor pool, and a barbecue area. Rooms feature modern furnishings and the suites have kitchens; from $85 s or d.

Holiday Inn Sunspree Resort is in Apex Mountain Village, 33 km west of the city, tel. (250) 292-8121. It's designed for skiers—and priced accordingly; from $64.50 per person. In summer low season, the rooms go for just $70 s or d—a bargain considering the rooms are large and modern and each has a kitchen.

Hostel
Penticton International Hostel, 464 Ellis St., tel. (250) 492-3992, occupies a historic residence close to the heart of downtown. Facilities include a kitchen, laundry, bike rentals, and an outdoor barbecue area; $14 per night for members of Hostelling International, $19 for nonmembers.

Campgrounds
All Penticton's commercial campgrounds are south of downtown around the north end of

Penticton Marina

JANE AND BRUCE KING

Skaha Lake. They're very popular in summer, so make reservations in advance if possible. The least-crowded seems to be **Wright's Beach Camp RV Park,** Hwy. 97, tel. (250) 492-7120, which is a little bit surprising as it's right on the lake and many sites are shaded. Sites are $20-30 per night. Across from Sudbury Beach and adjacent to Hwy. 97 is **South Beach Gardens,** 3815 Skaha Lake Rd., tel. (250) 492-0628, which charges $16 for an unserviced site and $18-22 for hookups. RV hookups are also offered year-round up at Apex Mountain Village, 33 km west of Penticton. The cost is $15 per vehicle, but you'll need plenty of quarters for the showers.

OTHER PRACTICALITIES

Food
Upstairs in the Slumber Lodge is the **Wild Goose Cafe,** 274 Lakeshore Dr., tel. (250) 492-0554, with views across Lake Okanagan. It's open daily 7 a.m.-3 p.m. A cooked breakfast costs a reasonable $5-7, although you may have to wait for a table in summer. The rest of the day it's the usual cafe fare of hamburgers, sandwiches, and salads.

For home cooking at inexpensive prices, try the family-style **Elite Restaurant,** right downtown at 340 Main St., tel. (250) 492-3051. Good-value daily specials (soup or salad, main course, dessert, and coffee) go for around $7-8. Open daily 7 a.m.-9 p.m.

On Main Street between Okanagan and Skaha Lakes are a number of decent eateries. **Lord Chumley's,** 2156 Main St., tel. (250) 492-4884, serves delicious fish and chips from $6. In the same vicinity, **Pistol and Burnes,** 2210 Main St., tel. (250) 490-8720, perches on the edge of a large supermarket parking lot. The casual cafe offers a row of outside tables and serves up good coffee and light snacks. For delicious Tex-Mex cuisine, head downtown to **Sandusky's,** 314 Main St., tel. (250) 493-3939, featuring a wide range of starters from $3, great chili for $4, and entrees from $7.

Transportation
Visitors flying into the Okanagan usually use Kelowna Airport, but **Air BC,** tel. (250) 492-2165, and **Canadian Regional,** tel. (250) 493-2900, have agents in Penticton. The **Greyhound Bus Depot** is at 307 Ellis St., tel. (250) 493-4101. Greyhound offers daily buses south to Osoyoos, linking up with services along Hwy. 3, and north through the Okanagan Valley to Salmon Arm on the TransCanada Highway.

Getting around town is easy on **Penticton Transit System,** tel. (250) 492-5602. Rental cars are available from **Avis,** tel. (250) 493-8133; **Budget,** tel. (250) 493-0212; **National Tilden,** tel. (250) 493-7288; and **Thrifty,** tel. (250) 493-2588. **Riverside Bike Rental,** on Riverside Dr. by Riverside Park at the west end of Okanagan lakefront, tel. (250) 493-1188, rents mountain bikes, six-speeds, or cruisers; $8 for the first hour, $6 for the second hour, $27 a day. They also rent a variety of other two- or four-wheeled contraptions. Open daily late May through September.

Services and Information

Penticton Regional Hospital is on Carmi Ave. (east off Main St.), tel. (250) 492-4000. The **post office** is on the corner of Winnipeg St. and Nanaimo Avenue.

You can't miss the **Penticton Visitor Info Centre** north of downtown right on the shore of Okanagan Lake, tel. (250) 493-4055 or (800) 663-5052. It's open in summer daily 8 a.m.-8 p.m.; the rest of the year Mon.-Fri. 9 a.m.-5 p.m., Sat.-Sun. 10 a.m.-4 p.m. If it's closed when you're there, you can still orient yourself to local surroundings with the gigantic town map and directory outside the entrance.

NORTH OF PENTICTON

To Okanagan Mountain Provincial Park

A 14 km secondary road runs northeast out of Penticton, skirting the east side of Okanagan Lake and passing through the small community of **Naramata**. Two farm wineries lie off Naramata Road. Stop by **Hillside Cellars**, just outside Penticton, tel. (250) 493-4424, and **Lang Vineyards**, near Naramata on Gammon Rd. (follow the signs from Naramata Rd.), tel. (250) 496-5987, to sample or buy quality wines available only at the vineyards.

Continue through Naramata and up into the mountains, where the road fizzles out near the south border of undeveloped 10,461-hectare Okanagan Mountain Provincial Park. The only way to get into this piece of untouched wilderness is to walk or boat over. Hike in for the day for a picnic, some fishing, or to explore the 24 km of trails. Be sure to bring warm clothes—it gets cold up here even when it's warm and balmy down in Penticton. The park has no facilities.

Summerland

Back on Hwy. 97 heading north from Penticton, you'll pass **Sun-Oka Beach Provincial Park,** which offers trees galore, picnic tables, beaches, and good swimming. As you enter Summerland, nestled between Giants Head Mountain and the lake, you'll be amazed how the road is lined with orchards and fruit stands. Stop for a free tour of the **Summerland Sweets** factory on Canyon View Rd., tel. (250) 494-0377, to see syrups, jams, and candy being made from fresh and frozen fruit; from Hwy. 97 take the Dunn St. or Arkell Rd. exit west, turn right on Gartrell Rd., left on Happy Valley Rd., right on Hillborn St., then left on Canyon View Road.

At **Sumac Ridge Estate Winery and Golf and Country Club,** one km north of Summerland, tel. (250) 494-0451, you can enjoy a round of golf followed by a winery tour and winetasting. The free tours and tastings are offered May-October, daily 10 a.m-4 p.m.

Continuing toward Kelowna

On the way to Kelowna you'll pass two entrances to **Okanagan Lake Provincial Park,** a grassy, tree-shaded, beach-fringed park popular for boating and swimming. The park holds numerous picnic tables, as well as tent and RV sites (from $15.50 a night April-Oct.; busy in summer).

Farther along is the community of **Peachland.** Crammed between a rocky bluff and Okanagan Lake, Peachland was founded in 1808 by Manitoba entrepreneur and newspaperman John Robinson, who came to the Okanagan in search of mining prospects but turned his talents to developing the delicious locally grown dessert peaches. While you're in this neck of the woods, tour and taste the wines of **Chateau St. Clair Winery,** tel. (250) 767-3113, which overlooks Summerland from its hilltop perch on Trepannier Bench Road. In summer it's open daily 10 a.m.-4:30 p.m. In winter hours vary; call for more information.

KELOWNA

British Columbia's fourth-largest city, Kelowna (pop. 95,000) lies on the shores of 170-km-long Okanagan Lake, approximately halfway between Penticton in the south and Vernon in the north. The city has boomed in recent years, mostly through improved access from the west; the Coquihalla Highway and Okanagan Connector cut travel time between Vancouver and Kelowna from around six hours to under four hours.

The town combines a scenic location among semiarid mountains with an unbeatable climate of long, sunny summers and short, mild winters. The low rolling hills around the city hold lush terraced orchards, and the numerous local vineyards produce some excellent wines. Visitors flock here in summer to enjoy the area's sparkling lakes, sandy beaches, and numerous provincial parks; in winter they come for great skiing at nearby Big White Ski Resort.

History

For thousands of years before the arrival of the first Europeans, the nomadic Salish peoples inhabited the Okanagan Valley, hunting (Kelowna is a Salish word for grizzly bear), gathering, and fishing. The first European to settle in the valley was an oblate missionary, Father Pandosy, who established a mission on the southern outskirts of present-day Kelowna in 1859. Since the first apple trees were planted at the mission, Kelowna has thrived as the center of the Okanagan fruit, vegetable, and vineyard industry (the valley is Canada's largest fruit-growing region). Tourism is also important to the local economy, and the city is full of lakeside resorts, golf courses, and visitor services.

SIGHTS

City Park

Right downtown, beautiful City Park is the largest of Kelowna's many parks. Its 14 lakefront hectares hold lots of flowers and large shady trees, expansive lawns, and a public beach. If you feel like taking to the water, you can rent a boat, houseboat, and fishing equipment at one of several marinas. Water-skiing and parasailing are also popular activities here. Near the entrance to the park you'll see the large, sparkling-white, attention-grabbing Dow Reid sculpture *Sails,* and a replica of the famed lake-dwelling serpent, Ogopogo (see the Special Topic).

At the south end of the park is one end of the 1,400-meter-long **Okanagan Lake Bridge.** Built in 1958, this amazing pontoon drawbridge is Canada's longest floating bridge.

Other Downtown Sights

Kelowna Museum, 470 Queensway Ave., tel. (250) 763-2417, is opposite the post office; look for the brightly painted totem pole marking the entrance. The museum holds a mishmash of fascinating displays, including: horse-drawn carriages; fossils found in the Princeton area; indigenous arts, crafts, clothing, jewelry, beads, and furs; children's books and games; radio equipment; pioneer artifacts; re-creations of an 1861 Kelowna trading post and a Chinese store; and a display of the interior of a Salish winter dwelling. It's open in summer, Mon.-Sat. 10 a.m.-5 p.m.; the rest of the year, Tues.-Sat. 10 a.m.-5 p.m. Admission is by donation.

Behind the museum is **Kasugai Gardens.** Built with the cooperation of Kelowna's Japanese sister city, Kasugai, the gardens are a quiet retreat from the downtown business district; admission is free and the gates are locked at dusk. **Kelowna Art Gallery,** 1315 Water St., tel. (250) 762-2226, is a modern facility hosting touring exhibitions and maintaining a permanent collection of contemporary and historical works by artists from throughout the province. It's open Tues.-Sun. 10 a.m.-5 p.m.; admission is by donation.

The **B.C. Orchard Museum,** 1304 Ellis St., tel. (250) 763-0433, tells the story of the local orchard industry through rare photographs, displays, and a hands-on discovery corner. It's open in summer, Mon.-Sat. 10 a.m.-5 p.m.; the rest of the year, Tues.-Sat. only.

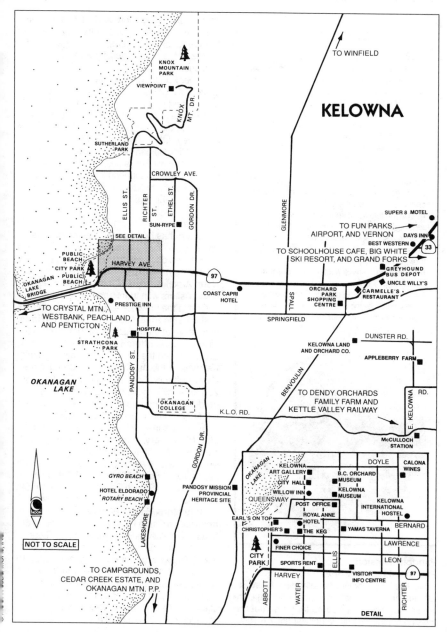

OGOPOGO

Ogopogo is the friendly Loch Ness–style sea serpent that allegedly lives on the bottom of "bottomless" Lake Okanagan. Local natives told the first white settlers who came to live in the Okanagan Valley that a fast-swimming monster called N'ha-a-tik, meaning "Devil of the Lake," lived in a deep part of the lake near present-day Kelowna. Whenever they had to canoe near that particular point, they unceremoniously threw an animal overboard as a sacrifice.

Since 1942, when the mysterious monster became known as Ogopogo, thousands of sightings have allegedly been made, and the creature has been the subject of feature stories on the television shows, *Unsolved Mysteries* and *Inside Edition.* Consensus is that Ogopogo is a snakelike creature with small humps, green skin, and a nice big smile, the latter feature confirmed by enterprising locals who print his image on T-shirts, posters, and postcards.

Although a million dollars has been put up for anyone providing definitive proof of Ogopogo's existence, no one has yet claimed the reward. Anyway, keep your eyes open and your camera at hand; you just never know, you may be one of the few (sober) ones to spot him.

BOB RACE

Pandosy Mission
Provincial Heritage Site

Drive south from downtown along Pandosy St., turn left on K.L.O. Rd., then right on rural Benvoulin Rd., and you'll come to the site of the mission established by Father Pandosy in 1859.

The route meanders through lush irrigated farmlands and orchards, past nurseries, fields of grass-munching horses, and large country homes with picture-perfect flower and vegetable gardens.

Father Pandosy, an oblate priest, operated a church, school, and farm here, ministering to natives and whites until his death in 1891. His mission claimed a lot of "firsts"—first white settlement in the Okanagan Valley, first school in the valley, first fruit and vine crops in the valley, and first Roman Catholic mission in the B.C. interior. The mission is open daily from 8 a.m. to dark, and the $2 donation includes an informative tour of the buildings, grounds, and antique farming equipment.

Wineries

Viticulture has been a mainstay of the Okanagan's economy for almost a century, but has really taken off in the last decade. Today, many producers here export their wines throughout North America. Most of the local wineries welcome visitors with tours and free tastings.

One of the province's oldest wineries, in operation since the 1930s, is **Calona Wines,** downtown at 1125 Richter St., tel. (250) 762-9144. Calona offers tours through summer, every hour on the hour 9 a.m.-5 p.m. South of Kelowna is the much-heralded **Cedar Creek Estate Winery,** 5445 Lakeshore Dr., tel. (250) 764-8866, where the vineyards and extensive gardens overlook Lake Okanagan. Tours are offered in summer, daily 11 a.m.-4 p.m.

Across Okanagan Lake from Kelowna is **Mission Hill Winery,** 1730 Mission Hill Rd., Westbank, tel. (250) 768-7611, offering tours through summer, daily 10 a.m.-7 p.m. Also find out what's happening at **Hainle Vineyards Estate Winery,** 5355 Trepanier Bench Rd., Peachland, tel. (250) 767-2525; tours through prior arrangement.

Gray Monk Estate Winery, 22 km north of Kelowna on Camp Rd., Winfield, tel. (250) 766-3168, offers daily tours May-Dec., on the hour 11 a.m.-4 p.m.; the rest of the year by appointment. The winery's retail shop is open daily 10 a.m.-5 p.m. Also in Winfield, **Hiram Walker & Sons,** Jim Bailey Rd., tel. (250) 766-2431, provides one-hour tours combined with tastings of Canadian Club whiskey, vodka, gin, rum, and liqueurs, daily 9:30 a.m.-3 p.m.

Other Agricultural and Industrial Tours

You could probably spend a couple of weeks taking one tour a day around Kelowna—orchard tours, vineyard tours, fruit-factory tours, forestry tours, and industrial tours. One that all tour-lovers will enjoy is the free 30-minute tour of the **Sun-Rype Fruit-processing Plant,** 1165 Ethel St., tel. (250) 470-6417, which shows you how apple juice, applesauce, and pie fillings are created. Tours are offered June-Sept., Mon.-Fri. 9 a.m.-3 p.m. **Kelowna Land and Orchard Co.,** Dunster Rd., tel. (250) 763-1091, offers the choice of a self-guided tour or one aboard a tractor-drawn wagon. The tours through the large orchard are available daily through summer.

The valley's largest cherry producer, **Dendy Orchards Family Farm,** off K.L.O. Rd. at 3690 Pooley Rd., tel. (250) 763-8057, opens its gate for tours in July, with plenty of delicious cherries for sale in the adjacent shop. If you have your own transportation, take the self-guided **Mc-Culloch Forest Tour** along a short forest route southeast of Kelowna; pick up a brochure with a map to various points of interest at the information center.

RECREATION

On the Lake

During the warm and sunny months of summer, Okanagan Lake comes alive with a colorful array of watercraft, fishermen, and swimmers out on the water, and sunbathers dotting the surrounding sandy beaches.

Gyro Beach and adjacent **Rotary Beach** are beautiful stretches of sand south of downtown along Lakeshore Drive. Less-crowded are the beaches in **Okanagan Mountain Provincial Park,** farther south. The paddlewheeler **MV *Fintry Queen,*** tel. (250) 763-2780, is moored at the foot of Bernard Ave., and makes a fun and stylish way to see some of Lake Okanagan. Two-hour cruises are offered in summer, on Sundays at 2 p.m. and on weekday evenings at 7:30 p.m.; adults $12, children $8. **Sports Rent,** 3000 Pandosy St., tel. (250) 861-5699, rents kayaks for $20 per day, canoes for $25 per day, and sailboards for $30 per day.

Hiking and Biking

Now abandoned, the **Kettle Valley Railway** grade that winds around the back of Kelowna was constructed in 1914 to connect the Kootenays city of Nelson to the main CPR line. Today it's a great destination for hikers or those with reliable mountain bikes. To get there take K.L.O. Rd. to McCulloch Rd., turn south (right) and then south (right) again following Myra Forest Service Rd. for 8.5 km. From the parking lot at this point, it's one km to the first of many trestles spanning 12-km-long Myra Canyon, where the rail line was carved into the mountainside.

The cacti-covered top of **Knox Mountain** offers great lake and city views. A hiking trail and a paved road popular with bicyclists both lead to

Ogopogo keeps a friendly eye on the MV Fintry Queen.

JANE AND BRUCE KING

the summit. To get there head north out of town along the lakeshore, passing pretty, lakeside Sutherland Park (good views of Crown Forest Mill and log rafts), then take Knox Mountain Dr. up to Knox Mountain Park, stopping at Crown Viewpoint on the way to the top.

Trails lead off the summit in all directions, and in May the mountain swarms with activity as cars and motorcycles race up the mountain during the **Knox Mountain Hill Climb.**

Fun Parks

Flintstones Bedrock City, 6.5 km north on Hwy. 97 at 990 McCurdy Rd., tel. (250) 765-3733, is a large theme park with a variety of rides and a theater. Open daily May-Oct.; adults $17, children $12. Next door is the water-slide haven of **Wild Waters,** tel. (250) 765-9453, open daily late May to September; admission $10. Farther north on Hwy. 97 is **Malibu Grand Prix,** tel. (250) 765-1434.

Over in Westbank, **Wild 'n Wet Waterslide Park,** tel. (250) 768-5141, is open May-Sept. daily; adults $14, children 4-6 $9, three and under free. Also in Westbank is **Old MacDonald's Farm,** on Hwy. 97, tel. (250) 768-5167, where you'll find a variety of farm animals and exotic animals, as well as mini-golf and pony rides. Open May-Sept.; adults $8, seniors and children $7.

Ski Areas

Near Kelowna are two downhill ski areas. Largest by far is **Big White Ski Resort,** 57 km east of Kelowna on Hwy. 33. One of the Okanagan's three major ski resorts, Big White has seen much expansion over the last couple of years. Construction of a new high-speed detachable quad chairlift on the Westridge face almost doubled the skiable terrain to 900 hectares and added over 100 meters to the area's vertical rise, now at over 725 meters. The resort is served by five quad chairs, two other chairs, and a T-bar. Lifts operate December through mid-April, daily 8:30 a.m.-3:30 p.m., and for night skiing Tues.-Sat. 5-9 p.m. Lift tickets are adults $42, seniors $30, over 70 and under five free. The area also offers a snowboard park, cross-country trails, and an ice-skating rink. On-mountain facilities in the large base village include rental shops, a ski school, accommodations, restaurants and cafes, and

a large mall. For general resort information call (250) 765-3101; for Big White Central Reservations call (250) 765-8888 or (800) 663-2772; for snow conditions call (250) 765-7669.

Since 1967 when the first chairlift was installed, **Crystal Mountain,** 28 km west of Kelowna, tel. (250) 768-5189 or 768-3753, has grown to be a favorite family ski area. With 20 runs over a 182-meter vertical rise, most of the slopes are suitable for beginners and intermediates. The small area also features a snowboard park with a half-pipe and jumps. Other facilities include a rental shop, ski school, and cafeteria. Tickets are adults $25, seniors $12.50, children $20. The lifts operate Tues.-Sun., with night skiing open Wed.-Sat. until 9 p.m.

Nightlife

Enjoy a drink overlooking Okanagan Lake in the stylish lounge at the **Eldorado Hotel,** 500 Cook Rd., tel. (250) 763-7500. Right downtown, **Sgt. O'Flaherty's,** in the Royal Anne Hotel at 348 Bernard Ave., tel. (250) 860-6409, is a friendly pub with bands churning out a variety of music styles nightly from 9 p.m. For loads of atmosphere, good beer, and inexpensive meals, visit the **Schoolhouse Cafe,** on Hwy. 33 east toward Big White, tel. (250) 491-1020. A unique two-story watering hole, part of the complex is in an old turn-of-the-century schoolhouse that's been partly restored with a principal's office, chalkboards, and lockers. The cafe features its own brewery, two large bar areas, and great pizza.

Sunshine Theatre, tel. (250) 763-4025, puts on three to four plays throughout the summer; pick up a schedule at the information center. The **Uptown Cinema Centre** screens films at 1521 Water St., tel. (250) 762-0099.

Festivals and Events

On the first weekend of May, the **Apple Blossom Festival** coincides with the beginning of the apple-picking season. The event features fun family events out at the Kelowna Land and Orchard Company on Dunster Road. Also in May is the **Knox Mountain Hill Climb,** North America's longest paved motor-vehicle hill climb.

Throughout July, the events of the **Mozart Festival** take place at various city venues, with classical performances by artists from throughout the province.

The second weekend of July, wander down to the marina at the Hotel Eldorado to admire watercraft displayed at the **Antique and Classic Boat Show.** Fall is ushered in with a **Salmon Barbecue and Mini Pow Wow,** which includes a buffet barbecue as well as native drumming displays. Held on streets, in parks, and at venues through the city, the **Kelowna Fringe Festival** brings eclectic modern theater productions to town the first week of September.

One of the biggest events on Kelowna's calendar is the **Okanagan Wine Festival,** held annually the first full week in October. Tastings and various activities take place throughout the valley. Celebrate **Snowfest** up at Big White Ski Resort in late January; the event features a parade, cross-country ski and snowmobile races, ice sculptures, the Frostbite Fishing Derby, a casino, and dances.

ACCOMMODATIONS AND CAMPING

Hotels and Motels

Downtown, and close to the lake, **Willow Inn,** 235 Queensway Ave., tel. (250) 762-2122 or (800) 268-1055, offers large, elegantly furnished rooms, each with a writing desk and lounge. Rates are $55-75 s, $65-75 d, including breakfast.

Highway 97 (also known as Harvey Ave,) north of downtown holds many motels tucked between shopping malls, gas stations, and fast-food restaurants. The least expensive is **Western Budget Motel,** 2679 Hwy. 97 N, tel. (250) 763-2484, which charges from $40 for a basic room. Another inexpensive choice is **Wayside Motor Inn,** 2639 Hwy. 97 N, tel. (250) 860-4454. **Super 8 Motel,** 2592 Hwy. 97 N, tel. (250) 762-8222, also has cheap rates in the low season, and regular rates at $68 s, $74 d.

Days Inn, 2469 Hwy. 97 N, tel. (250) 868-3297 or (800) 337-7177, offers large, modern rooms decorated in Santa Fe style, as well as an outdoor pool and hot tub; from $86 s or d, including a light breakfast. **Best Western Inn Kelowna,** 2402 Hwy. 97 N, tel. (250) 860-1212 or (888) 860-1212, features rooms of a high standard, a restaurant and lounge, complimentary coffee, and an outdoor pool; $99 s, $109 d. If you're looking for comfort and all the added extras, head for the **Coast Capri Hotel,** 1171 Hwy.

97 N, tel. (250) 860-6060 or (800) 663-1144, a full-service hotel with a heated pool, hot tub, sauna, coffee shop, licensed restaurant, pub, and nightclub. Rates range $99-119 s or d.

Hotel Eldorado, 500 Cook Rd., just off Lakeshore Rd., tel. (250) 763-7500, may be a bit above many travelers' budgets but is well worth the splurge. This delightful lakeside accommodation offers just 20 rooms, each furnished with antiques and many offering a lake view and private balcony. Hotel facilities include a lakefront cafe, a restaurant, a lounge, and a marina with boat rentals. Summer rates range $119-159 s or d, but ask about less expensive rates through the off-season. Also along the lake south of downtown is **Prestige Inn Kelowna,** 1675 Abbott St., tel. (250) 860-7900, which has a fancy restaurant and lounge, an exercise room, and an indoor pool; from $89 s, $99 d.

Snazzy **Lake Okanagan Resort,** on the west side of Okanagan Lake 17 km north along Westside Rd., tel. (250) 769-3511 or (800) 663-3273, offers tennis courts, a par-three golf course, swimming pools, a full-service marina, and horseback riding. From May to October, rates start at $175 for one to four people in a kitchen-equipped room.

Hostel

Kelowna International Hostel, 730 Bernard Ave., tel. (250) 763-9800, is only a five-minute walk from downtown and the beach. It has a kitchen, a TV room, and a barbecue. Dorm beds are $15 per night for members of Hostelling International, $19 for nonmembers. Weekly rates are slightly cheaper per night.

Campgrounds

The closest private campground to Kelowna on the east side of the lake is **Hiawatha RV Park,** 3787 Lakeshore Rd., tel. (250) 861-4837. It has a tenting area, showers, a laundromat, games room, and playground; tent sites $20, hookups $27-35. Just off the same road, but farther south, is **Lakeside RV Park,** 654 Cook Rd., tel. (250) 860-4072, charging $25-32 per site.

Most of the other commercial campgrounds are on the west shore of Okanagan Lake at Westbank. They include: **Happy Valley Resort,** 4026 Pritchard Dr., tel. (250) 768-7703; **Green Bay Resort,** 1375 Green Bay Rd., tel. (250)

768-5543; and **West Bay Beach Campground,** 3745 West Bay Rd., tel. (250) 768-3004. All offer coin-operated showers and full hookups and charge around $20 per site.

Two provincial parks in the vicinity of Kelowna offer camping. The closest is **Bear Creek Provincial Park,** nine km west of Kelowna on Westside Road. With 80 lakeside sites, hot showers, and a few short hiking trails, this park is a world away from the busy nearby commercial campgrounds, but you'll need to arrive early in the day to ensure a site; $15.50 per night. **Pennask Lake Provincial Park** lies along a gravel track north off Hwy. 97C (the Okanagan Connector), 60 km west of Kelowna; $9.50 per night.

FOOD

Family-style Dining

The Keg, downtown at 1580 Water St., tel. (250) 763-5435, is open daily 4-11 p.m., offering a 60-item salad bar, steaks, seafood, prime rib, and steak or chicken fajitas. Expect to pay $8-19 for a main course.

Opposite City Park, **Earl's,** upstairs at 211 Bernard Ave. (corner of Abbott St.), tel. (250) 763-2777, does a booming business, deservedly. The atmosphere features a shiny, black-and-white decor with flashy neon lighting (nothing beats a neon palm tree), a profusion of plants, and '60s background music. Grab a table on the rooftop garden patio and absorb the lake view, or just pretend you're outside (not hard to do with all the plants). The menu offers a wide variety of delicious soups, salads, gourmet burgers, chicken, seafood, steak, and pasta dishes—even tapas. Lunch ranges $5-12, dinner $6-20. At the cappuccino bar you can get all kinds of liqueur-laced coffee drinks for $2-5. For a quiet atmosphere, go to dinner before 6 p.m. Earl's is open Sun.-Mon. 11:30 a.m.-11 p.m., Tues.-Sat. 11:30 a.m.-midnight.

If you're looking for fast food, Hwy. 97 N (Harvey Ave.) will delight you—it's lined with fast-food restaurants and shopping malls. The best buffet along the strip is **Uncle Willy's,** in Dillworth Shopping Centre at 2339 Hwy. 97, tel. (250) 862-5866. The inexpensive all-you-can-eat lunch buffet is served daily 11:30 a.m.-2:30 p.m., and dinner is served daily 4-9 p.m.

Local Produce

For a delicious good time, tour **Appleberry Farm,** a working orchard at 3193 Dunster Rd., tel. (250) 868-3814. After the tour, relax in the wicker chairs for an afternoon tea featuring old-fashioned preserves. Or try the homemade buffet lunch with cheeses, salads, vegetables, desserts, beverages, and fresh fruit from the orchard. The farm is open April-Dec., daily in summer, closed Monday in spring and fall. Hours are 10 a.m.-5 p.m. To get there follow K.L.O. Rd. east past McCulloch Station, then turn left on E. Kelowna Rd. to Dunster Road.

Crepes

Carmelle's Restaurant, 1862 Benvoulin Rd., next to the Orchard Park Petrocan, tel. (250) 762-6350, gives you the option of sitting in the bright nonsmokers' room with picture windows and a view of orchards and hills across the road, or the darker smokers' room with a large open fireplace. A relaxing atmosphere, plenty of candles, and low-hanging orange-tassled lampshades suspended over each table invite quiet conversation while you tuck in to a variety of tantalizing crepes for $11-19, other main dishes for $8-19, and sinful dessert crepes for $4-7. Open for lunch Mon.-Fri. 11:30 a.m.-2 p.m. and for dinner daily from 5 p.m.

Greek

For tangy Greek food downtown, locals recommend **Yamas Taverna,** 1630 Ellis St., tel. (250) 763-5823. The authentic Greek atmosphere features blue-and-white furnishings and plenty of greenery. Open daily for a lunch buffet and from 5:30 p.m. for dinner; $9-14 for dinner entrees. A belly dancer performs on Saturday nights.

Other Restaurants

The **Finer Choice,** 237 Lawrence Ave., tel. (250) 763-0422, is an elegant restaurant decorated with antiques and oozing old-world charm. The waitpersons are attentive and the food well-prepared; expect to pay $14-21 for dinner entrees. Open Mon.-Fri. for lunch, and daily for dinner.

The atmosphere at **Christopher's,** 242 Lawrence Ave., tel. (250) 861-3464, is much different, with a light and breezy decor. But the steak and seafood dishes are also excellent. Open daily for lunch and dinner. The **Vintage**

Dining Room, in the Coast Capri Hotel, 1171 Hwy. 97 N, tel. (250) 860-6060, offers a particularly memorable Sunday brunch.

SERVICES AND INFORMATION

Transportation

Kelowna Airport, the province's third busiest, is 15 km north of downtown along Hwy. 97. It's served by **Air B.C.,** tel. (250) 861-8441, and **Canadian Regional,** tel. (250) 763-6620, both of which offer daily flights to and from Vancouver, Calgary, and Edmonton; and by **Central Mountain Air,** tel. (250) 765-1161, which links Kelowna to Kamloops and points further north. **Greyhound,** 2366 Leckie Rd., tel. (250) 860-3835 or (800) 661-8747, provides bus service throughout the Okanagan and beyond.

Local buses are run by **Kelowna Regional Transit System.** Get schedule and route information from the downtown terminal, Bernard Ave. at Ellis St., tel. (250) 860-8121. For a taxi, call **Kelowna Cabs,** tel. (250) 762-2222, or **Checkmate Cabs,** tel. (250) 861-1111. Rental car agencies include: **Avis,** tel. (250) 762-5500; **Budget,** tel. (250) 765-2299; **Hertz,** tel. (250) 765-3822; **National Tilden,** tel. (250) 762-0622; **Rent-a-wreck,** tel. (250) 763-6632; and **Thrifty,** tel. (250) 765-1633. All these agencies have vehicles out at the airport, but call in advance to ensure availability, especially in midsummer and during the ski season. **Sports Rent,** 3000 Pandosy St., tel. (250) 861-5699, rents mountain bikes for $7-10 per hour and $21-30 per day.

Other Services

The **post office** is right downtown on Queensway Avenue. **Kelowna General Hospital** is on the corner of Strathcona Ave. and Pandosy St., tel. (250) 862-4000. Note: Parking meters downtown are 50 cents per hour, free on Sunday.

Information

Kelowna Visitor Info Centre is at 544 Harvey Ave. (Hwy. 97 N), tel. (250) 861-1515. It's open in summer, daily 8 a.m.-8 p.m.; the rest of the year, daily 9 a.m.-5 p.m. Coming into town from the south on Hwy. 97, continue up Harvey Ave. for five blocks, then turn left on Richter St. at the traffic lights and go back one block (free parking). A good map for immediate orientation is posted outside the center; it also incorporates a legend of motels and attractions. On the west side of Lake Okanagan is **Westbank Visitor Info Centre,** 2375 Pamela Rd., tel. (250) 768-3378.

NORTH TOWARD VERNON

Along the 50-km stretch of Hwy. 97 between Kelowna and Vernon are several lake lookouts, resorts, and provincial parks, as well as gorgeous **Kalamalka Lake.** Enthusiastic scuba divers should make a point of stopping at **Ellison Provincial Park,** about a 15-minute drive south of Vernon, to experience B.C.'s first freshwater marine park. Enjoy shallow-water snorkeling and diving, weed beds full of life, underwater rock formations, a plastic bubble "communication center," a deep-water wreck, beach showers, and a number of campsites from $12 a night. As the highway approaches Vernon, it climbs through treeless grass-covered hills with the lake down below. **Kalamalka Lake Viewpoint,** five km south of Vernon on Hwy. 97, is worth a stop to appreciate the continuously changing emerald and turquoise water of the "Lake of a Thousand Colors," the Coldstream Valley, and the surrounding mountain panorama.

VERNON AND VICINITY

The city of Vernon (pop. 35,000) lies between Okanagan, Kalamalka, and Swan Lakes, at the north end of the Okanagan Valley. The city itself holds little of interest; the surrounding area boasts the main attractions. Among the area highlights: many sandy public beaches; Silver Star Mountain Resort, a year-round recreation paradise east of the city (see below); fishing in over 100 lakes within an hour's drive of the city; and spectacular views of Kalamalka Lake from **Kal Lake Lookout,** just south of town.

History

When gold was discovered at Cherry Creek (now Monashee Creek), east of Vernon, a small gold-rush resulted. But some of the miners noticed the agricultural potential of the Vernon area and decided to plant instead of pan. Forbes George Vernon, after whom the town was named in 1887, was one of these early settlers. Another, Cornelius O'Keefe, was bound for gold in the Cariboo when he noticed the area's lush growth of bunchgrass—prime feed for cattle and horses—and decided to stay put and establish a ranch. Between the 1860s and '70s, a number of large ranches sprang up. By 1890 over 4,000 head of cattle were mowing the bunchgrass on the rangelands around Vernon.

When construction began on the Shuswap and Okanagan Railroad connecting Vernon with the Canadian Pacific Railway mainline at Sicamous, Vernon began to grow. By 1891, the year the first passenger train puffed into town, Vernon had evolved from a sleepy little cattle community into a thriving town of 500 residents. That same year, Lord Aberdeen bought the Coldstream Ranch from Forbes George Vernon, subdivided it, and sold the parcels at affordable prices, thereby encouraging settlement. He also promoted the idea of growing trees in the area. Vernon became a city in 1892, which makes it the oldest city in the B.C. interior and fifth-oldest in the province.

SIGHTS

Historic O'Keefe Ranch

Established in 1867, the O'Keefe Ranch, 13 km north of Vernon toward Kamloops on Hwy. 9, tel. (250) 542-7868, was one of the Okanagan's first cattle ranches. Today you can tour the opulent, fully furnished O'Keefe Mansion and a number of noteworthy outbuildings, including a furnished old log house that was the O'Keefes' original home; a working blacksmith's shop; the still-in-use St. Ann's Church, where services have been held since 1889; a fully stocked general store where you can buy postcards and old-fashioned candy; and the Chinese cook's bunkhouse. If you worked up an appetite in your explorations, visit the **Homestead Restaurant,** open daily for lunch and weekends for dinner.

The ranch is open mid-May to early October, daily 9 a.m.-5 p.m., until 7 p.m. in July and August; admission adults $5.50, seniors $4.50, children $4.

In Town

Greater Vernon Museum and Archives, 3009 32nd Ave. (corner 31st St., behind the clock tower and fountain), tel. (250) 542-3142, holds photos from the early 1900s and a large collection of pioneer and native artifacts. Displays cover natural history, recreation, period clothing, and steamships. It's open in summer, Mon.-Sat. 10 a.m.-5 p.m.; the rest of the year, Tues.-Sat. 10 a.m.-5 p.m.

In the same vicinity is **Vernon Public Art Gallery,** 3216 31st Ave., tel. (250) 545-3173, featuring works by local artists as well as touring exhibitions. Open Mon.-Fri. 10 a.m.-5 p.m., Saturday noon-4 p.m. Good for children is **Vernon Science Centre,** 3203 30th Ave., tel. (250) 545-3644, with hands-on displays, mind-boggling optical illusions, and boards describing local industry. It's open Mon.-Sat. 10 a.m.-3 p.m.

Polson Park, off Hwy. 97 at 25th Ave., has a Chinese teahouse and Japanese garden, but

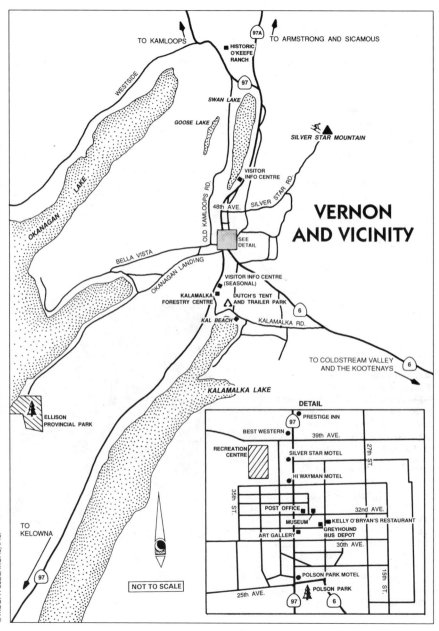

most people go to stare at the spectacular floral clock—nine meters wide, made up of more than 3,500 plants, and the only one of its kind in western Canada. Farther south on Reservoir Rd. is the **Kalamalka Forestry Centre,** one of four facilities in the province engaged in research aimed at improving forest management and production techniques. It's open to the public weekdays 8 a.m.-3 p.m.; call (250) 549-5674 for tour information.

EVENTS

The annual **Creative Chaos** craft fair held in early June always has an impressive turnout of both craftspeople and customers; admission is free. Over the second week of September, Armstrong (just north of Vernon) hosts the **Interior Provincial Exhibition and Stampede.** In early February, the town springs to life to celebrate **Vernon Winter Carnival** with parades, sleigh rides, ice sculptures, stock car races on ice, dances, and the "Over the Hill Downhill" team ski race at Silver Star. Get all the event information and dates at the Visitor Info Centre.

PRACTICALITIES

Accommodations and Camping
Polson Park Motel, 3201 24th Ave., tel. (250) 549-2231 or (800) 480-2231, is the least expensive of Vernon's 20-odd motels. Adjacent to Polson Park, the three-story motel has an outdoor pool and rooms from $30 s, $40 d. Along Hwy. 97 (32nd St.) through the center of Vernon are more motels, including inexpensive **Silver Star Motel,** 3700 32nd St., tel. (250) 545-0501, which charges from $35 s, $40 d, $45 for a kitchenette; and similarly priced **Hi Wayman Motel,** 3500 32nd St., tel. (250) 545-2148. **Best Western Vernon Lodge,** 3914 32nd St. tel. (250) 545-3385 or (800) 663-4422, has many rooms overlooking an enclosed three-story tropical atrium. Other facilities include an indoor pool with a whirlpool, a cafe, a restaurant, and a pub; $90 s, $95 d. The **Prestige Inn,** 4411 32nd St., tel. (250) 558-5991, offers a high standard of rooms, each comfortable and stylishly furnished; from $90 s, $100 d.

Dutch's Tent and Trailer Park, three km south of downtown on Kalamalka Rd., tel. (250) 545-1023, is only 400 meters from Kal Beach and Kalamalka Lake. The park has hot showers, a laundromat, and a snack bar. Tent sites are $16, hookups $17-21. Sixteen km southwest of town is **Ellison Provincial Park,** on the east shore of Okanagan Lake; sites are $12.

Food
One of the local favorites and one of the busiest restaurants in town is the **Sundowner,** 2501 53rd Ave., tel. (250) 542-5142. The menu includes steak, seafood, and pasta dishes, and an extensive salad bar. At dinner, main courses run from $8. Sunday brunch, 10:30 a.m.-2:30 p.m., costs adults $11, seniors $9, children $5. And the Mon.-Sat. lunch buffet is adults $8, seniors $6, children $5. On Thursday nights the Sundowner puts on a seafood buffet, and on Sunday nights a continental buffet.

At **Kelly O'Bryan's Restaurant,** 2905 29th St., tel. (250) 549-2112, tuck in to burgers, steak,

skiing at Silver Star Mountain Resort

DON WEIXL/SILVER STAR

seafood, salads, and pasta; open daily 11 a.m.-midnight. For more of a dinnertime splurge try the **Courtyard Garden Restaurant** at the Best Western Vernon Lodge, 3914 32nd St., tel. (250) 545-3385. The dining room is set in a lush tropical garden with a stream flowing through the middle, and the menu features Continental cuisine with nightly specials. Open daily, for lunch from 11 a.m. and dinner from 5 p.m.

Services and Information
The **Greyhound** bus depot is on the corner of 30th St. and 31st Ave., tel. (250) 545-0527. For local bus information and schedules, contact **Vernon Transit System,** 4210 24th Ave., tel. (250) 545-7221.

The **post office** is on the corner of 31st St. and 32nd Avenue. **Vernon Visitor Info Centre** is at 6326 Hwy. 97 N, tel. (250) 542-1415; open daily 8:30 a.m.-6 p.m., till 6:30 p.m. in summer. Stock up on printed material on the entire area here, or at the seasonal Info Centre on Hwy. 97 at the south end of town (open May-Sept.).

SILVER STAR MOUNTAIN RESORT

For summer or winter recreation, head up to Silver Star Mountain Resort, 22 km northeast of Vernon (take 48th Ave. off Hwy. 97). The views of Vernon as you climb the mountain are worth the fairly long, steep drive, and the resort at the top offers great skiing, a variety of summer recreation, and a colorful fully self-contained village.

Summer Activities
Silver Star offers the biggest range of summer recreation of any ski resort in the interior. Starting at the end of June, a chairlift runs from the village to the top of Silver Star Mountain (1,915 meters) for terrific views of Vernon and surrounding lakes, and good hiking in alpine meadows. The summer lift operates until September, daily 10 a.m.-4 p.m.; $7.50 per ride, or buy an all-day pass for $15. To learn more about the mountain's natural history, take the naturalist-led wildflower tour each Sunday at 1 p.m.; $16 per person, which includes a chairlift ride. Mountain-bike rentals are $9.50 for one hour, $15.50 for two hours, and $27 for four hours. All these rates include a Trail Pass, which is needed to ride the trails around the mountain. If you have your own bike, the Trail Pass is $5.

Silver Star Mountain Bike Tours, tel. (250) 542-0224, offers a three-hour bike tour down the steep road from Silver Star Mountain to Vernon. The price of $45 per person includes the use of a mountain bike, helmet, safety vest, and gloves, a souvenir water bottle, a chairlift ride, the guided descent, and return transportation.

Also in summer you can go horseback riding on beautiful trails adjacent to the village. A one-hour ride is $22 per person, two hours $38, and a supper ride is $50.

Skiing
From November through April, Silver Star is mobbed by downhill skiers, who come for great skiing and the facilities of an outstanding on-hill village. The two main faces—Vance Creek, good for beginners, and Putnam Creek, for intermediates and experts—are served by five chairlifts and a couple of T-bars. The resort's 80 runs cover 480 hectares with a vertical rise of 760 meters. Lift tickets are adults $42, seniors $29, children $22; those over 70 and under six ski free. For further resort information call (250) 542-0224; for snow reports call (250) 542-1745. Through winter a shuttle bus operates between Kelowna Airport and the mountain; book through Central Reservations, tel. (800) 663-4431.

Silver Star Cross-country Centre features 35 km of groomed and set tracks, while beyond these are 50 km of backcountry trails. A day pass is $10 per person; rentals are available for an additional $15.

Accommodations
The base village contains seven hotels; book year-round through Central Reservations, tel. (800) 663-4431, or contact each accommodation directly. Least expensive are **Kickwillie Inn,** tel. (250) 542-4548, and **Lord Aberdeen Hotel,** tel. (250) 542-1992, where each room features a fully equipped kitchen. In summer rooms go for $90 per night, rising to $160 during the height of the season. Rates at the **Silver Lode Inn,** tel. (250) 549-5105, are similar, but most rooms don't have kitchens. The most luxurious on-mountain lodging is **Vance Creek Hotel,** tel. (250) 549-5191, which offers large rooms, a rooftop hot tub, and full dining facilities; from $145 s or d.

THE KOOTENAYS

The wild and rugged Kootenays region of British Columbia lies east of the Okanagan Valley and south of the TransCanada Highway and is bordered by the United States to the south and Alberta to the east. Three north-south-trending mountain ranges—the **Monashees, Selkirks,** and **Purcells**—run parallel to each other across the region and are separated by lush green valleys and narrow lakes up to 150 km long. The snowcapped mountains and forested valleys abound with wildlife, including large populations of deer, elk, moose, black bear, and grizzly bear.

Europeans first entered the Kootenays in the late 1800s, searching for precious metals such as gold, silver, lead, and zinc, all of which were found in large quantities. While many of the boomtowns from this era have slipped into oblivion, others live on; **Sandon** is a ghost town, **Fort Steele** survives as a heritage theme park complete with costumed performers, and the grand old city of **Nelson** is today a heritage masterpiece, its streets lined with restored buildings.

At the southern end of the Monashee Mountains in the West Kootenays, delightful **Rossland** perches on the flanks of an extinct volcano and was once home to one of the world's richest gold mines. In the East Kootenays, highways follow the Rocky Mountain Trench north from the population center of **Cranbrook** to the Bavarian city of **Kimberley** and on to wilderness areas, hot springs, and the famous national parks of the Canadian Rockies.

Recreational opportunities abound throughout the Kootenays in all seasons. In summer, anglers flock to the lakes and rivers for trout, char, kokanee salmon, freshwater cod, and bass. Other visitors enjoy canoeing, swimming, or sunbaking on the beaches, or take to the mountains for hiking and wildlife-viewing. Much of the region's higher elevations are protected in a variety of rugged and remote parks, including the spectacular **Valhalla, Kokanee Glacier,** and **Top of the World Provincial Parks,** and the **Purcell Wilderness Conservancy.** While these natural preserves offer plenty of opportunities for day-trippers, it takes extended backcountry trips to fully experience their beauty.

In colder months the mountains of the Kootenays catch a phenomenal amount of snow, turning the whole region into a winter wonderland. You won't find any major ski resorts here, however three small but legendary ski areas—**Red Mountain, Whitewater,** and **Fernie Snow Valley**—attract adventurous powderhounds with some of North America's highest snowfalls and steepest lift-served slopes.

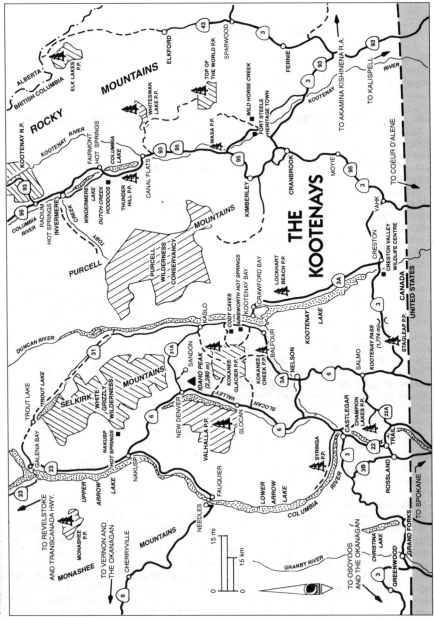

WEST KOOTENAYS

Clustered on the edge of the Monashee Range in the western Kootenays lie several communities that seem a world away from the hustle and the bustle of the nearby Okanagan Valley. Grand Forks, Rossland, Trail, and Castlegar all boomed at the turn of the 20th century, when thousands of gold-hungry prospectors descended on the slopes of Red Mountain. Today Red Mountain draws more skiers than prospectors, and lakes, rivers, parks, and peaks are the area's main attractions.

In addition to its mining history, the West Kootenays are also known as the home of the Dhoukobars, a religious sect of Russian immigrants who arrived in the early 1900s to till the land and practice their faith in peace. Aspects of their unique culture and lifestyle can be seen today in Grand Forks and elsewhere in the region.

GRAND FORKS

Perched above the confluence of the Granby and Kettle Rivers, Grand Forks (pop. 4,200) started out as a Hudson's Bay Company trading post and later became a mining town, home to the largest nonferrous smelter in the British Empire. At the turn of the 20th century, the rough-and-ready town was full of miners, ranchers, and land speculators. But then a very different group of people arrived in the valley.

The Doukhobors, a religious sect practicing pacifism and vegetarianism, fled persecution in their Russian homeland and set up communes in British Columbia in the early 1900s. They kept a low profile—farming, making everything they needed, and operating many successful communal enterprises. The sect added a contrasting element to the area's social mix until Doukhobor leader Peter Verigin died in 1924. After his death, the sect's way of life deteriorated and the communes dispersed. Today many Doukhobor descendants live in Grand Forks. Although they no longer live in communal villages, they still follow their beliefs and speak Russian, which is taught in local schools. To find out more about the intriguing Doukhobor

lifestyle, visit **Mountain View Doukhobor Museum,** a 1912 Doukhobor communal farmhouse on Hardy Mountain Rd., tel. (250) 442-8855, or **Fructova Heritage Centre,** 6110 Reservoir Rd., tel. (250) 442-3523, with similar displays.

Grand Forks also features a mix of historic turn-of-the-century homes and restored civic buildings. Downtown's **Boundary Museum,** 7370 5th St., tel. (250) 442-3737, displays mining artifacts, historic photos, and pioneer memorabilia. It's open June-Oct., daily 10:30 a.m.-4:30 p.m. Next door is **Grand Forks Visitor Info Centre,** 7362 5th St., tel. (250) 442-2833; open year-round, Mon.-Fri. 9:30 a.m.-4:30 p.m.

Accommodations and Camping
In a pleasant setting on the west edge of town, **Pinegrove Motel,** 209 Central Ave., tel. (250) 442-8203, offers rooms from $55 s, $65 d. Another option would be to head out to 19-km-long **Christina Lake,** 25 km east of town. The lake is a summer mecca for folks from throughout the West Kootenays, who come for the lake's warm waters and fishing for rainbow trout, bass, and kokanee. Around the lake are a couple of motels and 11 commercial campgrounds, many with cabins for rent. Right on the lake is **Cascade Cove RV Park,** 1290 River Rd., tel. (250) 447-6662, which offers tent sites for $14, and serviced sites for $18-21. To the north, at the opposite end of the lake, is **Texas Creek Provincial Park,** with 48 unserviced sites for $9.50.

ROSSLAND

Clinging to the slopes of an extinct volcanic crater deep in the tree-covered Monashee Mountains, Rossland (pop. 4,000) was once a goldrush boomtown known as the "The Golden City." The precious yellow metal was discovered on 1,580-meter-high Red Mountain by Joe Moris in 1890. Moris, like thousands of other prospectors unaware of the nearby wealth, had been traveling eastward on the Dewdney Trail to goldfields further afield. He nevertheless staked five claims on Red Mountain, the richest of which, Le Roi, later sold for $3 million. When word got out, thousands of diggers rushed in and the township of Rossland was born. The town's population peaked at 7,000 in 1897. At that time, the city boasted four newspapers, 40 saloons, and daily rail service south to Spokane. By 1929, the mountain had yielded six million tons of ore worth $165 million. Today, tourism supplies the bulk of Rossland's gold; the town serves as a mecca for mountain-bike enthusiasts and adventurous skiers.

Sights
Downtown Rossland is a picturesque place full of historic buildings and old-fashioned street lamps. Pick up a *Heritage Walking Tour* pamphlet from the museum, library, or downtown shops, and hit the streets.

Fire razed Rossland three times during its heyday, so it's ironic that the city is home to the **B.C. Firefighters Museum,** Queen St. and First Ave., tel. (250) 362-5514. Housed in the 1900 fire hall, the museum is open weekdays 10 a.m.-4 p.m.

One km west of downtown, **Rossland Historical Museum,** Hwy. 3B and Columbia Ave., tel. (250) 362-7722, stands at the entrance to the famous Le Roi mine and offers exhibits on the area's lustrous geological and human history. The museum also holds the Western Canada Ski Hall of Fame, which honors such luminaries as Olaus Jeldness—instigator of the local ski craze—and champion skier Nancy Greene, a local heroine who won a gold medal in the 1968 Olympics. The museum is open summers, daily 9 a.m.-5 p.m. Admission is adults $4, seniors $3, children $1.50.

To experience the day-to-day life of the early hardrock miners, tour the **Le Roi Gold Mine,** next to the museum complex. Outside the mine you'll see a gigantic compressor, a simulated mine shaft, and large pieces of mining machinery. The gold mine itself, just up the path, provides an introductory course in local geology with its displays of mineral veins, dikes, faults, and old and new mining equipment. The 45-minute tour includes detailed explanations of how ore is mined, trammed, drilled, and blasted, and tells you how to differentiate igneous, metamorphic, and sedimentary rocks. Museum admission is included in the tour cost of adults $8, seniors $5, children $3.

Kick up your heels (or watch the cancan girls and singing gamblers kick up theirs) at **Gold Fever Follies,** a live musical in the historic 1898 Miners Hall on Columbia Avenue. Performances take place throughout summer, Tues.-Sat. 3 p.m. and 7 p.m.; adults $5, children $3.

Mountain Biking
Each spring, Rossland comes alive with pedal power as mountain-bike enthusiasts take advantage of the maze of old logging and mining trails surrounding the city. Now known as the "Mountain Bike Capital of Canada," Rossland has hosted both the Canadian and North American championships. Rent bikes from **The Powderhound,** 2040 Columbia Ave., tel. (250) 362-5311. The best source of trail information is the brochure, *How to find your way around the twisting, hilly, scenic, tree-lined, and sometimes confusing (because it's situated on the side of a mountain—which is really what makes this place so great) streets and trails of Rossland,* available from all the town's bike shops.

Red Mountain Ski Area
The site of what was once one of the world's richest gold mines is now part of Red Mountain Ski Area, which offers some of North America's most challenging lift-served skiing. Last century, after the first frantic summer of mining on Red Mountain, a group of prospectors put on a winter carnival, including a ski race down the slopes of Red Mountain. The organizer was Olaus Jeldness, a legendary Norwegian who had prospected all over the western U.S. before moving north of the border. Jeldness admitted that the mountain was "far too steep and the snow conditions too extreme" for a proper race. But it went ahead nevertheless. First the competitors hiked all the way to the summit. Then Jeldness gave the signal to go before strapping on his own skis and schussing off after the rest of the field. Despite their head start, Jeldness easily passed the other racers to become Canada's first national champion. His wooden skis and trophies are housed in the Western Canada Ski Hall of Fame in the Rossland Historical Museum (see "Sights," above).

Facilities on the mountain have certainly improved since those early days, but Red Mountain is no megaresort. Nevertheless, the skiing is still world-class. While two mountains provide opportunities for skiers of all ability levels, the resort holds most appeal for experts. The heart-stopping face of Red Mountain is the star of the show. But adjacent Granite Mountain offers a vertical rise of 850 meters and almost unlimited intermediate and expert skiing, mostly on unmarked trails through powder-filled glades. Lift tickets are $35. For resort information call (250) 362-7700.

Across the road from the downhill ski area, **Blackjack** nordic area offers 50 km of groomed tracks. Cross-country skiers can also explore the many old logging roads in the area.

Ram's Head Inn

One of Canada's premier small lodges lies in the woods at the base of Red Mountain. Primarily designed for skiers, the Ram's Head Inn offers 12 guest rooms—each with private bath—a dining area, games room, sauna, outdoor hot tub, and a spacious communal lounge with luxurious chairs and a large fireplace. In winter (book well ahead), weekend packages go for $270 s, $204-240 per person/d, including two nights accommodations, breakfasts, and ski passes. A five-night midweek package costs $600 s, $465-545 per person d. In summer, the lodge charges $45 s, $52-68 d, with breakfast extra. For reservations write P.O. Box 636, Rossland, BC V0G 1Y0, or call (250) 362-9577.

Other Accommodations

Also up at the ski hill is the **Red Shutter Inn,** tel. (250) 362-5131, a cozy little bed and breakfast with shared bathrooms, a lounge area, and hot tub; summer rates are $39 s, $49 d. The premier downtown accommodation is the **Uplander Hotel,** 1919 Columbia Ave., tel. (250) 362-7375, with a restaurant and lounge; $53-99 s or d.

Food

Each morning, locals converge on the **Sunshine Cafe,** 2116 Columbia Ave., tel. (250) 362-7630, for hearty cooked breakfasts from $6. The rest of the day, the cafe offers a diverse menu including Mexican and Indian dishes. **Goldrush Books and Expresso,** 2063 Washington St., tel. (250) 362-5333, sets a few tables around bookshelves full of local and Canadian literature. For more substantial fare, head up the hill to **Elmer's Corner Cafe,** 1999 2nd Ave., tel. (250) 362-5266, where you can dine inside or out on the deck. Specialties include pizza and healthy sandwiches.

TRAIL AND VICINITY

Sprawling along both sides of the mighty Columbia River, Trail (pop. 8,000) lies 10 km and 600 vertical meters below Rossland. It's probable that neither your first nor your subsequent impression of Trail will be positive. The world's largest lead and zinc smelter dominates the downtown area, its 120-meter-high smokestacks belching thick plumes of smoke into the atmosphere 24 hours a day. The smelter is the foundation of Consolidated Mining and Smelting Co. (Cominco), one of the world's largest mining companies, and poor Trail is often described as "Cominco with a town built around it." Free tours of the **Cominco complex** show you the area where ores are melted and separated and tell you about the byproducts, such as fertilizers, converted from the wastes. The tours depart from the main gate on Aldridge Ave., Mon.-Fri. at 10 a.m. To book a tour, call (250) 368-3144.

Trail District Visitor Info Centre, west of downtown at 843 Rossland Ave., tel. (250) 368-3144, is open 9 a.m.-5 p.m., daily in summer, weekdays only the rest of the year.

Champion Lakes Provincial Park

Escape the smokestacks in this 1,408-hectare park, 23 km east along Hwy. 3B toward Nelson, then a few km farther along the access road. The park encompasses three large lakes nestled in the Bonnington Range. Hiking trails connect the lakes; First Lake, accessed from a trail at road's end, is the least busy. Camping is $9.50.

Salmo toward Creston

East of Trail on Hwy. 3, the small village of Salmo (pop. 1,100) features old-fashioned wooden buildings, a small museum (open in summer, daily 1-5 p.m.), and streets decorated in summer with huge hanging flower baskets bursting with brilliant color. The promise of quick fortune brought prospectors to gold diggings in the Salmo River watershed through the 1860s, but like so many other boomtowns in the Kootenays, the riches were short-lived. Those who stayed in the area turned to logging cedar and pine from the surrounding Selkirk Mountains as a source of income.

About 35 km east of Salmo lies 1,133-hectare **Stagleap Provincial Park,** where travelers can pause to picnic by Bridal Lake or go for a short hike.

Continuing east from there, you'll crest 1,774-meter **Kootenay Pass** (the highest paved highway pass in the country) and drop down the other side into Creston (see "Kootenay Lake and Creston," below).

CASTLEGAR

Though endowed with the rich history of the Doukhobors, Castlegar (pop. 7,300) is not a particularly attractive place. Spread out along the barren Columbia River Valley, it's a real crossroads town. Here the Kootenay River drains into the much larger Columbia River, Hwy. 3 passes through east to west, Hwy. 3A leads north to Nelson, and Hwy. 22 leads south

to Rossland and Trail. The town is also the major air gateway for the Kootenays.

The area's first nonnative residents, the Doukhobors, arrived in 1908. These pacificist Russian immigrants planted orchards, built sawmills, and even operated a jam factory while living in segregated villages along the valley floor. Many of their descendants still live in the area. Today, mining, transportation, and hydroelectric-power production sustain the local economy.

Doukhobor Sights

Castlegar's major attraction is the **Doukhobor Village Museum,** on the east side of the river along Hwy. 3A, tel. (250) 365-6622. The reconstructed village allows a glimpse of the traditional lifestyle of these intriguing Russian immigrants. The $3 admission includes a guided tour, led by Doukhobor descendants, through the main building and the simply furnished brick dwellings and outbuildings. Along the way you'll see some of the sect's artifacts, including hand-woven clothing, crocheted bedspreads and shawls, and carved wooden spoons and ladles. Also featured is a historic photo collection of the

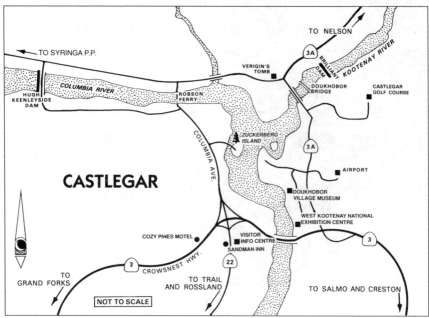

© MOON PUBLICATIONS, INC.

original Doukhobor settlements in Saskatchewan and British Columbia. The museum is open daily 9 a.m.-5 p.m.

Zuckerberg Island, at the confluence of the Kootenay and Columbia Rivers, was the home of Russian immigrant Alexander Zuckerberg, who came to Castlegar to teach Doukhobor children in 1931. Connected to the mainland by a 150-meter suspension bridge, the tree-covered two-hectare island is interesting to explore. A one-km trail passes a full-scale model of a *ckukuli* (native winter pit house), as well as a Hiroshima memorial, Russian orthodox chapel house, cemetery, log house, and many other Zuckerberg creations. To get there, turn off Hwy. 22 at 9th St., turn left on 7th Ave., then immediately right.

While you're in a Russian frame of mind, visit the old **Doukhobor Bridge,** which crosses the Kootenay River along Hwy. 3A. The remains of the old hand-poured cement suspension bridge built in the early 1900s can still be seen today. On the north side of the river just west of the

suspension bridge to historic Zuckerberg Island

ANDREW HEMPSTEAD

bridge lies **Verigin's Tomb,** the final resting place of the Doukhobors' spiritual leader.

Other Sights
Along the same road as the Doukhobor Village Museum is West Kootenay National Exhibition Centre, housing the **Kootenay Gallery of Art, History, and Science,** tel. (250) 365-3337. The gallery displays a good variety of artworks, often including elaborate exhibits from larger national galleries. It's open year-round, Tues.-Fri. 10:30 a.m.-4:30 p.m., and on summer weekends noon-4:30 p.m. Admission is adults $4, seniors $3.

North of town off Hwy. 3A, the enormous **Hugh Keenleyside Dam** spans the Columbia River to form Lower Arrow Lake. The structure features a lock system that allows boats to pass from one side of the dam to the other, despite the differing water levels.

Accommodations and Camping
The comfortable and reasonably priced **Cozy Pines Motel,** 2100 Crestview Cres. (on Hwy. 3 at the west entrance to Castlegar), tel. (250) 365-5613, offers spotless rooms with kitchenettes starting at $38 s, $45 d. Most other motels, restaurants, and other services are along Columbia Ave., which links downtown to Hwy. 3. Opposite the information center is **Sandman Inn,** 1944 Columbia Ave., tel. (250) 365-8444, with an indoor pool and restaurant; $70 s, $75 d. Campers should head north out of town toward Nelson and turn west off Hwy. 3A to **Syringa Provincial Park,** on the banks of Lower Arrow Lake. Sites are $12.

Services and Information
Castlegar Airport, along Hwy. 3A, is the Kootenays' air transportation hub. It's served by **Air B.C.,** tel. (800) 663-3721, and **Canadian Regional,** tel. (250) 365-5525 or (800) 665-1177.

Castlegar Visitor Info Centre is off Hwy. 22 (Columbia Ave.) at 20th St., tel. (250) 365-6313. It's open daily 8 a.m.-7 p.m. in summer, Mon.-Fri. 9 a.m.-5 p.m. the rest of the year.

THE SLOCAN VALLEY

The historically rich Slocan Valley, or "Silvery Slocan," nestles snugly between the Slocan and Valhalla Ranges of the Selkirk Mountains. In the 1890s the valley sprang into the limelight when silver was discovered at Sandon. It's much quieter today, and offers many picturesque towns and an abundance of outdoor-recreation opportunities.

Lemon Creek Lodge

If you're planning on staying in the Slocan Valley, this unique and comfortable lodge is an easy way to do it. It's about seven km south of Slocan (1.6 km west off the main highway at the sign, on Kennedy Rd.), close to both Valhalla and Kokanee Glacier Provincial Parks. Hosts provide all the necessary information on the local backcountry and can advise on activities to suit all interests. Rates of $45 s, $50 d include breakfast; a full meal plan is available. A couple of cabins are available for small groups, and you can camp for $15-19 per site. In winter the lodge offers ski packages ranging from a day-trip (cross-country ski instruction, lunch, and sauna/hot tub for $35 per person) to a five-day adventure (telemark instruction, a trip to Nakusp Hot Springs, accommodations, all meals, and transportation from $270 per person). Shuttles to and from Castlegar airport or Nelson bus depot can be arranged. For reservations call (250) 355-2403.

New Denver

Western gateway to "Silver Country," this picturesque town of 600 is on Slocan Lake, opposite Valhalla Provincial Park. Originally called Eldorado and renamed after Denver, Colorado, the town reached its mining peak in the 1890s.

Today the main street is lined with funky false-front stores and pioneer-style buildings left over from the prosperous silver days. Visit the **Silvery Slocan Museum** to find out all about New Denver's heyday. It's on the corner of 6th St. and Bellevue Dr., tel. (250) 358-2201; open July to early September.

Down on the lake within easy walking distance of the main street, **Sweet Dreams Guesthouse,** 702 Eldorado St., tel. (250) 358-2415, offers large rooms and a cooked breakfast for $50 s, $70 d. Campers can head to a **municipal campground** with full hookups on the south side of the town ($12-15), or to **Rosebery Provincial Park,** on Wilson Creek six km north of town ($9.50).

Opposite the headquarters of the Valhalla Wilderness Society is **Silver Spoon Bakery/Cafe,** 310 6th Ave., tel. (250) 358-2855, serving scrumptiously fresh cakes and pastries and good homestyle cooking at reasonable prices. Closed Mondays. Down the hill a bit you'll find **Apple Tree Restaurant,** 210 6th Ave., tel. (250) 358-2691, with a more extensive menu and an outside deck.

New Denver Visitor Info Centre is on the main highway next to Thrifty Gas, tel. (250) 358-2544; open July-Aug., daily 9 a.m.-5 p.m.

Valhalla Provincial Park

This 49,600-hectare park preserves the high peaks, deep valleys, and magnificent alpine lakes between the Valhalla Range of the Selkirk Mountains on the west and the west shores of Slocan Lake on the east. The most imposing peaks are in the south of the park, where spectacular spires rise above alpine meadows to a height of 2,800 meters.

Roads come to an abrupt end at the north and south end of the park, so the most popular access is by boat from New Denver or Slocan, across the lake. An eight-km lakeshore trail also connects Slocan with the west shore. Once there, you'll find hiking trails leading into the heart of the park. The most rewarding and popu-

---

VALHALLA WILDERNESS SOCIETY

Originally founded to lobby for the establishment of Valhalla Provincial Park, the Valhalla Wilderness Society has more recently been instrumental in convincing the B.C. government to designate the Khutzeymateen Valley, north of Prince Rupert, as Canada's first grizzly bear sanctuary. Closer to home, the small organization also successfully campaigned for the creation of the White Grizzly Wilderness.

The society's headquarters, in New Denver at 307 6th St. (under the Valhalla Trading Post sign), holds a small retail outlet selling books, posters, calendars, and shirts. For more information on the society and its latest crusade, write Valhalla Wilderness Society, P.O. Box 329, New Denver, BC V0G 1S0, or call (250) 358-2333.

lar is the **Beatrice Lake Trail,** 12.5 km each way. Like all trails starting from the lake, elevation gain is steady; you'll climb just under 1,000 vertical meters as you pass Little Cahill and Cahill Lakes and enter the massive cirque in which Beatrice Lake lies. From the backcountry campground at the lake, a vast wilderness is yours to explore. Another trail, one of the park's steepest, begins across Slocan Lake from New Denver and climbs **Sharp Creek.** Elevation gain is 1,400 meters, most of it made in the final push to a point overlooking **New Denver Glacier.**

Based in New Denver, **Kingfisher Water Taxi,** tel. (250) 358-2334, offers hiker drop-offs to the park and day tours on Slocan Lake. At the north end of the lake, **Slo-as-u-can,** tel. (250) 358-7789, rents canoes. The best source of trail and transportation information is **Valhalla Wilderness Society,** 307 6th Ave., New Denver, tel. (250) 358-2333, a group of local environmentalists who were instrumental in the establishment of the park and have gone on to crusade for further parks throughout the province. At the Society's office you can pick up a copy of the detailed *Trail Guide to Valhalla Provincial Park.*

Sandon

The original Slocan Valley boomtown, Sandon once was a thriving town of 5,000 people. After the discovery of silver on the slopes of Idaho Peak, Sandon grew quickly and at one time boasted 24 hotels, 23 saloons, banks, general stores, mining brokers' offices, and a newspaper. Its main link to the outside world was the Kaslo & Slocan Railway, built in 1895 to connect Sandon with sternwheeler transportation on Kootenay Lake.

Sandon was destroyed by fire in 1902, but quickly rebuilt and incorporated as a city in 1908. The Great Depression of 1929 put an end to the heyday, but the town remained the "soul of the Silvery Slocan" until the spring of 1955. That year the creek running through town flooded, sweeping away most of the city and leaving a ghost town. Today you can count the population on two hands.

The best place to start a visit to Sandon is the 1900 city hall, where the *Sandon Walking Tour Guide* is sold ($1). The brochure details all the original structures—only a fraction of which remain—with a map that makes exploring on foot more enjoyable. Up the creek from city hall are **Sandon Museum,** where exhibits bring the old town back to life, and **Silversmith Mine Powerhouse,** which still supplies power to the few remaining residents and retains its title as western Canada's oldest operating hydroelectric plant. Also on this side of the creek is the road to 2,280-meter **Idaho Peak.** The road is very rough, and passable only in July and August. From the end of the 12-km road, a steep one-km trail leads to the summit and spectacular 360-degree views of the Kootenays.

Along the north side of Carpenter Creek, a string of buildings in various states of disrepair

the Tin Cup Cafe in Sandon

lines a road leading to the mining area of Cody. On the same side of the creek, the **K&S Historic Trail** follows the route taken by the old wood-burning engines of the Kaslo & Slocan Railway as they carried rich silver ore from Sandon to Kaslo. The railway was destroyed by fire in 1910. The hiking trail, 5.6 km each way, passes several mining sites and provides fabulous views of the **New Denver Glacier,** across Slocan Lake in Valhalla Provincial Park.

The only services in Sandon are a souvenir shop in the old city hall and the **Tin Cup Cafe,** which was built as a private home in 1895 and is now open for coffee and light snacks. It's on the north side of Carpenter Creek at the far end of town.

NAKUSP

Forty-eight km northwest of New Denver, Nakusp (pop. 1,800) was established during the mining-boom years. Today the small town is best known for its hot springs and its stunning location on Upper Arrow Lake at the foot of the Selkirk Mountains.

Nakusp Museum, on 6th Ave., features an odd but intriguing collection of items, including pre-dam photos of the towns that now lie flooded beneath the Arrow Lakes. It's open July and August only, daily 9 a.m.-5 p.m.; admission $1.

Favorite summer activities here include mountain biking along surrounding logging roads, fishing and swimming in Upper Arrow Lake, and golfing at **Nakusp Centennial Golf Course,** tel. (250) 265-4531. In winter, you can head to the slopes of small **Summit Lake Ski Area,** 15 km southwest of town on Hwy. 6.

Nakusp Hot Springs
To get to these hot springs take Hwy. 23 north out of town for one km, then follow the signposted road along Kuskanax Creek for 12 km. Admission is adults $5, seniors $4, children $3. The pools are open in summer, daily 9:30 a.m.-10 p.m.; the rest of the year, daily 11 a.m.-9:30 p.m. For information call (250) 265-4528.

To see the source of the springs, take the sandy 500-meter trail that starts behind the pools. You'll cross the river and clamber through damp rainforest crammed with ferns and mosses, then come to an impressive waterfall where you can smell the sulphur from the springs.

Practicalities
Tenderfoot Lodge, 515 Broadway, tel. (250) 265-3618 or (800) 663-0100, is a brand new accommodation with large well-furnished rooms; $89 s or d. The lodge also offers rooms next door in the original, older wing for around $55. **Nakusp Recreation Park Campsite,** on 8th Ave., tel. (250) 265-4234, has shaded sites and hot showers and is within walking distance of the beach and the main street; $12-14 per night. Campers can also head 10 km south of town to **McDonald Creek Provincial Park,** which has fewer facilities but a better location; $9.50.

Accommodations are also offered up at the hot springs, but it can get busy during summer. The campground, tel. (250) 265-4528, features a grassy tent area and wooded vehicle campsites beside Kuskanax Creek; sites are $12-14. At **Nakusp Hot Springs Cedar Chalets,** tel. (250) 265-4505, each of the units has a kitchen and private bathroom. Rates are $48-62 per unit; book well ahead.

The place to be seen in Nakusp is the **Broadway Deli Bistro,** tel. (250) 265-3767, where you'll find great coffee and a constant stream of muffins coming out of the oven. Sit by the door to catch all the gossip as the locals wander in. It's open daily at 7 a.m. **Manor Restaurant,** 311 Broadway, tel. (250) 265-4433, serves Canadian and Chinese food ($5-10). Open daily 7:30 a.m.-9 p.m.

Nakusp Visitor Info Centre occupies the small building with the big yellow paddlewheel at 92 6th Ave., tel. (250) 265-4234 or (800) 909-8819. It's open in summer, daily 8 a.m.-4 p.m.; the rest of the year on weekdays only.

WEST TO THE OKANAGAN

From Nakusp, Hwy. 6 follows Lower Arrow Lake south to Fauquier, where it jumps the lake (you'll take the free ferry) and continues northwest to Vernon, a total distance of 195 km.

Fauquier consists of a gas station, golf course, and **Arrow Lake Motel,** tel. (250) 269-7622, featuring lake views and small but comfortable rooms for $38 s, $46 d. The ferry across

Lower Arrow Lake operates every 30 minutes 5 a.m.-10 p.m., crossing the lake to **Needles,** a ferry landing and nothing more.

From this point, Hwy. 6 ascends steeply to the high peaks of the Monashee Mountains. At Cherryville, 35-km Sugar Lake Rd. leads north to the remote wilderness of **Monashee Provincial Park.** This 7,513-hectare park is totally isolated; the only access is on foot along a 12-km trail. From the heights of the Monashees, Hwy.

6 descends to the **Coldstream Valley,** where you'll see field crops, orchards, and low, rolling hills; paddocks where horses frolic in fluorescent-green grass; rustic old barns in various degrees of disrepair; and well-loved old homes. At **Lumby** a road leads 37 km northeast to **Mabel Lake Provincial Park,** with a tree-shaded picnic area and camping for $9.50 per night.

For information on Vernon, see the Okanagan Valley chapter.

NELSON

The elegant city of Nelson (pop. 9,700) lies in a picturesque setting on the West Arm of Kootenay Lake, 660 km east of Vancouver. Its relaxed pace, hilly tree-lined streets, and turn-of-the-century architectural treasures have helped attract an eclectic mix of jaded big-city types and counterculture seekers. But while the city itself is uniquely charming, the surrounding wilderness of the Selkirk Mountains is Nelson's biggest draw. The area's many lakes provide excellent fishing, sailing, canoeing, and some of British Columbia's best inland beaches. Kokanee Glacier Provincial Park's alpine reaches are laced with trails suitable for hikers of all fitness levels. Old logging and mining trails attract happy hordes of mountain-bikers. And nearby hot springs provide a welcome relief at the end of a hard day's play. In addition, when the snow starts flying, powderhounds flock to **Whitewater**

Ski Resort for some of North America's best lift-served powder skiing.

History

After the discovery of copper and silver deposits on Toad Mountain in 1886, Nelson sprang up as a small mining camp along the banks of Ward Creek. The early mines proved profitable and the town expanded rapidly. Construction of a smelter began at the end of 1895, and wagon roads, railroads, and steamboat routes were developed to serve the local mining boom. Soon Nelson became the commercial and cultural center of the Kootenays, at its peak boasting 23 hotels and six saloons. Although mining operations waned by the turn of the century, silver had left a grand impact on Nelson. It was the first city in the province to operate an electric power plant (on Cottonwood Creek), and the smallest

Nelson's historic buildings today hold many cafes and restaurants.

ANDREW HEMPSTEAD

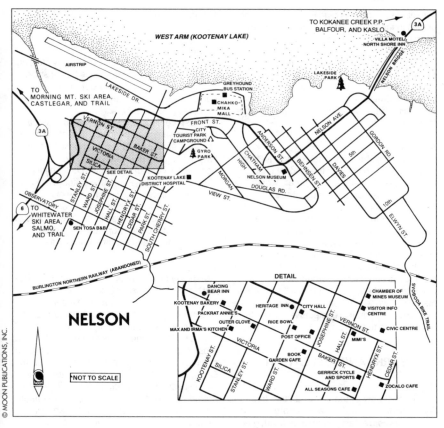

city in the country to have a streetcar system. Today the city retains its grandeur, which can be noted in the Steve Martin movie, *Roxanne,* filmed here in 1987.

SIGHTS

Architecture
Nelson has more heritage buildings per capita than any other city in British Columbia, save Victoria. Most can be viewed by walking around the downtown core between Baker and Vernon Streets. Pick up the detailed *Heritage Walking Tour* or *Heritage Motoring Tour* brochures from the information center. The walking-tour brochure details 25 downtown buildings, including the 1909 courthouse on Ward St. and the impressive stone-and-brick 1902 city hall on the corner of Ward and Vernon Streets.

Museums
Nelson's two museums are both worth visiting. **Nelson Museum,** 402 Anderson St., tel. (250) 352-9813, concentrates on local history, with displays covering native peoples, explorers, miners, traders, early transportation, Nelson's contribution to WW I, and the Doukhobors (a Russian religious sect who settled in the Kootenays). It also contains the *Ladybird,* a record-breaking

© MOON PUBLICATIONS, INC.

speedboat designed prior to the advent of hydro-planes in the 1950s. The museum is open daily 1-6 p.m. in summer, and Mon.-Sat. 1-4 p.m. the rest of the year. Admission is $2.

To absorb some of Nelson's mining history, cruise past the mining artifacts, mineral displays, and historic photos at the free **Chamber of Mines Museum,** next to the information center on Hall St., tel. (250) 352-5242. It's open Mon.-Fri. 1-5 p.m.

Artwalk

Organized by the local arts council, Nelson's annual Artwalk highlights the work of up to 100 local artists. Throughout summer, works are displayed city-wide at various venues such as restaurants and the theater. On the last Friday of every month, receptions are held at each of the venues. The receptions feature live entertainment, refreshments, and the artists themselves, on hand to discuss their work. A brochure available at the information center and motels and galleries around town contains biographies of each featured artist, tells where his or her work is displayed, and provides a map showing you the easiest way to get from one venue to the next.

PARKS AND RECREATION

City Parks

For a good view of the city and lake, head to **Gyro Park,** beyond the east end of Vernon Street. **Lakeside Park,** another pleasant green spot, is by Nelson Bridge and has a sandy beach, tennis courts, and a picnic area.

Hiking and Biking

The best nearby hiking is in **Kokanee Glacier Provincial Park** (see "Highway 3A to Balfour" under "Kootenay Lake and Creston," below), but the bed of the Burlington Northern Railway, built in 1893, provides an interesting nine-km trek right on Nelson's back doorstep. Access the railway from the top end of South Cherry Street. The many old logging and mining roads surrounding the city are great for mountain biking; one favorite is the **Svoboda Bike Trail,** accessed along Elwyn St. beyond the college. For bike rentals and a trail map, head to **Gerrick**

Cycle and Sports, 702 Baker St., tel. (250) 354-4622.

Fishing

Kootenay Lake holds kokanee, Dolly Varden, and rainbow trout, and the lake's feeder streams also provide good fishing opportunities. For guided fishing, contact **Split Shot Guiding Service,** tel. (250) 229-5262.

Those content to view fish rather than catch them can watch spawning kokanee at the mouth of **Kokanee Creek,** 20 km northeast of town on Hwy. 3A, and at **Redfish Creek,** five km farther northeast, where an interpretive center offers displays describing the kokanee's lifecycle. Kokanee are landlocked salmon. Instead of migrating in from the ocean like their anadromous cousins, kokanee spend their lives in the larger lakes of British Columbia's interior, spawning each summer in the rivers and streams that feed the lakes.

Skiing

Legendary powder makes **Whitewater Ski Resort** a mecca for ski bums in the know. The small ski area 19 km south of Nelson sits beneath a string of 2,500-meter-high peaks. The peaks catch an amazing amount of snow and deposit it in enough bowls and glades to keep most experts happy for days. Three double chairlifts access 18 marked trails; the Summit Chair, with a vertical rise of 430 meters, opens up the best powder-packed slopes. The area's abundant snowfall makes for a long season, but conditions are best in February and March. Whitewater has no on-mountain accommodations—just the lifts and a day lodge with a cafeteria, rental shop, and ski school. Lift tickets are adults $34, seniors $27; children under six ski free. For resort information call (250) 354-4944; for snow reports call (250) 352-7669; for accommodations packages call (800) 666-9420.

Morning Mountain Ski Area, tel. (250) 352-9969, provides good family skiing, with runs geared to beginning and intermediate skiers. Facilities include a T-bar, day lodge, rental shop, and ski school. The area offers night skiing Tues.-Fri. and day skiing Sat.-Monday. To get there, head out toward Castlegar and take Blewitt Ski Hill Road. **Apex-Busk Cross-country Ski Area** offers 25 km of groomed trails. It's off Hwy. 6, 12 km south of Nelson.

ACCOMMODATIONS AND CAMPING

Hostel
Right downtown, the **Dancing Bear Inn,** 171 Baker St., tel. (250) 352-7573, offers clean and comfortable accommodations at a very reasonable price. Affiliated with Hostelling International, the nicely renovated inn features a cozy lounge area with a television, reading material, information on local attractions and restaurants, and a cupboard full of board games. Other facilities include a kitchen, laundry, and lockers. The dorm-style rooms are spacious, with a maximum of six beds in each. A few doubles and a single room are also available. All beds are the same price; members of Hostelling International pay $17 per night, nonmembers $20.

Hotels and Motels
The best choice, right downtown, is the old-fashioned **Heritage Inn,** 422 Vernon St., tel. (250) 352-5331, which provides attractive, recently refurbished rooms, some with lake views, for $52-68 s, $58-68 d. Across Nelson Bridge from downtown are **Villa Motel,** tel. (250) 352-5515, and **North Shore Inn,** tel. (250) 352-6606, both offering rooms of a high standard for $55 s, $60 d. If you don't mind being away from town, check out **Duhamel Motel,** eight km northeast of Nelson on Hwy. 3A, tel. (250) 825-4645. Each of the eight units has a kitchenette and across the road is a good beach; $45 s, $50 d.

Bed and Breakfasts
Uphill from downtown, **Sen Tosa B&B,** 402 Observatory St., tel. (250) 354-1993, offers three comfortable guest rooms and particularly delicious breakfasts (the owners also operate one of Nelson's favorite restaurants). Guests have use of a communal living area and a pleasant garden with an outdoor hot tub. Rates are $55 s, $65 d. If you don't mind being out of town, **Crystal Springs B&B,** 2290 Crystal Springs Rd. (take Hwy. 3A northeast out of town), tel. (250) 825-3495, is a good choice. It's right beside a wildlife corridor and surrounded by a natural bushland setting, so complete privacy is guaranteed. The guest area includes a private bathroom and living area. Rates are $75 s or d.

Campgrounds
Right downtown, **City Tourist Park** on the corner of High and Willow Sts., tel. (250) 352-9031, isn't particularly impressive. It's surrounded by houses and its sites are closely spaced; $13-20 per night, open in summer only. A much better choice is the lakeside **Kokanee Creek Provincial Park,** 20 km northeast of Nelson on Hwy. 3A, tel. (250) 825-4421. Although the large park offers more than 100 sites, it's often full; the beautiful location makes this one of the Kootenays' most popular campgrounds. Unserviced sites are $12. If the park is full, continue eight km further northeast to Balfour, where you'll find two commercial campgrounds.

FOOD AND DRINK

Breakfast at Mimi's
Nelson's reputation as a center of good eating has come ahead in leaps and bounds during recent years, but for breakfast, old habits die hard. And everyone heads for Mimi's, 702 Vernon St., tel. (250) 352-7113, an old old-style place with fast and friendly service and eggs, bacon, hash browns, and toast for $6.

Cafes
Book Garden Cafe, 556 Josephine St., tel. (250) 352-1812, combines a bookstore with an outdoor patio cafe serving a variety of coffees and healthy meals. Sandwiches or soup and salad go for $6 while Sunday brunch, served 10 a.m.-4 p.m., runs $6-8. Open daily from 9 a.m. The counterculture of Nelson is evident at **Packrat Annie's,** 411 Kootenay St., tel. (250) 354-4722, where a wide cross-section of the local community wanders in for herbal tea, muffins, or lunch; and **Kootenay Bakery,** 295 Baker St., tel. (250) 352-2274, which offers a great selection of breads and cakes.

Restaurants
For the cheapest meal in town and the chance to view Nelson's alternative-lifestylers, head to the **Rice Bowl,** 459 Ward St., tel. (250) 354-4299, where you can get six pieces of sushi for $4 or the delicious Thai noodle salad for $6. The freshly squeezed juices are also good. The **Outer Clove,** 536 Stanley St., tel. (250) 354-1667, is typical of

Nelson's new batch of restaurants, appealing to modern tastes but in a relaxed, low-key environment. The emphasis is on garlic, with tapas from $5 (you'd need three for a filling meal) and dinners $10.50-16. Most lunch items are under $8. It's open Mon.-Sat. 11:30 a.m.-9:30 p.m.

Tucked into a back alley behind the main street is **All Seasons Cafe,** 620 Heritage Lane, tel. (250) 352-0101, a small yet stylish place known for its wine list. Lunch is well-priced, but dinner is most popular, with a menu ranging from vegetarian Japanese to West Coast salmon. The best pizza in town comes straight from the wood-fired oven at **Max & Irma's Kitchen,** 515 Kootenay St., tel. (250) 352-2332, a stylish place open for lunch and dinner. Order your favorite off the standard menu ($10 and up) or pay $6 for a base and build-your-own from a large assortment of mouthwatering toppings. For Mexican cuisine, try **Zocalo Cafe,** in an old church at 802 Baker St., tel. (250) 352-7223. Start with freshly made guacamole for $5, then devour a Mexican main meal—cooked American-style—for $10-14.

Drink

The Heritage Inn, 422 Vernon St., tel. (250) 352-5331, is the center of Nelson's after-dark scene. Within this old hotel you'll find the **Boiler Room,** a bar that comes alive with a disco Wed.-Sat. from 10 p.m.; and the elegant **Library,** with tapestried chairs by a fireplace, books to read, and an elaborate draped ceiling—the perfect place to head for a quiet drink.

SERVICES AND INFORMATION

Transportation

Although a prime chunk of lakeside real estate, right in town, is taken up by a small airstrip, no scheduled flights serve Nelson. The closest commercial airport is at Castlegar, 45 km away. Among charter companies using the local strip is **Nelson Mountain Air,** tel. (250) 354-1456, which offers flightseeing over Kokanee Glacier (around $70 per person).

Long-distance bus transportation is provided by **Greyhound.** The depot is at the Chahko-Mika Mall, 1112 Lakeside Dr., tel. (250) 352-3939. From Vancouver, buses come into Nelson via Castlegar, then continue east to Cranbrook via Salmo.

Local car rental agencies include: **Rent-a-wreck,** tel. (250) 352-5122; **Thrifty,** tel. (250) 352-2811; and **Whitewater Motors Ltd.,** tel. (250) 352-7202. For details of local bus transportation, call **Nelson Transit System** at (250) 352-8228.

Other Services

Kootenay Lake District Hospital is immediately east of downtown at 3 View St., tel. (250) 352-3111. The **post office** is at 514 Vernon Street. For quality arts and crafts, drop by the **Craft Connection,** 441 Baker St., tel. (250) 352-3006, a co-op owned and operated by local artists and craftspersons; closed Sunday. **Packrat Annie's,** 411 Kootenay St., sells books, tapes, and CDs, and offers good peoplewatching opportunities.

Information

All the information you'll need on Nelson and the Kootenays is available at **Nelson Visitor Info Centre,** 225 Hall St., tel. (250) 352-3433. It's open in summer, Mon.-Fri. 8:30 a.m.-6 p.m.; Sat.-Sun. 10 a.m.-6 p.m.; the rest of the year, Mon.-Fri. 8:30 a.m.-4:30 p.m. For information on the Kootenays' provincial parks, head north 20 km to the large **visitor center** at Kokanee Creek Provincial Park, tel. (250) 825-4421.

KOOTENAY LAKE AND CRESTON

Heading first north, then east from Nelson, Hwy. 3A follows a narrow arm of Kootenay Lake before coming to the main body of water at Balfour. From there, you have a choice of routes. You can cross Kootenay Lake by ferry and follow the east shore of the lake down to Creston, or you can continue north up the west shore of the lake, passing through Ainsworth Hot Springs and Kaslo before arcing back west to Slocan Valley and Arrow Lake.

HIGHWAY 3A TO BALFOUR

Kokanee Creek Provincial Park

This 257-hectare park 20 km northeast of Nelson features a great beach and one of the Kootenays' most popular campgrounds. Short trails crisscross the park, and kokanee—a landlocked species of salmon—spawn in Kokanee Creek at the end of summer. The large campground's sites are unserviced, but fill fast through summer; $12 per night. A visitor center, open in summer 9 a.m.-9 p.m., holds displays on local ecosystems, trail reports for Kokanee Glacier Provincial Park (see below), and other useful information.

Kokanee Glacier Provincial Park

Straddling the highest peaks of the Selkirk Mountains, this 32,035-hectare mountain wilderness park can be seen from downtown Nelson. The steep and narrow gravel roads into the park are often impassable until late June, and the hiking trails remain snow-covered even later; check road and trail conditions at the visitor center in Kokanee Creek Provincial Park before setting off. But don't let these things discourage you from visiting. This is one of B.C.'s premier provincial parks, filled with magnificent scenery and abundant wildlife and providing some unrivaled opportunities for backcountry travel.

The park is named for a massive glacier that, along with two other glaciers and 30 lakes, feeds dozens of creeks and rivers flowing west to Slocan Lake and east to Kootenay Lake. Lying almost entirely above 1,800 meters, the park's environment—dominated by barren peaks and, for a few short weeks in the middle of summer, meadows of lush subalpine wildflowers—is very different than the valley floor.

The heart of the park is too steep and rugged to be penetrated by roads, so all the best features must be reached on foot. The main access is via an unsealed road that spurs off Hwy. 3A 20 km from Nelson and follows Kokanee Creek 16 km to **Gibson Lake.** A 2.5-km trail circles the lake, but the best hiking is further afield. From Gibson Lake, it's four km uphill to beautiful **Kokanee Lake.** There the trail flattens out, continuing three km to Kaslo Lake and a further two km to a backcountry campground ($2 per person) and **Slocan Chief Cabin,** a century-old structure that sleeps 12 ($10 per person). Total elevation gain along this trail is 600 meters, but most of this is gained in the moderately steep ascent to Kokanee Lake. From the cabin, those experienced in alpine travel have many opportunities for exploring surrounding peaks and Kokanee Glacier.

The park can also be accessed from a rough 24-km unsealed road that begins six km west of Kaslo and ends at the **Joker Millsite** trailhead. Here you can pick up a steep five-km trail to Slocan Chief Cabin or a five-km trail (elevation gain 450 meters) to a backcountry campground at **Joker Lakes,** two beautiful bodies of water in a glacial cirque surrounded by towering peaks.

Because of the park's remote location, it's vital to pick up information on road and hiking-trail conditions at the **visitor center** in Kokanee Creek Provincial Park, tel. (250) 825-4421; open in summer 9 a.m.-9 p.m. The center can provide you with detailed directions to other park access points and give you up-to-the-minute information on which trails, if any, are closed due to bear activity.

Balfour

The picturesque village of Balfour lies at the junction of the north, south, and west arms of Kootenay Lake. Here you can easily while away the better part of a day, enjoying beautiful lake views from a waterfront cafe or watching the local community of partially tame Canada geese honking for handouts down on the beach.

Back in the 1890s, sternwheelers plied the lake, dropping off prospectors and supplies at isolated mining camps and settlements along its shores. But completion of the railway in the early 1900s quickly put most of the sternwheelers out of action. Today one public ferry remains, and it's "North America's longest free ferry ride." The 45-minute trip across Kootenay Lake from Balfour to Kootenay Bay offers majestic lake and mountain scenery and makes a good route to Creston and points east (see "Across Kootenay Lake," below).

AINSWORTH HOT SPRINGS

Overlooking Kootenay Lake from a hillside 17 km north of Balfour, these springs were discovered in the early 1800s by local natives who found that the hot, odorless water (high in magnesium sulphate, calcium sulphate, and sodium carbonate) helped heal their wounds and ease their aches and pains. Today the springs have been commercialized, and include a main outdoor pool, a jacuzzi, steam bath, and cold plunge pool. Rates are $6 for a single entry or $10 per day. The pools are open year-round, with summer hours 8:30 a.m.-9:30 p.m.

If you want a bit more pampering, stay at **Ainsworth Hot Springs Resort,** tel. (250) 229-4212 or (800) 668-1171, which features exercise and massage rooms, a lounge, and a licensed restaurant overlooking the main pool and beautiful Kootenay Lake. Room rates are $89-154 s or d, plus an extra $10 for a kitchenette. Rates start at $70 in the off-season. Another good accommodation choice in the vicinity of the hot springs is **Woodbury Resort,** three km to the north, tel. (250) 353-7717. Facilities include a heated swimming pool, restaurant, pub, grocery store, and a marina with boat rentals and fishing supplies. Accommodations are in kitchenette units ($50 s, $54 d) or cabins ($60 s, $64 d). Camping is $15-18.

Cody Caves Provincial Park
High above the hot springs, this cave system was discovered by prospector Henry Cody in the 1890s. Made up of several large chambers totalling 800 meters in length, the caves also hold an underground creek that drops over 11-meter Cody Falls. Experienced spelunkers can explore the caves unguided, but others will want to join a tour with **Hiadventure Corp.,** tel. (250) 353-7425. Based at the caves' entrance, this company offer tours through summer 10 a.m.-5 p.m. Cost is $12 per person. To get to the caves, turn off Hwy. 31 just north of Ainsworth Hot Springs, follow a narrow 15-km gravel road to a trailhead, then hike 20 minutes.

KASLO AND VICINITY

Tree-lined streets graced by elegant turn-of-the-century architecture, lake and mountain views from almost every street, and the world's oldest passenger sternwheeler tied up at the wharf make Kaslo (pop. 1,000), 70 km north of Nelson, a worthwhile stop. Another of the Kootenays' great boomtowns, Kaslo began as a sawmill community in 1889. But nearby silver strikes in 1893 quickly turned the town into a bustling city of 3,000 and an important commercial hub; a railway brought silver down from Sandon to Kaslo, where it was loaded onto steamers and shipped out to Creston and the outside world. The town's 1898 city hall is one of only two wooden buildings in the country that are still the seats of local government.

Sights
Drydocked by the lakefront stands the 50-meter-long **SS** *Moyie,* the last Canadian Pacific Railway sternwheeler to splash up Kootenay Lake. Built in 1897 and launched the following year at Nelson, the grand old red-and-white vessel was used for transportation of passengers, freight, and mail right up until its retirement in 1957. Today the ship serves as a museum containing a fine collection of photos, antiques, and artifacts of the region. It's open daily in summer 9:30 a.m.-4:30 p.m.; admission adults $5, seniors $4, children $3.

Another place to step back in time is the **Kootenay Mining Heritage Centre,** in the old fire hall on 3rd Street. Admission is $2. Open in summer, daily 10 a.m.-5 p.m.

and climbing into the Selkirks. Along the way it passes a number of provincial park campgrounds.

The highlight of the road is **Trout Lake,** a narrow body of water surrounded by 2,000-meter-high peaks. At the lake's extreme southern end is a small provincial park and camping. From this point the road gets pretty rough, climbing high above the lake and winding around steep gullies. At the north end of the lake is the remote community of Trout Lake, the center of a short-lived gold rush. In a ramshackle old building dating to 1892, the **Windsor Hotel,** tel. (250) 369-2244, offers basic rooms from $35 s, $40 d. Meals are available.

White Grizzly Wilderness
Straddling the Selkirk Mountains north of Hwy. 31A, this newly created area protects 137,000 hectares of mountainous terrain that is prime territory for grizzly bears. The best way to visit the area is on a guided hike with Erica Mallam of the Valhalla Society in New Denver, 307 6th Ave., tel. (250) 358-7789. The full-day trip begins with a one-hour slide show teaching species identification and safe travel in bear country. Then it's out into the field to visit an uninhabited black bear den and hike along the Whitewater Glacier Trail, from which grizzlies can often be seen at a safe distance across the valley. Tour cost is adults $40, children $20. For further information on the area, including a topographical map showing trails ($4), head to the Valhalla Society headquarters in New Denver.

ACROSS KOOTENAY LAKE

From Balfour, the world's longest free ferry ride takes you across Kootenay Lake to **Kootenay Bay.** An interesting stop there, four km from the ferry, is **Kootenay Forge,** a traditional blacksmith shop where you can watch artisans practicing this ancient trade; open weekdays 9 a.m.-5 p.m. Continue down the road to western Canada's only traditional broom manufacturer. The raw materials (from California and Mexico) used by **North Woven Broom Company** are handcrafted into brooms using 19th-century methods. Stop in anytime and you're likely to find Janet and Rob Schwieger hard at work and

ANDREW HEMPSTEAD

The SS Moyie *was the last sternwheeler on Kootenay Lake.*

Practicalities
Right downtown, the inexpensive **Kaslo Motel,** 330 D Ave., tel. (250) 353-2431, charges $42-48 s or d; some rooms have small kitchens. Across the inlet from downtown, **Beachcomber's Marina,** 551 Rainbow Dr., tel. (250) 353-7777, offers kitchenette units from $50 and a small camping area with sites $11-14.

Rosewood Cafe, tel. (250) 353-7673, occupies a restored house at the top of 4th Street. It's open all day, and you can stop by for just coffee and cake or for the hearty home-style cooking; lunches from $6.

Kaslo Visitor Info Centre, 311 4th St., tel. (250) 353-2525, is open in summer only, daily 9 a.m.-8 p.m.

North from Kaslo
Highway 31 leads north from Kaslo to **Galena Bay,** 50 km south of Revelstoke. The road parallels Kootenay Lake before turning to gravel

eager to share their knowledge of this lost art. The workshop is crammed with brooms of all shapes and sizes, ranging in price from $24-58.

From here, it's 80 km of lake-hugging road to Creston. Along the way you'll pass small clusters of houses and a number of resorts. The pick of local accommodations is **Wedgwood Manor,** just south of Crawford Bay, tel. (250) 227-9233. Set on 20 beautiful hectares adjacent to a golf course and within walking distance of a beach, this 1910 home offers six heritage-style rooms, each with a private bathroom. Guests can relax in the library or in the extensive gardens. Rates are $79 s, $89-105 d. **Lockhart Beach Provincial Park,** 18 km south of Crawford Bay, has a small campground with sites for $9.50 per night.

CRESTON

In a wide, fertile valley at the extreme southern end of Kootenay Lake lies Creston, a thriving agricultural center of 4,900. Although the town is south of the Kootenays' most spectacular mountains, the scenery is still impressive; the valley is flanked by the Selkirk Mountains to the west and the Purcell Mountains to the east. No mineral riches have been found around Creston, but the lure of gold and silver further afield drew hopefuls through the valley, turning it into a prime transportation link across British Columbia's remote southern interior. As the town grew, agriculture became the mainstay of the local economy. Fruit stands lining Hwy. 3 as it enters Creston from the west are a sign of the district's most obvious industry; apples, strawberries, apricots, plums, and peaches are all sold at roadside stands.

Sights
Creston Valley Wildlife Centre, 10 km west of town, tel. (250) 428-3259, is part of a 7,000-hectare wildlife reserve extending from Kootenay Lake to the Canada/U.S. border. Protecting vital resting grounds along the Pacific flyway, the site provides a haven for over 250 species of birds, including a large population of osprey, a flock of the rare Forester's tern, and a nesting colony of western grebe. Displays in the wildlife center, open May-Oct., daily 8 a.m.-6 p.m., focus on the abundant birdlife, as well as on mammals and reptiles present in the reserve. From the center, hiking trails lead along areas of wetland to a 10-meter-high birdwatching tower. Admission to the center is $3, and you can take a canoe trip or join a guided hike for $5 per person.

Creston is home to **Columbia Brewery,** 1220 Erickson St., tel. (250) 428-9344, producer of British Columbia's popular Kokanee beer. Tours are offered in summer, Mon.-Fri. at 11:30 a.m., 1 p.m., and 2:30 p.m. Out of town to the west, **Kootenay Candles,** 1511 Northwest Blvd., tel. (250) 428-9785, makes handcrafted candles that are sold at their factory retail outlet. Tours are offered.

Practicalities
Right downtown, the aptly named **Downtowner Motor Inn,** 1218 Canyon St., tel. (250) 428-2238 or (800) 665-9904, sports an easily recognized blue and white exterior; $43 s, $48 d. West of Creston, right by the wildlife sanctuary, is **Summit Creek Campground,** tel. (250) 428-7441; $12.50 per site, hot showers available.

The busiest place in town each morning is **Creston Valley Bakery,** 113 10th Ave., tel. (250) 428-2661, where you'll find plenty of tables and a large selection of freshly baked cakes and pastries. Formerly specializing in just fine coffees, **Kootenay Rose,** 129 10th Ave., tel. (250) 428-7252, is now open for dinner Mon.-Saturday. The menu is packed with healthy vegetarian dishes.

Creston Visitor Info Centre is at the east end of town at 1711 Canyon St., tel. (250) 428-4342. It's open in summer, daily 9 a.m.-6 p.m.; the rest of the year, weekdays 9 a.m.-4:30 p.m.

EAST KOOTENAYS

This stunning chunk of British Columbia encompasses the Purcell Mountains and the Rocky Mountain Trench, immediately west of the Rocky Mountains. On the northern end of this wide valley, **Radium Hot Springs** serves as the western gateway to the national parks of the Rocky Mountains. On the south end, **Cranbrook** is the region's largest population center. The mighty Columbia River flows down the valley between the two cities.

History

For 2,000 years before the first Europeans arrived, the Kootenay tribe lived in this beautiful valley, hunting, gathering, and making horseback trips over the Rockies to hunt buffalo on the Albertan plains. In 1807 David Thompson, an explorer for the fur-trading North West Company, found his way over Howse Pass and set up Kootenay House trading post at the north end of Windermere Lake.

During the next 50 years the region was explored and mined, its animals trapped by fur traders, its people preached to and baptized by missionaries. But it wasn't until 1863 that settlers showed much interest in the rugged, mountainous terrain. At the shout of "Gold!" along Wild Horse Creek, miners swarmed into the area. First the town of **Fisherville** sprang up along the banks of the gold-bearing creek, then **Galbraith's Ferry** was established nearby on the edge of the Kootenay River. In 1888, Galbraith's Ferry was renamed **Fort Steele** to honor NWMP Superintendent Sam Steele, who built the first NWMP post west of the Rockies on the site.

In 1893 North Star Mine opened in **Kimberley** and began yielding riches in the form of lead, zinc, and silver. Fort Steele was the commercial center of the region until 1898, when the Canadian Pacific Railway (CPR) bypassed it in favor of Cranbrook. Fort Steele then declined as Cranbrook flourished.

Today Fort Steele has been reconstructed as a heritage park. It's worth a visit, especially in summer when park staff reenacts the town's vivid history.

EAST FROM CRESTON

From Creston, the Crowsnest Highway (Hwy. 3) crosses the **Purcell Mountains** and descends to Cranbrook, the region's largest town. The distance between the two towns is a little over 100 km.

Yahk

Yahk grew into a thriving lumber town in the 1920s, but was abandoned by the 1930s. Today empty houses and hotels line the streets, but the pioneer **museum** keeps history alive with its displays of household artifacts and costumes from the past. Tiny nine-hectare **Yahk Provincial Park** lies beside the rushing Moyie River east of town. Fishing in the river is good for rainbow trout and Dolly Varden; camping is $9.50 per night.

South of Yahk is the **Kingsgate port of entry,** open daily 24 hours.

Moyie

Once boasting a population of 1,500, Moyie today holds nothing more than a few historic buildings along deserted streets; the church on Tavistock St. and the fire hall beside the highway are among the survivors. Miners working the nearby St. Eugene Mine for lead and silver were the first settlers. To get to the mine site, take Queens Ave. east out of town and look for tailings.

Moyie has no accommodations, but 13 km north of town is 91-hectare **Moyie Lake Provincial Park,** which offers fishing and swimming and the chance to view kokanee spawning on gravel river beds. The large campground has hot showers; $14.50 per site.

CRANBROOK

Crossroads of the eastern Kootenays, Cranbrook (pop. 19,000) is nestled at the base of the Purcell Mountains and provides spectacular views eastward to the famous Canadian Rockies. The city itself has few tourist attractions, but with

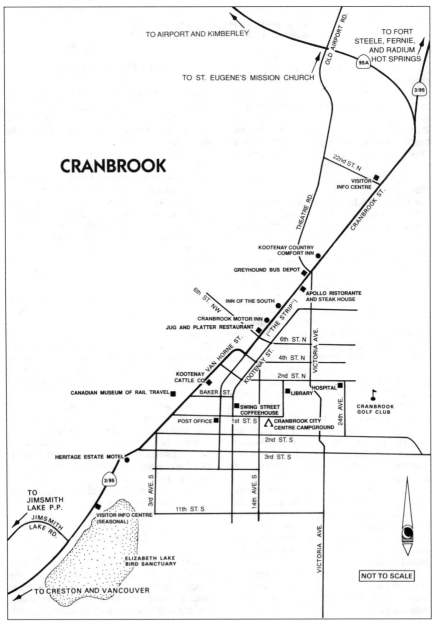

CRANBROOK

TO AIRPORT AND KIMBERLEY

TO FORT STEELE, FERNIE, AND RADIUM HOT SPRINGS

OLD AIRPORT RD.

95A

3/95

TO ST. EUGENE'S MISSION CHURCH

22nd ST. N

VISITOR INFO CENTRE

THEATRE RD.

CRANBROOK ST.

KOOTENAY COUNTRY COMFORT INN

GREYHOUND BUS DEPOT

APOLLO RISTORANTE AND STEAK HOUSE

6th ST. NW

INN OF THE SOUTH

CRANBROOK MOTOR INN

JUG AND PLATTER RESTAURANT

("THE STRIP")

6th ST. N

4th ST. N

2nd ST. N

VAN HORNE ST.

KOOTENAY ST.

VICTORIA AVE.

KOOTENAY CATTLE CO.

CANADIAN MUSEUM OF RAIL TRAVEL

BAKER ST.

SWING STREET COFFEEHOUSE

LIBRARY

HOSPITAL

24th AVE.

CRANBROOK GOLF CLUB

POST OFFICE

1st ST. S

CRANBROOK CITY CENTRE CAMPGROUND

2nd ST. S

HERITAGE ESTATE MOTEL

3rd ST. S

3/95

TO JIMSMITH LAKE P.P.

JIMSMITH LAKE RD.

3rd AVE. S

14th AVE. S

11th ST. S

VISITOR INFO CENTRE (SEASONAL)

ELIZABETH LAKE BIRD SANCTUARY

VICTORIA AVE.

NOT TO SCALE

TO CRESTON AND VANCOUVER

© MOON PUBLICATIONS, INC.

all the surrounding wilderness and nearby Fort Steele Heritage Town, it's a good base for exploring further afield.

History
Originally a campsite for Kootenay natives, the area's first European landowners were the Galbraiths, who ran the ferry across the Kootenay River at Fort Steele. In the 1880s the family sold their holdings to Col. James Baker, who met with little success in his initial attempts to establish a townsite here. But Baker's fortunes turned around quickly when the Canadian Pacific Railway ran its line right through the struggling settlement. The town rapidly grew and in 1905 the city of Cranbrook was incorporated. Today this service and transportation center is the region's major city and has an economy based on forestry, mining, and ranching.

Canadian Museum of Rail Travel
Cranbrook's main attraction, this museum is on a siding of the main CPR line directly opposite downtown on Van Horne St., tel. (250) 489-3918. It features the only surviving and restored set of special railway cars from the Trans-Canada Limited, a luxury train (also called "The Millionaires' Train") built for the Canadian Pacific Railway in 1929. The dining, sleeping, and solarium lounge cars sport inlaid mahogany and walnut paneling, plush upholsteries, and brass fixtures. Restoration displays, a viewing corridor, a model railway display, a slide show, and a 45-minute guided tour of the interiors of cars are included in the price of the Grand Tour Ticket; adults $5, seniors $4, children $3. Buy your ticket at the restored 1900 Elko Station. After the tour, head for the **Dining Car Tearoom** to enjoy scones and tea (served 11:30 a.m.-2 p.m.) and to see, but not use, the railway's silver, china, and glassware collection. The museum is open in summer, daily 8 a.m.-8 p.m.; fall and spring, daily 10 a.m.-6 p.m.; winter, Tues.-Sat. noon-5 p.m.

Heritage Walking Tour
The locals are proud of their downtown heritage buildings, which you can view on a self-guided walking tour by picking up the handy *Cranbrook Heritage Tour* brochure from either information center or the railway museum (stop number one

on the tour). Start at the Rotary Clock Tower in Cranbrook Square—the tower is an exact replica of the old post office tower that stood across Baker St. at the corner of 10th Avenue. The original tower was demolished in 1971, much to the dismay of Cranbrook preservationists, but the clock from the old tower was incorporated into the replica. You can still see the home of Colonel Baker—the original Cranbrook developer for whom downtown's main street is named—in Baker Park off 1st St. S; the Interpretation Room is open weekdays 9 a.m.-5 p.m. Many other heritage homes are found between 10th and 13th Aves. and 1st and 4th Sts. South.

If you're still in a heritage mood and heading for Kimberley, take Old Airport Rd. (a continuation of Theatre Rd.) north to **St. Eugene's Mission Church,** between Cranbrook and Kimberley. Built in 1897, this is the finest Gothic-style mission church in the province and features beautiful, hand-painted Italian stained-glass windows.

Elizabeth Lake Bird Sanctuary
Beside the highway at the southern city limits (park at the information center), this large area of wetlands is a haven for many species of waterfowl, including Canada geese, and teal, ring-neck, scaup, redhead, bufflehead, goldeneye, and ruddy ducks. You can also see coots, grebes, black terns, and songbirds. Mammals present include muskrats, white-tailed deer, and occasionally moose.

Entertainment and Events
Jughead's, 807 Baker St., tel. (250) 426-8662, is the place to head for live music each weekend. **Inn of the South,** 803 Cranbrook St., tel. (250) 489-4301, and **Town and Country Hotel,** 600 Cranbrook St., tel. (250) 426-6683, also both hold nightclubs.

The annual four-day **Sam Steele Days** festival is held on the third weekend in June and honors the commander of the first North West Mounted Police post in this region. Expect a huge parade, the Sweetheart Pageant, loggers' sports, bicycle and wheelchair races, a truck rodeo, a variety of sporting events, live theater, and whatever else the Sam Steele Society comes up with each year. Find out all the details by calling (250) 426-4161.

Accommodations and Camping

All motels are along Hwy. 3 through town. The highway is known as Van Horne St. south of 4th St. N, and Cranbrook St. to the north. On average, motel prices here are among the lowest in the province, making it a good spot to rest overnight. The flower-basket-adorned **Heritage Estate Motel,** 362 Van Horne St., tel. (250) 426-3862 or (800) 670-1001, has large rooms at $45 s, $49 d. It's usually busy, so book ahead in summer. An inexpensive option in the heart of the commercial strip is **Cranbrook Motor Inn,** 621 Cranbrook St., tel. (250) 426-8231; from $39 s, $44 d. Slightly more expensive and just as good value is **Kootenay Country Comfort Inn,** 1111 Cranbrook St., tel. (250) 426-2296. **Inn of the South,** 803 Cranbrook St., tel. (250) 489-4301, offers deluxe rooms and an indoor pool, jacuzzi, sauna, dining room, cocktail lounge, and nightclub; $69-77 s, $76-86 d.

One of the area's most attractive campgrounds is in 12-hectare **Jimsmith Lake Provincial Park,** four km off the main highway at the southern outskirts of the city. The park's wooded campsites rent for $9.50 per night; open May-September. Downtown, **Cranbrook City Centre Campground,** in Baker Park at the corner of 14th Ave. and 1st St. S, tel. (250) 426-2162, provides grassy tent sites for $13 and hookups for $15-20. A stream and waterfall flow nearby, and hot showers are available.

Food

All the plants inside the **Jug and Platter Restaurant,** on the main commercial strip at 611 Cranbrook St., tel. (250) 489-5515, more than make up for the lack of greenery outside. This is the place for breakfast, with the daily special $4-5. The rest of the day, it's sandwiches and hamburgers for $3-8 and Ukrainian specials (borscht, pyrogies, and other delicacies) for around $7-9. For good coffee, fresh muffins, and light snacks head to **Swing Street Coffeehouse,** 16 11th Ave., tel. (250) 426-5358; open daily from 8:30 a.m.

Cranbrook lacks outstanding restaurants, but a few longtime favorites offer reliable food and service. One of these is the **Kootenay Cattle Co.,** in a nondescript building at 40 Van Horne St. N, tel. (250) 489-5811. Head here for steak dinners, a variety of other dishes, and an excellent salad bar. It's open Tues.-Fri. for lunch ($7-10) and daily for dinner ($10-25). Another good choice, **Apollo Ristorante and Steak House,** 1012 Cranbrook St., tel. (250) 426-3721, offers a salad bar, steaks, seafood, Italian dishes, and 25 varieties of pizza. Expect to pay $6 and up at lunch, $12 in the evening. Open daily.

Transportation

Cranbrook Airport, on the north side of town off Hwy. 95A, is served by **Air B.C.,** tel. (250) 489-1114, and **Canadian Regional,** tel. (250) 426-7719. Both fly daily between Cranbrook and Vancouver. The **Greyhound** bus depot is at 1229 Cranbrook St., tel. (250) 426-3331 or (800) 661-8747. Bus service runs at least once daily: east to Fernie, Sparwood, and into Alberta; west to Creston and Castlegar; and north to Kimberley, Radium Hot Springs, and through Kootenay National Park to Banff and on to Calgary. **Dewdney Coach Lines,** tel. (250) 426-4662, runs daily (except Sunday) between Cranbrook and Golden.

Rental car agencies include: **Avis,** tel. (250) 426-3331 or (800) 879-2847; **Budget,** tel. (250) 489-4371 or (800) 268-8900; **National Tilden,** tel. (250) 489-0911 or (800) 387-4747; and **Rent-a-wreck,** tel. (250) 426-3004. For a cab call **Star Taxi** at (250) 426-5511.

Services and Information

Cranbrook Regional Hospital is off 2nd St. on 24th Ave. N, tel. (250) 426-5281. The **post office** is downtown on the corner of 10th Ave. and 1st St. South.

Cranbrook has two information centers, one at each end of the city. The main **Cranbrook Visitor Info Centre** is at 2279 Cranbrook St. N, tel. (250) 426-5914. It's open in summer, daily 9 a.m.-6 p.m.; the rest of the year, Mon.-Fri. 9 a.m.-5 p.m. At the southern entrance to the city is a seasonal center open in summer, daily 9 a.m.-5 p.m.

FERNIE AND VICINITY

Fernie (pop. 5,200) lies nestled in the Elk Valley 100 km east of Cranbrook on Hwy. 3. The town itself is a coal-mining and forestry center offering little of visitor interest. But in winter one of British Columbia's great little ski resorts comes alive nearby. Town center is a couple of blocks south of the highway, and holds the usual array of historic buildings and small-town shops. Look for an impressive red brick courthouse on 4th Ave. and a good bakery on 2nd Avenue. About 12 km south of town is 259-hectare **Mount Fernie Provincial Park,** where hiking trails lead along a picturesque creek and to a waterfall.

Fernie Snow Valley

This is another of British Columbia's legendary ski areas, boasting massive annual snowfalls, exciting skiing, and uncrowded slopes. The lifts lie under a massive ridge that catches an incredible 10 meters of snow each year, filling a wide open bowl with enough of the white fluffy stuff to please all powderhounds. A few runs are groomed, but the steeper stuff—down open bowls and through trees—is the main attraction. The resort's total vertical is 730 meters, with many of the challenging slopes at higher elevations and in Cedar Bowl. Rentals are available at the hill or from **Fernie Sports,** on the main drag through town, tel. (250) 423-3611. Lift tickets cost adults $34, seniors $26, children $12; under six ski free. The resort is open mid-December through mid-April, but the best conditions are in January and February. Accommodations are available on the hill (see below), and visitors with RVs are offered hookups and shower facilities for $12. The resort is 14 km south of Fernie. For information call (250) 423-4655; for snow reports call (250) 423-3555.

Practicalities

Fernie's least expensive accommodations are at **Sundown Budget Motel,** 892 6th Ave., tel. (250) 423-6811. Rooms are basic, but for $25 s, $30 d what do you expect? The motel is also an associate of Hostelling International (listed as Fernie Hostel) and offers dorm beds for $12-15 per person. Facilities for hostellers include a communal kitchen and laundry. During winter, inquire about ski packages. At **Park Place Lodge,** 742 Hwy. 3, tel. (250) 423-6871, amenities include air-conditioned rooms, a restaurant and pub, and a large courtyard surrounding a heated pool. Summer rates are $55 s, $69 d. Fernie's newest accommodation is **Super 8 Motel,** one km west of downtown at 2021 Hwy. 3, tel. (250) 423-6788 or (800) 800-8000; $60 s, $66 d.

Up at the ski resort, **Griz Inn,** tel. (250) 423-9221, offers 45 kitchen-equipped suites, an indoor pool, hot tub, and restaurant. Ski packages start at $85 per person per day while off-season rates (outside the ski season) drop to $70 s or d. All winter accommodations can be booked through **Fernie Central Reservations,** tel. (250) 423-9284. The best bet for campers is 12 km south at **Mount Fernie Provincial Park.** Facilities are limited, but the treed setting more than makes up for it; $9.50 per night.

Overlooking the Elk River at the west end of town, **Rip and Richard's Restaurant,** tel. (250) 423-3002, serves standard fare, including hearty cooked breakfasts from $5, burgers from $6, and dinners from $9. From the deck, you'll enjoy panoramic views all the way across to the ski hill.

Fernie Visitor Info Centre is through town to the north, tel. (250) 423-6868. It's open Mon.-Fri. 8:30 a.m.-4:30 p.m.

Akamina-Kishinena Recreation Area

Bordering Glacier National Park (U.S.) and Waterton Lakes National Park (Alberta), this remote tract of 10,922 hectares protects the extreme southeastern corner of British Columbia. The only access to the park is on foot from one of two trailheads. The most popular and easiest access is via Akamina Parkway in Waterton Lakes National Park. From near the end of the road (the trailhead is signposted) it's 1.5 km to the recreation-area border, from where trails lead past stunning alpine lakes to the park's more remote corners. You can also access the area at the end of an unsealed road that leaves Hwy. 3 16 km south of Fernie. The road leads 110 km into the Flathead River Valley, where trails climb along Akamina Creek into the recreation area.

Sparwood

Thirty kilometers northeast of Fernie, Sparwood (pop. 4,300) began as three separate coal-mining towns: Michel, Middletown, and Natal. In the 1960s, a resurgence of civic pride saw the old towns demolished and replaced by the new center of Sparwood.

The coal seams and part of the mining operations can be seen on the ridge high above Sparwood, but a more eye-catching element of the local industry is the world's largest truck,

Sparwood is home to the world's largest truck.

ANDREW HEMPSTEAD

which sits beside Hwy. 3 in the center of town. Beside the truck is **Sparwood Visitor Info Centre,** tel. (250) 425-2423, where you can arrange a tour of the mines. **Mountain Shadows Campground,** set among trees immediately south of town, tel. (250) 425-7815, adjoins the local golf course and holds the trailhead for a four-km hiking trail. Unserviced sites are $10, hookups $15, which includes the use of hot showers.

Elkford

Surrounded by towering peaks, this small coalmining community of 2,800 lies 35 km north of Sparwood on Hwy. 43, which continues north to remote Elk Lakes Provincial Park. Abundant recreation opportunities in the area include fishing in the Elk River, wildlife viewing, and hiking and mountain biking on hundreds of kilometers of logging and mining roads. In winter, these same roads are a mecca for snowmobilers. The community has few services, but you'll find a small **municipal campground** within walking distance of downtown. At the corner of Hwy. 43 and Michel Rd. is **Elkford Visitor Info Centre,** tel. (250) 865-4362, a good source of local road and trail information.

Elk Lakes Provincial Park

This park and the adjacent **Elk Lakes Recreation Area** encompass over 17,000 hectares of rugged wilderness 87 km north of Elkford. Glaciers shaped the terrain here; their remnants can still be seen along the park's west border.

The main access road ends in the provincial park, which borders Kananaskis Country in Alberta. From the main parking lot, a trail leads one km to Lower Elk Lake and another kilometer or so to Upper Elk Lake. At the lower lake, a narrow trail climbs 135 meters to a lookout. The stunningly beautiful upper lake is surrounded by steep snowcapped peaks, and several avalanche paths end right at water's edge. The park's only facility is a primitive campground at the main trailhead. For further information contact the local BC Parks office at (250) 422-3212.

FORT STEELE AND VICINITY

Gold miners first poured into the Kootenay River Valley when gold was discovered in Wild Horse Creek in 1865. The miners crossed the Kootenay River by ferry at a site that became known as Galbraith's Ferry. The fare to cross the river was a steep $5 per person and $10 per loaded pack animal.

In 1887, a year before the first bridge was constructed, the North West Mounted Police established a post on the riverbank. Superintendent Sam Steele and his 75 Mounties settled land-ownership disputes between local natives and new ranchers, easing friction and maintaining order. When silver and lead discoveries were made in the East Kootenays in the 1890s, Fort Steele grew rapidly. The town became a social, administrative, and supply center for the region, and served as a busy river-traffic hub for sternwheelers carrying ore and supplies to American refineries. However, the glory and bustle were short-lived. When the railway bypassed the town in 1898, putting Cranbrook on the map instead, Fort Steele's population plummeted—to a miserable 500 people by 1905.

Fort Steele Heritage Town

Today Fort Steele lives again. At Fort Steele Heritage Town you'll see over 60 restored, reconstructed, fully furnished buildings, including log barracks, hotels, a courthouse, jail, museum, dentist's office, ferry office, printing office, and a general store crammed to the rafters with intriguing historical artifacts. In summer, the park staff brings Fort Steele back to life with appropriately costumed working blacksmiths, carpenters, quilters, weavers, bakers, ice-cream makers, and many others. Hop on a stagecoach or a steam train, heckle a street politician, witness a crime and testify at a trial, watch a silent movie, and view operatic performances presented in the Opera House.

The grounds are open year-round. From late June to early September, the action takes place daily 9:30 a.m.-5:30 p.m. Admission is adults $5.50, seniors and youths $3.25, children $1.50, families $10.75. Once inside, some shows cost extra. One of the highlights is Fort Steele Follies, a professional 1880s'-style live-theater company performing at the Wild Horse Theatre, tel. (250) 426-5682. Showtimes are summer only, Tues.-Sun. at 2 p.m. and 8 p.m. Afternoon shows cost adults $7, seniors $5.50, while the evening shows are slightly more expensive.

For more information call (250) 489-3351 or for a recorded message of current hours and activities call (250) 426-7352.

A few commercial facilities surround the main entrance to Fort Steele. The largest is **Fort Steele Resort and RV Park,** tel. (250) 489-4268, which offers a heated pool, showers, laundry, and a barbecue and cooking facility. Unserviced sites are $16, serviced sites $20-22.

Wild Horse Creek

To get to the original Wild Horse Creek diggings, continue north from Fort Steele and take the logging road to Bull River and Kootenay Trout Hatchery. Fisherville—the first township in the East Kootenays and once home to over 5,000 miners—was established at the diggings in 1864, but was relocated upstream when it was discovered that the richest seam of gold was right below the main street.

About five km from the highway is Wild Horse Graveyard. From this point you can hike a section of Wild Horse Creek to see a number of historic sites, including the Chinese burial ground, the site of the Wild Horse post office, the remains of Fisherville, and the diggings. It takes about two hours to do the trail, allowing for stops at all the plaques along the way. Hikers here can also saunter down the last 2.5 km of the Dewdney Trail, imagining all the men and packhorses, loaded to the hilt, that once struggled from the Fraser Valley to the East Kootenays in search of fortune.

KIMBERLEY

Kimberley, 31 km north of Cranbrook on Hwy. 95A, stands 1,117 meters above sea level in the Purcell Mountains, surrounded by steep, permanently snow-covered peaks—you can hike up to the snow at any time of year. Although named for a famous South African diamond mine, Kimberley boomed as a result of the silver and lead deposits unearthed on nearby North Star Mountain. The deposits were discovered in 1892, and by 1899 over 200 claims had been staked. As was so often the case, only operations run by larger companies proved profitable. One of these, Cominco's **Sullivan Mine,** is still in operation today and is one of the world's largest lead and zinc mines.

The town is also known as the "Bavarian City of the Canadian Rockies." Most of the local shops and businesses, and many of Kimberley's homes, have been "Bavarianized"—decorated Bavarian-style with dark wood finish and flowery trim, steep triangular roofs, fancy balconies, brightly painted window shutters, and flower-filled window boxes. The Bavarianization occurred in the 1970s when a group of local businesspeople devised the idea to attract tourists. They did such a good job of luring visitors that many Europeans found Kimberley appealing and joined the town's resident population of 7,000—the European-style delis and restaurants you see downtown are mostly authentic. Strolling the pedestrian-only Bavarian Platzl, you'll feel as though you've just driven into a village high in the Swiss Alps. Even the local car dealership looks like a chalet where you'd expect to find bell-wearing cows and brightly dressed milkmaids rather than cars.

Bavarian Platzl

Follow signs to Kimberley city center and the Platzl on Spokane Street. This is the focus of downtown—a cheerful, red brick, pedestrian plaza complete with babbling brook, ornamental bridges, and the "World's Largest Cuckoo Clock" ("Happy Hans" pops out and yodels on the hour). The plaza is lined with shops and many German restaurants and delis selling European specialties. At the far end of the Platzl, **Kimberley Heritage Museum,** tel. (250) 427-7510, houses mining-history exhibits, a stuffed grizzly bear, a hodgepodge of artifacts, and displays relating to all the locally popular outdoor sports. One of the latter exhibits honors Kimberley hero Gerry Sorensen, the world's fastest downhill skier in 1982. The museum is open in summer, Mon.-Sat. 9 a.m.-4:30 p.m.; the rest of the year, Mon.-Sat. 1-4 p.m.

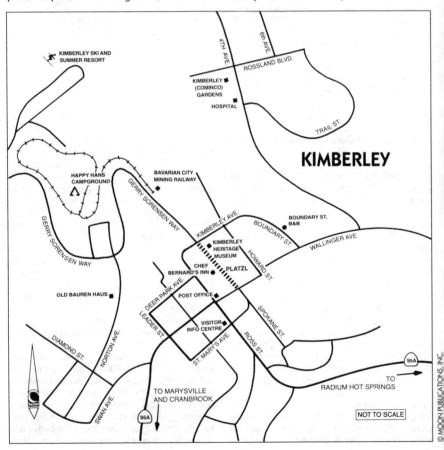

Other Sights

Kimberley Gardens, also known as Cominco Gardens, brightens up 4th Ave. next to the hospital. Originally planted in 1927 to test the value of a fertilizer developed by Cominco, the one-hectare gardens now hold close to 50,000 flowers. Admission is $2.50. After a stroll through the flower garden, refresh yourself next door at **Greenhouse Tea Garden** (see "Food," below).

The **Bavarian City Mining Railway,** tel. (250) 427-2929, was constructed from materials salvaged from mining towns around the province. The seven-km track circles Happy Hans Campground, descends a steep-sided valley, and crosses a 70-meter-long trestle into downtown Kimberley. Along the way, the train makes stops at particularly impressive mountain views, the original townsite, the Sullivan mine entrance, and other points of interest. It operates through summer; $3.50 per person.

On the southern outskirts of Kimberley is the community of **Marysville,** where you can stop and stretch your legs at **Marysville Falls.** From the parking lot at the bridge, walk downstream 800 meters through the woods—passing wild roses and other assorted wildflowers—to a series of small waterfalls and one large fall.

Kimberley Ski and Summer Resort

From early December to early April, four lifts here provide great family skiing on a wide variety of slopes. The resort, four km west of downtown Kimberley, offers 50 designated runs covering 480 hectares, with a maximum vertical rise of 700 meters. The longest run covers more than six kilometers. Most beginners and intermediates will be content on the well-groomed main slopes, while more experienced skiers will want to head to the expert terrain served by the Easter Chair. Night skiing is offered Tues.-Sat. and ski rentals and lessons are available. Additional facilities at the resort include two snowboard parks, a cross-country ski area, an ice-skating rink, accommodations, and restaurants. Lift tickets are adults $35, seniors $25, children $16 (children eight and younger ski free). In summer, the resort stays open for chairlift rides, hiking, summer luge, go carting, and mini-golf.

For general information call (250) 427-4881; for snow reports call (250) 427-7332; for ski packages call (800) 667-0871.

Events

Several annual events in Kimberley draw crowds. Look for **Winterfest** in mid-February; an **International Old Time Accordion Championship** the second week of July, followed a week later by **Julyfest** (soccer, arm wrestling, horseshoe throwing, and a parade); and **B.C. Days in the Platzl** in August. On the long Labour Day weekend, Kimberley kicks up its heels at the **Alpine Folk Dance Festival.** Get a complete list of local events from the information center.

Accommodations and Camping

On the Platzl, right downtown, **Chef Bernard's Inn,** tel. (250) 427-4820 or (800) 905-8338, offers basic but comfortable rooms for $54 s or d. Many of Kimberley's best restaurants are right downstairs. **Travellaire Motel,** toward Marysville at 2660 Warren Ave., tel. (250) 427-2252, has rooms for $40 s, $45 d. One block from downtown, **Boundary St. B&B,** 89 Boundary St., tel. (250) 427-3510, offers a small room for $45 s, $55 d, and two larger rooms—one with a view—for $55 s, $60 d. All rates include a cooked breakfast.

Amenities at the vast **Happy Hans Campground,** two km north of city center on the way to the ski hill, tel. (250) 427-2929, include a swimming pool, miniature golf, attractive tree-lined campsites, and spotlessly clean bathrooms. Rates are $15-18 per vehicle. The Bavarian City Mining Railway terminal is on the grounds.

Food

European gourmet specialties, predominantly German, are available all around town. The **Gasthaus,** in the Platzl, tel. (250) 427-4851, features German lunches such as goulash, from $5, and German dinner specialties such as bratwurst, rheinischer sauerbraten, wiener-schnitzel, and kassler rippchen for $10-16. It's open daily except Tuesday, 11:30 a.m.-10 p.m. For breakfast, head to **Chef Bernard's,** also in the Platzl, tel. (250) 427-7461. It's inexpensive and servings are hearty. **Kimberley City Bakery,** a Swiss bakery, tea room, and sidewalk cafe in the Platzl, tel. (250) 427-2131, is open daily from 8:30 a.m. Away from the Platzl, **Old Bauren Haus,** 280 Norton Ave., tel. (250) 427-5133, features Bavarian specialties and plenty of atmosphere. It's in a post-and-beam building originally constructed about 350 years ago in southern Bavaria. The building was taken apart, shipped to Canada, and painstakingly rebuilt.

If you've had enough of the old Bavarian theme, head to the **Crossing Pub** in the Hotel Kootenay, tel. (250) 427-7744, where you'll find Canadian-style pub meals and live entertainment most nights.

The **Greenhouse Tea Garden,** next to Kimberley Gardens, tel. (250) 427-4885, serves a classic afternoon tea, accompanied by desserts and delectables such as fresh-baked scones with jam. Prices are reasonable and the atmosphere, inside a real greenhouse, is delightful; the stunning pink-and-green interior is complemented by hanging plants, flowery tablecloths, and views of the distant mountains and gardens. Hours are 10:30 a.m.-7 p.m. daily.

Information
For more information on Kimberley and the surrounding area, drop by **Kimberley Visitor Info Centre,** 350 Ross St., tel. (250) 427-3666. It's open in summer, daily 9 a.m.-7 p.m.; the rest of year, Mon.-Fri. 9 a.m.-5 p.m.

NORTH TOWARD RADIUM HOT SPRINGS

This stretch of highway passes through a deep valley chock-full of commercial facilities such as world-class golf courses, resorts, and hot springs. The low elevation makes for relatively mild winters and an early start to the summer season. And with the Purcell Mountains on one side and the Rockies on the other, the valley certainly doesn't lack for scenery.

Wasa Provincial Park
Unlike the several backcountry parks in the area, 144-hectare Wasa Provincial Park, 30 km north of Kimberley, is easily accessible off the main highway. Facilities include picnic tables, a nature trail, and swimming and water-sports areas. Fishing is possible, but only so-so. The park is open year-round, but the $12 camp fee is collected only May-September.

Whiteswan Lake Provincial Park
Continuing north, the Rockies close in and the scenery becomes unbelievably beautiful. Twenty-eight km north of Skookumchuck, an unsealed old logging road takes off east into the mountains, leading first to 1,994-hectare Whiteswan Lake Provincial Park, then to Top of the World Provincial Park (see below). The road climbs steadily from Hwy. 93/95, entering Lussier Gorge after 18 km. Within the gorge, a steep trail leads down to undeveloped **Lussier Hot Springs.** Whiteswan Lake and smaller Alces Lake attract abundant birdlife; loons, grebes, and herons are all common. Fishing in both lakes is excellent for rainbow trout. The main road skirts the lakes and passes four campgrounds; $9.50 per site, no showers.

Top of the World Provincial Park
If you thought the scenery around Whiteswan Lake was wild and remote, wait till you see this 8,790-hectare wilderness a rough 52 km from Hwy. 95 (turn off the Whiteswan Lake access road at Alces Lake). You can't drive into the park, but it's a fairly easy six-km hike from the end of the road to picturesque **Fish Lake,** the park's largest body of water. The trail climbs alongside the pretty Lussier River to the lake, which is encircled with Engelmann spruce and surrounded by peaks up to 2,500 meters high. The hike to the lake gains just over 200 vertical meters and makes a good day-trip. Those keen on exploring further afield or trying their luck for cutthroat trout and Dolly Varden in the lake can stay overnight in a trailside cabin or camp at one of four designated areas.

Canal Flats
The small lumber-mill town of Canal Flats lies between the Kootenay River and Columbia Lake. David Thompson, the first European explorer in this neck of the woods, crossed from the lake to the river in 1808, naming the flat McGillivray's Portage. In 1889 the two waterways were connected by a canal with a single lock, but the passage was so narrow and dangerous that only two steamboats ever got through.

North of Canal Flats, the highway passes 44-hectare **Thunder Hill Provincial Park,** which overlooks turquoise-and-blue Columbia Lake, then approaches and passes the weirdly shaped **Dutch Creek Hoodoos,** a set of photogenic rock formations carved over time by ice, water, and wind.

Fairmont Hot Springs

Kootenay natives used these springs as a healing source for eons prior to the arrival of Europeans, but they wouldn't recognize the place today. Four-star resorts, golf courses, a ski resort, and an airstrip long enough to land a Boeing 737 on now surround the site. Despite all the commercialism, the hot springs are still the main attraction. Their appeal is simple; unlike most other springs, the hot water bubbling up from underground here contains calcium, but no sulfur with its attendant smell.

The pools are a magical experience, especially in the evening. Lazily swim or float around in the large warm pool, dive into the cool pool, or sit 'n' sizzle in the hot pool and watch the setting sun color the steep faces of the Rocky Mountains immediately behind the resort. Admission is adults $5.50, children $4, with discounts after 9 p.m. The pools are open daily 8 a.m.-10 p.m.

Behind the hot springs is **Fairmont Hot Springs Ski Area,** where one chairlift and a platter serve a vertical rise of 304 meters. You wouldn't go out of your way to ski here, but the mountain vistas and the unique opportunity to soak in hot springs after a day on the slopes make a winter trip to Fairmont worthwhile. The resort offers rentals and a ski school, and is also a trailhead for many cross-country ski trails.

A large resort with lodge accommodations and a campground makes up part of the hot springs complex. Rooms at the lodge are $109-154 s, $117-161 d. Some have lofts and kitchens (a kitchen costs $25 extra). Discounted multinight packages and ski and golf packages are often available, especially in the off-season. Campers have a choice of nearly 300 sites spread around tree-shaded grounds, all just a one-minute stroll from the hot pools. Unserviced sites are $15, hookups range $20-35. The campground is open year-round and offers discounts outside of the busiest summer months. For all bookings call (250) 345-6311 or (800) 663-4979.

Windermere Valley

The next area to lure travelers off Hwy. 93/95 is **Windermere Lake,** a popular spot for swimming and water sports. On the northwest shore of the lake, **Invermere** (pop. 2,500) serves as the valley's business and commercial center. Site of a 1807 post set up by David Thompson to trade with Kootenay natives, today the town holds motels, eateries, grocery stores, gas stations, the Greyhound bus depot, and a laundry. The motels downtown are a bit overpriced; the best option is **Delphine Lodge,** tel. (250) 342-6851, a couple of kilometers north in the small village of Wilmer. Restored to its turn-of-the-century glory, the lodge offers six rooms decorated in early-Canadian style and features extensive gardens out back. Rates of $50 s, $60-80 d include a light breakfast.

Back in Invermere, on the corner of 5th St. and 7th Ave., is **Invermere Visitor Info Centre,** tel. (250) 342-6316; open July-Aug., daily 9 a.m.-5 p.m.

Based at Panorama Resort, R.K. Heli-ski offers heli-skiing daytrips into the Purcell Mountains.

R.K. HELI-SKI

Panorama Resort

Panorama boasts the third-highest vertical rise of all North American ski areas, behind only Whistler/Blackcomb, also in British Columbia, and Big Sky, Montana. Yet despite the impressive relief, Panorama offers slopes suitable for all levels of expertise. For current lift prices call (250) 345-6311; for snow reports call (250) 345-6413.

During the warmer months, **Purcell River Odysseys** leads two- to three-hour whitewater-rafting trips for $34-44 and rents kayaks for $25 per day. To book a river trip or on-mountain accommodations, call the Panorama Resort Activities Centre, tel. (250) 342-6941.

Purcell Wilderness Conservancy

If you take the road west from Invermere beyond Panorama Resort, you'll end up nine km from the boundary of Purcell Wilderness Conservancy, a 198,180-hectare wilderness straddling the heart of the rugged Purcell Mountains. No roads and few trails penetrate the preserve. The end of the road is the trailhead for a 61-km hike—up Toby Creek, over 2,256-meter Earl Grey Pass, and along the Hamill Creek watershed. The trail ends on Kootenay Lake, six km east of Hwy. 31, 40 km north of Kaslo.

ROCKY MOUNTAINS
INTRODUCTION

The high peaks of the Continental Divide form British Columbia's eastern boundary, separating the province from neighboring Alberta. Along this lofty border lie four contiguous national parks—**Kootenay, Yoho, Banff,** and **Jasper.** Declared a World Heritage Site by UNESCO, these parks encompass close to 20,000 square kilometers of Mother Nature's finest offerings.

Many factors combine to make the mountains here so beautiful. The peaks themselves exhibit drastically altered sedimentary layers visible from miles away, especially when accentuated by a particular angle of sunlight or a dusting of snow. Between the peaks lie numerous cirques—basins gouged into the mountains by glaciers. These cirques fill with glacial meltwater each spring, creating lakes that shimmer a trademark translucent green. And thanks to a climate that keeps the treeline low and the vegetation relatively sparse, fantastic views of the wide sweeping valleys are assured.

The best-known of the four parks are Banff and Jasper, both of which lie across the Continental Divide in Alberta and are therefore covered only fleetingly in this handbook; for more detailed coverage, see Moon Publications' *Al-*

berta and the Northwest Territories Handbook. On the British Columbia side of the divide, Kootenay and Yoho National Parks may lack the famous glaciated lakes and bustling resort towns of their neighbors, but they boast the same magnificent mountain vistas, glacially fed streams and rivers, unlimited hiking opportunities, and abundant wildlife.

All four parks are open year-round. When the snow falls, Banff and Jasper stay busy with downhill skiers, while the parks on the British Columbia side become a much quieter winter wonderland for cross-country skiers and snowshoers.

A furor arose in the summer of 1996 when park entrance fees were raised considerably, but the bottom line is that you can still visit one of the most beautiful landscapes on the face of the earth for less than the price of a movie ticket. A one-day permit good for all four parks is $5 per person to a maximum of $10 per vehicle. An annual Great Western Pass good for entry to all 11 of western Canada's national parks is $35 per person to a maximum of $70 per vehicle. Both are available from all park gates and information centers.

THE LAND

The Rocky Mountains extend the length of the North American continent; north of the 49th parallel they are most commonly known as the **Canadian Rockies**. Although the mountains are composed of bedrock laid down up to one billion years ago, it wasn't until 100 million years ago that forces below the earth's surface transformed western Canada from a lowland plain into the varied, mountainous topography seen today.

The western ridges of the mountains drop dramatically into the Rocky Mountain Trench. The **front ranges** lie to the east, in Alberta, and slope to the foothills. The **main ranges** are older, higher, and not as severely disturbed as the front ranges; most glaciers are found among these mighty peaks. The spine of the main range is the **Continental Divide**. To the east of the divide all waters flow to the Atlantic Ocean; those to the west flow into the Pacific.

Since rising above the surrounding plains these mountains have been eroding. At least four times in the last million years sheets of ice have covered much of the land, filling valleys and rounding off lower peaks. As the ice retreated it carved massive U-shaped valleys, the distinctive **Bow** and **Kootenay Valleys** being prime examples. In addition, glacial meltwater carved deep channels into the valleys and many rivers changed course.

FLORA

Over 700 species of plants have been recorded in the four parks. Each species falls into one of three distinct vegetation zones: the **montane zone** covers the valley floors; the higher **subalpine zone** covers most of the forested area; and the highest **alpine zone** is found among the peaks, where climate is severe and vegetation limited.

Montane-zone vegetation is usually found at elevations below 1,350 meters, but can grow at higher elevations on sun-drenched, south-facing slopes. As fires frequently affect this zone, **lodgepole pine** is the dominant species; its tightly sealed cones open only with the heat of a forest fire, thereby regenerating the species quickly after a blaze. **Douglas fir** is the zone's climax species and is found in open stands throughout the four parks. **Aspen** is common in older burn areas, while **limber pine** thrives on rocky outcrops.

Dense forests of **white spruce** and **Engelmann spruce** typify the subalpine zone. White spruce dominates to 2,100 meters, while Engelmann spruce takes over at elevations between 2,100 and 2,400 meters. Lodgepole pine occurs in dense stands in areas affected by fire. In 1968 a fire burned 2,500 hectares near Vermilion Pass in Kootenay National Park; today it's a good area to view early stages of regeneration. **Subalpine fir** grows above 2,200 meters and is often stunted by the high winds at such lofty elevations.

The transition between the subalpine and alpine zones is gradual and usually occurs around 2,300 meters. The alpine zone's severe climate sees temperatures averaging below zero, strong winds, and a very short summer. Alpine plants adapt by growing low to the ground with long roots. Mosses, mountain avens, saxifrage, and an alpine dandelion all thrive in this environment. The best places to view brightly colored carpets of alpine wildflowers are Kindersley Summit in Kootenay National Park and Sunshine Meadows in Banff.

FAUNA

The Canadian Rockies provide a spectacular backdrop for viewing a great variety of mammals, many of which can be spotted from the roadside. Spring and fall are the best times of year for wildlife viewing. The big-game animals have moved below the snow cover of the higher elevations and the crowds have thinned out. Winter also has its advantages. Although bears are hibernating, herds of elk winter at lower elevations, coyotes are often seen roaming around highways, bighorn sheep have descended from the heights, and wolf packs can occasionally be seen along Kootenay River Valley. In summer, with the onslaught of millions of visitors, the larger mammals tend to move away from

Besides people, elk are the most common large mammals in the Canadian Rockies.

the more heavily traveled tourist areas. It then becomes a case of knowing when and where to look for them.

Ungulates

Five species of deer inhabit the Canadian Rockies. **Elk** can be seen along the highways through Kootenay and Yoho National Parks, but they're more common in Banff and Jasper. **White-tailed deer** can be seen throughout the mountains. **Mule deer** are less common but are easily recognized by their large floppy ears. A small herd of **woodland caribou** roams Jasper National Park; they are most commonly seen during late spring, feeding in river deltas. **Moose,** although not common, can occasionally be seen feeding on aquatic plants along the major drainage systems.

In summer, **mountain goats** feed in alpine meadows. A good place to spot them is Goat Lookout on the Icefields Parkway. Unlike most large mountain-dwelling mammals, these sure-footed creatures don't migrate to lower elevations in winter but stay sheltered on rocky crags where wind and sun keep the vegetation snow free. Often confused with the goat is the darker **bighorn sheep.** The thick horns on the males of this species often curl 360 degrees.

Predators

Coyotes are widespread along all major valley corridors, where they find an abundance of small game. The **lynx** population fluctuates greatly; look for them in the backcountry during winter.

Cougars, the largest local members of the cat family, are very shy. **Wolves** had been driven close to extinction by the early 1950s, but today at least 10 packs have been reported through the four parks.

Bears

Black bears are common in all four parks. They are most often seen in spring, when they first come out of hibernation. At that point, snow blankets much of the mountains and the bears are forced to lower elevations to feed, often along the edge of the highway. During late spring **grizzlies** are occasionally seen crossing highways at higher elevations. For the most part they remain in remote mountain valleys, and if they do see, smell, or hear you they'll generally move away.

The chance of encountering a bear face-to-face in the backcountry is remote. To lessen chances of an encounter even further, follow these simple precautions: never hike alone or at dusk; make lots of noise when passing through heavy vegetation; keep a clean camp; and read the pamphlet *You are in Bear Country,* available at all park information centers. At each center, daily trail reports list recent bear sightings. Report any bears you see to the nearest park information center.

Birds

Over 260 species of birds have been recorded in the area, but most are shy and live in heavily wooded areas. One species that definitely isn't shy is the **gray jay.** This fearless marauder haunts campgrounds and picnic areas, scavenging food right off your picnic table. Similar in color, but larger, is the **Clark's nutcracker,** which lives in higher, subalpine forests. Other common residents include the jet-black **raven** and the black-and-white **magpie.**

Several species of grouse inhabit the area. Most common is the **downy ruffled grouse,** seen in montane forest. The **blue grouse** and **spruce grouse** are seen at higher elevations, as is the **white-tailed ptarmigan,** which lives above the treeline (watch for them along higher elevations of the Stanley Glacier Trail in Kootenay National Park. **Woodpeckers** can often be heard drilling for dinner in the subalpine forests.

Although raptors are not common in the Canadian Rockies, **bald eagles** and **golden eagles** are present part of the year, and Alberta's provincial bird, the **great horned owl,** lives in the mountains year-round.

KOOTENAY NATIONAL PARK AND VICINITY

Shaped like a lightning bolt, this narrow 140,600-hectare park follows Hwy. 93 between Radium Hot Springs and Banff. The 94-km-long highway provides spectacular mountain vistas, and along the route you'll find many short and easy interpretive hikes, scenic viewpoints, picnic areas, and roadside interpretive exhibits. The park isn't particularly noted for its day-hiking opportunities, but backpacker destinations such as the Rockwall and Kaufmann Lake rival almost any other area in the Canadian Rockies.

The park is open year-round, although you should check road conditions in winter, when avalanche-control work and snowstorms can close Hwy. 93 for short periods of time. Permits are required for entry into the park; they're available from both of the park information centers and from the Radium Hot Springs information center. A one-day permit is $5 per person to a maximum of $10 per vehicle, and an annual Great Western Pass, good for entry to all 11 of western Canada's national parks, is $35 per person to a maximum of $70 per vehicle.

Kootenay has the fewest services of the four contiguous mountain national parks. Day-use areas, a gas station and lodge, and three campgrounds are the only roadside services inside the park. The small service town of Radium Hot Springs, at the junction of Hwys. 93 and 95 near the park's west gate, has a population under 600 but offers a range of accommodations, cafes and restaurants, gas stations, and grocery stores.

HISTORY

Although their traditional home was along the river valley to the south, the indigenous Kootenay people regularly came to this area to enjoy the hot springs—a meeting place for mountain and Plains bands—and to collect ocher from the Paint Pots area for ceremonial painting purposes.

European explorers and fur traders, among them legendary geographer David Thompson, first entered the valley in the early 1800s. In search of a viable path through the mountains, they found a well-traveled corridor that remained a major transportation route into the 20th century.

In 1905 Randolph Bruce, an Invermere businessman, persuaded the Canadian government and Canadian Pacific Railway to build a road linking the Kootenay River Valley to the prairie transportation hub of Calgary so that western produce could get out to eastern markets. Construction of the difficult Banff-Windermere Rd. began in 1911. But with three mountain ranges to negotiate and deep, fast-flowing rivers to cross, the money ran out after the completion of only 22 kilometers. In order to get the highway project going again, the provincial government agreed to hand over an eight-km-wide section of land along both sides of the proposed highway to the federal government. Originally called the Highway Park, the land became known as Kootenay National Park in 1920. The highway was finally completed

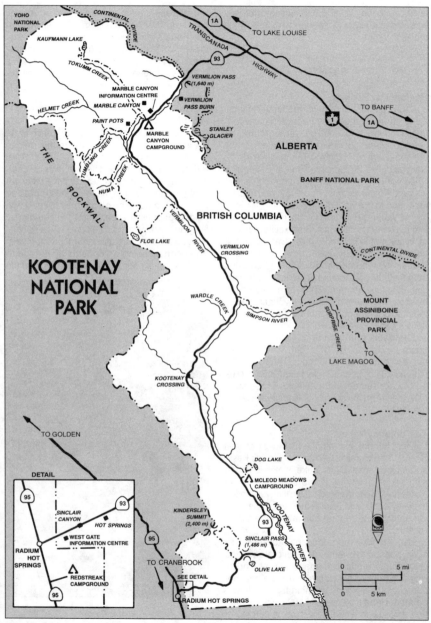

in 1922 and the official ribbon-cutting ceremony was held at Kootenay Crossing in 1923; a plaque marks the spot.

SIGHTS

Radium Hot Springs

Just inside the boundary of Kootenay National Park, the road squeezes through narrow Sinclair Canyon and emerges at Radium Hot Springs, where odorless mineral water gushes out of the foot of Redstreak Mountain at 45° C. Natives called the springs Kootemik, meaning "Place of Hot Water." Early European visitors warped "Kootemik" into "Kootenay" and applied the name to the local residents.

The water is diverted from its natural course into the commercial pools. Steep cliffs tower directly above the hot pool, whose waters are colored a milky blue by dissolved salts, including calcium bicarbonate and sulfates of calcium, magnesium, and sodium. The hot pool is particularly stimulating in winter when it's edged by snow and covered in steam—your head is almost cold in the chill air, but your submerged body melts into oblivion.

The pools are open year-round. Summer hours are daily 9 a.m.-10:30 p.m.; shorter hours the rest of the year. Admission is adults $3 (day pass $5.50), children $2 (day pass $3.50). Towel and locker rentals are available. Three short trails lead from the springs to Redstreak Campground.

To Kootenay Valley

Leaving the hot springs, the highway parallels Sinclair Creek, crests 1,486-meter Sinclair Pass, and passes small **Olive Lake,** which is ringed with bright yellow wildflowers in summer. At **Kootenay River Viewpoint** you'll have a splendid view of the wild Kootenay River Valley and the snowcapped mountains along the Continental Divide.

The highway then descends to the valley floor, passes two riverside picnic areas, and crosses the pretty Kootenay River at **Kootenay Crossing.** This was where the official ribbon-cutting ceremony opening the Banff-Windermere Road took place in 1923. Today you'll find a roadside historical exhibit, a number of

hiking trails, and a warden's station. As you cross the river and pass small, green **Kootenay Pond,** your eyes will revel in views of milky-green rivers, lush grassy meadows, tree-covered hills, and craggy, snowcapped peaks; keep your eyes peeled for mountain goats. A bit further on, you'll come to a particularly nice picnic spot at **Wardle Creek.**

Paint Pots

A scenic one-km trail (20 minutes each way) leads over the Vermilion River to this unique natural wonder: three circular ponds stained red, orange, and mustard yellow by oxide-bearing springs. The natives, who believed that animal spirits resided in these springs, collected ocher from around the pools. They mixed it with animal fat or fish oil then used it in ceremonial body and rock painting. The ocher had a spiritual association and was used in important rituals. Europeans, seeing an opportunity to "add to the growing economy of the nation," mined the

Marble Canyon

ocher in the early 1900s and shipped it to paint manufacturers in Calgary.

Several much longer hiking trails lead off the Paint Pots trail, including one of many routes to the **Rockwall** (see "Hiking," below).

Marble Canyon

Be sure to stop and take the enjoyable self-guided trail, one km each way, that leads along this ice-carved, limestone-and-dolomite, marble-streaked canyon. The walk takes only about 30 minutes or so, yet as one of several interpretive plaques says, it takes you back over 500 million years.

From the parking lot, the trail follows a fault in the limestone and marble bedrock through Marble Canyon, which has been eroded to depths of 37 meters by fast-flowing **Tokumm Creek.** As the canyon narrows, water roars down through it in a series of falls. The trail ends at a splendid viewpoint where a natural rock arch spans a gorge. Marble Canyon is also the trailhead for the **Kaufmann Lake Trail** (see "Hiking," below).

East to the Continental Divide

Continuing eastward from Marble Canyon, Hwy. 93 climbs steadily to the **Vermilion Pass Burn.** Lightning started the fire that roared through this area in 1968, destroying thousands of hectares of trees. Lodgepole pines, which require the heat of a fire to release their seeds, and fireweed were the first plant species to sprout up through the charred ground. From the highway everything seems pretty dead, but along the 0.8-km **Fireweed Trail** you'll see the growth of a new forest on the floor of the old.

The burn area is immediately west of the Continental Divide, which the highway crosses at an elevation of 1,640 meters. The divide marks the border between Kootenay National Park to the west and Banff National Park in the province of Alberta to the east.

HIKING

Some 200 km of trails lace Kootenay National Park. Hiking opportunities range from short interpretive walks (see "Sights," above) to challenging treks through remote backcountry. All trails start from Hwy. 93 on the valley floor, so

you'll be facing a strenuous climb to reach the park's high alpine areas, especially those in the south. For this reason, many hikes require an overnight stay in the backcountry.

Juniper Trail

- Length: 3.2 km (one hour) roundtrip
- Elevation gain: 90 meters
- Rating: easy

Named for the abundance of juniper along one section, this trail traverses a variety of terrain in a relatively short distance. You'll pass Sinclair Creek, an avalanche slope, and a lookout offering views of the Windermere Valley and the Purcell Mountains. The trail begins on the north side of the road just beyond the park information center and rejoins the highway 1.5 km farther into the park. There you can retrace your steps back to the start or return along the highway.

Kindersley Summit

- Length: 10 km (four hours) one-way
- Elevation gain: 1050 meters
- Rating: difficult

The elevation gain on this strenuous day-hike will be a deterrent for many, but views from the summit will make up for the pain endured along the way. The trailhead is 10 km up Hwy. 93 from the park's west gate. From this point the trail climbs through a valley for about three km, then switchbacks up across a number of avalanche paths and through more forest before emerging at an alpine meadow on Kindersley Pass. The final two-km slog gets you 200 meters higher, to an elevation of 2,400 meters at Kindersley Summit, a saddle between two slightly higher peaks. This is where the scenery makes the journey worthwhile. You'll enjoy views west to the Purcell Mountains, east to the Continental Divide, and, most spectacularly, north over the Kootenay River Valley. An alternate return route to the valley floor follows Sinclair Creek down from Kindersley Summit. This cuts a couple of kilometers off the return distance.

Dog Lake

- Length: 2.6 km (40 minutes) one-way
- Elevation gain: 80 meters
- Rating: easy

Dog Lake is no Mona Lisa, but it is a popular and easily reached destination, especially for those

ANDREW HEMPSTEAD

The trail to Dog Lake takes about 40 minutes each way.

staying in McLeod Meadows Campground (if you're not camping, park at the picnic area 500 meters to the south). The trail first crosses the wide Kootenay River by footbridge. Then it hops a low ridge over to the shallow lake, which is fringed by marshes at the north end.

Floe Lake
- Length: 10.4 km (3.5 hours) one-way
- Elevation gain: 730 meters
- Rating: moderate/difficult

Of all the lakes in Kootenay National Park, this would have to be the most beautiful. Unfortunately, reaching it requires a strenuous day-trip or an overnight expedition. From the parking lot 70 km up Hwy. 93 from Radium Hot Springs, the trail follows Floe Creek, ascending the watershed through a forest of lodgepole pine and making many switchbacks before leveling off 400 meters before the lake. Nestled in a glacial cirque, the gemlike lake's aquamarine waters

reflect the Rockwall, a sheer limestone wall rising 1,000 meters above the far shore. In fall, stands of stunted larch around the lakeshore turn brilliant colors, adding to the incredible beauty.

The Rockwall
- Length: 54 km (three days) roundtrip
- Elevation gain: 760 meters
- Rating: moderate/difficult

This is one of the classic hikes in all the Canadian Rockies. The Rockwall is a 30-km-long east-facing escarpment that rises over 1,000 meters from an alpine environment. Four different routes provide access to the spectacular feature; each begins along Hwy. 93 and traverses a steep valley to the Rockwall's base.

The most popular trail starts at the Paint Pots and follows Helmet Creek 12 km to spectacular 365-meter **Helmet Falls**. A further 2.4 km takes you to the beginning of the Rockwall trail and a campground, the first of five along the route. The trail then follows the Rockwall in a southeasterly direction for 30 km, passing magnificent glaciers, waterfalls, and lakes, before ending at **Floe Lake** (see above), 10.4 km from the highway.

The Tumbling Creek and Numa Creek drainages provide alternative access routes to the Rockwall and require similar elevation gains. The elevation gain noted above is for the initial climb from the highway; along the route ascents are made to four additional passes, with elevation gains ranging 280-830 meters.

Hikers will need to make arrangements for shuttle transportation between the beginning and end of this route—about 13 km apart—or allow extra time to hike back. As elsewhere in the park, all hikers spending the night in the backcountry must register and pick up a permit ($6 per person per night) at either of the park information centers.

Kaufmann Lake
- Length: 15 km (five hours) one-way
- Elevation gain: 570 meters
- Rating: moderate

The overnight backpack trip to this beautiful lake in the extreme north end of the park begins at Marble Canyon parking lot. The trail follows Tokumm Creek the entire distance, passing through a forest of lodgepole pine before entering an open meadow and crossing many small waterways. Most elevation gain is made in the final two km, as the trail switchbacks up to the glacial cirque holding Kaufmann Lake. The exquisite lake is surrounded by peaks jutting as high as 3,400 meters. Two campgrounds lie at the end of the trail.

Stanley Glacier
- Length: 4.6 km (two hours) one-way
- Elevation gain: 365 meters
- Rating: moderate

Although this glacier is no more spectacular than those alongside the Icefields Parkway just a few kilometers away, the sense of achievement of traveling on foot makes this trail well worth the effort. From the trailhead on Hwy. 93, three km west of the park's eastern boundary, the trail crosses the higher reaches of the Vermilion River. It passes through an area burned by devastating fires in 1968 and climbs steadily until reaching a narrow rock-filled basin and the main glacier viewpoint. It's possible to continue another kilometer up the valley to within 500 meters of the glacier's toe, but the going gets rough.

OTHER RECREATION

The town of Radium Hot Springs is a base of operations for recreation opportunities outside the park. In summer, fishing and boating on nearby Windermere Lake are locally popular activities. Whitewater-rafting trips are offered by **Kootenay River Runners,** tel. (250) 347-9210; from $58 for a half-day trip, $85 full day. Horse fanciers can rent a ride at **Longhorn Stables,** one km north of town, tel. (250) 347-9755.

ACCOMMODATIONS AND CAMPING

Kootenay Park Lodge
This small lodge at Vermilion Crossing, 65 km from Radium Hot Springs, tel. (403) 762-9196, is the only accommodation actually within the park. The lodge comprises 10 log cabins, a restaurant, and a gas station/grocery store. Rates are $75-97 s or d, depending on cabin size.

Motels in Radium Hot Springs
Kootenay Motel is along Hwy. 93, up the hill from the junction of Hwy. 95, tel. (250) 347-9490. The air-conditioned rooms are decorated simply; from $39 s, $44 d. Along the same stretch of road, and similarly priced, is **Valley View Motel,** tel. (250) 347-9565, with a pleasant outdoor barbecue area.

At the top end of the scale, **Radium Hot Springs Resort,** tel. (250) 347-9311 or (800) 667-6444, features as well as one of the province's top golf courses as well as a health club, indoor pool, restaurant, and lounge. Regular motel rooms range $120-145 while kitchen-equipped condos sleeping up to six people start at $185 per night. Golf and ski packages lower rates considerably, especially before and after summer's peak season.

Campgrounds
The park's largest camping area is **Redstreak Campground** at Radium Hot Springs (vehicle access from Hwy. 93/95 on the south side of Radium Hot Springs township), which holds 242 sites, showers, and kitchen shelters. Trails lead from the campground to the hot springs, town, and a couple of lookouts. Unserviced sites are $13, hookups $16-18. Fire permits cost $3 per site per night. This facility is open mid-May through September.

The park's two other campgrounds—**McLeod Meadows,** 27 km from the west gate, and **Marble Canyon**—are much smaller and offer fewer facilities (no hookups or showers). They're open June-Aug. and all sites are $13. Hikers planning overnight trips in the backcountry must register at either of the park information centers and pick up a permit ($6 per person per night).

Canyon Camp, on Hwy. 95, 300 yards north of the Hwy. 93/95 junction, tel. (250) 347-9564, is open year-round. Sites are spread along a pleasant creek and all facilities are provided; sites are $16-21 per night.

FOOD

The town of Radium Hot Springs holds several good choices for a food break. Give all the fast-food places out by the highway junction a miss and head to **Springs at Radium Restaurant,** at the golf course on Stanley St. (on the west side of the highway), tel. (250) 347-6441. The view from the deck, overlooking the Columbia River and Purcell Mountains, is nothing short of stunning. The food is good and remarkably inexpensive; in the morning, for example, an omelette with hash browns and toast is just $6. Lunch and dinner are also well-priced, with a massive Caesar salad for $6 and main meals $9-16.

As always, **Husky House Restaurant,** at the corner of Hwys. 93 and 95, tel. (250) 347-9811, serves a good solid menu of typical Canadian fare at reasonable prices. This one is open daily 6:30 a.m.-10:30 p.m. Just across the road is **Screamer's,** the place to hang out with an ice cream on a hot summer's afternoon.

INFORMATION

West Gate Information Centre, one km from Radium Hot Springs, tel. (250) 347-9615, is an essential first stop. Here you can collect a free map with hiking-trail descriptions; find out about trail closures and campsite availability; get the weather forecast; buy topographical maps ($10 each) and national park fishing licenses ($6 for seven days); and register for overnight backcountry trips. The center is open mid-May to mid-June, weekends 8 a.m.-8 p.m., and the rest of summer daily 8 a.m.-8 p.m.

Marble Canyon Information Centre, at the eastern end of the park, is open July-Aug., daily 8 a.m.-5 p.m. For further park information, write the Superintendent, Kootenay National Park, P.O. Box 220, Radium Hot Springs, BC V0A 1M0, or call (250) 347-9615.

On the west side of the Hwy. 93/95 junction is **Radium Hot Springs Visitor Info Centre,** tel. (250) 347-9331. It's open weekdays year-round and in the busier summer months Mon.-Thurs. 9 a.m.-5 p.m., Friday 9 a.m.-8 p.m., Sat.-Sun. 10 a.m.-6 p.m.

In the peak summer season free slide shows and talks are presented by park naturalists five nights a week at **Redstreak Campground** (see "Campgrounds" under "Accommodations and Camping," above). The programs usually start around dusk, and typically feature topics such as wolves, bears, the park's human history, or the

effect of fire. Dates and details are posted at campgrounds and information centers.

VICINITY OF KOOTENAY NATIONAL PARK

Mount Assiniboine Provincial Park
Named for one of the Canadian Rockies' most spectacular peaks, this 38,600-hectare park is a haven for experienced hikers, offering alpine meadows, lakes, glaciers, and many peaks over 3,000 meters to explore. The park's highest peak, 3,618-meter **Mount Assiniboine,** is known as the "Matterhorn of the Rockies" for its resemblance to that famous Swiss landmark. Native peoples—including the Assiniboine tribe for whom the peak is named—ventured into this section of the Canadian Rockies many thousands of years prior to European exploration.

The roughly triangular park lies northeast of Radium Hot Springs, sandwiched between Kootenay National Park to the west and Banff National Park to the east. It's inaccessible by road; access to the park is on foot or by helicopter.

Three trails provide access to **Lake Magog,** the park's largest body of water. The most popular comes in from the northeast, starting at Sunshine Village in Banff National Park and leading 29 km via Citadel Pass to the lake. Not only is this trail spectacular, but the relatively high elevation of the trailhead (2,100 meters) makes for a less strenuous approach. From the west, a 32-km trail leads off Hwy. 93 at Simpson River in Kootenay National Park. This trail climbs the Simpson River and Surprise Creek drainages and crosses 2,270-meter Ferro Pass to the lake. The third approach is from Kananaskis Country (Alberta) to the southeast. At 27 km, this is the shortest approach, but its elevation gain is greater than the other two trails.

If these long approaches put visiting the park out of your reach, there's one more option: you can fly in by helicopter from Canmore, Alberta. Helicopter access is restricted to 2-3 days per week and costs $60-70 per person each way. For details contact **Assiniboine Heli Tours,** tel. (403) 678-5459, **Canadian Helicopters,** tel. (403) 678-2207, or **Canmore Helicopters,** tel. (403) 678-4802.

At Lake Magog you'll find the main trailhead for a variety of day-hikes, as well as the park's main facility area. Not that the park offers *that* many facilities. A designated camping area on the lake's west shore provides a source of drinking water and pit toilets. Open fires are prohibited. Sites are $7 per night. Also at the lake are the **Naiset Cabins,** $10 per person per night, and the more luxurious **Mount Assiniboine Lodge,** P.O. Box 1527, Canmore, AB T0L 0M0; tel. (403) 678-2883. The lodge offers basic but comfortable guest cabins for $120 per person per day, all meals included.

For further park information write P.O. Box 118, Wasa, BC V0B 2K0, or call (250) 422-3212. For information on the condition of trails leading into the park contact the Kootenay or Banff park information centers.

Bugaboo Glacier Provincial Park and Alpine Recreation Area

Inaccessible to all but the most experienced hikers and climbers, this vast tract of wilderness in the Purcell Mountains northwest of Radium Hot Springs is reached along a 45-km gravel road west from Brisco. At road's end, a trail climbs steeply to a glaciated area that rivals the Canadian Rockies in beauty.

Aside from the icefields covering half the park, the most dominant features here are spectacular granite spires rising to elevations above 3,000 meters. While the Purcell Mountains are an ancient range 1.5 billion years old, the spires formed as intrusions thrust skyward only about 70 million years ago. Since then, erosion has shaped them into today's granite needles towering over the surrounding icefields.

For nearly 100 years the Bugaboos have been a mecca for climbers, but first ascents have been made as recently as the 1970s. In 1972, the Alpine Club of Canada built the **Conrad Kain Hut** as a base for hikers and climbers wanting to explore the park. The hut, equipped with stoves and bunk beds for 50 people, is named for the first mountaineer to climb the highest spire. It's located a strenuous five-km hike from the end of the road, up a valley carved by the retreating Bugaboo Glacier. The trail gains around 700 meters in elevation; allow at least two hours. Camping is also possible near the hut. No set trails lead from the hut to the spires or icefields and you'll need climbing and glacier-travel experience to continue deeper into the park. For further information write Bugaboo Glacier Provincial Park, P.O. Box 118, Wasa, BC V0B 2K0, or call (250) 422-3212.

In summer, the world's largest heli-skiing operation, **C.M.H. Heli-skiing,** P.O. Box 1660, Banff, AB T0L 0C0, tel. (403) 762-7100 or (800) 661-0252, opens its Bugaboo lodge for heli-hikers. The company offers weekend and week-long packages.

YOHO NATIONAL PARK AND VICINITY

Yoho, a Cree word of amazement, is a fitting name for this 1,313-square-kilometer park on the western slopes of the Canadian Rockies. It's the smallest of the four contiguous parks, but its wild and rugged landscape holds spectacular waterfalls, extensive icefields, a lake to rival those in Banff, and one of the world's most intriguing fossil beds. In addition, you'll find some of the finest hiking in all of Canada on the park's 300-km trail system.

The park is open year-round, although road conditions in winter can be treacherous and occasional closures occur on Kicking Horse Pass. The road out to Takakkaw Falls is closed through winter, and often doesn't reopen until mid-June.

Park-entry permits are required and can be bought at the park information center. A one-day permit is $5 per person to a maximum of $10 per vehicle, and an annual Great Western Pass, good for entry to all 11 of western Canada's national parks, is $35 per person to a maximum of $70 per vehicle. Within the park are four lodges, four campgrounds, and the small railway town of **Field,** where you'll find basic services.

HISTORY

The Kootenay and Shuswap tribes of central British Columbia were the first humans to travel

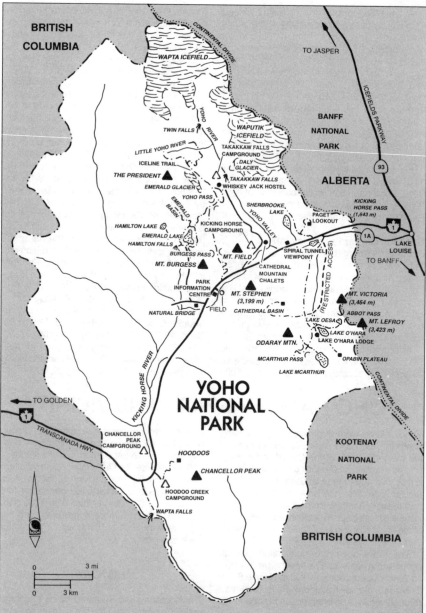

BURGESS SHALE

In 1909, Smithsonian Institute paleontologist Charles Walcott was leading a pack train along the west slope of Mt. Field, on the opposite side of the valley from the newly completed Spiral Tunnel. There he stumbled across fossil beds that have helped refine scientific understanding of life in the early Cambrian period. Encased in a layer of sedimentary rock known as the Burgess Shale, the fossils here are of marine invertebrates around 530 million years old. Some freak event—probably a mud slide—suddenly buried the ancient creatures. Walcott excavated an estimated 65,000 specimens from the site. Today, paleontologists continue to uncover the perfectly preserved fossils—albeit in far fewer numbers than in Walcott's day.

The world-renowned site is open only to those accompanied by a licensed guide. The only access is along a very strenuous 10-km trail that gains 880 meters in elevation. Through summer, tours are led to "Walcott's Quarry" ($35 per person) and the more easily reached Mt. Stephen Fossil Beds ($25 per person). For details call the Yoho National Park Information Centre at (250) 343-6324.

through the rugged area that is now the national park. It's believed the men hid their families in the mountains before crossing over to the prairies to hunt buffalo and to trade with other tribes. On their return they set up seasonal camps along the Kicking Horse River to dry the buffalo meat and hides.

The first Europeans to explore the valley of the Kicking Horse River were members of the Palliser Expedition of 1858. The unfortunate expedition geologist, Dr. James Hector, inadvertently gave the river its name. Bucked from his horse at the river's edge, he was kicked unconscious and took two hours to come to.

Soon more Europeans arrived and set up trading posts throughout the West. By 1880 the buffalo herds had been eradicated, forcing a change in the traditional lifestyle of the indigenous people.

Like adjacent Banff, the coming of the railway was a prime catalyst in the formation of Yoho National Park. The railbed was laid across the Continental Divide and down along the Kicking Horse River in 1884. Upon opening of the line in 1886, 16 square km of land around the base of lofty 3,199-meter Mt. Stephen was set aside as a reserve. In 1911 the reserve was expanded and made into a national park. That put an end to the lead, zinc, and silver mining on the faces of Mt. Stephen and Mt. Field, but remnants of the Monarch and Kicking Horse mines can still be seen.

The small township of Field started as a railway maintenance depot at the bottom of treacherous "Big Hill." The Canadian Pacific Railway operated a hotel and restaurant in town until 1918. To encourage visitors to this side of the mountains, the CPR also built lodges at several natural attractions, including **Emerald Lake Lodge** in 1902, **Lake O'Hara Lodge** in 1913, and **Wapta Lodge Bungalow Camp** in 1921. The segment of road that later became part of the TransCanada Highway was built in 1927 and followed the railway's route.

SIGHTS

As with the other three mountain parks, you don't need to travel deep into the backcountry to view the most spectacular features here—many are visible from the roadside. The sights below are listed from east to west, starting at the park boundary (the Continental Divide).

Spiral Tunnel Viewpoint

The joy CPR President William Van Horne felt upon completion of his transcontinental rail line in 1886 was tempered by massive problems along a stretch of line west of Kicking Horse Pass. "Big Hill" was less than five km long, but its gradient was so steep that runaway trains, crashes, and other disasters were common occurrences. A trail from Kicking Horse Campground takes you past the remains of one of those doomed trains.

Nearly a quarter century after the line opened, railway engineers and builders finally solved the problem. By building two spiral tunnels down through two km of solid rock to the valley floor, they lessened the grade dramatically and the terrors came to an end. Today, the TransCanada Highway follows the original railbed.

Along the way is a viewpoint with interpretive displays telling the fascinating story of Big Hill.

Yoho Valley

Fed by the Wapta Icefield in the far north of the park, the **Yoho River** flows through this spectacularly narrow valley, dropping more than 200 meters in the last kilometer before joining the Kicking Horse River. The road leading up the valley passes the park's main campground, climbs a *very* tight series of switchbacks, and ends 14 km from the main highway at **Takakkaw Falls,** the most impressive waterfall in the Canadian Rockies.

Meaning "Wonderful" in the language of the Cree, Takakkaw tumbles 400 meters over a sheer rock wall, creating a spray bedecked by rainbows. It's one of Canada's highest falls and can be seen from the parking lot. But it's well worth the easy 10-minute stroll over the Yoho River to appreciate the sight in all its glory. For all the hiking opportunities in this area see "Hikes in Other Areas of the Park," below.

PROVINCE OF BRITISH COLUMBIA

Takakkaw Falls

Natural Bridge

Three km west of Field is the turnoff to famous Emerald Lake (see below). On your way out to the lake, you'll first pass another intriguing sight. At Natural Bridge, two km down the road, the Kicking Horse River has worn a narrow hole through a limestone wall, creating a bridge. Over time, the bridge will collapse and, well, it won't be such an intriguing sight any more. A trail leads to several viewpoints—try to avoid the urge to join the idiots clambering over the top of the bridge.

Emerald Lake

One of the jewels of the Canadian Rockies, this beautiful lake is surrounded by a forest of Engelmann spruce, as well as by some of the park's highest peaks. Covered in ice for most of the year, for a few short months in summer it comes alive with activity as hikers, canoeists, and horseback riders take advantage of the magnificent surroundings. **Emerald Lake Lodge** is the grandest of Yoho's accommodations, offering a restaurant, cafe, lounge, and recreation facilities for both guests and nonguests (see "Other Recreation" and "Accommodations and Camping," below).

LAKE O'HARA HIKING

The area around Lake O'Hara is one of the premier hiking areas in the Canadian Rockies. Trails radiate from the lake in all directions, passing high alpine meadows, spectacular snowcapped peaks, and more than 20 other lakes. The longest of the trails is just over seven km, making Lake O'Hara an especially fine hub for day-hiking. Trail maps are available for $8 at the Lake O'Hara Lodge or the park information center. Facilities at the lake include a warden's station, lodge, and campground (see "Accommodations and Camping," below).

Access to the lake is by shuttle bus from a parking lot 15 km east of Field and three km west of the Continental Divide. Buses run four times daily through summer; reservations are taken up to 30 days in advance at the Park Information Centre, tel. (250) 343-6433. The reservation fee is $10 and the fare is $11 per person roundtrip. Six places are allotted each day on a first-come, first-served basis and there's usually a line for these tickets. You can also walk up the 11-km access road to the lake in about 3.5-4 hours; the elevation gain is 420 meters.

Lake Oesa
- Length: three km (one hour) one-way
- Elevation gain: 250 meters
- Rating: easy/moderate

With the Continental Divide peaks of Mt. Victoria (3,464 meters) and Mt. Lefroy (3,423 meters) as a backdrop, this small aqua-colored lake surrounded by talus slopes is one of the area's gems. The trail begins on the north side of Lake O'Hara, nearly directly opposite the lodge, and climbs past a number of small lakes before entering the cirque in which Lake Oesa lies.

Opabin Plateau Circuit
- Length: 5.9 km (two hours) roundtrip
- Elevation gain: 250 meters
- Rating: easy/moderate

Separated from Lake Oesa by 2,848-meter Mt. Yukness, this plateau high above treeline is dotted with small lakes. The time given above is an absolute minimum, for it's easy to spend an entire day exploring the alpine plateau and scrambling around the surrounding slopes. From the trailhead, 300 meters southeast of Lake O'Hara Lodge, the trail passes Mary Lake, climbing steeply and reaching the plateau in a little over two km. The trail loops through the plateau before descending back into the subalpine forest and finishing on the Lakeshore Trail 600 meters from the lodge.

Lake McArthur
- Length: 3.5 km (80 minutes) one-way
- Elevation gain: 300 meters
- Rating: easy/moderate

This trail begins along the main access road, 200 meters north of Lake O'Hara Lodge. It crosses an open meadow, disappears into a dense forest of Engelmann spruce and subalpine fir, then climbs up to Schäffer Lake. At a junction beyond that lake, the left fork leads to Lake McArthur and the right fork to McArthur Pass. It's a steep final ascent to the lake, but the trail levels off and slopes gently down for the final 400 meters. Surrounded on two sides by

steep cliffs, the large lake is fed by McArthur Glacier and reaches depths of over 80 meters.

Odaray Plateau
- Length: 2.6 km (one hour) one-way
- Elevation gain: 280 meters
- Rating: easy/moderate

For a panoramic overview of the Lake O'Hara area with a minimum of energy output, it's hard to beat Odaray Plateau, immediately west of the lodge. From the warden's cabin the trail crosses open meadows and climbs steadily the entire distance to the lofty perch below Odaray Mountain.

Cathedral Basin
- Length: 7.5 km (2.5 hours) one-way
- Elevation gain: 300 meters
- Rating: moderate

The trail out to Cathedral Basin is the longest in the Lake O'Hara area, yet is still an easy day-trip for most people. From the Lake O'Hara campground the trail heads northwest, crossing Morning Glory Creek at the 2.4-km mark then passing large Linda Lake. The final ascent to Cathedral Basin makes a wide loop through an area of ancient rockslides. From this point, the magnificent panorama of the Lake O'Hara area and the backdrop of the Continental Divide are laid out to the southeast.

HIKES IN OTHER AREAS OF THE PARK

While the park's premier hiking area is around Lake O'Hara, 300 km of trails wind through other parts of the park. Generally, these trails gain considerable elevation, so a degree of fitness is required. Most of the hikes detailed below are along the Yoho Valley and in the vicinity of Emerald Lake. The hike to the world-famous Burgess Shale is detailed in the Special Topic.

Paget Lookout
- Length: 3.5 km (90 minutes) one-way
- Elevation gain: 520 meters
- Rating: moderate

Beginning from a trailhead at the Wapta Lake picnic area five km west of the Continental Divide, the trail to this viewpoint is moderately strenuous but worthwhile for the panorama of the Kicking Horse River Valley. The first kilometer traverses a forest of Engelmann spruce. Then the trail breaks out above treeline just below the lookout, the site of an abandoned fire tower. As an alternative, branch right 1.4 km along the trail and continue two km to **Sherbrooke Lake,** which is fed by the Waputik Icefield.

Yoho Pass

- Length: 4.7 km (two hours) one-way
- Elevation gain: 530 meters
- Rating: moderate

The Yoho Valley provides many fine opportunities for serious day-hikers to get off the beaten track. The trail to Yoho Pass, which can be combined with the Iceline Trail (see below), begins on the west side of Whiskey Jack Hostel, 500 meters before the Takakkaw Falls parking lot. It leads 3.7 km to picturesque, spruce-encircled Yoho Lake, then continues another easy kilometer to the pass. The pass is below treeline, so views are limited. But from this point, it's 5.5 km and an elevation loss of 530 meters down to Emerald Lake; six km and an elevation gain of 300 meters to spectacular Burgess Pass; or 2.4 km north, with little elevation gain or loss, to an intersection with the Iceline Trail.

Iceline Trail

- Length: 6.4 km (2.5 hours) one-way
- Elevation gain: 690 meters
- Rating: moderate/difficult

Constructed in 1987, this is one of the most spectacular day-hikes in the Canadian Rockies. The length given above is from the trailhead at Whiskey Jack Hostel to the highest point along the trail. In the middle of this stretch you'll reach the trail's highlight—the four-km traverse of a moraine below Emerald Glacier. Views across the valley improve as the trail climbs to its 2,220-meter crest. Many day-hikers return from this point, although officially the trail continues into Little Yoho River Valley. Another option is to continue beyond Celeste Lake and loop back to Takakkaw Falls and the original trailhead, a total distance of 18 km.

Twin Falls

- Length: eight km (2.5 hours) one-way
- Elevation gain: 300 meters

- Rating: moderate

This trail takes over where the road through the Yoho River Valley ends. Starting at the Takakkaw Falls parking lot, it continues upriver to Twin Falls, passing many other waterfalls along the way. At spectacular Twin Falls, water from the Wapta Icefield divides in two before plunging off an 80-meter-high cliff. Mother Nature may work in amazing ways, but some times she needs a helping hand—or so the Canadian Pacific Railway thought. In the 1920s, the company dynamited one of the channels to make the falls more symmetrical.

Emerald Lake Loop

- Length: 5.2 km (1.5-2 hours) roundtrip
- Elevation gain: minimal
- Rating: easy

One of the easiest yet most enjoyable walks in Yoho is around the park's most famous lake. The trail encircles the lake and can be hiked in either direction. The best views are from the western shoreline, where a massive avalanche has cleared away the forest of Engelmann spruce.

Hamilton Falls

- Length: 800 meters (40 minutes) one-way
- Elevation gain: 60 meters
- Rating: easy

The trail to these falls begins from the Emerald Lake parking lot, down the hill from the bridge to the lodge. It's an easy walk through a forest of Engelmann spruce and subalpine fir to a viewpoint at the base of the falls. A little farther along, the trail begins switchbacking steeply and offers even better views of the cascade. The trail ends at **Hamilton Lake,** which lies in a small glacial cirque a steep 880 vertical meters above Emerald Lake. Total distance from Emerald Lake to Hamilton Lake is 5.5 km (2.5 hours) one-way.

Emerald Basin

- Length: 4.3 km (two hours) one-way
- Elevation gain: 280 meters
- Rating: easy/moderate

The trail to the delightful Emerald Basin begins from the west shore of Emerald Lake, 1.5 km from the main parking lot. From there it's a steady three-km climb through a subalpine forest to the basin, which, chances are, you'll have to yourself. The most impressive sight awaiting you there is the south wall of the President Range, towering 800 vertical meters above.

Hoodoo Trail

- Length: three km (60-90 minutes) one-way
- Elevation gain: 460 meters
- Rating: moderate

Hoodoos are found in varying forms throughout the Canadian Rockies. They are formed by the erosion of relatively soft rock from beneath a cap of harder, more weather-resistant rock. Although these examples require some effort to reach, their intriguing appearance makes the trip worthwhile. The trail begins from Hoodoo Creek Campground, 23 km southwest of Field. The first half of the trail is relatively flat, leaving all the elevation gain to be made in the last, painful 1.5 km.

Wapta Falls

- Length: 2.4 km (45 minutes) one-way
- Elevation loss: minimal
- Rating: easy

This trail begins from the end of a two-km access road leading south off the TransCanada Hwy. in the park's extreme southwestern corner. It follows an old fire road for a bit then narrows for the easy stroll through thick forest to a viewpoint above the falls. A steep descent leads to a lower viewpoint.

OTHER RECREATION

Whitewater Rafting

Anyone looking for whitewater-rafting action will want to run the Kicking Horse River. The rafting season runs May-Aug., with river levels at their highest in late June.

Whitewater Voyageurs, based beside the Husky gas station in Golden, tel. (250) 344-7335 or (800) 667-7238, departs daily at 9 a.m. for an exciting trip through the river's lower canyon. Lunch is included in the price of $90 per person. A half-day trip is $50. From Banff, trips with this operator can be booked through **Adrenalin Descents,** in the Banff Ptarmigan Inn, 339 Banff Ave., tel. (403) 762-8177; transportation from Banff is provided. Also operat-

ing from Golden is **Alpine Rafting Company,** tel. (250) 344-5016 or (800) 663-7080.

In Lake Louise, **Wild Water Adventures,** tel. (403) 522-2211, leads full-day trips down the river for $89, including a narrated bus trip to the put-in point and a gourmet lunch. The company also offers half-day trips from Lake Louise at 8:30 a.m. and 1:30 p.m.

Boating and Fishing

No river or stream is particularly well known for fishing, mainly because most of the water is glacially derived and therefore heavily silt-laden. A national parks **fishing permit** costs $6 for seven days or $13 annually. **Emerald Sports,** on the shore of Emerald Lake, tel. (250) 343-6377, rents canoes and small boats for $26 per hour or $40 all day. Fishing in Emerald Lake mightn't be world class, but there are some trout in the waters and Emerald Sports offers a range of fishing tackle for rent or sale.

Horseback Riding

Emerald Lake Stables, at the lake of the same name, rents horses. A one-hour trip around Emerald Lake costs $22. Two-hour rides are $35, three-hour rides $45, lunch rides $62, and all-day rides with dinner go for $85.

Wintertime

The TransCanada Highway through the park is open year-round, but facilities are only open June through mid-September. Some of the trails at higher elevations are impassable until July. Wintertime attracts cross-country skiers who happily slide along the Yoho Valley to frozen Takakkaw Falls, or follow the Lake O'Hara trails.

ACCOMMODATIONS AND CAMPING

Kicking Horse Lodge

In the small railway town of Field (pop. 240), elegant Kicking Horse Lodge, 100 Centre St., tel. (250) 343-6303 or (800) 659-4944, offers 14 well-furnished rooms, a large comfortable lounge, and a restaurant (open in summer only). Rates are $106 s or d, $108 with a kitchenette, off-season discounts available. Across the road is a small general store that serves passable food to eat in or take out.

Emerald Lake Lodge

The extensive grounds of this grand accommodation lie along the southern shore of one of the Canadian Rockies' most magnificent lakes. Originally known as Mt. Stephen House, the lodge was built in 1911 in the same tradition as the Chateau Lake Louise and Banff Springs Hotel—as a playground for wealthy railway travelers. In 1986 the lodge underwent considerable renovation and expansion and now boasts 85 units. Guest facilities include a hot tub and sauna, swimming pool, restaurant, lounge, and cafe. Guests can also go horseback riding, or go boating and fishing on Emerald Lake. Rooms are large and many of the more expensive ones are on the lakefront. Rates range $260-410 per night, with sharp discounts in the off-season. For bookings call (250) 343-6321 or (800) 663-6336.

Overlooking Emerald Lake, the lodge cafe features magnificent views from tables inside and out. The menu is varied—you can sit and

the cafe at Emerald Lake

ANDREW HEMPSTEAD

sip a coffee or have a full lunch. Hot meals range $7-12, sandwiches and salads $6-10. Within the main lodge you'll find a more formal dining room and a bar offering live entertainment on Friday and Saturday nights.

Lake O'Hara Lodge

This lodge set around beautiful Lake O'Hara allows hikers not equipped for overnight camping the opportunity to explore the backcountry on leisurely day-hikes. Located 11 km from the road, the lodge transports guests via shuttle bus to and from a parking lot three km west of the Continental Divide and 15 km east of Field. The 23 cabins, some with private bathrooms, are spread around the lakeshore. Rates are $150-220 per person, including all meals. The lodge books up well in advance; for reservations call (250) 343-6418. In the off-season call (403) 678-4110.

Cathedral Mountain Lodge and Chalets

Comprising 20 rustic cabins alongside the Kicking Horse River, this is the most basic of the park's accommodations. Each unit has a fully equipped kitchen and some have private bathrooms. A restaurant and grocery store are on the premises. The chalets are open in summer only; rates range $69-135 per unit. For bookings call (250) 343-6442. In the off-season call (403) 762-0514.

Hostel

Hostelling International operates **Whiskey Jack Hostel** near Takakkaw Falls. Formerly staff quarters for a privately run lodge that was destroyed by an avalanche, the hostel provides basic dormitory accommodations and a communal kitchen. Members of Hostelling International pay $11 per night, nonmembers $15. Book through Banff International Hostel at (403) 762-4122.

Campgrounds

The park's main camping area is **Kicking Horse Campground,** five km northeast of Field along the road to Takakkaw Falls. Facilities include showers, flush toilets, and kitchen shelters. Unserviced sites are $13, hookups $17. The campground is open mid-May to mid-October. Back toward the TransCanada Hwy., an overflow area with more limited facilities is also open for winter camping. At the end of the same road, **Takakkaw Falls Campground** is designed for tent campers only. Park at the very end of the road and load up the carts with your gear for a pleasant 400-meter walk along the valley floor. No showers are provided, and the only facilities are pit toilets and picnic tables; $12 per site.

Hoodoo Creek Campground, along the TransCanada Hwy. 23 km southwest of Field, provides sheltered private spots among the trees; $14 per night. A few hundred meters farther west is the turnoff to **Chancellor Peak Campground,** beside the Kicking Horse River; $12 per night.

Just north of Lake O'Hara is a 30-site campground with two kitchen shelters and woodstoves. Camping is $6 per person per night plus a daily fee of $3 per site for firewood. Reservations for sites can be made at (250) 343-6433 up to 30 days in advance. A few sites are left open on a first-come, first-served basis.

Primitive wilderness campsites are scattered throughout the backcountry. Users must obtain a permit from the Park Information Centre; $6 per person per night.

INFORMATION

The main source of information about the park is the **Park Information Centre** on the Trans-Canada Hwy. at Field, tel. (250) 343-6324. This is also the place to book the bus trip up to Lake O'Hara, pick up backcountry camping permits, buy topographical maps, and find out schedules for the interpretive programs. The center is open in peak summer season, daily 9 a.m.-7 p.m.; May-June and September, daily 9 a.m.-5 p.m. For more information write Superintendent, Yoho National Park, P.O. Box 99, Field, BC V0A 1G0.

GOLDEN

From the park's western boundary, the Trans-Canada Highway meanders down the beautiful Kicking Horse River Valley to the railway and ser-vice town of Golden (pop. 4,100). The town doesn't offer much in the way of sights, although you might check out the small museum on 14th Street.

Recreation

Whitewater-rafting companies based in town include **Whitewater Voyageurs,** at the Husky gas station, tel. (250) 344-7335 or (800) 667-7238; and **Alpine Rafting Company,** 1020 N. TransCanada Hwy., tel. (250) 344-5016 or (800) 663-7080. Both offer full-day trips down the Kicking Horse River in nearby Yoho National Park for around $90 per person including lunch.

The local ski resort, **Whitetooth Ski Area,** spreads across the lower slopes of the Purcell Mountains. The main runs are easily spotted across the valley as you enter town from the east. Whitetooth has only one chairlift and a short T-bar, but the vertical rise is a respectable 580 meters and the longest run is well over one kilometer. The snow is generally good and crowds are always at a minimum. Lift tickets are adults $25, seniors $18, children $11. The lifts operate Fri.-Mon. only. For snow reports and further information call (250) 344-6114.

Accommodations and Camping

Over 20 motels, most strung out along the highway, make finding a place to stay in Golden easy. **Ponderosa Motor Inn,** on the Trans-Canada Hwy. at the west entrance to town, tel. (250) 344-2205, is one of the least expensive and boasts impressive views from the grounds. Rates for the air-conditioned rooms start at $48 d. Similarly priced, and on the same side of town, is **Swiss Village Motel,** tel. (250) 344-2276. Room rates at **Prestige Inn,** Trans-Canada Hwy., tel. (250) 344-7990, may be higher than the other motels in town, but the standard is better and amenities such as an indoor pool, hot tub, fitness center, and restaurant make it a comfortable place to stay. Rates start at $90 s, $100 d.

Down beside the Columbia River you'll find **Golden Municipal Campground,** on 9th St. S (turn at the one traffic light in town), tel. (250) 344-5412. It's a quiet place with adequate facilities, including a pool and tennis court next door. Unpowered sites are $11, powered sites $13.50.

Food
Last time I passed through Golden I had a great meal at **Legendz Diner,** on the west side of the TransCanada Hwy., tel. (250) 344-5059. As the name suggests, it's a 1950s'-style diner complete with attentive staff and good filling meals from $7.

Information
Golden Visitor Info Centre, downtown at 500 10th Ave., tel. (250) 344-7125, is open year-round, weekdays 8:30 a.m.-4:30 p.m. Out on the highway opposite the Esso gas station is a seasonal information center open in summer, daily 9 a.m.-7 p.m.

BANFF NATIONAL PARK

Canada's most famous national park lies east of British Columbia, across the Continental Divide in the province of Alberta. But since most visitors to Kootenay and Yoho National Parks include Banff in their itinerary, it's included in this book.

Most famous of the four contiguous parks, Banff encompasses some of the world's most magnificent scenery. The snowcapped peaks of the Rocky Mountains form a spectacular backdrop for glacial lakes, fast-flowing rivers, and endless forests. The park's vast wilderness is home to deer, moose, elk, mountain goats, bighorn sheep, black and grizzly bears, wolves, and cougars. Many of these species are commonly sighted from roads in the park.

The human species is concentrated mainly in the picture-postcard town of **Banff,** located in the south of the park, 122 km east of Radium Hot Springs and 128 km west of Calgary. Northwest of Banff along the TransCanada Highway is **Lake Louise,** regarded as one of the seven natural wonders of the world. It's rivaled for sheer beauty only by **Moraine Lake,** just down the road. North of Lake Louise, the **Icefields Parkway** begins its spectacular course to Jasper National Park, running right alongside the Continental Divide.

Banff National Park is open year-round, although occasional road closures occur on mountain passes along the park's western boundary in winter, due to avalanche-control work and snowstorms. Permits are required for entry into the park; they're available from all park gates as well as the park information center in Banff. A one-day permit is $5 per person to a maximum of $10 per vehicle, and an annual Great Western Pass, good for entry to all 11 of western Canada's national parks, is $35 per person to a maximum of $70.

HISTORY

Working its way west, the Canadian Pacific Railway's transcontinental rail line reached the Rocky Mountains in the summer of 1883. By that fall, tracks had been pushed through to Laggan, now known as Lake Louise. On 8 November 1883, three young railway workers—Franklin McCabe, and William and Thomas McCardell—went prospecting for gold on their day off. They didn't find gold, but instead found something just as precious—a hot mineral spring that in time would attract wealthy customers from around the world.

The 25-square-km reserve established around the springs was later expanded and renamed **Rocky Mountains Park.** At the turn of the century Canada had an abundance of wilderness; it certainly didn't need a park to preserve it. The only goal of Rocky Mountains Park was to draw wealthy patrons of the railway and generate income for the government and the Canadian Pacific Railway. Luxurious lodgings such as the Banff Springs Hotel were constructed, and golf courses, the hot springs themselves, and manicured gardens were developed. Banff soon became Canada's best known tourist resort, attracting visitors from around the world. The park's present boundaries, encompassing 6,641 square km, were established in 1964.

SIGHTS

Town of Banff
This bustling commercial center of 7,000 permanent residents enjoys a magnificent setting alongside the Bow River. The towering face of

Mt. Rundle looms over town to the south, while **Cascade Mountain** dominates the northern skyline. A strip of hotels and motels lines the north end of Banff Ave., while a profusion of shops, boutiques, cafes, and restaurants hugs the south end. Over the Bow River you'll find **Cascade Gardens,** a formal flower garden, and the Park Administration Building.

The park is known worldwide for natural beauty, so it's ironic that the most-recognizable landmark here is man-made. The **Banff Springs Hotel,** a mix of Scottish castle and French country chateau, perches on a terrace above a bend in the Bow River. Built in 1888, it's one of the world's largest, grandest, and most opulent mountain-resort hotels. But budget travelers shouldn't let the hotel's highbrow ambience discourage them from spending time here; sightseeing is encouraged. Tours are offered in summer, daily at 5 p.m. Tickets are $5 per person. Call (403) 762-2211 for details. Below the hotel is **Bow Falls,** a small cascade but a spectacular one during high water in late spring.

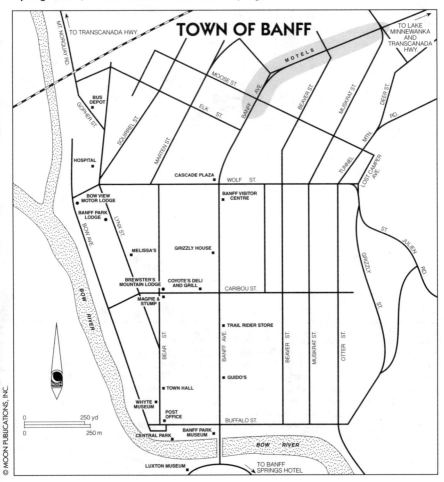

© MOON PUBLICATIONS, INC.

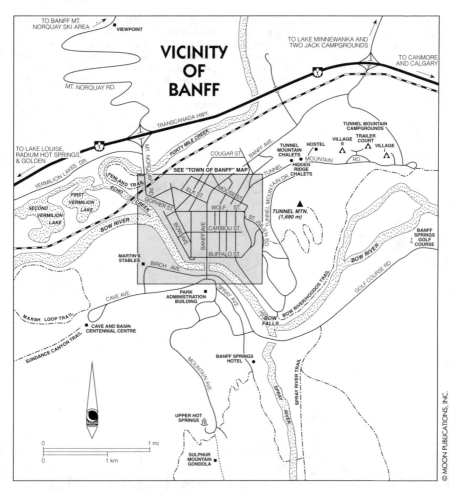

TO BANFF MT. NORQUAY SKI AREA

VIEWPOINT

VICINITY OF BANFF

MT. NORQUAY RD.

TRANSCANADA HWY.

TO LAKE LOUISE, RADIUM HOT SPRINGS, & GOLDEN

TO LAKE MINNEWANKA AND TWO JACK CAMPGROUNDS

TO CANMORE AND CALGARY

TUNNEL MOUNTAIN CAMPGROUNDS

FORTY MILE CREEK

BANFF AVE.

COUGAR ST.

TUNNEL MOUNTAIN CHALETS

HOSTEL

MOUNTAIN

VILLAGE II

TRAILER COURT

VILLAGE

HIDDEN RIDGE CHALETS

SEE "TOWN OF BANFF" MAP

FENLAND TRAIL

MT. NORQUAY RD.

ECHO CREEK

FIRST VERMILION LAKE

SECOND VERMILION LAKE

BOW RIVER

GOPHER ST.

ELK ST.

MOOSE ST.

WOLF ST.

BANFF AVE.

CARIBOU ST.

BOW AVE.

TUNNEL MOUNTAIN DR.

ST. JULIEN RD.

TUNNEL MTN. (1,690 m)

BANFF SPRINGS GOLF COURSE

BOW RIVER

MARTIN'S STABLES

BIRCH AVE.

BUFFALO ST.

CAVE AVE.

PARK ADMINISTRATION BUILDING

SPRAY AVE.

BOW RIVER/HOODOOS TRAIL

GOLF COURSE RD.

MARSH LOOP TRAIL

SUNDANCE CANYON TRAIL

CAVE AND BASIN CENTENNIAL CENTRE

BOW FALLS

BANFF SPRINGS HOTEL

SPRAY RIVER TRAIL

MOUNTAIN AVE.

SPRAY RIVER

MOON

0   1 mi

0   1 km

UPPER HOT SPRINGS

SULPHUR MOUNTAIN GONDOLA

© MOON PUBLICATIONS, INC.

If rainy weather forces you indoors, check out Banff's excellent museums. **Banff Park Museum,** 93 Banff Ave., tel. (403) 762-1558, provides insight into the park's early history and displays stuffed specimens of local wildlife. The museum building dates from 1903. Tours are offered daily at 3 p.m. One block away is the **Whyte Museum of the Canadian Rockies,** 111 Bear St., tel. (403) 762-2291, housing the world's largest collection of Canadian Rockies literature and art. Across the Bow River

from these two museums, **Luxton Museum,** 1 Birch Ave., tel. (403) 762-2388, is dedicated to the native peoples who once inhabited the Canadian Rockies and surrounding prairies. The three museums are open daily year-round and an admission of $2.50-5 is charged at each.

Cave and Basin Centennial Centre, at the end of Cave Ave., tel. (403) 762-1557, marks the site of the hot springs that sparked the park's development. Although the pools are now closed to bathers, the center is still one of Banff's most popular attractions. Interpretive displays describe the how's and why's of the springs. A narrow tunnel winds into the dimly lit cave, and a number of short trails lead from the center to the entrance of the cave and through a unique environment created by hot spring water.

Vicinity of Banff

The easiest way to get high above town without raising a sweat is on the **Sulphur Mountain Gondola,** at the end of Mountain Ave., tel. (403) 762-2523. The gondola rises 700 meters in eight minutes to an elevation of 2,285 meters. Views from the observation deck are breathtaking, and for even better views you can continue along the **Vista Trail** to a restored weather observatory. The gondola runs in summer, 7:30 a.m.-9 p.m., shorter hours the rest of the year, closed in December; $10 per person. Along the road up to the gondola is **Upper Hot Springs,** tel. (403) 762-1515, open daily for public swimming and soaking; $7 per person.

The shallow **Vermilion Lakes** form an expansive montane wetland supporting a variety of mammals and 238 species of birds. Get there on Vermilion Lakes Dr., which parallels the Trans-Canada Hwy. immediately west of Banff.

One of the best car-accessible views of town is on Mt. Norquay Rd., which switchbacks steeply to the base of **Banff Mt. Norquay,** the local ski area. On the way up are several look-outs, including one near the top where bighorn sheep often graze.

Meaning "Lake of the Water Spirit," **Lake Minnewanka** is the largest body of water in Banff National Park. The reservoir was first constructed in 1912, and additional dams were built in 1922 and 1941 to supply hydroelectric power to Banff. Easy walking trails lead along the western shore, and a 90-minute cruise departs from the dock every two hours. **Brewster** offers this cruise combined with a bus tour from Banff for $40 per person. To get to the lake head six km down Lake Minnewanka Rd., which begins where Banff Ave. ends at the northeast end of town.

Bow Valley Parkway

Two roads link Banff to Lake Louise. The Trans-Canada Highway is the quicker route, popular with through traffic. The other is the more scenic 51-km Bow Valley Parkway, which branches off the TransCanada Highway five km west of Banff. Along this route are a number of impressive viewpoints, interpretive displays, picnic areas, hiking trails, great opportunities for viewing wildlife, three lodges, campgrounds, a hostel (Castle Mountain), and one of the park's best restaurants (Baker Creek Bistro).

Among the road's highlights: **Johnston Canyon,** where Johnston Creek drops over a series of spectacular waterfalls deep within a chasm; **Silver City,** once a boomtown of five

ANDREW HEMPSTEAD

Castle Mountain

mines and 2,000 residents; and distinctive **Castle Mountain.**

Lake Louise

Regarded as one of the world's seven natural wonders, this magnificent body of water 51 km north of Banff is framed by glaciated 3,459-meter **Mt. Victoria** at one end, and one of the world's most photographed hotels, **Chateau Lake Louise,** at the other. Down in the valley, the hamlet of Lake Louise comprises a small mall, hotels, and restaurants. In 1882, outfitter Tom Wilson became the first European to lay eyes on the lake. Soon after, a rail spur was brought in off the main CPR line and in 1890 a hotel was built on the lakeshore. The lake gets *very* busy in summer; try to arrive at dawn, when the first rays of sunlight hit the top of Mt. Victoria, casting magnificent reflections across the water. And don't miss the views from the two-km **Louise Lakeshore Trail** traversing the lake's north side.

As impressive as Lake Louise, **Moraine Lake** nestles in a rugged setting in the Valley of the Ten Peaks, 14 km from Lake Louise. Walter Wilcox, the first white man to reach its shore, said "no scene has given me an equal impression of inspiring solitude and rugged grandeur." Those thoughts are mirrored by the thousands of tourists who visit today.

Across the Bow Valley from Lake Louise is **Lake Louise Summer Sightseeing Lift,** tel. (403) 522-3555, part of the massive Lake Louise Ski Area. The lift operates June-Sept.; $9.50 per person. Of course, the lift also runs in winter for skiers; see "Winter Activities" under "Other Recreation," below.

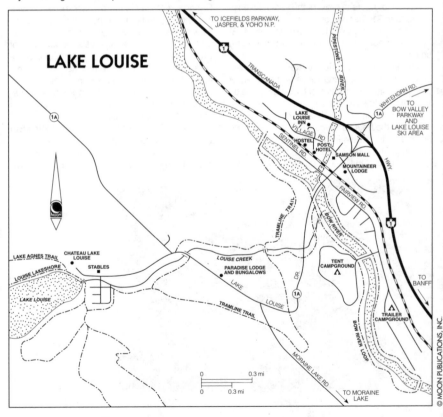

Icefields Parkway

The 230-km Icefields Parkway linking Lake Louise and Jasper is one of the most scenic, exciting, and inspiring mountain roads ever built. From Lake Louise it parallels the Continental Divide, following in the shadow of the highest, most rugged mountains in the Canadian Rockies for 122 km to Sunwapta Pass, the boundary between Banff and Jasper National Parks.

The sparkling, translucent waters of **Bow Lake,** 25 km north of Lake Louise, are among the most beautiful that can be seen from the Icefields Parkway. The lake is fed by various glaciers, including aptly named **Crowfoot Glacier,** at the lake's south end. The glacier sits on a wide ledge near the top of Crowfoot Mountain, its glacial "claws" clinging to the mountain's steep slopes. The retreat of this glacier has been dramatic; only 50 years ago two of the claws extended to the base of the lower cliff. The road leaves Bow Lake and climbs to 2,069-meter **Bow Summit,** one of the highest points crossed by a public road in Canada. From the parking lot at Bow Summit, a short paved trail leads to one of the most breathtaking views imaginable. Far below the viewpoint is **Peyto Lake,** whose impossibly intense greens and blues change from one hue to the next, according to season.

From Bow Pass the parkway follows the Continental Divide, crossing numerous streams and passing many peaks, lakes, and viewpoints. The **North Saskatchewan River** posed a major problem for early travelers and later for the builders of the Icefields Parkway. One km past the Saskatchewan River crossing, a viewpoint provides panoramic vistas of the entire valley and numerous peaks to the west. On the north side of the North Saskatchewan River you'll see the towering hulk of **Mt. Wilson** (3,261 meters), as well as Cirrus Mountain's **Weeping Wall,** where a series of waterfalls tumbles 100 meters over a long gray limestone cliff. In winter this wall of water freezes, becoming a mecca for ice climbers. The road then begins its long climb to **Sunwapta Pass** (2,023 meters).

HIKING

The park's 80-some trails range from short interpretive walks to overnight backcountry op-

portunities. Day-hikers will find many easy trails leading to spectacular vistas. Before attempting any hikes you should visit the **Banff Visitor Centre,** 224 Banff Ave., tel. (403) 762-1550, or **Lake Louise Visitor Centre,** beside Samson Mall, tel. (403) 522-3833, for advice on the condition of trails and closures. Those planning an overnight trip into the backcountry *must* pick up a permit from one of the visitor centers before heading out; $6 per person per night.

Fenland

- Length: two km (30 minutes) roundtrip
- Elevation gain: none
- Rating: easy

This short interpretive trail begins at the Forty Mile Creek Picnic Area, 300 meters north of the rail line along Mt. Norquay Rd., within easy walking distance of downtown Banff. The trail traverses terrain in all stages of transition between wetland and floodplain forest. It's also a popular shortcut for joggers and cyclists heading to Vermilion Lakes.

Tunnel Mountain

- Length: 2.3 km (30-60 minutes) one-way
- Elevation gain: 300 meters
- Rating: easy/moderate

Accessible from downtown Banff, this short hike is an easy climb to one of the park's lower peaks. The trailhead is on St. Julien Rd., 350 meters south of Wolf Street. The trail ascends the western flank of Tunnel Mountain through a forest of lodgepole pine, switchbacking past some viewpoints before reaching a high ridgetop. Here the trail turns northward, climbing through a forest of Douglas fir to the summit (which is partially treed, preventing 360-degree views).

Western Slope of Mount Rundle

- Length: 5.4 km (two hours) one-way
- Elevation gain: 500 meters
- Rating: moderate

At 2,950 meters, Mt. Rundle is one of the park's dominant peaks. An easy-to-follow trail ascends the mountain's western slope but ends some 1,000 vertical meters beneath the summit. Continuing to the top from there is possible without ropes, but previous scrambling experience is advised.

The trail begins at the golf course behind the Banff Springs Hotel; look for it in back of the first hole you come to on the right side of Golf Course Road. It branches off the Spray River Trail after 700 meters, climbing steadily through dense forest for 2.5 km. At that point it breaks out above the treeline and continues to its end in a gully, from where the undefined route to the summit begins.

Cascade Amphitheatre
• Length: 6.6 km (2-3 hours) one-way
• Elevation gain: 610 meters
• Rating: moderate/difficult

This enormous meadow-filled cirque directly behind Cascade Mountain is one of the most rewarding destinations for hiking in the Banff area. The trail begins by the Banff Mt. Norquay day lodge at the end of Mt. Norquay Road. Skirting the base of a number of ski lifts, it follows an old road to the floor of Forty Mile Valley and crosses Forty Mile Creek. The trail then switchbacks up the western flank of Cascade Mountain, levels off, and enters a magnificent U-shaped valley where the amphitheater-like topography soon becomes apparent. The trail becomes indistinct in the subalpine meadow, which is carpeted with colorful wildflowers in summer. The most popular route to the summit of 2,998-meter Cascade Mountain is along the southern ridge of the amphitheater wall. The route entails a long scramble up scree slopes and should be attempted only by experienced scramblers.

Cory Pass
• Length: 5.8 km (2.5 hours) one-way
• Elevation gain: 920 meters
• Rating: moderate/difficult

This strenuous hike from the Fireside Picnic Area at the Banff end of Bow Valley Parkway has a rewarding objective—a magnificent view of dogtoothed Mt. Louis. The towering slab of limestone rises over 500 meters from the valley below. Just over one km from the trailhead the trail divides. The left fork climbs steeply across an open slope to an uneven ridge that it follows before ascending yet another steep slope to Cory Pass—a wild, windy, desolate area surrounded by jagged peaks and dominated by Mt. Louis. An alternative to returning along the same trail is to continue into **Gargoyle Valley,**

following the base of Mt. Edith before ascending to Edith Pass and returning to the junction one km from the picnic area. Total distance for this trip would be 13 km, a long day considering the steep climbs and descents involved.

Sunshine Meadows
• Length: reached by bus
• Elevation gain: minimal
• Rating: easy

Sunshine Meadows, straddling the Continental Divide, is a unique and beautiful spot. Heavy precipitation creates a lush cover of vegetation during the short summer season—over 300 species of wildflowers have been recorded, including fireweed, glacier lilies, mountain avens, white mountain heather, and forget-me-nots. Mount Assiniboine, known as the "Matterhorn of the Rockies," is easily distinguished to the southeast. (For further details of hiking in this area, see "Mount Assiniboine Provincial Park" under "Kootenay National Park and Vicinity," earlier in this chapter).

The meadows are along a 6.5-km road that's closed to public vehicles. In summer, **White Mountain Adventures** offers a shuttle service for a limited number of hikers. Pick up the shuttle to the meadows from Banff (daily at 9:30 a.m., $35 roundtrip) or the Sunshine Village parking lot, 18 km from Banff (daily at 10 a.m., 11 a.m., and 1 p.m., $15 roundtrip). On the 9:30/10 a.m. shuttle, a two-hour guided hike is included in the rate. Advance reservations are required; call (403) 678-4099.

As an alternative to the shuttle, you can walk up the service road from the end of Sunshine Village Rd.; allow two hours each way.

Rockbound Lake
• Length: 8.4 km (2.5 hours) one-way
• Elevation gain: 760 meters
• Rating: moderate/difficult

The trailhead for this strenuous hike is just east of Castle Junction on the Bow Valley Parkway. For the first five km it follows an old fire road along the southern flanks of Castle Mountain. Early in the season or after heavy rain, this section can be boggy. Glimpses of surrounding peaks ease the pain of the steady climb as the trail narrows. After eight km you'll come to **Tower Lake.** The trail skirts it to the right and climbs a steep slope. From the ridge, Rockbound Lake comes into view and the reason for its name immediately becomes apparent. Scramble up any of the nearby slopes for panoramic views.

Plain of the Six Glaciers

• Length: 5.3 km (90 minutes) one-way
• Elevation gain: 370 meters
• Rating: easy/moderate

Hikers along this trail are rewarded not only with sweeping views of glaciated peaks but with a rustic, trail's-end teahouse serving homemade goodies baked on a woodstove. The trail begins in front of Chateau Lake Louise. Branching off the Louise Lakeshore Trail, it climbs steadily through a subalpine forest and traverses a wasteland of moraines produced by the Victoria Glacier. Views are awesome. From the teahouse, continue another km to the summit of a low ridge for an incredible panorama taking in 10 nearby peaks.

Lake Agnes

• Length: 3.6 km (90 minutes) one-way
• Elevation gain: 400 meters
• Rating: moderate

This strenuous hike is one of the park's most popular. It begins in front of Chateau Lake Louise and climbs steeply to tiny Mirror Lake. Then it passes Bridal Veil Falls before making a final ascent into the glacial cirque in which Lake Agnes lies. A rustic teahouse in the cirque makes a nice rest stop. From this point, trails lead to the rock formations **Little Beehive** (one km) and **Big Beehive** (2.1 km). From Big Beehive, you'll have spectacular views of Lake Louise.

Paradise Valley

• Length: 18 km (six hours) roundtrip
• Elevation gain: 380 meters
• Rating: moderate

This aptly named trail makes for a long dayhike, but you can break it up by overnighting at the backcountry campground at the far end of the loop. From the trailhead 3.5 km down Moraine Lake Rd., the trail climbs steadily, crossing **Paradise Creek** numerous times and passing the junction of a trail to **Saddleback,** a high pass. After five km the trail divides, looping eight km around either side of the valley. **Lake An-**

nette lies 700 meters down the left fork. It's a typical subalpine lake in an atypical setting—nestled against the near-vertical 1,200-meter north face of snow- and ice-capped **Mt. Temple** (3,549 meters), one of the 10 highest peaks in the Canadian Rockies. This difficult face was successfully climbed in 1966, relatively late for mountaineering "firsts." The lake is a worthy destination in itself—allow yourself four hours roundtrip from the trailhead.

To complete the entire loop, continue beyond the lake into an open avalanche area affording views across Paradise Valley. Look and listen for pikas and marmots among the boulders. The trail then passes through **Horseshoe Meadow,** crosses Paradise Creek, and starts back down the valley. Keep to the left at all trail crossings and you'll quickly arrive at a series of waterfalls known as the **Giant Steps.** From the base of these falls it's eight km back to the trailhead.

Consolation Lakes

• Length: three km (one hour) one-way
• Elevation gain: 65 meters
• Rating: easy/moderate

This short trail begins from the bridge over Moraine Creek, near the Moraine Lake parking lot, and ends at a pleasant subalpine lake. The first section of the trail traverses a boulder-strewn rock pile—the result of rock slides on the imposing Tower of Babel (3,101 meters)—before entering a dense forest of Engelmann spruce and subalpine fir. It then follows babbling **Babel Creek** to the lower lake. The wide valley affords 360-degree views of the surrounding jagged peaks, including Mt. Temple back down the valley and Mt. Bident and Mt. Quandra at the far end of the lakes.

Larch Valley

• Length: 2.9 km (60-90 minutes) one-way
• Elevation gain: 450 meters
• Rating: moderate

In autumn, when the larch trees have turned a magnificent gold and the sun is shining, few spots in the Canadian Rockies can match the beauty of this valley. But don't expect to find much solitude. The trail begins just past Moraine Lake Lodge and climbs fairly steeply, then passes through an open forest of larch and into a meadow beyond.

Larch Valley

Keen hikers will want to continue through the meadows to **Sentinel Pass** (2,608 meters), one of the park's highest passes. From the end of the meadow the trail switchbacks 1.2 km up a steep slope to the pass, which is sandwiched between Pinnacle Mountain (3,067 meters) and Mt. Temple (3,549 meters). Most hikers opt to return from the pass along the same trail, but you can also continue into Paradise Valley.

Bow Glacier Falls
- Length: 3.4 km (one hour) one-way
- Elevation gain: 130 meters
- Rating: easy/moderate

This hike, beginning from the north end of beautiful Bow Lake along the Icefields Parkway, skirts the lake and continues—albeit in a somewhat sketchy fashion—to narrow but spectacular Bow Glacier Falls. The trail follows the lakeshore past Num-ti-jah Lodge to a gravel outwash area at the end of the lake. From this point the trail climbs steeply before leveling out at the edge of

a vast moraine of gravel, scree, and boulders. This is the end of the maintained trail; to reach the base of the falls you'll need to pick your way through another 800 meters of rough ground.

Parker's Ridge
- Length: 2.4 km (one hour) one-way
- Elevation gain: 210 meters
- Rating: easy/moderate

This short trail into the alpine begins from a parking lot at the north end of the park, just four km south of the park boundary. From the trailhead on the west side of the road, the path gains elevation quickly through open meadows and scattered stands of subalpine fir.

During the short alpine summer, the high meadows are carpeted with red heather, white mountain avens, and blue alpine forget-me-nots. This fragile environment is easily destroyed, so it's very important that you stay on the trail. From the summit of the ridge, you look down on the two-km-wide Saskatchewan Glacier spreading out below.

OTHER RECREATION

Mountain Biking
Banff is a great place for cycling. The roads to Lake Minnewanka and Mt. Norquay, the Bow Valley Parkway, and the Lake Louise area are all popular with pedallers. And a number of trails radiating from Banff townsite and ending deep in the backcountry have been designated as bicycle trails. Before heading into the backcountry, pick up the *Trail Bicycling Guide* from the Banff or Lake Louise visitor centers. **Bactrax Bike Rentals,** in the Banff Ptarmigan Inn, 339 Banff Ave., tel. (403) 762-8177, rents high-standard mountain bikes for $5-7 per hour and $17-25 per day, the best deal in town.

Horseback Riding
This traditional form of mountain transportation is offered by **Warner Guiding & Outfitting,** tel. (403) 762-4551. Their main office is in Trail Rider Store at 132 Banff Ave., but most trips depart from either **Martin's Stables,** tel. (403) 762-2832, behind the recreation grounds on Birch Ave., or **Banff Springs Corral,** tel. (403) 762-2848, along Spray Avenue. One-hour rides

(Sidebar, rotated) ANDREW HEMPSTEAD

are $21, two hours $36, three hours $46. **Brewster Lake Louise Stables,** tel. (403) 522-3511, offers hour-long rides (departing on the hour) for $21.40, rides to the end of Lake Louise for $32.10, half-day rides for $48.15, and all-day rides up Paradise Valley for $85.60.

Whitewater Rafting and Canoeing

While the closest commercially run river is the Kicking Horse, over the border in British Columbia (see "Yoho National Park and Vicinity," earlier in this chapter), many whitewater outfitters are based in Banff and Lake Louise. These include: **Wild Water Adventures,** tel. (403) 522-2211; **Kootenay River Runners,** 204 Caribou St., tel. (403) 762-5385; **Rocky Mountain Raft Tours,** tel. (403) 762-3632; and **Whitewater Voyageurs,** 339 Banff Ave., tel. (403) 762-8177. All offer transportation between Banff and the Kicking Horse River.

Banff Canoe Rentals, on the corner of Wolf St. and Bow Ave., rents canoes for use on the Bow River, Vermilion Lakes, or Lake Minnewanka. **Adrenalin Descents,** in the Banff Ptarmigan Inn at 339 Banff Ave., tel. (403) 762-8177, rents whitewater kayaks and offers various kayaking courses.

Golfing

Banff Springs Golf Course, spread out along the Bow River between Mt. Rundle and Tunnel Mountain, is considered one of the world's most scenic courses. Designed by Stanley Thompson in 1928, the course challenges all levels of golfer. Each fall hundreds of elk gather on the course, and there's always the chance of seeing coyotes, deer, or black bears scurrying across in front of you. Green fees are $74 for 18 holes including a cart, $30 for nine holes with no cart. Club rentals are $25. To book tee times call (403) 762-6801.

Winter Activities

Within Banff National Park are three world-class ski resorts. The small but steep slopes of **Banff Mt. Norquay,** tel. (403) 762-4421, overlook the town of Banff. Canada's first chairlift was installed on this mountain in 1948 and quickly attracted expert skiers. But the resort widened its appeal in 1990 with the opening of new intermediate terrain. Lift tickets cost $35. A free shuttle bus runs between the resort and Banff hotels.

Sunshine Village, tel. (403) 762-5561, 18 km northwest of downtown Banff, boasts over six meters of snow annually and a season stretching nearly 200 days. The village is accessed by gondola from the valley floor and is best suited to intermediate skiers. Lift tickets cost $42 per day.

Lake Louise, tel. (403) 522-3555, Canada's largest ski area, spreads over four distinct mountain faces and provides something for everyone. Look for a vertical rise of 1,000 meters on the front face and endless powder-filled bowls over the back. Lift tickets run $45 per day.

Downhill skiing isn't the only winter activity around here. Many hiking trails are perfect for cross-country skiing. Pick up a copy of *Cross-country Skiing—Nordic Trails in Banff National Park* from one of the information centers. Also available in the area: sleigh rides, ice-skating, snowshoeing, and dogsledding.

ACCOMMODATIONS AND CAMPING

Banff

Right downtown, **Brewster's Mountain Lodge,** 204 Caribou St., P.O. Box 2286, Banff, AB T0L 0C0, tel. (403) 762-2900 or (800) 691-5085, features an eye-catching log exterior and an equally impressive lobby. Summer rates start at $170 s or d. Like most other accommodations in town, rates are slashed by up to 50% the rest of the year.

Two blocks off Banff Ave., **Bow View Motor Lodge,** 228 Bow Ave., P.O. Box 339, tel. (403) 762-2261 or (800) 661-1565, offers rooms for $120-130 s or d. Continuing north along Banff Ave. you'll come to a motel strip where **Spruce Grove Motel,** 545 Banff Ave., P.O. Box 471, tel. (403) 762-2112, offers basic rooms for $80 s or d—the least expensive rate in the area. A step up in standard is **Rundle Manor Apartment Hotel,** 348 Marten St., P.O. Box 1077, tel. (403) 762-5544 or (800) 661-1272, which charges $115 for one-bedroom suites and $175 for two-bedroom suites, each with a full kitchen. **Rundlestone Lodge,** 537 Banff Ave., P.O. Box 489, tel. (403) 762-2201 or (800) 661-8630, features a whirlpool, sauna, and laundry. Rooms start at $160, and many of them have balconies, fireplaces, and/or kitchenettes. The full-service

Banff Ptarmigan Inn, 337 Banff Ave., P.O. Box 1840, tel. (403) 762-2207 or (800) 661-8310, features tastefully decorated rooms, down comforters on all beds, and mountain views. Rooms are $164 s, $171 d.

The town's most expensive accommodation is also its best-known. The **Banff Springs Hotel,** P.O. Box 960, tel. (403) 762-2211 or (800) 441-1414, is one of the world's great mountain resorts, offering 825 guest rooms in 80 different configurations. The hotel also boasts 16 eateries, a health club, pool, outdoor jacuzzi, library, 27-hole golf course, tennis courts, and horseback riding. Standard rooms begin at $190 s or d in high season; view rooms are $290-350, and suites begin at $425.

Lake Louise

The best-known accommodation here is **Chateau Lake Louise,** P.O. Box 96, Lake Louise, AB T0L 1E0, tel. (403) 522-3511 or

Moraine Lake, near Lake Louise

ANDREW HEMPSTEAD

(800) 441-1414. Views at this historic 511-room lakeshore hotel are the equal of any mountain resort in the world. But all this historic charm and mountain scenery comes at a price. Summer rates start at $220 s or d for a standard room, $380 if you want a lake view. A much better deal, especially for those who like privacy, is **Paradise Lodge and Bungalows,** on the road up to the lake, P.O. Box 7, Lake Louise, AB T0L 1E0, tel. (403) 522-3595. Spread out around its well-manicured gardens are kitchen-equipped cabins ranging $140-190 per night and newly built suites for $210 s or d.

Down on the valley floor and within walking distance of Samson Mall are: **Mountaineer Lodge,** P.O. Box 150, tel. (403) 522-3844, open in summer only, $150 s or d; **Lake Louise Inn,** P.O. Box 209, tel. (403) 522-3791 or (800) 661-9237, where rooms start at $155 per night; and the elegant **Post Hotel,** P.O. Box 69, tel. (403) 522-3989 or (800) 661-1586, with stylish rooms from $240 s or d.

Hostels

Banff International Hostel, tel. (403) 762-4122, is just off Tunnel Mountain Rd. three km from downtown Banff. Facilities in this large modern hostel include a lounge area, recreation room, bike and ski workshop, large kitchen, self-service cafe, and laundry. Members of Hostelling International pay $19 per night, nonmembers $24. Of a similar high standard, and with an inexpensive cafe, is **Lake Louise International Hostel,** on Village Rd., one km from Samson Mall, tel. (403) 522-2200. Hostel members pay $19 per night in a four- or six-bed dorm, or $23.50 in a two-bed dorm. Nonmembers pay $25 and $29, respectively. Book well ahead to be assured of a bed at both these hostels.

Also within the park are four rustic hostels with outside toilets, no showers, and only basic kitchen facilities. They include: **Castle Mountain Hostel,** 32 km from Banff along the Bow Valley Parkway; **Mosquito Creek Hostel,** 24 km along the Icefields Parkway; **Rampart Creek Hostel,** a further 64 km along the Icefields Parkway; and **Hilda Creek Hostel,** near Sunwapta Pass at the park's north end. Rates range $9-11 for members, $15-16 for nonmembers. Reservations can be made at the hostels in Banff or Lake Louise.

Campgrounds

Although the park's 11 campgrounds hold well over 1,500 sites, all fill by early afternoon. Closest to Banff are **Tunnel Mountain Village II** and **Tunnel Mountain Trailer Court,** 3.5 km along Tunnel Mountain Road. The former has electrical hookups and is the only serviced campground in the park open year-round. The latter has full hookups. Both have hot showers but little privacy. Sites are $19-22 and no tents are allowed. Less than one km farther along the road is **Tunnel Mountain Village I,** which offers hot showers, private sites, firewood, and kitchen shelters, but no hookups. Sites are $16. Toward Lake Minnewanka northeast of town you'll find **Two Jack Lakeside,** $16 per night, and **Two Jack Lake Main,** $13 a night. **Johnston Canyon Campground, Castle Mountain Campground,** and **Protection Mountain Campground** are all along Bow Valley Parkway; $13-16 per night.

Lake Louise Campground, within easy walking distance of the village, is divided into two areas by the Bow River. One side has unserviced sites, the other serviced. The sites are close together, but some privacy and shade is provided by towering lodgepole pines. The unserviced (tent camping) sites have flush toilets, kitchen shelters, fire rings, and free firewood; $14 per night. Serviced (trailer camping) sites have power and flush toilets; $18.

Campgrounds along Icefields Parkway include **Mosquito Creek** (Km 24; $10), **Waterfowl Lake** (Km 57; $13), and **Rampart Creek** (Km 88; $10). Each has pit toilets, kitchen shelters, firewood, and fire rings, but no showers or hookups. All three are open from mid-June to early September, and Mosquito Creek stays open for winter camping.

FOOD

Banff

With over 100 restaurants to choose from, you're sure to find something that suits your taste and budget. The biggest concentration of eateries is along Banff Avenue. The **Cake Company,** 220 Bear St., tel. (403) 762-2330, serves great coffee, as well as a delicious range of pastries, muffins, and cakes baked daily on the premises.

A town favorite that has faithfully served locals for many years is **Melissa's,** 218 Lynx St., tel. (403) 762-5511, with huge breakfasts from $5 and typical Canadian-style lunches and dinners. **Bumper's,** 603 Banff Ave., tel. (403) 762-2622, is one of the town's busiest restaurants; large cuts of Alberta beef ($11-19), efficient service, and great prices attract the crowds. **Magpie & Stump,** 203 Caribou St., tel. (403) 762-4067, serves no-frills authentic Mexican food at reasonable prices. Lunch is priced from $5, dinner from $8.

The bistro-style **Coyote's Deli and Grill,** 206 Caribou St., tel. (403) 762-3963, emphasizes the health conscious—broiled chicken, vegetarian lasagna, and tempting desserts are favorites.

Guido's, 116 Banff Ave., tel. (403) 762-4002, serves homemade pasta topped with a variety of sauces. The **Grizzly House,** 207 Banff Ave., tel. (403) 762-4055, isn't cheap, but its eclectic decor and bizarre menu provide Banff's most unusual dining experience. Try the fondues of buffalo, rattlesnake, and alligator.

Among the 16 different eateries at the **Banff Springs Hotel** you'll find: **Koffie Haus,** serving reliable and reasonably priced meals; the **Alhambra Room,** a Spanish-style restaurant serving continental dishes; the **Alberta Room,** home of a $10.50 breakfast buffet; and the **Rob Roy Room,** a fine-dining restaurant renowned for its excellently prepared Alberta beef. For further dining information and reservations at the hotel, call (403) 762-2211.

Lake Louise

Down on the valley floor, **Samson Mall** houses a grocery store, a take-out pizza place, a bar, and the not-to-be-missed **Laggan's Mountain Bakery,** tel. (403) 522-2017, which is *the* place to hang out with a coffee and a freshly baked muffin. Another inexpensive place is **Bill Peyto's Cafe,** in the hostel on Village Road.

Diners often drive in from Banff specially to eat at **Lake Louise Station Restaurant,** in the old railway station at 200 Sentinel Rd., tel. (403) 522-2600. Its well-prepared main dishes average $16. **Chateau Lake Louise** features a choice of eateries, including: the **Poppy Room,** where a continental buffet breakfast is $9 and a pizza and pasta dinner buffet is $15; the **Edel-**

weiss Room, featuring great views of Lake Louise and the chateau's most elegant dining; and **Glacier Saloon,** a Western-style bar and grill serving light meals.

SERVICES AND INFORMATION

Transportation

The closest airport is an hour and a half away in Calgary. **Brewster,** tel. (403) 762-6700, operates an airporter service that leaves Calgary International Airport four times daily for Banff ($30 one-way) with three of those runs continuing to Lake Louise ($12.50 from Banff). **Greyhound,** tel. (403) 762-6767 or (800) 661-8747, offers scheduled daily service from the Calgary bus depot at 877 Greyhound Way SW, to Banff ($17.92 one-way) and Lake Louise ($19.45) and continuing along the TransCanada Hwy. to Vancouver. The trip between Vancouver and Banff takes 14 hours and costs $97.32 each way.

Getting around both Banff and Lake Louise is easiest on foot, although the **Banff Explorer** bus serves parts of Banff and both towns have cab services and outlets of major rental car companies.

Brewster, 100 Gopher St. (ticket office), tel. (403) 762-6700, offers a three-hour tour of Banff ($35), a four-hour tour of Lake Louise ($38), and a nine-hour tour from Calgary to Banff ($65).

Information

Banff Visitor Centre, 224 Banff Ave., houses information desks for **Parks Canada,** tel. (403) 762-1550, and the **Banff/Lake Louise Tourism Bureau,** tel. (403) 762-8421. Head to the Parks Canada side for details of Banff's natural wonders, advice on hiking trails, and permits for overnight backcountry travel. The tourism bureau is the place to find out about local accommodations, restaurants, and other practicalities. **Lake Louise Visitor Centre,** Samson Mall, Lake Louise, tel. (403) 522-3833, features interpretive displays, video programs, and park staff on hand to answer questions, issue backcountry camping permits, and recommend hikes suited to your ability. Both centers are open July-Aug., daily 8 a.m.-8 p.m.; June and September, daily 8 a.m.-6 p.m.; the rest of the year, daily 9 a.m.-5 p.m.

For more information on the park write to: Superintendent, Banff National Park, P.O. Box 900, Banff, AB T0L 0C0. For general tourism information write to: Banff/Lake Louise Tourism Bureau, P.O. Box 1298, Banff, AB T0L 0C0.

JASPER NATIONAL PARK

Like Banff National Park to its south, Jasper National Park is not in B.C. but across the border in Alberta. Nevertheless, it will be briefly covered here as a convenience to travelers making the circuit of all four contiguous Rocky Mountain parks. Northernmost of the four parks, 10,900-hectare Jasper is a stunning counterpart to its sister parks. Within its boundaries lie snow-capped peaks, vast icefields, beautiful glacial lakes, abundant hot springs, thundering rivers, and the most extensive backcountry trail system of any Canadian national park.

The park extends from the headwaters of the Smoky River in the north to the Columbia Icefield and Banff National Park in the south. To the east are rolling foothills; to the west, the Continental Divide. The park is bisected by two roads. The **Yellowhead Highway** runs east-west, from Edmonton to British Columbia, while the spectacular **Icefields Parkway** runs north-south, connecting Jasper to Banff. The main service center in the park is the town of **Jasper,** a smaller, less-commercial version of Banff, where you'll find a number of motels and restaurants.

Permits are required for entry into the park; they're available from all park gates as well as the park information center in Jasper. A one-day permit is $5 per person, and an annual Great Western Pass, good for entry to all 11 of western Canada's national parks, is $35 per person.

HISTORY

The first white man to enter what is now Jasper National Park was David Thompson, one of Canada's greatest explorers. He was looking for a pass through the mountains as part of a route to the Pacific Ocean. After a viable route was found, the North West Company built a post named Jasper's House (named after post proprietor Jasper Hawse) near the present townsite. Leading up to the end of the fur-trading era, many visitors came to the area and returned home with accounts of the region's natural splendor. Although at the turn of the 20th

century only seven homesteaders lived in the valley, the federal government foresaw a population explosion on the way—the railway was due to come through in 1910. To protect the valley from being overrun, the government established the boundaries of Jasper Forest Park in 1907. As a forest park, mining and logging were still allowed. Much of this activity was centered at **Pocahontas** (near the park's east gate), where a township was established and thrived. The Pocahontas mine closed in 1921 and many families relocated to Jasper's House, which had grown from a railway camp into a popular tourist destination. Jasper was officially designated a national park in 1930.

SIGHTS

Icefields Parkway

One of the world's great mountain drives, the 230-km Icefields Parkway runs astride the Continental Divide between Lake Louise and Jasper townsite. About halfway along the route, the road crests **Sunwapta Pass,** marking the boundary between Banff and Jasper National Parks. From there it's 108 km north to Jasper, past the Columbia Icefield (see below), the Sunwapta River, various glacial viewpoints, and **Sunwapta Falls.** At these falls 48 km north of Sunwapta Pass, the Sunwapta River abruptly changes direction and drops into a deep canyon. Two km farther downstream, the river flows into the much-wider **Athabasca River.**

Continuing north up the parkway you'll pass **Goat Lookout,** where mountain goats can occasionally be seen searching for salt licks along the riverbank, and **Athabasca Falls,** where the Athabasca River is forced through a narrow gorge and over a cliff into a cauldron of roaring water.

Columbia Icefield

The largest and most accessible of 17 glacial areas along the Icefields Parkway is 325-square-km Columbia Icefield at the south end of the park. It's a remnant of the last major glaciation

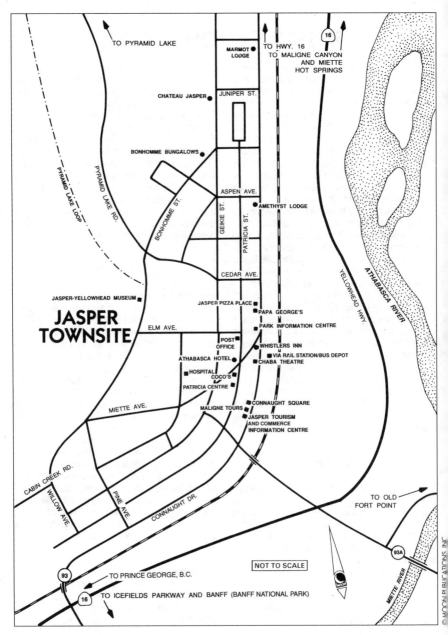

JASPER TOWNSITE

that covered most of Canada 20,000 years ago. The icefield has survived because of the elevation (1,900-2,800 meters above sea level), cold temperatures, and heavy snowfalls.

From the main body of the ice cap, which sits astride the Continental Divide, glaciers creep down three main valleys. **Athabasca Glacier,** visible from the Icefields Parkway, is the most accessible. A path to its toe traverses glacial till—a mixture of rock, sand, and gravel deposited by the retreating glacier. The speed at which glaciers advance and retreat varies with the long-term climate. Athabasca Glacier has retreated more than 1.5 km in the last 100 years. Currently it retreats two to three meters per year. The safest way to experience the icefield up close is with **Brewster,** at the VIA rail station, 607 Connaught Dr., tel. (403) 852-3332, which drives Snocoaches (specially developed tour vehicles with balloon tires) right onto the Athabasca Glacier. The 90-minute tour, which includes time spent walking on the glacier, costs $21.50 per person and operates mid-May to early October.

Overlooking Columbia Icefield is the **Icefield Centre,** a magnificent new facility featuring accommodations (see the listing for Columbia Icefield Chalet under "Accommodations and Camping," below) and a large display area detailing the story of glacier formation and movement. It's open May and September, daily 10 a.m.-5 p.m.; June-Aug., daily 10 a.m.-7 p.m.

Jasper Townsite

Jasper (pop. 3,800) is the park's main service center and an important crossroads. Highway 16 leads east from town to Edmonton and west to Prince George, while the Icefields Parkway leads 280 km south to Banff. Run by Parks Canada, the town is in a less dramatic setting than Banff but it's also quieter and less commercial.

At the back of town, the excellent, relatively new **Jasper-Yellowhead Museum and Archives,** 400 Pyramid Lake Rd., tel. (403) 852-3013, displays a collection of artifacts cataloguing the park's human history. The museum's extensive archives hold photos, documents, and maps. It's open June-Sept., daily 10 a.m.-9 p.m. If you like taxidermy, visit **The Den Wildlife Museum,** which exhibits stuffed animals in their "natural setting." It's down a dark stairway beneath the Whistlers Inn. Open year-round, daily 9 a.m.-10 p.m.; admission $2.50.

Vicinity of Jasper

For a thrilling ride to an unbeatable view, take the **Jasper Tramway,** located three km south of town on Icefields Parkway then another three km up Whistlers Road. The tramway's two 30-passenger cars climb 1,000 vertical meters up the steep north face of **The Whistlers,** taking seven minutes to reach the top. At the upper terminal, a one-km trail leads to a 2,470-meter summit. The tram operates in summer, daily 8 a.m.-10 p.m., shorter hours April-May and Sept.-Oct., closed the rest of the year. Roundtrip fare is $14.95. For more information call (403) 852-3093.

Mount Edith Cavell (3,363 meters) can be seen from the townsite and many other vantage points in the north end of the park. But the most impressive view of the peak could be from directly below it. To get there, head south on Hwy. 93A, then take a 14.5-km road leading to a parking area below the peak's northeast face.

Several lakes lie close to Jasper townsite. Take Pyramid Lake Rd. to **Patricia** and **Pyramid Lakes,** formed when glacial moraines dammed shallow valleys. Pyramid is backed by **Pyramid Mountain.** Both lakes are popular for picnicking, fishing, and boating. Boat rentals are available at **Pyramid Lake Resort,** tel. (403) 852-4900. East of town are **Edith** and **Annette Lakes,** perfect places for a picnic, swim, or pleasant walk. South of these lakes, and overlooking **Lac Beauvert,** is **Jasper Park Lodge,** the park's premier accommodation since 1921.

Maligne Canyon and Maligne Lake

One of the most spectacular canyons in the four contiguous parks lies 11 km north of Jasper townsite. Maligne Canyon has been eroded by the fast-flowing Maligne River. It's up to 50 meters deep, but is so narrow that squirrels often jump across. At the top of the canyon, opposite the teahouse, you'll note large potholes in the riverbed. These potholes are created when rocks and pebbles become trapped in what begins as a shallow depression. Under the force of the rushing water, the captive stones carve jug-shaped hollows into the soft bedrock. Explore the canyon from an interpretive trail that winds down from the parking lot, crossing the canyon

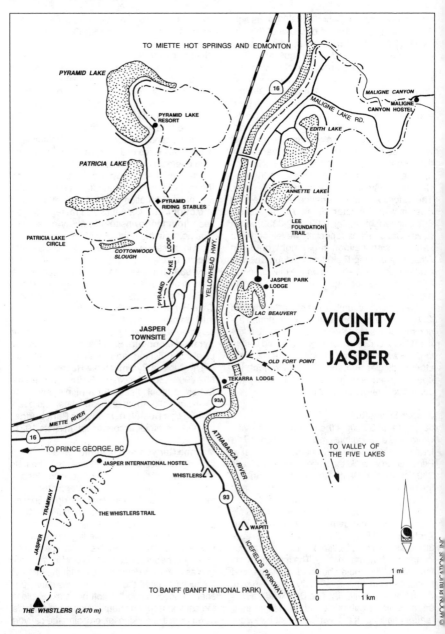

PYRAMID LAKE

TO MIETTE HOT SPRINGS AND EDMONTON

16

MALIGNE CANYON

MALIGNE CANYON HOSTEL

PYRAMID LAKE RESORT

MALIGNE LAKE RD.

EDITH LAKE

PATRICIA LAKE

ANNETTE LAKE

PYRAMID RIDING STABLES

LEE FOUNDATION TRAIL

PATRICIA LAKE CIRCLE

COTTONWOOD SLOUGH

PYRAMID LAKE LOOP

YELLOWHEAD HWY.

JASPER PARK LODGE

LAC BEAUVERT

JASPER TOWNSITE

VICINITY OF JASPER

OLD FORT POINT

TEKARRA LODGE

93A

MIETTE RIVER

ATHABASCA RIVER

16

TO PRINCE GEORGE, BC

TO VALLEY OF THE FIVE LAKES

JASPER INTERNATIONAL HOSTEL

WHISTLERS

93

THE WHISTLERS TRAIL

WAPITI

JASPER TRAMWAY

0   1 mi

0   1 km

TO BANFF (BANFF NATIONAL PARK)

ICEFIELDS PARKWAY

THE WHISTLERS (2,470 m)

MOON

© MOON PUBLICATIONS, INC.

six times. The most spectacular sections of the canyon can be seen from the first two bridges, at the upper end of the trail.

From the canyon, Maligne Lake Rd. climbs to **Medicine Lake,** which does a disappearing act each year—the water level fluctuates due to an underground drainage system. At the end of the road, 48 km from Jasper, is Maligne Lake, the largest glacier-fed lake in the Canadian Rockies and second-largest in the world. Here you can take a glass-enclosed boat on a 90-minute narrated cruise to oft-photographed **Spirit Island.** Cruises leave in summer, every hour on the hour 10 a.m.-5 p.m., with fewer sailings in May and September; $35 per person. Make bookings at the Maligne Tours office, 626 Connaught Dr., tel. (403) 852-3370.

Miette Hot Springs

These hot springs are at the end of an access road in the far east of the park. Water flowing into the pools is artificially cooled from 54° C to a soothing 39°. The pools are open mid-May to mid-June, daily 10:30 a.m.-9 p.m.; mid-June to September, daily 8:30 a.m.-10:30 p.m. Admission is $4.50, a towel $1, and lockers 25 cents. For more information call (403) 866-3939. The source of the springs is 200 meters from the back of the picnic area.

HIKING

For experienced hikers, Jasper's thousand kilometers of interconnecting backcountry trails can provide a wilderness adventure rivaled by few areas on the face of the earth. Opportunities are more limited for casual day-hikers. Most trails in the immediate vicinity of the townsite have little elevation gain and lead through montane forest to lakes. The trails at the base of Mt. Edith Cavell, in the Tonquin Valley, around Maligne Lake, and along the Icefields Parkway have more rewarding objectives and are more challenging.

Before setting off on any hike, whatever the length, go to the **Park Information Centre** in Jasper townsite for a trail map and information on trail conditions and closures. To prevent overuse, many longer trails operate on a quota system and you *must* pick up a permit before heading out; $6 per person per night.

Pyramid Lake Loop

• Length: 17 km (five hours) roundtrip
• Elevation gain: 150 meters
• Rating: easy/moderate

Numerous official and unofficial hiking trails web the benchland immediately west of Jasper townsite. From the parking lot opposite the Aquatic Centre on Pyramid Lake Rd., a well-marked trail climbs to a bluff overlooking the Athabasca River Valley. Bighorn sheep can often be seen grazing here. If you return to the trailhead from here, you will have hiked seven km. The trail continues north, disappearing into the montane forest until arriving at Pyramid Lake. Various trails lead back to town from the lake.

Patricia Lake Circle

• Length: five km loop (90 minutes roundtrip)
• Elevation gain: minimal
• Rating: easy

This trail begins across the road from the riding stables on Pyramid Lake Road. It traverses a mixed forest of aspen and lodgepole pine—prime habitat for elk, deer, and moose—and skirts Cottonwood Slough, where you'll see a number of beaver ponds.

Valley of the Five Lakes

• Length: 2.3 km (one hour) one-way
• Elevation gain: 60 meters
• Rating: easy

These small lakes nestled in an open valley make a worthwhile destination. From the trailhead 10 km south of Jasper townsite along the Icefields Parkway, the trail passes through a forest of lodgepole pine, crosses a stream, and climbs a ridge from where you'll have a panoramic view of surrounding peaks. As the trail descends to the lakes, turn left at the first intersection to a viewpoint between two of the lakes. These lakes are linked to Old Fort Point by a tedious 10-km trail through montane forest.

Jacques Lake

• Length: 12 km (3-3.5 hours) one-way
• Elevation gain: 100 meters
• Rating: moderate

This trail begins from a parking lot along Maligne Lake Rd., at the southeast end of Medicine Lake. It skirts numerous small lakes as it climbs gently through a narrow valley. On either side, the severely faulted Queen Elizabeth Ranges rise steeply above the valley floor, their strata tilted nearly vertical.

Lake Trail (East Side)
- Length: 3.2-km loop (one hour roundtrip)
- Elevation gain: minimal
- Rating: easy

This short trail begins at Maligne Lake, from the back of Parking Lot 2. From there it traverses the eastern shore of the lake to **Schäffer Viewpoint,** named for the first white person to see the valley. After dragging yourself away from the spectacular panorama, follow the trail into a forest of spruce and subalpine fir before looping back to the trailhead.

Opal Hills
- Length: 8.2-km loop (three hours roundtrip)
- Elevation gain: 455 meters
- Rating: moderate

This trail begins at the back of Parking Lot 1, climbing steeply for 1.5 km to a point where it divides. Both options end in the high alpine meadows of the Opal Hills; the trail to the right is shorter and steeper. Once in the meadow, you'll enjoy views of the entire Maligne Valley. Across Maligne Lake are the rounded Bald Hills, the Maligne Range, and, to the southwest, the distinctive twin peaks of Mts. Unwin (3,268 meters) and Charlton (3,217 meters).

Cavell Meadows
- Length: four km (90 minutes) one-way
- Elevation gain: 350 meters
- Rating: easy/moderate

This trail begins from the parking lot beneath Mt. Edith Cavell, 14.5 km from the Icefields Parkway. It climbs steadily through a forest of Engelmann spruce and subalpine fir to emerge facing the northeast face of Mt. Edith Cavell and Angel Glacier. The trail continues to higher viewpoints and an alpine meadow, filled with wildflowers in mid-July.

Astoria River
- Length: 19 km (6-7 hours) one-way
- Elevation gain: 450 meters
- Rating: moderate

Beginning opposite the hostel on Mt. Edith Cavell Rd., this trail descends through a forest on the north side of Mt. Edith Cavell for five km, then crosses the Astoria River and begins a long ascent into spectacular Tonquin Valley. Amethyst Lakes and the 1,000-meter cliffs of the Ramparts first come into view after 13 km. At the 17-km mark, a trail to the left climbs into Eremite Valley where there is a campground. The right fork continues, following the Astoria River to Tonquin Valley, Amethyst Lakes, and a choice of four campgrounds.

OTHER RECREATION

Mountain Biking
While the Icefields Parkway between Banff and Jasper attracts cyclists from around the world, the shorter, unpaved bike trails radiating from town are most popular with day-trippers. The brochure *Trail Bicycling Guide* lists the designated bike trails; it's available from Freewheel Cycle, 611 Patricia St., tel. (403) 852-3898.

Horseback Riding
Pyramid Riding Stables, on Pyramid Lake Rd., tel. (403) 852-3562, offers one-, two-, and three-hour guided rides for $18.50, $30, and $40, respectively. The one-hour trip follows a ridge high above town, providing excellent views of the Athabasca River Valley. **Sunrider Stables,** at Jasper Park Lodge, tel. (403) 852-4215, offers guided rides around Lake Annette; the one-hour trip is $22. **Ridgeline Riders,** at Maligne Lake, offers 3.5-hour guided rides high into the Bald Hills for $45. Book through Maligne Tours at 626 Connaught Dr., tel. (403) 852-3370.

Overnight pack trips are also available. They generally consist of four to six hours of riding per day, and one or more nights spent at a remote mountain lodge where you can hike, boat, fish, or ride. Rates start at $140 per person per day. For details contact **Skyline Trail Rides,** P.O. Box 207, Jasper, AB T0E 1E0, tel. (403) 852-4215; or **Tonquin Valley Packtrips,** P.O. Box 550, Jasper, tel. (403) 852-3909.

Canoeing and Whitewater Rafting
Half a dozen outfitters in Jasper offer river-running trips ranging from an easy float down the Athabasca River to a wild ride through the boulder-strewn rapids of the Maligne River. Most companies offer

a choice of rivers and provide transportation to and from downtown hotels. Expect to pay $35-45 for a two-hour trip on the Athabasca and $55 for a three-hour trip on the Maligne. For details and reservations contact **Jasper Adventure Centre,** in the Chaba Theatre, tel. (403) 895-5595; **Jasper Raft Tours,** tel. (403) 852-3612; **Maligne Tours,** tel. (403) 852-3370; **Rocky Mountain River Guides,** tel. (403) 852-3777; or **White Water Rafting,** tel. (403) 852-7238.

Fishing

Fishing in the park's many alpine lakes—for rainbow, brook, cutthroat, and lake trout, as well as pike, whitefish, and Dolly Varden—is excellent. Maligne Lake is the most popular fishing hole; in 1981 a record 10-kilogram rainbow trout was caught in its deep waters. Boats, bait, and tackle are available from the Boathouse at Maligne Lake, tel. (403) 852-3370. You'll also need a National Park fishing license ($6 per week, $13 per year), available from the park information center or On-line Sport & Tackle at 600 Patricia Street.

Several outfitters offer guided fishing trips on the lake. **Maligne Tours,** tel. (403) 852-3370, charges $80 a half day, $150 a full day. **Currie's Guided Fishing,** 414 Connaught Dr., tel. (403) 852-5650, leads trips to Maligne Lake (full day $149), as well as hike-in trips to other lakes (from $139). Currie's shop sells and rents tackle and rents canoes and fishing boats. **On-line Sport & Tackle,** 600 Patricia St., tel. (403) 852-3630, also offers guided trips, sells tackle, and rents canoes and boats (from $25 per day).

Climbing and Mountaineering

Jasper Climbing Schools & Guide Service runs two-day beginner's rock-climbing classes covering technique, safety, and use of equipment. Everything is supplied except lunch, gloves, and boots; $80. They also lead two-day courses for intermediates ($110), snow- and ice-climbing trips to Columbia Icefields ($90), and ascents of nearby summits. For dates and details contact Hans Schwarz, P.O. Box 452, Jasper, AB T0E 1E0, tel.(403) 852-3964.

Golfing

The world-famous **Jasper Park Lodge Golf Course** was designed by renowned golf-course architect Stanley Thompson. The 18-hole championship course follows the contours of the Athabasca River Valley and hugs the banks of turquoise-colored Lac Beauvert. The 6,598-meter course is a true test of accuracy, and with holes named "The Maze," "The Bad Baby," and "The Bay" you'll need lots of balls, literally. Green fees for 18 holes vary with the season; $75 in summer, $60 mid-May to June and mid-Sept. to mid-October. Club rentals are $30 and an electric cart is $32. For a tee time call (403) 852-6090.

Winter Activities

Winter is quiet in the park, but there's still plenty to do. **Marmot Basin Ski Area,** tel. (403) 852-3816, provides downhill skiers with 400 hectares of varying terrain served by seven lifts. The area is generally uncrowded and the snowfall high. The season runs from early December to late April. Lift tickets are $35.

Maligne Canyon becomes a unique attraction in winter, when the Maligne River freezes between the deep limestone walls and remarkable ice formations transform the canyon into a magical frozen world. **Maligne Tours,** 626 Connaught Dr., tel. (403) 852-3370, offers two-hour guided tours into the depths of the canyon throughout winter; $22 per person.

Also in winter, many snow-covered hiking trails are groomed for cross-country skiing (the booklet *Cross-country Skiing in Jasper National Park,* available at the park information center, details each trail and its difficulty); portions of Lac Beauvert and Pyramid Lake are cleared for ice-skating; and horse-drawn sleighs jingle their way around town.

ACCOMMODATIONS AND CAMPING

Hotels and Motels

The least expensive and most centrally located lodging within walking distance of downtown is the **Athabasca Hotel,** 510 Patricia St., P.O. Box 1420, Jasper, AB T0E 1E0, tel. (403) 852-3386. Rates are $75-129 s or d; the low-end rooms share bathrooms. Also downtown, **Whistlers Inn,** 105 Miette Ave., P.O. Box 250, tel. (403) 852-3361 or (800) 282-9919, features spacious rooms and a rooftop jacuzzi; $109 s, $119 d.

Marmot Lodge, 86 Connaught Dr., P.O. Box 687, tel. (403) 852-4471 or (800) 661-6521, features modern and stylishly decorated rooms, many with mountain views. Summer rates are from $138 s or d, from $80 the rest of the year. Closer to downtown and in the same price range is **Amethyst Lodge,** 200 Connaught Dr., P.O. Box 1200, tel. (403) 852-3394 or (800) 661-9935.

Chateau Jasper, 96 Geikie St., P.O. Box 1418, tel. (403) 852-5644 or (800) 661-9323, is one of Jasper's nicest lodgings. Rooms are large and the low ceilings give them a cozy feel; $250 s or d. Downstairs is an excellent restaurant. The town's best-known accommodation is **Jasper Park Lodge,** P.O. Box 40, tel. (403) 852-3301 or (800) 441-1414, on Lac Beauvert. It's the park's original resort, and boasts four restaurants, three lounges, horseback riding, tennis courts, a championship golf course, and Jasper's only covered shopping arcade. Basic rooms start at $354 s or d; off-season rates begin at $115.

Summer Lodging

Scattered around the park are a number of lodgings open summers only. **Bonhomme Bungalows,** on Bonhomme St., P.O. Box 700, tel. (403) 852-3209, offers basic cabins, each with TV, bathroom, and coffee-making facilities; $95-145 s or d. **Tekarra Lodge,** P.O. Box 669, tel. (403) 852-3058, is 1.5 km southeast of the townsite at the confluence of the Miette and Athabasca Rivers. Rooms in the lodge are $95 s or d; cabins, each with a kitchenette and wood-burning fire-

place, begin at $125. Down on the Icefields Parkway, four km south of the townsite, **Jasper House Bungalows,** P.O. Box 817, tel. (403) 852-4535, offers basic sleeping units for $80 and units with cooking facilities from $150. Spread along a picturesque bend on the Athabasca River, six km south of the townsite, is **Becker's Roaring River Chalets,** P.O. Box 579, tel. (403) 852-3779. One-bed sleeping rooms are $70, and chalets—each with a kitchenette, fireplace, and double bed—are $95 (or $120 for those on the riverfront). The park's newest lodging also has the most spectacular views. Opened in 1996, **Columbia Icefield Chalet,** tel. (403) 852-6550, features 32 standard rooms each with private bathroom. Summer rates range $120-155 s or d, while in May and the first couple of weeks of October rates start at $70.

Private Home Accommodations

At last count, more than 70 private residences in Jasper opened their doors to guests. The owners often offer nothing more than a room with a bed, but the price is right; $40-70 s or d. Usually the bathroom is shared with other guests or the family. Few have kitchens, and breakfast is not included; park bylaws prohibit private-home lodgings from serving breakfast. The positive side, apart from the price, is that your hosts are usually knowledgeable locals and town is only a short walk away. For a full listing that includes the facilities at each, write to Jasper Home Accommodation Association, P.O. Box

Athabasca Falls is just a short walk from one of the park's hostels.

ANDREW HEMPSTEAD

758, Jasper, AB T0E 1E0; use the association's brochure to book ahead.

Hostels
Hostelling International operates five hostels within Jasper National Park. The largest and most modern is **Jasper International Hostel,** on the road to the tramway, seven km from downtown Jasper ($10 by cab). It features 80 beds, a large kitchen, a common room, showers, an outdoor barbecue area, and mountain-bike rentals. Members of Hostelling International pay $17, nonmembers $22.

The other four hostels are more rustic; none have showers, but all have kitchens and prime locations. Rates are $10 for members, $15 for nonmembers. Closest to town is **Maligne Canyon Hostel,** beside the Maligne River and a short walk from the canyon. Also close to town, and with million-dollar views, is **Mt. Edith Cavell Hostel,** 13 km up Mt. Edith Cavell Road. Along the Jasper section of the Icefields Parkway, **Beauty Creek Hostel** is at Km 144 (from Lake Louise), just 17 km from Columbia Icefield, and **Athabasca Falls Hostel** is a further 54 km toward Jasper townsite at Km 198, its namesake falls only a few minutes' walk away. Reservations for all the above hostels can be made by calling (403) 852-3215.

Campgrounds
The 781-site **Whistlers Campground,** at the base of Whistlers Rd., three km south of Jasper townsite, is the largest campground in the Canadian Rockies. Prices vary with the services available—unserviced sites $15, powered sites $18, full hookups $22. The campground is open June to mid-October and has showers. Two km farther south is **Wapiti Campground,** which stays open year-round and also has showers; unserviced sites $15, powered sites $18. Northeast of the townsite, along Hwy. 16, are the smaller, more primitive **Snaring River Campground,** 17 km from Jasper, $10; and **Pocahontas Campground,** 45 km northeast, $13.

Six more campgrounds line the Icefields Parkway. **Wilcox Creek** and **Columbia Icefield Campgrounds** lie within two km of each other at the extreme southern end of the park. Both are primitive campgrounds with toilets, cooking shelters, and fire rings; sites are $10. Traveling north

from there, you'll come to **Jonas Creek, Honeymoon Lake,** and **Mt. Kerkeslin Campgrounds** along the next 50 km stretch of road. Each charges $10 per site per night. **Wabasso Campground** is along Hwy. 93A, 16 km south of Jasper townsite; $13.

FOOD

Cafes
Soft Rock Cafe, in Connaught Square at 622 Connaught Dr., tel. (403) 852-5850, starts the day by dishing up plates of waffles topped with cream and your choice of fresh fruit for $3.95. **Spooner's,** in the Patricia Centre at 610 Patricia St., tel. (403) 852-4046, is a second-floor cafe with stunning mountain views and a good range of coffees and light meals. A couple of doors away, **Coco's Cafe,** 608 Patricia St., tel. (403) 852-4550, is another coffee-lovers' meeting place.

Restaurants
Large and noisy **Jasper Pizza Place,** 402 Connaught Dr., tel. (403) 852-3225, is filled with bright furnishings and photos from Jasper's earliest days. Regular-size pizzas from the wood-fired oven start at $8.75; smaller pita pizzas, perfect for a lunchtime snack, are $3.25. **Papa George's,** 406 Connaught Dr., tel. (403) 852-3351, is a locals' favorite and one of Jasper's oldest restaurants. Breakfast is $3-6, lunch and dinner feature burgers, pasta, and steaks; daily specials are $10-15 and include soup and salad. Upstairs in the Patricia Centre, **Miss Italia Ristorante,** 610 Patricia St., tel. (403) 852-4002, features mountain views from tables indoors and out. Pastas average $10, with Taste of Italy choices, featuring a sampling of cuisine from three regions, for $15.

At **Fiddle River Seafood Company,** 620 Connaught Dr., tel. (403) 852-3032, upstairs in Connaught Square, the seafood is fresh, but expect to pay around $40 per person for a three-course meal. Six km south of town, the intimate and relaxing **Becker's Gourmet Restaurant,** tel. (403) 852-3535, offers inspiring views of Mt. Kerkeslin and the Athabasca River, along with well prepared steak and seafood dishes.

Jasper Park Lodge offers a choice of casual or elegant dining in four restaurants and three lounges. These include: **Obsessions,** with tempting French pastries, gourmet coffee, and homemade truffles and chocolates; **Spike Lounge Deck,** overlooking the golf course; the outdoor **La Terrasse,** overlooking Lac Beauvert; rustic **Moose's Nook,** featuring inexpensive Canadian fare; and the **Edith Cavell Room,** Jasper's finest fine-dining restaurant. For all lodge restaurant reservations call (403) 852-3301.

SERVICES AND INFORMATION

Transportation
The **VIA rail station** is at 607 Connaught Dr., tel. (800) 561-8630. Jasper is on the "Canadian" route, the only remaining transcontinental passenger rail route in the country. Trains run either way three times weekly. To the west the line divides, going to both Prince Rupert and Vancouver; to the east it passes through Edmonton and all points beyond. **Greyhound,** tel. (403) 852-3926 or (800) 661-8747, offers buses departing Jasper for most points in Canada, including Vancouver (three times daily, 12-13 hours, $97.50 one-way), and Edmonton (five times daily, 4.5 hours, $47.08 one-way) with connections to Calgary, and Prince Rupert (once daily, 18 hours, $123.64 one-way). Between June and the end of September, **Brewster,** tel. (403) 852-3332 or (800) 661-1152, operates an airporter service between Jasper and Calgary International Airport ($56 one-way), picking up passengers in Banff ($42 one-way to Jasper), and Lake Louise ($36 one-way to Jasper).

Public transportation within the park is limited. The **Maligne Lake Shuttle** runs out to Maligne Lake eight times daily ($20 roundtrip) and will make drops at Maligne Canyon; tel. (403) 852-3370. **Avis, Budget,** and **National Tilden** have car rental outlets in town. Another way to get around is on a tour with **Brewster,** tel. (403) 852-3332; a three-hour Discover Jasper tour is $32. **Maligne Tours,** tel. (403) 852-3370, offers a variety of tours including one to Maligne Lake; $50. **Jasper Adventure Centre,** in the Chaba Theatre at 604 Connaught Dr., tel. (403) 895-5595, is the agent for a number of local tour operators.

Information
The Parks Canada **Park Information Centre,** tel. (403) 852-6786, occupies a beautiful old stone building in Athabasca Park on Connaught Drive. The staff provides general information on the park and can direct you to hiking opportunities and issue backcountry permits. Maps, books, and local publications are for sale in back, and the day's interpretive programs are posted out front. The center is open in summer, daily 8 a.m.-8 p.m.; the rest of the year, daily 9 a.m.-5 p.m. For more information on the park write to Superintendent, Jasper National Park, P.O. Box 10, Jasper, AB T0E 1E0.

At **Jasper Tourism and Commerce Information Centre,** 632 Connaught Dr., P.O. Box 98, Jasper, AB T0E 1E0, tel. (403) 852-3858, the friendly staff never seems to tire of explaining that all the rooms in town are full. They will happily ring around to find accommodations for you. The center also stocks brochures on activities, shopping, and restaurants. It's open in summer, daily 8 a.m.-8 p.m.; the rest of the year, Mon.-Fri. 9 a.m.-5 p.m.

BOB RACE

CENTRAL BRITISH COLUMBIA

Ranging from the western slopes of the Rocky Mountains to the Pacific Ocean, central British Columbia holds such varied natural features as the massive Fraser River, the lofty peaks of the Cariboo and Coast Mountains, and the deeply indented coastal fjords around Bella Coola.

The region's history is dominated by colorful sagas of Canada's biggest gold rush, when over 100,000 miners and fortune seekers passed through the area on their way to the gold fields. But the best remembered man in these parts was not a miner but an explorer. In 1773, Alexander Mackenzie left the Fraser River for the final leg of his epic transcontinental journey. Fourteen days later he reached the Pacific Ocean, becoming the first person to cross the continent.

Today the most heavily traveled route through Central B.C. is the TransCanada Highway, which for the purposes of this book also forms the region's southern boundary. In the east of the province, the highway bisects **Glacier National Park,** a small but spectacular park of glaciers and towering peaks. Heading west from the park, the highway passes the heli-skiing haven of **Revelstoke** and the watery playground of **Shuswap Lake** before coming to the large population center of **Kamloops.**

From Kamloops, two highways lead north. Highway 5 accesses **Wells Gray** and **Mount Robson Provincial Parks,** the former a vast forested wilderness and the latter named for one of the most spectacular mountain peaks in all of Canada. The other route, Hwy. 97, runs through **Cariboo Country,** best-known for the 1860s' gold-rush town of **Barkerville,** now completely restored and one of the highlights of a trip north.

GLACIER NATIONAL PARK

Encompassing 135,000 hectares of the Selkirk Mountains west of the Rocky Mountain Trench, this park is a wonderland of snowcapped peaks, vast icefields, thundering waterfalls, steep-sided valleys, and fast-flowing rivers. The TransCanada Highway bisects the park, cresting at 1,327-meter **Rogers Pass.** From the summit, Golden is 80 km east and Revelstoke is 72 km west.

Those from south of the 49th parallel probably associate the park's name with the American

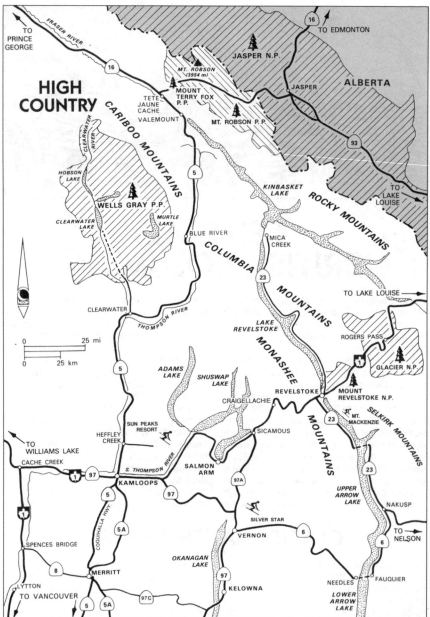

© MOON PUBLICATIONS, INC.

national park in Montana. The two parks share the same name and glaciated environment, but the similarities end there. In the "other" park, buses shuttle tourists here and there and the backcountry is crowded with hikers. Here in the Canadian version, commercialism is almost totally lacking and use of the backcountry is blissfully minimal.

The best place to start a visit to the park is **Rogers Pass Information Centre.** Looking south from the center, you can see the **Illecillewaet, Asulkan,** and **Swiss Glaciers.** As far as actual "sights" go, driving through the park you'll be surrounded by one of the most awe-inspiring panoramas visible from any Canadian highway. Each roadside viewpoint seems to outdo the last. You can also get out of the car and go hiking to get a better feeling for the park, but most of the trails here entail strenuous climbs.

Through-traffic excepted, permits are required for entry into Glacier National Park; they're available from the information center. A one-day permit is $5 per person to a maximum of $10 per vehicle, and an annual Great Western Pass, good for entry to all 11 of western Canada's national parks, is $35 per person to a maximum of $70 per vehicle.

THE LAND

Regardless of whether you approach the park from the east or west, you'll be climbing from a valley only 600 meters above sea level to 1,327-meter Rogers Pass in under 15 kilometers. The pass is not particularly high, but it's impressive. Surrounding peaks, many topping 3,000 meters, rise dramatically from the pass and draw massive amounts of precipitation from eastward-moving clouds. The resulting heavy snows feed more than 400 glaciers and permanently cloak some 14% of the park's landscape in snow and ice. Most of the glaciers lie in the park's southern half. Notable among them are Deville Icefield, which surrounds 3,393-meter Mt. Dawson, the park's highest peak, and Illecillewaet Icefield, whose glacial arms can be viewed up close from hiking trails starting at the Illecillewaet Campground.

Flora

Three distinct vegetation zones can be seen within the park—montane (600-1,300 meters), subalpine (1,300-1,900 meters), and alpine (1,900 to 3,000-plus meters). The montane forest supports a lush variety of tree species, including mountain hemlock, subalpine fir, Engelmann spruce, western red cedar, western hemlock, lodgepole pine, whitebark pine, western white pine, black cottonwood, Douglas fir, aspen, and white birch.

Flower lovers will be impressed by the 600 species of flowering plants that have been identified within the park. The best time to see wildflowers in the high meadows and forests is early August, though an amazing profusion of color sweeps through the lower elevation forests starting in June, and in July the edge of the high-

JANE AND BRUCE KING

Daisies carpet Glacier National Park's lower elevations in summer.

way and avalanche paths turn bright yellow with wild lilies.

Fauna

The rugged terrain and long hard winters in Glacier National Park mean that resident mammals are a tough and hardy bunch. Healthy populations of both black and grizzly bears inhabit the park. The black bears often feed along the roadside in late spring. Grizzlies are less common and tend to remain in the backcountry, but early in the season, lingering snow can keep them at lower elevations; look for them on avalanche slopes. As is the case throughout the mountains, smaller mammals are most common. Columbia ground squirrels hang around campgrounds and picnic areas, and hoary marmots inhabit rocky areas at higher elevations. The only other common mammals in the park are moose, which live along Beaver Valley, and mountain goats, which live on and around all major peaks.

HISTORY

In a scenario familiar throughout western Canada, the proclamation of Glacier National Park was influenced by the Canadian Pacific Railway's desire to see tourists use its rail line. For CPR engineers, finding a passable train route through the Columbia Mountains proved a formidable challenge. The major obstacle was not the elevation, but the threat of avalanche; extremely high snowfalls in the area were coupled with narrow valleys and steep approaches from both east and west, all attributes spelling danger.

In 1881 Maj. A.B. Rogers, chief engineer of the CPR, scaled Rogers Pass from the west, along the Illecillewaet River. The following year he climbed the pass again, this time from the east. His success in reaching the pass from both directions led him to declare the route feasible for a railway. Through the next three summers rail workers toiled with picks and shovels, finally completing a railbed on 7 November 1885. The last spike was driven into the ground at Craigellachie, 100 km to the west, and the transcontinental rail line was opened, with Rogers Pass an integral link in the vital transportation corridor.

To coincide with the opening, a national park was proclaimed, protecting the pass and surrounding wilderness and, much to the delight of the cash-strapped CPR, bringing visitors to the area—by rail of course. For the next three decades the CPR operated passenger and freight services over the pass, thrilling thousands of pioneer passengers. Unfortunately, despite railway engineering ingenuity, frequent and devastating avalanches took their toll on the tracks, forcing the CPR to tunnel under Mount Macdonald and the pass in 1916. The rerouted line bypassed the park's most spectacular scenery, and the number of visitors to the park dropped dramatically.

TransCanada Highway

In the early 1950s, a new team of engineers tackled the same problem—this time in an effort to build a highway across the pass. The tunnel approach that had worked for the railway was deemed impractical for a highway, so a new solution to the avalanche danger was required. In 1962 a route through the national park and over the pass was completed—this time with the addition of concrete snowsheds over sections of the highway. At the same time, the world's largest mobile avalanche-control program was created to stave off danger here. Experts constantly monitor weather and snow conditions so they can accurately predict when and where avalanches will occur. Then they close the highway and dislodge potential slides with mobile howitzers, thereby stabilizing the slopes.

HIKING

The park's 21 hiking trails cover 140 km and range from short interpretive walks to long, steep, and difficult climbs. Aside from the interpretive trails, most gain a lot of elevation, rewarding the energetic hiker with outstanding views. Along flat ground, reasonably fit hikers can usually cover three kilometers (or more) in an hour. But on Glacier National Park's steep trails, up to double that time should be allowed. Opportunities for long-distance backcountry trips are limited to the far east end of the park. If you're planning an overnight trip into the backcountry you'll need to register and pick up a permit ($6 per person

ANDREW HEMPSTEAD

The snowcapped peaks of Glacier National Park can be seen from the highway.

per night) from the information center. Remember, many of the park's high-elevation trails are covered in snow until well into July.

The two most popular interpretive trails are the **Abandoned Rails Interpretive Trail** (one km; 20 minutes roundtrip), which starts at the information center, and the **Meeting of the Waters Trail** (one km; 25 minutes roundtrip), which starts behind Illecillewaet Campground, four km south of the information center. The first four trails detailed below also start at Illecillewaet Campground.

Avalanche Crest
- Length: 4.2 km (2.5 hours) one-way
- Elevation gain: 800 meters
- Rating: moderate/difficult

This trail begins behind the Illecillewaet Campground, four km south of Rogers Pass Information Centre. As you face the large information board, the trail leads off to your left, climbing steeply through a subalpine forest for the first three km, then leveling out and providing stunning views below to Rogers Pass and south to Illecillewaet and Asulkan Glaciers.

Great Glacier
- Length: 4.8 km (two hours) one-way
- Elevation gain: 320 meters
- Rating: easy/moderate

Of the trails beginning from the Illecillewaet Campground, the Great Glacier Trail has the least elevation gain. But hard-core hikers will get the opportunity to scramble up rocky slopes to the toe of the Illecillewaet Glacier, 340 vertical meters higher.

Asulkan Valley
- Length: 6.5 km (four hours) one-way
- Elevation gain: 930 meters
- Rating: moderate/difficult

While elevation on this trail is similar to others in the steep-sided Illecillewaet River Valley, it is gained over a longer distance, meaning a less strenuous outing. Nevertheless, a full day should be allowed roundtrip. From the back of Illecillewaet Campground, the trail follows Asulkan Brook through a valley of dense subalpine forest. Whereas other trails lead to panoramic overlooks, the highlight of this trail's final destination is a view of the immense icefield rising high above you.

Abbott Ridge
- Length: five km (3.5 hours) one-way
- Elevation gain: 1,040 meters
- Rating: difficult

Winding up the west slope of a steep valley, this trail is for the physically fit; the gradient averages 20%. For the first 2.5 km, wide switchbacks lead up to Marion Lake. The trail then continues upward to a high treeless ridge offering views extending eastward across the Illecillewaet Icefield and adjoining glaciers. The ridge itself rises a further 150 meters to the 2,454-meter summit of Mt. Abbott.

Balu Pass
- Length: five km (3.5 hours) one-way
- Elevation gain: 1,020 meters
- Rating: difficult

From the information center parking lot, this trail climbs steeply and steadily between 2,606-meter Mt. Cheops to the south and a ridge of 2,700-meter peaks to the north. As elevation is gained, the valley closes in and the trail becomes steeper, finally ending at a pass 2,300 meters above sea level.

Hermit
- Length: 2.8 km (two hours) one-way
- Elevation gain: 940 meters
- Rating: difficult

This trail begins from the west side of the highway one km north of the information center. It climbs *very* steeply through a subalpine forest, breaking out above the treeline and ending at a view of glaciated peaks towering 1,000 meters above. Snow lingers on this trail well into July, so check conditions before heading out.

Copperstain
- Length: 16 km (seven hours) one-way
- Elevation gain: 1,225 meters
- Rating: difficult

The Beaver Gravel Pit, 12 km northeast of Rogers Pass Information Centre, is the trailhead for two overnight hikes, including this one to alpine meadows flanked by 2,320-meter Bald Mountain and 2,606-meter Copperstain Mountain. The climb is steady at first, ascending the Beaver River Valley for four km, then branching north along Grizzly and Copperstain Creeks for the final, painful ascent to the meadows. Also from the gravel pit, a 42-km trail leads up the Beaver River Valley to the park's extreme southeast corner. Backcountry camping is allowed anywhere along these two trails, but register first at the information center.

ACCOMMODATIONS AND CAMPING

Glacier Park Lodge
This lodge at Rogers Pass is a Best Western affiliate and the only motel in the park. It offers 50 midsize rooms, a restaurant, cafe, and heated outdoor pool. Summer rates are from $115 s,

$125 d; off-season rates are lower. For bookings call (250) 837-2126. Motels of a similar standard but with much lower rates can be found in Golden, 80 km to the east, and Revelstoke, 72 km to the west.

Campgrounds
Illecillewaet Campground, 3.5 km south of Rogers Pass, is open year-round, although the snow is not cleared in winter. Facilities include kitchen shelters, flush toilets, picnic tables, and firewood ($3 per site). Sites are not particularly private and the surrounding peaks and towering cedar trees mean little sunshine before noon, but the campground is the perfect base for exploring as it's the trailhead for the park's main concentration of hiking trails. All sites are $13. Smaller **Loop Brook Campground** holds just 20 sites, and also costs $13 per night. It's three km beyond the Illecillewaet Campground toward Revelstoke; open July-September.

With just 77 campsites in the entire park and no reservations taken, chances are good that both campgrounds will be full if you arrive late in the afternoon. If that's the case, head either 40 km west to **Canyon Hot Springs Resort,** tel. (250) 837-2420, where you'll find hot springs, showers, a laundry, restaurant, and sites for $17-21 per night; or 30 km east to **Kinbasket Lake Resort,** tel. (250) 344-6693, which offers similar facilities (but no hot springs) and sites for $16-19.

INFORMATION

Rogers Pass Information Centre, tel. (250) 837-6274, is 1.2 km north of the actual pass and resembles the old-fashioned snowsheds that once protected the railroad from avalanches. The center's fascinating displays focus on the

---

TIME TRAVEL

Glacier National Park falls within two time zones. If you pass through the park westbound, turn your watch *back* one hour to **Pacific standard time.** If you're eastbound, turn it *forward* one hour to **mountain standard time.**

park's natural and human history. Videos on various aspects of the park are shown on the television (the viewing area by the fireplace is a great spot to whittle away time while waiting for the clouds to lift), and the center's theater screens *Snow War,* an award-winning documentary on avalanche protection. Staff members provide information on trail conditions and closures, conduct interpretive programs, and lead guided hikes.

The center is also the only place in the park to buy park passes, necessary for those planning on any hiking or camping. (Rangers regularly check for passes at all trailheads.) If you already have an annual pass, it must be presented for admission to the information center. Hours are 8 a.m.-8 p.m. daily during the peak summer season, 9 a.m.-5 p.m. daily in late spring and early fall, and Mon.-Fri. 9 a.m.-4 p.m. the rest of the year.

REVELSTOKE TO SALMON ARM

REVELSTOKE

Revelstoke lies at the confluence of the Illecillewaet River and the mighty Columbia, and is surrounded by mountains—the Monashees to the west and the Selkirks to the east. The setting couldn't be more spectacular.

An 1850s' gold rush along the Columbia River brought the first Europeans to the area, but the town really began to grow with the coming of the railroad in the 1880s. In fact, the city is named for Lord Revelstoke, who provided funding for completion of the Canadian Pacific Railway's line through town. Finally, the TransCanada Highway came to town earlier this century, helping turn Revelstoke into today's midsize city of 6,500.

The historic downtown core has been rejuvenated and centers around the appealing, all-brick Grizzly Plaza. The town holds a couple of museums, but the main attractions are further afield, including two massive dams and a national park on the back doorstep (see "Mount Revelstoke National Park," below).

Museums
Railway buffs shouldn't miss **Revelstoke Railway Museum,** a re-creation of an early Canadian Pacific Railway station. Reflecting the importance of this mode of transportation in Revelstoke's history, the museum centers around a massive 1948 steam locomotive and Business Car No. 4, the ultimate in early rail-travel luxury. Admission is adults $4, seniors $3, children $2. Open in summer, daily 9 a.m-7 p.m.; the rest of the year, Mon.-Fri. 1-4 p.m. It's on Victoria Rd., between the TransCanada Hwy. and downtown, tel. (250) 837-6060.

Revelstoke Museum, in an old post office building on the corner of Boyle Ave. and 1st St., preserves plenty of pioneer memorabilia and a great collection of historical black-and-white photos, and offers displays on local industries, early Chinese miners, and skiing at Mt. Mackenzie. Upstairs is the local **art gallery.** Open in summer, Mon.-Fri. 1-5 p.m.; the rest of the year, Monday, Wednesday, Friday 1-4:30 p.m. Admission is by donation.

Dams
The Columbia River, North America's third-longest, is controlled by many dams. Four of these are in British Columbia and two are in the vicinity of Revelstoke. The dams are also used to generate hydroelectric power.

Revelstoke Dam, eight km north of the city on Hwy. 23, was completed in 1985. It's 470 meters wide, 175 meters high, and contains over two million cubic meters of concrete. The massive reservoir behind the dam stretches over 100 km and covers 11,000 hectares.

Nestled in the valley downstream of the dam is the generating station, capable of producing over two million kilowatts of electricity. Exhibits at the two-story **Revelstoke Dam Visitor Centre,** above the generating station, explain the valley's history and the operation and impact of the dams. From the center, a high-speed elevator whisks visitors to the top of the dam for an excellent view. The center is open weekdays only, in summer 8 a.m.-7 p.m., the rest of the year 9 a.m.-5 p.m. Admission is free.

Upstream of Revelstoke Dam is **Mica Dam and Generating Station,** at **Mica Creek,** 140 km by road to the north. This dam is much larger, rising 200 meters, stretching 800 meters across the Columbia River Valley, and containing 14.8 trillion cubic meters of water in **Kinbasket Lake.** The lake extends north to Valemount and south to a point just north of Golden. **Mica Dam Visitor Centre** is open in summer, daily 10:30 a.m.-4:30 p.m.; tours of the powerhouse are offered at 11 a.m. and 1:30 p.m. A gas station and a commercial campground, both 74 km north of Revelstoke, are the only facilities along this stretch of Hwy. 23.

Skiing

The interior mountain ranges of British Columbia attract heli-skiers from around the world, and Revelstoke, nestled between the Selkirk and Monashee Mountains, is the center of much of the action. **Selkirk Tangiers Heli-skiing,** P.O. Box 1409, Golden, BC V0A 1H0, tel. (250) 344-5016 or (800) 663-7080, operates from town, of-

fering all-inclusive packages—including seven days heli-skiing (over 30,000 vertical meters), accommodations, and meals—from around $4,000. Three- and five-day packages are also offered and early-season discounts apply.

C.M.H. Heli-skiing, P.O. Box 1660, Banff, AB T0L 0C0, tel. (403) 762-7100 or (800) 661-0252, has heli-skiing lodges scattered throughout the remote backcountry of British Columbia, but in Revelstoke, the company's guests stay right downtown at the Regent Inn and are whisked off daily for the mountains.

Snowcat skiing can get you some prime powder at a fraction of the price of heli-skiing. The folks at **CAT Powder Skiing,** P.O. Box 1479, Revelstoke, BC V0E 2S0, tel. (250) 837-5151 or (800) 991-4455, are the local experts, using their own lodge in downtown Revelstoke as a base. Each day begins with a bus trip out to

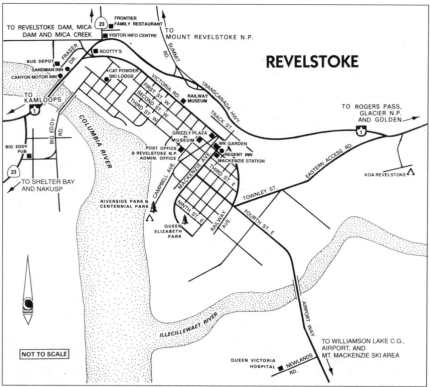

Revelstoke Dam

JANE AND BRUCE KING

the Mt. Mackenzie Ski Area. From there the snowcat takes skiers high into the Monashee Mountains for an average 4,000-5,000 vertical meters of powder skiing a day. Packages include skiing, accommodations, and all meals, and cost around $700 for two days, $1,000 for three days.

The only lift-served skiing near Revelstoke is **Mt. Mackenzie Ski Area,** six km south of downtown. Rumors of massive expansions have been rife for years, but nothing has happened yet. The resort's two chairlifts, one T-bar, and one rope tow serve a vertical rise of 680 meters. Facilities include ski rentals, a ski school, cafeteria, and bar. The season generally lasts from mid-December to late March. Closed Tuesday and Wednesday. For snow reports or further information call (250) 837-5268.

Selkirk Lodge

Operated by Selkirk Tangiers Heli-skiing, this lodge is high on the Albert Icefield, many miles from the nearest road. In winter it's accessible only by helicopter. Once the helicopter drops you at the lodge, you're free to cross-country ski or telemark to your heart's desire; the diverse terrain is suitable for skiers of all ability levels. The lodge itself is rustic but comfortable. On-site hosts lead ski tours and cook all meals. Seven-night packages are around $1,000, including accommodations, all meals, and helicopter transfers from Revelstoke.

Entertainment

In July and August, entertainment takes place most evenings at the **Grizzly Plaza bandshell**—look for singing, dancing, comedy, or magic shows. For music and dancing, the young crowd heads for **Big Eddy Pub,** 2108 Big Eddy Rd., tel. (250) 837-9072. For a quieter evening, head to the **One Twelve Lounge,** in the Regent Inn at 112 1st St., tel. (250) 837-2107, or the poolside lounge at the **Sandman Inn** on the TransCanada Hwy., tel. (250) 837-5271.

Accommodations

Between the highway and downtown, **CAT Powder Ski Lodge,** 1601 3rd St., tel. (250) 837-5151 or (800) 991-4455, is a recently renovated motel with comfortable beds in well-furnished rooms, a large indoor whirlpool, and a restaurant. It's a base for a snowcat skiing operation (see "Skiing," above), so summer is the off-season and rooms are great value at $48 s, $53 d; golf packages are also a good deal. Right downtown, the restored **Regent Inn,** 112 1st St., tel. (250) 837-2107, serves as the wintertime base of C.M.H. Heli-skiing. The inn offers comfortable and well-furnished rooms, a restaurant, cafe, bar, and lounge. Rates are $99 s, $114 d, including breakfast.

Out on the highway are many more motels, including the **Canyon Motor Inn,** 1911 Fraser Dr., tel. (250) 837-5221, $49 s, $59 d; and the **Sandman Inn,** 1821 Fraser Dr., tel. (250) 837-5271, with a heated pool and a 24-hour restaurant, $85 s, $90 d.

Camping

Campgrounds are plentiful in and around Revelstoke. **KOA Revelstoke** is off the Trans-Canada Hwy. six km east of downtown, tel. (250) 837-2085. The well-kept campground offers grassy sites, lots of trees, a swimming pool, propane-filling facilities, a well-stocked store, free hot showers, laundry facilities, and a main lodge that looks like a Swiss chalet. Unserviced sites are $20.50, full hookups $25. It's open mid-April to mid-October.

Quiet **Williamson Lake Campground** lies on the edge of a warm lake perfect for swimming. Shaded grassy sites, hot showers, a picnic shelter, and fire pits are all just above the shoreline. Sites are $13-18. The campground is seven km south of town on Airport Way, tel. (250) 837-5512. Finally, along Hwy. 23 between Revelstoke and Shelter Bay are three provincial parks offering sites for $9.50.

Food

For breakfast, head to **Scotty's,** behind the Shell gas station, tel. (250) 837-4464. The service is fast and efficient, and five bucks will get you the daily special or most any cooked meal on the menu. Also out on the highway is the **Frontier Family Restaurant,** tel. (250) 837-5119, a typical roadside diner with an atmosphere that lives up to its name. The wood interior is decorated with red-and-white checkered curtains, cowboy boots, hats, antlers, and cattle horns; the waitresses wear jeans; and a sign outside says "Y'all come back, y'hear!" On top of all that, the food is good. Huge breakfasts cost around $6 (try the "Hide-yer-plate-flapjacks"). Lunch is similarly priced, and dinner is $11-15.

Downtown, **Mackenzie Station,** 212 Mackenzie Ave., tel. (250) 837-5040, is a small cafe/bakery open for lunch. On the next block is **WK Garden,** 119 Mackenzie Ave., tel. (250) 837-2082, which offers a good selection of well-priced Chinese dishes; lunch specials from $6. The stylish decor and relaxed atmosphere of **One Twelve Restaurant,** at the Regent Inn, 112 1st St., tel. (250) 837-2107, make it a popular place to go if you're in the mood for a bit of a splurge. Closed Sunday. In the same inn, and open daily, is **Dapper Dan's,** offering a choice of Mexican food, burgers, soups, and salads for $6-8.

Services and Information

Greyhound buses come through Revelstoke four to seven times daily in both directions along the TransCanada Highway. The depot is by the Sandman Inn at 1899 Fraser Dr., tel. (250) 837-5874.

Queen Victoria Hospital is on Newlands Rd. (off Airport Way), on the southeast side of town, tel. (250) 837-2131. The **post office** is a couple of blocks from downtown at 313 3rd Street.

Revelstoke Visitor Info Centre is on the TransCanada Hwy. by the Hwy. 23 N turnoff, tel. (250) 837-5345. It's open in summer, daily 8 a.m.-8 p.m., the rest of the year Mon.-Fri. 8:30 a.m.-4:30 p.m. The **Revelstoke National Park administration office** is in the post office building at 313 3rd St., tel. (250) 837-7500. It's open year-round, Mon.-Fri. 8:30 a.m.-4:30 p.m.

MOUNT REVELSTOKE NATIONAL PARK

Visitors to this 26,000-hectare national park can experience a high alpine environment without any strenuous hiking; the main access road into the park, Meadows in the Sky Parkway, climbs abruptly from the valley bottom, gaining nearly 1,500 meters of elevation before reaching a high alpine meadow over 2,000 meters above sea level.

The park protects the highest peaks of the **Clachnacudiann Range,** a northern arm of the Selkirk Mountains. The forested slopes of the range come to an icy apex around the Clachnacudiann Glacier and surrounding peaks, such as **Mt. Coursier** and **Mt. Inverness,** both 2,637 meters high. The park's diverse vegetation includes forests of ancient cedar along the Illecillewaet River, subalpine forests of Engelmann spruce and fir on higher slopes, and finally, above the treeline, meadows of low-growing shrubs that come alive with color for a few weeks in midsummer.

As with all Canadian national parks, a permit is required for entry; in this case it only applies for travel on the Meadows in the Sky Parkway (see below). Permits are issued at the park gate, at the lower end of the parkway. A one-day permit is $5 per person to a maximum of $10 per vehicle, and an annual Great Western Pass, good for entry to all 11 of western Canada's national parks, is $35 per person to a maximum of $70 per vehicle.

Meadows in the Sky Parkway

East of Revelstoke the TransCanada Highway follows the Illecillewaet River, the park's southern boundary. Along this 25-km stretch you'll pass a couple of short interpretive trails, but the park's beauty is best appreciated from Meadows in the Sky Parkway, a 26-km road that leaves the highway and climbs to a high alpine meadow—the most spectacular part of the park.

The road is very steep, gaining well over one kilometer of elevation as it climbs seemingly endless hairpin bends through a subalpine forest of Engelmann spruce, hemlock, and the odd towering cedar. The summit area is snowed in until July, so try to plan your trip after this time. Over the years, high usage of the summit area created problems, so a few years back the final kilometer to the summit was blocked to private vehicles and a free shuttle-bus service established. The bus runs between a parking lot at Balsam Lake and the end of the road at Heather Lake. It operates daily 10 a.m.-6 p.m. in summer, starting as soon as the snow melts off the road—usually late July at the earliest. It's also possible to walk this final stretch; the trail climbs 90 meters in elevation and takes around 20 minutes each way. From the top, the panoramic view takes in the Columbia River Valley and the distant Monashee Mountains.

Hiking

The park doesn't have an extensive network of hiking trails—just 10 marked trails totaling 65 km in length. Most take under an hour and are posted with interpretive panels. Along the TransCanada Hwy., the 500-meter-long **Giant Cedars Interpretive Trail** (allow 15 minutes) traverses a meadow before disappearing into an ancient cedar forest and then along a sparkling creek. Farther west along the highway is the trailhead for **Skunk Cabbage Interpretive Trail,** which leads down to the Illecillewaet River.

The park's most demanding trail is the 10-km **Summit Trail,** which begins—or, more sensibly, ends—at the entrance to the park and runs to the Balsam Lake warden's cabin. The

trail makes an elevation gain of 1,200 meters so allow at least 3.5 hours for this strenuous uphill slog. The eight-km **Lindmark Trail** is equally strenuous, gaining 950 meters in elevation as it traverses up to Balsam Lake from the lookout eight km from the park gate.

Heather Lake is the trailhead for the one-km (roundtrip) **Meadows in the Sky Interpretive Trail,** which features signs explaining the flora of the fragile alpine environment. From the east side of Heather Lake, a nine-km trail leads through alpine meadows to the **Jade Lakes.** Along the route, short side trails lead to **Miller** and **Eva Lakes.**

Mountain Bike Tours

Summit Cycle Tours, tel. (250) 837-3734, takes the hard part out of a mountain-biking trip through the national park. The company's tours start with a van ride to the summit of Meadows in the Sky Parkway, where you'll spend some time exploring the alpine environment. Then the tour proceeds downhill on a ride back to the valley floor. The tour lasts 2-3 hours and costs $38-47 per person.

Practicalities

The park's main gate is closed from 10 p.m. until 7 a.m., prohibiting access. Although backcountry camping is allowed in designated areas (permit required; $6 per person per night), no campgrounds or services lie within the park. Revelstoke, at the base of Meadows in the Sky Parkway, has campgrounds, other accommodations, restaurants, and all other services. The city is also home to the park's **administration office,** in the post office building at 313 3rd St., tel. (250) 837-7500. It's open year-round, Mon.-Fri. 8:30 a.m.-4:30 p.m. Another source of information is **Rogers Pass Information Centre,** in nearby Glacier National Park.

WEST TOWARD SALMON ARM

Continuing west along the TransCanada Highway from Revelstoke, it's 104 km to the major center of Salmon Arm. The first stop along the way should be intriguing, black **Summit Lake,** lying in a heavily forested ravine and fed by a waterfall that plunges over a cliff face high above. A few km farther west is similarly black **Victor Lake,** also fed by a waterfall. Shoreside **Victor Lake Provincial Park** makes a good spot for a picnic.

Tourist Trap Valley

Several attractions on the next stretch of road compete for your tourist dollar. On the shore of Three Valley Lake is the well-marked **Three Valley Gap** ghost town, a rebuilt pioneer community with more than 20 historic buildings moved to the site from around the province. The town is open April-Oct., 8 a.m.-dusk; admission $6. In the same complex you'll find a lakeside motel (from $75 s, $80 d), restaurant, and cafeteria. For more information or reservations, call (250) 837-2109.

The next commercial attraction, eight km west, is **Enchanted Forest,** tel. (250) 837-9477, where a trail through towering trees meanders past more than 250 handcrafted figurines to fairyland buildings. It's open daily through summer; admission is adults $6, children $4.

The next venture along the highway, **Beardale Castle Miniatureland,** tel. (250) 836-2268, takes miniature appreciators through several European towns and villages, into the world of nursery rhymes and fairy tales, and on into the world of trains. It's open daily May-Sept.; admission is adults $6, children $4.

The Last Spike

At **Craigellachie,** signs point off the highway to the Last Spike. It was here on 7 November 1885 that a plain iron spike joined the last two unjoined sections on Canadian Pacific's transcontinental rail line, finally connecting Canada from sea to sea. A cairn with a plaque and a piece of railway line marks the spot. Nearby are picnic tables and **Craigellachie Station,** an information center open May-October.

Shuswap Lake

Protected waterways, secluded beaches, and more than 1,000 km of shoreline make enormous Shuswap Lake a busy water-sports haven during summer. Houseboating is the number-one activity in these parts, and **Sica-**

mous (pop. 3,000) is known as the "Houseboat Capital of Canada." Rental agencies in Sicamous include: **Blue Water Houseboats,** tel. (250) 836-2255 or (800) 663-4024; **Admiral Houseboats,** tel. (250) 836-4611; **Three Buoys Houseboat Vacations,** tel. (250) 836-2403 or (800) 663-2333; and **Twin Anchors Houseboat Rentals,** tel. (250) 836-2450 or (800) 663-4026. Expect to pay from $100 per boat per day, more for those that sleep more than four people.

The lake takes its name from the Shuswap tribe, the northernmost of the great Salish family and once British Columbia's largest tribe.

SALMON ARM

Known as the "Gem of the Shuswap," Salmon Arm (pop. 15,000) lies along the Salmon Arm of Shuswap Lake, surrounded by lush farmland and forested hills. Legend has it that the name was coined in the days when the rivers here were chockablock with salmon. Farmers used to spear the fish with pitchforks and use them for fertilizer.

Sights

From downtown, follow the Salmon Arm Wharf signs to lakeside **Marine Park,** where picnic tables dot the lawns and colorful flowerboxes hang from the lampposts. The attractive **Salmon Arm Wharf,** the largest marina structure in British Columbia's interior, lures you out over the water, past a boat-launching area, a snack bar, and businesses renting motorboats and houseboats.

Two km east of Salmon Arm on Hwy. 97B, the **Salmon Arm Museum,** tel. (250) 832-5243, relates the town's early history through a slide show, photo albums, and the adjacent **Haney House,** a turn-of-the-century farmhouse on beautiful, parklike grounds. The museum also offers a self-guided tour describing Salmon Arm's historic sites and buildings. It's open July-Aug., daily 10 a.m.-8 p.m.; June and September, weekdays 10 a.m.-6 p.m. Admission is $3.

For excellent views of Shuswap Lake, take **Fly Hills Scenic Drive,** which starts almost opposite the Salmon River Motel and Campground on the Trans-

KAREN MCKINLEY

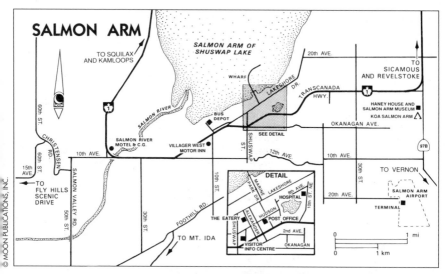

© MOON PUBLICATIONS, INC.

Canada Hwy. west of town. From the highway, turn onto 40th St. and follow the scenic route signs: right on 10th Ave., left on Salmon Valley Rd., right on Christensen Rd., left on 5th Ave., left on 60th St., right on 15th Ave., then on up a forest-service road into the Fly Hills. The road gets pretty rough in sections, but the higher you go, the better the views become.

Accommodations and Camping

Salmon River Motel and Campground, one km west of Salmon Arm, tel. (250) 832-3065, offers rooms of a reasonable standard for $54 s, $59 d, $5 extra for a kitchenette. Out back are a few tree-shaded campsites with hookups; $16.50-19.50. Closer to town is **Villager West Motor Inn,** 61 10th St. SW, tel. (250) 832-9793, with an indoor pool; $70-80 s or d. The landscaped **KOA Salmon Arm,** at the junction of the TransCanada Hwy. and Hwy. 97B, tel. (250) 832-6489, features hot showers, a laundry, heated pool and hot tub, store, miniature golf, playground, and petting zoo. Tent sites are $22, full hookups $31, and rustic cabins $40.

Food

The **Eatery,** right downtown at 361 Alexander St. NE, tel. (250) 832-7490, does a brisk soup-and-sandwich business. **Orchard House**

Restaurant, 720 22nd St. NE, off the Trans-Canada Hwy. east of town, tel. (250) 832-3434, is where the locals splurge—main courses of eclectic North American fare start at $15.

Services and Information

The **Greyhound** bus depot is at the Village West Mall on the TransCanada Hwy., tel. (250) 832-3962. **Shuswap Air,** tel. (250) 832-8830, offers flightseeing and scheduled flights between Salmon Arm, Kelowna, and Vancouver. All flights arrive and depart from the airport at the east end of 20th Avenue.

Salmon Arm Visitor Info Centre, 751 Marine Park Dr., tel. (250) 832-2230, is open in summer, daily 9 a.m.-6 p.m.; the rest of the year, Mon.-Fri. 9 a.m.-5 p.m.

WEST TOWARD KAMLOOPS

Squilax

Squilax lies at the turnoff to Roderick Haig-Brown Provincial Park, 48 km west of Salmon Arm. The town's one remaining building was originally a general store and is now the Hostelling International–affiliated **Squilax Hostel,** tel. (250) 675-2977. The hostel office, kitchen, and lounge area are in the building, while the dorm beds are in three railway carriages out back. The carriages sit on a short stretch of rail line and overlook the west end of Shuswap Lake. Rates are $13.50 for members and $17.50 for nonmembers.

Roderick Haig-Brown Provincial Park

Turn off at the Squilax Bridge to get to this 988-hectare park named for noted British Columbian conservationist and writer Roderick Haig-Brown. The mostly forested park flanks the Adams River between Adams Lake and Shuswap Lake, protecting vital spawning grounds of the sockeye salmon. After an arduous 500-km swim from the Pacific Ocean, the salmon spawn here during the first three weeks of October. You can see them along the entire river, although viewing platforms behind the main parking lot provide the best overlook. The salmon runs occur annually, but every four years a dominant run sees up to a million fish congregating in the river. The next such run will be in 1998.

Outside of October, the park is still worth visiting. Large mammals are common, interesting canyons dot the riverbank, fishing is good, and hikers will find a 40-km network of trails.

KAMLOOPS

Kamloops (pop. 80,000) is the province's fifth-largest city and a main service center along the TransCanada Highway. The city holds a few interesting sights but is certainly no scenic gem—the surrounding landscape is dominated by barren parched rolling hills. The downtown area, however, lies along the south bank of the Thompson River and is set off by well-irrigated parkland.

Entering the city from the west, the Trans-Canada Highway descends the Aberdeen Hills, passing shopping malls, motels, and Kamloops Visitor Info Centre. The highway bypasses downtown; take Columbia St. W to get to the city center. From the east, the TransCanada Highway parallels the Thompson River through almost 20 km of industrial and commercial sprawl.

History

Shuswap natives were the first people to live in this region, basing their lifestyle on hunting and salmon fishing. But the city of Kamloops wasn't established until 1812, when the North West Company established a fur-trading post at the confluence of the north and south branches of the Thompson River. Over the years all kinds of colorful characters have passed through or lived in Kamloops—fur traders, explorers, gold miners, cattle ranchers, railway builders, and farmers. Around the time of the town's founding, sternwheelers plied the Thompson River, dropping off passengers and collecting lumber. But the arrival of the railway in Kamloops contributed the most to the region's development; the Canadian Pacific Railway line was completed in 1885. Settlers flocked in on the trains; lumber and cattle were chugged out. The Canadian Northern Railway (now the Canadian National Railway) was completed in 1915, and Kamloops became a major transportation center. Today the local economy revolves around the forest-products industry, copper mining, cattle and sheep ranching, and tourism.

SIGHTS

Kamloops Museum and Art Gallery

Two attractions share the same address at 207 Seymour St., tel. (250) 828-3576. The museum's excellent displays cover local native culture, the fur trade (peek in the reconstructed fur trader's cabin), pioneer days, natural history (many stuffed and mounted critters), industry, and transportation. You'll see a furnished turn-of-the-century living area, a stable complete with tack and carriage, a blacksmith shop, paddle-wheels, old wall clocks and cameras, and a 15-minute slide presentation on the city's history. Kamloops Art Gallery features works by contemporary artists in all sorts of media—quite a contrast to the museum. Both the museum and gallery are free. Summer hours are Mon.-Fri. 9 a.m.-8 p.m., Saturday 10 a.m.-5 p.m., Sunday 1-5 p.m.; the rest of the year, Tues.-Sat. 9:30 a.m.-4:30 p.m.

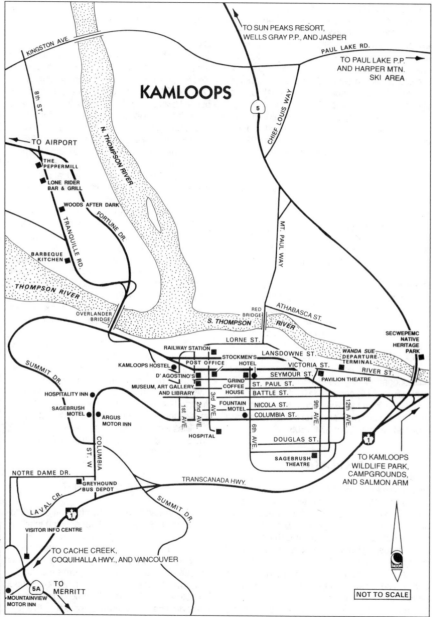

KAMLOOPS

TO SUN PEAKS RESORT, WELLS GRAY P.P., AND JASPER

PAUL LAKE RD.

TO PAUL LAKE P.P. AND HARPER MTN. SKI AREA

KINGSTON AVE.

8th ST.

5

CHIEF LOUIS WAY

TO AIRPORT

THE PEPPERMILL

LONE RIDER BAR & GRILL

WOODS AFTER DARK

N. THOMPSON RIVER

FORTUNE DR.

TRANQUILLE RD.

MT. PAUL WAY

BARBEQUE KITCHEN

THOMPSON RIVER

OVERLANDER BRIDGE

RED BRIDGE

S. THOMPSON RIVER

ATHABASCA ST.

SECWEPEMC NATIVE HERITAGE PARK

LORNE ST.

RIVER ST.

Railway Station

POST OFFICE

STOCKMEN'S HOTEL

LANSDOWNE ST.

WANDA SUE DEPARTURE TERMINAL

KAMLOOPS HOSTEL

VICTORIA ST.

D'AGOSTINO'S

SEYMOUR ST.

PAVILION THEATRE

MUSEUM, ART GALLERY, AND LIBRARY

"GRIND" COFFEE HOUSE

ST. PAUL ST.

BATTLE ST.

SUMMIT DR.

HOSPITALITY INN

3rd AVE.

FOUNTAIN MOTEL

NICOLA ST.

9th AVE.

12th AVE.

SAGEBRUSH MOTEL

ARGUS MOTOR INN

1st AVE.

2nd AVE.

COLUMBIA ST.

6th AVE.

HOSPITAL

DOUGLAS ST.

COLUMBIA ST. W

SAGEBRUSH THEATRE

TO KAMLOOPS WILDLIFE PARK, CAMPGROUNDS, AND SALMON ARM

NOTRE DAME DR.

TRANSCANADA HWY.

GREYHOUND BUS DEPOT

1

LAVAL CR.

SUMMIT DR.

VISITOR INFO CENTRE

TO CACHE CREEK, COQUIHALLA HWY., AND VANCOUVER

5A

TO MERRITT

MOUNTAINVIEW MOTOR INN

MOON

NOT TO SCALE

© MOON PUBLICATIONS, INC.

Secwepemc Native Heritage Park

A living-history museum dedicated to the Shuswap tribe, Secwepemc Park offers numerous exhibits focusing on the Shuswaps' traditions and rich mythology. Among the highlights are an archaeological site dating back 2,000 years, a re-created Shuswap winter village, a salmon-fishing station, and a model of a traditional summer shelter. To get to the park, follow Hwy. 5 north across the Thompson River and take the first right. It's open Mon.-Fri. 8:30 a.m.-4:30 p.m. Admission is adults $5, seniors and children $3. For more information call (250) 828-9801.

Kamloops Wildlife Park

Among this park's more than 150 furry inhabitants are many species of mammals from western Canada, including a couple of grizzly bears. The park is beside the TransCanada Hwy.,16 km east of Kamloops, tel. (250) 573-3242. Admission is adults $6, seniors and children $3. Open daily through summer 8 a.m.-8 p.m.

River Cruise

One of the best ways to appreciate the city and some of its history is to take a cruise down the Thompson River in the *Wanda Sue,* a reconstructed sternwheeler. The boat departs several times a day, May-Sept., from the terminal at the Old Yacht Club Public Wharf on River Street. Light meals and alcoholic beverages are available onboard during the two-hour cruise. Tickets cost adults $14, seniors $10, children $7; get your ticket from the wharf ticket office up to one hour before sailing. For current times and more information, call (250) 374-1505.

RECREATION

Paul Lake Provincial Park

This small 402-hectare provincial park northeast of Kamloops is a relaxing, grassy, tree-shaded spot to take a picnic, go swimming in warm Paul Lake, or camp. And the drive out there, following Paul Creek past scrub-covered rolling hills and flower-filled meadows, is an enjoyable ramble through the countryside. At the park's picnic area and beach you'll find picnic tables, toilets, and changing rooms. The campground offers basic sites for $9.50. To get there,

head north of Kamloops five km on Hwy. 5, then 17 km east on Paul Lake Road.

Skiing

Two downhill ski areas are near the city, to the north off Hwy. 5. Larger of the two is **Sun Peaks Resort** (formerly known as Tod Mountain), tel. (250) 578-7222, which has seen ongoing development both on the slopes and at the base village. From the main village, two high-speed lifts whisk skiers up the mountain. One of these—the Sunburst Express—links up with three more lifts that access intermediate and expert terrain above the treeline as well as an easy eight-km cruising run back to the village. The total vertical rise is 935 meters. Facilities at the resort include a variety of eateries, a rental shop, a ski school run by Olympic-medalist Nancy Greene, and a variety of accommodations. Lift tickets are adults $42, seniors $27, children $23; discounted multiday and half-day tickets available. On-mountain accommodations packages are good value—from $70 per person per night including a lift ticket. For room reservations call (800) 807-3257. For snow reports call (250) 578-7232.

Smaller and closer to the city is **Harper Mountain,** 23 km from downtown along the road out to Paul Lake Provincial Park, tel. (250) 372-2119. It's a family-oriented area with a vertical rise of 425 meters served by three lifts. The resort is open in winter daily, and for night skiing Wed.-Fri. until 10 p.m. On weekdays, the main chairlift only operates after 12:30 p.m. On weekends, lift tickets are adults $25, seniors and children $17. During the week they're a little cheaper. Facilities include a day lodge, rentals, ski school, and groomed cross-country-ski trails. For daily ski reports call (250) 828-0336.

ENTERTAINMENT

Head to **Jukebox Jive,** downtown at 322 Victoria St., tel. (250) 374-5909, for dancing to all the rock 'n' roll classics; open Wed.-Sat. from 8 p.m.

The amateur and professional musicians of the **Kamloops Symphony Society** regularly present classic and pop performances at the **Sagebrush Theatre,** in the Senior High School on 10th Ave., tel. (250) 372-5000. The **Western Canada Theatre Company** presents live theatrical productions by top Canadian actors, producers, and designers. Performances take place in the **Pavilion Theatre,** down by the river at 1025 Lorne St., tel. (250) 372-3216.

ACCOMMODATIONS AND CAMPING

Hotels and Motels

Kamloops has a large number of reasonably priced motels. Least expensive downtown is the **Fountain Motel,** 506 Columbia St., tel. (250) 374-4451 or (800) 253-1569, with older-style rooms from $38 s, $44 d and kitchenettes an extra $8. For something a bit more fancy, stay at **Stockmen's Hotel,** in the heart of the city at 540 Victoria St., tel. (250) 372-2281 or (800) 663-2837. Summer rates are from $110 s, $120 d, but rates are considerably lower the rest of the year. Ski packages are offered in winter.

On the western approach to the city are many brand-new accommodations aimed at the passing highway traveler. These offer clean and comfortable no-frills accommodations but no particular bargains. Among them, **Alpine Motel,** 1393 Hugh Allan Dr., tel. (250) 374-0034 or (800) 270-1260, offers standard rooms from $60, or suites with kitchen and jacuzzi for a few dollars more. Also in the area is **Mountainview Motor Inn,** 1225 Rogers Way, tel. (250) 374-4788 or (800) 667-8868, a three-story complex with a pool, exercise room, jacuzzi, and laundry; $75 s, $80 d.

To save a few bucks head down Columbia St. W from the TransCanada Hwy. to a wide sweeping bend holding a cluster of older motels. Least expensive of these is **Sagebrush Motel,** 660 Columbia St. W, tel. (250) 372-3151, with a pool and restaurant; $40 s, $45 d. Similarly priced and directly across the road is the **Argus Motor Inn,** 625 Columbia St. W, tel. (250) 374-6944. Of a higher standard, and with more facilities is the **Hospitality Inn,** 500 Columbia St. W, tel. (250) 374-4164 or (800) 663-5733. Rates here start at $89 s, $98 d, and for a few extra bucks you get a view.

Hostel

Built in 1909, the Old Courthouse is now home to **Kamloops Hostel,** 7 W. Seymour St., tel. (250) 828-7991, one of the grandest hostels in Canada. The building has been renovated to make hostellers feel a little more comfortable than the original "guests," yet the historic charm remains in the vaulted ceilings, winding staircases, stained glass windows, and Canadian flags. Upstairs in the main courtroom you can write letters in the witness stand, sit in the judge's seat to sign the guest register, or relax in the jury seats. The original jail cells now hold bathrooms. And if you try to do any ironing, you'll be sent to solitary confinement—where the ironing board is. Dorm beds are $14.50 for members, $19.50 for nonmembers.

Campgrounds

Heading out of Kamloops to the east are two commercial campgrounds. The first, eight km from downtown, is **Kamloops Riverview RV**

Kamloops Hostel

Park, 4395 TransCanada Hwy., tel. (250) 573-3255. Facilities include coin-operated showers, a laundry, and a heated pool; $22 per site. Eight km farther east is **Kamloops Waterslide and RV Park,** 9115 TransCanada Hwy., tel. (250) 573-3789, which offers full hookups, coin-operated showers, a laundry, hot tub, and grocery store, and is next door to the wildlife park. Unserviced sites are $15, hookups $18-25.

The town's most scenic campground is at **Paul Lake Provincial Park,** north of Kamloops five km on Hwy. 5, then 17 km east on Paul Lake Road. Facilities are basic, but the setting makes up for it. All sites are $9.50.

FOOD

Downtown

Sitting at one of the city's busiest downtown intersections is the **Grind Coffee House,** 476 Victoria St., tel. (250) 828-6155. Aside from the usual array of gourmet coffees, the health-conscious menu offers sandwiches and other fare from $5. Enjoy your meal at tables set around a courtyard. Across from Kamloops Museum, **D'Agostino Restaurant,** 275 Seymour St., tel. (250) 372-1111, offers a lunch menu featuring burgers from $6, salads from $3, and pasta dishes from $5.50. The dinner menu offers more of the same at a slightly higher price, as well as steaks, seafood, and all-you-can-eat specials (under $10).

Tranquille Road

Aside from downtown, the next biggest concentration of restaurants is along Tranquille Rd., heading north toward the airport. Most are family-style restaurants with relaxed atmosphere and plenty of parking. Pick of the bunch is the **The Peppermill,** 755 Tranquille Rd., corner of Renfrew Ave., tel. (250) 376-7344, which specializes in "buffet extravaganzas" for $10-17 and a soup-and-salad-bar lunch for $7. The **Lone Rider Bar and Grill,** 501 Tranquille Rd., tel. (250) 554-2600, serves Sante Fe–style food in a Mexican atmosphere. This place is trendy, with prices to match. Sandwiches and burgers start at $5, main meals from $10. Friday is Rib Night. **Barbecue Kitchen,** 273 Tranquille Rd., tel. (250) 376-0333, is noted locally for its particularly good traditional Chinese fare. Dishes range $6-12 and you get ample por-

tions for the price. Open Tues.-Sat. noon-9 p.m., Sunday 5-9 p.m.

SERVICES AND INFORMATION

Transportation

Kamloops Airport is on Airport Rd., seven km northwest of city center; follow Tranquille Rd. through the North Shore until you come to Airport Rd. on the left. **Air B.C.,** tel. (250) 828-1118, and **Canadian Regional,** tel. (250) 376-5721, both offer scheduled flights between Kamloops and Vancouver. Kamloops is also a hub for **Central Mountain Air,** serving destinations throughout northern British Columbia; book through Air Canada at (800) 663-3721.

The railway station is right downtown at the north end of 3rd Avenue. **VIA Rail,** tel. (800) 561-8630, runs scheduled service three times weekly west to Vancouver and east to Jasper. Kamloops is also the overnight stop for **Rocky Mountaineer Railtours,** tel. (800) 665-7245, a summer-only luxurious rail trip between Vancouver, Jasper, and Banff.

The **Greyhound** bus depot is at 725 Notre Dame Dr., off Columbia St. W at the west end of town, tel. (250) 374-1212 or (800) 661-8747. Greyhound provides daily service to most parts of the province.

Local bus transportation is provided by **Kamloops Transit System;** adult fare is $1.25, a day pass is $3. For a schedule and route information, call (250) 376-1216. Taxi companies include: **Kami Cabs,** tel. (250) 554-1377, and **Yellow Cabs,** tel. (250) 374-3333. For a rental car, call **Budget,** tel. (250) 374-7368 or (800) 268-8900; **Hertz,** tel. (250) 376-3022 or (800) 263-0600; **National Tilden,** tel. (250) 374-5737 or (800) 387-4747; or **Rent-a-wreck,** tel. (250) 374-7788 or (800) 327-0116.

Other Services and Information

The **Royal Inland Hospital** is at the south end of 3rd Ave. at 311 Columbia St., tel. (250) 374-5111. The **post office** is at 301 Seymour Street. **Kamloops Visitor Info Centre** is beside the TransCanada Hwy. on the western outskirts of town (at Hillside Rd. opposite the Aberdeen Mall), tel. (250) 374-3377 or (800) 662-1994. It's open in summer daily 8 a.m.-8 p.m.; the rest of the year, Mon.-Fri. 8:30 a.m.-4 p.m.

NORTH TO MOUNT ROBSON

From Kamloops, Hwy. 5 follows the North Thompson River to Tete Jaune Cache on Hwy. 16. This stretch of highway is part of the most direct route between Vancouver and Jasper National Park, and is also worthwhile for two excellent provincial parks—**Wells Gray,** a vast wilderness of rivers and mountains, and **Mount Robson,** protecting a spectacular peak that is the highest point in the Canadian Rockies.

Clearwater

The small town of Clearwater (pop. 1,700), 125 km north of Kamloops, is the gateway to Wells Gray Provincial Park. A few motels, restaurants, gas stations, services, and an information center are on the highway; the rest of the community is off the highway to the south.

Jasper Way Inn Motel, on the old highway, two blocks north of Hwy. 5, tel. (250) 674-3345, lies on the shores of beautiful Dutch Lake. You'll have bucolic views of the wildflower-edged, glassy lake in the foreground, tree-covered hills on the far shore, and snow-covered mountains in the distance. Rooms start at $50 s, $55 d, with kitchenettes an extra $5.

Camping is most pleasant within the nearby provincial park, but an alternative is **Dutch Lake Resort,** tel. (250) 674-3351, where unserviced sites are $14, and hookups are $16-21.

The only place to really recommend for food in town is **Ice Cream Adventure,** tel. (250) 674-3303, at the turnoff to Wells Gray Provincial Park; an enormous cone topped with whipped cream and a cherry is only $2. At the same intersection is **Clearwater Visitor Info Centre,** tel. (250) 674-2646; open daily through summer 8 a.m.-6 p.m., the rest of the year weekdays 9 a.m.-5 p.m.

WELLS GRAY PROVINCIAL PARK

Snow-clad peaks, extinct volcanoes, and ancient lava flows. Amazing waterfalls—so many the park is often referred to as the "Waterfall Park." Icy mineral springs, subalpine forest, and flower-filled meadows. An abundance of lakes and rivers where anglers can fish to their heart's content for rainbow trout and Dolly Varden.

With so much to see and do, Wells Gray Provincial Park is a must-see detour on the route between Kamloops and Jasper. The main access road into the 530,000-hectare park leads north from Clearwater for 36 km to the park boundary. From there it continues 11 km to one of the park's highlights, Helmcken Falls, where it turns to gravel and continues another 16 km to its end at Clearwater Lake. Apart from three campgrounds, the park has no services.

Sights and Hikes

Before reaching the park boundary on the road up from Clearwater, you'll first pass 270-hectare **Spahats Creek Provincial Park.** Here a short trail leads to a colorful lava canyon where 61-meter-high **Spahats Creek Falls** plummets over multicolored bedrock. The narrow ribbon of water flows into a wide pool before merging with the Clearwater River.

Just inside the park boundary, take a gravel road to the west to **Green Viewing Tower** atop Green Mountain. The viewpoint provides panoramic views of a volcanic cone and many spectacular, rugged peaks, including snow-capped Garnet Peak, highest in the park.

Wells Gray is best known for its waterfalls, the two most spectacular of which are accessible by road. Southernmost is **Dawson Falls,** four km into the park, where the **Murtle River** cascades over a 90-meter-wide and 20-meter-high ledge. A little farther along the main road is the **Mush Bowl** (or Devil's Punchbowl), where the river has carved huge holes in the riverbed. But save some film for incredible **Helmcken Falls,** British Columbia's fourth-highest falls, where the Murtle River cascades off the edge of Murtle Plateau in a sparkling, 137-meter-high torrent to join the Clearwater River. In winter, the frozen falls create an enormous ice cone as tall as a 20-story building.

For an enjoyable short walk from the road (20 minutes each way), hike the one-km trail out to **Ray Farm,** former home of one of the area's first settlers. John Bunyon Ray cleared his

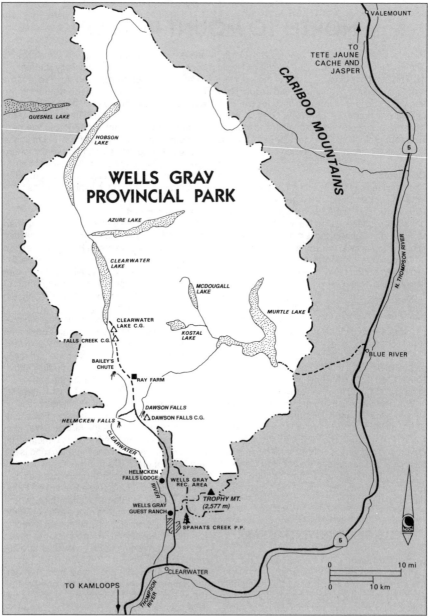

TO VALEMOUNT

TO
TETE JAUNE
CACHE AND
JASPER

CARIBOO MOUNTAINS

QUESNEL LAKE

HOBSON
LAKE

WELLS GRAY
PROVINCIAL PARK

AZURE LAKE

CLEARWATER
LAKE

MCDOUGALL
LAKE

MURTLE LAKE

KOSTAL
LAKE

CLEARWATER
LAKE C.G.

FALLS CREEK C.G.

BAILEY'S
CHUTE

RAY FARM

BLUE RIVER

N. THOMPSON RIVER

DAWSON FALLS

HELMCKEN FALLS

DAWSON FALLS C.G.

CLEARWATER

HELMCKEN
FALLS LODGE

WELLS GRAY
REC. AREA

TROPHY MT.
(2,577 m)

WELLS GRAY
GUEST RANCH

RIVER

SPAHATS CREEK P.P.

CLEARWATER

TO KAMLOOPS

THOMPSON
RIVER

0   10 mi
0   10 km

Helmcken Falls

farm out of the wilderness in 1912, and he and his wife raised a family in this isolated spot. The picturesque abandoned farm buildings sit among rolling meadows full of wildflowers. From the farm, another short trail leads to a mineral spring.

Continuing north up the road, a 500-meter trail (10 minutes each way) winds through a stand of towering cedar trees to **Bailey's Chute,** a narrow rapids-filled passage between two lakes. In fall, large numbers of chinook salmon battle the torrent, trying in vain to leap up the chute. After a number of valiant attempts, they're washed back downstream to the gravel beds where they spawn and die.

Back out on the road and continuing north, you'll soon come to **Clearwater Lake** at road's end. One of the park's six major lakes, Clearwater Lake was created when an ancient lava flow blocked the valley. In summer, **Clearwater Lake Tours,** tel. (250) 674-2121, runs a four-hour motorboat cruise from Clearwater Lake Campground to the north end of the lake, where you'll have views of adjacent **Azure Lake.** Tours depart at 10 a.m.; adults $40, seniors $34, children $27. The company also rents canoes for those who would rather propel themselves the 50 km to Azure Lake; $30 a day or $150 a week, drop-offs available via water taxi anywhere on Clearwater Lake. This overnight trip is popular with paddlers, the only hitch being a 500-meter portage between the two lakes. Numerous wilderness campsites line the shores of both lakes.

The center of the park and the rugged northern reaches are accessible only on foot, and contain a vast wilderness of tall peaks, dense forests, and lakes and rivers. This is where the animals like to hang out—mountain goats, caribou, moose, mule deer, and black and grizzly bears. Access into the east side of the park is by a 24-km gravel road off Hwy. 5, just north of the community of Blue River. From the trailhead at the end of the road it's a 2.5-km hike (40 minutes) to **Murtle Lake,** the park's largest freshwater lake.

Accommodations and Camping
Between Clearwater and the park boundary, **Wells Gray Guest Ranch,** tel. (250) 674-2792, is surrounded by grassy meadows full of wildflowers and grazing horses. Activities organized for guests include horseback riding, canoeing, whitewater rafting, and fishing. Well-furnished, kitchen-equipped cabins rent for $105 per night, and camping is available for $12, no hookups. The ranch has a restaurant and saloon. **Helmcken Falls Lodge,** tel. (250) 674-3657, is also on the park access road, and offers similar activities and accommodations; $112-135 per night.

Each of the three campgrounds inside the park has drinking water, toilets, and picnic tables; $9.50 per site. Heading up the road from the village of Clearwater, you'll pass, in order, **Dawson Falls Campground, Falls Creek Campground** (with spacious riverside sites), and finally **Clearwater Lake Campground,** which is almost at the end of the road, right on the lake, and is the first to fill each night.

Information
Park information is available at **Clearwater Visitor Info Centre** in Clearwater, tel. (250) 674-2646. The center sells two invaluable guidebooks to the park: *Exploring Wells Gray Park* and *Nature Wells Gray.*

BLUE RIVER AND VALEMOUNT

Blue River

Although right on busy Hwy. 5, this one-time railway division point has remained small, holding just a couple of hundred residents along with services for passing travelers. But with the Cariboo Mountains to the north, Wells Gray Provincial Park to the west, and the northern reaches of the North Thompson River just to the east, the town makes a great base for exploring British Columbia's unspoiled interior wilderness. Closer in, Lake Eleanor offers a good beach and swimming right in the heart of town. And just over the rail line from downtown, at the confluence of the Blue and North Thompson Rivers, you'll find a myriad of hiking trails.

Mike Wiegele Helicopter Skiing, based at **Mike Wiegele Resort** at the north end of town, offers heli-skiing in the Monashee and Cariboo Mountains. The company has been featured in many ski movies and attracts an international clientele. During summer, the resort is a base for heli-hiking in the same mountain ranges. Freestanding lakeside units at the resort rent from $105 s, $125 d in summer. The main lodge holds a restaurant, gym, sauna, and spa. For heli-skiing information write P.O. Box 249, Banff, AB T0L 0C0, or call (403) 762-5548 or (800) 661-9170. For information on accommodations or summer heli-hiking call (250) 673-8381 or (800) 661-9170.

A less expensive option to the resort is **Blue River Campground,** tel. (250) 673-8203, where sites range $12-20 per night. The campground is within walking distance of Lake Eleanor and the town's services.

Valemount and Vicinity

North of Blue River, Hwy. 5 follows the North Thompson River through the Cariboo Mountains to Valemount, 30 km south of the Yellowhead Highway. Valemount is the base for **CMH Heli-hiking,** tel. (403) 762-7100, which offers packages including transportation to a remote lodge, helicopter flights to the hiking area high above treeline, hiking gear, and a gourmet lunch, all for $235 per person per day. Trips leave at 8 a.m. from Valemount's **Alpine Inn,** tel. (250) 566-4471, which is therefore the best place to stay if you're going heli-hiking. Rates at the inn are $60 s, $70 d.

From the Yellowhead Highway junction north of Valemount, Prince George is 270 km to the west and the British Columbia/Alberta border is 77 km east. Although most of the distance to the border is through Mount Robson Provincial Park (see below), two worthwhile stops lie between the highway junction and the park. The first of these is **Rearguard Falls,** a one-km hike (20 minutes each way) from the highway. Eight km downstream from the falls—some 1,200 km up the Fraser River from the Pacific Ocean—is a spawning grounds for Pacific salmon; many of the hardy fish make it all the way to the falls. Continuing east along the highway is a viewpoint for 2,650-meter **Mount Terry Fox,** off to the south and protected by a provincial park. The mountain was named after a 22-year-old British Columbian who lost his leg to cancer and subsequently raised funds for cancer research by courageously running 5,375 km across Canada on an artificial limb.

MOUNT ROBSON PROVINCIAL PARK

Spectacular Mount Robson Provincial Park encompasses 217,200 hectares of steep canyons and wide forested valleys; icy lakes, rivers and streams; and rugged mountain peaks permanently blanketed in snow and ice. Towering over the park's western entrance is magnificent 3,954-meter **Mt. Robson,** highest peak in the Canadian Rockies.

Local Shuswap natives called the peak Yuh-hai-hs-hun ("Mountain of the Spiral Road") for its layered appearance. Historians guess that the peak's European name honors a member of the Hudson's Bay Company, though details of the christening have been lost to history.

Mountaineers were attracted to the challenge of climbing Mount Robson at the very beginning of this century, but the first official ascent took place in 1913, the same year the park as we know it today was created. Led by Swiss guide Conrad Kain, the first ascent party was made up of members of the Alpine Club of Canada. Although this was the first official summit climb, the summit had been attempted four years earlier by Rev. George Kinney and friends. Kinney

Mt. Robson

thought he'd made the summit, but he was climbing the summit ridge in a heavy fog; a cairn and a message recording the names of the members of Kinney's climbing team was later found on the ridge about 100 vertical meters from the top.

Roadside Sights

As you approach the park from the west, you'll see Mount Robson long before you reach the park boundary, provided the weather is cooperating. It's impossible to confuse this distinctive peak with those that surround it—no wonder it's known as the "Monarch of the Canadian Rockies." Views of the mountain improve all the way to the main facility area, where you'll find a visitor center, three campgrounds, a gas station, and a restaurant. On a clear day the panorama from this lump of commercialism is equal to any sight in British Columbia. The sheer west face of Mount Robson slices skyward just 11 km away across a flower-filled meadow. This is as close as you can get to the peak in your car.

From the visitor center, it's 60 km along Hwy. 16 to the park's eastern boundary. The highway follows the Fraser River most of this distance, passing a short trail to **Overlander Falls,** then paralleling photogenic **Moose Lake.** Waterfalls on the far side of the lake create a deliciously scenic backdrop. The Moose River drains into the Fraser River at **Moose Marsh,** a good spot for wildlife watching at the southeast end of Moose Lake. Moose often feed here at dawn and dusk, and waterfowl are present throughout the day.

Continuing eastward, the highway crosses the Fraser River before reaching long and narrow **Yellowhead Lake** at the foot of 2,458-meter **Yellowhead Mountain.** From this point, the highway climbs to small and picturesque **Portal Lake,** then crests 1,066-meter **Yellowhead Pass** on the British Columbia/Alberta border. It's the lowest highway pass over the Continental Divide.

Berg Lake Trail

- Length: 19.5 km (eight hours) one-way
- Elevation gain: 725 meters
- Rating: moderate

This is the most popular overnight hike in the Canadian Rockies, but don't let the crowds put you off—the hike is well worth it. Beautiful aqua-colored Berg Lake lies below the north face of Mount Robson, which rises 2,400 meters directly behind the lake. Glaciers on the mountain's shoulder regularly calve off into the lake, resulting in the icebergs that give the lake its name. It's possible to traverse the trail's first section and return the same day, but to get all the way to Berg Lake and back you'll need to stay in the backcountry overnight. Along the route are seven primitive campgrounds, including three along the lakeshore. Overnight hikers must register at the visitor center and pay a camping fee of $6 per person per night.

From the trailhead two km north of the visitor center along a narrow access road, the trail follows the Robson River 4.5 km through dense subalpine forest to glacially-fed **Kinney Lake.** There the trail narrows, crossing the fast-flowing river at the eight-km mark and climbing alongside it. The next four km, through the steep-sided Valley of a Thousand Falls, are the most demanding, but views of three spectacular waterfalls ease the pain of the 500-vertical-meter climb. The first glimpses of Mount Robson come soon after reaching the head of the valley, from where it's a further one km to the outlet of Berg Lake, 17.5 km from the trailhead. The first of three lakeside campgrounds is two km from this point.

While the panorama from the lake is stunning, most hikers who have come this far will want to spend some time exploring the area. From the north end of the lake, trails lead to Toboggan Falls and more mountain views, up Snowbird Pass and to the head of Robson Glacier, and to Robson Pass, which opens up the remote northern reaches of Jasper National Park.

Other Hikes in the Park
Aside from the busy trail to Berg Lake, the park holds only two other established trails. The shortest of the two ascends the slopes of 2,458-meter **Yellowhead Mountain.** From the trailhead across the rail line at Yellowhead Lake it's a steady climb through subalpine forest to the first viewpoint at the one-km mark. Another three km and a total elevation gain of 720 meters brings you to flower-filled meadows and panoramic views extending east to the Continental Divide and west to the Selwyn Range. Allow two hours each way for this hike.

The other option is the 13-km (each way) **Fitzwilliam Basin Trail,** which requires an overnight stay in the backcountry. Elevation gain is 950 meters, so it's a fairly demanding trail. From the trailhead on the south side of Hwy. 16, three km east of Lucerne Campground, the trail climbs steadily for six km to the confluence of Rockingham and Fitzwilliam Creeks. Although easy to follow, the remaining seven km along the northern slopes of 2,911-meter Mt. Fitzwilliam are rough going. After ascending a steep ridge the trail all but dissipates, but many camping spots can be found in the wide lake-filled basin.

Other Recreation
Mount Robson Adventure Holidays, based at Mount Robson Adventure Centre (by the vis-

itor center), tel. (250) 566-4386 or (800) 882-9921, conducts a number of "gentle adventure" tours within the park. These include rafting ($40), a naturalist-led bus tour ($40), canoeing on Moose Lake ($45), and a guided hike to Kinney Lake ($40). **Premier Air,** based in Valemount, tel. (250) 566-4901, offers flightseeing over the area for $65 per person for 40 minutes, $115 for 70 minutes.

Accommodations and Camping
Mount Robson Guest Ranch, south of the visitor center on Hargreaves Rd., tel. (250) 566-4370, offers comfortable kitchen-equipped units from $80 s, $100 d, as well as a few campsites for $14-18. Similarly priced, but with no camping, is **Mount Robson Lodge,** seven km west of the visitor center, tel. (250) 566-4821.

Within the park are four campgrounds with road access. Three of these are operated by the park. Closest to the visitor center is **Robson River Campground,** while across the road is **Robson Meadows Campground.** Both have flush toilets and showers but no hookups; $14.50 per site. In the east of the park is the more rustic **Lucerne Campground,** where sites are $9.50. **Emperor Ridge Campground,** tel. (250) 566-8438, is a commercial facility right behind the visitor center; $13.50 per site including hot showers but no hookups.

Information
At the park's western entrance, **Mount Robson Visitor Centre,** tel. (250) 566-9174, features informative natural-history slide shows, an evening interpretive program, and trail reports updated daily. The center stocks the brochure, *Mount Robson Provincial Park,* which provides sufficient information if you're only driving through the park. Hikers and climbers can pick up more detailed trail descriptions and topographical maps ($11) at the center. Hours are mid-June to mid-September, daily 8 a.m.-8 p.m.; mid-May to mid-June and mid-September to mid-October, daily 8 a.m.-5 p.m.; closed the rest of the year.

CARIBOO COUNTRY

The wild, sparsely populated Cariboo region extends from Kamloops north to Prince George and west to the Pacific Ocean. Its most dramatic natural features are the mountain ranges that rise like bookends to either side. In the west, the **Coast Mountains** run parallel to the coast and rise to a height of 4,016 meters at **Mt. Waddington.** In the east, the **Cariboo Mountains** harbor numerous alpine lakes, high peaks, and several provincial parks.

Between the two ranges flows the **Fraser River,** which is flanked to the west by expansive plateaus that are home to British Columbia's biggest ranches. This is cowboy country, where horseback holidays and the famous Williams Lake Stampede are the main visitor drawcards. This was once gold-rush country—most of the

region's towns began as stopping places along the Gold Rush Trail. Those such as **100 Mile House** owe their names to the trail but have remained small, while others such as **Williams Lake** and **Quesnel** have continued to grow and are service centers for the ranching and forestry industries. The only coastal access in Cariboo Country is via Hwy. 20, which runs through **Tweedsmuir Provincial Park** to **Bella Coola,** at the head of a long fjord.

CACHE CREEK AND LILLOOET

Cache Creek

A town born with the fur trade at a spot where traders cached furs and food supplies, Cache

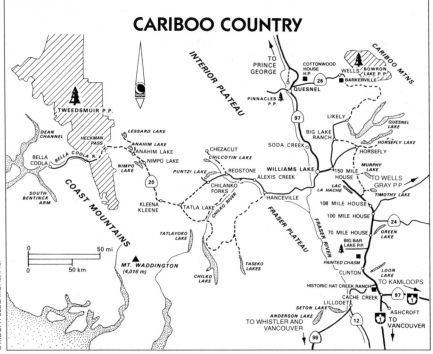

CARIBOO COUNTRY

along the Thompson River south of Cache Creek

Creek was once the largest town between Vancouver, 337 km to the south, and Kamloops, 80 km to the east. But since the new Coquihalla Highway opened, the town is but a shadow of its former self. It still lies on the most direct route between the south and north ends of the province, and travelers not willing to pay the $10 toll on the Coquihalla Highway still pass through, even though it will cost them at least an extra $5 in gas.

The surrounding desertlike climate is intriguing; sagebrush and cacti grow on the relatively barren volcanic landscape and tumbleweeds blow through town. Due to the town's former highway prominence, the main drag is lined with motels, roadside diners, and gas stations.

The **Castle Inn Motel,** 1153 TransCanada Hwy., tel. (250) 457-9547, may have seen better days, but it's one of the few places in the province where you can get a double room for under $40. A step up is the **Desert Motel,** 1069 Trans-Canada Hwy., tel. (250) 457-6226 or (800) 663-0212, which is air-conditioned and has an outdoor pool; $50 s, $55 d. The best campground in town is **Brookside Campsite,** at the base of steep cliffs east of town, tel. (250) 457-6633. Facilities are excellent and sites are $12-17.

Historic Hat Creek Ranch

Between 1885 and 1905, the Cariboo Wagon Road bustled with stagecoaches and freight wagons. One of the few sections of the original road still open to the public is at Hat Creek Ranch, 11 km north of Cache Creek on Hwy. 97. Many of the original buildings—some dating as far back as 1861—still stand, and visitors can watch the blacksmith at his forge, appreciate a collection of antique farm machinery, enjoy a picnic lunch in the orchard, or take a guided tour of the ranch house. Admission to the ranch is free, but a donation is requested after touring the house. The ranch is open through summer, daily 10 a.m.-6 p.m. For more information call (250) 457-9722.

Lillooet

This historic town of 2,000 was founded as Mile 0 of the 1858 Cariboo Wagon Road—also known as the Gold Rush Trail—that led north to the Barkerville and Wells goldfields. Several towns along the Gold Rush Trail—70 Mile House, 100 Mile House, and 150 Mile House, among them—were named for their distance up the wagon road from Lillooet.

With thousands of prospectors passing through in the mid-1800s, Lillooet was the scene of its own gold rush. Originally known as Cayoosh Flat, the town was renamed in the mid-1860s. The new name was a misspelling of Leelwat, a tribe of natives who lived to the north. By the time of this name change the city held some 16,000 residents, making it the second-largest population center north of San Francisco and west of Chicago. But like all other boomtowns, the population explosion was short-lived. As all the most productive local goldfields were worked dry, prospectors continued north on the Cariboo Wagon Road or east on the Dewdney Trail.

Saunter along wide Main Street and pretend you're back in the gold-rush era—which won't be hard if you happen to be here in June during **Only in Lillooet Days.** During this week-long celebration, the town re-creates the Old West with all sorts of entertaining events.

A row of rusty farming relics out front marks **Lillooet Museum,** on Main St. at 8th Ave., tel. (250) 256-4308. Inside are ore samples and details about the one-time boomtown's mining history and growth. It's open May through mid-October, daily 11 a.m.-4 p.m. Also in the museum, and open the same hours, is **Lillooet Visitor Info Centre,** tel. (250) 256-4308.

One block up the hill from the museum, **4 Pines Motel,** 108 8th Ave., tel. (250) 256-4247, charges $42 s, $46 d. **Cayoosh Creek Campground** is a barren spot near the south end of town, where Cayoosh Creek drains into the much larger Fraser River. Facilities include hot showers and hookups. Sites are $13-15. For a meal, head to **Lillooet Inn Restaurant,** 687 Main St., tel. (250) 256-0028, open every day from 6:30 a.m.

CLINTON TO 100 MILE HOUSE

Clinton

Originally called 47 Mile House, the old-fashioned town of Clinton lies 40 km north of Cache Creek on Hwy. 97. The original roadhouse, opened in 1861 at the junction of the original Cariboo Wagon Road and the new route north from Yale, burned down in 1958. Until the fire, the roadhouse was the site of the annual **Clinton Ball,** a fancy-dress wingding that attracted people from all over the area each May. The ball continues to this day but in other locations.

South Cariboo Historical Museum, on the main drag through town (Hwy. 97), tel. (250) 459-2442, occupies an old schoolhouse made of handmade bricks fired locally in the 1890s. The museum contains pioneer belongings, guns, historical photos, native and Chinese artifacts, freight wagons, and all sorts of items from the gold-rush days. It's open in summer, Mon.-Fri. 10 a.m.-6 p.m.

A nearby natural attraction worth seeing is Painted Chasm, in 3,068-hectare **Chasm**

Provincial Park, eight km north of town. Here glacial meltwater has carved a deep box canyon out of mineral-laden volcanic bedrock. It's quite a spectacle when the sunlight brings out the color and sparkle of the minerals.

The huge log structure on the main street is **Cariboo Lodge,** tel. (250) 459-7992, featuring eight comfortable rooms ($50 s, $60 d), a restaurant, cafe, and pub. Another place for a meal is the **Wolf's Cry Inn,** also on the main street, tel. (250) 459-2610, featuring Southwestern-style dishes; closed Tuesday. **Clinton Visitor Info Centre** occupies a beautiful 1910 house on the main street of town, tel. (250) 459-2640; open May-Aug., daily 9 a.m.-5 p.m.

North to 100 Mile House

Continuing north from Clinton, you'll come to a gravel road that leads west off the highway into the ranch country of the Fraser Plateau. Up this road about 40km is 332-hectare **Big Bar Lake Provincial Park,** which offers fishing and swimming in both the lake and the adjacent river; campsites $9.50. Also in the vicinity is the enormous **Gang Ranch.** Started in the 1860s, the ranch was at one time North America's largest.

Back on the main highway, between 70 Mile House and 100 Mile House are several turnoffs leading to hundreds of lakes, big and small. All information centers in Cariboo Country stock the invaluable *Cariboo-Chilcotin Fishing Guide.* Updated annually, the booklet features essential fishing information (the where, when, and with what) for many of the lakes, plus maps, camping spots, and even recipes for the ones that didn't get away. The other provincial park between Clinton and 100 Mile House is at 32-km-long **Green Lake,** 19 km east of Hwy. 97. The lake lies along an old Hudson's Bay Company fur-brigade trail; you can see traces of the trail along the lake's shoreline. The park has a shaded lakeside picnic area and a campground ($9.50 per night).

Passing through 100 Mile House, it's difficult to miss the **South Cariboo Visitor Info Centre,** tel. (250) 395-5353. Look for the world's largest cross-country skis out front. The center is open year-round, Mon.-Fri. 8:30 a.m.-4:30 p.m.; longer hours in summer. At the north end of town, one of the original Cariboo stagecoaches is on display. And birdwatchers might want to detour a couple of kilometers west of town to an eight-hectare wetlands reserve where waterfowl are prolific.

Continuing toward Williams Lake

Three km north of 100 Mile House, a road heads east off the highway, leading 30 km to **Ruth Lake;** 44 km to six-hectare **Canim Beach Provincial Park,** with campsites for $9.50; 70 km to **Mahood Falls,** between Canim and Mahood Lakes; and 86 km to the western border of **Wells Gray Provincial Park** (see "Wells Gray Provincial Park" under "North to Mount Robson," earlier this chapter), where you'll find a primitive campsite.

Back out on the highway and continuing north, you'll come to 19-km-long **Lac La Hache,** named for a trader who dropped his axe in the water. This is one of the most picturesque bodies of water in Cariboo Country and is known for its large concentrations of kokanee and lake trout. At the lake's south end is the small community of Lac La Hache, where you'll find a small museum and information center on the east side of the highway. At the lake's north end, a provincial park offers campsites for $9.50.

The next main turnoff, at **150 Mile House,** takes you on a 65-km scenic drive northeast to

Horsefly Lake Provincial Park, which offers swimming, campsites ($9.50), and, in late August, a sockeye salmon run. In 1859, the first gold strike in the Cariboo region was made nearby. Continuing out to the end of the access road you'll come to the much larger **Quesnel Lake.**

WILLIAMS LAKE

Originally bypassed by the builders of the Cariboo Wagon Road because of protests from a stubborn landowner, Williams Lake (pop. 11,500) has ironically become the Cariboo region's largest city. No one knows for sure how the city got its name, but the most popular theory is that it was named after Shuswap chief Willyum, who kept the peace as best he could between the valley's indigenous people and early white settlers. Today the ranching and forestry center is best known for the Williams Lake Stampede, one of Canada's biggest rodeos.

History

When gold seekers poured into the Cariboo in 1860, Williams Lake became a regional postal center and headquarters for the gold commis-

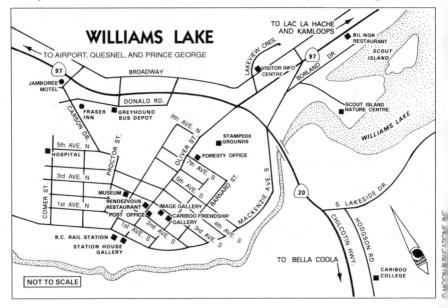

WILLIAMS LAKE

TO LAC LA HACHE AND KAMLOOPS

BIL-NOR RESTAURANT

SCOUT ISLAND

TO AIRPORT, QUESNEL, AND PRINCE GEORGE

LAKEVIEW CRES.

97

VISITOR INFO CENTRE

97

BORLAND DR.

BROADWAY

JAMBOREE MOTEL

DONALD RD.

SCOUT ISLAND NATURE CENTRE

FRASER INN

GREYHOUND BUS DEPOT

8th AVE. N.

WILLIAMS LAKE

CARSON DR.

PROCTOR ST.

OLIVER ST.

STAMPEDE GROUNDS

5th AVE. N

HOSPITAL

FORESTY OFFICE

7th AVE. S

3rd AVE. N

5th AVE. S

BARNARD ST.

MACKENZIE AVE. S

20

S. LAKESIDE DR.

COMER ST.

MUSEUM

1st AVE. N

RENDEZVOUS RESTAURANT

IMAGE GALLERY

POST OFFICE

CARIBOO FRIENDSHIP GALLERY

1st AVE. S

2nd AVE. S

3rd AVE. S

4th AVE. S

B.C. RAIL STATION

STATION HOUSE GALLERY

CHILCOTIN HWY.

HODGSON RD.

TO BELLA COOLA

CARIBOO COLLEGE

NOT TO SCALE

sioner. It was destined for boomtown status until the Cariboo Wagon Road bypassed the town in 1863, thus terminating the small community's reason for being.

Despite the town's uncertain future, William Pinchbeck decided to stay in the valley. He and fellow settler William Lyne started a large farm that supplied the gold camps with bacon, ham, fresh vegetables, and flour, as well as whiskey from their own distillery. In addition to being a farmer, Pinchbeck acted as the local judge, lawyer, and doctor.

In September 1919 the Pacific Great Eastern Railway (now B.C. Rail) ran tracks around the lake and Williams Lake came back to life. To celebrate the event, the town held a large picnic and rodeo—the first Williams Lake Stampede. By 1920 the town had hotels, stores, and homes, and ranchers were thrilled to be able to put their cattle on the train instead of herding them south on cattle drives.

Sights

Exhibits at the large **Museum of the Cariboo Chilcotin,** 113 4th Ave. N, tel. (250) 392-7404, include historical photos, remains of the Chinese settlement at Quesnel Forks, the story of the Stampede, and all kinds of picks, pans, and axes from the gold-mining days. The museum is open in summer, Mon.-Sat. 10 a.m.-4 p.m.; the rest of the year, Tues.-Sat. 11 a.m.-4 p.m.

Many stores in town sell the painting, pottery, weaving, photography, and jewelry of local artisans. These include: **Station House Gallery,** in the historic British Columbia Railway depot at 1 Mackenzie Ave. N, tel. (250) 392-6113; **Cariboo Friendship Society,** 99 3rd Ave. S, tel. (250) 398-6831, featuring native artwork; and **Image Gallery,** 85 3rd Ave. S, tel. (250) 392-6360.

On the eastern outskirts of the city, **Scout Island Nature Centre,** tel. (250) 398-8532, is surrounded by wetlands that serve as a staging area for migratory waterfowl. Colorful displays inside the center catalog the surrounding ecosystem, but the idea is to get out into the wetlands. Wander along one of the short hiking trails or climb the observation tower for a bird's-eye view of the wild landscape. The center is open in summer, Mon.-Fri. 9 a.m.-4 p.m., Sunday 1-4 p.m.

Outdoor Recreation

Opportunities for outdoor recreation abound in the area. One of many ranches offering horseback riding is **Springhouse Trails Summer Resort,** on Dog Creek Rd., about 20 km southwest of town off Hwy. 20, tel. (250) 392-4780. Horse rental is $18 an hour and you can stay out on the ranch overnight (see "Accommodations and Camping," below).

The region's diverse waterways provide plenty of opportunities for boating. Numerous gently flowing streams and serene lakes make perfect spots for canoe and kayak discovery trips, while the Fraser River provides opportunities for exciting rafting trips. Fishing in these same waters is also rewarding, yielding trout, steelhead, Dolly Varden, and kokanee. The booklet *Cariboo-Chilcotin Fishing Guide,* available at the information center, details the region's most productive lakes.

Plenty of winter activities are available here to keep locals and passers-through from getting cabin fever. Cross-country skiers use 30 km of wooded trails on **Bull Mountain,** about 20 km north on Hwy. 97. Downhill skiers head to **Mt. Timothy Ski Area,** 25 km east of Lac La Hache, tel. (250) 395-3772, which offers 25 runs and a vertical rise of 250 meters. Snowmobiling and ice fishing are two other locally popular winter pastimes.

Williams Lake Stampede

On the first weekend of July, the town comes alive as the best cowboys in the land compete in the Williams Lake Stampede, one of Canada's largest rodeos. The whole town dresses up for the occasion; the locals put on Western garb and the shopfronts are decorated accordingly. The highlight of each day's action is the rodeo, when cowboys compete for big bucks in bareback riding, saddle-bronc riding, calf-roping, steer-wrestling, and the crowd favorite, bull riding. Scheduled around these traditional events

DOVER PUBLICATIONS, INC.

are cow-milking contests, barrel racing, tractor pulls, chariot races, raft races, a parade, barn dances, all-you-can-eat breakfasts and steak-outs, and a host of other decidedly Western-flavored activities.

For the month preceding the rodeo, the British Columbia Forestry Association building on 7th Ave. S becomes Stampede headquarters, where you can purchase tickets and Stampede memorabilia; many of the event posters have become collectors' items. For general stampede information, call (250) 392-6585; for tickets, call (250) 398-8388.

Accommodations and Camping

The least expensive motels are along Hwy. 97 on the city's northeastern and western outskirts. Pick of the lot is **Drummond Lodge Motel,** on Hwy. 97 east of downtown, tel. (250) 392-5334 or (800) 667-4555. It's set picturesquely on extensive grounds overlooking the lake, and each of the well-decorated rooms comes with complimentary coffee and plenty of television channels. Rates are $56 s, $61 d. RVers can set up their rigs out back for $23-26 per night. Barbecue facilities are available.

Off the highway at the north end of town is **Jamboree Motel,** 845 Carson Dr., tel. (250) 398-8208, which charges $48 s, $51 d. One block closer to downtown is **Fraser Inn,** 285 Donald Rd., tel. (250) 398-7055 or (800) 452-6789, a full-service hotel with a whirlpool, sauna, exercise room, gift shop, pub, and restaurant. Rooms are $69-85 s or d.

If a ranching vacation is more your style, consider **Springhouse Trails Summer Resort,** 20 km southwest of town on Dog Lake Rd., tel. (250) 392-4780, where horseback riding is $20 an hour. The basic but comfortable rooms are $57 s, $64 d, and all-inclusive package deals are available from $120 per person per day. You can also camp here for $18 a night, with hookups.

The best campground in the area is **Wildwood Campsite,** about 13 km north of the city center, tel. (250) 989-4711. Facilities include full hookups, washrooms and showers, a laundry, and a general store; $13-16 per site. During the Stampede, camping is permitted on the Stampede Grounds.

Food

Williams Lake lacks outstanding eateries, but has no shortage of typical family-style restaurants. One of these is **Rendezvous,** right downtown at 240 Oliver St., tel. (250) 398-8312. Its lunch menu features a soup and salad bar for $6.50, and burgers, sandwiches, pizza, and pasta dishes for around $5.50-8. At dinner the main dishes (fish, chicken, and steak, primarily) range $11-21, including a delicious salad from the salad bar. Hours are Mon.-Thurs. 11 a.m.-10 p.m., Fri.-Sat. 11 a.m.-10:30 p.m., Sunday 4:30-10 p.m.

The **Great Cariboo Steak Company,** in the Fraser Inn at 285 Donald Rd., tel. (250) 398-7055, is open on weekdays from 6 a.m., Saturday from 7 a.m., Sunday from 8 a.m. Breakfast ranges $5-10; all-you-can-eat lunch buffets are $9; sandwiches, croissants, and burgers run $6.50-9; and dinner prices range from $8.50 for the all-you-can-eat salad bar to around $13 for steak, prime rib, chicken, seafood, and pasta dishes.

For Chinese food try the locally recommended **Bil-Nor Restaurant,** east of the information center on Hwy. 97 S, tel. (250) 392-4223.

Services and Information

Williams Lake Airport, 13 km northwest of downtown, is served by **Air B.C.,** tel. (800) 663-3721, offering flights to and from Prince George, Vancouver, and Kamloops; and **Wilderness Airline,** tel. (800) 665-9453, which links Williams Lake to Bella Coola, Vancouver, and Campbell River.

The **Greyhound** bus depot is just off Hwy. 97 at 215 Donald Rd., tel. (250) 398-7733. Daily services run north to Prince George and south to Vancouver. Williams Lake is also on the **B.C. Rail** route between Vancouver and Prince George; for reservations call (250) 398-3799. Local car rental companies include **Budget,** tel. (250) 398-7522, and **National Tilden,** tel. (250) 392-2976.

Williams Lake Visitor Info Centre is beside Hwy. 97 at 1148 Broadway, tel. (250) 392-5025. It's open in summer, daily 8 a.m.-6 p.m.; the rest of the year, Mon.-Fri. 9 a.m.-5 p.m.

WEST ON HIGHWAY 20

Highway 20 west of Williams Lake leads 485 km to Bella Coola, the only road-accessible town along the 500 km of coastline between Powell River and Prince Rupert. The highway is paved less than half its length; the rest of the way it's mostly all-weather gravel and can be slow going in spots. But experiencing the vast and varied wilderness of the **Chilcotin Coast** is worthy of as much time as you can afford. And with the 1996 resumption of ferry service between Bella Coola and Port Hardy, you'll only need to make the trip one-way. Services along Hwy. 20 are spaced at regular intervals, but don't take the trip too lightly; make sure your vehicle is in good condition and carry tools and spare tires to alleviate the necessity of an expensive tow-truck ride.

Williams Lake to Heckman Pass

The road west from Williams Lake meanders through the Fraser River Valley before beginning a steady climb to the **Chilcotin Plateau,** the heart of British Columbia's ranching country. The landscape is open—most of the land has been cleared by generations of ranchers.

The first community with accommodations is **Alexis Creek,** 114 km west of Williams Lake. Stay and eat at the **Chilcotin Hotel,** tel. (250) 394-4214, which charges $46 s or d. Beside the Chilcotin River, 10 km west of Alexis Creek, is **Bull Canyon Provincial Park,** with campsites for $9.50 a night. Continuing west, the highway follows the Chilcotin River, passing a turnoff to beautiful **Chilko Lake,** 100 km southwest of the highway.

At Chilanko Forks, 58 km west of Alexis Creek, a spur road leads 10 km north to **Puntzi Lake.** At this picturesque body of water are a number of low-key fishing resorts, including **Poplar Grove Resort,** tel. (250) 481-1186, which features small lakeside cabins, each with basic cooking facilities and shared washrooms. Rates are from $34 s or d.

Continuing west, the road narrows and turns to gravel, passing the small community of Tatla Lake then climbing steadily to **Nimpo Lake,** where you'll find more small resorts. **Stewart's Lodge,** tel. (250) 742-3388 or (800) 668-4335, offers 10 units on Nimpo Lake from $50, as well as eight other cabins at remote lakes throughout the Chilcotin region.

From this point, it's 10 km west to the small community of Anahim Lake, then a steady climb

of another 30 km to 1,524-meter **Heckman Pass** over the Coast Mountains. Continuing west across the pass, you'll be faced with **"The Hill."** This infamous descent from Heckman Pass to the Bella Coola Valley drops nearly the full 1,524 meters in less than 10 km. Be prepared for numerous switchbacks and a gradient as steep as 18%.

Tweedsmuir Provincial Park

At nearly a million hectares, this is British Columbia's largest provincial park. Roughly triangular, the park is bounded by Ootsa Lake on the north, the high peaks of the Coast Mountains on the west, and the Rainbow Range—so named for its colorful volcanic formations—on the east. Within these boundaries lies an untouched landscape, wild and remote, holding numerous river systems, forested valleys, alpine meadows, waterfalls, and glaciers. Most of those park highlights are accessible only on foot.

Although the park's resident populations of large mammals are high, viewing opportunities are limited. Black and grizzly bears, mountain goats, caribou, wolves, and moose are all present, but tend to remain well away from the highway. In early fall, grizzlies can occasionally be seen feeding on spawned-out salmon along

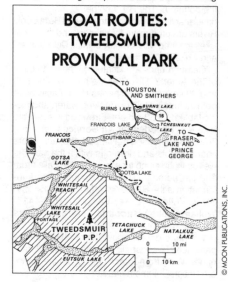

BOAT ROUTES: TWEEDSMUIR PROVINCIAL PARK

© MOON PUBLICATIONS, INC.

the Atnarko River. Highway 20 meanders through the southern section of the park, but aside from two campgrounds and a handful of picnic areas along this route, the park is devoid of facilities.

The park's trail system is not extensive, and most established routes require an overnight stay in the backcountry. One exception is a trail to a series of kettle ponds formed by a receding glacier that stalled many thousands of years ago. This trail is four km (70 minutes) each way, beginning from a picnic area 16 km west of Atnarko River Campground. At the other end of the spectrum, the 16.5-km trek to **Hunlen Falls** is a park highlight for experienced backcountry hikers. These falls tumble 260 meters into a narrow canyon from the north end of Turner Lake. The trail is steep, gaining around 1,500 meters and snaking through more than 60 switchbacks in one six-km section. To get to the trailhead, take the gravel road south from the bottom of The Hill. Another popular activity is fishing; Atnarko and Bella Coola Rivers are productive for salmon, and the larger lakes are filled with a variety of trout, Dolly Varden, and whitefish.

Campgrounds are located on the north bank of the Atnarko River (at the base of The Hill) and 30 km west at Fisheries Pool. Facilities at both include pit toilets, drinking water, and picnic tables; $9.50 a night. Firewood is available for a fee. **Tweedsmuir Air Services,** tel. (250) 742-3388, is based at Nimpo Lake, and offers charter flights and drop-offs within the park, as well as flightseeing trips over Hunlen Falls (from $80 per person). The best source of park information is the **BC Parks office** at 640 Borland St. in Williams Lake, tel. (250) 398-4414. **Williams Lake Visitor Info Centre** also offers park information.

For more details about the north end of the park, see "Tweedsmuir Provincial Park (North)" under "West from Prince George" in the Northern British Columbia chapter.

BELLA COOLA

The urge to see what's at the end of the road brings many travelers over The Hill and down to Bella Coola (pop. 800). Here the Bella Coola River drains into North Bentinck Arm, a gateway to the Inside Passage and the Pacific Ocean. The town lies in a coastal valley that was originally the home of the Bella Coola tribe. On 22 July 1793, Alexander Mackenzie reached the coast here, simultaneously becoming the first nonnative to see the area and the first person to cross continental North America. The latter feat earned him a place in history as one of the world's greatest explorers.

Although the Hudson's Bay Company established a post at Bella Coola in 1869, it wasn't until 1894 that permanent settlement of Bella Coola Valley began in earnest. That year a group of Norwegians arrived and, seeing the fjords and snowcapped peaks, were reminded of home. They settled 15 km inland at a spot on the river they named Hagensborg.

BOB RACE

Sights

Bella Coola Historic Museum, housed in a schoolhouse and surveyor's cabin, features artifacts of early Norwegian settlers and the Hudson's Bay Company; open June-September. Over in Hagensborg, the many hand-hewn timber buildings still standing are testament to the construction skills of the early settlers. Aside from these historic sites, there's plenty of outdoor recreation to keep visitors busy. Unfortunately, most of the action is out on the water and requires the services of a boat charter company (not cheap). Fishing is the most popular activity; expect to pay from $75 per hour for four persons. Those with a sense of history will want to visit **Mackenzie Rock,** in the Dean Channel, where Alexander Mackenzie, in his own words, "mixed up some vermillion and melted grease and inscribed in large characters on the face of the rock on which we slept last night, this brief memorial: Alexander Mackenzie, from Canada, by Land, the Twenty Second of July, One Thousand Seven Hundred and Ninety Three."

Practicalities
Right on the river is **Bella Coola Motel,** Clayton St., tel. (250) 799-5323, with clean and comfortable rooms each with a full kitchen for $59 s, $64 d. A few bucks more is the **Cedar Inn,** Mackenzie St., tel. (250) 799-5316. In Hagensborg, **Bay Motor Hotel,** tel. (250) 982-2212 or (888) 982-2212, was renovated in 1995 and has a restaurant and bar; $60 s, $65 d. Also in Hagensborg is Bella Coola's only campground, **Gnome's Home Campground and RV Park,** tel. (250) 982-2504, where unserviced sites are $12 and serviced sites are $13-15. Both Bella Coola and Hagensborg have a couple of restaurants.

Bella Coola Visitor Info Centre, tel. (250) 799-5919, is open in summer daily from 9 a.m. to around 7 p.m. Other services in Bella Coola include gas stations, a post office, and a hospital. The airport, 15 km east of Bella Coola is served by **Wilderness Airline,** tel. (800) 665-9453, which offers scheduled flights to and from Williams Lake, Vancouver, and Campbell River.

Discovery Coast Passage
In 1996, **BC Ferries** opened up a route linking Bella Coola to Port Hardy on Vancouver Island. The *Queen of Chilliwack* makes the 20-hour crossing June-Sept., with departures from Bella Coola and Port Hardy approximately every three days. Peak one-way fare for adult passengers is $110, children 5-11 $55, cars $220, canoes and kayaks $40.75, bicycles $15. To book, call BC Ferries at (250) 386-3431 or, toll-free in B.C., (888) BCFERRY.

QUESNEL AND VICINITY

Quesnel (pop. 8,700) began during the Barkerville gold rush of the 1860s. Prospectors traveling north on the Fraser River disembarked at the confluence of the Fraser and Quesnel Rivers and a town sprang up on the site. Today the town's economy revolves around ranching, mining, and especially forestry; Two Mile Flat, east of downtown, is North America's most concentrated wood-products manufacturing area.

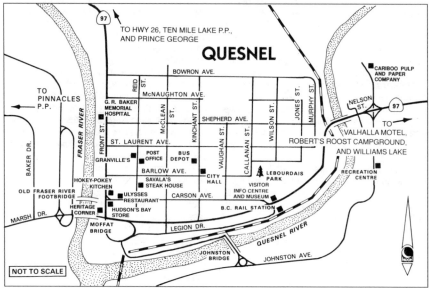

Cottonwood House
Provincial Historic Park

About 28 km east of Quesnel on Hwy. 26, this park preserves a former roadhouse built in 1864. In addition to the old guesthouse, structures at the site include a barn, stable, and other outbuildings. You'll also find an interpretive center and displays of old farming equipment. In summer, carriage rides are a main attraction. The park is open early June to mid-September, daily 8 a.m.-8 p.m. Admission is free. For more information call (250) 992-8716.

Barkerville Historic Park

In 1862 Billy Barker struck gold on Williams Creek, in the north of Cariboo Country. One of Canada's major gold rushes followed, as thousands of prospectors streamed in to what soon became known as Barkerville. The area turned out to be the richest of the Cariboo mining districts, yielding over $40 million in gold. By the mid-1860s Barkerville's population had peaked at over 10,000. But fortunes began to fade after the turn of the century. In 1916 Barkerville was destroyed by fire. Although the town was quickly rebuilt, the gold played out soon thereafter and many of the miners lost interest and moved on.

A hundred years after the first strike, the provincial government decided to make the town a heritage site and re-create its boomtown atmosphere. Today Barkerville, 85 km east of Quesnel, holds over 120 authentically restored buildings. Historic reenactments take place throughout summer, when the town's shops, stores, and restaurants all operate in a century-old time warp. Highlights include the town bakery, which sells some of the most mouthwatering baked goods in the province; the stagecoach rides, a big hit with the kids; and the musical comedy performances at the Theatre Royal, presented two to three times daily (adults $8).

In summer the park is open daily 8 a.m.-8 p.m., although many of the attractions and rides operate shorter hours; admission is adults $6, seniors and children $4, families $15. From Labour Day until the third weekend in June, admission to the park is free but most of the attractions are closed, re-opening late in May. For more information call (250) 994-3332.

BC Parks runs three campgrounds (with hot showers) within the historic site; sites are $12 a night. The nearest lodging is the **Hub Motel,** in the community of Wells a few km back toward Quesnel, tel. (250) 994-3313. Rates are $42 s, $45 d.

Bowron Lake Provincial Park

Best known for its wilderness canoe circuit, Bowron Lake Provincial Park encompasses 121,600 magnificent hectares of forests, lakes, and rivers in the Cariboo Mountains. To get there, take Hwy. 26 east of Quesnel toward Barkerville, but just past Wells take a signposted gravel road to the north.

The park boundary follows a chain of six major lakes—Indianpoint, Isaac, Lanezi, Sandy, Spectacle, and Bowron—and some smaller lakes and waterways that, roughly, form a diamond-shaped circuit. Campsites, cabins, and cooking shelters are strategically spaced along the way. To circumnavigate the entire 116-km route takes 7-10 days of paddling and requires seven portages, the most difficult being a 2.5-km hike uphill from the starting point. As well as being proficient in the use of canoes, those attempting the route should be well prepared for backcountry travel and wet weather. July and August are the most popular months; try to avoid departing on a weekend if you like solitude. September is one of the most colorful months, with lakeside trees in their fall colors.

Before setting out on the circuit, paddlers must obtain a permit from the BC Parks registration center at the end of the park access road. Permits cost $55 (plus tax) for one person or $70 for two. Groups of six or more are required to make advance reservations; contact BC Parks, Cariboo District, 540 Borland St., Williams Lake, BC V2G 1R8; tel. (250) 398-4414.

Bowron Lake Lodge and Resorts, tel. (250) 992-2733, and **Beckers Lodge,** tel. (250) 992-8864, are privately owned lodges near the end of the park access road. Both are right on Bowron Lake and offer a variety of accommodations as well as canoe rentals, full outfitting services for those doing the lake circuit, and meals. Rates start at $48 s, $55 d. At the very end of the access road is a small provincial park campground with sites for $9.50 (no hot showers).

Sights around Town

At **Heritage Corner,** Carson Ave. and Front St., you can see the Old Fraser Bridge, the remains of the steamer *Enterprise,* a Cornish waterwheel used by gold miners, and the original Hudson's Bay Store. To learn all about Alexander Mackenzie or the gold-rush days, head to **Quesnel and District Museum,** Hwy. 97 at Carson Ave., tel. (250) 992-9580. It's open in summer, daily 8 a.m.-4:30 p.m.; admission $2. Eight-km west of Quesnel on Baker Dr. are the geologically intriguing, glacially eroded hoodoos at the small, day-use **Pinnacles Provincial Park.**

Billy Barker Days
The main event in Quesnel is the Billy Barker Days celebration, named for the prospector who made the first gold strike in the Cariboo. Over the third weekend of July, downtown streets are closed to traffic in favor of an outdoor crafts fair, parade, and dancing. Residents casually stroll around town in period costumes from the gold-mining days—men in cowboy hats, women in slinky long dresses with brightly feathered hats. The Quesnel Rodeo is one of some 150 events staged during the festival; a detailed schedule is available at the information center or by calling the organizing committee at (250) 992-1234.

Accommodations and Camping
Quesnel's best-value accommodation is the **Valhalla Motel,** on Hwy. 97 three km south of downtown, tel. (250) 747-1111. All rooms are air-conditioned and feature comfortable beds and tea- and coffee-making facilities. Other amenities include a laundry, pleasant gardens, and a restaurant. Rooms are $50 s, $55 d. **Quesnel Airport Inn, Motel, and RV Park** on the north side of town about one km south of the Barkerville turnoff, tel. (250) 992-5942, offers standard rooms from $40 s, $43 d, kitchenettes for an extra $5, and RV hookups for $15-21.

For campers, the best bet is to head north 11 km to 260-hectare **Ten Mile Lake Provincial**

Park, where sites are $11 a night. Closer to town is **Robert's Roost Campground,** on the west side of Dragon Lake, tel. (250) 747-2015. To get there, take Hwy. 97 south, turn east on Gook Rd., and go to the end. Amenities include showers, a laundry, boat rentals, and a beach with swimming. Unserviced sites are $14, serviced sites $15-19, kitchenette units $55.

For a light meal or just a coffee and cake, head to the **Hokey-pokey Kitchen,** in a historic log building right downtown at 102 Carson Ave., tel. (250) 992-2700. Prices are right, and everything served is fresh and healthy. Another popular coffeehouse is **Granville's,** 383 Reid St., tel. (250) 992-3667, open daily from 8 a.m. **Savala's Steak House,** 240 Reid St., tel. (250) 992-9453, offers an extensive salad bar as well as steaks, spareribs, pizza, and a variety of other Italian dishes. The salad bar alone is $6.50, while entrees start at $9. **Ulysses Restaurant,** 122 Barlow Ave., tel. (250) 992-6606, specializes in southern European cuisine. A hearty plate of pasta or souvlaki is around $10-14.

Services and Information
Quesnel is served by air, rail, and bus transportation. **Air B.C.,** tel. (800) 663-3721, flies daily between Quesnel and Vancouver. The airport is off Hwy. 97 on the northern outskirts of town. **B.C. Rail** trains stop at Quesnel daily on their run between Vancouver and Prince George. The station is on Carson Ave., directly opposite the information center. And then there's **Greyhound,** which offers daily bus service to and from everywhere; the depot is at 365 Kinchant St., tel. (250) 992-2231.

Quesnel Visitor Info Centre is beside Lebourdais Park at 703 Carson Ave., tel. (250) 992-8716 or (800) 992-9922. It's open daily 8 a.m.-8 p.m. in summer, and Mon.-Fri. 8:30 a.m.-4:30 p.m. the rest of the year.

BOB RACE

NORTHERN BRITISH COLUMBIA

Northern British Columbia is a wild and remote region extending from the Yellowhead Highway (Hwy. 16) north to the 60th parallel. Its mostly forested landscape is broken by two major mountain ranges—the Rockies and the Coast Mountains—and literally thousands of lakes, rivers, and streams. Wildlife is abundant here; the land is home to moose, deer, black and grizzly bears, elk, Dall's sheep, and mountain goats.

The region's largest city is **Prince George,** a forestry and service center 780 km north of Vancouver in the heart of a recreational paradise. From Prince George, the Yellowhead Highway runs west to the towns of **Vanderhoof, Burns Lake, Smithers,** and **Terrace,** all jumping-off points for fishing and boating adventures on surrounding lakes and rivers.

The western terminus of the Yellowhead Highway is **Prince Rupert,** a busy coastal city at the north end of the BC Ferries network and, international politics permitting, at the south end of the Alaska Marine Highway. (See "Alaska

Marine Highway" under "Transportation" in the Prince Rupert section below.) It's northern B.C.'s sole major coastal city; north of here the coastline is part of Alaska.

Off the coast from "Rupert" are the **Queen Charlotte Islands,** part of British Columbia yet entirely unique. The islands beckon adventure, with legendary fishing, great beachcombing, ancient Haida villages, and a typical laid-back island atmosphere.

Two routes head north off the Yellowhead Highway. The **Stewart-Cassiar Highway** begins west of Prince George and parallels the Coast Mountains, passing the twin towns of **Stewart** and **Hyder** and a number of remote provincial parks. It ends at its junction with other route north—the famous **Alaska Highway.** Mile Zero of the Alaska Highway is at **Dawson Creek,** northeast of Prince George. From there the highway winds through kilometer after kilometer of boreal forest, past lakes and mountains to the great northland of Alaska.

PRINCE GEORGE

British Columbia's sixth-largest city, Prince George (pop. 78,000) lies roughly at the geographical center of the province, at the confluence of the historically important Fraser and Nechako Rivers. The 1,360-km-long Fraser is the province's longest river, while the Nechako is the Fraser's third-largest tributary. Together the two rivers flow for 50 km within the city limits.

Early trappers and explorers used the rivers as transportation routes into the northern reaches of the province. When they discovered the region's wealth of wolf, fox, lynx, mink, wolverine, otter, and muskrat, they quickly established forts and trading posts by rivers and lakes so that furs could be sent out and supplies could be brought in. In 1807, Simon Fraser of the North West Company began construction of Fort George—named after then-reigning King George III of England—near the confluence of the Fraser and Nechako Rivers. The North West Company merged with the Hudson's Bay Company in 1821, and Fort George was operated as a Hudson's Bay Company post until 1915.

The railroad reached the area in 1908, and in 1915 the Grand Trunk Pacific Railway platted the townsite of Prince George a few km south of the original Fort George. The new town went on to become a major logging, sawmill, and

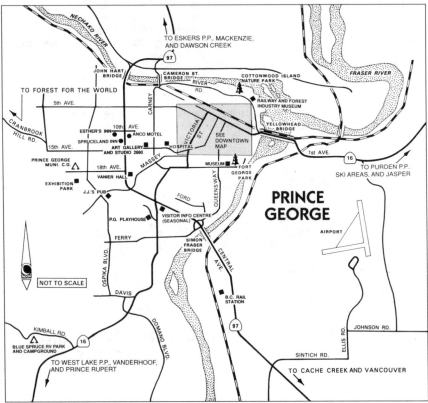

© MOON PUBLICATIONS, INC.

pulp-mill town, the center of the white spruce industry in British Columbia's central interior. Hundreds of sawmills started cutting local timber, and Prince George became the self-proclaimed "Spruce Capital of the World." The city has continued from strength to strength, and has grown to become northern British Columbia's economic, social, and cultural center.

SIGHTS

Connaught Hill Park
The best place to start a Prince George sightseeing trip is the top of Connaught Hill, which affords a panoramic view of the city. To get there from downtown, take Queensway St. south, turn right on Connaught Dr., then right again on Caine Drive. At the summit are grassy tree-shaded lawns, picnic spots, and several well-kept gardens bursting with color in summer.

Fort George Park
The site where Simon Fraser established Fort George in 1807 is today preserved as 36-hectare riverside Fort George Park. Trails lead through the park, along the Fraser River and to the Indian Burial Grounds. Park highlights include the Fraser Fort George Regional Museum (see below), and the original **Fort George Railway Station**, just across from the museum, where on summer weekends and holidays noon-4 p.m., weather permitting, a miniature steam train provides rides along a kilometer or so of track; $2 per person. Next to the rail station is an old schoolhouse—if it's locked, peek in through the window at row after row of old-fashioned desks.

Fort George Park is the venue for the city's July **Folkfest** celebrations and **Simon Fraser Days,** held in late July or early August. To get to the park, take Queensway St. south from downtown and turn left (east) on 20th Avenue.

Fraser Fort George Regional Museum
This museum in Fort George Park, tel. (250) 562-1612, is an excellent place to discover the fascinating natural and human history of Prince George and the lifestyle and culture of the indigenous Carrier tribe. The self-guided-tour pamphlet available at the main entrance gives you the opportunity to explore the museum at your own pace; allow at least an hour. Among the items on display are many stuffed and mounted specimens of wild animals and birds native to British Columbia—including two towering grizzly bears in the foyer—fine crafts of the local Carrier people, an impressive sternwheeler anchor, snowshoes, guns, horrific ani-

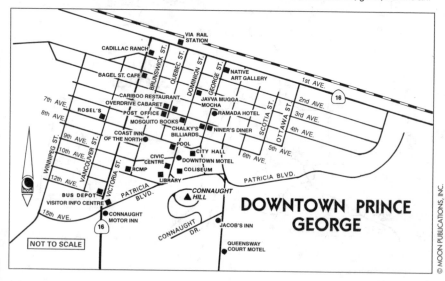

DOWNTOWN PRINCE GEORGE

NOT TO SCALE

© MOON PUBLICATIONS, INC.

mal traps and other relics of the fur trade, artifacts from early sawmilling days, an old buggy, mock-ups of early business establishments, and a hands-on Science Centre. The museum is open mid-May to mid-September, Tues.-Fri. 10 a.m.-7 p.m., Sat.-Mon. 10 a.m.-5 p.m.; the rest of the year, Tues.-Sun. noon-5 p.m. Admission is adults $4, seniors $3, children $2.

Prince George Railway and Forest Industry Museum

Here's one railway buffs shouldn't miss. Take a self-guided tour through some of the antiquated railway cars and buildings, clamber on retired railway equipment, and chug back in time via the black-and-white photo displays and assorted memorabilia. It's open May-Sept., Thurs.-Sun. 10 a.m.-5 p.m. Admission is adults $3, seniors $2.50, children $1.50. To get there from downtown, take Hwy. 16 east to the River Rd. exit (just before the Yellowhead Bridge over the Fraser River) and continue north down River Rd. one km to the museum. For more information call (250) 563-7351.

RACHEL TAYLOR

Cottonwood Island Nature Park

Just down River Rd. from the railroad museum is the entrance to beautiful 33-hectare Cottonwood Island Nature Park—one of Prince George's 116 city parks and a beautiful spot for a quiet stroll or picnic. The park lies beside the Nechako River, which overflows each spring; over time, sediment from the overflow has built up an island. The park's dominant feature is an extensive forest of northern black cottonwood trees. In spring the cottonwoods are covered with sticky buds, and in summer the air is thick and the ground white with seed-bearing tufts of fluff. You'll see all sorts of birds, and might spy the occasional beaver, fox, or moose. The park's trail system is extensive; the short walk between the main parking lot and the river is popular.

Eskers Provincial Park

This 1,600-hectare park 40 km northwest of Prince George (access is off Hwy. 97 along Pine Marsh Rd.) is named for the park's main features. The eskers, or long gravel ridges, were deposited by a receding glacier at the end of the last ice age. Ten km of hiking trails lead around Circle Lake, to two viewing platforms, and through forests of aspen, lodgepole pine, and Douglas fir.

Forestry Sights

Forestry is the heart and soul of Prince George's economy. In summer, **Northwood Pulp and Timber** offers various tours of its operations. The most popular is a four-hour tour that takes in the climate-controlled seedlings nursery; the sawmill, where logs are processed into dimension lumber; and the pulp mill, where high-quality pulp is produced for paper manufacturers around the world. The tour is free, but visitors are required to wear long pants and closed-toe shoes for safety. Tours depart from the seasonal Visitor Info Centre (corner of Hwys. 16 and 97) weekdays at 1 p.m.—they're very popular, so book ahead at (250) 563-5493.

Forest for the World, a 106-hectare recreation area set aside for forest demonstrations, hiking, and cross-country skiing, was established in 1986 to commemorate Prince George's 75th anniversary. To get there, take 15th Ave. to the west end of the city, continue onto Foothills Blvd., and turn left on Cranbrook Hill Rd., which steeply climbs Cranbrook Hill. At the signs for Forest for the World, turn left on Kueng Rd. and continue to the end. From the parking lot, trails lead to Shane Lake (10 minutes one-way), where beavers and waterfowl are present, and to a hilltop viewpoint northwest of Shane Lake (15 minutes one-way).

Galleries

Two-story **Prince George Art Gallery,** 2820 15th Ave., tel. (250) 563-6447, maintains a large permanent collection and also puts up temporary shows that change every four to five weeks. It's a good place to buy high-quality local artwork at a reasonable price. Look for paintings, sculpture, pottery, beadwork, woven and painted silk items, and jewelry. Hours are Tues.-Sat. 10 a.m.-5 p.m., Sunday 1-5 p.m. Next to the gallery is Studio 2880, where you can catch artists in the act of creation.

To see and buy all sorts of native arts and crafts, head for the **Native Art Gallery** in the Native Friendship Centre, 144 George St., tel. (250) 562-7385. Throughout summer you can watch experienced carvers and painters teaching their students. Moccasins, jewelry, carvings, hand-printed cards, and sweatshirts with native designs are all for sale. The gallery is open year-round, Tues.-Sat. 10 a.m.-4:30 p.m.

RECREATION

Summer Activities
Prince George is a convenient base for a wide range of outdoor pursuits. Anglers probe the area's lakes and rivers for trout, char, salmon, steelhead, Dolly Varden, whitefish, sturgeon, and grayling. The lakes also provide enjoyable canoeing and boating. Wildlife watchers will have a field day scanning the woods for black and grizzly bears, elk, mountain goats, bighorn sheep, woodland caribou, wolves, deer, and moose. In spring, autumn, and winter, visit the unique **moose viewing area** near Tabor Mountain to see these enormous wild vegetarians in their natural habitat.

Hikers can follow the **Heritage River Trail** through the city, past interpretive signs detailing local natural history. The clearly marked gravel trail, open to hikers, joggers, cyclists, and cross-country skiers, runs between Cameron Street Bridge and Carrie Jane Gray Park. You can make an 11-km loop of it if you complete the circuit by following Carney Street. Ask for the *Heritage River Trails* pamphlet at the information centers.

Those who prefer to get off the beaten track should instead request the *Prince George and Area Hiking Guide,* which describes seven trails in the area. One of the most popular of those listed in the guide is **Fort George Canyon Trail,** a 4.5-km path through a canyon (striking in autumn) southeast of **West Lake Provincial Park.** To get there go west along Hwy. 16, turn south (left) on Blackwater Rd., then east (left) on West Lake Road.

Skiing
The closest downhill skiing to Prince George is 30 km east at **Tabor Mountain,** while **Purden Lake Ski Area** is a further 25 km east. Both are small family-oriented resorts with under 300 meters vertical rise and no overnight accommodations. Both have ski schools and ski rentals. Near Pine Pass, 192 km north of the city along Hwy. 97, is **Powder King Ski Village,** tel. (250) 997-6323. Snowfall at this small ski area is among the highest of any North American resort, but the resort's remote location makes it a destination for only the very keenest skiers and boarders. The season lasts from mid-November to late April. Skiers enjoy a vertical rise of 700 meters and a longest run of three kilometers. The base village holds a ski school, rentals, and a restaurant.

Cross-country skiers can find beautiful spots to ski just about anywhere in the area—try **Fort George Park** or **Cottonwood Island Nature Park** downtown, any of the nearby abandoned logging roads, or an overnight ski to **Raven Lake.** Get more details at the main Prince George Visitor Info Centre.

Indoor Activities
Four Seasons Pool, 700 Dominion St. (corner of 7th Ave.), tel. (250) 561-7636 or 564-7665, is open daily 6:30 a.m.-11 p.m.; admission of adults $4.50 allows use of the pools, saunas, jacuzzi, and water slide, as well as participation in several daily aqua-fitness classes. Waterslide fanatics will want to head to **Fantasy North Waterslide,** at Esther's Inn, 1151 Commercial Dr., tel. (250) 562-4131.

To shoot pool in a clean and bright setting, head to **Chalky's Billiards,** 511 George St., tel. (250) 564-1283. Prince George also offers bowling alleys, roller rinks, and curling rinks.

ENTERTAINMENT

Performing Arts
Excellent live-theater productions are regularly staged at **Prince George Playhouse,** junction of Hwys. 16 and 97, tel. (250) 563-8401. **Studio 2880,** 2880 15th Ave., tel. (250) 562-4526, is the local arts center, operated by the Community Arts Council. It hosts many cultural activities,

acts as a ticket office for events, and organizes workshops, art classes, concerts, ballets, special events, and two major craft markets each year. In 800-seat **Vanier Hall,** at Prince George Secondary School, 2901 Griffiths, tel. (250) 562-6441, you can take in a concert by the **Prince George Symphony Orchestra** or one of many visiting performers. Touring musicians and other entertainers perform in the **Civic Centre,** 855 Dominion St., tel. (250) 561-7723.

Large events such as Octoberfest, rodeos, and sports tournaments are held in the 2,500-seat **Coliseum,** 888 Dominion St., tel. (250) 561-7635, by the library and Four Seasons Pool.

To find out what's going on in town, pick up the local newspaper or inquire at one of the information centers.

Drinking and Dancing

Of the city's many pubs and nightclubs, one of the most popular is **Steamers,** 2595 Queensway St., tel. (250) 562-6654. **Overdrive Cabaret,** 1192 5th Ave., tel. (250) 564-3773, has a DJ playing top-40 hits, as does **Club 770** in the Coast Inn of the North, 770 Brunswick St., tel. (250) 563-0121. **Cadillac Ranch,** 1380 2nd Ave., tel. (250) 563-7720, features live bands—usually country and western. If you're just looking for a friendly pub and a quiet drink, try **Coach's Corner Pub** in the Ramada Hotel, 444 George St., tel. (250) 563-0055.

FESTIVALS AND EVENTS

Prince George is certainly not short on year-round celebrations and goofy seasonal events; ask at the information centers for a free events calendar. In early January, the **Prince George Winter Carnival** features logging sports, scuba diving, dogsledding, and car races on the ice at nearby Tabor Lake. One month later the city goes berserk with a 10-day **Mardi Gras,** featuring a snow ball and snowgolf in bright crazy costumes, knurdling (jousting using padded poles), bed races on ice, and other hog-wild events. It's all finished off with a fireworks display.

In May, the warmer half of the annual events calendar kicks off with **Elks May Days,** the biennial **Forestry Exhibition,** and the **Northern Children's Festival.** Summer brings the big

Folkfest to Fort George Park. At this early-July bash, Prince George celebrates its ethnic heritage through song, dance, food, and dress. **Simon Fraser Days** is a citywide celebration held around the beginning of August. During this week and a half of madness, you'll witness just about everything: the Sandblast (when skiers test their skills down the sandy slopes of a local riverbank), mudbowl volleyball, raft races, a rodeo, and a triathlon. The only fall celebration is **Octoberfest,** which rocks the Coliseum for days with Bavarian oom-pah-pah.

ACCOMMODATIONS AND CAMPING

Hotels and Motels

Least expensive of the accommodations downtown is **Downtown Motel,** 650 Dominion St., tel. (250) 563-9241, which offers small, basic rooms from $45 s or d. The full-service **Coast Inn of the North,** 770 Brunswick St., tel. (250) 563-0121 or (800) 663-1144, charges $89 s, $99 d. Of a similar standard is **Ramada Hotel,** 444 George St., tel. (250) 563-0055 or (800) 272-6232, an unattractive but distinctive redbrick building in the heart of downtown. Amenities include a restaurant, lounge, pub, pool, sauna and whirlpool, casino, gift shop, and covered parking. Rooms start at $129.

A few blocks south from downtown, where the Yellowhead Hwy. crosses Patricia Blvd., is **Connaught Motor Inn,** 1550 Victoria St., tel. (250) 562-4441 or (800) 663-6620. It's a large place, with close to 100 air-conditioned rooms and a pool, sauna, and restaurant. Rates are $55 s, $60 d. South of downtown on Queensway St. are a couple of old two-story motels with budget rates: **Jacob's Inn,** 1401 Queensway St., tel. (250) 563-9236; and **Queensway Court Motel,** 1616 Queensway St., tel. (250) 562-5068. Both offer basic rooms from $40.

The most concentrated area of accommodations is along the Hwy. 97 bypass west of downtown. The best value of these, with comfortable rooms and a load of extras at a reasonable price, is **Esther's Inn,** 1151 Commercial Cres., tel. (250) 562-4131 or (800) 663-6844. Rooms are set around a lush tropical atrium packed with palms and philodendrons, waterfalls, Polynesian artifacts, swimming pools, a water slide,

and a thatched-roof restaurant. Rooms range $55-80 s, $60-85 d. For an extra $10 you can have a room with a kitchen. Another good choice is the modern **Spruceland Inn,** 1391 Central St., tel. (250) 563-0102, which charges $52 s, $58 d. To save a few bucks, consider **Anco Motel,** 1630 Central St., tel. (250) 563-3671, which charges from $44 s or d.

Campgrounds

Privately operated **Blue Spruce RV Park and Campground** is on Kimball Rd., five km west on Hwy. 16 from the junction of Hwy. 97, tel. (250) 964-7272. It's a popular spot, filling up each night during the busy summer months. Each site has a picnic table and a barbecue grate, and the facilities include spotlessly clean heated bathrooms, a coin-operated laundry, a swimming pool, mini-golf, and a playground. Unserviced sites are $15, hookups $18-22.50. Closer to the city is treeless **Prince George Municipal Campground,** at 4188 18th Ave. (take the Hwy. 97 bypass). Sites are $12-17. The closest provincial park to Prince George is at **Purden Lake,** 55 km east of the city on Hwy. 16. The picturesque lake has a small stretch of sandy beach and offers fishing for rainbow trout and burbot. Sites are $12 a night.

FOOD

Coffeehouses

Javva Mugga Mocha, 304 George St., tel. (250) 562-3338, is a stylish, big-city type of coffeehouse right downtown. A few blocks from downtown is **Bagel Street Cafe,** 1493 3rd Ave. at Victoria St., tel. (250) 563-0671. It's small—just one long row of stools—and gets crowded when workers from the government offices across the road are on a break, but it's inexpensive; coffee $1.50, hearty lunches from $5.

Restaurants

An excellent place for lunch is **Papaya Grove Restaurant** in Esther's Inn, 1151 Commercial Cres., tel. (250) 562-4131. You can choose from among three different seating areas: under a thatched roof, around the pool, or in the bar. All are enclosed within a massive tropical indoor atrium. A set menu is offered, but the buffet is the most popular choice. The daily lunch buffet (11 a.m.-2 p.m.) is around $9, with a different theme each day. Sunday brunch is particularly good; for $12.95 you get all the usual breakfast choices, along with salmon, prawns, roast beef, and a staggering number of desserts. The dinner buffet is $12.95 Sun.-Thurs., and $16.95 on Friday and Saturday when prime rib is served.

Right downtown are a couple of good-value restaurants. **Niner's Diner,** 508 George St., tel. (250) 562-1299, features an intriguing green-and-gray 1950s' diner decor. All the waitpersons are garbed in shiny shirts and small green aprons. On the menu are chicken dishes for $10-12 (the stir-fry is huge); sandwiches and burgers from $6; pasta, seafood, steaks, and prime rib ranging $9-18; and desserts $4-6. It's open Mon.-Sat. 11:30 a.m.-11:30 p.m. Another popular spot, similarly priced, is **Cariboo Steak and Seafood Restaurant,** 1165 5th Ave., tel. (250) 564-1220.

When locals feel like dressing up and splashing out a little, they head for **Rosel's,** 1624 7th Ave., tel. (250) 562-4972. Occupying a heritage house with a pleasant outdoor patio, Rosel's offers a varied menu including veal, prawns, cabbage rolls, Viennese schnitzel, pasta, European sausages, and sandwiches. Lunch runs $8-12, dinners are $12-28, and at either one you have the option of selecting small or regular portions of the main dishes—handy for the diet-conscious. It's open for lunch Mon.-Sat. 11 a.m.-3 p.m. and for dinner daily from 5:30 p.m.

Another spot for a splurge is the **Log House Restaurant,** on the Yellowhead Hwy. nine km east of downtown, tel. (250) 963-9515. It's decorated in a typical northern style—the walls are crammed with antiques and trophy heads. Both the food and service are excellent.

TODD CLARK

TRANSPORTATION

Air

The airport is about 18 km east of town and is served by **Air B.C.,** tel. (250) 561-2905; **Canadian Regional,** tel. (250) 563-0521; and **Central Mountain Air,** tel. (250) 693-9022 or (800) 663-3905. The **Airporter** bus, tel. (250) 563-2220, provides shuttle service between the airport and downtown. One-way fare is $12.

Train

VIA Rail operates transcontinental service from Prince George west to Prince Rupert and east through Jasper and Edmonton to Toronto and beyond. The VIA Rail station is on 1st Ave. between Brunswick and Quebec Sts., tel. (250) 564-5233 or (800) 561-8630.

. **B.C. Rail** runs the Cariboo Prospector, a summer-only train between Vancouver and Prince George via Whistler. The station is out of town on the southeast side of the city, off Terminal Blvd., tel. (250) 564-9080 or (800) 663-8238.

Bus

The **Greyhound** bus depot is at 1566 12th Ave. (corner of Victoria St.), just across from Tourism Prince George, tel. (250) 564-5454 or (800) 661-8747. Greyhound runs regularly scheduled services from Prince George south to Kamloops and Vancouver (via Williams Lake and Quesnel); west along the Yellowhead Hwy. to Terrace and Prince Rupert; north to Dawson Creek via Chetwynd; and east along the Yellowhead Hwy. to Jasper and Edmonton.

Getting Around

The **Prince George Transit System** operates buses throughout the city daily except Sunday. Pick up a current *Prince George Rider's Guide* from the information centers or call (250) 563-

0011. Prince George **handyDART,** tel. (250) 562-1394, provides door-to-door transportation for disabled passengers unable to use the regular bus service.

For a cab call **Emerald Taxi,** tel. (250) 563-3333, or **Prince George Taxi,** tel. (250) 564-4444. Car-rental agencies in town include: **Avis,** tel. (250) 562-2847; **Budget,** tel. (250) 960-4200; **Hertz,** tel. (250) 963-7454; **National Tilden,** tel. (250) 564-4847; **Rent-a-wreck,** tel. (250) 563-7336; and **Thrifty,** tel. (250) 564-3499.

SERVICES AND INFORMATION

Services

Prince George Public Library, 887 Dominion St., tel. (250) 563-9251, also has a good display of native art and artifacts; open Mon.-Thurs. 10 a.m.-9 p.m., Fri.-Sat. 10 a.m.-5:30 p.m., Sunday (in winter only) 1-5 p.m. **Mosquito Books,** 1209 5th Ave., tel. (250) 563-6495, features a great selection of local and northern British Columbia literature; closed Sunday.

The main post office is on the corner of 5th Ave. and Quebec Street. Prince George Regional Hospital is at 2000 15th Ave., tel. (250) 565-2000 (routine calls) or 565-2444 (emergencies). A private health clinic deals with walk-in problems; turn off 15th Ave. on Edmonton by the hospital. The RCMP is on the corner of Brunswick and 10th Ave., behind the library, tel. (250) 562-3371.

Information

Tourism Prince George, tel. (250) 562-3700 or (800) 668-7646, operates two information centers. The main one is at the corner of Victoria St. and Patricia Blvd; open year-round, Mon.-Fri. 8:30 a.m.-5 p.m., Saturday 9 a.m.-4 p.m. The other one is at the corner of Hwys. 16 and 97, handy if you're coming into the city from the south or west; open summers only, daily 9 a.m.-8 p.m.

WEST FROM PRINCE GEORGE

VANDERHOOF

The first town west of Prince George is Vanderhoof (pop. 4,500), a service center for the Nechako Valley and British Columbia's geographical center (the exact spot is marked by a cairn five km east of town). Vanderhoof grew as a stop on the Grand Trunk Pacific Railway. Today it's a prosperous farming and logging town.

Sights
The 1914 building at the corner of Hwy. 16 and Pine Ave. houses **Vanderhoof Community Museum,** tel. (250) 567-2991. The museum displays mounted specimens of birds and animals, pioneer equipment, blacksmithing tools, a rock collection, and plenty of local history from gold-rush and pioneer days. It's open daily 10 a.m.-5 p.m.; admission $1. The museum is on the grounds of a **Heritage Village,** which consists of 11 restored heritage buildings, among them a jail, 1922 schoolhouse, and a restored gambling room. Also in the village is the **OK Cafe,** where you can tuck in to hearty homemade soup and rolls, salads, and tasty pie and ice cream. It's inside a heritage-style building decorated with old-fashioned wallpaper and frilly curtains.

Vanderhoof's town symbol is the Canada goose. You can see these beautiful birds and a variety of other waterfowl in spring and fall at their transient home, **Nechako Bird Sanctuary,** along the banks of the Nechako River. Access is via the wooden bridge at the north end of Burrard Ave., the town's main street.

If you want to get away from the main highway for a couple of hours, take a 100-km detour south along a good gravel road (Nechako Ave., then Kenney Dam Rd.) to **Kenney Dam,** once the world's largest earth-filled dam. From the far side of the dam, a 1.2-km trail (20 minutes each way) leads downriver to 18-meter-high **Cheslatta Falls** and a picnic area.

Recreation
Rivers and lakes dot the region, making fishing a prime local pastime. Pick up a copy of the local *Recreation and Fishing Guide* from the information center. Another must-have for those who want to escape the main highway is the free *Forest Service Recreation Sites* brochure and map for Vanderhoof-Kluskus. It details the Nechako River watershed south of Vanderhoof, including forest roads, trails, recreation sites, campsites, and other facilities. If you're heading north to Fort St. James, also collect the free Forest Service brochure and map for Stuart Lake.

In July, some 20,000 spectators flock into Vanderhoof to enjoy the spectacular **Vanderhoof International Airshow,** one of the largest airshows in North America and a three-day camp-out. Planes putt and zoom in from just about everywhere to see military jet aerobatic displays, civilian stunt flying, experimental aircraft, and antique fighters and warbirds parked on the tarmac. Admission is adults $18, seniors and students $11 (tickets are cheaper if bought in advance). Campsites are $10 per night. For more information write P.O. Box 1248, Vanderhoof, BC V0J 3A0, or call (250) 567-3144.

Practicalities
Inexpensive accommodations are available at the **Hillview Motel,** tel. (250) 567-4468, and the **Coachlight Motel,** tel. (250) 567-2296. Both are on Hwy. 16 at the east side of town and charge from $45 s, $50 d. The Coachlight also offers RV hookups for $12. Much nicer, and only a few dollars more, is **North Country Inn,** downtown at 2575 Burrard Ave., tel. (250) 567-3047.

Riverside Park Campground enjoys a pleasant setting beside the Nechako River. Turn north off Hwy 16 onto Burrard Ave. and continue through town; the campground is to the west side of Burrard Avenue. Showers and firewood are supplied; $13 per night. **Vanderhoof Municipal Campground** is beside Stony Creek, along Hwy. 16 on the west side of town. Facilities are fairly grim, but sites are only $9; no hookups or showers.

For delicious food at reasonable prices head to the comfortable log-cabin **North Country Inn,** 2575 Burrard Ave., tel. (250) 567-3047.

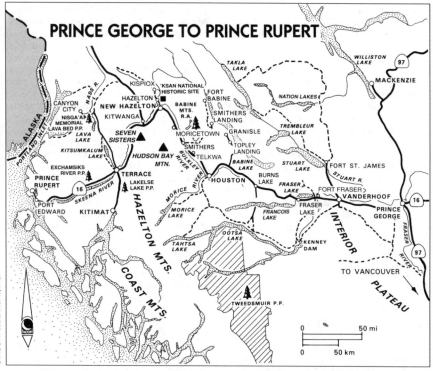

PRINCE GEORGE TO PRINCE RUPERT

Burgers and sandwiches are $5-9; soup and salad bar is around $8; steak, seafood, and pasta dinners run $10-29. Try the delicious chicken lasagna. Another good choice is the **Chuckwagon Cafe,** 2466 Burrard Ave., tel. (250) 567-2220; closed Sunday.

Vanderhoof Visitor Info Centre is at 2353 Burrard Ave., tel. (250) 567-2124. It's open daily 8:30 a.m.-6 p.m. in summer, and Mon.-Fri. 9 a.m.-5 p.m. the rest of the year.

FORT ST. JAMES

A sealed road leads 60 km north from Vanderhoof to Fort St. James (pop. 2,200), the earliest nonnative settlement on the Pacific Slope of British Columbia. It's worth a detour up from the Yellowhead Highway to check out several sights of interest in the area.

Fort St. James National Historic Site
In the early 1800s, Fort St. James was the chief fur-trading post and capital of the large and prosperous district of New Caledonia—the name originally given to central B.C. by Simon Fraser.

When Fraser first arrived at Stuart Lake he was working for the North West Company, expanding the fur trade west of the Rockies and trying to find a water route to the Pacific. He established the fort among the cooperative local Carrier tribe in 1806. The natives did not fear the white man—they desired his iron, tools, weapons, and exotic jewelry. But establishment of the fort changed their lifestyle forever. In 1821, the fort became a Hudson's Bay Company outpost and continued to operate until the early 20th century.

Today the beautifully restored fort forms the centerpiece of a historic park at the southeast end of Stuart Lake. Enter the fort through the Visitor Reception Centre, which holds displays on

© MOON PUBLICATIONS, INC.

pioneer explorers, fur traders, and the indigenous Carrier people. An audio recording and a map trace the route of the early explorers, and a slide show fills you in on the restoration of the fort's original buildings. Free guided walking tours leave from the center May-September. In July and August, characters dressed in pioneer garb lurk in the log-constructed general store, the fish cache, the single men's bunkhouse, the main house, and the veggie garden. You're actively encouraged to get into the spirit of things and play along. Tell them you've just arrived by canoe, want to stay the night in the men's house, and need a good horse and some provisions . . . then see what happens!

Most of the park is open only in the summer season, mid-May through September, daily 9 a.m.-5 p.m. The reception center, tel. (250) 996-7191, is open the rest of the year as well, Mon.-Fri. 8:30 a.m.-4:30 p.m. Admission to the park is free.

Other Local Sights

Aside from the historic park, you can cruise west along the lakefront, first along Stuart Dr., then Lakeshore Drive. You'll pass Our Lady of Good Hope Catholic Church, built in 1873, and the Russ Baker Memorial (Baker was a local bush pilot who founded Pacific Western Airlines). Bush pilots played an important role during the early days of mining, fur trapping, and forestry in this area; find out more at the information center. Pictographs are found along the lake's northern shore but can only be reached by boat.

The area's natural attractions also make the side trip to Fort St. James worthwhile. Start with **Stuart Lake** itself, the province's seventh largest body of water. The lake is more than 90 km long and up to 13 km wide. It's known to produce rainbow trout up to seven kilograms and lake char up to 13 kilograms, as well as lake trout, whitefish, and kokanee. So break out the rod and reel, or go swimming, sailing, or windsurfing.

North of Fort St. James, Germanson Landing North Rd. (well-maintained gravel) leads to the **Takla-Nation Lakes** region—a favorite with hikers and campers in search of untouched wilderness, and with anglers wanting to pull grayling, char, rainbow trout, and Dolly Varden from the region's dozens of fish-filled lakes. Others canoe or take small putt-putt boats along waterways used by pioneer explorers. Canoeists often travel the

100-km route through the Nation Lakes chain. And locals say it's possible, using a small motorboat, to travel 290 km through the Takla Lake system from Fort St. James, taking 7-10 days; you'll need experience handling rough water and weather and should contact the local Forest Service office for advice about natural land and water hazards, weather patterns, and other pertinent conditions. The third very popular way of getting into the backcountry is by floatplane—to rustic lodges and remote fishing camps.

Many good hiking trails wander away from the local area—try the three-km (one hour) each way **Mt. Pope Trail** northwest of town, which takes you to the summit for views of Stuart Lake and surrounding mountains. Get details on this and other trails at the local information center.

In winter, **Murray Ridge Ski Hill,** 30 km north of Fort St. James, offers 19 designated runs on a 570-meter vertical rise, as well as a day lodge, ski-rental shop, ski school, and snack bar. The season runs from mid-December to mid-April, with lifts operating Friday through Monday. Other winter activities popular in the area include cross-country skiing, snowmobiling, and ice fishing.

Practicalities

The best place to stay in the area is **Stuart Lodge,** Stones Bay Rd., tel. (250) 996-7917, on the shore of Stuart Lake five km west of Fort St. James. The complex's six kitchenette units are well-priced at just $55 s, $61 d. If you'd prefer to be in town, stay at the **New Caledonia Motel,** 167 Douglas Ave., tel. (250) 996-8051, which charges $45 s, $50 d.

Paarens Beach Provincial Park and **Sowchea Bay Provincial Recreation Area,** west of Fort St. James, both offer lakeside tent and vehicle camping, swimming, fishing, picnic areas, and washrooms; open May-Sept. with an $9.50 nightly fee for campers. **Stuart River Campground** on Roberts Rd. (cross Stuart River where many floatplanes are moored), tel. (250) 996-8690, features river fishing, boat launching and rentals, showers, and a laundromat; unserviced sites $12, hookups $14.

Dining opportunities in Fort St. James are limited. Head north of town to **Whiskey Jack Restaurant,** tel. (250) 996-8828, for lunch and dinner served in a relaxed atmosphere and a pleasant setting.

To get the scoop on the entire area, stop at **Fort St. James Visitor Info Centre,** 115 Douglas Ave., tel. (250) 996-7023. It's open Mon.-Fri. 8:30 a.m.-4:30 p.m. in May, June, and September, and daily 8 a.m.-6 p.m. in July and August.

FORT FRASER TO FRASER LAKE

Heading west from Vanderhoof, the Yellowhead Highway passes through low rolling terrain to **Fort Fraser,** one of the province's oldest communities; Simon Fraser established the former fur-trading post in 1806.

Continuing west, the highway crosses the wide Nechako River, passing the turnoff to 191-hectare **Beaumont Provincial Park.** The park offers boating on Fraser Lake and a campground open May-Oct.; $12 per site. It also marks the eastern edge of an area known as the **Lakes District,** comprising over 300 fish-filled lakes. Traveling this stretch of the highway in summer you'll notice all the vehicles hauling canoes, kayaks, or small fishing boats.

The town of **Fraser Lake** (pop. 1,400), 60 km west of Vanderhoof, lies on a chunk of land sloping gently down to its namesake lake. In winter, trumpeter swans settle in at each end of the lake. In summer, a salmon run on the **Stellako River**—a short stretch of water between Fraser and Francois Lakes—draws scores of eager anglers.

Overlooking Fraser Lake, **Pipers Glen Resort,** tel. (250) 690-7565, features a grassy lakeshore camping area with full hookups and showers; $12-15 per night. **Fraser Lake Visitor Info Centre,** along the highway through town, tel. (250) 699-8941, offers tourism information and a small museum out back. It's open July-Aug., daily 8 a.m.-6 p.m.

Just west of Fraser Lake, a turnoff leads south to **Francois Lake,** another popular fishing hole. **Glenannan Tourist Area,** at the lake's east end, boasts a handful of resorts providing everything an angler could possibly desire. **Birch Bay Resort,** tel. (250) 699-8484, rents motorboats and offers small rustic cabins for $35-45 per night and campsites for $13-16 per night. In same vicinity is **Nithi on the Lake,** tel. (250) 699-6675, featuring similar accommodations at similar rates.

BURNS LAKE AND VICINITY

The first thing you see when you enter Burns Lake is an enormous chainsaw-carved trout with the inscription "Three Thousand Miles of Fishing!" That pretty much sums up what attracts visitors to the town and surrounding Lakes District.

Like other towns along the Yellowhead Highway, Burns Lake (pop. 2,000) grew after construction of the Grand Trunk Pacific Railway. Many buildings from those early railroad days remain, and **Deadman's Island** in Burns Lake got its name from an accident that killed two workers during the railway's construction. The one-hectare island is the province's smallest provincial park.

Sights
Continue west along the highway through town for about one kilometer until you come to the green-and-white **Heritage Centre,** comprising a museum and the local information center. The museum is housed in a 1919 home whose furnished rooms contain an odd assortment of articles, including a collection of foreign currency, memorabilia from an old ship (viewed through a porthole), and a number of typewriters that have seen better days. Open daily 1-5 p.m.; admission $2.

Ask at the adjacent information center for a map showing the location of all the heritage buildings around town. Of particular note is the **Bucket of Blood,** a historic fur-trading depot and gambling den where a murder occurred during a poker game. It's on the corner of Hwy. 16 and 5th Avenue. You'll also discover many gift shops where paintings and beadwork by the local Carrier bands are on display.

For a wonderful view of the area, follow 5th Ave. up the hill out of town, then take the turnoff to **Boer Mountain Forestry Lookout.** Rockhounds might prefer to head 6.5 km south of town to **Eagle Creek Agate Opal Site,** one of the province's few opal deposits. From the parking lot, a four-km trail (one hour each way) leads to the creekside deposit and an intriguing outcrop of hoodoos.

Fish Fantasies
More than 300 lakes dot the high country between the Fraser and Skeena watersheds, and

all are renowned fishing spots. To even mention all the lakes and their fishing possibilities would take a whole other book. Ask at the information center for the free *Burns Lake 3,000 Miles of Fishing* map and information sheet. The center also stocks brochures on local fishing resorts and guides, boat rentals, and floatplane adventures.

Burns Lake itself offers excellent fishing for rainbow, eastern brook, and cutthroat trout, as well as kokanee, chinook, steelhead, lake char, and other species. The area between Burns Lake and Tweedsmuir Provincial Park is dotted with resorts and rustic lodges, most catering primarily to fishermen.

Practicalities
Wanakena Motel, on the east end of town before Hwy. 16 descends to the main street, tel. (250) 692-3151, is an older place but rooms are clean; $45 s, $50 d, kitchenettes an extra $5. For something a bit more upmarket, stay at **Burns Lake Motor Inn,** Hwy. 16 W, tel. (250) 692-7545, which charges $70s, $75 d.

KOA Burns Lake is off Hwy. 16 on Freeport Rd., about seven km east of Burns Lake, tel. (250) 692-3105. Its picturesque tent sites lie up in a forested area, and each site has a picnic table. The large RV section below is out in the open, and has full hookups, free showers, a laundromat, store, and gift shop. Unserviced sites are $14, hookups $18-24. The nearest provincial parks with campgrounds are along a gravel road north of Burns Lake. **Ethel F. Wilson Provincial Park** is on Pinkut Lake, 24 km along this road, and **Pendleton Bay Provincial Park** is 15 km farther up the same road.

A locally recommended eatery is the **Panhandle Restaurant,** 710 Yellowhead Hwy., tel. (250) 692-3316, serving reasonably priced Chinese dishes; open daily for dinner. Across the highway from Lakeview Mall, **Mulvaney's Pub,** tel. (250) 692-3078, offers salads, burgers, and hearty pub-style meals at reasonable prices.

Burns Lake Visitor Info Centre is in the Heritage Centre west of downtown, tel. (250) 692-3773. It's open through summer, Mon.-Fri. 8 a.m.-7 p.m., Sat.-Sun. 9 a.m.-5 p.m. As well as town information, the staff provides hints on the best fishing spots and directions to Tweedsmuir Provincial Park.

TWEEDSMUIR PROVINCIAL PARK (NORTH)

The town of Burns Lake is not only near British Columbia's smallest provincial park (Deadman's Island in Burns Lake), it also happens to be the northern gateway to the largest: 981,000-hectare Tweedsmuir Provincial Park. The park extends over 200 km from north to south. Its northern boundary, formed by **Ootsa** and **Whitesail Lakes,** is accessed along a network of gravel roads south from Burns Lake. The only road *within* the park is Hwy. 20 (see "West on Highway 20" under "Cariboo Country," in the Central British Columbia chapter).

Most of the park's northern section is made up of the **Quanchus Mountain Range,** holding many peaks topping 1,900 meters, and the **Nechako Plateau,** which is riddled with lakes and streams. Wildlife abounds. If you're in the right place at the right time you can see caribou, mountain goats, moose, black and grizzly bears, mule deer, wolves, smaller mammals such as hoary marmots and wolverines, and many birds. The lakes are filled with fish, including rainbow trout, kokanee, mountain whitefish, and burbot, among others.

Aside from fishing, the most popular activity in the park's northern reaches is boating, canoeing, or kayaking the circular route through Ootsa, Whitesail, Eutsuk, Tetachuck, and Natalkuz Lakes. Some portaging is required. Ootsa Lake is the main access to the park but the shoreline has been described as a forest of drowned trees and floating hazards—very dangerous, with few places to land when frequent strong winds funnel across the lakes. Some channels have been cut through the dead trees to emergency landing areas; follow the large yellow diamond signs. Because of the strong winds, keep as close to the shoreline as possible. May is the windiest month here.

Practicalities
Wilderness campsites are sprinkled around some of the lakes within the park. To get to Ootsa Lake, follow Hwy. 35 for 16 km south from Burns Lake to Francois Lake, take the free vehicle-ferry across Francois Lake, then continue south another 44 km to the settlement of Ootsa Lake. To

get *into* the park itself, you'll need a canoe, kayak, or motorboat, or be willing to charter a floatplane. **Lakes District Air Services,** based along Francois Lake Rd., tel. (250) 692-3229, flies charters year-round—on floats in summer and skis in winter. Rates are $350 per hour for the three-passenger Cessna 185, and $460 per hour for the six-passenger Beaver. This company also owns a cabin in the park at Tesla Lake. The cabin sleeps four, and comes equipped with cooking facilities, hot showers, and a couple of small motorboats. It rents for $1,800 for four people for four days, including the flight out; you supply your own food, sleeping bags, and fishing gear.

Before visiting the park, write BC Parks, District Manager, Bag 5000, Smithers, BC V0J 2N0, tel. (250) 847-7320, or stop by Burns Lake Visitor Info Centre.

TOPLEY TO TELKWA

Babine Lake

At Topley, 51 km west of Burns Lake, a side road leads north to 177-km-long Babine Lake, the province's largest natural lake and yet another spot known for producing trophy-size rainbow trout, Dolly Varden, kokanee, coho salmon, and whitefish. The rivers flowing in and out of the lake also splash with fish, including rainbow trout, steelhead, and salmon.

Topley Landing, 30 km from the Yellowhead Hwy., is a former trapping and trading center

dating back to the 1700s. Beyond the landing, over the Fulton River, is 148-hectare **Red Bluff Provincial Park,** named for iron-impregnated cliffs nearby. The park's small campground enjoys a picturesque riverside location, but facilities are limited; $9.50 per night.

The road terminates at **Granisle,** formerly a company town where life revolved around a copper mine. In 1992 the mine closed, many residents moved out, and a developer moved in, attempting to attract retirees and holidaymakers. The preexisting mining-employee accommodations were refurbished to be sold as condominiums, and the former Granisle Village Inn was revamped and renamed the **Grande Isles Resort.** The resort, tel. (250) 697-6322 or (800) 671-4475, is excellent value, with comfortable, kitchenette units from $60 s or d. Another option is to head down to the cafe and ask around for George Johnson, who rents out basic rooms complete with lake views and kitchens for $45. The sockeye salmon run here in August and September, but other than that there's little reason to come out here.

Houston

Like Burns Lake, Houston's welcoming sign also proudly bears a carved fish—this time a steelhead. Houston calls itself "Steelhead Country." The forestry town lies at the confluence of the Bulkley and Morice Rivers in the stunning Bulkley Valley, which enjoys the snowcapped Telkwa and Babine Ranges for a backdrop. As in the

Fishing draws many visitors to Babine Lake.

rest of this region, the local fishing is superb. At the information center you can pick up a copy of the *Northwood Pulp and Timber Limited Forest Operations* recreation map, which shows all the area's rivers and lakes. The best steelhead fishing is in the Morice River—take the highway west toward Smithers, turn left at the Northwood Pulp Mill sign, and continue about 1.6 km to the end. At the dirt road turn right (at the bridge). Both bait fishing and fly-fishing are popular here.

Motels in town include **Houston Motor Inn**, tel. (250) 845-7112, and **Pleasant Valley Motel**, tel. (250) 845-2246. Both are on the highway and both charge from $52 s, $55 d. Right downtown on 14th St. is **District of Houston Campground**, little more than a parking lot; $4 per night.

Houston Visitor Info Centre is on the highway at Benson Ave., tel. (250) 845-7640—look for the huge fishing rod in the parking lot. It's open in summer, daily 9 a.m.-5 p.m., weekdays only the rest of the year.

Telkwa

As you continue west, the scenery just keeps getting better. You'll pass open fields and rolling, densely forested hills, all the while surrounded by snowcapped mountains peeking tantalizingly out of clouds. The neat little village of Telkwa lies at the confluence of the Bulkley and Telkwa Rivers. Several species of anadromous fish make spawning runs up the rivers here at various times of year—spring chinook salmon in late June, coho salmon in August, and steelhead between fall and freeze-up. The area also appeals to canoeists, offering stretches of water to suit novices through intermediates.

Many of the buildings in the village were put up between 1908 and 1924. The Telkwa Museum Society puts out a *Walking Tour Through Historic Telkwa* brochure, which describes each of the buildings. Nearby **Tyhee Lake Provincial Park** has a good swimming beach, picnic facilities, and a campground with hot showers ($12 per site, May-Sept.; free the rest of the year).

SMITHERS AND VICINITY

The town of Smithers (pop. 5,800) is surrounded by the Coast Mountains, with splendid 2,560-meter Hudson Bay Mountain towering directly

above. It's a vibrant community with some excellent accommodations, fine restaurants, and a variety of interesting arts-and-crafts shops. Hiking trails close to town lead to a magnificent glacier, intriguing fossil beds, and a remote recreation area.

Town Sights

With a backdrop of magnificent towering mountains, it's no surprise that Main Street is done up in a Bavarian theme. Visitors shop here for native crafts and tourist paraphernalia. The grand old 1925 courthouse, at the junction of the Yellowhead Hwy. and Main St., is home to **Bulkley Valley Museum**, tel. (250) 847-5322, and **Smithers Art Gallery**, tel. (250) 847-3898. The museum spotlights the valley's history with plenty of black-and-white photos and pioneer equipment. The gallery exhibits local artwork. Both the museum and gallery are open in summer, Mon.-Sat. 11 a.m.-5 p.m. **Adam's Igloo Wildlife Museum**, on the left side of the highway about 10 km west of town, tel. (250) 847-3188, displays a large number of stuffed North American animals exhibited in simulated natural habitats. It's open in summer, Tues.-Sun. 9 a.m.-6 p.m.

Driftwood Canyon Provincial Park

Many millions of years ago, the Bulkley Valley had a subtropical climate. The area north of where Smithers now lies was a low wetland of swamps and shallow lakes. Over eons, deposited sediments covered and preserved the remains of the plants and animals that died in the water. Around a million years ago, a lava flow covered the entire region. But then during the last Ice Age, melting ice carved out a canyon that sliced right through the ancient wetlands, exposing the fossil beds.

Most of the fossils here are from plants, but insect and fish fossils have also been uncovered, including some of the world's oldest known trout fossils. A short walk from the road leads to a viewing platform over the east bank of Driftwood Creek, where interpretive panels describe the site's significance. Excavated specimens can be viewed in the Bulkley Valley Museum. The park is 17 km northeast of town; take Hwy. 16 three km east, head north on Babine Lake Rd., turn left on Telkwa High Rd., then right on Driftwood Road.

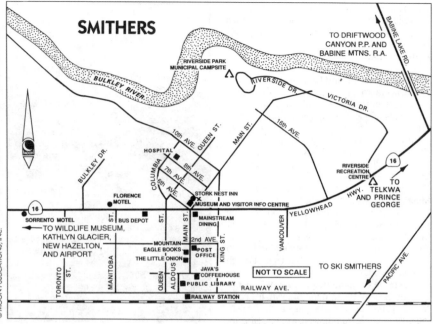

Babine Mountains Recreation Area

From Driftwood Canyon, Driftwood Rd. continues five km to a parking lot—the trailhead for a variety of trails leading into Babine Mountains Recreation Area. The area protects 32,000 hectares of the Skeena Mountains, a remote wilderness dominated by rugged peaks and glacier-fed lakes and rivers. The park is accessible only on foot, but you don't need to travel too far into the park to reach the best parts. From this trailhead, the **McCabe Trail** leads eight km (three hours) one-way to the alpine meadows between Mts. Hyland and Harvey, while the **Silver King Basin Trail** climbs steadily through a subalpine forest for nine km (three hours) one-way to another alpine meadow. The wildflower-filled meadows come alive with color in mid-July.

Kathlyn Glacier and Vicinity

About eight km west of Smithers on the Yellowhead Hwy., take the **Hudson Bay Mountain Lookout** turnout for magnificent views of the mountain and the quickly receding Kathlyn Glacier on its north face. In the same vicinity,

turn south off the highway at Lake Kathlyn Rd. to the trailhead for **Glacier Gulch,** a strenuous 1,000 vertical meters above the parking lot. The trail is only six km one-way, but allow at least three hours to reach the toe of Kathlyn Glacier. Just 500 meters along the trail is dramatic **Twin Falls,** a worthy destination in itself. Beyond the Glacier Gulch trailhead, Lake Kathlyn Rd. ends, appropriately enough, at **Lake Kathlyn,** a photogenic body of water at the base of Hudson Bay Mountain.

Ski Smithers

This 120-hectare ski resort on Hudson Bay Mountain is mostly geared to beginners and intermediates, but a few of the 19 designated runs challenge more experienced skiers. Three lifts serve a vertical rise of 600 meters. Facilities include two day lodges, a rental shop, and a ski school. A day pass is adults $32, children $21; those under six and over 60 ski free. For resort information call (250) 847-2058 or, within B.C., (800) 665-4299. Cross-country skiers can choose from a 2.5-km marked trail on the mountain or the 10-km **Pine Creek Loop** on the road to the ski area. To get to the mountain take either Main St. or King St. south onto Railway Ave. and turn left; the base area is 23 km from downtown.

Accommodations and Camping

Since skiers from throughout the north flock to the slopes of Hudson Bay Mountain when the snow falls, the local lodgings are apt to be as busy in winter as in summer. The upscale **Stork Nest Inn,** north of the highway at 1485 Main St., tel. (250) 847-3831, is styled on a Bavarian lodge. It features comfortable rooms, a cooked breakfast, and airport transfers; $55 s, $62 d. Don't be put off by the exterior of the **Sorrento Motel,** on the west side of town at 3800 Hwy. 16, tel. (250) 847-2601. It has clean rooms, each with a kitchen, for $38 s, $40 d, or $55 s or d in the new wing. Another inexpensive option on the same side of town is **Florence Motel,** 4160 Hwy. 16, tel. (250) 847-2678, but it's a bit rough around the edges.

Riverside Park Municipal Campsite is beside the Bulkley River, north of town. It's open May-Oct., providing shaded sites and river fishing only minutes from downtown. Facilities include coin-operated showers but no hookups; sites are $7 per night. **Riverside Recreation Centre,** along the Yellowhead Hwy. east of town, tel. (250) 847-3229, has better facilities and is within the bounds of a golf course; unserviced sites $14, serviced sites $17.

Food

Specialty coffees and a fine selection of light meals draw locals to the cavernous **Java's Coffeehouse,** 3735 Alfred Ave., tel. (250) 847-5505. **The Little Onion,** 1089 Main St., tel. (250) 847-6121, is a great little restaurant with a stylish yet uncomplicated decor. The short but varied menu is priced similarly to big-city restaurants of similar standard. It's open weekdays for lunch, and Mon.-Sat. for dinner.

At busy **Mainstream Dining,** 1338 Main St., tel. (250) 847-4567, you'll find pizza (the large "small" starts at around $12), a good salad bar (try the tangy house dressing), and an assortment of tasty Italian dishes, ribs, steaks, and seafood. Main courses range around $8-17. Finish it off with gourmet Italian ice cream.

Moricetown Canyon was named after Father Morice, a pioneer missionary.

Services and Information

Smithers Airport, right beside Hwy. 16, four km west of town, is served by **Canadian Regional,** tel. (250) 847-2252, and **Central Mountain Air,** tel. (250) 847-5000. The **Greyhound** bus depot is on Hwy. 16, west of the information center next to the Bread and Butter Stop, tel. (250) 847-2204.

Smithers Visitor Info Centre is upstairs in the museum building at the corner of Main St. and the Yellowhead Hwy., tel. (250) 847-9854 or (800) 542-6673. It's open daily 9 a.m.-6 p.m. in summer, and Mon.-Fri. 8:30 a.m.-4:30 p.m. the rest of the year. A good source of northern literature is **Mountain Eagle Books,** 1237 Main St., tel. (250) 847-5245.

Continuing West from Smithers

The next place to stop and stretch your legs is the viewpoint at **Moricetown Canyon,** where the 500-meter-wide Bulkley River funnels and roars its way down through a 15-meter-wide canyon. Salmon desperately hurl themselves up these spectacular rapids in autumn. Below the canyon the river pours into a large pool, one of the best fishing spots in the area.

The canyon is part of **Moricetown Indian Reserve,** which recognizes an area that has been a Carrier village site for more than 5,000 years. Villagers still fish the canyon using traditional spears and nets; look for the locals congregated around the canyon in summer.

Continuing west, you'll notice the scenery change dramatically; suddenly pine trees line the Bulkley River and cover the hills and mountains. About 50 km from Smithers, a four-km gravel road to the north leads to **Ross Lake Provincial Park,** one of those wonderful discoveries you'll always remember. The lake has good swimming, crystal-clear waters full of trout, salmon, and Dolly Varden, and a backdrop of forested hills and spectacular snowcapped peaks. In the early mornings you can hear loon; in the evenings beaver slide into the water, slapping their tails. Facilities include a boat-launching area (no power boats allowed), barbecue pits, picnic tables, and pit toilets. The park is a day-use area only, with no campsites.

NEW HAZELTON AND VICINITY

It's easy to be confused by the three Hazeltons—Hazelton, New Hazelton, and South Hazelton—situated at the most northerly point on the Yellowhead Highway. As usual, the arrival of the Grand Trunk Pacific Railway caused the confusion. The original Hazelton (called Old Town) was established 50 years or so before the railway came. The other two Hazeltons were founded because each of their respective promoters thought he owned a better spot for a new railway town. Today the largest of the three small communities is New Hazelton (pop. 1,000), a service center watched over by spectacular Mount Rocher Deboule (French for "Mountain of the Rolling Rock").

Hazelton

From New Hazelton, Hwy. 62 leads about eight km northwest to Hazelton. Along the way it crosses the one-lane **Hagwilget Suspension Bridge,** 79 meters above the turbulent Bulkley River. Stop and read the plaque about the original footbridge—made from poles and cedar rope—that once spanned the gorge here and you'll be glad you live in modern times.

At the junction of the Bulkley and Skeena Rivers, Hazelton has retained its unique 1890s-style architecture and pioneer settlement atmosphere. Along the waterfront you'll find a museum (open daily 10 a.m.-5 p.m.), a landing with river views, and a cafe.

'Ksan National Historic Site

'Ksan, which means "Between the Banks," is an authentically reconstructed Gitksan village on the outskirts of Hazelton, tel. (250) 842-5544. To best appreciate the history and culture of

burial house at 'Ksan National Historic Site

JANE AND BRUCE KING

the village, join one of the fascinating one-hour guided tours; admission to the grounds is free but tours are adults $6, seniors $4, children $3. Tours leave every hour on the hour, visiting the burial house, food cache, smokehouse, community houses, and the 'Ksan artists' carving shop and studio. You'll see traditional northwest coast carved interiors, paintings and painted screens, totem poles, and fine examples of native artifacts, arts and crafts, tools and implements, and personal possessions. And you'll learn how the people lived and all about their beliefs and legends.

Finish up in the **Northwestern National Exhibition Centre and Museum,** which features cedar boxes and cedar-bark mats, woven and button blankets, masks, coppers (the most valuable single object a chief possessed), rattles used by shamans, and an art gallery with changing exhibitions. In the gift shop are the works of on-site artists. The village is open May to mid-October, daily 9 a.m.-6 p.m. On Friday nights from mid-July to mid-August, performances of traditional Gitksan song and dance take place starting around 8 p.m. Admission is adults $7, children $5.

Kispiox

The traditional Gitksan village of Kispiox lies 16 km north of Hazelton along Kispiox Valley Rd. (turn off on the Smithers' side of Hazelton). Sights here include a large group of red cedar **totem poles** near the confluence of the Skeena and Kispiox Rivers, and the locally operated, log-constructed **Kispiox Salmon Hatchery.** The hatchery can rear 500,000 salmon fry per year. It's open daily 8 a.m.-5 p.m.

This area is another fishy one; the Kispiox River is full of steelhead Sept.-Nov., and coho in August and September.

The Seven Sisters

These impressive peaks lie west of New Hazelton, immediately south of the junction of the Yellowhead Hwy. and Hwy. 37. From the highway you'll get only occasional glimpses of the range; for the best panorama take Hwy. 37 north across the Skeena River, turn west (left) toward Cedarvale and stop after about 10 km at the picnic area by Sedan Creek.

Several trails also lead to good views of the peaks. The one-km **Gull Creek Trail** climbs about 200 vertical meters from the trailhead at Gull Creek, which is signposted along Hwy. 16. Serious hikers can take any of a number of routes up into the heart of the range, but each is a strenuous slog. The easiest to follow is **Coyote Creek Trail,** an old mining road beginning from where Hwy. 16 crosses Coyote Creek. The nine-km road ends at a few cabins that are often used by climbers. From there it's a six-km climb along a rough trail that becomes increasingly difficult to follow. The trail ends on a high alpine ridge at the base of a large icefield.

Practicalities

Along the highway through New Hazelton is the **28 Inn,** tel. (250) 842-6006, a new motel complex with large rooms, a restaurant, and a pub. Rooms in the new wing are $44 s, $48 d. **'Ksan Campground,** tel. (250) 842-5940, adjacent to the 'Ksan National Historic Site, is right beside the river and offers outstanding views of the Babine Range. It's also very popular with anglers—dangle a line from the back of your tent site, or join the others on an early-morning or late-evening trek along the riverside trail to the best spots. Tent sites are grassy, and the vehicle campsites are large and separated by trees and bushes; $11 per night. Serviced sites with full hookups are available, but provide less privacy; $14 per night.

Between the highway and "Old" Hazelton is the log **Hummingbird Cafe,** tel. (250) 842-5628, the best spot for a meal in all the Hazeltons. The wood interior is decorated with etched glass and hanging lamps, and you'll be dazzled by the million-dollar picture-window view of Mount Rocher Deboule. Tiny hummingbirds flit back and forth between the feeders outside the windows. At lunch, expect to pay around $6-9 for sandwiches, hamburgers, or a huge taco salad. At dinner choose from steaks, chicken, and pasta dishes, all for around $14. It's open daily from 11 a.m. until at least 10 p.m.

New Hazelton Visitor Info Centre, is at the intersection of Hwys. 16 and 62, tel. (250) 842-6071. It's open June-Sept., daily 8 a.m.-7 p.m., and holds a display detailing local history.

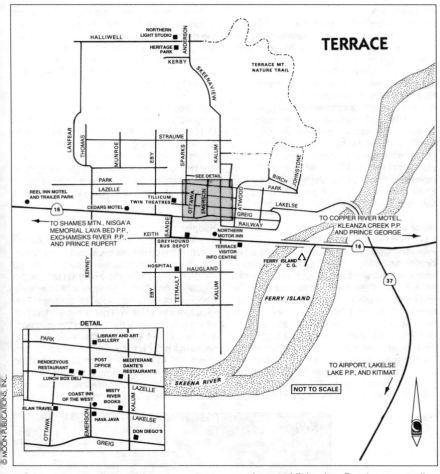

TERRACE AND VICINITY

Terrace (pop. 13,500) lies on the Yellowhead Highway, 581 km west of Prince George and 140 km east of Prince Rupert. The city is built on a series of steep terraces along the beautiful Skeena River, the province's second-largest river system, and is completely surrounded by the spectacular Hazelton and Coast Mountains. The town offers basic tourist services and little else. But the surrounding area makes up for it with a mix of intriguing sights, beautiful parks, and outstanding recreation opportunities.

Originally home of the Tsimshian, "those who taste the rain," the site that is now Terrace was founded by George Little in 1911. Little's sawmill operation got a boost with the arrival of the railway in 1914; his logs were used for railroad ties. Today the forestry industry still forms the basis for the city's economy.

Heritage Park

At this outdoor-indoor museum, 4113 Sparks St. (north of downtown up Skeenaview St.), tel. (250) 635-2508, a one-hour guided tour takes you through an old, beautifully furnished log hotel, a dance hall, a barn, and six authentic log cabins dating from between 1910 and 1955. Some of the cabins are furnished, others contain historical artifacts or collections of antique farming and mining equipment. The guide fills you in on the early history of Terrace—covering gold, copper, and lead mining, fur trading, construction of the telegraph line, logging, and the homesteaders of the late 1800s and early 1900s. Admission is adults $2.50, students and seniors $1.50. It's open 10 a.m.-6 p.m., Wed.-Sun. in summer, Tues.-Sat. the rest of the year.

Nisga'a Memorial Lava Bed Provincial Park

Protecting Canada's youngest lava flow, the fascinating landscape of this 17,683-hectare park is unique within the province. The flow is about 18 km long and three km wide; experts think the molten rock spewed through the earth's crust between 1650 and 1750. You can see all different types of lava, as well as crevasses, spiky pinnacles, sinkholes, craters, and bright blue pools where underground rivers have risen to the surface. Explore the lava with caution—in some parts the surface may be unstable, and it's very hard on footgear. The only facilities are a day-use area and a couple of short hiking trails.

To get to the park, take Hwy. 16 west out of town for three km, then head north around the back of the sawmill on Kalum Lake Drive. The park is 78 km along this road; watch for logging trucks during the week. The information center in Terrace has an interesting brochure on the lava beds.

Lakelse Lake Provincial Park

This 362-hectare park at the north end of beautiful Lakelse Lake offers good swimming beaches, boating, fishing, and a hiking trail through an old-growth forest of towering spruce, cedar, and hemlock. Also here are a large campground (see "Camping," below) and a shaded picnic area. To get there, take Hwy. 37 south toward Kitimat for 26 km.

Hiking

In addition to those at the parks mentioned above, many other trails in the area tempt hikers. For an easy stroll, take the three-km path (50 minutes or less) around **Ferry Island,** in the middle of the Skeena River east of downtown (reached via Hwy. 16). More demanding is **Terrace Mountain Nature Trail,** a five-km trail providing great views of the city and the surrounding area. It takes about two hours roundtrip, because much of it is uphill. Start at the intersection of Halliwell Ave. and Anderson St. (by Heritage Park), climbing the lower slopes of Terrace Mountain to a cleared area where views are best, then descending to the end of Johnstone

sandy beach at Lakelse Lake Provincial Park

JANE AND BRUCE KING

THE ELUSIVE KERMODEI

Little known outside British Columbia is the Kermodei (pronounced kerr-MO-dee), an elusive subspecies of black bear inhabiting only the vast tract of wilderness north of Terrace and uninhabited Princess Royal Island south of Kitimat.

First studied by Francis Kermode, director of the provincial museum at the turn of the 20th century, the bear was originally thought to be a distinct species. It's slightly larger than other black bears, has a different jaw structure, and, although its color varies, some individuals are pure white. These white bears are not albinos, merely the lightest-colored members of the species.

The Tsimshian called the Kermodei "Spirit Bear," and often rendered it in human form in their artwork. Once close to extinction, the Kermodei is now fully protected.

Street. Complete the circle by walking down Johnstone St., turning right on Park Ave., right again on Kalum Ave., then continuing straight onto Skeenaview Ave. back to the trailhead.

Further afield, consider scenic **Clearwater Lakes Trail,** which begins from Hwy. 37, 27 km south of Terrace. The trail leads 1.8 km to Little Clearwater Lake, then another 0.7 km to Big Clearwater Lake. The two lakes are linked by a shallow creek, along the banks of which are many good picnic spots and berries to pick in season. From the same parking lot, a trail leads 1.8 km to a lookout with outstanding views of Lakelse Lake.

To get the rundown on all the best hikes in the area, ask for the handy *Terrace Hiking Trails* brochure at the information center.

Fishing

The Skeena River is chock-full of salmon, as well as a variety of other fish. Steelhead can be caught April-May and Aug.-October. Chinooks make their upstream migration in late May and again July through August. Coho salmon run from August to early fall. Be sure to get a license and read up on the latest rules and regulations before hitting the rivers and lakes. You can pick up a list of local guides and outfitters from the information center.

Skiing

British Columbia's newest ski area, **Shames Mountain,** offers a vertical rise of 550 meters and virtually guaranteed good snow coverage. In the opening season (1990-91) an amazing 2,400 cm of snow fell at the resort—nearly twice as much as at any other resort in North America. Current facilities include a day lodge, ski school, chairlift, T-bar, and rope tow, but Shames Mountain has big expansion plans for the future. For further resort information, phone (250) 635-3773 or call the Snowphone at (800) 663-7754.

Galleries

Northern Light Studio, 4820 Halliwell Ave., tel. (250) 638-1403, is an art studio, gallery, and shop featuring custom framing, stained glass, native art, British Columbia jade, fine silver jewelry, and original paintings. It's open Mon.-Sat. 9:30 a.m.-5:30 p.m. Behind the studio is a small Japanese garden. The basement floor of **Terrace Public Library,** 4610 Park Ave., tel. (250) 638-8177, holds a community art gallery offering exhibitions that change monthly. It's open Tues.-Sat. noon-3 p.m. and 7-9 p.m., Sunday 1-4 p.m.; closed Monday.

Accommodations

The less expensive motels are strung out along Hwy. 16 on the eastern and western outskirts of the city. To the west, your best bet is **Cedars Motel,** 4830 Hwy. 16, tel. (250) 635-2258, which is nothing special but charges only $42 s, $45 d. Another popular place—judging by the large number of fishing boats in the parking lot—is **Reel Inn Motel and Trailer Park,** 5508 Hwy. 16, tel. (250) 635-2803, which is only slightly more expensive. An inexpensive choice on the other side of town is **Copper River Motel,** three km east at 4113 Hwy. 16, tel. (250) 635-6124. It's clean and has coffee- and tea-making appliances, friendly owners, a store, and everything you need. On the down side are the paper-thin walls. Rates are from $45 s, $50 d; a kitchen is available for an extra $10.

Right downtown is the luxurious **Coast Inn of the West,** 4620 Lakelse Ave., tel. (250) 638-8141 or (800) 549-3939, where each of the 60 air-conditioned rooms is decorated in stylish pastel colors. Facilities include a restaurant, lounge, and a nearby aquatic center open to guests. Rooms are $105 s, $115 d.

Camping

On Ferry Island in the Skeena River, just over three km east of downtown, **Ferry Island Campground,** tel. (250) 638-4750, offers sheltered sites set among birch and cottonwood trees, berry bushes, and wildflowers. A few sites have excellent views of the river and mountains, and a hiking trail runs through the woods and around the island. Facilities include picnic tables and shelters, fire grates, firewood, and pit toilets, but no showers. A few sites have electrical hookups. Unserviced sites are $9 per night, serviced sites are $11-13.

A short drive from Terrace are three provincial parks with campgrounds. **Kleanza Creek Provincial Park,** site of a short-lived gold rush, is 20 km east of Terrace on Hwy. 16; $9.50 a night. In the opposite direction, 50 km west of the city on Hwy. 16 is **Exchamsiks River Provincial Park;** $9.50 a night. **Lakelse Lake Provincial Park,** 16 km south of Terrace along Hwy. 37, is the most developed of the three parks, offering a sandy beach, safe swimming, an interpretive amphitheatre, hot showers, and flush toilets. Sites are $14.50 a night. The gates of this park close 11 p.m.-7 a.m.

Food

One of the most popular places to go for breakfast is the **Northern Motor Inn,** near the Chevron gas station on Hwy. 16 just east of Terrace, tel. (250) 635-6375. Large omelettes, hash browns, toast, and coffee run around $7-8. The rest of the day, head to **Hava Java,** 4621 Lakelse Ave., tel. (250) 638-7877, for your daily quota of caffeine in a big-city coffeehouse atmosphere. Just down the street is the **Lunch Box Deli,** 4716 Lazelle St., tel. (250) 635-3696, good for sandwiches.

For delicious Mexican food, head downtown to **Don Diego's,** 3212 Kalum St., tel. (250) 635-2307, where many tables catch the evening sun. It's a small, bright restaurant with lots of plants and Mexican wall hangings. Lunch is $6-8 (the shrimp crepes are superb). Dinner entrees start at around $9. It's always busy so you may have to wait for a table. Hours are Mon.-Sat. 11 a.m.-9 p.m., Sunday 10 a.m.-2 p.m. and 5-9 p.m. For excellent Southern European cuisine, try **Mediterane Dante's Restaurante,** 4606 Lazelle St., tel. (250) 635-7229. It's a small place, but has an outdoor patio with umbrella-covered tables. Hours

are Mon.-Sat. 11 a.m.-11 p.m., Sunday 4-11 p.m. **Rendezvous Restaurant,** also on Lazelle St., tel. (250) 635-5944, features steak, seafood, pizza, pasta, and a good salad bar. Expect to pay around $8-15 for a main course. It's open Mon.-Thurs. 11 a.m.-11 p.m., Fri.-Sat. 11 a.m.-midnight, Sunday 4-10 p.m.

In summer, it's worth the drive up Shames Valley to the ski resort's **Tea-Bar.** It's open weekends 1-5 p.m. for lunch and afternoon teas, and affords spectacular views of the surrounding mountainscapes.

Transportation

Terrace and Kitimat Airport is on Hwy. 37 eight km south of Terrace. Both **Canadian Regional,** tel. (800) 665-1177, and **Air B.C.,** tel. (800) 663-3721, offer daily scheduled flights from the airport to Vancouver. **VIA Rail** trains pass through town three times a week en route to Prince Rupert or Toronto. The train station is just a small building on Railway Rd. that opens only when a train arrives or leaves. Purchase tickets at **Elan Travel,** 4741 Lakelse Ave., tel. (250) 635-6181. For more rail information, call VIA Rail direct at (800) 561-8630. The **Greyhound** bus depot is at 4620 Keith Ave., tel. (250) 635-4428. Greyhound offers daily service west to Prince Rupert and east to Prince George. The only northward public transportation is with **Seaport Limousine,** tel. (250) 635-7676, which makes runs to Stewart.

Information

Terrace Visitor Info Centre, 4511 Keith Ave., tel. (250) 635-2063, is beside Hwy. 16 on the east side of town. It's open through summer Mon.-Fri. 8:30 a.m.-8 p.m., Sat.-Sun. 9 a.m.-8 p.m.; the rest of the year Mon.-Fri. 9 a.m.-5 p.m. The helpful staff will happily lead you down with brochures and pamphlets and tell you everything there is to do in the area. For local literature and a good selection of Canadiana, head downtown to **Misty River Books,** 4606 Lakelse Ave., tel. (250) 635-4428.

SOUTH TO KITIMAT

The planned industrial community of Kitimat (pop. 12,000), at the northern end of Douglas

Channel 62 km south of Terrace, was founded by the aluminum giant **Alcan** (Aluminum Company of Canada) in the 1950s. Canada's largest industrial endeavor at the time, the project included one of the world's largest aluminum smelters, a company town to serve the workers, and a massive hydroelectric scheme on the Nechako River. The hydroelectric project intended to redirect the river's course to a power station at Kemano, then use the electricity generated there to run the Kitimat smelter. The government kicked in millions of dollars upgrading the region's infrastructure, but only the first stages of the hydroelectric project were ever completed. Intense pressure from environmentalists and native organizations forced the provincial government to cancel the rest of the project in 1995.

Tours

The highlight of a visit to B.C.'s self-proclaimed "Aluminum City" is a guided industrial tour. The Alcan **aluminum smelter** here produces 270,000 tons of aluminum products worth $500 million annually. Two-hour tours, offered in summer Mon.-Fri. at 10:30 a.m. and 1:30 p.m., start with an audio-visual presentation, then it's into a bus for a drive around the works and down to the wharf. Tours are free, but book ahead at (250) 639-8259.

Methanex Corporation, Kitimat's newest industry and northern British Columbia's only **petrochemical plant,** offers tours Mon.-Thurs. at 10 a.m. Check first for specific safety restrictions. Book at (250) 639-9292. Eurocan's **pulp and paper mill** tour is conducted Tuesday and Thursday at 10 a.m. and 2 p.m. No children under 12; tel. (250) 632-6111.

If all this industrial hooey gives you a headache, get back to nature at **Kitimat River Fish Hatchery,** tel. (250) 639-9616, which conducts tours Mon.-Fri. four times daily.

Other Sights

In **Radley Park,** along the Kitimat River, you'll see the province's largest living tree, a 500-year-old giant Sitka spruce. It's behind the Riverlodge Recreation Centre. The **Centennial Museum,** 293 City Centre, tel. (250) 632-7022, displays historic and native artifacts, and a gallery features locally produced artwork. It's

open June-Aug., Tues.-Fri. 10 a.m.-5 p.m., Sat.-Sun. noon-5 p.m.; the rest of the year Tues.-Sat. 11 a.m.-5 p.m.

Practicalities

City Centre Motel, right downtown at 480 City Centre, tel. (250) 632-4848 or (800) 663-3391, features comfortable rooms, each with a fully equipped kitchen and tea- and coffee-making facilities. Rates run a reasonable $46 s, $48 d. Similarly priced is **Kitimat Motel,** 656 Dadook Cres., tel. (250) 632-6677, in a pleasant parklike setting. **Radley Park Campground** has a riverside setting, showers, a few hookups, and a kitchen shelter; $14.50 a night.

For the best breakfast in town, head to **The Chalet,** 852 Tsimshian Blvd., tel. (250) 632-4615. The **Cloverpatch,** 633 Dadook Cres., tel. (250) 632-2000, serves healthy lunches, while **Rosario's,** 607 Legion St., tel. (250) 632-4980, makes pizza. **Kitimat Visitor Info Centre** is at the north entrance to town at 2109 Forest Ave., tel. (250) 632-6294 or (800) 664-6554.

WEST TOWARD PRINCE RUPERT

The 147-km stretch of the Yellowhead Highway between Terrace and Prince Rupert rivals any stretch of road in the province for beauty. For almost the entire distance, the highway hugs the north bank of the beautiful Skeena River. On a fine day, views from the road are stunning—snow-dusted mountains, densely forested hillsides, ponds covered in yellow water lilies, and waterfalls like narrow ribbons of silver, snaking down vertical cliffs from the snow high above. In some sections the highway shrinks to two extremely narrow lanes neatly sandwiched between the railway tracks and the river—drive defensively.

Exchamsiks River Provincial Park, on the north side of the highway 50 km west of Terrace, features a grassy picnic area where the deep green Exchamsiks River drains into the much larger Skeena River. Camping is $9.50 a night. As the highway continues westward, the Skeena widens, eventually becoming a tidal estuary. Sandbars and marshes, exposed at low tide, are a mass of colorful mosses, and wading birds can be seen feeding in shallow pools. Keep an eye out for bald eagles on the sandbars or perched in the trees above the highway.

Just over 110 km from Terrace, the highway leaves the river and meanders inland past high forested cliffs to **Prudhomme Lake,** on the north side of the highway. The lake holds a number of forested islands, and is flanked by a small provincial park; campsites $9.50.

PRINCE RUPERT

Prince Rupert (pop. 17,800) lies on hilly Kaien Island 720 km west of Prince George. It's one of Canada's major west-coast ports, and life here revolves around the ocean. The city boasts a large fishing fleet and is a major water transportation hub; from here you can catch ferries south to Vancouver Island, west to the Queen Charlotte Islands, or, with any luck, north to Alaska (see "Alaska Marine Highway" under "Transportation," below).

The city itself holds an odd but intriguing mixture of cultural icons—Pacific Northwest native totem poles, old English coats of arms and street names, modern high-rise hotels and civic buildings—all crammed together on the edge of the Pacific Ocean. Plan to spend at least a day in the area, visiting the excellent museum, exploring an old cannery village, or maybe taking a harbor tour.

History

For at least 5,000 years, Kaien Island and the vicinity have been inhabited by the Coast Tsimshian, whose lives were traditionally dominated by fishing and food gathering. They followed the spring and summer salmon and oolichan runs, returning every season to the same village sites. Trade networks were established, artistic traditions emerged, and a class system evolved. Before 1790 the region was among the most heavily populated area on British Columbia's coastline.

When Europeans arrived on the northwest coast, the local Tsimshian, eager to cash in on fur trading, moved to Fort Simpson, a Hudson's Bay Company post north of Prince Rupert. For a time, they continued to hold their traditional potlatches—days-long festivals filled with feasting, storytelling, and dancing in elaborate costumes and masks. But in 1884, the government, swayed by church lobbyists who claimed the practice was evil, banned potlatching, and this crucial, millennia-old element of the Tsimshians'

economic, trade, and social structure effectively died out.

Prince Rupert was the brainchild of Charles M. Hays, general manager of the Grand Trunk Pacific Railway. In 1902, Hays devised a plan to build a rail line from North Bay, Ontario, to a new port on the central B.C. coast—a port he hoped would rival Vancouver and become *the* Pacific port for Canada. In 1914 the railway was completed, but unfortunately, Hays never saw it. He went down with the Titanic in 1912. The new city was named after pioneer English business magnate and adventurer Prince Rupert, cousin of Charles II.

After WW I, fishing and fish processing became important parts of the city's economy, and during WW II Prince Rupert became a shipbuilding center and an American army

---

PORT ESSINGTON

Port Essington, originally a Tsimshian site called Spokeshute, was established as a shipping settlement at the mouth of the Skeena River south of Prince Rupert. The settlement was serviced by sternwheelers and riverboats, and supplied Hudson's Bay Company brigades and ports. As the fur trade declined through the 1800s, the salmon industry here grew. The area soon had 12 canneries—mainly staffed by Chinese, Japanese, and native laborers.

The town flourished during fishing seasons and boasted hotels, restaurants, stores, and a red-light district. In the 1890s, miners stopped in on their way to northern Canadian goldfields, and the inevitable missionaries came to try to enforce Christianity. The port's boom days lasted until the arrival of the Grand Trunk Pacific Railway, when canneries were built near the railhead at Prince Rupert and Port Essington was abandoned. Today only charred fragments remain.

PRINCE RUPERT

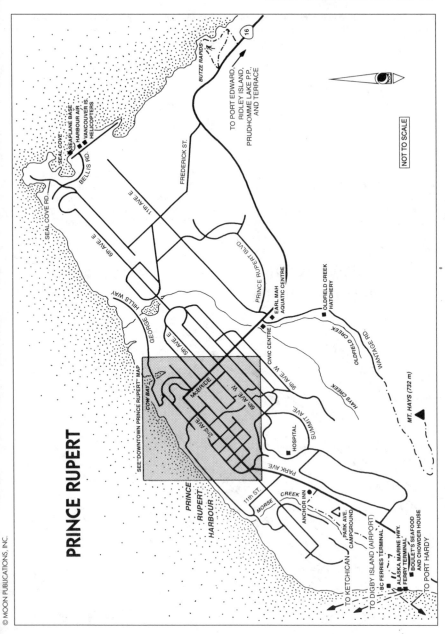

NOT TO SCALE

© MOON PUBLICATIONS, INC.

16

TO PORT EDWARD, RIDLEY ISLAND, PRUDHOMME LAKE P.P., AND TERRACE

BUTZE RAPIDS

SEAL COVE
SEAPLANE BASE
HARBOUR AIR
VANCOUVER IS. HELICOPTERS

SEAL COVE RD.

BELL'S RD.

FREDERICK ST.

11th AVE E

6th AVE E

HILL'S WAY

GEORGE

PRINCE RUPERT BLVD

EARL MAH AQUATIC CENTRE

OLDFIELD CREEK HATCHERY

OLDFIELD CREEK

WANTAGE RD.

HAYS CREEK

MT. HAYS (732 m)

9th AVE E

5th AVE E

CIVIC CENTRE

9th AVE W

6th AVE W

McBRIDE

2nd AVE W

SUMMIT AVE.

SEE "DOWNTOWN PRINCE RUPERT" MAP

COW BAY

HOSPITAL

PARK AVE.

PRINCE RUPERT HARBOUR

11th ST.

MORSE CREEK

ANCHOR INN

PARK AVE. CAMPGROUND

TO KETCHIKAN

TO DIGBY ISLAND (AIRPORT)

BC FERRIES TERMINAL

ALASKA MARINE HWY. FERRY TERMINAL

BOULET'S SEAFOOD AND CHOWDER HOUSE

TO PORT HARDY

base. Tourism started in the '60s with the commencement of the B.C. and Alaska ferry services. Today, fishing is still the mainstay of the economy; up to 2,000 fishing vessels cruise the coast in search of salmon, herring, lingcod, sole, and halibut. Their total annual catch averages some 7,000 tons. Prince Rupert also boasts four fish-processing plants, extensive deepwater-port facilities, grain and coal terminals, and a thriving wood-products industry.

SIGHTS

Museum of Northern British Columbia

You can easily spend several hours at this fascinating museum, which occupies the distinctive log building on the corner of 1st Ave. W

and McBride St., tel. (250) 624-3207. Exhibits trace the history of Prince Rupert from 5,000-year-old Tsimshian settlements through fur-trading days to the founding of the city in 1914 as the western terminus of the Grand Trunk Pacific Railway. Many of the most fascinating displays spotlight the Coast Tsimshian natives—their history, culture, traditions, trade networks, and potlatches. Among the Tsimshian artifacts on display: totem poles, pots, masks, beautiful wooden boxes, blankets, baskets, shiny black argillite carvings, weapons, and petroglyphs.

Admission to this excellent museum is just $3. The museum and the information center out front are both open early June through early September, daily 9 a.m.-8 p.m.; the rest of the year, Mon.-Sat. 10 a.m.-5 p.m.

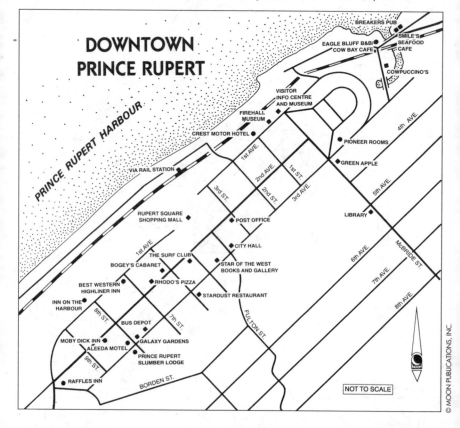

DOWNTOWN PRINCE RUPERT

PRINCE RUPERT HARBOUR

BREAKERS PUB
SMILE'S SEAFOOD CAFE
EAGLE BLUFF B&B/
COW BAY CAFE
COWPUCCINO'S
VISITOR INFO CENTRE AND MUSEUM
FIREHALL MUSEUM
CREST MOTOR HOTEL
PIONEER ROOMS
GREEN APPLE
VIA RAIL STATION
LIBRARY
RUPERT SQUARE SHOPPING MALL
POST OFFICE
CITY HALL
1st AVE.
THE SURF CLUB
BOGEY'S CABARET
STAR OF THE WEST BOOKS AND GALLERY
BEST WESTERN HIGHLINER INN
RHODO'S PIZZA
STARDUST RESTAURANT
INN ON THE HARBOUR
BUS DEPOT
MOBY DICK INN
GALAXY GARDENS
ALEEDA MOTEL
PRINCE RUPERT SLUMBER LODGE
RAFFLES INN
BORDEN ST.
FULTON ST.

1st AVE. W, 2nd AVE., 3rd ST., 1st ST., 2nd ST., 3rd AVE., 4th AVE., 5th AVE., 6th AVE., 7th AVE., 8th AVE., McBRIDE ST., 8th ST., 7th ST., 9th ST.

NOT TO SCALE

© MOON PUBLICATIONS, INC.

North Pacific Cannery Village Museum

South of Prince Rupert in Port Edward is the oldest remaining cannery village on North America's west coast. Dating to 1889, the village is now classified as a historic site. Here you can find out everything you've ever wanted to know about fish, the fishing industry, canning—even which fish tastes the best (locals say it's red snapper every time). On entering the village, a guide takes you on a tour of the museum, then you're free to stroll at your own pace along the boardwalk through the riverside cannery settlement with its many original buildings. Included in the admission charge is the Skeena River Story, a live performance and slide show presented through summer daily at 11:30 a.m., 1 p.m., 2:30 p.m., and 4 p.m. The village is open May-Sept., daily 10 a.m.-7 p.m.; the rest of the year, Wed.-Sat. 10 a.m.-4 p.m. Admission to the museum and village is $7, good for credit on purchases of $7 or more in the cannery stores. For further information, call (250) 628-3538.

To get to the village, head out of Prince Rupert on the Yellowhead Hwy. and take the first road to the right after leaving Kaien Island. **Farwest Bus Lines,** tel. (250) 624-6400, runs a bus from downtown Prince Rupert to Port Edward several times a day on weekdays, twice a day on weekends. Fare to Port Edward proper is $2 each way, but to get to the cannery—another 6.5 km down the road—you have to specifically tell the driver your destination when you board in Rupert and pay an extra $1.

Other Sights

If you find buildings interesting, you may want to walk around the modern **Civic Centre,** corner McBride St. and Wantage Rd.—look for the three brightly painted totem poles out front. Adjacent to the Civic Centre is the ultramodern **Prince Rupert Performing Arts Centre,** also worth a visit. You can take a guided tour through its muted purple-and-orange interior, by appointment; call (250) 627-8888.

The **Firehall Museum,** beside the new fire hall on Stiles Place, tel. (250) 627-4475, features a 1925 REO Speedwagon along with various other firefighting memorabilia. It's open Tues.-Sat. 9 a.m.-5 p.m., except when there's a fire being fought in town.

totem poles outside the Prince Rupert Civic Centre

Along Wantage Rd. is **Oldfield Creek Hatchery,** tel. (250) 624-6733, a salmon-raising facility open for tours. On the same side of the city but a little further out (just south of the industrial park) is **Butze Rapids.** The churning water of these reversing tidal rapids produces lots of floating foam that local Tsimshian natives called "kaien"—hence the name Kaien Island, upon which the city of Prince Rupert stands.

Harbor Tours, Ferries, and Boat Charters

The best way to see the harbor is on a boat tour operated by the Museum of Northern British Columbia, corner 1st Ave. W and McBride St., tel. (250) 624-3207. The 2.5-hour tour starts with a slide show in the museum and then boards a small, enclosed ferry. The first stop is the historic fishing village of **Dodge Cove** on Digby Island, which has been inhabited for over 5,000 years. Then the ferry takes you to the native village of **Metlakatla,** allowing time for a stroll through the village or along the beach.

Throughout the tour, guides point out historical sites along the shoreline and pass around archaeological artifacts for your examination. Tours depart the museum in summer, daily at 1 p.m.; adults $20, children $12, under five free.

BC Ferries runs all sorts of shuttle services around the harbor to communities with no road connections. Times vary. Head down to the small docks at the bottom of McBride St. for route and schedule information, or call (250) 624-3337. The shortest trip is a 15-minute run to **Dodge Cove** on Digby Island. There's not much to do on the island but it's a nice cruise there and back, and just $5 roundtrip. A ferry also cruises along the Portland Inlet to **Kincolith,** a small isolated native village; $16 roundtrip. Also ask down at the docks about ferries to **Port Simpson,** where a small native village occupies the former site of a Hudson's Bay Company fort, and to Metlakatla.

Seashore Charters, tel. (250) 624-5645, keeps a list of all the local charter operators, their vessels, tours, and rates, and can provide more information on fishing tours, harbor tours, and adventure tours. Some of the options available include yacht trips; day-long cruises looking for eagles, waterfowl, seals, otters, porpoises, and killer whales; and fishing trips for salmon, halibut, or cod, with gear and bait supplied. Expect to pay from $75 per person for a fishing trip.

Industrial Tours

Prince Rupert's main industrial terminals—a **grain terminal** and a **coal terminal**—are on Ridley Island, a small island south of Kaien Island. Access is off Hwy. 16 via Ridley Island Industrial Road. Ninety-minute tours of both fully automated terminals are offered in summer. Make arrangements through the Prince Rupert Visitor Info Centre, tel. (250) 624-5637.

RECREATION

Hiking

A variety of hiking opportunities exist around the city. Right in town you can take the **Heritage Walking Tour** to see the town's historical buildings and sites. Other trails lead from town to Cow Bay, Hays Creek, Morse Creek, the ferry terminals, and the low summit of Mt. Oldfield. Pick up a map and descriptions for all the local trails at the information center.

For views of Prince Rupert, the sound, southeastern Alaska, and plenty of bald eagles soaring through updrafts, you'll need to ascend 732-meter-high **Mount Hays.** To get to the base of this local landmark take Wantage Rd. south off the Yellowhead Hwy. at the civic center. A gondola used to operate up to the mountain, opening up alpine hiking in summer and skiing in winter, but it hasn't operated for a few years. Today you can reach the summit by hiking up a gravel road that provides panoramic views of Digby Island and the town.

Indoor Recreation

Prince Rupert has a number of sports venues at the corner of McBride St. and Wantage Road. In the **Civic Centre** building you can have a game of squash, or watch badminton, basketball, or volleyball in action. In the **Arena** you'll find a roller-skating rink in summer and an ice-skating rink in winter; skate rental is available. Next door is the **Earl Mah Aquatic Centre,** tel. (250) 627-7946, which has two pools, a sizzling whirlpool, two saunas, and a fitness area; admission is adults $4, seniors or children $2.

Arts and Entertainment

In the same complex as the recreation facilities listed above is the ultramodern **Prince Rupert Performing Arts Centre,** corner McBride St. and Wantage Rd., tel. (250) 627-8888, where just about anything could be happening. Symphony concerts, plays, lectures, and operas are among the events scheduled here.

The most popular spot in town for a beer is **Breakers Pub,** 117 George Hills Way, tel. (250) 624-5990. This popular local pub boasts plenty of atmosphere, an outdoor deck with harbor views, and a bistro-style restaurant; open daily noon-midnight. Many rowdy bars can be found downtown—just follow your nose and ears. For the cabaret atmosphere and dancing into the wee hours, try **Bogey's Cabaret** on 2nd Ave. between 6th and 7th Sts., or the **Surf Club** at 200 5th St., tel. (250) 624-3050.

Most of the hotels also have licensed lounges with some form of entertainment, particularly on weekends. The **Moby Dick Inn,** 935 2nd Ave. W, tel. (250) 624-6961, and **Raffles Inn,** 1080 3rd Ave. W, tel. (250) 624-9161, have nightclubs.

Festivals and Events

The major annual celebration here is June's **Seafest.** All sorts of wacky events involving the sea are scheduled—a canoe-dunking contest (the water's icy so no one wants to lose), bathtub races, and fish-filleting competitions, to name a few. Another event held in June is **Culture Days,** featuring a salmon feast and plenty of authentic native dancing and singing.

ACCOMMODATIONS AND CAMPING

Prince Rupert has a great campground within easy walking distance of the ferry terminals. On the other hand, motel accommodations are generally overpriced and will need to be booked well in advance during the busy summer months.

Hotels and Motels

The bright blue and green **Pioneer Rooms,** 167 3rd Ave. E, tel. (250) 624-2334, is mostly full of "steadies" in winter, but in summer the manager makes available daily or weekly accommodations. Facilities include small rooms with shared bathrooms, an outside yard with a barbecue, a living room with television, and a microwave and fridge for guest use; $24 per person. Rooms rapidly fill with ferry arrivals and departures. Reservations can be made over the phone a day or two ahead, but you'd be wise to check the place out before committing yourself.

Prince Rupert's most reasonably priced motel is the **Aleeda Motel,** on the west side of downtown at 900 3rd Ave. W, tel. (250) 627-1367. The small and basic rooms go for $53 s, $65 d. On the same block, and with a better standard of rooms, is **Moby Dick Inn,** 935 2nd Ave. W, tel. (250) 624-6961 or (800) 663-0822; $65 s, $75 d. Also in the area are **Raffles Inn,** 1080 3rd Ave. W, tel. (250) 624-9161 or (800) 663-3207, with rooms for $60 s, $65 d, and the **Prince Rupert Slumber Lodge,** 909 3rd Ave. W, tel. (250) 627-1711, which charges $60 s, $65 d.

The massive red-brick building right downtown is the 10-story **Best Western Highliner Inn,** 815 1st Ave. W, tel. (250) 624-9060 or (800) 668-3115, which has a downstairs restaurant and many rooms with harbor views. Rates are $78-115 s or d. A few blocks from downtown is **Inn on the Harbour,** 720 1st Ave. W, tel.

(250) 624-9107 or (800) 663-8155, where you'll pay $72 s, $77 d, most of that for the view.

In a prime harborside location, the full-service **Crest Motor Hotel,** 222 1st Ave. W, tel. (250) 624-6771, holds a glass-enclosed waterfront cafe, a dining room, and a lounge with nightly entertainment. Rates for the the stylishly decorated rooms—most with water views—start at $139 s or d. The closest accommodation to the ferry terminal is **Anchor Inn,** 1600 Park Ave., tel. (250) 627-8522, an ugly three-story place that looks as if it's been built back-to-front; $75 s, $85 d.

Bed and Breakfast

If you're looking for something a little different, stay at **Eagle Bluff Bed and Breakfast,** 201 Cow Bay Rd., tel. (250) 627-4955. The house is built out over the water, overlooking the marina and harbor, and lies within easy walking distance of a number of cafes and restaurants. Rates are $40 s, $50 d for a shared bath; $50 s, $60 d for a private bath; and $90 for a large suite sleeping five. A cooked breakfast—complete with freshly baked muffins—is included.

Camping

Like the rest of Rupert's accommodations, **Park Avenue Campground,** 1750 Park Ave., tel. (250) 624-5861, fills and empties on a daily basis with the arrival and departure of the ferries. If you know when you're arriving in the city, phone ahead to avoid any hassles. The campground is a one-km hike from both the city center and ferry terminals. Facilities include hot showers, cooking shelters, a grassy tenting area, pay phones, a mail drop, and visitor information. For a rundown on what's happening in town, ask Wayne, the friendly caretaker. Unserviced sites are $9-12, full hookups $16. The other alternative is **Prudhomme Lake Provincial Park,** along the Yellowhead Hwy. 16 km east of downtown; $9.50 per night.

FOOD

Breakfast

Most of Rupert's larger motels have restaurants, but the place to head for substantial and inexpensive breakfasts is the **Moby Dick Inn,** 935 2nd Ave. W, tel. (250) 624-6961. You can order anything from a bowl of fruit and a muffin ($4) to eggs, bacon, and toast (under $5) or steak and eggs ($7.50). It's always crowded, and service can be slow. Just around the corner, the **Raffles Inn,** 1080 3rd Ave. W, tel. (250) 624-9161, offers similar fare.

Cow Bay Cafes

East of downtown is Cow Bay, originally a fishy-smelling, rough-and-tumble part of town that was home to a large fishing fleet. The boats are still there, moored in a marina, and a few old buildings still stand. But for the most part, the bay is a changed place. Rowdy dives have been replaced by trendy art and crafts shops, restaurants, and two of the city's best cafes.

Cowpuccino's Coffee House, 25 Cow Bay Rd., tel. (250) 627-1395, is a great little place with freshly-brewed coffee, newspapers and magazines to read, and a laid-back atmosphere. It's open daily from 7:30 a.m. to 10 or 11 p.m. each night. On the waterfront is the popular **Cow Bay Cafe,** 205 Cow Bay Rd., tel. (250) 627-1212, where you can sit at an outside table and take in the smells of the ocean, or stay inside and enjoy the greenery. Good home-cooked meals and daily specials start at $5. It's open Tues.-Sun. 11 a.m.-8 p.m.; around lunchtime the tables fill up fast.

Seafood

Ask a local where to go for good seafood and the answer is invariably **Smile's Seafood Cafe,** 113 Cow Bay Rd., tel. (250) 624-3072. This diner-style cafe, decorated with black-and-white fishing photos and colored-glass floats, has been serving seafood since 1934. It's always busy, mobbed by local fishermen, residents, and visitors no matter what time of day. The extensive menu includes seafood salads and sandwiches, burgers, fish and chips, shellfish, and seafood specialties. Prices range $5-25 per plate. Smile's is open daily 9 a.m.-10 p.m. in July and August, and 11 a.m.-8 p.m. the rest of the year.

Another notable place for fresh seafood is the casual **Boulet's Seafood & Chowder House,** at the end of the Yellowhead Hwy. near the ferry terminals, tel. (250) 624-9309. Especially good is the lunchtime clam chowder, served with a small loaf of bread, dessert, and

tea or coffee for $8. Boulet's is open Mon.-Sat. 11 a.m.-9 p.m. For delicious takeout fish and chips try the **Green Apple,** 301 McBride St., tel. (250) 627-1666.

Other Restaurants

Stardust Restaurant, 627 3rd Ave. W, tel. (250) 627-1221, serves large helpings of good Chinese food at reasonable prices. The average price for one dish is $8, combo plates are $8-10. It's open daily 10:30 a.m.-10:30 p.m. Takeout orders available. **Galaxy Gardens,** 844 3rd Ave. W, tel. (250) 624-3122, boasts a flashier decor with lots of wicker and bamboo. On the menu are tasty chow meins, prawn and chicken dishes, and special combos. **Rhodos Pizza,** 716 2nd Ave., tel. (250) 624-9797, serves up pizza, steak, and delicious Greek specialties from $9. On the walls are Greek plates and artifacts, and the background music is, naturally, Greek.

TRANSPORTATION

Air

Prince Rupert Airport is west of town on Digby Island, and linked to the city by a ferry that takes buses and foot passengers only—no cars. Airlines provide free bus transportation between the airport and downtown, via the ferry, but bus passengers must still must pay the ferry fare of $10 per person each way. **Air B.C.,** 112 6th St., tel. (250) 624-4554, and **Canadian Regional,** 500 2nd Ave. W, tel. (250) 624-6292, both provide daily flights between Vancouver and Prince Rupert via Terrace.

Developed by the Royal Canadian Air Force in 1941, **Seal Cove Air Base** lies at the east end of town and serves as the seaplane base for Prince Rupert. To get there, take 5th Ave. east from McBride St. and follow the signs to Seal Cove. The largest operator is **Harbour Air,** tel. (250) 627-1341, which makes scheduled flights to Port Simpson ($35 each way), Kitkatla ($65), Kincolith ($69.16), Masset ($116), and Sandspit ($170). The company also offers flightseeing excursions, from a 20-minute flight over the city for $69 per person, to an hour-long trip to the Khutzeymateen Valley grizzly bear sanctuary for $189 per person. **Vancouver Island Helicopters,** also at the seaplane base, tel. (250) 624-2792, offers chopper charters, which are more expensive than the floatplane variety. Call for rates.

Rail

Prince Rupert is the western terminus of Canada's transcontinental rail system, which runs east from here to Prince George and Edmonton, across the prairies to Toronto, and on to the Atlantic provinces. The route through British Columbia is the highlight of the trip, especially the couple of hundred kilometers just outside Prince Rupert, where the line follows the Skeena River. To get to the **VIA Rail** station take 2nd St. north over the rail line, tel. (250) 624-3291 or (800) 561-8630. Trains arrive in Prince Rupert on Monday, Thursday, and Saturday at 8 p.m., and depart on Wednesday, Friday, and Sunday at 8 a.m. The station, which could do with a coat of paint, is only open a couple of hours either side of arrivals and departures.

Bus

The **Greyhound** bus depot is at 822 3rd Ave. W (opposite Overwaitea), tel. (250) 624-5090 or (800) 661-8747. Reservations are not taken—just turn up and buy your ticket on the day you want to go. From Prince Rupert, buses travel east along the Yellowhead Hwy. to Terrace and Prince George, then either north to the Alaska Hwy., east to Jasper National Park and Edmonton, or south through Cariboo Country to Kamloops and onto Vancouver. The run between Prince George and Prince Rupert leaves twice daily.

BC Ferries

Prince Rupert is the northern terminus of the BC Ferries network, which offers regular services south to Port Hardy on Vancouver Island, and west to the Queen Charlotte Islands. The terminal is two km from downtown, right alongside the Alaska Marine Highway terminal. Ferries serving Prince Rupert have both day rooms and sleeping cabins, shower facilities, food service, and plenty of room to sit back and relax. During the busy summer months it's imperative that you book well in advance, especially if you plan to transport a vehicle. For reservations call BC Ferries, tel. (250) 386-3431 or, toll-free in B.C., (888) BCFERRY. You can also look them up on the internet at http://bcferries.bc.ca/ferries.

The 15-hour ferry trip from Prince Rupert to Port Hardy is a beautiful ride on the well-equipped *Queen of the North,* which departs at 7:30 a.m. on odd-numbered days in June, July, and September, and on even-numbered days in August, arriving in Port Hardy at 10:30 p.m. The rest of the year sailings are less frequent. The peak one-way fares are: adults $102; children 5-11 $51, cars $210, kayaks and canoes, $17.50, bicycles $6.50. Discounts are available for B.C. seniors, and cabins are available by reservation.

Through summer the *Queen of Prince Rupert* cruises to Skidegate on the Queen Charlotte Islands between five and six times a week, less frequently the rest of the year. Departure times vary, but most often it's 11 a.m. from Prince Rupert (arriving Skidegate at 5:30 p.m.) and 11 p.m. from Skidegate (arriving Prince Rupert at 6 a.m.). Peak one-way fares: adults $23, children 5-11 $11.50, cars $87, kayaks and canoes $7, bicycles $6. Discounts are offered to B.C. seniors. Cabins are available.

Alaska Marine Highway

The Alaska Marine Highway operates an extensive network of ferries through southeast Alaska and, subject to the caveat mentioned in the next paragraph, down to Prince Rupert. The first stop north from Prince Rupert is Ketchikan, six hours away. Walk-on passengers need not make reservations, but if you require a cabin or have a vehicle, make reservations as far in advance as possible (up to one year), especially for sailings between May and September.

Travelers hoping to catch the Alaska Marine Highway ferry in Prince Rupert should note that the service has been subject to suspension in the recent past due to a dispute between the U.S. and Canada over fishing rights. The ferry was blockaded in Prince Rupert harbor by hundreds of Canadian fishing boats in July 1997, after which the Alaska Marine Highway pulled that ferry from its schedule. Contact the company for the current status of the Prince Rupert ferry.

Alaska Marine Highway ferries serving Prince Rupert include the *Taku, Matanuska,* and *Malaspina,* which together offer sailings five to six times weekly. Each of the comfortable boats offers a variety of cabins, a cafeteria, restaurant, bar, lounge areas, and showers. If you don't want to pay the extra for a cabin, sleep in one of the many lounge areas or out on the back of the boat. You can even pitch a tent in the Solarium if you want.

Sample one-way fares (in $US) from Prince Rupert are as follows: To Ketchikan—adult, $38; child 2-11, $18; vehicle up to 15 feet, $75; canoe, kayak, or bicycle, $10; cabin, $38-63. To Juneau—adult, $104; child 2-11, $52; vehicle up to 15 feet, $240; canoe, kayak, or bicycle, $20; cabin, $83-145. To Haines—adult, $118; child 2-11, $60; vehicle up to 15 feet, $273; canoe, kayak, or bicycle, $22; cabin, $98-164.

Check-in time is three hours ahead of sailing time—it takes up to two hours to go through Customs and one hour to load up. Foot passengers must be there one hour ahead of sailing.

For reservations or schedule information, contact Alaska Marine Highway, P.O. Box 25535, Juneau, AK 99802-5535, tel. (907) 465-3940 or (800) 642-0066, fax (907) 277-4829. You can also call the Prince Rupert terminal direct at (250) 627-1744. This terminal and ticket office is open daily 9 a.m.-4 p.m. and for up to two hours before and after arrival and departure of vessels.

Getting Around

Local bus service is provided by **Prince Rupert Transit System,** 2nd Ave. W, tel. (250) 624-3343. Adult fare starts at $1.50. All-day passes cost $3.50 and are available from the driver. Have exact fare ready—drivers don't carry change. The only car-rental agencies in town are **Budget,** tel. (250) 627-7400, and **National Tilden,** tel. (250) 624-5318. For a cab call **Skeena Taxis,** tel. (250) 624-2185.

SERVICES AND INFORMATION

Prince Rupert Regional Hospital is south of downtown at 1305 Summit Ave., tel. (250) 624-2171. The **post office** is on 2nd Ave. at 3rd Street. **Laundromats** are located at 226 7th St. and 745 2nd Ave. West.

The **library** is just off McBride Ave. at 101 6th Ave., tel. (250) 627-1345. If you're looking for books, especially on B.C. native art or history, spend some time at **Star of the West Books and Gallery,** 518 3rd Ave. W, tel. (250) 624-9053. A gallery in the back of the store features local wildlife, native art, and photography. Hours are Mon.-Fri. 9 a.m.-9 p.m., Saturday 9 a.m.-6 p.m.

Prince Rupert Visitor Info Centre is at the corner of 1st Ave. and McBride St., tel. (250) 624-5637 or (800) 667-1994. It's one of the best information centers around, with a knowledgeable staff and lots of printed material on Prince Rupert sights, walking tours, restaurants, services, and ferry schedules. Hours are daily 9 a.m.-9 p.m. from early June to early September; Mon.-Sat. 10 a.m.-5 p.m. the rest of the year. Beside the information center is a pleasant park with views across to Digby Island.

QUEEN CHARLOTTE ISLANDS

Wild. Quiet. Mysterious. Primordial. The Queen Charlotte Islands lie like a large upside-down triangle approximately 100 km off the northwest coast of mainland British Columbia, 48 km south of Alaska. Of the chain's 150 mountainous and densely forested islands and islets, the main ones are **Graham Island** to the north and **Moresby Island** to the south, separated by narrow **Skidegate Channel.** The islands stretch 270 km from north to south and up to 85 km across at the widest spot. Running down the west side of the islands are the rugged **Queen Charlotte** and **San Christoval** ranges, which effectively protect the east side from Pacific battering. Nevertheless, the east coast, where most of the population lives, still receives over 1,000 millimeters of rain annually.

Life on the islands is very different from elsewhere in the province. Isolated from the mainland by stormy Hecate Strait, the residents share an island cameraderie and laid-back, away-from-it-all temperament. Visitors can ex-

pect a friendly reception and adequate services. Motel-style accommodations are available in each town, but bed and breakfasts provide a closer glimpse of the island lifestyle. Groceries are also available, though choices can be limited. Gasoline is slightly more expensive than on the mainland, and raging nightlife is nonexistent.

Island Fauna

The only land mammal indigenous to the islands is the Queen Charlotte otter, a subspecies of the mainland otter. The world's largest black bears call the Queen Charlottes home. Though they're a lot heftier than their mainland cousins, they're not a distinct subspecies. Their size comes from a short hibernation and a summer-long salmon feast. No grizzlies live on the islands, but black-tailed deer are common. They were introduced as a meat source and have multiplied many times over. Other mammals present include elk (also introduced), squirrels, beavers, and muskrats.

Stare out to sea to spot killer whales, dolphins, seals, sea lions, otters, and tufted puffins. If you visit between late April and June, you might spot gray whales feeding in Hecate Strait on their way from Mexico to Alaska. The best places to whalewatch are along Skidegate Inlet near the museum, or at the northernmost tip of Rose Spit.

The Haida

The Haida people have lived on the Queen Charlottes since time immemorial. Fearless warriors, expert hunters and fishermen, and skilled woodcarvers, they owned slaves and threw lavish potlatches. They had no written language, but carved records of their tribal history, legends, and important events on totem poles ranging from three to 104 meters high. Living in villages scattered throughout the islands, they hunted sea otters for their luxuriant furs, fished for halibut and Pacific salmon, and collected chitons, clams, and seaweed from tidepools.

The first contact the Haida had with Europeans occurred in 1774, when Spanish explorer Juan Perez discovered the Charlottes. The islands weren't given a European name until 1787, when British captain George Dixon arrived and began trading with the Haida. He named the islands after his queen, the wife of George III. The whites gave the Haida goods, liquor, tools, blankets, and firearms in exchange for sea otter furs; over a 40-year period the otters were hunted almost to extinction. In addition, the white traders brought European diseases that ravaged the Haida population.

At the turn of the 19th century, white settlers from the mainland began moving over to the Charlottes to live along the low-lying east coast and the protected shores of Masset Inlet. By the 1830s the traditional lifestyle of the Haida was coming to an end. The governments on the mainland prohibited the Haida from owning slaves and throwing potlatches—an important social and economic part of their culture—and forced all Haida children to attend missionary schools. The Haida abandoned their village sites and moved onto reserves at Skidegate and Masset on Graham Island.

Today totem poles are rising once again on the Queen Charlottes, as a renewed interest in Haida art and culture is compelling skilled elders to pass their knowledge on to younger generations. The first totem pole to be erected in 90 years was put up in 1969 in Masset, followed by one in 1978 at Skidegate. In 1986 a 50-foot dugout canoe, created out of a single huge cedar log, was commissioned for Vancouver's Expo86, and a second canoe was launched in Old Massett.

For many years the Haida struggled alongside the Island Protection Society to preserve their heritage. Their longtime efforts paid off in two major events: in 1981 the best-known of the abandoned Haida Villages, **Ninstints,** was declared a UNESCO World Heritage Site, and in 1988 the southern section of the archipelago was proclaimed **Gwaii Haanas National Park Reserve.**

TRANSPORTATION

Air

Canadian Regional, tel. (604) 279-6611, (800) 665-1177 in Canada, or (800) 426-7000 from the U.S., flies daily between Vancouver and

Sandspit ($354 one-way). **Harbour Air,** tel. (250) 627-1341, offers daily service from Prince Rupert to Masset ($116 one-way) and Sandspit ($170 one-way). Rental cars are available at each airport, and from Sandspit you can hop aboard an Airporter bus to Queen Charlotte City for $12. **Harbour Air,** tel. (250) 627-1341, flies a floatplane right to Queen Charlotte City harbor from Prince Rupert; $170 each way.

Ferry

In summer, **BC Ferries** operates the *Queen of Prince Rupert* between Prince Rupert and Skidegate five or six times a week, less frequently the rest of the year. Departure times vary, but most often it's 11 a.m. from Prince Rupert (arriving Skidegate at 5:30 p.m.) and 11 p.m. from Skidegate (arriving Prince Rupert at 6 a.m.) Peak one-way fares are: adults $23, children 5-11 $11.50, cars $87, kayaks and canoes $7, bicycles $6. B.C. seniors get a discount. Cabins are available. For more information call BC Ferries, tel. (250) 386-3431 or, toll-free in B.C., (888) BCFERRY. The company is also on the internet at http://bcferries.bc.ca/ferries.

The ferry terminal is five km east of Queen Charlotte City at Skidegate. Taxis usually wait at the terminal when the ferry arrives; expect to pay around $10 to get into town.

Getting Around

A ferry connects Graham and Moresby Islands, departing hourly in each direction 7 a.m.-10 p.m.; peak roundtrip fare is adults $3.50, children $1.75, cars $9.50, canoes and kayaks $2, bicycles free. Apart from that, the islands have no public transportation. The least expensive car rentals are available at **Rustic Car Rentals** in Queen Charlotte City, tel. (250) 559-4641, which charges from $48 a day plus 20 cents a kilometer for the smallest vehicles. Other agencies include **Budget,** with offices in Queen Charlotte City (tel. 250-559-4675), Masset (tel. 250-626-5571), and Sandspit (tel. 250-637-5688); **National Tilden,** in Masset (tel. 250-626-3318); and **Thrifty,** with offices in Queen Charlotte City (tel. 250-559-8837) and Sandspit (tel. 250-637-2299). Book well ahead.

To get around by floatplane, including to Gwaii Haanas National Park Reserve, call **South Moresby Air Charters,** tel. (250) 559-4222.

QUEEN CHARLOTTE CITY

Perched along the shores of Bearskin Bay, five km west of the dock for the mainland ferry, picturesque Queen Charlotte City is not really a city at all but a small laid-back fishing village of 1,000 people. Several heritage buildings in town date back to 1909; most of them are along the main road. For good photographic possibilities, wander out onto the marina and look back at the village.

The town is also home to the Queen Charlotte division of **MacMillan Bloedel Industries,** the

Gracie's Place

JANE AND BRUCE KING

logging giant that leases much of the land on Graham Island. In summer, the company runs a four-hour bus tour that details all stages of logging. If you don't have your own transportation and don't mind a bit of pro-logging propaganda, the tour is a good way to see some of Moresby Island. Free tours (take your own food and drinks) depart from Queen Charlotte City Information Centre and Port Clements Museum on Tuesday at 10 a.m. Book at (250) 557-4212.

Accommodations and Camping

Rustic **Gracie's Place,** 3113 3rd Ave., tel. (250) 559-4262, is delightful lodging islands-style. Decorated with sea treasures and flowering plants, the four cozy guest rooms each have their own toilet, shower, and entrance. Rates are $50 s, $60 d for the two standard rooms; $70 s or d for one of the two kitchen-equipped units.

Even better value is **Dorothy and Mike's Guest House,** 3125 2nd Ave., tel. (250) 559-8439, which features gardens and water views, use of a kitchen, and a cooked breakfast—all for $40 s, $50-60 d. **Spruce Point Lodging,** 609 6th Ave., tel. (250) 559-8234, has a great downtown location with superb water views and offers bed-and-breakfast lodging for $55 s, $65 d. Built in 1910, the old Premier Hotel has been totally renovated and now operates as **Premier Creek Lodging,** 3101 3rd Ave., tel. (250) 559-8415. Its "sleeping rooms" with shared facilities cost $30 per person, but worth the extra money are the rooms with balconies and harbor views for $65 s, $75 d.

The motels in town may lack the atmosphere of the above accommodations, but they offer higher-standard rooms and more amenities. Try **Sea Raven Motel,** 3301 3rd Ave., tel. (250) 559-4423 or (800) 665-9606, for $50 s, $70 d, or similarly priced **Hecate Inn,** 321 3rd Ave., tel. (250) 559-4543 or (800) 665-3350.

Haydn Turner Park, through town to the west, has toilets, picnic tables, and fire rings for campers, but no showers or hookups; $7 per night.

Food

The place to go for breakfast is **Margaret's Cafe,** 3223 Wharf St., tel. (250) 559-4204. All the locals congregate here. This place has plenty of atmosphere, and the food is good and plentiful for the price (muffin and coffee, $3), but be pre-

pared to wait for a table. It's open Mon.-Sat. 6:30 a.m.-3 p.m., Sunday 8 a.m.-3 p.m. For something more substantial, head to **Sea Raven Restaurant,** in the motel of the same name at 3301 3rd Ave., tel. (250) 559-4423. Specializing in local seafood, the Sea Raven is open nightly from 6 p.m. Another local favorite for seafood is **Claudette's Place,** corner 3rd Ave. and 2nd St., tel. (250) 559-8861. It's on the pricey side—most entrees run $17-22. Open daily 9 a.m.-10 p.m. The **Oceana Restaurant,** 3119 3rd Ave., tel. (250) 559-8633, specializes in Chinese dishes, and the service is fast and friendly.

Services and Information

Emergency services in Queen Charlotte City include **Queen Charlotte Islands General Hospital,** 3209 3rd Ave., tel. (250) 559-4300, and the **RCMP,** tel. (250) 559-4421. The **post office** and a **laundromat** are in the City Centre Building off 2nd Avenue. For island and North Coast literature, head to **Observer Books,** 623 7th St., tel. (250) 559-4680. **Rainbows Gallery,** 3201 3rd Ave., tel. (250) 559-8420, also sells books, along with a good selection of locally crafted souvenirs.

Queen Charlotte Visitor Info Centre, 3220 Wharf St., tel. (250) 559-4742, offers a wide variety of brochures and information on everything that's going on around the islands. Don't leave without buying a copy of the latest edition of the *Guide to the Queen Charlotte Islands,* which includes maps, details on all the villages, and more—all for $3.95.

NORTH TO PORT CLEMENTS

From Queen Charlotte City, Graham Island's main road follows the eastern coastline past the ferry terminal and Haida Gwaii Museum to the Haida community of Skidegate Village, from where it's a pleasant 65 km coastal drive to Port Clements.

Haida Gwaii Museum

While totem poles and other ancient Haida art can be seen in various places around the islands, this museum on the north side of the Skidegate Landing ferry terminal allows visitors the opportunity to see a variety of such art under one roof.

Inside are striking Haida wood and argillite carvings, pioneer artifacts, a beautiful woven blanket, jewelry, historic black-and-white photos, stunning prints by Haida artist Robert Davidson, ancient totems from Tanu and Skedans dating to 1878, the skull of a humpback whale, shells galore, and a collection of stuffed birds. The museum is open in summer, Tues.-Fri. 10 a.m.-5 p.m., Sat.-Sun. 1-5 p.m.; closed Sunday and Tuesday the rest of the year. Admission is $2.50. For further information call (250) 559-4643.

When you leave the museum, be sure to wander up the road and visit the longhouse-style **cedar carving shed** where the fantastic 15-meter-long canoe *Loo Taas* (which means "Wave Eater") is housed. The striking red-and-black vessel was commissioned for Expo86 in Vancouver, after which it was paddled to the Queen Charlottes.

Between mid-April and early June, migrating gray whales rest and feed on shallow gravel bars in front of the museum. A wooden deck overlooking the water is a great vantage point to watch these magnificent creatures.

Skidegate Village and Vicinity

Continuing north from the museum you'll soon come to Skidegate Village, a Haida reserve of 600 residents. A 100-year-old weathered totem pole still stands here, and you'll see another new totem—this one carved by Haida artist Bill Reid—in front of the longhouse facing the beach. The longhouse is the Skidegate Haida Band Council House, where local artisans fashion miniature totem poles, argillite ornaments, and jewelry in traditional designs.

From Skidegate, the road follows the shoreline of Hecate Strait, past driftwood-strewn beaches, an attractive old graveyard, and **Balance Rock,** one km north of Skidegate Village. A highway sign and turnout mark the start of a short trail down to the rock. Continuing north, the scenery becomes rural, as the road skirts land cleared by early settlers for cattle-grazing; watch for black-tailed deer in this area. Near **Lawn Hill** look for tree stumps that have been carved in the shapes of animals and birds.

Tlell and Vicinity

This small ranching community is the northernmost settlement on the east coast before the road swings inland toward Port Clements and Masset. Sandwiched between the Tlell River and the beach, Tlell has recently become a haven for artisans; look for signs pointing the way to their outlets, which are concentrated on Richardson Rd. off Wiggins Road. The Tlell River is favored by local anglers for its huge runs of coho salmon and steelhead.

Tlell River House, on Beitush Rd., tel. (250) 557-4211 or (800) 667-8906, overlooks the river and is a short walk from the beach. Basic rooms go for $70 s, $75 d; downstairs is a good restaurant. Attractive **Tlell River Farm and Lodge,** on the west side of the main road, tel. (250) 559-4569, offers seven rooms, each with private bathroom, for $60-90 per person daily including three meals. Also on the highway is **Cacilia's B&B,** tel. (250) 557-4664, whose rustic main lodge lies in a Sitka spruce forest behind the beach. Rooms are basic but reasonably priced at $35 per person. For those willing to rough it, space on the floor is $10 per person; supply your own sleeping bag. Bike and kayak rentals are available.

Just north of Tlell is the southern tip of Naikoon Provincial Park. While the park's main entrance is farther north out of Masset (see the full listing below) vistors exploring the Tlell area will find interesting things to see and do here in the park's south end as well. The main attraction down here is the wreck of the *Pezuta,* a wooden log barge that ran aground in 1928. To get there, park at the picnic area on the north side of the Tlell River and follow the river to its mouth, then walk north along the beach. It's about 10 km (2.5 hours) each way. Keen hikers may want to attempt the **East Beach Hike,** a 94-km trail that leads all the way north from the Tlell River to Tow Hill via Rose Spit. For trail and other park details, stop in at **park headquarters** beside the highway in Tlell, tel. (250) 557-4390. **Misty Meadows Campground,** immediately north of park headquarters, is uncrowded and costs only $9.50 per site for scenic campsites. Facilities include a picnic area, pit toilets, and beach trails.

Port Clements

Weatherbeaten houses decorated with driftwood, shells, fishing floats, and other sea-washed treasures line the streets of this logging

BEACHCOMBING ON THE CHARLOTTES

Beachcombing on the Queen Charlotte Islands is popular year-round, but is especially good after heavy winter storms. You may find fishing floats from countries around the Pacific (glass balls from Japan are especially prized), bottles, rope, driftwood, shells, whale bones, semi-precious agate, or just about anything that floats. A few years back, a container of Nike runners broke apart somewhere in the Pacific; they were found scattered on beaches throughout the Charlottes and as far south as the Oregon coast. Before that, an abandoned fishing boat from Japan washed ashore and caused excitement; it's now on display in Prince Rupert.

and fishing village on the northeast shore of Masset Inlet. **Port Clements Museum,** on Bayview Dr., tel. (250) 557-4443, houses an intriguing selection of pioneer artifacts and relics from the village, as well as black-and-white photos of logging camps and early village life. It's open through summer, daily 1-5 p.m.; weekends only the rest of the year.

If you're driving south from Port Clements, you might want to consider taking **Charlotte Main,** a logging road linking Port Clements and Queen Charlotte City. To get to it, take Bayview Dr. out of town and on past a couple of sights of interest. Six km from town, watch for a sign directing you to an extremely rare **golden spruce.** The tree, 50 meters tall and more than 300 years old, is a distinctive yellow color, standing out from all the other green trees surrounding it. It produces only green-boughed seedlings, making its color even more of a mystery. From the parking area, follow a beautiful five-minute trail through lush, second-growth forest to the Yakoun River; the golden spruce stands on the opposite bank. Farther down the road, a short trail leads through the forest to a **Haida canoe.** Many unfinished canoes lie in the bush, but this is the only one that can be easily reached.

Finally, you'll come to **Juskatla,** an old logging camp established in the 1940s to supply Queen Charlottes spruce for WW II airplanes. Here you'll find the start of the Charlotte Main logging road, as well as the main office for the MacMillan Bloedel logging company. The company actively logs off Charlotte Main, so travel along the road is safest outside of operating hours (Mon.-Fri. 6:30 a.m.-5:30 p.m.).

From Juskatla, the logging road continues south to Queen Charlotte City. A turnoff to the west (signposted) leads to **Rennell Sound,** the only point on the remote west coast accessible by road. At the end of the road you'll find great beachcombing opportunities and free primitive campsites. The final descent to the shore is a hair-raising 24% gradient, one of the steepest public roads in North America.

MASSET AND VICINITY

Originally named Graham City, Masset (pop. 1,400) is the largest and oldest town on the Queen Charlottes. The Graham Steamship, Coal, and Lumber Company founded the settlement in 1909, a few km east of a Haida community named Massett. Over time, Massett became known as Old Massett or Haida, and Graham City was incorporated as Masset (with one "t"). Today, about half the population works at the Canadian Armed Forces Station (built in 1971) and lives on the base. The other half is involved in the fishing industry—either as fishermen or as workers in the local crab cannery or fish-freezing plant.

As you enter town from the south, passing the information center and seaplane base, continue straight ahead to reach Naikoon Provincial Park or cross Delkatla Inlet for downtown Masset and Old Massett.

Town Sights

Masset makes a good base from which to explore the beautiful surrounding area and Naikoon Provincial Park, but there's not much to do in town. You might want to stroll around to see the **heritage buildings,** including the old schoolhouse and hospital, both on Collison Avenue, or head down to **government wharf,** where some interesting activity is almost always going on: boats coming and going, fishermen loading supplies or unloading their catch.

Delkatla Wildlife Sanctuary

Bordering Masset to the east is Delkatla Wildlife Sanctuary, where you can observe Canada geese, sandhill cranes, trumpeter swans, great blue herons, many varieties of ducks, and other waterfowl resting during migration. Several short walking trails wind through the preserve near town; follow Hodges Ave. west onto Trumpeter Dr. and continue alongside the inlet to the trailhead. For better views, drive along Tow Hill Rd. toward Naikoon Provincial Park, turning left at the sanctuary sign onto Masset Cemetery Road. Along this road, more signs point out trails or other points of interest. You'll first pass a turnout for the **Bird Walk Trail,** which winds along the edge of a marshy area for 500 meters. Then farther down the road, you'll come to **Simpson Viewing Tower.** The trail to the tower leads through a wide open meadow and marshes dotted with wildflowers, and the top of the lofty perch makes an excellent spot to watch the preserve's abundant waterfowl. You might also spy bald eagles, peregrine falcons, and other birds of prey, as well as four-legged marsh animals such as muskrats.

Back on Tow Hill Rd., continue east to a parking lot and a trail to the beach. Just across from the parking lot is beautiful **Masset Cemetery,** where the graves are marked by large aboveground mounds of moss planted with flowering bulbs and surrounded by bushes and trees. It's a peaceful place to ponder the beauty of the Charlottes.

Old Massett

If you're in search of Haida treasures, head for the village of Old Massett, also known as Haida. It's just a five-minute drive from Masset, west down the coastal road. Go as far as the road takes you and you'll end up at the old blue schoolhouse, now **Ed Jones Haida Museum.** Inside, exhibits include a large collection of fas-

cinating old photographs showing how the villages used to look, Haida art and prints, and some of the original totem poles from around the Queen Charlottes. Outside you'll find a partly completed canoe and a field sprinkled with more totems, these from a more recent era. The museum is open in summer, Sat.-Sun. 9 a.m.-5 p.m.; admission by donation. Across from the museum is a carving shed where artists can be seen working throughout summer.

Continue up behind the museum to **Adams Family House of Silver,** tel. (250) 626-3215, to view or buy carved-wood items and silver jewelry directly from the artist (who also has a fantastic Haida print collection). It's open daily 10 a.m.-noon and 1-6 p.m. Next door, the impressive weathered building with the tall totem pole out front is **Haida Arts and Jewellery,** tel. (250) 626-5560, open Mon.-Sat. 11 a.m.-5 p.m., Sunday noon-5 p.m. Here you can buy custom argillite carvings, silk-screen prints, handcrafted silver and abalone jewelry, books on native culture, printed sweatshirts, and greeting cards.

Langara Island

Langara Island, at the northwestern tip of the archipelago, is a rugged and remote place with wooded slopes ending at a rocky shoreline. A couple of small native villages, two lodges, and a beautifully restored 1913 lighthouse are the only human intrusions. The main attraction here is the salmon and halibut fishing; the provincial record-setting halibut, a 320-pounder, was pulled from local waters. Fishing is best April-Sept., when anglers book up the island's **Langara Fishing Lodge,** tel. (250) 873-5500, and **North Island Lodge,** tel. (250) 758-1616.

On the mainland, across a narrow strait from the island, are the abandoned Haida villages

TODD CLARK

of Kiusta and Yaku, where some of the earliest contacts occurred between native Haida and whites. Access is difficult by boat because of often-rough seas.

Accommodations and Camping

Several B&Bs in Masset provide lodgings and local flavor. **Harbourview Lodging,** 1608 Delkatla St., tel. (250) 626-5109, provides pleasant rooms (one with a view of the fishing pier), a shared bathroom, sauna, and optional breakfast. Rates start at $40 s, $50 d. Rustic **Copper Beech House,** next to the pier at 1590 Delkatla Rd., tel. (250) 626-5441, is decorated with sea treasures and has a beautiful flower garden. Rates of $50-70 per room include a delicious breakfast prepared by the enthusiastic host. **Alaska View Lodge** is 13 km from Masset on Tow Hill Rd., tel. (250) 626-3333, but has an excellent beachside location. Rooms with a balcony, beach views, and breakfast (when you want it) range $50-80.

The only motel right in Masset is the **Singing Surf Inn,** 1504 Old Beach Rd., tel. (250) 626-3318, with large rooms and a restaurant and bar downstairs; $74 s, $78 d. **Naikoon Park Motel,** Tow Hill Rd., tel. (250) 626-5187, near the entrance to Naikoon Provincial Park and walking distance from the beach, offers basic rooms at a good price—$40 s, $45 d. Rooms with a kitchen are $55, but you might not need it as guests also have use of a pleasant barbecue area.

Masset-Haida Lions RV Site and Campground is on Tow Hill Rd. two km north of Masset, opposite the Delkatla Wildlife Sanctuary. The campground features large, fairly private campsites with tables among the trees, and communal washrooms with coin-operated hot showers. Unserviced sites are $8, powered sites $10. Another option is to continue 20 km along the road into Naikoon Provincial Park (see below).

Food and Nightlife

Don't miss dining at the **The Path,** five km along the road to Tow Hill. It's a classic island restaurant, with no electricity, kerosene lighting, driftwood benches and tables, and a vegetarian menu that mirrors the simplicity of the restaurant decor. Dishes are mostly under $10 and the desserts are all delicious. Open daily in summer for dinner only.

Even though Masset has a large fishing fleet, most of the catch ends up in mainland canneries. Your best choice for seafood is **Cafe Gallery,** on the corner of Collison Ave. and Orr St., tel. (250) 626-3672, where the daily lunch specials are around $9 and dinner entrees range $14-20. The menu also includes steak, chateaubriand, and pasta dishes. Open Mon.-Sat. 8:30 a.m.-9 p.m.

Pearl's, on the corner of Main St. and Collison Ave., tel. (250) 626-3223, features Chinese cuisine. For around $10 you can get an enormous helping of chicken and vegetables in black bean sauce, along with a large bowl of steamed rice, tea, and the mandatory fortune cookie. Open Mon.-Sat. for lunch, and daily for dinner. Head to **High Tide Cappuccino Bar,** Delkatla Rd., tel. (250) 626-5140, for coffee and cakes along with water views and a casual atmosphere.

The town's nightlife—such as it is—is found at **Daddy Cool's Neighbourhood Pub,** on the corner of Collison Ave. and Main St., tel. (250) 626-3210, or the often-rowdy **Kilsli Lounge** in the Singing Surf Inn on Old Beach Rd., tel. (250) 626-3318.

Services and Information

Masset's link to the outside world is **Harbour Air,** tel. (250) 626-3225, which offers flights twice daily to Prince Rupert's Seal Cove Air Base from the seaplane base beside Tow Hill Rd.; $116 one-way. **Budget,** on Collison Ave., tel. (250) 626-5571, rents everything from compact economy cars to four-wheel drives. Small cars start around $65 a day plus 30 cents per kilometer. **National Tilden** is based in the Singing Surf Inn, tel. (250) 626-3318. Book well ahead to ensure a vehicle for September and October, when Masset is flooded with salmon fishermen.

Masset Visitor Info Centre is beside the main road as you come into town from the south, tel. (250) 626-3982. It's open mid-May through mid-September, daily 9 a.m.-4 p.m.

NAIKOON PROVINCIAL PARK

This spectacular park encompasses some 72,640 hectares along the northeast tip of Graham Island. Tlell marks the park's southern boundary, while access to the northern reaches is via the road out to Tow Hill, 26 km east of Masset. The

Tow Hill and the north end of Agate Beach

park's dominant features are its beaches, 97 kilometers of them, bordering Hecate Strait on the east and the turbulent Dixon Entrance on the north. Most of the rest of the park is lowlands, surrounded by stunted lodgepole pine, red and yellow cedar, western hemlock, and Sitka spruce. Wildlife is abundant; blacktail deer, black bear, marten, river otter, raccoons, red squirrels, beaver, muskrat, small herds of wild cattle, and many species of birds inhabit the park. Dolphins, orcas, harbor porpoises, and hair seals swim offshore year-round, and northern fur seals and California gray whales migrate north past the park in May and June.

Sights
The drive out to the park from Masset is superb, passing through kilometer after kilometer of moss-draped trees. Along the way you'll pass **Tow Hill Ecological Reserve,** a beautiful spruce forest where birds tweet from the treetops and the ground and most of the trees are completely cushioned in spongy yellow moss.

At the end of the road, long sandy **Agate Beach** is a beachcomber's delight strewn with shells, driftwood, and shiny, sea-worn pebbles of every color under the sun. Walk along the shores of McIntyre Bay and scramble over the rocks at the base of 109-meter-high **Tow Hill** to find more treasures and small sea creatures in the tidepools. Here you might see bald eagles soaring on the updrafts caused by the near-vertical cliffs.

Trails lead in a number of directions—to the summit of Tow Hill, along the Hiellen River, to Cape Fife (see below), and along North Beach to **Rose Spit,** a narrow five-km-long point of land that gave the park its name (*Naikoon* is the Haida word for "Long Nose").

Cape Fife Trail
The Cape Fife Trail (three hours each way) passes boglands and stunted pine trees on its 10-km route to **Fife Point,** overlooking Hecate Strait. Here the shore above the high-tide line is blanketed by a mass of driftwood logs, crushed together during the fierce storms that regularly lash this coast. A rough shelter at the end of the trail provides some protection from the elements. Backcountry camping is also permitted; hide among the trees on especially windy days. From this point you can hike north along the beach to Rose Spit, at the northeastern tip of the Charlottes, then continue back along North Beach to the parking lot at Hiellen River—a total of 34 km and an easy two-day trip. Well-equipped adventurers can continue south from Fife Point along **East Beach** to finish at Tlell, a total distance of 72 km. This has become a popular hike—take your time (allow 4-5 days) and bring adequate food and water.

Practicalities
Agate Beach Campground is near Tow Hill, about 26 km from Masset. The campsites lie

along the back of the beach and offer out-standing views. A shelter and pit toilets are pro-vided, but no showers. In summer you need to nab a spot early in the day—by late afternoon they're all taken. The campground is open year-round. Sites cost $9.50 per night May-Sept.; the rest of the year they're free. The **park head-quarters,** tel. (250) 847-7320, and another campground are to the south at Tlell (see "Tlell and Vicinity," under "North to Masset," above).

SANDSPIT AND VICINITY

Across Skidegate Channel, Sandspit (pop. 750) is the only community on Moresby Island. It oc-cupies a low-lying, windswept spit overlooking Shingle Bay, 15 km east of the ferry dock. The rest of the island is wilderness. The north half is largely given over to logging, and holds a num-ber of remote logging camps. The south half and over 100 outlying islands fall within Gwaii Haanas National Park Reserve (see below), which protects a high concentration of aban-doned Haida villages.

Logging drives Sandspit's economy. **Timber-West,** tel. (250) 637-5436, holds leases to much of Moresby Island. The company operates an in-formation center on the road into Sandspit; stop in for details of sights along logging roads, hints on driving, and a short film presentation. Be-tween mid-May and mid-September, the com-pany offers free half-day forest tours, leaving from the information center Wednesday and Friday at noon.

Into the Bush
Those determined to tour the forests in their own vehicle can make an enjoyable loop trip south out of Sandspit. Logging roads lace the forest, leading to beaches strewn with driftwood, streams alive with salmon and steelhead, and beautiful Skidegate and Mosquito Lakes (good trout fish-ing). Free campgrounds are available at Gray Bay and Mosquito Lake. Before heading out, pick up a local map and route advice from the Tim-berWest Information Centre on Alliford Bay Road.

Accommodations and Camping
Sandspit lacks the appeal of communities on Graham Island, but services are available. **Sea-port B&B,** 371 Alliford Bay Rd., tel. (250) 637-5698, features three basic rooms in a water-front home. Rates of $30 s, $40 d include a self-serve breakfast and use of kitchen facilities. Friendly **Moresby Island Guest House,** 385 Alliford Bay Rd., tel. (250) 637-5300, is a popu-lar kayakers' hangout offering rooms with shared baths and kitchens; $30 s, $60 d, including a light breakfast and laundry privileges. **Sandspit Inn,** across from the airport, tel. (250) 637-5334, charges from $70 s, $80 d, and has Sandspit's only restaurant and bar.

Free campgrounds are located at **Gray Bay** and **Mosquito Lake** (named after the Mosquito airplane, not the pesky insects), both on the log-ging roads detailed under "Into the Bush," above.

Services and Infomation
Sandspit Airport, the main airport for the Queen Charlotte Islands, is on the east side of town beside Hecate Strait. It's served by **Canadian Regional,** tel. (250) 637-5388, and **Harbour Air,** tel. (250) 637-5350. The **Airporter** bus meets all flights, transporting passengers to Queen Charlotte City for $12 per person. **Bud-get,** tel. (250) 637-5688, and **Thrifty,** tel. (250) 637-2299, have car rental agencies in Sandspit.

Get all the information about Moresby Island, its sights and facilities, and the interior logging roads at the **TimberWest Information Centre** on Alliford Bay Rd., tel. (250) 637-5436. The center is open Mon.-Fri. 9 a.m.-5 p.m.

GWAII HAANAS
NATIONAL PARK RESERVE

Renowned around the world for its ancient Haida villages dotted with totem poles, this park en-compasses the southern half of Moresby Island as well as 137 smaller islands in the south of the archipelago—a total of 1,480 hectares of land and 1,600 km of coastline. It's a remarkable place. Ancient brooding totems and remnants of mighty Haida longhouses stand against a back-drop of lush wilderness—dense trees, thick spongy moss, and rock-strewn beaches with incredibly clear water. Colonies of nesting seabirds and an abundance of marinelife—killer and minke whales, sea lions, tufted puffins—all add to the atmosphere.

Jointly managed by Parks Canada and the Haida nation, the park was established in 1988 after a long and bitter struggle between the Haida and forestry companies. The area now protected was home to seafaring Haida for almost 10,000 years, but within 100 years after their first contact with whites their communities were wiped out. Over 500 historic sites were left behind—from burial grounds to entire villages.

Ninstints, on tiny Anthony Island near the south end of the park, is the world's best-preserved totem village. Anthony Island was declared a UNESCO World Heritage Site in 1981, just 97 years after the last Haida families had abandoned their remote home. **Hotspring Island,** site of another village, holds hot springs and unique flora. Other well-known villages include **Skedans** (closest to Sandspit), **Tanu,** and **Windy Bay.**

Park Practicalities

The only access to the park is by air or sea. Before heading in you need to make a reservation through Parks Canada, tel. (250) 559-6319, and obtain a free permit from the Skidegate Haida Band Council House in Skidegate Village.

Several guides and outfitters on the islands can help you with your visit. **Moresby Explorers,** tel. (250) 637-2215 or (800) 806-7633, and **Queen Charlotte Adventures,** tel. (250) 559-8990 or (800) 668-4288, both offer guided kayak trips and can also provide drop-offs and pick-ups for those heading into the park unguided. **Moresby Mountain Sports** in Queen Charlotte City, tel. (250) 559-8234, rents sea kayaks, which come with paddles, lifejackets, and splash skirts. Single kayaks are $50 a day or $220 a week; doubles are $60 a day or $340 a week.

Ecosummer Expeditions, 1516 Duranleau St., Vancouver, BC V6H 3S4, tel. (604) 669-7741 or (800) 465-8884, has been conducting sailing trips through the south end of the archipelago since well before the proclamation of a park. You'll board the company's 67-foot *Ocean Light* for eight days of sailing, visiting all the best-known abandoned Haida villages, exploring the waterways, and searching out land and sea mammals. All meals and accommodations aboard the boat are included in the rate of $1,995 per person.

South Moresby Air Charters, at the wharf in Queen Charlotte City, tel. (250) 559-4222, offers flightseeing trips to the park, including visits to Ninstints and the hot springs. Rates start at $350 per hour of flying time plus $50 for each hour of waiting time. **Vancouver Island Helicopters,** based at Sandspit Airport, tel. (250) 637-5344, offers pricey chopper tours to the park. Rates begin at $100 per person for four passengers to fly down the coast to Skedans and back, with a quick village tour included.

THE STEWART-CASSIAR HIGHWAY

An alternative to the Alaska Highway, this route turns off the Yellowhead Highway 45 km west of New Hazelton and leads north to the Yukon, joining the Alaska Highway just west of Watson Lake. The route opens up a magnificent area of northern wilderness that in many ways rivals that along the more famous Alaska Highway.

The highlight of the Stewart-Cassiar Highway is definitely the side trip west to the twin coastal villages of **Stewart** and **Hyder.** But the route also passes the remote river town of **Telegraph Creek** and jumping-off points for various wilderness adventures.

From the Yellowhead Highway it's 155 km north to Meziadin Junction, then 65 km west to **Stewart,** official beginning of the Stewart-Cassiar Highway. Total length of the trip between the Yellowhead and Alaska Highways is 733 km. Add another 130 km roundtrip for the jaunt out to Stewart.

Be Prepared

The highway is mainly paved, but improved gravel sections are found on the 80-km stretch north of Meziadin Junction, the 40-km stretch south of Kinaskan Lake, and for around 30 km each side of Dease Lake. Be prepared for washboard conditions on these sections, especially after heavy rain. Dust and mud can also be problematic, and many narrow, one-lane bridges call for extra caution.

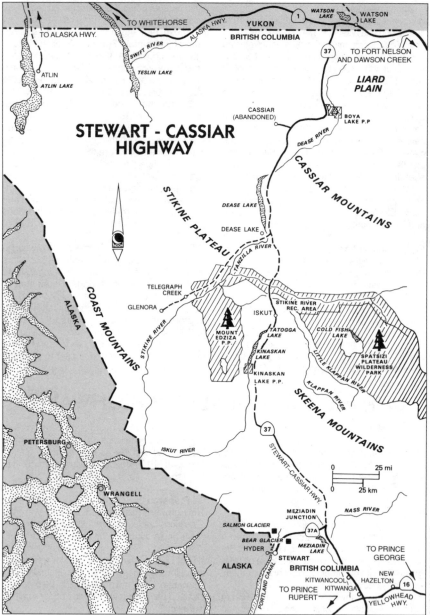

© MOON PUBLICATIONS, INC.

lakeside camping
along the Stewart-
Cassiar Highway

Gas stations and services can be found along the highway, but it's not a bad idea to fill up with gas wherever and whenever you get the opportunity. And to be on the safe side, take spare tires, belts, hoses, bailing wire, a strong adhesive, and spare parts. In summer, lots of RVs and logging trucks take this route, so if you do get stranded it shouldn't be too long before someone comes along.

FROM YELLOWHEAD HIGHWAY TO MEZIADIN JUNCTION

Tree-covered hills, dense patches of snow white daisies, banks of pink-and-white clover and purple lupine, craggy mountains and distant peaks, beautiful lakes covered in yellow water lilies, and lots of logging trucks flying along the road—these are images of the 155 km between the Yellowhead Highway and Meziadin Junction, the turnoff to Stewart.

Kitwanga

This small village just north of the Yellowhead Highway is home to **Kitwanga Fort National Historic Site,** the first national historic site commemorating native culture in western Canada. The site protects 13-meter-high Battle Hill, where 200 years ago a native warrior named Nekt fought off attacks from hostile neighbors. A trail leads from the parking lot down to the flat area around the bottom of the hill, where you can read dis-

play panels describing the hill's history. The site is on Kitwanga Valley Rd., overlooking the Kitwanga River, and is open year-round; admission free.

Kitwancool Totem Poles

Continuing north, you're paralleling what was commonly called the Grease Trail, the route coastal natives took to the interior to trade their greasy oolichans (minuscule fish) with other tribes. At the native village of Kitwancool, 25 km from Kitwanga, you can see an outstanding group of totem poles, most more than 100 years old. The oldest, "Hole in the Ice," is approximately 140 years old; some say it's the oldest standing totem pole in the world. It tells the story of a man preventing his people from starving by chopping a hole in the ice and doing a spot of ice fishing.

Meziadin Junction toward Stewart

At the junction is a gas station and a small information center, open July-Aug. only. Just south of the junction is 335-hectare **Meziadin Lake Provincial Park,** lying along the northeast shore of Meziadin Lake, two km from the highway. It's open June-Oct. and has a boat launch, pit toilets, and mostly gravel campsites, some on the lake's edge; $9.50 per night May-Sept., free the rest of the year.

From Meziadin Junction, Stewart is 65 km west along a spectacular stretch of highway that crosses the glaciated Coast Mountains. The first 40 km is all uphill, through thick subalpine forests, and past lakes, waterfalls, and a string of glaciers sitting like thick icy slabs atop almost-vertical mountains. Suddenly, and quite unexpectedly, the highway rounds a corner and there in front of you is magnificent, eggshell blue **Bear Glacier.** The glacier tumbles down into deep blue **Strohn Lake,** where large icebergs float across the surface in the breeze. From Bear Glacier it's downhill all the way to Stewart. Keep an eye out for three mighty waterfalls on the north side of the highway, one after another. One plummets down into a large buildup of ice, complete with blue ice cave. This stretch of road is good for wildlife viewing; numerous mountain goats wander the hillsides, and black bears nose around the avalanche slopes in search of their next meal.

STEWART

The twin towns of Stewart, British Columbia, and Hyder, Alaska, straddle the International Boundary at the headwaters of **Portland Inlet,** the world's fourth-longest fjord. Canada's most northerly ice-free port, Stewart (pop. 1,000) enjoys a stunning setting; snowcapped peaks rise over 2,000 meters from the fjord.

Two brothers, Robert and John Stewart, were the first permanent settlers at the head of Portland Canal, arriving shortly after the turn of the 20th century. Prospecting through the surrounding mountains, they came across incredible wealth. Word got out and by 1910, Stewart's population had boomed to 10,000. The main street was lined with busy shops, the city had four daily newspapers, and at least every second day a steamer loaded with new arrivals and supplies would dock at one of two long wharves. But the boom was short-lived, especially after the Grand Trunk Pacific Railway decided to build its western terminus at Prince Rupert. By the end of WW I the population had dwindled to 20.

Today a massive lode of copper keeps the local economy alive. The Granduc Mining Co. began operations in 1964, drilling a record 16-km-long tunnel into the Coast Mountains. The mining operation has not been without its problems. During the initial year of operations, an avalanche killed 27 workers. And financial difficulties forced the mine's closure for a few years in the mid-1980s.

STEWART AND HYDER: SOME QUICK FACTS

The twin towns of Stewart (Canada) and Hyder (United States) are separated by an international border, but you'd hardly know it. None of the formalities or checkpoints you'd expect at a border exist here, and residents of both towns, as well as visitors, are free to wander from country to country at will.

Residents of both towns:
• send their kids to school in Canada
• are supplied power by B.C. Hydro
• use the Canadian phone system (area code 250)
• are policed by the R.C.M.P.
• never have to wait for a drink—Hyder has one bar for every 30 residents

Notes for the traveler:
• leave your passport at home—no border checks are made
• buy your booze in Hyder—it's cheaper
• fill your gas tank in Hyder—it's also cheaper
• use Canadian currency in both towns
• post your mail on whichever side of the border saves the cost of international postage
• don't miss the drive to Salmon Glacier

To get the lowdown on the town's interesting past, head to **Stewart Historical Society Museum,** in the original city hall on Columbia St. between 6th and 7th Sts., tel. (250) 636-2568. Displays include a tool collection and exhibits on the town's boom-and-bust mining industry; admission $2. It's open in summer, daily 9:30 a.m.-4:30 p.m.

Locals here brag about throwing the **longest birthday party in North America.** The annual cross-cultural festival starts on 1 July (Canada Day) in Stewart and ends on 4 July (U.S. Independence Day) in Hyder. One of the event's highlights: the **International Bed Race,** beginning in Alaska and ending in British Columbia.

Practicalities
King Edward Hotel, on 5th Ave., tel. (250) 636-2244 or (800) 663-3126, offers basic rooms for

$60 s, $70 d. Across the road is the affiliated **King Edward Motel** (register at the hotel), where rooms are of a similar standard, but are slightly larger and have kitchenettes, $75 s, $85 d.

Nestled below the towering peaks of the Coast Mountains at the back of town is **Stewart Lions Campground,** on 8th Ave., tel. (250) 636-2537. Facilities are basic, and you need quarters for the showers; $12-15 a night. If this place is full, continue through town to Hyder, where you'll find two more campgrounds.

The small but ever-busy **Brothers Bakery,** on 5th Ave., serves delicious cakes and breads at reasonable prices. Next door in an old three-story building is **Bitter Creek Cafe,** serving light meals at lunchtime. The only place open for dinner is the restaurant in the **King Edward Hotel,** tel. (250) 636-2244, but it's nothing special. Also in the hotel is a coffee shop open for breakfast and lunch.

Stewart Visitor Info Centre overlooks the mudflats at the north end of 5th Ave., tel. (250) 636-9224. The staff offers a wealth of local information, including directions out to Salmon Glacier, hiking-trail brochures, and history sheets. It's open mid-May through mid-September, daily 8:30 a.m.-7 p.m. The main street (5th Ave.) also holds a small grocery store, drug store, post office, bank, and laundromat.

HYDER AND VICINITY

Continue through Stewart along the Portland Canal and, next thing you know, you're in Hyder, Alaska, U.S.A. (pop. 90)—without all the formalities and checkpoints you'd expect at an international border. The "Friendliest little ghost town in Alaska" is a classic end-of-the-road town, its main drag lined with a motley assortment of buildings, some boarded up. Hyder is best-known for its three bars, each licensed to be open 23 hours a day. Join the tradition and tack a dollar bill to the wall of **Glacier Inn** to ensure that you won't return broke, then toss back a shot of pure grain alcohol ($2) in one swallow to qualify for your "I've been Hyderized" card.

Settled by prospectors in the late 1890s, Hyder was called Portland City until the U.S. Postal Authority told residents there were too many cities already named Portland. The town thrived for many years, but today few of the original structures remain. Fires destroyed much of the old town, and no one ever bothered to rebuild. The most recent fire was the night before the 1995 Fourth of July celebrations. Fireworks stored for the occasion in the back of the fire hall exploded, burning that building to the ground and preventing locals from getting to the fire truck to stop the library and post office from suffering a similar fate.

Fish Creek and Salmon Glacier

Turn right at the end of Hyder's main street and follow the gravel road through town and along Fish Creek. Several kilometers beyond, at **Fish Creek Viewing Platform,** you can watch bears fishing and feasting at the all-you-can-eat salmon buffet. Generally, the black bears arrive first, usually around the end of July. During August the grizzlies move down from higher elevations to feed. This is a unique opportunity to watch a number of bears at once—one that

ANDREW HEMPSTEAD

Salmon Glacier

costs many hundreds of dollars in southwestern Alaska—but keep your distance.

From the creek, the road narrows considerably and becomes increasingly steep, winding around the side of a mining operation and up a steep-sided valley. Eventually it crosses back into Canada, and after about 20 km, **Salmon Glacier** comes into view. This glacier is one of British Columbia's most awesome sights, snaking for many kilometers through the highest peaks of the Coast Mountains.

Practicalities

Most services are back in Stewart, but Hyder does have accommodations, a couple of places to eat, and cheap gas. Canadian money is used in all Hyder businesses except the post office, where only U.S. currency is accepted.

The **Sealaska Inn,** on Premier Ave., tel. (250) 636-2486, is an old two-story hotel with a row of basic rooms on the top floor. Rooms with shared bathroom facilities are $28 s, $32 d, while those with private facilities are $42 s, $48 d. Sites at adjacent **Camp-run-a-muck** are $14 a night; book at the Inn. The campground has showers and a laundry, and an overflow area on the road out to Fish Creek has water and electricity hookups (same rates). Also head to the Sealaska Inn if you're hungry; the kitchen serves Mexican food, pizza, and hamburgers. For local information, head to any of the gift shops.

NORTH OF MEZIADIN JUNCTION

Kinaskan Lake Provincial Park

For the first 200 km north from Meziadin Junction, the highway follows a valley bordered by the Coast Mountains to the west and the Skeena Mountains to the east. At the 200-km mark is 1,800-hectare Kinaskan Lake Provincial Park, known for its hungry rainbow trout. It's also the gateway for hikers heading west into much larger Mount Edziza Provincial Park. (The 24-km Mowdade Lake Trail connects the two parks.) In the south of the park, a trail leads one kilometer to great fishing at **Natadesleen Lake,** then a further kilometer along an overgrown trail to beautiful, tiered **Cascade Falls.** Camping at the park is $9.50 a night.

Tatogga Lake

About 25 km farther north is **Tatogga Lake Resort,** where lodging, camping, food, and gas are available. Rustic cabins cost $30-55 per night, tent sites are $7-9, and sites with hookups are $11-17. You can't miss the moose rack-adorned restaurant, which offers good food at reasonable prices and a decor of mining and trapping memorabilia. The big, thick slices of banana bread for a couple of bucks are a great deal. Before you leave, fill up with gas and get your free cup of coffee; the next gas station north is at Dease Lake.

Red Goat Lodge

Continuing north you'll come to Red Goat Lodge, a bed and breakfast, hostel and campground overlooking Eddontenajon Lake. The tenting area is up the hill in a secluded area among trees. Campsites, most overlooking the lake, cost $8-12. The hostel is an associate of Hostelling International. It offers 10 dorm beds, a kitchen, and a lounge area that comes alive at night with stories past and present, slide shows, and impromptu musical performances from guests gathered around the log fire. Beds are $13 per night for HI members, $16 for non-members. Showers ($1 for five minutes) and laundry facilities (take lots of quarters) are available to campers and hostellers alike.

Also in the lodge are four tastefully decorated B&B rooms, each with private bath; rates of $65 s, $85 d include a delicious home-cooked breakfast served in the "Breakfast Room," which boasts beautiful lake and mountain views. The hosts, 20-year veterans of the local river systems, also rent canoes by the hour, evening, or week, and will enthusiastically help with the planning of guest expeditions. For reservations or more information, call (250) 234-3261 or (888) 733-4628.

Iskut and Vicinity

The small Tahltan town of Iskut has a post office, gas station, and grocery store (open daily 8 a.m.-9 p.m.). North of Iskut are two popular lodgings. **Mountain Shadow Guest Ranch,** tel. (250) 234-3333, boasts its own private lake with great trout fishing and good potential for moose-watching. Campsites with panoramic valley and mountain views are $14-20 per night; rustic cabins are $55 s, $60 d. A few km farther north is **Bear-paw Ranch,** where cabins are $55 s or d and rooms in the adjacent Alpine Hotel (same owners) are $89 s or d. The ranch offers horseback riding, fishing, guided hiking, and amenities including a restaurant, hot tub, and sauna. For information and reservations write P.O. Box 69, Iskut, BC V0J 1V0, or call the operator and ask to be connected to Meehaus Channel 2M3-858.

Spatsizi Plateau Wilderness Park

This wilderness park is just that—over 675,000 hectares of total wilderness. Access is by foot or floatplane only. The park's varied topography includes broad plateaus, stunning peaks, glaciers, rivers, and lakes. Wildlife abounds; watch for grizzly bears, moose, wolves, wolverines, mountain goats, woodland caribou, and over 100 species of birds.

Backcountry canoeing draws many, if not most, visitors to the park. The most popular trip begins with a floatplane flight to Tuaton Lake, at the headwaters of the Stikine River in the heart of the park. After putting in at the lake, you'll paddle the Stikine down to a pullout where the river crosses the Stewart-Cassiar Hwy., a 250-km journey with two short portages. Another popular trip begins with a five-km portage from an old (and in some places rough) B.C. Rail grade that follows the park's southwestern boundary for 80 km. Reach the signposted trail-head via Eulue Lake Rd., which spurs east from the Stewart-Cassiar Hwy. one km north of Tatogga Lake. The portage takes you to the upper reaches of the Spatsizi River, a tributary of the Stikine. This route passes Cold Fish Lake, where you'll find eight cabins, a rustic sauna, and a cookhouse; $10 per person per night. At least seven days should be allowed for either trip.

For more information on canoe routes, as well as general park information, contact BC Parks, Area Supervisor, General Delivery, Dease Lake, BC V0C 1L0, tel. (250) 771-4591. Tony Shaw, owner of the Red Goat Lodge (see above), can arrange transportation to the park and canoe rentals, and can show you slides of the various trips.

Between Iskut and Dease Lake

On this stretch, the highway runs through the **Stikine River Recreation Area,** a narrow park straddling the Stikine River and linking Spatsizi Plateau Wilderness Park and Mount Edziza Provincial Park. The bridge over the Stikine River is used as a pull-out point for canoe trips that start in Spatsizi Plateau Wilderness Park. Downstream from the bridge, the river flows in a torrent of whitewater through the **Grand Canyon of the Stikine,** an 85-km-long canyon with vertical rock walls towering more than 300 meters. Only a few teams have successfully kayaked the canyon. In early September 1992, an unassuming 37-year-old man from Montana quietly slipped his kayak into the water at the Hwy. 37

Black bears inhabit the north woods.

bridge and became the first person to success-fully descend the canyon solo.

Dease Lake

The small community of Dease Lake, on the shores of its namesake lake 65 km north of Iskut, provides basic tourist services and a bit more. Here you'll find a summer air service, Central Mountain Air, tel. (800) 663-3905, to Terrace and Smithers, as well as guides and outfitters to help with your expeditions to the two nearby provincial parks.

Dease Lake's only accommodation is the **Northway Motor Inn,** tel. (250) 771-5341, charging $64 s, $68 d for a basic room, plus $5 for a kitchen. The town has no campgrounds, but 10 km south, where the highway crosses the **Tanzilla River,** is a rest area with picnic tables and pit toilets. The individual pull-through spots are large enough for most RVs.

The best place to eat is the **Boulder Cafe,** where an always-busy waitress will serve you breakfast ($4-8), lunch, or dinner (burgers $7, main dishes from $9) while you admire the old photographs lining the walls; open daily 8 a.m.-9 p.m. For takeout pizza and delicious soft-serve ice cream, head for the small Atco trailer beside the gas station. Dease Lake also has a laundromat and an intriguing gift shop.

Telegraph Creek

From Dease Lake an unsealed road leads 119 km west along the Tanzilla River to Telegraph Creek (pop. 300), which lies on a terraced hill overlooking the Stikine River. The road pass-es through the Stikine River Recreation Area, where it drops over one incredibly steep and scary section.

Telegraph Creek, originally home of the Tahltan people, was on the first leg of the "Trail to the Interior" used during the Klondike Gold Rush. Gold-seekers started in Wrangell, Alas-ka, continued up the Stikine River by steamer as far as was navigable, then continued over-land through Telegraph Creek to Dease Lake and on to the Liard River. Later, Telegraph Creek grew as an important stopover point along the Yukon Telegraph Line, the main over-land route between the Yukon and all points south before the construction of the Alaska Highway.

The town boasts friendly people, gorgeous scenery, and heritage buildings dating back to the 1860s. Riverboat charters are popular—by the hour or day, or right through to Wrangell or Petersburg, Alaska (book through Stikine Riversong Lodge, tel. 250-235-3196). A 20-km road leads west from town to **Glenora,** which had 10,000 residents in its gold-rush heyday. Nowadays, only one or two of the origi-nal buildings remain.

Originally a Hudson's Bay Company store, the **Stikine Riversong Lodge,** tel. (250) 235-3196, has a cafe, general store, gas station, and rooms from $46 s, $50 d. The owners can arrange transportation to Mt. Edziza Provincial Park. Alternatively, you'll find two Forest Service campgrounds along the road out to Glenora.

Mount Edziza Provincial Park

This 232,698-hectare wilderness west of the Stewart-Cassiar Highway is one of the province's most inaccessible parks, but it's also one of the most magnificent and intriguing. The long and narrow park is bordered to the north by the road out to Telegraph Creek, to the west by Mess Creek, and to the east by Little Iskut River and a string of four lakes. Within these boundaries lies a moonlike volcanic landscape, above the tree-line and dominated by 2,787-meter **Mt. Edziza,** an extinct volcano whose glaciated crater is over two km wide. Rather than blowing out in one massive and spectacular eruption, this volcano oozed periodically over the course of four million years, eventually covering 1,600 square kilo-meters with lava. Small eruptions in the vicinity of the central cone have created dozens of cinder cones, some perfectly symmetrical.

Access to the park is on foot, on horseback, or via a charter floatplane from Dease Lake or Telegraph Creek. The easiest overland access is from Kinaskan Lake Provincial Park, 55 km south of Iskut; from the west bank of the lake (accessed by boat), it's 24 km by trail to Mow-dade Lake, then a further 25 km to the first of the cinder cones, directly south of the main peak. This trail continues northward around Mt. Edziza to Buckley Lake, ending across the Stikine River from Telegraph Creek. Charter-flight operators can drop hikers at any of the main lakes, but Mowdade is most popular for its vicinity to the park's most spectacular volcanic features.

Continuing to the Alaska Highway

As you continue north from the turnoff to Telegraph Creek, the road parallels the east shore of Dease Lake. Good campsites are found by the lake, along with the occasional chunk of jade on the lakeshore—the area has been called the jade capital of the world. From Dease Lake to the Alaska Highway it's clear sailing for 235 km along the northern slopes of the Cassiar Mountains.

Cassiar, 115 km north of Dease Lake, was once a company town for Cassiar Asbestos Mine. The booming little burg held a thousand residents, a grocery store, liquor store, bank, supermarket, and a multimillion-dollar school. But in March 1992, the company pulled out and the residents followed suit. The following year the town was auctioned off right down to the last fence post. To get there head 16 km along the Cassiar Spur road, passing a few old cabins and the back of a monstrous pile of green tailings. Don't expect any services.

The next worthwhile stop is 4,597-hectare **Boya Lake Provincial Park,** 150 km north of Dease Lake and 85 km from the Alaska Highway. The lake is clear, icy-cold, well stocked with fish, and ringed by white claylike beaches. Campsites are $9.50 per night.

From Boya Lake, the highway continues north, paralleling the Dease River for around 20 km and traversing the Liard Plain across the border and into the Yukon. From the border it's another four km to the junction of the Alaska Hwy., then 21 km east to Watson Lake or 423 km west to Whitehorse.

NORTH FROM PRINCE GEORGE

The landscapes and lifestyles in the area northeast of Prince George are closely aligned with neighboring northwest Alberta. The region's dominant natural feature, the **Peace River,** flows east from B.C.'s northern Rockies across the border into Alberta, lacing the two provinces together both topographically and economically. Rich farmland flanks the river on both sides of the border, creating a common agricultural zone whose hub is Grande Prairie, Alberta. This region of B.C. also shares Alberta's mountain time zone.

Most travelers use the route north from Prince George to access Mile Zero of the Alaska Highway at Dawson Creek. But this direct route, a distance of 405 km, bypasses the region's highlight at **Hudson's Hope,** halfway between Chetwynd and Fort St. John. Whichever route you take, there's plenty to see and do, with a number of interesting provincial parks and towns offering northern hospitality.

ALONG THE CROOKED RIVER

Heading north out of Prince George, Hwy. 97 climbs through low rolling hills to the Nechako Plateau before descending alongside the Crooked River to massive Williston Lake. Pastoral farmland lines much of the route, and in summer the roadside is ablaze with red-orange Indian paintbrush and purple lupine.

The first worthwhile stop is 873-hectare **Crooked River Provincial Park,** 80 km north of Prince George. It's only a small park, but adjacent Bear Lake is good for rainbow-trout fishing, swimming, and canoeing, and the large campground ($9.50 a night) usually has sites available.

Carp Lake Provincial Park

This 19,344-hectare park lies 140 km north of Prince George on Hwy. 97, then 32 km west (turn off at McLeod Lake) along a sometimes rough unsealed road. Over 6,000 hectares of the park is taken up by Carp Lake, a picturesque body of water dotted with islands and filled with fish, although you won't catch carp; the lake was named by explorer Simon Fraser who noted Carrier Indians journeyed to the lake for fish "of the carp kind."

You really need a watercraft of some kind to truly appreciate the many coves and islands and to take advantage of the fishing opportunities. Boatless visitors can sunbake and swim at the sandy beaches of Kettle Bay at the end of the road, or hike a number of short trails. A one-km trail (20-minutes each way) leads to Rainbow Lake, and another short trail, along the access road in the park's northeast cor-

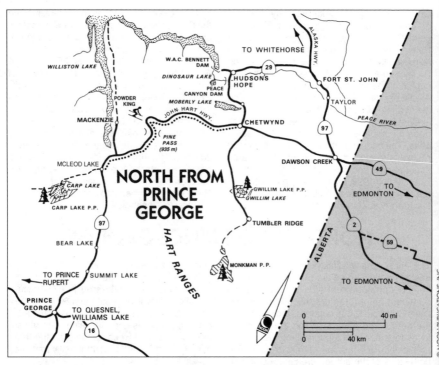

NORTH FROM PRINCE GEORGE

ner, leads past 12-meter-high **War Falls** to **War Lake,** where you can drop a line for rainbow trout.

At the main facility area, **Carp Lake Campground** holds 90 lakeshore sites, each with a fire ring and picnic table. Back toward the park entrance is **War Lake Campground,** offering similar facilities. Both campgrounds charge $9.50 per site per night.

Mackenzie

The forestry town of Mackenzie (pop. 6,200) lies 180 km north of Prince George on the southern arm of massive Williston Lake, a reservoir created by the W.A.C. Bennett Dam. The town was founded in the 1960s as a base for the massive logging operation that cleared the way for construction of the dam. At the town's entrance is the world's largest tree crusher, used during that logging operation. Nearby **Morfee Lake** is a great swimming and boating spot,

while the logging road to the summit of Morfee Hill offers lake views.

Tourist facilities in town are limited. The nicest place to stay, catering mostly to business travelers, is the **Alexander Mackenzie Hotel,** on Mackenzie Blvd., tel. (250) 997-3266 or (800) 663-2964. All rooms are air-conditioned and the complex includes a pub and restaurant. Rates are $70 s or d. Less expensive is **Timberman Inn,** also on Mackenzie Blvd., tel. (250) 997-6464; $45 s, $50 d. On the town's southern outskirts, **Mackenzie Municipal RV Park** is little more than a gravel parking lot, but holds a few grassy tent sites. Picnic tables, firewood, hot showers, and hookups are all supplied for $10-16 a night.

Out at the junction of Hwys. 97 and 39 is **Mackenzie Visitor Info Centre,** open summers only, daily 9 a.m.-6 p.m. For local information the rest of the year, head to the **Mackenzie Chamber of Commerce,** 86 Centennial Dr., tel. (250) 997-5459; open Mon.-Fri. 8:30 a.m.-4:30 p.m.

Over Pine Pass

Continuing east toward Chetwynd, the landscape becomes more dramatic as the highway climbs steadily up the western slopes of the Rocky Mountains. Look for signs to the west for 40-hectare **Bijoux Falls Provincial Park,** a small day-use area where the Misinchinka River plummets over a rocky outcrop. From the park, the highway meanders over one of its most scenic stretches—935-meter Pine Pass, atop the Continental Divide. From the pass, it's downhill all the way, following the Pine River to Chetwynd.

CHETWYND AND VICINITY

Chetwynd (pop. 3,200) lies at the relatively busy junction of Hwys. 97 and 29. The community was first established in 1912, when it was known as "Little Prairie." With the arrival of the railway in 1958 its name was changed to Chetwynd to honor a director of the P.G.E. Railway—a pioneer who had great faith in the future of the Peace River Country. Today Chetwynd is a forestry town and a center for artistic log-carving. The town promotes itself as the "Chainsaw Sculpture Capital of the World."

The one main road through town is lined with services. **Pinecone Motor Inn,** 5224 53rd Ave., tel. (250) 788-3311 or (800) 663-8082, charges $60 s, $65 d for large rooms with comfortable beds. Campers can head five km south of town to **Wildmare Grove Campsite,** tel. (250) 788-2747, with showers and hookups, $8-15 a night; or 29 km north of town to **Moberly Lake Provincial Park,** with over 100 sites for $9.50 a night.

Chetwynd Visitor Info Centre is in a railway caboose beside the highway, tel. (250) 788-3345. It's open in summer, daily 8 a.m.-6 p.m.

Tumbler Ridge

Tumbler Ridge, 94 km south of Chetwynd, is a modern boomtown that sprang up much the same way gold-rush towns did a hundred years ago. Back in the early 1980s the provincial government struck a deal with several Japanese coal companies. The government agreed to improve regional infrastructure, including constructing a new railhead and coal-loading dock at Prince Rupert, if the companies would construct mines and a township at the site of the rich Northeast Coal Deposits. Tumbler Ridge (pop. 4,000) was created virtually overnight to allow the employees of the Northeast Coal Project to settle in quickly and comfortably. From the start it held all the creature comforts, services, and recreational facilities you'd expect in a long-established town.

The mining operation here is massive. The **Quintette Mine** moves 120 million tons of earth annually, from which 4.3 million tons of coal are extracted. From the mine, a 13-km-long conveyor belt transports raw coal to a railhead from where it's shipped to the port city of Prince Rupert. Tours of the mine are offered in July and August. Book through the Visitor Info Centre, tel. (250) 242-4702.

The town's only motel is **Tumbler Ridge Inn,** right downtown, tel. (250) 242-4277. Basic rooms are $56 s or d, and the complex includes a coffee shop, pub, and restaurant. **Lions Flatbed Creek Campground** enjoys a pleasant riverside setting three km south of town. Facilities include hot showers and a cooking shelter; sites are $7.50. The other option for campers is **Gwillim Lake Provincial Park,** halfway between Tumbler Ridge and Chetwynd; $9.50.

Tumbler Ridge Visitor Info Centre, on Southgate Rd., tel. (250) 242-4702, is open year-round, Mon.-Fri. 8:30 a.m.-4:30 p.m.

Monkman Provincial Park

One of the most inspiring sights in the northern interior is **Kinuseo Falls,** where the Murray River cascades 60 meters in a spectacular fan-shaped arc to the valley floor below. The falls are at the north end of 32,000-hectare Monkman Provincial Park. From Tumbler Ridge a rough gravel road leads 60 km (90 minutes each way) southwest, ending at the northern entrance to this wild and mountainous wilderness. From the picnic area a short trail leads to the falls viewpoint. **Kinuseo Falls Campground** offers 42 sites alongside the Murray River; $9.50 a night. The park has no other facilities.

Moberly Lake Provincial Park

North of Chetwynd, the 65-km-long stretch of Hwy. 29 to Hudson's Hope passes **Moberly Lake,** a long and narrow body of water encircled by a typical boreal forest. Moberly Lake Provincial Park, at the lake's eastern end, has a day-use area and a primitive campground where sites are $9.50 a night.

HUDSON'S HOPE

Human habitation of the Peace River Valley predated Alexander Mackenzie's 1793 journey along the river by many thousands of years. But Mackenzie's detailed reports encouraged an influx of white settlers to the valley. In 1805, fur traders founded Hudson's Hope at a picturesque riverside site. Today the town's population is just over 1,000.

W.A.C. Bennett and Peace Canyon Dams

These two dams are the area's main attractions, their sheer size an awe-inspiring sight. Together the two facilities generate almost 40% of the hydroelectricity used in the province.

Larger of the two, the W.A.C. Bennett Dam, seven km west of town, is one of the world's largest earth-filled structures. It backs up 164,600-hectare **Williston Lake,** British Columbia's largest lake, which extends more than 300 km along three flooded valleys. At the top of the dam's control building is **Bennett Dam Visitor Centre,** tel. (250) 783-5211, where displays catalog the construction tasks, a film celebrates the dam's opening, and the uses of electricity are detailed. Free guided tours of the dam are scheduled on weekends in summer, 9:30 a.m.-4:30 p.m., and are available the rest of the year by appointment. The visitor center is open in summer, daily 8 a.m.-6 p.m.; the rest of the year, Mon.-Fri. 8 a.m.-4 p.m.

The much smaller Peace Canyon Dam is downstream from Bennett Dam, five km south of Hudson's Hope on Hwy. 29. **Peace Canyon Dam Visitor Centre,** adjacent to the powerhouse, focuses on the fascinating natural history, exploration, and pioneers of the area, and the building of the Peace Canyon Project. You can also see the central control system, powerhouse, and switchgear station. Don't miss a trip up to the outside observation deck. This center is open in summer, daily 8 a.m.-8 p.m.; the rest of the year, Mon.-Fri. 8 a.m.-4 p.m.

DINOSAURS IN THE PEACE RIVER VALLEY

During construction of Peace Canyon Dam, fossilized remains of the **plesiosaur,** a marine reptile, were discovered. This wasn't the first time evidence of prehistoric life had been discovered in the Peace River Valley. As early as 1922, dinosaur footprints over 100 million years old were found in the area where Hudson's Hope now lies. The footprints belonged to several species of dinosaurs, most common among them the **hadrosaur.** This plant-eater was around 10 meters long and weighed about four tons. It was amphibious, but preferred the land, walking around on its hind legs ever-alert for the ancestors of the dreaded tyrannosaurus.

Footprints are as important as skeletons in unraveling the mysteries of dinosaurs. They provide clues about the ratios of various dinosaurs in a particular area, and information on herds and how they traveled.

Most dinosaur footprints discovered in the valley have been excavated and transported to museums throughout Canada (a couple are on display in the Hudson's Hope Museum). Plant and shell fossils can still be found. The best time for searching them out is after heavy rain—try looking downstream from the dam (a few short trails lead from the highway into the canyon but it's a bit of a scramble). The best opportunity to learn more about local dinosaurs is in the **Peace Canyon Dam Visitor Centre.**

Heritage Park

Across from Hudson's Hope Visitor Info Centre, this small chunk of parkland is dotted with historic buildings moved to the site from throughout the Peace River Valley. The site itself is of some historical significance—Simon Fraser spent the winter of 1805-06 here. The main displays are housed in **Hudson's Hope Museum,** tel. (250) 783-7535, which is crammed with geological specimens, dinosaur bones and casts of footprints discovered during dam construction, and historical artifacts that belonged to trappers, miners, and early homesteaders. The park also holds a trapper's cabin and fur cache, a log replica of a 1900 Hudson's Bay Company trading post, a furnished home from 1935, and the tiny log-walled St. Peter's Church. The grounds are open year-round; the museum (admission $2.50) is open in summer, daily 9:30 a.m.-5:30 p.m.

Practicalities

Neither of the town's two accommodations is outstanding. The choices are: **Peace Glen Hotel,** at the south end of town on Dudley Dr., tel. (250) 783-9966; and **Sportsman Inn,** downtown at 10501 Carter Ave., tel. (250) 783-5523. Both have an in-house pub and restaurant and charge from $50 s or d a night.

The town's three municipal campgrounds ask for a donation of only $5 a night (don't abuse the system—most municipal campgrounds charge $9-16 per night). Closest to

civilization is **Gething Park,** on the south end of town, which has flush toilets, coin-operated showers, and plenty of firewood. **Alwin Holland Park,** west of town, is more primitive (pit toilets) but is off the main highway and has some nice hiking trails. The third, **Peace Canyon Dam Campground,** has pit toilets, firewood, and good fishing and swimming.

Northwoods Flying Service, tel. (250) 783-9121, offers 20-minute sightseeing flights over the dams and local area for $35 per person. **Hudson's Hope Visitor Info Centre** is at 10507 105th Ave., tel. (250) 783-9154; open in summer, daily 9 a.m.-6 p.m. The staff provides information on local attractions and offers a couple of brochures on nearby hiking opportunities. (The trails are enjoyable but not well marked.)

THE ALASKA HIGHWAY

When the Japanese threatened invasion of Canada and the United States during WW II, the Alaska Highway was quickly built to link Alaska with the Lower 48. It was the longest military road ever constructed in North America—an unsurpassed road-construction feat stretching 2,288 km between Dawson Creek, B.C. and Delta Junction, Alaska.

Construction began 9 March 1942 and was completed, incredibly, on 20 November that same year. In less than nine months troops had bulldozed a rough trail snaking like a crooked finger through almost impenetrable muskeg and forest, making literally hundreds of detours around obstacles and constructing 133 bridges.

At a cost of more than $140 million, the highway was the major contributing factor to the growth of the northern British Columbia in the 1940s. At the height of construction, the region's population boomed. Dawson Creek's population alone rose from 600 to over 10,000, and Whitehorse replaced Dawson City as a more-convenient capital of the Yukon.

The highway was notoriously difficult in its earliest days. Highway travelers returned with tales of endless mud holes and dust, washed-out bridges, flat tires, broken windshields and smashed headlights, wildlife in the road, mos-

quitoes the size of hummingbirds, and sparse facilities. But they also sported "I drove the Alaska Highway" bumper-stickers as though they'd won a prize. Nowadays the route doesn't merit quite the bravado—it's paved most of the way, has roadside lodges fairly frequently, and can easily be driven in three days, or two at a pinch. What hasn't changed is the scenery. You'll still see kilometer after kilometer of unspoiled wilderness, including boreal forests of spruce and aspen, the majestic, snow-dusted peaks of the northern Canadian Rockies, and a number of gorgeous rivers and streams.

Although official signage along the Alaska Highway is in kilometers, many services are marked in miles, a legacy of imperial measurement. This only becomes confusing when you consider that highway improvements have shortened the original route. For example, Liard River Hot Springs is still marked as Mile 496, though it's now only 754 km (462 miles) from Dawson Creek.

DAWSON CREEK

Although Dawson Creek (pop. 11,800) marks the southern end of the Alaska Highway, it's still a long way north—over 400 km northeast of Prince

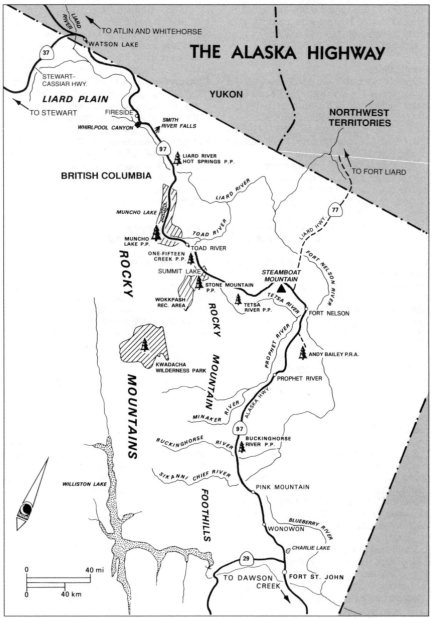

© MOON PUBLICATIONS, INC.

DAWSON CREEK

TO FORT ST. JOHN AND DELTA JUNCTION, ALASKA

GOLF COURSE

MILE ZERO RV PARK AND CAMPGROUND

20th ST.

97 ALASKA HWY.

9th ST.

MILE ZERO CAFE

HART HWY.

97

TUBBY'S RV PARK

ALAHART RV PARK

WALTER WRIGHT PIONEER VILLAGE

TO CHETWYND AND PRINCE GEORGE

PEACE VILLA MOTEL

BOSTON PIZZA

GREYHOUND BUS DEPOT

ALASKA AVE.

17th ST.

16th ST.

CITY HALL

12A ST.

N.A.R. PARK

MILE ZERO CAIRN

102nd AVE.

15th ST.

14th ST.

13th ST.

12th ST.

THE DYNASTY

ALASKA HOTEL/CAFE

MILE ZERO SIGNPOST

49

NORTHWINDS LODGE

TO PEACE RIVER (ALBERTA)

11th ST.

POST OFFICE

INDOOR POOL

LIBRARY

10th ST.

106th AVE.

108th AVE.

TO BEAR MTN. SKI AREA

110th AVE.

8th ST.

HOSPITAL

2

TO AIRPORT AND GRANDE PRAIRIE (ALBERTA)

NOT TO SCALE

© MOON PUBLICATIONS, INC.

George and 1,200 km north of Vancouver. While the city thrives on its historic location at Mile Zero, it's also an important service center whose economy is more closely tied to neighboring Alberta, a few km to the east, than to British Columbia.

Dawson Creek was named after Dr. George Mercer Dawson, a Canadian geologist who surveyed the prairie here in 1879. His report noted the area's fertility—thereby encouraging settlement—and led to the subsequent discovery of gas and oil fields.

The first wave of settlers came to the area in 1912, but the arrival of the Northern Alberta Railway (N.A.R.) in 1931 put Dawson Creek on the map, establishing the city as an agricultural service center. Agriculture is still the basis of Dawson Creek's economy; local products include wheat, oats, barley, canola, vegetables, specialty crops, cattle, dairy, hogs, sheep, poultry, and honey. Oil and gas rigs stand in the Elmsworth Basin south of the city, while pipelines and processing plants lie to the east.

Northern Alberta Railway (N.A.R.) Park

This park, on the corner of Hwy. 2 and the Alaska Hwy., makes a good first stop in town. Here you'll find Dawson Creek Visitor Info Centre, an art gallery, and **Dawson Creek Museum,** tel. (250)

*Dawson Creek
Art Gallery*

JANE AND BRUCE KING

782-9595. This marvelous and curious museum, housed in the original 1931 Northern Alberta Railway station, offers exhibits on a wide variety of topics including construction of the Alaska Highway, the area's railroad history, pioneer life, and local flora and fauna. Among the unusual items on display: a rack of antlers estimated to be several thousand years old, a gas pump from the 1920s, a 1941 Massey-Harris cream separator, and the largest mammoth tusks found in western Canada. The museum is open June-Sept., daily 8 a.m.-7 p.m.; the rest of the year, Tues.-Sat. 10 a.m.-noon and 1-4 p.m. Admission is $2.

In the towering grain elevator adjacent to the museum is **Dawson Creek Art Gallery,** tel. (250) 782-2601; open in summer Tues.-Sat. 10 a.m.-5 p.m. The elevator itself is fascinating. It was saved from demolition and redesigned with a spiral walkway around the interior walls to make the most of the building's height. Inside are high-quality paintings and locally made arts and crafts—for viewing and buying.

In front of the park is the Alaska Highway's official starting point, marked by a cairn. The original marker, a one-meter-high post, was mowed down by a car in the 1940s. Despite the cairn's official status, the Mile Zero signpost in the center of 102nd Ave. at 10th St. is more often photographed.

Walter Wright Pioneer Village

One km west of N.A.R. Park at the Hwy. 97 split, this village of historical buildings holds two pioneer churches, a furnished log house, a general store, the Napoleon Loiselle Blacksmith Shop (containing many of his inventions), a trapper's cabin with handmade furniture, and two old schoolhouses. Scattered around are pieces of old farm machinery, tools, and equipment used by the area's first homesteaders. The village is named for the man responsible for finding and bringing all the buildings together. It's open June-Sept., daily 10 a.m.-6 p.m.; admission is adults $3, seniors and children $1.50.

Recreation

Dawson Creek Golf Course and Country Club offers 18 challenging holes next to the Mile Zero City Campground, on the Alaska Hwy. west of town, tel. (250) 782-7882. **Centennial Swimming Pool,** on the corner of 10th St. and 105th Ave., tel. (250) 782-7946, provides a junior-Olympic-size pool, weight room, jacuzzi, tanning bed, and saunas. Wintertime recreation centers around **Bear Mountain,** south of downtown along 17th St., tel. (250) 782-4988. The small ski hill's one T-bar serves a 132-meter vertical rise. Rentals and lessons are available.

Festivals and Events

Dawson Creek holds plenty of celebrations and events throughout the year. Look for the **Mile Zero Mardi Gras** in February, the **Peace Country Arts Festival** in March, and the **Kiwanis Trade and Sports Show** in April. In May, **Mile Zero Days** features a fiddlers' contest, dart tournament, craft show, horse show, pig races, pancake breakfasts, cookouts, and a parade. In June, July, and August, the **Muskeg North Musical Revue** brings old-time dancing and music to Walter Wright Pioneer Village. Also in August, the city holds its **Fall Fair and Rodeo.** October's big event is the **Halloween Howl** at Walter Wright Pioneer Village, while December brings the **Rotary Carol Fest.** Schedules for all events are available at the information center.

Accommodations and Camping
Dawson Creek's oldest and most colorful accommodation is the **Alaska Hotel,** right downtown at 10209 10th St., tel. (250) 782-7998. Known as the Dew Drop Inn when it first opened in 1928, the hotel has been recently renovated in a heritage style. Rooms remain basic, with shared bathroom facilities; $40-55 s, $45-60 d. A popular cafe and a pub are downstairs. Similarly priced is **Northwinds Lodge,** 832 103rd Ave., tel. (250) 782-9181 or (800) 665-1759, a no-frills roadside motel with comfortable rooms, some with kitchenettes. In the opposite direction from downtown, along the road up to Alaska is **Peace Villa Motel,** 1641 Alaska Ave., tel. (250) 782-8175, which charges $55 s, $58 d.

Mile Zero RV Park and Campground, tel. (250) 782-2590, isn't at Milo Zero of the famous highway—it's about one km north from downtown—but it's the pick of Dawson Creek's numerous campgrounds. Sites are set around a large shaded grassy area, and each one has a picnic table. Facilities include hot showers and a laundry. Rates are $10-15 a night. Other RV parks in town include **Alahart RV Park,** at the junction of the Alaska Hwy. and Hwy. 97, tel. (250) 782-4702, and **Tubby's RV Park,** 800 meters west along Hwy. 97 from the Alaska Hwy. junction, tel. (250) 782-2584. Both offer full hookups.

Food
The best-known eatery in town is the **Alaska Cafe,** in the Alaska Hotel at 10209 10th St., tel. (250) 782-7040. The cafe is colorfully decorated in an old-fashioned style and serves tasty burgers, sandwiches, and croissants at lunch, and steak, chicken, seafood, and pork dishes ($12-18) at dinner. The desserts are delicious. Equally popular is **Mile Zero Cafe,** 1901 Alaska Ave., tel. (250) 782-1456, with similar fare

served in a casual setting. One of Dawson Creek's several Chinese restaurants, **Dynasty,** 1009 102nd Ave., tel. (250) 782-3138, also offers steak and seafood, a salad bar, and a buffet lunch.

Transportation
Dawson Creek Municipal Airport is south of town on Hwy. 2. It's served by **Air B.C.,** tel. (250) 782-1720, which operates daily scheduled flights between Dawson Creek and southern B.C. cities, and **Central Mountain Air,** tel. (250) 785-6100, serving northern centers. The **Greyhound** bus depot is at 1201 Alaska Ave. between 12th and 14th Sts., tel. (250) 782-3131; scheduled services run between Dawson Creek and Prince George, Grande Prairie (Alberta), and north along the Alaska Hwy. to Whitehorse (Yukon).

Information
An almost obligatory stop for travelers heading north on the famous highway is **Dawson Creek Visitor Info Centre,** in N.A.R. Park, tel. (250) 782-9595. It's open in summer, daily 8 a.m.-8 p.m.; the rest of the year, Mon.-Fri. 8:30 a.m.-4:30 p.m.

North toward Fort St. John
The initial 72 km of the Alaska Highway between Dawson Creek and Fort St. John skirts nearly flat croplands and fields of wildflowers brilliantly abloom in summer. **Kiskatinaw Provincial Park,** 28 km from Dawson Creek then four km off the highway, is only 58 hectares but offers a small campground ($9 a night) and fishing in the Kiskatinaw River. North of the park, the highway descends through a steep ravine to the Peace River and the small township of **Taylor,** site of a huge Petro-Canada Oil Refinery. Apart from this dominant man-made feature, Taylor is best known as home of the annual World Invitational Gold Panning Championships every August.

FORT ST. JOHN

Second-largest community along the Alaska Highway (only Whitehorse, Yukon, is larger), Fort St. John (pop.15,000) is an important service center for local industries, including oil, gas, and coal extraction, forestry, and agriculture. It's one

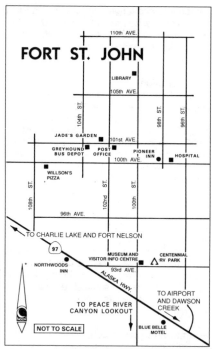

canoe, and the grizzly bear with claws big enough to send shivers up your spine. Other exhibits detail the geological and mining ventures that the town thrives on today.

The museum also houses over 6,000 restored and carefully cataloged artifacts; one display details the discovery in nearby Charlie Lake Cave of a bead and tools dating back some 10,500 years. Videos about the local area can be screened on request. The museum is open in summer, daily 8 a.m.-8 p.m.; the rest of the year, Mon.-Sat. 11 a.m.-4 p.m. Admission is adults $3, seniors $2, children $1.50.

Peace River Canyon Lookout
This lookout provides splendid panoramic views taking in the wide, deep-green Peace River, its rocky canyon walls, and the lush fields along the canyon rim. From the museum/information center head south along 100th St., crossing the Alaska Hwy. and continuing along the gravel road, which ends at the edge of the canyon. It's well worth the short drive.

Charlie Lake
This picturesque lake is just north of Fort St. John; follow signs off the Alaska Highway. It's a remnant of an enormous ice-dammed lake that covered this area and northern Alberta more than 10,500 years ago. At Charlie Lake Caves, animal bones and artifacts such as stone tools, a fluted spear point, and a handmade stone bead—the oldest found in North America—were discovered, leading archaeologists to postulate that this area was one of the earliest North American sites occupied by humans.

Today the lake is a popular recreation area known for its good fishing—for trout, arctic grayling, walleye, and northern pike. Swimming isn't quite so delightful, as the lake can clog with algae at times.

Two small provincial parks occupy sections of the lake's shoreline. **Charlie Lake Provincial Park,** at the junction of the Alaska Hwy. and Hwy. 29, is mainly a campground ($9.50 per site), while 312-hectare **Beatton Provincial Park,** on the lake's east shoreline, features beautiful aspen-lined hiking trails, a beach, boating, fishing, swimming, cross-country skiing, snowmobiling, ice fishing (with warm-up huts), and a campground ($9.50 per site).

of the province's oldest nonnative settlements— the Beaver and Sekani tribes both occupied the area when white traders arrived in the 1790s— and served as a fur-trading post until 1823. But it wasn't until construction of the Alaska Highway began that Fort St. John really boomed.

Fort St. John–North Peace Museum
You can't miss this museum complex at 9323 100th St. (the same building as the Fort St. John Visitor Info Centre), tel. (250) 787-0430. Just look for the unique exhibits outside, including a skyscraping 40-meter-high **oil derrick** that came from Mile 143 of the Alaska Highway. In the museum local history springs to life with reconstructed historical interiors. A trapper's cabin recalls the original Rocky Mountain fort and fur-trading days, while the pioneer days are commemorated in fully furnished rooms, including a kitchen, bedroom, schoolroom, dentist's office, post office, outpost hospital, and blacksmith's shop. Don't miss the fur press, the birchbark

Accommodations and Camping

Most motels in town are strung out along the Alaska Hwy. and 100th Street. One of the least expensive is **Blue Belle Motel,** 9705 Alaska Hwy., tel. (250) 785-2613, which charges $38 s, $40 d. Of a similar standard, but with a coffee shop, restaurant, and pub, is **Northwoods Inn,** 10627 Alaska Hwy., tel. (250) 787-1616. **Pioneer Inn,** 9830 100th Ave., tel. (250) 787-0521, is a full-service hotel with a variety of dining rooms, an indoor pool, a whirlpool and sauna, and an exercise room. Rates are $106-121 s or d.

Fort St. John Centennial RV Park, 9323 100th St., tel. (250) 785-3033, is close to the museum and information center, but it's small and doesn't offer much shade. Facilities include showers, a laundry, and hookups. Sites are $10-17 per night. A more pleasant option would be either one of the two provincial parks north of town on Charlie Lake (see above).

Food

Willson's Pizza, 10503 100th Ave., tel. (250) 785-8969, has the best pizza in town and good lasagna at reasonable prices. If you're in the mood for some tasty Chinese food, try **Jade's Garden,** 10108 101st Ave., tel. (250) 787-2585; the buffet is good value at around $12 per person, but all the dishes on the menu are reasonably priced. Open daily from 11 a.m. A few of the motels have dining rooms, including Northwoods Inn, where a cooked breakfast is $6-9.

Nightlife

For country music, locals flock to **Trappers Pub** in the Pioneer Inn. It's open till 2 a.m.; free admission. For rock 'n' roll try the cabaret **Northwoods,** on the Alaska Hwy. north of town; at "The Woods," as locals call it, you can expect to pay a couple of bucks cover charge on Friday and Saturday nights.

Services and Information

The airport is about nine km south of town and is serviced by **Air B.C.,** tel. (250) 787-6046, and **Central Mountain Air,** tel. (250) 785-6100. The **Greyhound** bus depot is at 10355 101st Ave., tel. (250) 785-6695.

The **hospital** is on 100th Ave., between 96th and 98th Sts.; the **post office** is on the corner of 101st Ave. and 102nd St.; the **library** is on 100th St. between 106th and 107th Avenues.

Fort St. John and District Visitor Info Centre is at 9323 100th St., tel. (250) 785-3033, in the same building as the museum. It's open May through mid-June, daily 8 a.m.-6 p.m.; mid-June through mid-September, daily 8 a.m.-8 p.m.; the rest of the year, Mon.-Fri. 8 a.m.-5 p.m.

WONOWON TO PROPHET RIVER

Wonowon

The 374-km stretch of the Alaska Highway between Fort St. John and Fort Nelson passes through boreal forest and a landscape that becomes more and more mountainous. The first services are at Wonowon, 83 km north of Fort St. John at Mile 102. The Husky gas station, tel. (250) 772-3288, offers rooms from $40 and a few campsites for $15, as well as gas and a restaurant.

Pink Mountain

From Wonowon, the highway climbs steadily to Pink Mountain, at Mile 147. Numerous services perch on the low summit, where snow can fall year-round. On the west side of the highway, **Pink Mountain Campsite,** tel. (250) 772-3234, provides tent and RV sites for $14 (no hookups) and rustic cabins for $25 s, $30 d (showers are an extra $2.50).

A few kilometers beyond the summit is **Mae's Kitchen,** tel. (250) 772-3215, where breakfasts are huge and the pancakes ($4.50) and blueberry muffins ($2.50) are especially good. For lunch, try the house special Buffalo Burger, complete with fries and salad for $7.50. The restaurant is open daily 7 a.m.-10 p.m. Mae's Kitchen also offers a few inexpensive motel units.

Continuing northward, look for the "maintained" airstrip to the west—how would you like to land on that one? Not far north of Pink Mountain the highway passes into Pacific standard time—set your clock back one hour.

Sikanni Chief to Prophet River

The next services are 30 km north of Pink Mountain at Sikanni Chief, where the highway passes through a low-lying area frequented by moose. The modern **Sikanni River RV Park,** tel. (250)

774-1028, offers sites with hookups for $11-16, and small cabins with basic cooking facilities for $30 s, $40 d.

Twenty km north from Sikanni Chief you'll pass the small 55-hectare **Buckinghorse River Provincial Park,** which offers camping ($9 a night) and good river fishing. From here north, a new and scenic stretch of the highway runs through **Minaker River Valley** then parallels the **Prophet River,** passing a rustic campground (open May-Sept.; campsites $7) where a hiking trail leads down to the river. Farther along, at Mile 217, is the tiny community of **Prophet River,** with all visitor services.

North toward Fort Nelson
The highway north to Fort Nelson was rerouted during 1991-92, eliminating 132 bends and curves. The next place worth a detour, about 30 km south of Fort Nelson and 12 km south of the highway along a dirt road, is 174-hectare **Andy Bailey Provincial Recreation Area.** Adjacent to Jackfish Creek (which reportedly offers good pike fishing), the area has a sandy beach with good swimming and a boat launch. Camping is $7.

FORT NELSON

At Mile 300 of the Alaska Highway, Fort Nelson (pop. 3,800) is the largest town between Fort St. John and the Yukon. The **Muskwa, Prophet,** and **Sikanni Chief Rivers** all flow together here to create the large **Fort Nelson River,** which in turn flows into the even larger **Liard River** at Nelson Forks to the northwest. Starting around 1800, many different trading posts were built on the site, but each was destroyed by either natives, fire, or flood.

Fort Nelson's economy is based on forestry, oil, and gas. The town holds North America's second-largest gas-processing plant, as well as the world's largest chopstick-manufacturing company.

Sights
Fort Nelson Historical Museum, on the west side of the highway at the north end of town, tel. (250) 774-3536, contains a great collection of Alaska Highway construction items and native

and pioneer artifacts. An interesting 30-minute movie, shown throughout the day, uses footage taken during the construction of the highway to effectively convey what a mammoth task the project was. The building is surrounded by machinery and vehicles used during the early days. Around back is a trapper's cabin crammed with antiques. The museum is open in summer, daily 8:30 a.m.-7:30 p.m. Admission is adults $3.50, seniors and children $2.

At the end of Mountain View Dr. is the **Native Trail,** a four-km self-guided interpretive trail that passes two native-style shelters and holds signs describing native foods, local wildlife, and trapping methods. Allow at least one hour roundtrip.

Accommodations and Camping
Fort Nelson has many hotels and motels spread out along the Alaska Highway. The nicest is **Blue Bell Motel,** 3907 50th Ave. (next to the Petro-Canada gas station), tel. (250) 774-6961 or (800) 663-5267. The modern two-story lodging has nice rooms, a laundry, and an adjacent 24-hour restaurant. Rates are $60 s, $70 d, kitchens an extra $10. A few bucks less expensive is **Mini Price Inn,** 5036 51st Ave., tel. (250) 774-2136, which has small rooms for $42 s, $47 d.

Beside the museum is **Westend Campground,** tel. (250) 774-2340, where you can choose from tent sites in an open area or individual sites surrounded by trees. The tent sites are $12, hookups are $17. Facilities include coin-operated showers, a laundromat, grocery store, and free firewood. It's open April to October. On either side of town along the Alaska Hwy., the closest camping is 20 km south at **Andy Bailey Provincial Recreation Area,** and 77 km west at **Tetsa River Provincial Park.**

Food
As you enter town from the south, modern **Dan's Neighbourhood Pub,** tel. (250) 774-3929, wouldn't look out of place in Vancouver—and it's always busy. All the usual fare is offered, with burgers $6-9, salads $4-8, and steak, chicken, and Mexican dishes from $10. Open daily 11 a.m.-midnight.

Services and Information
The **Greyhound** bus depot is at 5031 51st Ave., tel. (250) 774-6322. Daily scheduled service runs

south to Dawson Creek and north to Whitehorse. The **post office** is also on 51st Avenue. **Fort Nelson General Hospital** is at 5315 Liard St., tel. (250) 774-6916. The town also has plenty of gas stations, two banks, and a laundromat.

In the recreation center, through town to the north, is **Fort Nelson Visitor Info Centre,** tel. (250) 774-6400. Here you can get information on road conditions and find out the current topics for the Visitor Welcome Program—a series of entertaining talks on local subjects, offered each summer's evening at 6:45 p.m. The center is open daily 8 a.m.-8 p.m. in summer.

CONTINUING TO WATSON LAKE

Awaiting the traveler on this 525-km portion of the Alaska Highway are Rocky Mountain peaks, glacial lakes, mountain streams, provincial parks with some great scenery, and the mighty Liard River.

Soon after leaving Fort Nelson you'll come to a junction with the gravel **Liard Highway,** which runs north 175 km to Fort Liard in the Northwest Territories. From this junction, the Alaska Highway climbs the lower slopes of **Steamboat Mountain,** which, with a certain amount of imagination, resembles an upturned boat. Here you'll have tremendous views of the Rocky Mountains and the valley below. **Tetsa River Provincial Park,** 77 km west of Fort Nelson, offers grayling fishing in the river and short riverside hiking trails. A campground within the park has sites for $9.50 a night.

Summit Lake and Vicinity
This lake, 140 km west of Fort Nelson, is a popular stopping point for travelers. It lies at the north end of 25,691-hectare **Stone Mountain Provincial Park,** a vast wilderness of jagged peaks, lakes, and rivers named for the predominantly stony nature of the mountains. The best way to appreciate the surrounding panorama is by hiking the 2.6-km **Summit Peak Trail,** which ends in a treeless alpine area 1,000 vertical meters above the trailhead. The massive elevation gain means only the fittest of hikers should attempt the trail; allow at least two hours each way. The trailhead is on the north side of the highway, across from the campground. Much less strenuous is the 2.5-

km trail to **Flower Springs Lake,** nestled in alpine peaks south of the highway. Allow one hour each way. The trailhead is three km along Microwave Tower Rd., which spurs south at the cafe.

Wokkpash Recreation Area, 37,800 hectares of wilderness suitable only for experienced backcountry users, adjoins the southern boundary of Stone Mountain Provincial Park. Known for its hoodoos, deep gorges, and alpine meadows, the area is accessible on foot or by horseback along a 25-km route through the Wokkpash Valley to Wokkpash Lake.

At Summit Lake's eastern end is an exposed campground (expect snow at any time of the year) with pit toilets and picnic tables; $9.50 a night. The **Summit Cafe,** open daily 7 a.m.-10 p.m., is a popular truck stop; hearty breakfasts are $3-8, and sandwiches and burgers start at $5.

Just beyond the lake, the highway crosses 1,295-meter **Summit Pass,** highest point along the Alaska Highway. From this lofty summit, the highway continues to **One-fifteen Creek Provincial Park,** where a 300-meter trail leads to huge beaver dams. Camping in the park is $9. **Toad River,** 55 km from Summit Lake and at Mile 426 of the Alaska Hwy., is the next small service center. Here you'll find **Poplars Campground,** tel. (250) 232-5465, which has gas, a restaurant, cabins from $50 s or d, and campsites with hookups for $13-17.

Muncho Lake Provincial Park
Lying among mountains and forested valleys at the north end of the Canadian Rockies, this 88,420-hectare park surrounds stunning **Muncho Lake,** one of the highlights of the Alaska Highway.

Upon entering the park from the east, **Folded Mountain** comes into view to the north. This easy-to-recognize peak is representative of the area's geology; it was created by extensive folding and faulting of limestone bedrock. But it's the park's namesake lake that will grab your attention. The magnificent, 12-km-long body of water is encircled by a dense spruce forest, which gives way to barren rocky slopes at higher elevations. North of the lake, natural mineral licks attract Stone sheep and woodland caribou.

The small community of Muncho Lake spreads out along the eastern banks of the lake, providing services for park visitors. If you plan to overnight here, try to book ahead; motel rooms and campgrounds all fill up well in advance in July and August. **J & H Wilderness Resort,** tel. (250) 776-3453, offers motel rooms for $52 s or d, and campsites with clean and modern facilities, including free hot showers, for $16-18. The resort's restaurant is particularly good, and portions are served with the trucker's appetite in mind; breakfasts from $3.50, dinners from $7.50, a burger with a huge portion of fries is $6. It's open daily 7 a.m.-10 p.m.

Another lodging option is **Muncho Lake Lodge,** tel. (250) 776-3456, where basic motel rooms are $45 s, $50 d and camping is $12 a night. The most pleasant camping is found at the two campgrounds in the provincial park itself, north of the town. Sites at these two campgrounds are all $9.50 a night, but with only 15 sites in each one, they fill up fast.

Liard River Hot Springs Provincial Park
One of the most wonderful places to stop on the whole highway is this 668-hectare park, 40 km north of Muncho Lake. Most travelers understandably rush to soak their tired, dusty limbs in the hot pools. But the rest of the park is also worth exploring. The hot springs have created a microclimate around the overflow area. Over 80 plant species here are found nowhere else in northern British Columbia. Also inhabiting the area are many species of small fish, and mammals such as moose, woodland caribou, and black bear.

Early indigenous people no doubt discovered the springs, but workers on the Alaska Highway constructed the boardwalk and pools that exist today. The 500-meter-long boardwalk leads from the main parking lot over warm-water swamps to **Alpha Pool,** where water bubbles up into a long, shallow concrete pool. The pool area, surrounded by decking, has pit toilets and changing rooms. A rough trail leads 200 meters farther to undeveloped **Beta Pool,** which is cooler, much deeper, and not as busy.

At the entrance to the hot springs is a campground providing toilets, and showers. Firewood is available. Sites are $12 June-Aug., and $7 the rest of the year. The sites are often full by noon. Gates to the hot springs and campground are locked between 11 p.m. and 6 a.m.

Opposite the park entrance, at Mile 497, is **Trapper Ray's Liard Hot Springs Lodge,** tel. (250) 776-7349, which has rooms for $65 s, $70 d, campsites for $8-15, a small cafe, some grocery supplies, and gas. At Mile 496, **Lower Liard River Lodge,** tel. (250) 776-7341, offers rooms with shared facilities for $45 s, $50 d. This lodge has a great little cafe/restaurant and serves as the Greyhound bus stop.

To Watson Lake and Beyond
Anglers will find good fishing for grayling in the Liard River below **Smith River Falls,** 30 km or so northwest of the hot springs. Canyon and river views dot the highway heading north and west, and visitor services are available at **Coal River** and **Fireside.** The highway crosses the

signpost forest at Watson Lake

ANDREW HEMPSTEAD / NADINA PURDON

60th parallel and enters the Yukon just before Contact Creek Lodge (all services). It then meanders back and forth across the border six times before reaching the final crossing, 57 km farther west.

Watson Lake (pop. 1,800), a major service center along the highway, lies just north of the British Columbia/Yukon border. The town is best known for the famous **Signpost Forest** started by Carl K. Lindley, a GI who was working on the Alaska Highway. Instructed to repair a directional sign, he added a mileage sign to his home town of Danville, Illinois. Over the years others followed his lead, and today over 20,000 signs have been added. Behind the "forest" is the excellent **Alaska Highway Interpretive Centre,** tel. (403) 536-7469, open in summer, daily 9 a.m.-9 p.m. This facility provides visitors with historic information on the highway through extensive displays and an audiovisual presentation.

Twenty-one km west of Watson Lake, the Alaska Highway meets the Stewart-Cassiar Highway (see "The Stewart-Cassiar Highway," above), which leads south to the Yellowhead Highway between Prince George and Prince Rupert. The distance between Prince George and Watson Lake is almost identical via either the Alaska Highway or the Stewart-Cassiar Highway. The loop trip up one and back the other is around 2,450 km.

Continuing north on the Alaska Highway, it's 444 km to Whitehorse, capital of the Yukon; 524 km to Skagway, northernmost point of the Alaska Marine Highway; and 1,990 km to Delta Junction, Alaska, the official end of the Alaska Highway. The best source of information for those continuing north is Moon Publications' *Alaska-Yukon Handbook,* by Deke Castleman and Don Pitcher.

ATLIN

The small community of Atlin lies in the extreme northwest corner of British Columbia, 370 km west of Watson Lake along the Alaska Highway, then 100 km south along a mostly unpaved road. Isolated a long way from the rest of the province, it's one of British Columbia's most picturesque and intriguing communities. The glaciated peaks of the Coast Mountains form a stunning backdrop for the town, which is set on a gently sloping hill overlooking beautiful **Atlin Lake,** one of British Columbia's largest natural lakes. The lake's southern end and a massive chunk of the Coast Range are encompassed in 271,134-hectare **Atlin Provincial Park.**

Atlin was a boomtown with more than 5,000 people during the 1898 Klondike gold rush, when gold was discovered in nearby Pine Creek. Today they're still finding some color hereabouts, but the town's population has dwindled to about 500.

The highlight of Atlin is the surrounding scenery. The film adaptation of Farley Mowat's *Never Cry Wolf* was shot here, and it's easy to understand why. Wandering along the lakeshore you'll have outrageous views of sparkling peaks, glaciers, waterfalls, and mountain streams. Tied up on the lake in front of town is the **SS** *Tarahne,* a steamer built in 1916. The vessel plied the lake for 20 years, providing freight and transportation services. If you want to get out on the lake yourself, contact **Norseman Adventures,** tel. (250) 651-7535, which rents small motorboats (from $80 for eight hours) and houseboats (from $1,095 for seven days).

Atlin Historical Museum, housed in a 1902 schoolhouse at the corner of 3rd and Trainor Sts., tel. (250) 651-7522, lets you relive the excitement of the gold rush and Atlin's early days and view a display of Tlingit artifacts. It's open in summer, daily 9 a.m.-5:50 p.m.; admission is $3. Scattered through town are many historic buildings and artifacts pretty much untouched from the gold-rush era. The **Pioneer Cemetery,** two km east of town, reveals Atlin's pioneer history through stories and tales on weathered grave markers.

South of Atlin along Warm Springs Rd. are various lakes, camping areas, and, at the end of the road, **warm springs.** The springs bubble out of the ground at a pleasant 29° C into shallow pools surrounded by flower-filled meadows.

Practicalities

The main accommodation in town is the **Atlin Inn,** tel. (250) 651-7546. It's right in the center of town and has a cafe downstairs (open daily 7 a.m.-9 p.m.). The rooms are luxurious, and at $90 s, $100 d they're still reasonable value. The inn also offers a number of similarly priced kitchen-equipped cottages.

South of town, along the road to the warm springs, are a number of **campgrounds.** The first of these, Pine Creek, has pit toilets and firewood, and it's the only one with a fee; tents $5, RVs $7. The others at Palmer Lake, Atlin Lake, and at the warm springs are free. **Atlin Visitor Info Centre** is in the museum at the corner of 3rd and Trainor Sts., tel. (250) 651-7522. It's open July-August, daily 9 a.m.-5:30 p.m.; weekends only in June and September.

DOVER PUBLICATIONS, INC.

BOOKLIST

HISTORY

Duff, Wilson. *The Indian History of British Columbia: The Impact of the White Man*. Victoria: University of British Columbia Press, 1997.

Elliot, Gordon R. *Parkerville, Quesnel, and the Cariboo Gold Rush*. Vancouver: Douglas and McIntyre, 1978.

It Happened in British Columbia—A Pictorial Review 1871-1971. Victoria: B.C. Centennial '71 Committee, 1970.

Pethick, Derek. *British Columbia Recalled: A Picture History 1741-1871*. Surrey, BC: Hancock House Publishers Ltd., 1980.

Touchie, Rodger. *Vancouver Island: Portrait of a Past*. Vancouver: J.J. Douglas Ltd., 1974.

PEOPLE

Ashwell, Reg. *Indian Tribes of the Northwest*. Surrey, BC: Hancock House Publishers Ltd., 1989.

Malcolm, Andrew H. *The Canadians*. New York: Saint Martin's Press, 1991.

McFeat, Tom. *Indians of the North Pacific Coast*. Ottawa: Carleton University Press, 1989.

Tanner, Ogden. *The Canadians*. Alexandria, VA: Time-Life Books, 1981.

ARTS AND CRAFTS

Allen, D. *Totem Poles of the Northwest*. Surrey, BC: Hancock House Publishers Ltd., 1977.

Kew, Della, and P.E. Goddard. *Indian Art and Culture of the Northwest Coast*. Surrey, BC: Hancock House Publishers Ltd., 1997.

FLORA AND FAUNA

Hunter, Tom. *Wildlife of Western Canada*. Surrey, BC: Heritage House Publishing Co. Ltd., 1986.

Kunelius, Rick. *Animals of the Rockies*. Banff, Alberta: Altitude Publishing, 1983.

Lyons, C.P. *Trees, Shrubs, and Flowers to Know in British Columbia*. Edmonton: Lone Pine Publishing, 1995.

PARKS

Baird, D.M. *Banff National Park*. Edmonton: Hurtig Publishers, 1977.

Stephenson, Marylee. *Canada's National Parks: A Visitor's Guide*. Scarborough, Ontario: Prentice-Hall Canada, Inc., 1991.

GEOGRAPHY AND TRAVEL

British Columbia's Coast: The Canadian Inside Passage. Anchorage: Alaska Geographic Society, 1986.

Bryan, Liz, and Jack Bryan. *Country Roads Of British Columbia*. Vancouver: Sunflower Books, 1981.

Canadian Book of the Road: A Complete Motoring Guide to Canada. Westmont, Quebec: Reader's Digest Books (in conjunction with the Canadian Auto Association), 1991.

Castleman, Deke, and Don Pitcher. *Alaska-Yukon Handbook.* Chico: Moon Publications, 1997.

Farley, Albert. *Atlas of British Columbia.* Victoria: University of British Columbia Press, 1979.

Fryer, Harold. *Magnificent Yellowhead Highway.* Surrey, BC: Heritage House Publishing Co. Ltd., 1980.

Gadd, Ben. *Handbook of the Canadian Rockies.* Jasper: Corax Press, 1995.

Historic Fraser and Thompson River Canyons. Surrey, B.C.: Heritage House Publishing Co. Ltd., 1986.

Macaree, Mary, and David Macaree. *103 Hikes in Southwestern British Columbia.* Seattle: The Mountaineers, 1994.

Searby, Ellen. *Alaska Inside Passage Traveler.* Juneau: Windham Bay Press, 1996.

Shewchuk, Murphy. *Backroads Explorer: Similkameen and South Okanagan.* Surrey, B.C.: Hancock House Publishers Ltd. (Out of print.)

Wershlere, Terri. *Vancouver: The Ultimate Guide.* San Francisco: Chronicle Books, 1993.

ACCOMMODATIONS

B.C. Ministry of Tourism, Recreation, and Culture. *Accommodations.* Key Pacific Publishers Company Ltd. Printed every January, this free booklet is available at information centers throughout British Columbia.

Canadian Automobile Association. *Tour Book: Western Canada and Alaska.* Another free booklet available to members.

Pantel, Gerda. *The Canadian Bed and Breakfast Guide.* Toronto: Penguin Books Canada, 1996.

INDEX

Page numbers in **boldface** indicate the primary reference. *Italicized* page numbers indicate information in captions, charts, illustrations, maps, or special topics.

ABOUT THE AUTHORS

JANE KING

Born in Scotland, raised in England and Australia, then settling down in the United States, Jane King feels she has roots in three continents! After spending a year backpacking through Europe, then working as a registered nurse in Australia and the U.S., she turned her hand to travel writing. She wrote *New Zealand Handbook* and *British Columbia Handbook*, and is currently working on a guidebook to Tasmania. Living in Northern California with her husband Bruce, daughters Rachael and Stephanie, and a menagerie of pets, Jane enjoys flying small airplanes, cross-country skiing, photography, and escaping on "adventures" with her family whenever possible!

ANDREW HEMPSTEAD

Since beginning work for Moon Publications, Andrew Hempstead has worked on Moon Travel Handbooks to Alaska and New Zealand, and co-authored Moon's *Alberta and the Northwest Territories Handbook* and *Australia Handbook*. When not hanging out at home on the beach in New South Wales, Andrew can often be found enjoying his "home away from home" in Banff, Alberta.

MOON TRAVEL HANDBOOKS

LOSE YOURSELF IN THE EXPERIENCE, NOT THE CROWD

For 25 years, Moon Travel Handbooks have been the guidebooks of choice for adventurous travelers. Our award-winning Handbook series provides focused, comprehensive coverage of distinct destinations all over the world. Each Handbook is like an entire bookcase of cultural insight and introductory information in one portable volume. Our goal at Moon is to give travelers all the background and practical information they'll need for an extraordinary travel experience.

The following pages include a complete list of Handbooks, covering North America and Hawaii, Mexico, Central America and the Caribbean, and Asia and the Pacific. To purchase Moon Travel Handbooks, check your local bookstore or order by phone: (800) 345-5473 M-F 8 am.-5 p.m. PST or outside the U.S. phone: (916) 345-5473.

"An in-depth dunk into the land, the people and their history, arts, and politics."
—*Student Travels*

"Amazingly detailed in a style easy to understand, the Handbooks offer a lot for a good price."
—*International Travel News*

"Moon Travel Handbooks' line of travel guides adds wisdom to one's wanderings."
—*Excursions*

"Outdoor enthusiasts gravitate to the well-written Moon Travel Handbooks. In addition to politically correct historic and cultural features, the series focuses on flora, fauna and outdoor recreation. Maps and meticulous directions also are a trademark of Moon guides."
—*Houston Chronicle*

"Moon [Travel Handbooks] . . . bring a healthy respect to the places they investigate. Best of all, they provide a host of odd nuggets that give a place texture and prod the wary traveler from the beaten path. The finest are written with such care and insight they deserve listing as literature."
—*American Geographical Society*

"Moon Travel Handbooks offer in-depth historical essays and useful maps, enhanced by a sense of humor and a neat, compact format."
—*Swing*

"Perfect for the more adventurous, these are long on history, sightseeing and nitty-gritty information and very price-specific."
—*Columbus Dispatch*

"Moon guides manage to be comprehensive and countercultural at the same time . . . Handbooks are packed with maps, photographs, drawings, and sidebars that constitute a college-level introduction to each country's history, culture, people, and crafts."
—*National Geographic Traveler*

"Few travel guides do a better job helping travelers create their own itineraries than the Moon Travel Handbook series. The authors have a knack for homing in on the essentials."
—*Colorado Springs Gazette Telegraph*

www.moon.com

Enjoy our travel information center on the World Wide Web (WWW), loaded with interactive exhibits designed especially for the Internet.

ATTRACTIONS ON MOON'S WEB SITE INCLUDE:

HANDBOOK DESTINATIONS
Our award-winning, comprehensive travel guides cover destinations throughout North America and Hawaii, Central America and the Caribbean, and Asia and the Pacific.

PRACTICAL NOMAD
Extensive excerpts, a unique set of travel links coordinated with the book, and a regular Q & A column by author and Internet travel consultant Edward Hasbrouck.

TRAVEL MATTERS
Our on-line travel zine, featuring articles; author correspondence; a travel library including health information, reading lists, and cultural cues; and our new contest, **DESTINATION X,** offering a chance to win a trip to the mystery destination of your choice.

ROAD TRIP USA
Our best-selling book, ever; don't miss this award-winning Web guide to off-the-interstate itineraries.

Come visit us at: **http://www.moon.com**

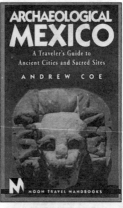

MEXICO

"These books will delight the armchair traveler, aid the undecided person in selecting a destination, and guide the seasoned road warrior looking for lesser-known hideaways."

—Mexican Meanderings Newsletter

"From tourist traps to off-the-beaten track hideaways, these guides offer consistent, accurate details without pretension."

—Foreign Service Journal

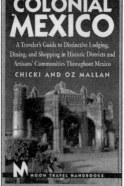

Archaeological Mexico	**$19.95**
Andrew Coe	450 pages, 25 maps
Baja Handbook	**$15.95**
Joe Cummings	380 pages, 44 maps
Cabo Handbook	**$14.95**
Joe Cummings	265 pages, 18 maps
Cancun Handbooks	**$13.95**
Chicki Mallan	270 pages, 25 maps
Colonial Mexico	**$16.95**
Chicki Mallan	300 pages, 38 maps
Mexico Handbook	**$21.95**
Joe Cummings and Chicki Mallan	1,200 pages, 232 maps
Northern Mexico Handbook	**$16.95**
Joe Cummings	590 pages, 68 maps
Pacific Mexico Handbook	**$17.95**
Bruce Whipperman	580 pages, 69 maps
Puerto Vallarta Handbook	**$14.95**
Bruce Whipperman	330 pages, 36 maps
Yucatan Handbook	**$15.95**
Chicki Mallan	470 pages, 62 maps

CENTRAL AMERICA AND THE CARIBBEAN

"Solidly packed with practical information and full of significant cultural asides that will enlighten you on the whys and wherefores of things you might easily see but not easily grasp."

—Boston Globe

Belize Handbook	**$15.95**
Chicki Mallan	390 pages, 45 maps
Caribbean Handbook	**$16.95**
Karl Luntta	400 pages, 56 maps
Ecuador Handbook	**$16.95**
Julian Smith	450 pages, 43 maps
Costa Rica Handbook	**$19.95**
Christopher P. Baker	780 pages, 74 maps
Cuba Handbook	**$19.95**
Christopher P. Baker	740 pages, 70 maps
Dominican Republic Handbook	**$15.95**
Gaylord Dold	420 pages, 24 maps
Honduras Handbook	**$15.95**
Chris Humphrey	330 pages, 40 maps
Jamaica Handbook	**$15.95**
Karl Luntta	330 pages, 17 maps
Virgin Islands Handbook	**$13.95**
Karl Luntta	220 pages, 19 maps

NORTH AMERICA AND HAWAII

"These domestic guides convey the same sense of exoticism that their foreign counterparts do, making home-country travel seem like far-flung adventure."

—Sierra Magazine

Alaska-Yukon Handbook	**$17.95**
Deke Castleman and Don Pitcher	530 pages, 92 maps
Alberta and the Northwest Territories Handbook	**$17.95**
Andrew Hempstead and Nadina Purdon	530 pages, 72 maps,
Arizona Traveler's Handbook	**$17.95**
Bill Weir and Robert Blake	512 pages, 54 maps
Atlantic Canada Handbook	**$17.95**
Nan Drosdick and Mark Morris	460 pages, 61 maps
Big Island of Hawaii Handbook	**$13.95**
J.D. Bisignani	370 pages, 23 maps
British Columbia Handbook	**$16.95**
Jane King and Andrew Hempstead	400 pages, 65 maps

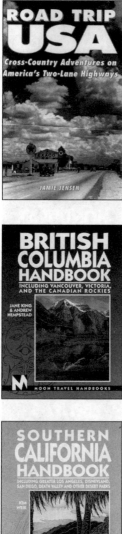

Colorado Handbook	**$18.95**
Stephen Metzger	480 pages, 59 maps
Georgia Handbook	**$17.95**
Kap Stann	370 pages, 50 maps
Hawaii Handbook	**$19.95**
J.D. Bisignani	1,030 pages, 90 maps
Honolulu-Waikiki Handbook	**$14.95**
J.D. Bisignani	380 pages, 20 maps
Idaho Handbook	**$18.95**
Don Root	610 pages, 42 maps
Kauai Handbook	**$15.95**
J.D. Bisignani	320 pages, 23 maps
Maui Handbook	**$14.95**
J.D. Bisignani	410 pages, 35 maps
Montana Handbook	**$17.95**
Judy Jewell and W.C. McRae	480 pages, 52 maps
Nevada Handbook	**$16.95**
Deke Castleman	500 pages, 40 maps
New Mexico Handbook	**$15.95**
Stephen Metzger	360 pages, 47 maps
New York City Handbook	**$13.95**
Christiane Bird	300 pages, 20 maps
New York Handbook	**$19.95**
Christiane Bird	780 pages, 95 maps
Northern California Handbook	**$19.95**
Kim Weir	800 pages, 50 maps
Oregon Handbook	**$16.95**
Stuart Warren and Ted Long Ishikawa	540 pages, 33 maps
Road Trip USA	**$22.50**
Jamie Jensen	800 pages, 165 maps
Southern California Handbook	**$19.95**
Kim Weir	750 pages, 30 maps
Tennessee Handbook	**$17.95**
Jeff Bradley	530 pages, 44 maps
Texas Handbook	**$17.95**
Joe Cummings	620 pages, 70 maps
Utah Handbook	**$17.95**
Bill Weir and W.C. McRae	490 pages, 40 maps
Washington Handbook	**$19.95**
Don Pitcher	870 pages, 113 maps
Wisconsin Handbook	**$18.95**
Thomas Huhti	590 pages, 69 maps
Wyoming Handbook	**$17.95**
Don Pitcher	610 pages, 80 maps

ASIA AND THE PACIFIC

"Scores of maps, detailed practical info down to business hours of small-town libraries. You can't beat the Asian titles for sheer heft. (The) series is sort of an American Lonely Planet, with better writing but fewer titles. (The) individual voice of researchers comes through."

—*Travel & Leisure*

Australia Handbook	**$21.95**
Marael Johnson, Andrew Hempstead, and Nadina Purdon	940 pages, 141 maps
Bali Handbook	**$19.95**
Bill Dalton	750 pages, 54 maps
Bangkok Handbook	**$13.95**
Michael Buckley	244 pages, 30 maps
Fiji Islands Handbook	**$13.95**
David Stanley	280 pages, 38 maps
Hong Kong Handbook	**$16.95**
Kerry Moran	370 pages, 39 maps
Indonesia Handbook	**$25.00**
Bill Dalton	1,380 pages, 249 maps
Japan Handbook	**$22.50**
J.D. Bisignani	970 pages, 213 maps
Micronesia Handbook	**$14.95**
Neil M. Levy	340 pages, 70 maps
Nepal Handbook	**$18.95**
Kerry Moran	490 pages, 51 maps
New Zealand Handbook	**$19.95**
Jane King	620 pages, 81 maps
Outback Australia Handbook	**$18.95**
Marael Johnson	450 pages, 57 maps
Pakistan Hanbdbook	**$19.95**
Isobel Shaw	660 pages, 85 maps
Philippines Handbook	**$17.95**
Peter Harper and Laurie Fullerton	670 pages, 116 maps
Singapore Handbook	**$15.95**
Carl Parkes	350 pages, 29 maps
Southeast Asia Handbook	**$21.95**
Carl Parkes	1,000 pages, 196 maps
South Korea Handbook	**$19.95**
Robert Nilsen	820 pages, 141 maps
South Pacific Handbook	**$22.95**
David Stanley	920 pages, 147 maps

Tahiti-Polynesia Handbook	**$13.95**
David Stanley	270 pages, 35 maps
Thailand Handbook	**$19.95**
Carl Parkes	860 pages, 142 maps
Tibet Handbook	**$30.00**
Victor Chan	1,104 pages, 216 maps
Vietnam, Cambodia & Laos Handbook	**$18.95**
Michael Buckley	720 pages, 112 maps

OTHER GREAT TITLES FROM MOON

"For hardy wanderers, few guides come more highly
recommended than the Handbooks. They include
good maps, steer clear of fluff and flackery, and offer
plenty of money-saving tips. They also give you the
kind of information that visitors to strange lands—on
any budget—need to survive."

—*US News & World Report*

Moon Handbook	**$10.00**
Carl Koppeschaar	141 pages, 8 maps
Moscow-St. Petersburg Handbook	**$13.95**
Masha Nordbye	259 pages, 16 maps
The Practical Nomad: How to Travel Around the World	**$17.95**
Edward Hasbrouck	575 pages
Staying Healthy in Asia, Africa, and Latin America	**$11.95**
Dirk Schroeder	197 pages, 4 maps

MOONBELT

A new concept in moneybelts.
Made of heavy-duty Cordura
nylon, the Moonbelt offers
maximum protection for your money
and important papers. This pouch,
designed for all-weather comfort, slips under your shirt or waistband, rendering it virtually
undetectable and inaccessible to pickpockets. It features a one-inch high-test quick-release
buckle so there's no more fumbling around for the strap or repeated adjustments. This
handy plastic buckle opens and closes with a touch but won't come undone until you want
it to. Moonbelts accommodate traveler's checks, passports, cash, photos, etc.
Size 5 x 9 inches. Available in black only. **$8.95**

THE PRACTICAL NOMAD

✈ TAKE THE PLUNGE

"The greatest barriers to long-term travel by Americans are the disempowered feelings that leave them afraid to ask for the time off. Just do it."

✈ TAKE NOTHING FOR GRANTED

"Even 'What time is it?' is a highly politicized question in some areas, and the answer may depend on your informant's ethnicity and political allegiance as well as the proximity of the secret police."

✈ TAKE THIS BOOK

With experience helping thousands of his globetrotting clients plan their trips around the world, travel industry insider Edward Hasbrouck provides the secrets that can save readers money and valuable travel time. An indispensable complement to destination-specific travel guides, *The Practical Nomad* includes:

airfare strategies

ticket discounts

long-term travel considerations

travel documents

border crossings

entry requirements

government offices

travel publications

Internet information resources

WHERE TO BUY MOON TRAVEL HANDBOOKS

BOOKSTORES AND LIBRARIES: Moon Travel Handbooks are distributed worldwide. Please contact our sales manager for a list of wholesalers and distributors in your area.

TRAVELERS: We would like to have Moon Travel Handbooks available throughout the world. Please ask your bookstore to write or call us for ordering information. If your bookstore will not order our guides for you, please contact us for a free catalog.

> **Moon Travel Handbooks**
> **P.O. Box 3040**
> **Chico, CA 95927-3040 U.S.A.**
> **tel.: (800) 345-5473, outside the U.S. (916) 345-5473**
> **fax: (916) 345-6751**
> **e-mail: travel@moon.com**

IMPORTANT ORDERING INFORMATION

PRICES: All prices are subject to change. We always ship the most current edition. We will let you know if there is a price increase on the book you order.

SHIPPING AND HANDLING OPTIONS: Domestic UPS or USPS first class (allow 10 working days for delivery): $4.50 for the first item, $1.00 for each additional item.

Moonbelt shipping is $1.50 for one, 50 cents for each additional belt.

UPS 2nd Day Air or Printed Airmail requires a special quote.

International Surface Bookrate 8-12 weeks delivery: $3.00 for the first item, $1.00 for each additional item. Note: We cannot guarantee international surface bookrate shipping. We recommends sending international orders via air mail, which requires a special quote.

FOREIGN ORDERS: Orders that originate outside the U.S.A. must be paid for with an international money order, a check in U.S. currency drawn on a major U.S. bank based in the U.S.A., or Visa or MasterCard.

TELEPHONE ORDERS: We accept Visa or MasterCard payments. Call in your order: (800) 345-5473, 8 a.m.-5 p.m. Pacific standard time. Outside the U.S. the number is (916) 345-5473.

INTERNET ORDERS: Visit our site at: www.moon.com